West's Law School Advisory Board

JESSE H. CHOPER
Professor of Law and Dean Emeritus,
University of California, Berkeley

JOSHUA DRESSLER
Professor of Law, Michael E. Moritz College of Law,
The Ohio State University

YALE KAMISAR
Professor of Law Emeritus, University of San Diego
Professor of Law Emeritus, University of Michigan

MARY KAY KANE
Professor of Law, Chancellor and Dean Emeritus,
University of California,
Hastings College of the Law

LARRY D. KRAMER
President, William and Flora Hewlett Foundation

JONATHAN R. MACEY
Professor of Law, Yale Law School

ARTHUR R. MILLER
University Professor, New York University
Formerly Bruce Bromley Professor of Law, Harvard University

GRANT S. NELSON
Professor of Law, Pepperdine University
Professor of Law Emeritus, University of California, Los Angeles

A. BENJAMIN SPENCER
Professor of Law,
Washington & Lee University School of Law

JAMES J. WHITE
Professor of Law, University of Michigan

INTRODUCTION TO LAW PRACTICE:

ORGANIZING AND MANAGING LEGAL WORK

Fourth Edition

By

Professor Gary A. Munneke
Professor of Law
Pace University School of Law

AMERICAN CASEBOOK SERIES®

WEST®
A Thomson Reuters business

Mat #41170046

Thomson Reuters created this publication to provide you with accurate and authoritative information concerning the subject matter covered. However, this publication was not necessarily prepared by persons licensed to practice law in a particular jurisdiction. Thomson Reuters does not render legal or other professional advice, and this publication is not a substitute for the advice of an attorney. If you require legal or other expert advice, you should seek the services of a competent attorney or other professional.

American Casebook Series is a trademark registered in the U.S. Patent and Trademark Office.

COPYRIGHT © 1991 WEST PUBLISHING CO.
© West, a Thomson business, 2002
© 2007 Thomson/West
© 2013 Thomson Reuters
    610 Opperman Drive
    St. Paul, MN 55123
    1–800–313–9378

Printed in the United States of America

ISBN: 978–0–314–27645–2

ABOUT THE AUTHOR

Gary A. Munneke is a professor of law at Pace University School of Law, in White Plains, New York, where he teaches courses in Professional Responsibility, Law Practice Management and a Seminar on the Legal Profession. He is an active leader of the American Bar Association, where he currently serves as Section Officers Conference Liaison to the Board of Governors. He is also the Co-Chair of the New York State Bar Association Committee on Law Practice Management, a member of the NYSBA Continuing Legal Education Committee and a member of the *New York State Bar Association Journal* Board of Editors. He was one of four subcommittee chairs of the New York State Bar Association Task Force on the Future of the Legal Profession.

From 2006–2009, Professor Munneke served on the ABA Board of Governors, after a two year term on the ABA Nominating Committee and a six-year term in the ABA House of Delegates. He has also served the ABA as Chair of the Law Practice Management Section and Chair of the LPM Publishing Board; as a member of the Standing Committee on Publishing Oversight; as Chair of the Finance Committee of the Section of Legal Education and Admissions to the Bar, and as a member of the ABA Diversity Center governing board.

He has previously served as President of the National Association for Law Placement, as New York State Chair of the Fellows of the American Bar Foundation, as well as a number of other committees for the ABA and other professional associations.

Professor Munneke is the author of numerous books and articles about current issues on the legal profession, the practice of law and legal career issues, including *Law Practice Management in a Nutshell, Seize the Future: Forecasting and Influencing the Future of the Legal Profession, The Essential Formbook: Comprehensive Management Tools for Lawyers The Legal Career Guide: From Law Student to Lawyer, Careers in Law, Nonlegal Careers for Lawyers, Barron's How to Succeed in Law School, Barron's Guide to Law Schools, Opportunities in Law Careers, and Careers in Law*. His upcoming book, *Disaster Planning and Recovery: Essential Forms for Law Firms*, updates his work in this area in The Essential Formbook. Professor Munneke is a frequent speaker at seminars and conferences on topics related to his teaching and writing.

A graduate of the University of Texas School of Law, Professor Munneke is a member of the Texas and Pennsylvania bars, and the New York State Bar Association. He is a Life Fellow of the American Bar Foundation, a Fellow of the College of Law Practice Management, the 2011 recipient of the Samuel S. Smith Award, presented by the ABA Law Practice Management Section for outstanding contributions to the field of law practice management, and the 2011 recipient of Pace Law School's Richard Ottinger Award for Outstanding Faculty Service.

ACKNOWLEDGEMENTS

This is the Fourth Edition of this casebook, and the list of those who have assisted me, reviewed materials and offered their thoughts has grown voluminous. They include deans at the three law schools where I have taught the course in Law Practice Management: Pace Law School, the University of Baltimore School of Law, and Widener University School of Law, professional colleagues in both the practicing bar and the academy, research assistants, and students in my classes. Without their help, it would not have been completed.

The author wishes to express his gratitude to all those who have assisted him, and although this list is undoubtedly incomplete, the following individuals deserve to be mentioned: Denise Acevedo, Dawn Addiego, Joe Aggozino, Ann Albert, Alan Alvarez, Professor Lisle Baker, Joel Bennett, Rebekah Binger, Tony Broccolo, Professor Donald Brodie, Beryl Brown, Scott Brown, Lesley Campbell, Tony Cherego, Janet Childs, Kaley Childs, Jennifer Chin, Sean Conway, Christine Cragg, Dean Leary Davis, Rhonda DiStephano, Lisa De Bock, Betty Donavan, Donna Drumm, Professor Barbara Durkin, Eileen Eck, Tasha Fasce, Rick Feferman, Tracy Fitzsimmons, Jay Foonberg, Elizabeth Fraser, Dean Steve Friedman, Bryn Fuller, Loni Gardner, Erica Gerlando, Terry Girolamo, Brittany Gold, Dean Steven Goldberg, Keith Goldstein, Richard Granat, Arthur Greene, Jonah Grossbardt, Linda Hahs, Dana Halber, Professor Al Hannon, Sherene Hannon, Susan Huot, Kristina Ivtindzioski, Cynthia Kasnia, Kay Ann King, Sameer Ladha, Christina Langella, Cindy Lerner, Rachel Littman, Professor Lou Lobenhoffer, Theresa Loscalzo, Michael Maggi, Adele Magnani, Fred Marasco, Dawn Mark, Lexi Maxwell, Deborah McCreery, Professor Gayle McKechnie, May Beth McManus, Denise Mobley, Loretta Musial, Jack O?Hara, Lucie Olejnikova, Dean Richard Ottinger, Justina Parrello, Rick Pescatore, Andrea Roberts, Professor Rick Rodgers, Marian Rothbart, Jane Ryan, Thomas Sciacca, Margaret Serrano, Dean Michelle Simon, Stephanie Skelly, Debbie Slowata, Mary Stagliano, Jennifer Stivrins, Dan Timins, Karen Tobias, Natalie Voevodkin, Sara Waranch, Professor Bill Weston, Debra Whitson, Lisa Widen, Dean Bob Yegge, and Jennifer Yuen. The author also wishes to recognize three deceased colleagues, who contributed significantly to the teaching of law practice management: Luther Avery, Dennis Murphy, and Tom Steele.

This acknowledgment section would not be complete without expressing the greatest thanks to the author's wife, Sharon Walla, not only for her continuing support of this work, but also for her indulgence in allowing her law firm to serve as a laboratory, example and working model for many of the concepts presented in the book.

GARRY A. MUNNEKE

October 2012

White Plains, New York

Summary of Contents

	Page
About the Author	iii
Acknowledgements	v
Table of Cases	xvii

PART 1. THE LEGAL SERVICES INDUSTRY

Chapter

1.	The Business of Law	2
2.	The Marketplace for Legal Services	16
3.	Business or Profession?	39
4.	The Truth about Law Firms	59
5.	Managing the Practice of Law	96

PART 2. MANAGING THE LEGAL ORGANIZATION

6.	Strategic Planning and Marketing Legal Services	128
7.	Managing Clients	158
8.	Managing Lawyers and Support Staff	172
9.	Managing the Law Office	211
10.	Managing Information and Technology Resources	238
11.	Managing Financial Resources	260

PART 3. MANAGING THE LEGAL WORK PRODUCT

12.	Providing Excellent Services	294
13.	Managing Substantive Law Practice Systems	313
14.	Practice System Components	329

PART 4. MANAGING YOURSELF AS A PROFESSIONAL

15.	Managing Your Professional Life	362
16.	Building a Successful Career	390

Appendices	417
Index	509

TABLE OF CONTENTS

	Page
ABOUT THE AUTHOR	iii
ACKNOWLEDGEMENTS	v
TABLE OF CASES	vii

PART 1. THE LEGAL SERVICES INDUSTRY

Chapter 1. The Business of Law 2
- A. Why Practice Management? 2
  - Problems and Questions 3
- B. Survival 3
  - Problems and Questions 7
- C. The Future of the Practice of Law 7
  - Executive Summary 8
  - Innovation and Change 10
  - When Law Firms Fail, Partners Feel Squeeze 12
  - Problems and Questions 15

Chapter 2. The Marketplace for Legal Services 16
- A. Lawyer Demographics 16
  - The U.S. Lawyer Population in 2000 18
  - Problems and Questions 20
- B. The Competition 21
  - Unauthorized Practice of Law Committee v. Parsons Technology 22
  - Problems and Questions 26
- C. Legal Employment 26
  - Race to the Finish Line: Legal Education, Jobs and the Stuff Dreams Are Made of 27
  - Practice Settings 31
  - Problems and Questions 34
- D. Economics of the Law Business 34
  - Problems and Questions 38

Chapter 3. Business or Profession? 39
- A. Professional Values 39
  - Practicing Law Across Geographic and Professional Borders: What Does the Future Hold? 40
  - Problems and Questions 45
- B. Multijurisdictional Practice 45
  - Birbrower v. Superior Court 46
  - Problems and Questions 49
- C. Cross–Professional Practice 50
  - Problems and Questions 51
- D. Specialization 52
  - Requiem for a General Practice: The End of an Era 52
  - Problems and Questions 58

Chapter 4. The Truth about Law Firms — 59

- A. What Is a Law Firm? — 59
  - 1. Generally — 59
  - 2. The Law Firm Pyramid — 61
    - *Problems and Questions* — 67
- B. The Relationship Among Partners — 68
  - 1. Partnership Principles — 69
  - 2. The Written Agreement — 71
  - 3. Implied Partnerships — 72
  - 4. Other Forms of Organization — 73
    - *Problems and Questions* — 75
- C. Compensating the Owners — 76
  - *Ten Terrible Truths About Law Firm Partner Compensation* — 77
  - *Compensation Systems: For the Love of Money or the Mission of the Firm* — 79
  - *Problems and Questions* — 83
- D. The Life Cycle of a Law Firm — 84
  - 1. From Growth to Maturity — 84
    - *PLCs Spur Strategies for Success* — 84
  - 2. Death and Retirement — 88
    - *A Loss in the Firm* — 88
    - *Problems and Questions* — 93
  - 3. Metamorphosis — 93
    - *Problems and Questions* — 94

Chapter 5. Managing the Practice of Law — 96

- A. Management and Lawyers — 96
  - *Problems and Questions* — 97
- B. Management Theory and Practice — 97
  - 1. B–School Thinking — 98
    - *The Coming of the New Organization* — 98
    - *Legal Strategy 101: It's Time for Law Firms to Re-think Their Business Model* — 99
  - 2. The Legal Perspective — 104
    - *The Function of Management* — 104
    - *An Overview* — 105
    - *Law Firms Embrace Business School 101: As Recession Bites, More Attorneys Attend Management Training and Take Mini–M.B.A. Courses* — 108
    - *Problems and Questions* — 110
- C. Management and Professional Failure — 110
  - 1. The Concept of Risk — 111
  - 2. Malpractice — 112
    - *Togstad v. Veseley, Otto, Miller & Keefe* — 112
  - 3. Malpractice Insurance — 115
  - 4. Discipline — 117
    - *Preamble, Model Rules of Professional Conduct* — 117
    - *Problems and Questions* — 120
- D. Paradigm for Studying Law Practice Management — 121
  - *Problems and Questions* — 123

PART 2. MANAGING THE LEGAL ORGANIZATION

Chapter 6. Strategic Planning and Marketing Legal Services 128
A. Background 128
    Alexander v. Cahill 130
    Problems and Questions 142
B. Developing a Strategic Marketing Plan 142
    1. General Principles 142
        Implementation of a Marketing Plan 143
    2. Create a Plan 149
        a. Analyze the Marketplace 149
        b. Assess the Competition 150
        c. Evaluate Yourself 151
        d. Identify a Niche 151
        e. Develop a Plan 152
        Problems and Questions 153
C. Implementing a Marketing Plan 153
    1. Marketing Mechanics 153
    2. The Economics of Marketing 155
    3. Reaching the Marketplace 155
    Problems and Questions 156

Chapter 7. Managing Clients 158
A. Clients and Lawyers 158
    1. Client–Centered Lawyering 158
    2. Managing Client Relations 160
    Problems and Questions 161
B. Fees and Billing 161
    1. Legal Fees 162
    2. Engagement Letters 164
        Using Engagement Letters 164
    3. Billing for Services 167
        Excerpt 167
    4. Fee Disputes 169
    Problems and Questions 170
C. Phone Calls 171
    Problems and Questions 171

Chapter 8. Managing Lawyers and Support Staff 172
A. Human Resources Management 172
    1. The Value of Employed Lawyers and Support Staff 172
    2. Lawyers as Managers 173
    3. Law Firms as Employers 174
        Legal Considerations 175
        Problems and Questions 178
B. Administrative and Support Staff 179
    1. Who Makes Up the Support Staff? 179
    2. Law Firm Administrators 180
        Why Hire Professional Managers? 181
    3. Paralegals 182
    4. Legal Secretaries 183
    5. Other Clerical Employees 185
    6. Consultants, Contract and Outsourced Services 185
    Problems and Questions 186

			Page
C.	Employed Lawyers		186
	1. Associate Lawyers		186
	2. Senior Employed Lawyers		188
	3. Administrative Lawyers		188
	Problems and Questions		189
D.	Elements of Human Resources Management		190
	1. Recruitment and Hiring		191
	How to Hire, Retain, and Motivate Your Staff		191
	2. Orientation and Training		201
	3. Feedback and Evaluation		202
	4. Compensation and Benefits		203
	5. Discipline and Termination		206
	Discipline and Termination		206
	Problems and Questions		209
E.	Getting the Most Out of Staff		210
	Problems and Questions		210

Chapter 9. Managing the Law Office 211

A.	The Law Office as a Place to Work		211
	Problems and Questions		213
B.	Office Design		213
	1. Core Functions		214
	2. The Information Resources Center		215
	3. Security		216
	4. Growth		217
	5. Lease or Purchase		217
	Problems and Questions		218
C.	Inside the Walls		219
	1. Office Equipment		219
	2. Computer Systems		220
	3. Other Technology		221
	4. Furnishings		224
	Go With the Flow: Tapping Into Positive Energy in Office Décor Through Feng Shui Principles		224
	5. Supplies		226
	Problems and Questions		226
D.	What Lies Ahead?		228
	The Mobile Law Office—From Lincoln to the Lincoln Lawyer		228
	The 21st Century Law Office . . . It's Not Your Father's Office Any More		232
	Problems and Questions		236

Chapter 10. Managing Information and Technology Resources .. 238

A.	The Information Business		238
B.	Computer Applications in the Law Office		240
	Technology and the Practice of Law		242
	Problems and Questions		252
C.	Knowledge Management		252
	1. Research		253
	2. Information Resources		254
	Implementing Technology in the Small Law Firm: How to Get Beyond an Unfulfilled Promise		255
	Problems and Questions		258

			Page
Chapter 11.	**Managing Financial Resources**		**260**
A.	Understanding the Basics		260
	Problems and Questions		264
B.	Law Firm Financial Management		264
	1. Capital		265
	2. Expenses		267
		a. Start-up Expenses	267
		b. Operating Expenses	268
	3. Income		269
	4. Profitability		269
	5. Billing, Collections and Realization		271
	6. Compensation		273
	7. Budgeting and Reporting		275
	8. Financial Planning		276
		It's That Time of Year: Some Tips to Help Manage Your Firm's Budgeting Process	277
		Problems and Questions	279
C.	Financing a Law Practice		280
	1. Introduction		280
	2. Partner Capital Contributions		281
	3. Borrowing		282
	4. Creating a Business Plan		288
		a. Overview	288
		b. Marketing Plan	289
		c. Resources Plan	289
		d. Financial Plan	289
	5. Selling the Plan		290
		Problems and Questions	291

PART 3. MANAGING THE LEGAL WORK PRODUCT

			Page
Chapter 12.	**Providing Excellent Services**		**294**
A.	The Yin and Yang of Excellence		294
	Problems and Questions		295
B.	Managing Quality		295
	1. Defining Quality Legal Services		296
	2. Measuring Quality		297
	3. Technology and Quality		299
		There's Just Something About Larry	301
	4. The Search for Excellence		304
		Dr. Deming's 1950 Lecture to Japanese Top Management	305
	5. Professional Standards		310
		Problems and Questions	311
Chapter 13.	**Managing Substantive Law Practice Systems**		**313**
A.	What Is Legal Work?		313
	Problems and Questions		314

		Page
B.	Legal Services Delivery Team	314
C.	Client Focus	319
	Problems and Questions	320
D.	Practice Systems	320
	1. What Is a System?	320
	2. Creating the System	322
	3. Implementing the System	324
	4. Improving the System	325
	Problems and Questions	325
E.	Macro–System Overview	325
	Problems and Questions	328

Chapter 14. Practice System Components — 329

A.	Administrative Support Systems	329
	Problems and Questions	330
B.	Document Assembly Systems	330
	Automating Document Systems Saves Time and Money	335
	Problems and Questions	336
C.	Administrative Support Systems	337
	1. Calendar and Tickler Systems	339
	Handheld Computers Keep Users Enthusiastic	341
	Skills and Systems: The Secrets to Better Law Office Management	343
	2. Filing and Retrieval Systems	344
	A 21st Century Law Office	345
	3. Conflict Checking Systems	348
	Conflict Management: Using Technology to Navigate the Minefield	349
	4. Timekeeping and Billing Systems	352
	Technology for Tightwads: Law Office Essentials on a Budget	352
	5. Client Trust Account Systems	353
	Excerpt From the ABA Guide to Lawyer Trust Accounts,	353
	Problems and Questions	355
D.	Litigation Management Systems	356
	Case Management for the Litigator	357
	Problems and Questions	359

PART 4. MANAGING YOURSELF AS A PROFESSIONAL

Chapter 15. Managing Your Professional Life — 362

A.	Personal Management Generally	362
	Problems and Questions	363
B.	Professional Skills	363
	Statement of Fundamental Lawyering Skills and Professional Values	363
	Standards for the Approval of Law Schools	365
	Problems and Questions	366
C.	Critical Management Skills	367
	1. Time Management	367
	2. Financial Management	370
	3. Organization	371
	How to Run Your Law Practice Without Letting It Run You	374
	4. Leadership and Supervision	378
	5. Communication	379
	6. Technology	382
	7. Rainmaking	382
	8. Substantive Legal Skills	384
	Problems and Questions	386

		Page
D.	Law School, CLE and the Real World	386
	1. Mandatory Continuing Legal Education	387
	2. Professional Competence	388
	Problems and Questions	389

Chapter 16. Building a Successful Career — 390

A.	Managing Your Career	390
	Paths Within the Legal Profession	390
	Problems and Questions	392
B.	The Legal Job Market	393
	What You Can Do With a Law Degree (Besides Practice Law)	393
	Problems and Questions	399
C.	Creating a Career Plan	399
	From The Legal Career Guide: From Law Student to Lawyer, 3d Edition	399
	Problems and Questions	404
D.	Balancing Life and Work	404
	Work Life Integration and the Practice of Law	405
	Reducing Stress: Understanding and Managing the Tigers in Our Heads	408
	Problems and Questions	412
E.	Epilogue	412
	Problems and Questions	415

APPENDICES

A.	Resources on Law Practice Management	417
B.	Selected Internet Resources	423
C.	Selected Model Rules of Professional Conduct	429
D–1.	Model LLP Agreement	443
D–2.	Model Partnership Agreement Checklist	455
E.	Law Firm Questionnaire	459
F.	Law Firm Marketing Questionnaire	461
G.	Human Resources Plan Checklist	463
H–1.	Physical Resources Plan (Law Office)	467
H–2.	Physical Resources Plan (Equipment and Furniture)	469
I.	Model Law Office Floor Plan	473
J.	Information Resources Plan Checklist	475
K.	Financial Plan Checklist	477
L.	Model Law Firm Financial Reports	483
M.	Substantive Practice System Checklist	499
N.	Student Experience and Skills Survey	501
O.	Career Plan Checklist	503
P.	Profile of Winters & Sommers, LLP	505

INDEX — 509

TABLE OF CASES

The principal cases are in bold type. Cases cited or discussed in the text are in roman type. References are to pages. Cases cited in principal cases and within other quoted materials are not included.

Adler, Barish, Daniels, Levin and Creskoff v. Epstein, 482 Pa. 416, 393 A.2d 1175 (Pa. 1978), 199

Alexander v. Cahill, 598 F.3d 79 (2nd Cir. 2010), **130**

Asam v. Alabama State Bar, 675 So.2d 866 (Ala.1996), 348

Bates & O'Steen v. State Bar of Arizona, 433 U.S. 350, 51 Ohio Misc. 1, 97 S.Ct. 2691, 53 L.Ed.2d 810, 5 O.O.3d 60 (1977), 4, 128, 132

Birbrower, Montalbano, Condon & Frank v. Superior Court, 70 Cal.Rptr.2d 304, 949 P.2d 1 (Cal.1998), **46**

Bushman v. State Bar, 113 Cal.Rptr. 904, 522 P.2d 312 (Cal.1974), 166

Castro, Matter of, 164 Ariz. 428, 793 P.2d 1095 (Ariz.1990), 119

Central Hudson Gas & Elec. Corp. v. Public Service Commission of New York, 447 U.S. 557, 100 S.Ct. 2343, 65 L.Ed.2d 341 (1980), 131

Collins v. Rizkana, 73 Ohio St.3d 65, 652 N.E.2d 653 (Ohio 1995), 176

E.E.O.C. v. Dowd & Dowd, Ltd., 736 F.2d 1177 (7th Cir.1984), 177

E.E.O.C. v. Sidley Austin Brown & Wood, 315 F.3d 696 (7th Cir.2002), 64

E.E.O.C. v. Sidley Austin LLP, 437 F.3d 695 (7th Cir.2006), 177

Foley, Hoag & Eliot, 229 NLRB No. 80, 229 NLRB 456 (N.L.R.B.1977), 177

Friedman v. Rogers, 440 U.S. 1, 99 S.Ct. 887, 59 L.Ed.2d 100 (1979), 136

Hishon v. King & Spalding, 467 U.S. 69, 104 S.Ct. 2229, 81 L.Ed.2d 59 (1984), 177

Ibanez v. Florida Dept. of Business and Professional Regulation, Bd. of Accountancy, 512 U.S. 136, 114 S.Ct. 2084, 129 L.Ed.2d 118 (1994), 132

In re (see name of party)

Komisarow v. Lansky, 139 Ind.App. 351, 219 N.E.2d 913 (Ind.App. 1 Div.1966), 73

Matter of (see name of party)

Myers v. Aragona, 21 Md.App. 45, 318 A.2d 263 (Md.App.1974), 72

Peel v. Attorney Registration and Disciplinary Com'n of Illinois, 496 U.S. 91, 110 S.Ct. 2281, 110 L.Ed.2d 83 (1990), 12, 132

Ranta v. McCarney, 391 N.W.2d 161 (N.D. 1986), 45

Redman v. Walters, 88 Cal.App.3d 448, 152 Cal.Rptr. 42 (Cal.App. 1 Dist.1979), 73

R. M. J., In re, 455 U.S. 191, 102 S.Ct. 929, 71 L.Ed.2d 64 (1982), 132

Shapero v. Kentucky Bar Ass'n, 486 U.S. 466, 108 S.Ct. 1916, 100 L.Ed.2d 475 (1988), 132

Spera v. Fleming, Hovenkamp & Grayson, P.C., 25 S.W.3d 863 (Tex.App.-Hous. (14 Dist.) 2000), 348

Togstad v. Vesely, Otto, Miller & Keefe, 291 N.W.2d 686 (Minn.1980), **112**

Unauthorized Practice of Law Committee v. Parsons Technology, Inc., 1999 WL 47235 (N.D.Tex.1999), **22**

Wagenmann v. Adams, 829 F.2d 196 (1st Cir. 1987), 298

Zauderer v. Office of Disciplinary Counsel of Supreme Court of Ohio, 471 U.S. 626, 105 S.Ct. 2265, 85 L.Ed.2d 652 (1985), 132

INTRODUCTION TO LAW PRACTICE:
ORGANIZING AND MANAGING LEGAL WORK
Fourth Edition

Part 1

The Legal Services Industry

■ ■ ■

CHAPTER 1

THE BUSINESS OF LAW

■ ■ ■

A. WHY PRACTICE MANAGEMENT?

It may seem like a simple question: Why practice management? The answer, however, is illusive. In part, it raises other questions: Why should lawyers care about management and learn to be effective managers? Why should law students learn about managing a law practice when their lot in life will be to work for partners who manage the law firm? Why should partners worry about management when they can hire MBAs and CPAs to take care of the office? Why should lawyers not just be lawyers and leave managing to the managers?

The answer to these questions is both simple and complex. In the most fundamental sense, lawyers have to manage their practices because they are responsible for the quality of services they deliver to clients. They might be able to hire people to help them, but the lawyers are responsible. They can be disciplined if they violate the Rules of Professional Conduct, which govern the relationships between lawyers and clients, and they can be sued for malpractice and other civil actions for failing to act with the care of an ordinary reasonably prudent lawyer. A majority of the mistakes that lawyers make, as we shall see, are related to management errors, so lawyers owe it to their clients, themselves and the profession to manage their practices professionally.

Law practice management is important in three interwoven ways: It involves management of the organization—the firm, the law department, the law office. It is common to refer to this kind of management as law firm management or law office management. Legal management also involves management of the legal work product, i.e., delivering services to clients. In this sense, every lawyer is a manager, whether she has a role in managing the firm or not. If we divide the working world into labor and management, lawyers fall squarely into the category of management. A third facet of management involves the acquisition and mastery of a set of professional skills, which allow lawyers to be effective managers in a wide variety of situations not limited to the practice of law. In this sense, management means managing yourself as a professional person.

Perhaps the most important reason that management is important for lawyers is that it is a critical key to professional success. Those who learn to become effective practice managers are more likely to find success and professional satisfaction in their careers and personal lives. Good management practices involve taking control of your life and making the most of opportunities that come your way.

Probably, law practice management should be a required subject for all law school students and an ongoing topic for the continuing legal education of lawyers. It is not. Law practice management courses are elective offerings at schools where they are offered, and they are not offered at all schools. Elements of law practice management may be taught in clinics and other skills classes, but most students leave law school with little or no preparation as practice managers. It does not improve when they go to work. At most firms, there is little or no management training, and the pressures of practice make it difficult for new lawyers to find time to learn management skills. Most lawyers pick up a little bit here and there, watch other lawyers, who may or may not be good managers, and muddle along as generations of their predecessors have. This course suggests that there is a better way.

PROBLEMS AND QUESTIONS

1. Throughout this book, you will find a section of "Problems and Questions" at the end of each section. These are intended to help you think about the materials you have just read. You may discuss some of them in class, but others may be left for your speculation on your own or in informal conversations with classmates. For instance, the title to this section, "Why Practice Management?" poses a central inquiry: Why does it matter if we as lawyers manage our practices? It may also imply that management is a practice in and of itself, leading to the question: What is involved in the practice of management in law? You get the picture.

2. A central theme in this course is that the practice of law is changing in response to a variety of forces. What are these forces? What do you see as the major changes in the practice of law? How have these changes reshaped the management of law firms?

B. SURVIVAL

Survive! No one ever told me in law school that the issue was survival—economic survival. No one ever said that anyone who knew how to "think like a lawyer" might fail at the practice of law, or explained the economic realities of practicing law that I would need to know in order to make it in my chosen profession. Students today may have more of a sense that they are entering a competitive environment, but with notable exceptions no one is talking about what they need to do to survive (and even thrive) as practitioners.

Lawyers tend to think of themselves as unique inhabitants of the world of work. The legal profession, with its Socratic method of education, arcane mores, and perquisites of self-regulation, views itself as ubiquitous. It is our strength and weakness. Not even doctors have the gall to refer to all those in the population who have not attended medical school as non-doctors. Lawyers perceive themselves as independent professionals, exempt from the laws of commerce and business, impervious to the depredations of economic cycles, and above the rules of the free market where providers of goods and services compete for patrons.

There may have been a time when the practice of law did not require lawyers to understand principles of business management. Private practice was conducted individually and inexpensively. Competition among lawyers and with other professions was limited. It was not difficult for a lawyer to earn a comfortable income, attain respect in the community and maintain control of his personal destiny.

Today, however, lawyers must regard law as a business, inasmuch as they earn their livelihood from the practice of law. The marketplace for legal services is a competitive one; not only has the size of the profession more than quadrupled in the past fifty years (See 2005 Lawyer Statistical Report, American Bar Foundation), but other professions and businesses have also begun to perform services traditionally restricted to lawyers. For example, accounting firms have encroached on tax litigation, banks in the trusts and estates area, and financial planners in estate planning. In a series of cases, the United States Supreme Court has made it clear that lawyers cannot prevent the development of this competition from both within and without the legal profession.

Furthermore, the technological advances of recent decades have forever changed the way lawyers deliver legal services to clients. If you were to look into a law office circa 1962, and compare it to a law office in 2012, the transformation would be mind-boggling. Hardly any aspect of the office would not have undergone major transformation (from telephones, to computers, to knowledge management systems). Lawyers who fail to understand this evolution cannot hope to succeed in the emerging practice of the future.

My first appreciation of the fact that the practice of law was undergoing a fundamental sea change occurred in 1974, when scarcely six months out of law school, I attended a conference called "Salvation for the Solo Practitioner." The speakers at that program talked about the delivery of legal services as a cottage industry, where most work was performed piecemeal by individuals, who operated much like tailors, cutting each suit individually. There was consensus among the speakers that lawyers needed to develop systems—routine ways to complete regularly recurring transactions—in order to practice efficiently and profitably. Their message, strangely prescient of the unregulated competitive marketplace ushered in by the U.S. Supreme Court's decision in *Bates v. State Bar of Arizona*, 433 U.S. 350, 97 S.Ct. 2691, 53 L.Ed.2d 810 (1977) just three years later, suggested that in order to survive in the future, lawyers needed to change the way they conduct business.

Even today, many practitioners seem to approach the future with their heels firmly planted in the past. They either ignore the changes that are transforming the practice of law, or they react slowly and resentfully to the evolving professional landscape. In truth, lawyers of all ages and experience levels deal with changes in the legal profession and society every day. Some just try to survive, while others try to excel by staying ahead of the curve.

This course is designed to help you do more than survive; its primary objective is to give you the tools to excel in the practice of law. If the average lawyer practices law for forty years, most law students today will be practicing well into the of the second half of the twenty-first century. Assuming that the changes of the past thirty years continue, it makes sense to prepare for the practice of law as it will become in thirty years, not as it was thirty years ago.

Law firms are changing in response to changing times. Large firms created to meet the legal needs of large corporations, are at a crossroads. They may choose (or be forced to) downsize in order to become leaner and meaner, as many corporations did in the nineties. They may outsource many services that were handled in-house in the past, such as libraries, information systems, printing or billing. They may utilize part-time or temporary workers in a variety of positions within the firm, where the work is cyclical, unpredictable, or simply not sufficient to support full-time positions. They may narrow the focus of their practice, divesting certain workgroups that do not fit with the firm's long-term strategic objectives, or bring in lateral expertise to bolster a practice group the firm wants to maintain or build. They may explore the feasibility of relationships with nonlawyer professionals, who can enhance the quality of services they provide to clients. They may review their mix of clients in order to shift the client base to a more favorable market position.

Notwithstanding such efforts to remain competitive, law firms face unprecedented challenges in the face of a rapidly changing economic environment. It is not clear that the economic model of law firms of today will remain sustainable in the future. In a world where more and more employees work online, from home or other locations, the need for immense (and expensive) offices is questionable. In an era when the fundamental relationship between the organization and worker is changing, the merit of retaining a large permanent staff has come under fire. At a time when client autonomy is on the rise, it is uncertain whether approaches that satisfied clients in the past will succeed in the new millennium.

This all leads to is a sense that the legal services industry will undergo a shakeout in the years ahead. Some practices will flourish and grow, while others will wither and fade. For older lawyers within a few years of retirement, it might be possible to escape having to deal with these inevitable changes. For the rest of the profession, the question is not whether to change, but how. The path of success is not altogether clear, and the environment continues to change. Lawyers will need to observe and anticipate—not just react to—trends in the marketplace; they will need to be innovative and creative in finding solutions to problems; they will need to be agile and quick in moving about the practice landscape.

Economic competition in the marketplace is sometimes characterized as a war. Lawyers often view the enemy as consisting of nonlegal competitors, rather than as competitors from within the profession. In truth, competition comes from both inside and outside forces. The war is very different, depending on whether it is viewed through the eyes of the legal profession as a whole, a law firm or other organization that delivers legal services, or an individual lawyer. all are competitors, but all have different stakes in the game.

This is a war that is defined by expectations as much as issues. A lawyer who wants a modest lifestyle and personal freedom will undoubtedly view the war in a different light than a large law firm fighting to hold onto its market niche, or a legal services website attempting to tap into the growing demand for online professional services. Winning this war is much more about figuring out goals for the future, mapping out a strategy, and then achieving success over time, in the face of change, competition and setbacks than it is about taking intellectual positions on issues such as MJP, MDP or the de-regulation of the legal marketplace.

As suggested above, law firms are changing in response to changing times. Large firms created to meet the legal needs of large corporations, are at a crossroads. They may choose (or be forced to) downsize in order to become leaner and meaner, as many corporations did in the nineties. They may outsource many services that were handled in-house in the past, such as libraries, information systems, printing or billing. They may utilize part-time or temporary workers in a variety of positions within the firm, where the work is cyclical, unpredictable, or simply not sufficient to support full-time positions. They may narrow the focus of their practice, divesting certain workgroups that do not fit with the firm's long-term strategic objectives, or bring in lateral expertise to bolster a practice group the firm wants to maintain or build. They may explore the feasibility of relationships with nonlawyer professionals, who can enhance the quality of services they provide to clients. They may review their mix of clients in order to shift the client base to a more favorable market position.

Notwithstanding such efforts to remain competitive, law firms face unprecedented challenges in the face of a rapidly changing economic environment. It is not clear that the economic model of law firm of today will remain sustainable in the future. In a world where more and more employees work online, from home or other locations, the need for immense (and expensive) offices is questionable. In an era when the fundamental relationship between the organization and worker is changing, the merit of retaining a large permanent staff has come under fire. At a time when client autonomy is on the rise, it is uncertain whether approaches that satisfied clients in the past will succeed in the new millennium.

PROBLEMS AND QUESTIONS

1. Have you read stories in the legal press about the dissolution of law firms that have been in practice for decades? *See, e.g,* James B. Stewart, "Dewey's Fall Underscores Law Firms' New Reality," *The New York Times*, May 4, 2012, describing the titanic demise of Dewey LeBoeuf, one of the largest and most prominent law firms in New York; William G. Johnston, "Anatomy of a Law Firm Breakup: A Look at Law Firm Dissolutions from 1998–2004," 84 N.C.L. Rev. 1691. How do you account for the fact that these law firms collapsed? Are they different in any fundamental ways from firms that have managed to stay in business?

2. You are the managing partner in the thirty-lawyer firm of Smith & Jones in a mid-size city. For the past three quarters, the financial reports have showed declining profits. At least part of the reason is attributable to the newly-opened branch office of Fyar & Brimstohn, the largest firm in the largest city in your state. You believe that that many S & J lawyers have become complacent about the importance of retaining current clients and bringing in new ones. It is clear that if things do not improve dramatically in the fourth quarter, partner bonuses for the year will have to be slashed. This could lead one or more of the firm's rainmakers to defect to Fyar, which, if office rumors are to be believed, is already courting them. You know that the firm could not survive such a loss. What can you do to save Smith and Jones?

3. What skills do you possess personally that will help *you* to thrive as a lawyer?

C. THE FUTURE OF THE PRACTICE OF LAW

The future of the legal profession, and by extension the practice of law, is a topic that inevitably provokes controversy in discussions among lawyers, as well as those who describe themselves as futurists. We all know that we cannot predict the future, but we all try to make educated guesses about how the future will be different, and the same as the present. More specifically, we seek to identify paths that will maximize the likelihood of our success in the future and minimize the risk of failure. In the context of this course, events of recent decades have demonstrated that dramatic changes have transformed society and the way lawyers practice. For law students, whose careers will span thirty to forty years, or more, taking the time to think about the future of the practice of law is not just idle pleasure. It is central to what you will be doing, where you will be doing it, who you will be doing it for, and what you will be compensated.

Various state and local bar associations have created task forces to study the future of the profession, and many have sponsored educational programs aimed at helping their members cope with the changing landscape for professional services. One notable inquiry was conducted by the New York Bar Association Task Force on the Future of the Legal Profession. Although their Report is not the first effort to assess the future of the legal profession and the practice of law, it is representative of many similar efforts.

EXECUTIVE SUMMARY
New York State Bar Association Task Force on the Future of the Legal Profession (2011).

The rapid pace of change in the legal profession, accelerated in part by the recent national economic downturn, prompted New York State Bar Association President Stephen Younger to form a task force to examine issues concerning the future of the profession ... [including]: (1) developments in the economics, structure, and billing practices of private law firms; (2) changes in the model for educating and training new lawyers; (3) the pressures on lawyers seeking to find balance between their professional and personal lives; and (4) the implications of technology on the practice of law.

Given the inherent difficulty in predicting the future with certainty, the Task Force studied current trends that are driving change. Understanding these trends provides insights into the probable future in various areas of the legal profession and enables lawyers to manage change as it unfolds.

There is strong evidence that unprecedented changes in practice are producing a restructuring in the way legal services are delivered. These changes include widespread access to legal information, the routinization of many legal tasks, demands by clients for more control of legal service delivery, and the emergence of an increasingly competitive marketplace. This restructuring in the way legal services are delivered affects all law firms—regardless of size, geographic location, and substantive practice area—although it may impact different firms in different ways. Clients are seeking more efficient services, predictable fees, and increased responsiveness to their needs, and they are willing to replace their lawyers if they are not satisfied with the services they receive.

In the area of billing for legal services, the hourly billing model has been strongly criticized by clients and commentators, leading to a shift away from hourly billing to alternative fee arrangements ("AFAs"). There are differing opinions among members of the Task Force as to how fundamental and pervasive this shift in billing practices will be. The Task Force believes, however, that AFAs will continue to expand over the course of the next decade, as a model for compensating lawyers and providing value to clients. The Task Force also believes that hourly billing will not disappear as a fee model in some practice areas.

The economic downturn of 2008–09 produced considerable economic fallout for law firms, including lower earnings, reduced hiring, more downsizing, and greater internal reorganization. As the economy recovers, it is apparent to many observers that the legal profession will not return to business as usual, and that to be successful in the post-recession era, law firms will need to engage in long-term restructuring to maintain sustainability and grow organically. Lawyers also will need to rethink the model and methodology of educating and training lawyers to deliver services and serve clients in the evolving law practice environment.

Competition for legal work will be intense, not only within the legal profession, but also among law firms and nonlegal service providers, foreign law firms, *pro se* litigators and self-help providers, as well as companies that use innovative delivery systems. Law firms that do not understand and address these changes will have difficulty competing in the emerging marketplace. Law firms will need to think more strategically, manage more effectively, and strive to be more client-centered than they have been in the past.

Technology is a driving force for many of these changes. Technology is a double-edged sword that helps lawyers to work faster and more efficiently, yet enables them to work constantly. It permits them to find better solutions to legal problems, yet increases the expectations of clients; assists them to compete more effectively in the marketplace, but opens the door to more competition. Technology has revolutionized the practice of law over the past quarter century. All signs indicate that technology will continue to impact the way lawyers are educated and practice, and will impact the traditional skills associated with lawyering and how lawyers interact with their clients.

. . .

In his book, *The End of Lawyers? Rethinking the Nature of Legal Services*, Oxford University Press (2008), Scottish law professor and futurist Richard Susskind ruminates about how lawyers and law firms will successfully manage the changing technological environment. He suggests that most lawyers practice law the way they always have, treating each case as if it were unique, when in fact much of what lawyers do is routine. Susskind argues that in a competitive technology-driven marketplace lawyers will not be able to pass off routine services as unique, and if lawyers do not figure this out other service providers will step in to do what lawyers presently do—hence the title, *The End of Lawyers*. He challenges lawyers to find ways to practice more quickly, cheaply and efficiently, warning that if they fail to do so, they will not survive in today's marketplace for professional services. Susskind has been widely heralded as a visionary, yet evidence suggests that lawyers have not heeded his call for change.

The future of the legal profession, and by extension the practice of law, is a topic that inevitably provokes controversy in discussions among lawyers, as well as those who describe themselves as futurists. We all know that we cannot predict the future, but we all try to make educated guesses about how the future will be different, and the same as the present. More specifically, we seek to identify paths that will maximize the likelihood of our success in the future and minimize the risk of failure. It is central to what you will be doing, where you will be doing it, who you will be doing it for, and what you will be compensated.

The American Bar Association has sponsored two national conferences, the National Conference on the Role of the Lawyer in the 1980s, held in January 1980, and Seize the Future: Forecasting and Influencing the Future of the Legal Profession, held in November 1999. The ABA also funded a Commission on the Future of the Legal Profession in the early 2000s. The following article comes from a book reporting on the Seize the Future conference. Innovation and change were identified by many of the speakers and participants as pervasive themes for the legal profession in the coming decades. This chapter reflects on how these twin swords can both assist us and entrap us as we contemplate the future of our professional practice.

INNOVATION AND CHANGE

From *Seize the Future: Forecasting and Influencing the Future of the Legal Profession.*
By Gary A. Munneke (American Bar Association 2001).

Change: Change is a constant. The world and everything in it is always changing. Stability is the illusion that the world of tomorrow will be similar enough to the world of today that we will not be totally disoriented when we wake up in the morning. Society seeks to reassure us that the assumptions we make about the way things work will be reliable. The legal system itself attempts to give citizens a sense of security in knowing that a predictable set of laws and rules of procedure will be used to resolve disputes equitably. There is no guarantee, however, that change will not outpace our ability to react. There is no certainty that our well-constructed world will continue to operate the way it always has.

There is a scene in the movie *Dr. Zhivago*, in which the lead character Lara and her suitor, a Russian prince, are dining in a beautiful upscale restaurant, enjoying the fruits of privilege and money. In the distance a rancorous noise can be heard above the diners' animated conversations. The sound gets louder, and soon restaurant patron and moviegoer alike can see that the sound is coming from a peasant mob, tattered and hungry marching through the street. A rock breaks the restaurant window; a melee follows; troops on horses arrive to brutally quell the disturbance. In the bloody aftermath of the riot, fine dining is the last thing on anyone's mind. We learn soon that the street battle was merely the opening round of a revolution that swept away all legacy, tradition and heritage in Imperial Russia. Are lawyers like the hapless protagonists of this film, sitting complacently in their comfortable offices while the revolution unfolds around them?

Trends: Any discussion of change should include an examination of trends. A trend may be defined as a general line of direction, movement or inclination; a statistical tendency. By looking at measurable phenomena over time, we hope to extrapolate statistically detectable movement of those phenomena in the future. If we can identify the trend, we can mold our behavior to maximize the advantage and minimize the risk to our interests in light of changing circumstances.

Trends lie: The problem, of course, is that trends can lie. Throughout the early 1920s, the economy grew steadily; prosperity increased. The trend line was consistently upward. Then, on October 23, 1927, the stock market crashed. In the wake of this crash, the economy collapsed; businesses failed; unemployment soared. The longest economic depression in U.S. history ensued. Many of those who thought that the good times of the roaring 20s would never end, lost their shirts (and everything else) because they relied on a trend that changed.

Trends change: A major mistake made by many roaring twenties prognosticators was to assume that the trend—economic boom—would go on forever. It is a common mistake to think that trends will never change. Almost any straight-line projection eventually changes direction. If a city's population grows at a rate of two percent per year, a straight-line projection would demonstrate that sometime in the future all the people on earth would live in that city. Of course, that is an absurd result; at some point in time the growth pattern slows down or reverses. In the twenties, projections told people that there would soon be a chicken in every pot. Inevitably, the trend reversed.

More information is better: Another mistake made by analysts back in the twenties was to not gather enough data to see the bigger picture. Yes, the economy blossomed throughout the 1920s, but research would have shown that economic cycles of expansion and depression had existed throughout the history of the United States. The real trend was that an economic downturn was highly probable after a period of prosperity. Had analysts obtained more information, they would have anticipated the economic downturn that occurred.

Garbage in, garbage out: On this point the computer guys have it right. In the 1920s, analysts relied on suspect information to base their predictions of continued economic boom. Unscientific anecdotal observations suggested that things would continue to improve. Economic indicators, such as stock prices, real estate prices, and employment rates all pointed to continued economic growth. But subjective observation is inherently myopic. And the economic indicators reflected an artificial expansion driven by behavior that was in turn fueled by the optimistic projections—a vicious and circular spiral. Other ominous signs that might have dictated more conservative behavior were ignored. Companies were over-valued. A growing segment of society did not reap the benefits of the good times. Economies abroad were failing. In retrospect, economists can demonstrate how the roaring twenties produced the great depression. The fact that so few people saw the crash coming should give pause to anyone living in the best of times. When it comes to the data upon which we make projections, if the information is bad, the projections are useless.

Complexity is complicated: A final thought about the 1920s collapse: the depression was not caused by one single triggering event. The stock market crash was a symptom, not a cause. In complex systems, a multitude of variables combine to influence what happens. Trends are the combined effect of the smaller trends in all these variables. Economic failure is a product of multiple negative trends that combine to change the course of events. Just as the depression was started by a complex set of circumstances, recovery in the late 1930s and early 1940s was produced by improvements on a variety of fronts.

At the end of the twentieth century, the American economy [was] strong, and has been healthy with the exception of minor economic recessions since World War II. Most of the people living in the United States today have known only good times. Will the trend continue? Will we experience another great depression? Can we discern in the tealeaves of economic analysis what the future may hold?

Innovation: . . . [I]n a rapidly changing environment, innovation is a key to survival. Those who adapt to change in their surroundings have a better chance of emerging unscathed by sea changes and paradigm shifts than those who try to hold on to old prerogatives, old ways of doing business, and old ideas. Innovation, by definition, rejects old ideas; innovation is radical, creative and dramatic. Incremental change and improved *process* are scant protection from fundamental shifts in the way business operates or people behave.

It may be tempting to regard thinking about the future something we would just rather not do. We all identify a little bit with Scarlett O'Hara, after Rhett Butler walks out the door, answering her question, "What will I do?" with the retort, "Frankly, my dear, I don't give a damn." Scarlett's lament, "I can't let him go. I can't. There must be some way to bring him back. Oh I can't think about this now! I'll go crazy if I do! I'll think about it tomorrow. . . . After all, tomorrow is another day!" *Gone With the Wind* (1939). So it might be useful to take a real-world look at a law firm that saw the world through Scarlett-colored glasses:

WHEN LAW FIRMS FAIL, PARTNERS FEEL SQUEEZE

From Wall Street Journal, by Jennifer Smith, May 21, 2012.

For many attorneys, a law-firm partnership provides a life of steady—and significant—income flow.

But for Andrew Ness and others who work at firms that fail, the road can be much bumpier.

Andrew Ness of Jones Day has lost three equity stakes in law firm partnerships over his career.

Over the course of his career, Mr. Ness, a partner who specializes in construction law in the Washington, D.C., office of Jones Day, has lost three equity stakes, the chunks of money often totaling hundreds-of-thousands of dollars that lawyers pay into a firm upon making partner.

Early on, the small boutique firm where Mr. Ness was first made partner dissolved, taking his money with it. Later Mr. Ness joined Thelen LLP and then Howrey LLP, two now-defunct firms that entered bankruptcy in 2009 and 2011, respectively.

"I did not see a dime of capital returned and don't expect to see a dime," Mr. Ness said.

To be sure, partners at big law firms are typically in a better position—and have a more ample financial cushion—than the legions of secretaries and associate attorneys who lose their jobs when such firms fail.

But partners who flee failing law firms such as Dewey & LeBoeuf LLP, which is heavily indebted and winding down its affairs after a rocky five-month run of partner exits, face a dilemma most job seekers don't. When those lawyers land a new gig, they have to pony up money to join the partnership, often without any guarantee that they will recoup their capital stakes from the previous firm.

The financial hit is magnified for partners like Mr. Ness unlucky enough to have hopped from one dying firm to another.

"These are huge sums of money," said one former Dewey partner. "It's kind of like your retirement fund ... You want to go someplace that's stable at this point, because you just can't afford to take another hit."

Like large medical practices or accounting firms, big law firms are jointly owned by partners. Each has a stake in the business: They invest money into the firm to help it operate, and take in a share of the profit.

Depending on the firm, capital requirements might range from 20% to as much as 60% of what a partner expects to earn in a given year. A young partner could be on the hook for $100,000 to $200,000.

But a seasoned lateral hire from another law firm who pulls in $1 million to $2 million a year might be asked to put in as much as half of what he or she expects to earn in a year. Often, the money is due upfront.

To smooth the path, many firms offer loan programs that allow partners to borrow money at attractive rates while they wait for their old firms to pay back their capital. Repayment can take anywhere from one to five years, depending on a firm's partnership agreement.

Law-firm lenders say capital-loan programs have expanded in recent years, as more firms ask partners to pay equity stakes in full, instead of deducting a portion each year from each partner's share of the profit.

Another boost to loan programs: Firms looking to tidy up their balance sheets and minimize bank debt also have been leaning on partners for additional infusions of cash.

Once a partner signs off on the loans, the money flows from the bank to the law firm. When that partner leaves, the firm sends capital payments straight to the bank until the loan is repaid.

But the lawyer is ultimately on the hook for the loan—and that can be a problem if law firms don't pay the money back as agreed.

Dewey & LeBoeuf has yet to pay return capital owed to dozens of partners who left Dewey Ballantine LLP before it merged with LeBoeuf, Lamb, Greene & MacCrae LLP in 2007, according to those former partners. Those who took out loans from Barclays Bank PLC's corporate-banking division say Dewey began skipping bank payments in 2008 and 2010, citing a lack of funds, then set up a new payment schedule that further delayed the return of capital.

In 2011, Dewey sent those partners quarterly statements indicating that money was being deducted from the firm's capital account and paid back to the bank.

But a former partner who contacted Barclays earlier this year was told that no payments on the loan principal had been made in 2011. In a February email shared with an online group of former partners, Dewey's general counsel, Janis Meyer, said the mix-up was because the statements didn't provide enough room to explain the situation, and promised to pay interest on the missed payments.

Representatives for Dewey & LeBoeuf and Barclays declined to comment.

Many of the partners who joined Dewey & LeBoeuf in 2011 took out loans to satisfy their capital contributions. That burden will likely weigh even more heavily on a number of partners who joined Dewey from Howrey as that firm collapsed. In essence, these partners are down two capital stakes.

Dewey leadership put "a lot of pressure on lateral partners during 2011 to pay their capital in advance," said former partner Henry Bunsow, one of several partners who joined the firm from Howrey.

Brad Hildebrandt, the chairman of Hildebrandt Consulting LLC, said partners whose firms have failed can face serious financial problems.

"It's unfortunate, because most partners didn't have control over the situation," Mr. Hildebrandt said.

When firms fail, he added, "Partners rarely get any capital back, they often have to write checks, and they rarely have any recourse."

PROBLEMS AND QUESTIONS

1. Do you agree with Richard Susskind's prognostications about the future of the practice of law? Do you think that change will be as dramatic as he predicts? What will you do to maximize your chances of success in the changing practice environment you enter? How will you avoid the pitfalls that await the unwary?

2. Suppose that you were appointed to a commission made up of experts charged with identifying the most salient trends affecting the practice of law for the next twenty-five years. What would those trends be? As you look at the predictions of the New York State Bar Association Task Force on the Future of the Legal Profession, do you agree or disagree with their predictions? What are your reasons? What is your evidence?

3. After the article in this chapter was published, Dewey ceased operations and filed for Chapter 11 bankruptcy on May 28, 2012. What happened to Dewey LeBoeuf? Could disaster have been averted?

4. What steps would you take now to assure that you would succeed in the emerging practice environment?

5. Some lawyers do not want to think about the future. They assume either that the future will be an extension of the past, or that whatever changes come along, they will be able to react appropriately. What are the risks and benefits of such a strategy?

CHAPTER 2

THE MARKETPLACE FOR LEGAL SERVICES

■ ■ ■

In this chapter, you will begin to look at the economic marketplace in which lawyers deliver their services to clients. It is a highly competitive marketplace, and the competitors are not only other lawyers but also professional service providers from a variety of different fields. In this changing marketplace, lawyers who do not cope with the demographic, technological, and other changes will not survive economically. Law students entering this environment need to think critically about what they can do to improve their opportunities.

A. LAWYER DEMOGRAPHICS

Starting from the assumption that law is a professional services business, the practice of law may be thought of as the legal services industry. Some lawyers resist thinking of the legal profession as an industry. Yet, in reporting statistics on the legal profession, the United States Department of Labor has referred to the "legal services industry" for over four decades now. The Department's Bureau of Labor Statistics releases periodic estimates of the amount of money Americans spend on professional services. This is the aggregation of legal fees paid by individuals and businesses to law firms and individual practitioners. The estimated gross national product for legal services is over $220.3 billion, according to the U.S. Bureau of Economic Analysis. *See* U.S. DEPARTMENT OF COMMERCE: BUREAU OF ECONOMIC ANALYSIS, Industry Data (2012), *available at* http://www.americanbar.org/content/dam/aba/migrated/marketresearch/PublicDocuments/lawyer_demographics_2012_revised.pdf-3k-2012-06-23.

According to the American Bar Association, there are just over 1,200,000 licensed lawyers in the United States today, of whom more than 74% are in private practice. *See*, AMERICAN BAR ASSOCIATION, *Lawyer Demographics* (2002), *available at* http://www.americanbar.org/content/dam/aba/migrated/marketresearch/PublicDocuments/abalawyer
demographics2012.authcheckdam.pdf. This means that there are approximately 880,000 lawyers delivering legal services to clients. A little quick math leads to the conclusion that the per capita income of lawyers in the United States is approximately $130,490 per lawyer according to the US

Department of Labor, Bureau of Labor Statistics. *See* US DEPARTMENT OF LABOR, BUREAU OF LABOR STATISTICS, *Occupational Employment Statistics, Occupational Employment and Wages May 2011, available at* http://www.bls.gov/oes/current/oes231011.htm#(2). Of course, not all lawyers earn precisely this statistical mean income. Partners in many large corporate firms earn over one million dollars annually, and a few plaintiffs' lawyers may obtain legal fees in seven or eight figures. However, many solo practitioners, especially those in small towns and cities saturated with practitioners, may have an annual income considerably below the national average. Salaried lawyers, including both new lawyers and salaried experienced lawyers (a group whose numbers are increasing), predominantly earn incomes below the national mean.

Law is a highly diversified industry. No single law firm accounts for more than 1% of the gross national legal product, and the largest 100 firms together control only a fraction of the legal business. In law, there is no predominant Microsoft, as there is in the computer software industry. There is no Big Four of law firms, as there is in accounting, although many observers wonder whether the future will produce aggregations of lawyers on a national level. Beginning in the 1970s, the largest law firms became increasingly larger. In 1972, the largest law firms in the United States included just over 100 lawyers each, whereas in 2012—a mere forty years later—there are several U.S. firms of more than 1,000, a truly exponential increase. In the 1970s, almost all law firms operated in one location; today all the largest firms and many smaller ones have offices in many different locations. In the 1970s, international practice was dominated by a handful of law firms that practiced international law, but in today's globalized marketplace for legal services cross-border practice, even for many small firms, has become commonplace.

It is interesting to note that the largest law firm in the world in 2012, Clifford Chance, LLP (with reported revenue in 2011 of $1.873 billion, approximately 6,700 employees today in 27 countries), is a small business organization when compared to other industries. Think about banks, insurance companies, retail conglomerates and industrial organizations. These companies may employ hundreds of thousands, or even millions of people worldwide. By contrast, the typical small law office has fewer than 10 people on staff, including both lawyers and support staff. Conventional wisdom holds that such small organizations inevitably deliver services to a limited number of individual and very small business clients. Conversely, large business organizations with a variety of complex, protracted legal concerns, require larger firms that can deliver services across a wide range of locations and needs. Although technology has made it possible for small service providers to break out of the limitations of localized practice, the broad axiom that small firms represent little people and big firms represent big companies has not changed over the years; what has changed is that the big firms are getting bigger, squeezing out mid-sized regional firms that in prior years filled the void between small and large. Despite the consolidation of law practice into larger and larger firms, small firms of 2–10 lawyers and solo practitioners remain the dominant professional models for law practice.

The American Bar Foundation, has studied lawyers for over forty years by looking at statistics derived from Martindale–Hubbell directory listings. The most recent report, *2000 Lawyers Statistical Report*, reveals some interesting facts about the demographics of legal practitioners.

THE U.S. LAWYER POPULATION IN 2000

From *The Lawyer Statistical Report: The U.S. Legal Profession in 2000.*
Edited by Clara N. Carson.

The United States lawyer population grew from almost 300,000 in 1960 to over one million by the year 2000. The most dramatic rise in lawyer numbers took place during the 1970s and 1980s. In each of those decades, the lawyer population increased by about fifty percent. Since 1951, the growth rate of the lawyer population has regularly exceeded that of the general U.S. population as reflected in declining population/lawyer ratios from 1 lawyer per 695 persons in 1951 to 1 per 264 in 2000. [The population to lawyer ratio has continued to drop. The 2010 U.S. Census places the national population at 308,745,536, while the lawyer population has increased to 1.2 million, for a 1 per 257 in 2010. Ed]

. . .

Components of Lawyer Population Growth

Over time, the growth (or decline) in lawyer population size is the result of an interaction between new admissions to the bar and mortalities among lawyers previously admitted. Yearly statistics are not available for initial/first-time bar admissions for mortalities among bar members. However, the combined effect of new admissions and mortalities on lawyer population growth may be inferred from a comparison of the number of law school degrees conferred in a given time frame with shrinkage during that same period in the number of previously admitted bar members.

An essential component of lawyer population growth in the period from 1960 to 2000 was the steady rise in law school enrollments and a consequent yearly increase in law degrees conferred. Law schools graduated less than 10,000 in the 1963–64 academic year; in academic year 1998–99, graduates numbered about 40,000.

. . .

The net effect of new bar admissions on lawyer population growth is moderated by mortalities. A total of about 750,000 law degrees were awarded between 1980 and 2000. A substantial proportion of this pool of potential bar admission applicants was eventually admitted to the bar. Over the same period (1980–2000), deaths among lawyers admitted prior to 1980 numbered about 110,000.

. . .

The size of the 2000 lawyer population, therefore, represents the outcome of the countervailing effects of new admissions and mortalities in prior years.

. . .

Increased Representation of Women in the Lawyer Population

A concomitant of lawyer population growth in the last three decades has been the rise in the number of women entering the profession. While no more than 3% of the lawyer population in the early 1970s were women, by the year 2000 women made up over one-quarter of the lawyer population.

. . .

As law school enrollments rose, the proportion of first year students who were women grew. In academic year 1963–64, 4% of the first year enrollment were women. From that time forward, women's representation in law school enrollment grew until by academic year 1998–99 women made up 47% of first-year enrollment.

. . .

Of lawyers in the 2000 lawyer population admitted prior to 1970, 3% were women and 97% were men; of admittees between 1970 and 1980, 13% were women and 87% men. In contrast, 39% of 1980–90 admittees were women and 61% were men. Of those lawyers admitted after 1990, 45% were women and 55% were men. As the lawyer population ages and mortalities rise among those older admission cohorts in which men predominate and if admission of women remains high, then the overall population of women in future lawyer populations will continue to grow.

. . .

The Age Distribution of the Lawyer Population

The age distribution of lawyers at first admission has remained stable over time. Since 1960 the median age at initial bar admission has been 26–27 years and the modal age 25 years. About 80% of all lawyers have been admitted by the age of 30 and 97% by age 40.

. . .

In contrast, the age composition of lawyer populations have varied over time in response to changes in the size of new admission cohorts. The median age of the lawyer population in 1960 was 46 years. By 1980, the median had declined to 39 years as the upsurge in new admissions during the 1970s swelled the ranks of young lawyers. The median age began to climb thereafter as the yearly rate of increase in the number of new admissions moderated. By the year 2000, the median age had risen to 45 years as new admission cohorts from the 1970s and 1980s entered their middle years.

. . .

As a result of the delayed entry of substantial numbers of women into the profession until the mid–1970s, the age distributions of the two groups [men and women] vary significantly. While the median age of men in the 2000 lawyer population was 48 and the mode 52 years, the median for women was 40 years and the mode 39 years. Almost one third (32%) of men were 55 years of age or older while less than one tenth (8%) of women were 55 or older.

The difference in the age distributions of men and women in the 2000 lawyer population is attributable to continuing escalation in yearly admissions of women to the bar over the last 30 years. While the male lawyer population in 2000 was 2.5 times the size it had been in 1970, the female lawyer population was 29 times larger than in 1970. As a result, the female population in 2000 was considerably younger than that of males. However, if yearly admissions of men and women continue at post 1990 levels, the differences in age distributions will diminish.

ABF statistics are consistent with those produced by other groups that collect data on lawyers, such as the legal consulting firms Hidebrandt International, PriceWaterhouseCoopers, and Altman & Weil. Despite the availability of these data, lawyers have been surprisingly understudied. There is no national census of lawyers, and very little empirical research. Those who wish to know more about how law is practiced must look at a variety of different sources to gather information.

The fact that many of these sources report similar results may provide a degree of confidence in assessments drawn from statistics, but in the absence of scientifically controlled studies, the validity of such conclusions remains at least partially in doubt. For instance, the *Martindale–Hubbell Legal Directory* used by the ABF to establish the population of lawyers, does not account for many law school graduates who work as lawyers inside business organizations. Such entities frequently do not require bar membership as a prerequisite to employment. Nor does the directory account for lawyers who dropped out of or never entered the practice of law. *The Statistical Report* claims that there were 500,000 lawyers in 1980, and since that time, 750,000 individuals have graduated from law schools. Even considering lawyers' mortality, there is clearly a discrepancy between the number of lawyers who have graduated from law school and the number who report themselves as such to Martindale–Hubbell.

PROBLEMS AND QUESTIONS

1. What do these statistics tell us about the practice of law? Are there lessons to be learned for lawyers that will help them to be more successful if they understand the marketplace in which they operate? What other information about the marketplace for legal services would you like to know?
2. Demographers sometimes talk about trends, such as the trend toward urbanization that occurred throughout the twentieth century, or the trend toward greater numbers of women in the profession. What demographic trends are having an impact on the practice of law today? Are

these trends likely to continue to affect the profession in the future, or will new trends emerge?

3. One trend that has caught the attention of some commentators is the increasing diversity of the population in the United States. Some demographers predict that by the mid-twenty-first century, Caucasians will make up less than 50% of the population, although at current rates, non-Caucasians will comprise only about 10% of the lawyer population. What are the implications of this dichotomy for the practice of law?

4. Take a look at the population of the area in which you think you will practice after graduation from law school. What are the salient features of this population? What significant demographic trends can you identify? How will these trends impact your firm's delivery of legal services in the marketplace?

B. THE COMPETITION

Lawyers practice in a variety of settings, including but not limited to private law firms. They provide many services, not all of which can be described as legal services. Many individuals who are not lawyers and organizations that are note law firms provide services similar to those provided by lawyers. Sometimes lawyers work for these nonlegal organizations and contribute to the delivery of "law-related" services. To make matters more confusing, states have laws prohibiting the unauthorized practice of law, although in many situations, such laws are never or sporadically enforced.

It might be an intriguing question to ask: "What are legal services?" and "What is a lawyer?" Is a lawyer a law school graduate, someone who has passed a bar exam, or someone who provides legal services to clients? Are judges and professors lawyers? What about computer consultants who provide specialized services to other lawyers? And what do we do with the legal press? Are they lawyers because they possess law degrees? These questions are relevant to any attempt describe the legal marketplace. If we define the legal services industry narrowly, we may fail to recognize that increasingly legally trained individuals are providing alternative forms of legal services through organizations that do not resemble traditional law firms at all.

The changing marketplace has produced an undoubted necessity for lawyers to reinvent themselves, their profession and the manner in which legal services are provided; in order to remain competitive in a world where the competitive forces are not only from other lawyers, but also from other industries that have infiltrated the legal services industry. For instance, in many states, title companies have driven practicing lawyers out of the residential real estate closing business. However, lawyers are now also mediators, counselors, financial planners, and agents.

Competition is the operative word for anyone entering the legal marketplace, as it is for members of all other professions. Every law student knows this is true anecdotally from the job-hunting war stories they tell and hear. The statistics bear out the experiences of law students. The legal profession has quadrupled in size since 1950, and almost doubled since 1980. At the same time, the legal services industry, which grew dramatically in the 1980s, consolidated in the 1990s. As a new century begins, competition for business from professional service firms outside the legal profession threatens to undermine the traditional economic base of the legal profession. It does not take a Nobel Prize winning economist to realize the consequence of an increased supply of qualified workers for a stable/unchanged/unchanging demand, namely employment positions.

In the early part of the century, bar associations created unauthorized practice of law ("UPL") committees and lobbied legislatures to pass unauthorized practice statutes. These efforts were designed to protect lawyers' professional monopoly from nonlegal competitors. Over the years, the UPL committees disappeared and states only enforced the most egregious forms of unauthorized practice. The result of this retrenchment was a shrinking of lawyers' monopoly to the giving of legal advice and representation of clients in court. It is not that lawyers are prohibited from engaging in other forms of client service, it is just that other types of organizations can do the same things. More than ever before, lawyers must convince potential clients that they provide valuable services for a reasonable price.

UNAUTHORIZED PRACTICE OF LAW COMMITTEE v. PARSONS TECHNOLOGY

United States District Court, N.D. Texas, 1999.
1999 WL 47235.

SANDERS, SENIOR JUSTICE. Before the Court are Plaintiff's Motion for Summary Judgment.... The Court heard oral argument on the cross-motions for summary judgment on December 17, 1998.

Having considered the motions, briefs, and arguments of both parties, and for the reasons set forth below, the Court concludes that there are no genuine issues of material fact and that Plaintiff Unauthorized Practice of Law Committee is entitled to judgment as a matter of law. Therefore, Plaintiff's Motion for Summary Judgment is granted and Defendant's Motion for Summary Judgment is denied.

I. BACKGROUND

The Plaintiff, the Unauthorized Practice of Law Committee ("the UPLC"), is comprised of six Texas lawyers and three lay citizens appointed by the Supreme Court of Texas. The UPLC is responsible for enforcing Texas' unauthorized practice of law statute, Tex. Gov't Code 81.101.106 (Vernon's 1998) ("the Statute").

The Defendant, Parsons Technology, Inc., ("Parsons") is a California corporation, whose principal place of business is Iowa, and is engaged in the business of developing, publishing and marketing software products, such as *Quicken Financial Software, Turbo Tax,* and *Webster's Talking Dictionary.* Parsons has published and offered for sale through retailers in Texas a computer software program entitled *Quicken Family Lawyer,* version 8.0, and its updated version *Quicken Family Lawyer '99* ("QFL").

QFL is the product at the center of this controversy. In its most recent version, QFL offers over 100 different legal forms (such as employment agreements, real estate leases, premarital agreements, and seven different will forms) along with instructions on how to fill out these forms. QFL's packaging represents that the product is "valid in 49 states including the District of Columbia;" is "developed and reviewed by expert attorneys;" and is "updated to reflect recent legislative formats." The packaging also indicates that QFL will have the user "answer a few questions to determine which estate planning and health care documents best meet [the user's] needs;" and that QFL will "interview you in a logical order, tailoring documents to your situation." Finally, the packaging reassures the user that "[h]andy hints and comprehensive legal help topics are always available."

The first time a user accesses QFL after installing it on her computer the following disclaimer appears as the initial screen:

> This program provides forms and information about the law. We cannot and do not provide specific information for your exact situation.
>
> For example, we can provide a form for a lease, along with information on state law and issues frequently addressed in leases. But we cannot decide that our program's lease is appropriate for you.
>
> Because we cannot decide which forms are best for your individual situation, you must use your own judgment and, to the extent you believe appropriate, the assistance of a lawyer.

This disclaimer does not appear anywhere on QFL's packaging. Additionally, it does not appear on subsequent uses of the program unless the user actively accesses the "Help" pull-down menu at the top of the screen and then selects "Disclaimer."

On the initial use of QFL, or anytime a new user name is created, QFL asks for the user's name and state of residence. It then inquires whether the user would like QFL to suggest documents to the user. If the user answers "Yes," QFL's "Document Advisor" asks the user a few short questions concerning the user's marital status, number of children, and familiarity with living trusts. QFL then displays the entire list of available documents, but marks a few of them as especially appropriate for the user based on her responses.

When the user accesses a document, QFL asks a series of questions relevant to filling in the legal form. With certain questions, a separate text box explaining the relevant legal considerations the user may want to take into account in filling out the form also appears on the screen. As the user proceeds through the questions relevant to the specific form, QFL either fills in the appropriate blanks or adds or deletes entire clauses from the form. For example, in the "Real Estate Lease—Residential" form, depending on how the user answers the question regarding subleasing the apartment, a clause permitting subleasing with the consent of the landlord is either included or excluded from the form.

If a user selects a "health care document" (i.e., a living will, an advance health care directive, or a health care power of attorney) the following screen appears:

> Health Care laws vary from state to state. Your state may not offer every type of health care document. Family Lawyer assumes that you wish to have a health care document based on the laws of your state. When you select a living will, health care power of attorney, or advance health care directive, Family Lawyer will open the appropriate document based on your state.

> When a Texas user selects a health care document a form entitled "Directive to Physicians and Durable Power of Attorney for Health Care" appears.

. . .

The UPLC filed this action in state court alleging that the selling of QFL violates Texas' unauthorized practice of law statute, Tex. Gov't Code § 81.101.

. . .

III. ANALYSIS

. . .

The UPLC moves for summary judgment because it claims, as a matter of law, the sale and distribution of QFL violates the Statute. The UPLC argues that QFL gives advice concerning legal documents and selects legal documents for users, both of which involve the use of legal skill and knowledge, and this constitutes the practice of law. Additionally, the UPLC argues that the Defendant's forms are misleading and incorrect. In sum, the UPLC alleges that QFL acts as a "high tech lawyer by interacting with its 'client' while preparing legal instruments, giving legal advice, and suggesting legal instruments that should be employed by the user." In other words, QFL is a "cyber-lawyer."

No one disputes that the practice of law encompasses more than the mere conduct of cases in the courts. *See In re Duncan,* 65 S.E. 210 (S.C.1909) (finding that the practice of law includes "the preparation of legal instruments of all kinds, and, in general, all advice to clients, and all action taken for them in matters connected with the law."). However, a comprehensive definition of just what qualifies as the practice of law is "impossible," and "each case must be decided upon its own particular facts." *Palmer v. Unauthorized Practice of Law Committee,* 438 S.W.2d 374, 376 (Tex.App.—Houston 1969, no writ); *see also State Bar of Michi-*

gan v. Cramer, 249 N.W.2d 1, 7 (Mich.1976) ("any attempt to formulate a lasting, all encompassing definition of 'practice of law' is doomed to failure.").

. . .

Based on the interpretations of the Statute by the Texas courts, QFL falls within the range of conduct that Texas courts have determined to be the unauthorized practice of law. For instance, QFL purports to select the appropriate health care document for an individual based upon the state in which she lives. QFL customizes the documents, by adding or removing entire clauses, depending upon the particular responses given by the user to a set of questions posed by the program. The packaging of QFL represents that QFL will "interview you in a logical order, tailoring documents to your situation." Additionally, the packaging tells the user that the forms are valid in 49 states and that they have been updated by legal experts. This creates an air of reliability about the documents, which increases the likelihood that an individual user will be misled into relying on them. This false impression is not diminished by QFL's disclaimer. The disclaimer only actively appears the first-time the program is used after it is installed, and there is no guarantee that the person who initially uses the program is the same person who will later use and rely upon the program.

QFL goes beyond merely instructing someone how to fill in a blank form. While no single one of QFL's acts, in and of itself, may constitute the practice of law, taken as a whole Parsons, through QFL, has gone beyond publishing a sample form book with instructions, and has ventured into the unauthorized practice of law.

Parsons attempts to avoid the conclusion that it is guilty of the unauthorized practice of law by arguing that the Statute requires personal contact or a lawyer-client relationship. Parsons bases its argument first on the language of the Statute, which it contends requires that the prohibited services must be provided "on behalf of a client" in order to be the practice of law.

Even assuming that Parsons is correct that paragraph (a) of the Statute requires the prohibited services to be completed "on behalf of" a client, paragraph (a) of the Statute is not an exclusive definition of the unauthorized practice of law. Paragraph (b) of the Statute gives the Court the authority to determine that other acts constitute the unauthorized practice of law. Therefore, a judge could legitimately determine, under the authority granted in paragraph (b), that services provided to the public as a whole, as opposed to a singular client, qualify as the practice of law.

. . .

Parsons' arguments to the contrary notwithstanding, QFL is far more than a static form with instructions on how to fill in the blanks. For instance, QFL adapts the content of the form to the responses given by the user. QFL purports to select the appropriate health care document for an individual based upon the state in which she lives. The packaging of QFL makes various representations as to the accuracy and specificity of the forms. In sum, Parsons has violated the unauthorized practice of law statute.

. . .

III. CONCLUSION

Plaintiff's Motion for Summary Judgment is GRANTED. Defendant's Motion for Summary Judgment is DENIED. . . .

PROBLEMS AND QUESTIONS

1. What is a lawyer? Does it matter how we define the term? If we assume that in many situations lawyers bring their legal skills and training to bear on the work they do, does it follow that they will bring a legal approach to occupations outside the law? For example, if a lawyer is employed by a bank as a trust officer, will the lawyer be more cognizant of drafting issues in documents, conflicts of interest, and other legal concerns than nonlawyers employed in the same position? Will the lawyer trust officer be more or less willing to refer legal issues to outside counsel for advice?

2. Should the marketplace for legal services be a competitive one, driven by supply and demand, or should the legal industry be regulated? If regulated, who should police the profession? If de-regulated, who will protect clients and the public from lawyer misconduct?

3. The Texas Legislature amended its UPL statute after the Parsons case to permit QFL, Nolo Press and other groups to operate legal Websites. What are the implications? Will law firms be forced to compete for business with a variety of nonlegal service providers? Assuming that nonlegal competitors can deliver services less expensively than lawyers, how do lawyers make the case that consumers should turn to licensed lawyers for their legal needs?

4. Can you think of other nonlawyers who compete with lawyers for legal business? What advantages do these providers have over lawyers? What advantages do lawyers have over the non-lawyer providers? Is it possible to regulate the delivery of legal services by nonlawyers, or is it too late to turn back the clock?

C. LEGAL EMPLOYMENT

The economy has had an impact on the job market for new and experienced lawyers alike. Beginning with the financial meltdown in 2008, law firms experienced a decline in legal work, as their clients felt pressure to reduce costs in order to survive a sagging economy. Less legal work meant fewer legal jobs. The situation was exacerbated by changes in the business model for law firms, mounting student debt for law school graduates and a backlog of unemployed lawyers competing in a shrinking job pool. The next article examines the job market circa 2012, as the economy improves.

RACE TO THE FINISH LINE: LEGAL EDUCATION, JOBS AND THE STUFF DREAMS ARE MADE OF

From New York State Bar Association Journal, by Gary Munneke, (February 2012).

For much of 2011, the legal press and b*law*gosphere produced a non-stop litany of negative stories about the dismal job market for lawyers and the failings of legal education in the United States. These critics argued that the law school value proposition no longer worked for students, who assumed significant student loan burdens and then entered a job market where many would not find legal jobs that paid the bills and serviced their debt. Anecdotal evidence suggested that graduates could make ends meet only by going to work for the most prestigious, highest-paying firms, despite declining job opportunities in that sector. Law schools, it was suggested, actively misrepresented their job-placement statistics in order to sustain a bankrupt system of legal education, which did not prepare graduates for the practice of law or the realities of the job market they would encounter. Commentators further noted that, over the past two decades, the cost of legal education had increased faster than the rate of inflation.

It is true that the recession of 2008–2009 seriously undermined the job market for both new and experienced lawyers. It is also true that legal education is expensive, and many students pay for it through loans that have to be repaid after graduation. And it is well documented that some law schools misstated employment and other statistics in the tight, competitive job market of recent years. But connecting the dots in this case does not lead to a conclusion that our system of legal education is bankrupt or that law school is not an excellent career choice for many students. This article will attempt to re-connect the dots in a way that more accurately reflects contemporary legal education and the job market for lawyers.

. . .

It has always been the case that not all law graduates will find employment with the highest-paying firms. Generally, the more elite the law school, the more likely are its graduates to snag those lucrative positions as associates in the largest firms. During the '80s and '90s, as the marketplace for legal services grew dramatically, more students from more schools were hired by top-tier firms. We should not kid ourselves; even in those heady days, not all graduates got those jobs. And, on some level, law students in that era knew the same thing my classmates knew: not everyone would.

Yes, the cost of legal education has risen astronomically since I was in law school. It is also true that the cost has increased in large measure because schools offered more clinics, more skills courses and smaller sections of traditional courses than they did when I was in law school. This does not negate the fact that it did get harder to pay for law school. Increasingly, students who lacked family financial resources have needed financial aid and loans in order to attend law school, and these loans have often been added to the burden of the loans that paid for undergraduate school. Even before 2008, observers lamented the fact that graduates could not afford to accept legal service and public interest jobs, because their student loans made such career choices infeasible—which again reminds us that the cost of legal education has been a growing issue for some time. Yet, many students did make the sacrifices needed to accept jobs in the public sector and in small Main Street firms that paid dramatically less than the salaries enjoyed by their Wall Street cousins. In fact, before the Great Recession, the overwhelming majority of graduates of most law schools did not go to work for BigLaw at big salaries.

When the Great Recession arrived in 2008, it affected the legal job market in a number of ways. Large law firms cut back on hiring, rescinded offers, told people to travel the world for a year, laid off "unproductive" associates and partners, and outsourced legal work to less-expensive providers. Evidence suggests that smaller firms did not behave with such draconian abandon and instead elected to hunker down and tighten their belts until things got better. These firms did not bring on new associates or lateral partners, but they did not engage in the same kind of downsizing that characterized large firm hiring. As a result of decreased hiring throughout the legal marketplace, the law school classes of 2008 and 2009 found limited opportunities. Even as things got better in 2010 and 2011, new graduates found themselves in competition with grads from the previous two classes. The outlook for 2012 appears better than it has been for several years, but graduating law students remain nervous about their prospects.

They have reason to be nervous. Even though the job market has improved, it has not returned to its pre–2008 vigor. In the world of corporate practice, general counsel were scrutinizing outside legal costs with an eye toward reducing expenses. They increasingly refused to pay to train start-up lawyers who did not possess the skills to handle legal work on their own. Many general counsel (individually and collectively through the Association of Corporate Counsel) called for an end to the inefficient hourly billing model. They experimented with Alternative Fee Arrangements, outsourcing legal work and requests for proposal before awarding legal bids. Companies explored non-litigation dispute resolution alternatives to reduce costs and increase predictability. On top of all this experimentation, the economy hung like a dark cloud, and the cold, hard reality was that there was just less legal work to go around.

Signs abound that the market for legal services is picking up, in concert with the general economy. Surveys and anecdotal reports tell us that there is once again more work for lawyers. It is not likely, however, that we will return to those halcyon days before 2008. The billable hour is equally inefficient in good times and bad, a fact well known to corporate counsel. New associates are no more practice-ready than they were before the recession. Some of the sheen has evaporated from the veneer of outsourcing—at least overseas—but the principle of contracting out work that can be done more economically seems rather recession-proof. Alternative dispute resolution is just as attractive in recovery as it was in recession. In short, corporate clients want a better deal, and we can expect them to pursue it.

In the world of individual and small-business representation, smaller firms have not experienced the same shakeout that has impacted the large-firm market. The threats to the viability of their firms have come more from online and non-legal service providers encroaching on work traditionally handled by lawyers, and pro se representation. To some extent, small firms and solo practitioners have faced increased competition from lawyers riffed by big firms, and by graduates who did not find employment in the large-firm market. The marketplace on Main Street has been more competitive than before the Great Recession, and the greatest shift has been the pressure to specialize in limited fields of practice in order to improve efficiency and profitability.

One other phenomenon affecting the legal job market (and which has gone largely unreported) is the increasing use of permanent staff by law firms of all sizes. In the past, most firms were divided into two classes of lawyers: partners and associates. Partners could leverage the work of associates to improve profitability. Firms were organized in such a way that, over time, associates were weeded out (or they left of their own volition), and some who stayed were eventually elevated to partnership. For whatever reason, losses in the associate ranks created new entry-level openings, and new law school graduates stood ready to fill those vacancies.

Now, however, a number of firms have eliminated the up-or-out system, converting experienced associates into "non-equity partners," "of counsel," "staff lawyers" or "permanent associates." By doing so, law firms could continue to leverage the expertise of these lawyers and save on the recruiting and training costs associated with hiring new lawyers. Thus, if the associates who go in do not go out, then there will be fewer new jobs for those eager to come in.

The point is that the economic model for law firms has been changing, and these changes often result in less entry-level hiring. The recent recession masked this evolution, because the faltering economy also produced a decline in job openings. What we will see, however, in the coming years as the economy improves is that law firms, going forward, will not look like law firms of the past. This trend is likely to be most pronounced in larger firms, but it will have an impact on small-firm hiring as well. To the extent that there is less hiring in large firms, more graduates can expect to earn lower salaries.

The American Bar Foundation reports that approximately 65% of all lawyers work in the private practice of law, and of these 20% (or 13% of all lawyers) work in large firms. The largest segment of the marketplace belongs to solo practitioners who account for more than 40% of all those in private practice (or 26% of all lawyers). Employment statistics for recent graduates are comparable, except that the number of graduates who go directly into solo practice has traditionally been less than 5%—although many lawyers become solos at some point in their careers. During the recession, fewer graduates found work in law firms and more decided to hang out a shingle. As the economy improves, the number of graduates who open their own practice will probably return to pre-recession levels, although law firm hiring will not reach pre-recession highs. This suggests two important developments in the job market.

First, more entry-level lawyers will earn salaries on the lower end of the spectrum. If the employment pattern projected above comes to pass, slightly more graduates will find themselves in the same situation as more than half of the graduates today, and before the Great Recession. With respect to graduates who go to work for small firms, government agencies, not-for-profits and other organizations, anecdotal evidence suggests that they do pay their bills and repay their loans. Chicken Littles who cry that it cannot be done are simply wrong. Thousands of law school graduates have been following this path for years. It may not be as easy to get by when you are making $60,000 compared to $160,000, but somehow you do it, and you survive.

As a profession, we should be working to create and support programs that permit restructuring of student loans and provide for loan forgiveness for graduates who accept public service/public interest jobs that pay less money. We should remind ourselves that one unchanged statistic over the past four decades (and probably more) is that 80% of the people in the United States do not have a regular lawyer, and many individuals either cannot afford a lawyer or do not have access to legal services. The same thing is true for many small businesses. There is plenty of legal work to go around; we need to find ways to fund these unmet legal needs....

Second, those who claim that there are not enough legal jobs to go around fail to understand that the job market for lawyers is incredibly elastic, because a law degree is incredibly malleable and flexible. In the early 1970s, the ABA created a Task Force on Professional Utilization to study what it called the "oversupply of lawyers." The thinking was that law schools were spewing out so many graduates that the legal job market could not absorb them. The final report of the Task Force concluded that while not all graduates could find work in law firms (especially the most prestigious ones), they did find work. Graduates also went to work in non-legal and non-law-related jobs in business, industry, government, education, private associations, NGOs, and virtually every other conceivable work environment. Every form of human endeavor encounters legal issues, and lawyers, whether they are practicing law or not, can address those legal issues. And lawyers bring with them a skill set that can be applied in a variety of different settings. What the Task Force found was that the job market could absorb law school graduates—when there were fewer law firm jobs, more lawyers pursued alternative careers; and vice versa. One might argue that if you are not going to practice law, why should you go to law school? The answer is that a legal education provides training that will give you an advantage in the job market—both in getting the job and performing the job. What the Task Force discovered in the 1970s remains true today.

Many lawyers who work in the legal services industry practice in small shops, alone or with one or two other lawyers (although computers now make home practice feasible). Some writers have referred to large firms as factories, and small firms as "mom and pop" shops, although the analogy is a flimsy one at best. For both large and small firms, technology and the routinization of legal work have imbued the practice of law with an assembly line quality, and profitability (or lack thereof) has become a dominant topic for partners in all types of law firms.

Size; however, is what truly characterizes the legal services industry in the United States. It is an oft-repeated statement that there are more lawyers in the U.S. today than any other country—now or at any time in the past. Such pronouncements often neglect to mention the point that American society is incredibly pluralistic and diverse; legal issues permeate every facet of society and may be either simple or very complex.

Changes in the demand for legal services and in the delivery of legal services also are having a profound effect on the legal services industry, as the legal profession evolves to accommodate demand. The following passage from *Seize the Future: Forecasting and Influencing the Future of the Legal Profession*, a book based on a 1999 American Bar Association Law Practice Management Section national conference on the future of the practice of law, captures a sense of this change:

PRACTICE SETTINGS

From *Seize the Future: Forecasting and Influencing the Future of the Legal Profession.*
By Gary A. Munneke (2001).

Prior to World War II, most lawyers practiced alone. Approximately eighty percent (80%) of all lawyers were in private practice, and three-fourths of those were solos. The largest firms in the country included between 25 and 50 lawyers. In-house corporate counsel positions were rare; at one time, some ethicists argued that it was improper for a lawyer to work in-house where his independent judgment could be compromised. Following the War, law school enrollments mushroomed with returning vets. This began a steady growth in the lawyer population from around 220,000 in 1950 to almost one million in 1999.

During the last half of the 20th century, the number of institutional multi-lawyer law firms increased dramatically. The largest firms grew to 100, 500, and eventually over 1,000 lawyers. Employment with corporations increased also as in-house positions became common. An expanded regulatory framework at federal, state and local levels led to more hiring of more lawyers by government entities. In addition, lawyers with greater frequency began to work in a variety of other settings where their legal skills were put to use outside traditional private practice settings.

The makeup of the profession has continued to change. Entering the 21st century, only about sixty percent (60%) of all lawyers are in private practice, and only about forty percent (40%) of these are solos (although the actual number of solo practitioners is not too different from what it was in 1950). More organizations now employ lawyers for a variety of activities, in lieu of hiring outside counsel.

The globalization of markets also means that an increasing number of American lawyers are working outside the boundaries of the United States. Although it is difficult to determine because there are no accurate records, it appears that significant numbers of law school graduates have abandoned the legal profession entirely for work organizations in unrelated fields. Some of these graduates never planned to practice law, while others left practice after a stint in the traditional profession.

After 1977, when the *Bates* decision triggered the deregulation of legal services marketing, lawyers began to develop creative variations on the traditional law firm model in order to become or remain competitive. Sophisticated practitioners attempted to define themselves in terms of a market niche. For some lawyers, this meant a shift from general to specialty practice, and an increasing number of lawyers now define themselves in terms of a substantive practice concentration. Other lawyers have developed a boutique practice area by catering to a narrow clientele or providing a very specific service. The concept of unbundling legal services contemplates that a lawyer or a law firm provide one particular part of a legal transaction (e.g., a lawyer who only handles appeals to the U.S. Supreme Court).

As the practice of law has become more complex, the emergence of multi-disciplinary practice has created waves within the legal profession. Interestingly, most lawyers today work with professionals from other fields in some way on a regular basis. Legal services and other professional services today are interwoven with increasing frequency. The organized bar, citing ethical concerns, has resisted the proliferation of multi-professional practice relationships.

Notwithstanding continued prohibition against law firms forming partnerships or sharing fees with non-lawyers, an increasing number of informal affiliations between lawyers and law firms and nonlegal enterprises have appeared. Many non-legal professional organizations have begun hiring lawyers to engage in work that would be considered practicing law in a law firm, but which is described as consulting or advisement by the non-legal service provider. Although lawyers retain the exclusive right to represent others in court, the limit of lawyers' professional monopoly has eroded over the past fifty years. Prosecution for the unauthorized practice of law has declined, and at least one state, Arizona, has decriminalized unauthorized practice.

The rise of the Internet further expands the reach of professional service providers, as well as blurs the line between practicing law and providing law-related information. Not only are many lawyers utilizing the Internet to provide services and attract clients, but other e-businesses are providing similar information and services. . . . [W]e can expect to see in the first few years of the 21st century, the rise of e-lawyering, the commoditization of online products as competition drives down prices, disintermediation that removes lawyers from many transactions, followed by e-bundling of legal services with other services. Thus, the combination of legal and nonlegal services in cyberspace will parallel the continued growth of multidisciplinary practice in the physical world.

The proliferation of information and services will give rise to the need for effective research and demand from clients for help in sorting through the morass of information. E-commerce will trigger a call for non-commodity expertise. The role of the lawyer as trusted advisor, one of the traditional bastions of legal service will regain prominence, as consumers struggle to make sense of a complex new world full of changing rules with legal implications.

These new rainmakers will distinguish themselves by bringing value to transactions. They will have the skill to sell themselves either in person on online. They will not require affiliation with a law firm or other formal organization in order to ply their trade. They may associate on an informal or short-term basis with a number of other organizations, both inside and outside the legal profession.

These changes will increase pressures to reduce jurisdictional barriers to practice. Although state licensing of lawyers for trial practice will continue to be common, the necessity for licensing in transactional activities will diminish. Despite calls for abolition of the bar exam, examination of candidates may become even stricter, with skills testing and greater focus on the professional responsibility issues, as well as substantive legal questions. Some states, in order to resist multidisciplinary and interstate practice, may use the licensing process to keep out interlopers.

Balanced against this reactionary response, more law school graduates will forego the bar examine entirely when they accept employment with organizations for which licensure is not a prerequisite. Law schools themselves will be forced to become more relevant to the practice of law, but because practice settings will become increasingly diverse, law schools will have to become more specialized. The law schools of the 21st century will be less cookie-cutter imitations of Harvard, and more unique institutions that serve a more clearly defined audience of practitioners. Law schools will foster multidisciplinary practice by continuing to build interdisciplinary studies programs.

The trend for law school graduates to accept positions in government, corporations, and other organizations outside the practice of law will continue. As multidisciplinary practice opportunities increase, many law school graduates will gravitate to those positions. Experienced lawyers will also abandon private practice for positions in business, industry and government. Multidisciplinary practices will recruit and hire legal talent from the ranks of experienced lawyers. The organized bar will have to work to incorporate these non-practicing lawyers into membership, or these lawyers will form their own specialized professional groups.

These examples are intended to make you think about the industry you will be entering soon. Consider the career options that are available, and the economics of the legal markets you are considering. Think about the geographic areas, substantive fields of practice and types of organizations that you are considering. You may seek help from your law school career service office, a lawyer mentor, a professor, or your own research. Most law students do not devote enough time to analyzing the economics of practice in light of their personal aspirations. This topic is taken up again in Chapter 13, and is discussed in more detail in *The Legal Career Guide From Law Student to Lawyer*, by Gary Munneke and Ellen Wayne (ABA, 2007).

PROBLEMS AND QUESTIONS

1. Practicing lawyers sometimes refer to "a glut of lawyers in the marketplace." Does this mean that there are too many lawyers or that lawyers in practice do not want any more competition? If there is an oversupply of lawyers, is it equally divided throughout the marketplace, or are some practice settings and geographic areas more saturated with legal talent than others?
2. What are the advantages and disadvantages of engaging in the private practice of law? Can you "practice law" without joining a law firm or opening your own office?

D. ECONOMICS OF THE LAW BUSINESS

The economics of law practice are fairly simple, for both large and small law firms. Lawyers in private practice deliver a legal work product—advice, representation, documents, research—to clients for money, in the form of legal fees. Although institutional practices such as government law offices, in-house counsel and public interest practices may not depend on selling their services on the open market in order to exist, private practitioners must market their services to potential clients in need of the services provided by the firm.

The law firm incurs costs associated with the delivery of legal services—for office space, equipment, staff and operations—that must be covered by the fees paid by clients. The partners, or owners of the firm are paid in the form of profit; thus, if there are no profits, the owners do not get paid. Unless the lawyers are independently wealthy and do not need to earn a living (something that is rare indeed), if the practice does not generate a profit, the firm will not stay in business for long.

A variety of surveys have explored how much money lawyers make from the practice of law. Recent law school graduates earn between $10,000 per year to more than $200,000, with a median of $93,748, in 2010, according to the National Association for Law Placement, an organization that has been surveying starting salaries for lawyer since the early 1970s (see http://www.nalp.org/salarycurve_classof2010). However, these numbers are somewhat deceptive. A graph of starting salaries shows a bimodal curve with one cluster of about 48% of all graduates between $40,000—$65,000, and another cluster of about 18% between $160,000–$165,000. These two clusters account for 76% of all graduates, leaving the remaining 24% scattered through the rest of the salary range. Generally, associates in the largest law firms in major cities earn the highest salaries, although corporate counsel and associates in mid-sized firms earn salaries above the median. Federal government lawyers and associates in smaller urban firms earn pay at or around the norm for the lower cluster. Lawyers who go to work for legal aid, public defenders, public interest organizations, and small town law firms are likely to earn salaries below the lower cluster.

Unlike the situation for starting salaries of recent graduates, it is more difficult to get a handle on the income levels of practitioners. Practically speaking, incomes for all lawyers include both the lowest associates to the highest paid partners—a considerable range to be sure. Moreover, there does not exist a single reliable source for information; however, the U.S. Bureau of Labor Statistics, various state and local bar association economic surveys, private consulting reports, research commissioned by the legal press and the American Bar Foundation *Lawyer Statistical Report* (see page 18) all provide information about how much money lawyers earn. A few generalizations follow:

- Average income has been reported between $70,000 and $150,000 depending on the survey. For instance, if the sample of respondents includes government and other institutional lawyers, the average is probably lower than a survey of private practitioners. Or if the respondents are not randomly selected, the results may be skewed toward the high end. A good estimate of the average lawyer's income is probably about $100,000.

- Law firm partners make more than associates and other employed lawyers. Associate salaries typically increase 4–5% per year above the starting salaries for 2–10 years of employment. The average for partners is harder to gauge, because there is great variance in partner income. The average has been reported at between $125,000 and $150,000.

- The larger the firm the more money partners earn. In some of the largest firms, partner draws exceed $1,000,000 per year. The lowest income levels are for solo practitioners; several surveys place their income levels at $75,000 or less annually. Interestingly, however, some of the most lucrative practices are highly successful solos and small firm plaintiffs personal injury practices (think of the income from one-third of ten $10,000,000 settlements).

- Lawyers in larger cities make more money than lawyers in small towns and rural areas. In fact, there is a strong positive correlation between population and lawyer income. However, other factors, such as proximity to natural attractions or the number of law schools in the area, may cause lawyer incomes to be higher or lower than those in other cities of similar population.

- Places that have institutional business, e.g., government and corporate offices, often have higher lawyer income levels, in part because of the availability of institutional legal work, and in part because the jobs created by these institutions often contributes to a strong economic base in the surrounding community.

- By limiting the number of owners (i.e., partners), and increasing the number of employed lawyers and support staff, the owners may be able to increase their income by means of leverage. For example, a solo practitioner may earn a gross income of $300,000 (1,500 hours @ $200/hour) and have overhead expenses of $150,000 (50% of gross). If the same practitioner hires an associate who generates $225,000 (1,500 hours @ $150/hour) and $112,500 incremental costs (50% of gross, including the associate's $65,000 salary), the additional profit of $112,500 accrues to the benefit of the owner, who now earns $262,500.

What all this means is that it is difficult to predict with certainty how much money an individual lawyer just graduating from law school will earn over the course of her career. It is highly probable that her income will be significantly higher than the median for the general population, and that she will earn a comfortable living. It should also be apparent that, for the most part, lawyers do not get rich practicing law; as an old family lawyer once quipped, "Rich lawyers were either born that way or went to work for their clients, but they didn't get rich practicing law." One might point to someone like Peter Angelos, a Baltimore practitioner who cashed in on asbestos litigation and then bought the Baltimore Orioles baseball team, but out of the million lawyers in the United States, Angelos is the exception not the rule.

In fact, most law students do not consider that if they go to work for $65,000 (typical for a small firm in New York City, the salary paid in the example above), and they work 3,000 hours (2,000 billable hours and 1,000 non-billable hours, assuming they can charge two-thirds of the time they are in the office to client matters), the hourly rate for 3,000 hours comes out to $21.67/hour. The 3,000 hours would come out to 60 hours per week

(50 weeks counting two weeks vacation), or six ten-hour days (not unusual at all for an associate workload). It is possible to insert different salaries and workloads, but any way you slice it, the hourly rate of pay for associates is much less than many think.

Another consideration is the opportunity cost of law school. In addition to the $50–100,000 cost of a legal education (which may be reflected in even larger student loans that cover living expenses), the law student postpones entry into the job market for at least three years. Let's take a look at what this might look like:

Assume that two college roommates each finished college in 2013. One of them goes to work for a bank at $30,000 per year and the other goes to law school paying out $25,000 per year. Assume also that the law student goes to work for the solo practitioner described above for $65,000 annually, and pays back $6,000 student loan debt each year, until the principal and interest are retired after 20 years. Finally, assume that the law graduate and the banker earn 5% raises annually, and that the lawyer's base increases to $100,000 upon making partner after six years. For the first ten years, the lawyer is behind the banker, and only catches up when the lawyer becomes a partner in the law firm. This is certainly an example of delayed gratification for the lawyer. Nor is it a choice without risk. Not all associates become partners, and not all small firm associates start at $65,000. Although a new lawyer in a large law firm might make more money and catch up sooner, most law graduates do not receive the most lucrative salaries, and a much smaller percentage of lawyers in larger firms ever make partner. Students might be able to avoid amassing student loans by working and going to law school part time, attending lower-cost state law schools, or pursuing career options with loan forgiveness programs, but the bottom line is that the economic realities for recent law school graduates can be intimidating, especially for those who came to law school with rose-colored glasses.

A continuing theme in this course will be the economic model for law firms. A law firm, whether it is a solo practice or a mega-firm of more than 1,000 lawyers delivers legal services to clients. It must pay the bills, including the salaries and benefits of employed lawyers and support staff. The profit—what is left after all the bills are paid—provides compensation to the owner(s) of the firm. If the firm cannot generate enough fees to produce a profit, the firm cannot stay in business, because the owners do not get paid.

Even in an institutional firm, like a corporate law department, where the general counsel's office is a cost center for the business, the operations of the department must come in at or under budget. Thus, although the general counsel does not have to earn his salary through profits from the delivery of legal services, managing expenses is critical to the efficient functioning of the department.

Unless you were born wealthy, or earned your fortune before entering law school, or your circumstances allow you to play at law, you are like the vast majority of all lawyers. You need to work to earn a living.

PROBLEMS AND QUESTIONS

1. What economic trends in the practice of law do you think will continue to influence the marketplace for legal services during your professional career? Would it make sense to offer narrow, highly-specialized services in a boutique practice? Will law offices in the future unbundle their services, offering only segments of a transaction, e.g., deposition services?

2. If there will be winners and losers in the war to claim the marketplace for legal work, how will you maximize your chances of attaining your personal and professional objectives?

3. Take a look at the description of Winters & Sommers, LLP, in Appendix P, page 505. What is your assessment of this firm's prospects for the future?

Chapter 3

Business or Profession?

■ ■ ■

A. PROFESSIONAL VALUES

In recent years, some commentators have argued that increased emphasis on business practices by lawyers has undermined the traditional values of the legal profession. These critics view the focus of law firms on marketing, economics, billing, efficiency and profitability as inconsistent with fundamental professionalism. They would take us back to simpler days when pursuit of the almighty dollar did not dictate decisions about client service and when greed did not trump integrity in the practice of law.

Other observers argue that professionalism and sound business practices go hand in hand, and that lawyers cannot attain true professionalism without effectively marketing their services to clients, managing the legal work product and operating their offices profitably. These pundits note that a high percentage of the complaints against lawyers are related to administrative mistakes, as opposed to substantive errors, and suggest that those who cut corners because they are not doing well financially are the most likely to engage in unprofessional conduct. They recognize that the profession and professional values evolve as society itself evolves and that professionalism is a product of the times.

Let us debunk one misconception up front. Those who say that Law cannot be a business and a profession at the same time are wrong. The truth is that law is both a business *and* a profession—a professional service business. Debates over whether law is a business or a profession sometimes obscure the underlying truth that lawyers must be good at business if they are to be professional. The question is not whether or not law is a money making trade, but whether or not lawyers can provide affordable, quality services to clients and make a decent living at the same time. It is not a question of choosing between business behavior and professional behavior, but a question of how the requirements of professionalism govern the way we lawyers do business.

This article addresses two of the most hotly debated issues in the practice of law today. Discussion in the ABA and other bar associations about the permissible scope of lawyer associations with other professionals permeated bar politics for the last half of the 1990s. Regardless of the issues, the choices lawyers make collectively continue to impact the way individual lawyers practice law.

PRACTICING LAW ACROSS GEOGRAPHIC AND PROFESSIONAL BORDERS: WHAT DOES THE FUTURE HOLD?

From Loyola Law Review, by Ann L. MacNaughton and Gary A. Munneke.
47 Loy. L. Rev. 665, Summer 2001.

In the 1960 musical comedy Please Don't Eat the Daisies, Doris Day sings, "When I was just a little girl, I asked my mother, What will I be? Will I be pretty? Will I be rich? Here's what she said to me: Que sera, sera. Whatever will be, will be." Lawyers, like the protagonist of the 1960 film Please Don't Eat the Daisies, seem to be asking what the future will bring to the practice of law. As players in a competitive marketplace for professional services, however, the simplistic answer, que sera, sera, is not very helpful. Perhaps the phrase epitomizes the futility of seeking 1950s wisdom to address fundamental practice questions in the twenty-first century. In order to succeed in the new millennium, practitioners will need to come to grips with a number of critical issues. "What will be, will be," will simply not be enough.

A new global business reality is transforming the practice of law. Nowhere is this transformation more apparent than in the areas of multijurisdictional and multidisciplinary practice. These two trends, towards practice across jurisdictional boundaries on the one hand and across professional boundaries on the other, are engaging the attention of lawyers at the American Bar Association, the Canadian Bar Association, the American Corporate Counsel Association, the International Bar Association, as well as numerous other state and local, international, and specialty bar associations. This article describes that new business reality, those trends, and some of the ethical constraints presented by current rules of professional conduct.

An Evolving Marketplace

Four aspects of the new economy are changing how business enterprises perceive and manage legal and business risks. First, a context of constant rapid change combined with widely differing values around the world is producing an evolution in business mores. This shift, in turn, contributes to conflicting standards governing business conduct worldwide. What this means to lawyers is that they face an increased risk of inadvertently violating jurisdictional laws, professional standards, administrative rules, or client expectations. Business transactions increasingly do not fall neatly within the geographic boundaries of a single jurisdiction; business in today's world typically crosses state lines and, increasingly, international boundaries. The advent of e-commerce promises, or threatens, depending on one's point of view, to produce a marketplace without geographic boundaries.

Second, globalization of business and a parallel consolidation of marketplaces create a business environment in which today's competitor may be tomorrow's joint venturer, partner, or merged entity. When such events combine with revolutionary changes in technology, old models for solving problems, like yesterday's computers, can become obsolete. Business venturers in the interconnected global marketplace of the twenty-first century will increasingly emphasize dispute avoidance strategies, cooperative business solutions, sophisticated models for cost-shared dispute resolution, and systems for creating competitive advantage through collaborative conflict management.

The Chinese symbol for "crisis" may be useful in understanding the transformational changes occurring in today's networked business world and how they impact the role of lawyers. That symbol is made up of two pictographs that, taken individually, mean "danger" and "opportunity." Both danger and opportunity are present to lawyers serving business enterprises that are redesigning themselves with new strategies, structures, and systems to compete by "working beyond their boundaries." Organizational charts are continuing to flatten, non-core businesses are being divested or out-sourced, and entrepreneurial activity is being stimulated inside and outside corporate corridors. The resulting network of merged entities, joint ventures, strategic alliances, and global trading sectors brings together a community of people with sharply differing values, experiences, and expectations. Managed well, this diversity can generate new solutions and tremendous productivity. Managed poorly, the conflict creates fertile soil for misunderstandings, disagreements over how best to accomplish even agreed objectives, polarized disputes that consume massive quantities of time and money; and ultimately failed ventures and lost opportunities.

Third, commercial and regulatory complexities often require interdisciplinary solutions from teams of professionals with an appropriate blend of business, legal, and relevant technical training and experience. In search of improved client service models, multidisciplinary solutions providers are creating new strategic alliances, and bright lines among professional services firms are beginning to blur.

Finally, the technology revolution continues to expand dramatically the interpersonal one-on-one, one-to-many, and many-to-one connectedness around the world. We can move our bodies, our voices, our images, and our information around the globe at will. E-mail has replaced telephone and fax as the preferred method of communication in many instances; now, video-conferencing is becoming as common today as e-mail was then. Attention is shifting to development of advanced web-based knowledge management and information sharing applications that enable more effective global compliance with regulatory requirements, transmission of advice and work product, paperless discovery, online dispute resolution, web-based marketing and sales, and myriad other purposes. Lawyers and others in firms of every size—the biggest of the big and the smallest of the small—are finding new ways every day to connect to clients, the public, and each other through the Internet.

Law practice today exists in an evolving global milieu in which practitioners encounter increased impact from multinational business enterprises and their needs for cooperative business solutions. For example, environmental practice has always been multidisciplinary in nature. Now, however, new competitors are offering integrated professional services to address problems that may have legal aspects through firms that are not necessarily owned by lawyers. Innovative solutions providers blend business, legal, and various types of technical expertise with common sense to help clients avoid disputes, resolve unavoidable ones efficiently, and create new value. Many other practice areas are experiencing the same kind of interdisciplinary evolution.

Current Events and Future Trends

Current events and future trends do not provide a basis for predicting the future, but they do provide a basis for helping to shape it. Although even careful study will not permit precognition, knowing and understanding economic, cultural, demographic, and technological trends can help observers identify and evaluate possible future developments, which in turn makes it possible to develop strategic plans that start with the preferred end in mind.

. . .

The practice of law is not immune to changes occurring throughout society. Although it is possible to argue the extent to which some of these changes will occur, or the timing of changes, it is difficult to deny that every aspect of society is dramatically different than it was fifty or one hundred years ago. Few among us are willing to stake our fortunes on an assumption that the bulk of the change is behind us. Instead, the more plausible assumption is that change will continue to occur in the short-term future and that the pace of change will accelerate....

Market dynamics creating our networked commercial world have profound implications for lawyers, for the delivery of legal services, and for the management of law practices. Most business lawyers, whether in-house or in private practice, are accustomed to providing a mix of legal and practical advice in conjunction with diverse other professionals whose expertise also is important in fashioning a solution for a particular problem. The question for professional service providers, including law firms, is not whether they will provide multidisciplinary services in this world, but whether they will be able to deliver such services efficiently, economically, and competently, while at the same time protecting ethical standards of confidentiality, loyalty to clients, and avoidance of interest conflicts.

. . .

The advice we give is almost always a mixture of practical or technical business advice, common sense, and experience, together with advice on the legality or legal consequences of the possible solution to the problem or the contemplated transaction or its structure. In functioning as such givers of advice many of us, or our firms, already have significant, established working relationships with other professionals, including not just accountants but engineers, property appraisers, financial consultants, and business and management consultants, to name just a few. At present these are informal relationships that do not involve sharing of legal fees or joint ownership of professional entities, a part of whose business is the practice of law; but all of us see the potential benefit to our clients and our own practices of being able to formalize these relationships, thus attracting and retaining the best members of other professions to work with us, or permitting us to join with them, and facilitating ever closer coordination of our join efforts in advising our clients on the wide range of considerations, both legal and non-legal, involved in avoiding or resolving legal, business, and personal problems or engaging in particular transactions.

. . .

Interdisciplinary Dispute Resolution Strategies

Twenty-five years ago, many corporate lawyers believed the best way to control litigation costs was through aggressive pursuit of legal rights and remedies with the objective of crushing the other side(s) to any controversy. Massive litigation—and massive litigation budgets—resulted. In 1976, the national Pound Conference was convened to consider problems of increased expense and delay in a crowded judicial system. It recommended public funding of pilot programs using mediation and arbitration, to direct disputants to various appropriate dispute resolution ("ADR") processes including for example litigation, arbitration, mediation, summary jury trial, and mini-trial.

. . .

Interdisciplinary teaming is common in business negotiations. International energy deals, for example, typically require a team of lawyers, managers, negotiators, geoscientists, economists, accountants, financial analysts, information management specialists, and other professionals. In-house teams may work with outside counsel, outside negotiators, outside litigation consultants, and/or other outside experts.

. . .

Only diverse professionals working together as a team could have created this innovative solution. Such interdisciplinary teaming is common for in-house lawyers working in nonlawyer owned business enterprises. Lawyers, however, are limited in the way that they can utilize interdisciplinary teams to reach innovative solutions. Current rules must change in order for outside professional services firms to provide similar value.

. . .

Conclusion

Our networked global community places high value on dispute avoidance strategies, and dispute resolution methodologies that preserve or enhance important relationships. Commercial and regulatory complexities often require interdisciplinary solutions.... These trends support the development of cooperative solutions through coordinated interdisciplinary teamwork among team members and stakeholders who may be geographically remote but work together closely through electronic communication and information-sharing tools and systems.

The legal profession is re-inventing itself in the face of increasing demands for integrated professional services and cooperative business solutions such as early case analysis, assisted negotiation strategies, and enterprise-wide solutions. International competition in global markets for client service is creating pressure for change. Delivery of legal services in the United States is restricted, at least as to United States lawyers, by economic constraints that have no counterpart in many other jurisdictions. Multijurisdictional interstate, international, and e-commerce transactions add to the complexity of the situation.

Important questions such as how to further the public interest without sacrificing or compromising lawyer independence, and how to protect the legal profession's tradition of loyalty to clients, are being addressed and will be answered as this process of change unfolds. As the State Bar of Texas Business Law Section Advisory Report pointed out, this will permit "attracting and retaining the best members of other professions to work with us, or permitting us to join with them, and facilitating ever closer coordination of our joint efforts in advising our clients on the wide range of considerations, both legal and non-legal, involved in avoiding or resolving legal, business, and personal problems or engaging in particular transactions."

In the final analysis, lawyers must remember that they bring something of value to transactions. The knowledge and skills of those trained in the law will always have a place in resolution of complex problems, because human problems by their nature have legal implications. Whether the legal profession finds ways to assure that lawyers can participate in and contribute to evolving problem solving models remains to be seen. Lawyers collectively can stick their heads in the sand, or sit back and sing, "Que sera, sera. What will be, will be," or they can choose to make choices about what the future looks like. The opportunity is ours, and the time is at hand.

PROBLEMS AND QUESTIONS

1. What is a profession? Why is important for lawyers to think of themselves as professionals? What do these considerations have to do with managing a law practice?

2. The article above talks about a networked global community in which countries, states, people and institutions are connected as they never have been before. What are the implications for the practice of law inherent in such an environment? In what ways do lawyers and law firms in the globalized community have to practice differently than their predecessors?

B. MULTIJURISDICTIONAL PRACTICE

Multijurisdictional practice (MJP) in the United States has followed an interesting path. Historically, a lawyer licensed in one state, let's say New York, was treated as a nonlawyer by states where she was not licensed, like New Jersey and Connecticut. As transportation and communication reduced the isolation of states, and national/uniform laws reduced jurisdictional differences, exceptions began to emerge. One of the first was for "pro hac vice" admission in litigation, by an out-of-state lawyer, often with a requirement by the court to retain "local counsel."

In other areas, however, the situation has been murkier. Prior to filing pleadings, for example, it was unclear whether a lawyer could go to another state to interview a potential witness to determine if litigation was permitted. If a lawyer advised a client in another state about matters that dealt with national, as opposed to state law, such as federal income taxation or Title VII civil rights, he risked charges of unauthorized practice. *See, e.g., Ranta v. McCarney*, 391 N.W.2d 161 (N.D. 1986). Corporate counsel, let's say a lawyer licensed in New York working for the IBM legal department there, risked UPL charges if she did the same work at IBM's facility in Austin, Texas. Questions were raised as to whether a lawyer from one state traveling to another state could conduct work for clients in her home state from the visiting state via computer or cell phone on a case back home.

Lawyers who practice in any of these situations work under a cloud. At worst they could be charged with the unauthorized practice of law, and at best treated like they are not "real" lawyers by members of the local legal community. The reality of modern practice, however, is that lawyers inevitably cross state borders daily. States appropriately desire to regulate predatory lawyers who would come into their jurisdictions to engage in the practice of law on a permanent and continuing basis without obtaining licensure, but the extension of this principle to purely temporary activities seems out of step with the evolving practice of law.

The situation was brought to a head in *Birbrower v. Superior Court of Santa Clara County* where the California court refused a New York firm's claim for legal fees from a California client, because the New York lawyers were not licensed to practice law in California. Although the law firm could recover on a *quantum meruit* basis fees for any work involving New York law, the New York lawyers were effectively engaged in the unauthorized practice of law when they advised a California client on matters involving California law. Considering the number of law firms that actively engaged in cross-jurisdictional representation at the time, *Birbrower* sent shock waves through the halls of more than a few law firms.

BIRBROWER v. SUPERIOR COURT

Supreme Court of California, 1998.
17 Cal.4th 119, 70 Cal.Rptr.2d 304, 949 P.2d 1.

HERLIHY, JUSTICE. This case involves the question of whether an out-of-state law firm, not licensed to practice law in this state, violated section 6125 when it performed legal services in California for a California-based client under a fee agreement stipulating that California law would govern all matters in the representation.

I. FACTS

Defendant Birbrower, Montalbano, Condon & Frank (Birbrower) is a professional law corporation incorporated in New York, with its principal place of business in New York. During 1992 and 1993, Birbrower attorneys, Kevin F. Hobbs and Thomas A. Condon (Hobbs and Condon), performed substantial work in California relating to the law firm's representation of ESQ. Neither Hobbs nor Condon has ever been licensed to practice law in California. None of Birbrower's attorneys were licensed to practice law in California during Birbrower's ESQ representation.

ESQ is a California corporation with its principal place of business in Santa Clara County. In July 1992, the parties negotiated and executed the fee agreement in New York, providing that Birbrower would perform legal services for ESQ, including "All matters pertaining to the investigation of and prosecution of all claims and causes of action against Tandem Computers Incorporated (Tandem)." The claims against Tandem, a Delaware corporation with its principal place of business in Santa Clara County, California, related to a software development and marketing contract between Tandem and ESQ dated March 16, 1990 (Tandem Agreement). The Tandem Agreement stated that "The internal laws of the State of California shall govern the validity of this Agreement, the construction of its terms, and the interpretation and enforcement of the rights and duties of the parties hereto."

While representing ESQ, Hobbs and Condon traveled to California on several occasions. In August 1992, they met in California with ESQ and its accountants. During these meetings, Hobbs and Condon discussed various matters related to ESQ's dispute with Tandem and strategy for resolving the dispute. Hobbs and Condon also met with Tandem representatives on four or five occasions during this trip to California. At the meetings,

Hobbs and Condon spoke on ESQ's behalf. Hobbs demanded that Tandem pay ESQ $15 million.

Around March or April 1993, Hobbs, Condon, and another Birbrower attorney visited California to interview potential arbitrators and to meet again with ESQ and its accountants. In August 1993, Hobbs returned to California to assist ESQ in settling the Tandem matter. Hobbs also met with Tandem representatives to discuss possible changes in the proposed agreement. Hobbs gave legal advice during this trip, including his opinion that ESQ should not settle with Tandem on the terms proposed.

ESQ eventually settled the Tandem dispute, and the matter never went to arbitration. Before the settlement, ESQ and Birbrower modified the contingency fee agreement. The modification changed the fee arrangement from contingency to fixed fee, providing that ESQ would pay Birbrower over $1 million. The original contingency fee arrangement had called for Birbrower to receive "one third (1/3) of all sums received for the benefit of the Clients ... whether obtained through settlement, motion practice, hearing arbitration, or trial by way of judgment, award, settlement, or otherwise ...."

II. Discussion

A. *The Unauthorized Practice of Law*

The California Legislature enacted section 6125 in 1927 as part of the State Bar Act, a comprehensive scheme regulating the practice of law in the state. J.W. v. Superior Court, 17 Cal. App.4th 958, 965, 22 Cal. Rptr.2d 527 (1993).... In our view, the practice of law "in California" entails sufficient contact with the California client to render the nature of the legal services a clear legal representation. In addition to a quantitative analysis, we must consider the nature of the unlicensed lawyer's activities in the state. Mere fortuitous or attenuated contacts will not sustain a finding that the unlicensed lawyer engaged in sufficient activities in the state, or created a continuing relationship with the California client that included legal duties and obligations. Our definition does not necessarily depend on or require the unlicensed lawyer's physical presence in the state. Physical presence here is one factor we may consider in deciding whether the unlicensed lawyer has violated section 6125, but it is by no means exclusive.

Exceptions to section 6125 do exist, but are generally limited to allowing out-of-state attorneys to make brief appearances before a state court or tribunal. They are narrowly drawn and strictly interpreted. For example, an out-of-state attorney not licensed to practice in California may be permitted, by consent of a trial judge, to appear in California in a particular pending action. (See In re McCue, 211 Cal. 57, 67, 293 P. 47 (1930)). In addition, with permission of the California court in which a particular cause is pending, out-of-state counsel may appear before a court as counsel pro hac vice. (Cal. Rules of Court, rule 983.)

B. *The Present Case*

The undisputed facts here show that our "sufficient contact" definition of "practice law in California" would not excuse Birbrower's extensive practice in this state. Nor would any of the limited statutory exceptions to section 6125 apply to Birbrower's California practice. As the Court of Appeal observed, Birbrower engaged in unauthorized law practice in California on more than a limited basis, and no firm attorney engaged in that practice was an active member of the California State Bar. In 1992 and 1993, Birbrower attorneys traveled to California to discuss with ESQ and others various matters pertaining to the dispute between ESQ and Tandem. Hobbs and Condon discussed strategy for resolving the dispute and advised ESQ on this strategy. Furthermore, during the California meetings with Tandem representatives in August 1992, Hobbs demanded Tandem pay $15 million, and Condon told Tandem that he believed the damages in the matter would exceed that amount if the parties proceeded to litigation. Also, in California, Hobbs met with ESQ for the stated purpose of helping to reach a settlement agreement and to discuss the agreement that was eventually proposed.

C. *Compensation for Legal Services*

The Court of Appeal found that Birbrower violated section 6125 when it engaged in the unlawful practice of law in California, and that its fee agreement with ESQ was unenforceable in its entirety. The Court of Appeal did not credit Birbrower for some services performed in New York, for which fees were generated under the fee agreement. The Court reasoned that the agreement was void and unenforceable because it included payment for services rendered to a California client in the state by an unlicensed out-of-state lawyer. We agree with the Court of Appeal to the extent it barred Birbrower from recovering fees generated under the fee agreement for the unauthorized legal services it performed in California. We disagree with the same court to the extent it implicitly barred Birbrower from recovering fees generated under the fee agreement for the limited legal services the firm performed in New York.

Section 6125 applies to the practice of law in California; it does not, in general regulate law practice in other states. Thus, although the general rule against compensation to out-of-state attorneys precludes Birbrower's recovery under the fee agreement for its actions in California, the severability doctrine may allow Birbrower to receive its New York fees generated under the fee agreement. Only if we conclude the illegal portions of the agreement pertaining to the practice of law in California may be severed from those parts regarding services Birbrower performed in New York. (11 A.L.R. at pp.908–909 . . .)

The law of contract severability is stated in Civil Code section 1599. Section 1599 states, "Where a contract has several distinct objects, of which one at least is lawful, and one at least is unlawful, in whole or in part, the contract is void as to the latter and valid as to the rest." Thus, the portion of the fee agreement between Birbrower and ESQ that includes payment for services rendered in New York may be enforceable to the extent that the illegal compensation can be severed from the rest of the agreement.

III. Disposition

We conclude that Birbrower violated section 6125 by practicing law in California. To the extent the fee agreement allows payment for those illegal local services, it is void, and Birbrower is not entitled to recover fees under the agreement for those services. The fee agreement is enforceable, however, to the extent it is possible to sever the portions of the consideration attributable to Birbrower's services illegally rendered in California from those attributable to Birbrower's New York services.

Birbrower raises issues for all situations where a lawyer licensed in one or more other states engaging in legal work in another state where she is not licensed, including the practice of law on the Internet, a medium that implicitly operates in a world without borders. Multijurisdictional practice (MJP) can include everything from e-mail to phone calls, as in *Birbrower*, to lawyers following their own clients' interests across state lines, to lawyers doing work on their laptops on vacations out-of-state, to lawyers opening permanent offices in states where they are not licensed.

Following the *Birbrower* decision, the ABA, after two years of extensive study and debate, adopted changes to Model Rule 5.5 on the Unauthorized Practice of Law, to include provision for MJP. These amendments allow a lawyer from one state to engage in legal work on a temporary basis in a state where she is not licensed, so long as the lawyer does not establish a permanent presence (such as an office) in the visiting state or hold herself out as admitted in that state. The ABA appears to have turned its sail in the direction of MJP, although not all states have immediately followed suit by adopting the ABA Rule, and not all of the questions have been answered.

PROBLEMS AND QUESTIONS

1. Do the proponents of MDP and MJP present convincing cases? What are the arguments by opponents for retaining the status quo? Suppose that the year is 2025, and all the prohibitions restricting lawyer involvement with nonlegal enterprises (i.e., Model Rules 5.4, 5.5 and 5.7) have been eliminated. What kind of organization would you create to deliver legal services to clients? Would it make sense to operate as a multidisciplinary professional services firm providing one-stop shopping for clients?

2. With the advent of e-commerce, considerably more information is now available on the Internet. many law firms as well as other information and service providers are entering this new business arena. What impact will e-lawyering will have on traditional law practice?

3. What should the *Birbrower* lawyers have done differently? Is it enough to say that an attorney who is not licensed in a state should not give legal advice in that state? Are jurisdictional practice barriers in an interconnected practice environment just another form of protectionism for local interests, or are there important policies that support protecting clients from out-of-state lawyers? What do the clients want? Was the client in *Birbrower* unhappy with the service or just trying to skip out on the bill? If the former, what could the attorney do to avoid the perception of inferior service? If the latter, what can the attorney do to protect herself from deadbeat clients?

4. The overarching question raised by *Birbrower* is whether there should be a national practice of law? Should law school graduates take one bar exam and be admitted to practice everywhere? Should a license to practice work like a driver's license, permitting licensed lawyers to enter other states, but presuming them, subject to sanction, to know the law and court rules? In a world dominated by telecommunications and the Internet, are jurisdictional boundaries less and less meaningful? Should clients of one state be denied counsel of their choice because local authorities want to keep the legal business in state? Will nationalization of the practice of law eventually lead to the end of mom and pop law shops to the domination of practice by coast-to-coast law businesses (think McLawFirm or Wal-Law)?

5. Does the concept of state control of the licensing process for lawyers make sense in a world where transactions, client interests, and legal work transcend not only state, but also national borders? How would you change or replace the present system? How will your law firm adapt to the realities of modern multijursidictional practice?

C. CROSS-PROFESSIONAL PRACTICE

The ABA and most state bar associations have taken a resolute stand in opposition to lawyers forming business arrangements with nonlawyers, both individual and institutional (see Model Rule 5.4). Notwithstanding this opposition, there is growing interest among some lawyers in the concept of cross-professional practice, including shared offices, ancillary businesses, joint marketing, cross-referrals, cooperative and controlled business arrangements, informal affiliated service networks, and other ventures. These practices provide synergies for a wider variety of professional services than available in traditional law firms, by bringing together teams of experts with different skills to solve clients' problems holistically. Such arrangements permit different professionals to share the costs of marketing services to common prospective clients, although they also tend to blur the distinction between legal and nonlegal work, as well as the separation between lawyer and nonlawyer partners or owners.

During the early 1990s, the ABA engaged in protracted debate over the issue of law firm diversification, that is, the degree to which law firms could own ancillary nonlegal businesses. Proponents argued that law firms needed to be able to respond to the needs of their clients by offering a wider range of services; opponents charged that ancillary businesses inescapably violated the ethical rules (See Model Rules 5.4, 5.5). These rules prohibit lawyers from entering into a partnership with a non-lawyer if any of the activities involves practicing law, sharing fees with a non-lawyer, allowing a non-lawyer to influence the lawyer's independent professional judgment and assisting a non-lawyer in the unauthorized practice of law. In the end, by adopting Model Rule 5.7, which permitted ancillary business with certain restrictions, the ABA acknowledged that ancillary businesses were not per se improper, but admonished that law firms needed to be sensitive to the ethical rules if they created nonlegal or law-related businesses. *See* Gary A. Munneke, *Dances with Nonlawyers: A New Perspective on Law Firm Diversification*, 61 FORDHAM L. REV. 559 (1992).

In 1999, the diversification problem resurfaced in the form of multi-disciplinary practice ("MDP"). Although the ancillary business debate pitted traditional practitioners against other lawyers who desired to practice law more creatively, the MDP issue emerged as other professionals, most notably accountants, began to encroach upon lawyers' turf by offering combined legal and nonlegal services, including tax advice, accounting, financial planning, and business management consulting.

In the case of multidisciplinary practice (MDP), the ABA voted in 2000 to reaffirm its longstanding prohibition in Model Rule 5.4 against lawyers forming partnerships or sharing fees with nonlawyers, thereby preventing lawyers from creating so-called one-stop shopping multidisciplinary practices (MDPs). Notwithstanding this action, the debate has continued, as lawyers and nonlawyers have experimented with the delivery of cross-professional services through relationships that do not involve formal partnerships or fee sharing. Undoubtedly, innovative approaches to service delivery will produce innovative forms of organization. Many of these new delivery systems will be controversial, and some may be challenged in court. All the evidence, however, points in the direction of lawyers practicing in increasingly diverse organizational settings as they strive to serve clients more efficiently and effectively.

PROBLEMS AND QUESTIONS

1. Proponents of lawyers practicing with nonlawyer professionals argue that such practices improve the quality of legal services by putting together a team of people who can help clients where the nature of the problems is seldom entirely legal? Is this true? Reformers also claim that lawyers oppose sharing legal fees and ownership of legal work for purely economic reasons, i.e., because they do not want the competition. Is this accurate?

2. Opponents of cross-professional practice insist that because nonlawyers are not subject to lawyer professional responsibility rules, arrangements where lawyers and nonlawyers work together and share fees are antithetical to the values of the legal profession. What do they mean by this?

3. ABA Model Rule 5.4 prohibits investment in law firms by nonlawyers, which means in effect that law firms cannot have nonlawyer limited

partners or sell stock to capitalize their organizations. Australia and the United Kingdom do allow nonlawyer investment in law firms. Does the UK/Aussie model create an advantage to firms from those countries in competition with U.S. firms in the globalized marketplace for legal services? Why or why not? Why would a law firm want to raise more capital anyway?

D. SPECIALIZATION

Another big trend in the delivery of legal services is the movement away from general practice and toward specialization. The legal profession has never embraced specialization like the medical profession. In fact, when a lawyer passes the bar exam, she is presumed to be competent to practice in all areas of the law. The absurdity of this proposition on its face should be enough to make the point, but the truth is that many lawyers and law firms describe themselves as being "General Practitioners."

ABA Model Rule 7.4 (which is followed by most states), dealing with claims of specialization, appears in the section of the Rules that deal with advertising legal services, reflecting the traditional view that specialization was merely a way to get clients, not a way to practice competently, efficiently or profitably. The following article takes on the conventional wisdom that lawyers can be all things to all people and suggests a new paradigm where practitioners are at least de facto specialists.

REQUIEM FOR A GENERAL PRACTICE: THE END OF AN ERA

From New York State Bar Association Journal, by Gary Munneke, (Feb. 2011).

Sometime in the mid-twenty-first century, an event will pass almost unnoticed in the public eye, a short announcement in *The Global Lawyer*, successor to the present day publication, *The American Lawyer*. It will read something like this:

Last GP Closes Doors

Harvey Witsworth, 79, of Elizabethtown, New York, shuttered his office door, handed over his few remaining files to other lawyers, and headed into the mountains for a well-earned retirement, photographing flora, fauna and landscapes of the Adirondacks. He leaves behind his secretary of fifty-two years, Mavis Blanchard, who it was said by locals ran both his office and his life. Witsworth, a general practitioner, once described himself as a "womb—to-tomb lawyer," adding that he could "handle every legal problem a person might have, from the day they were born 'til the day they died." Members of the North Country Bar Association recalled Witsworth as the last bastion of an era when lawyers took whatever cases came their way, regardless of the type of law or complexity. Ada Rondack, a tax lawyer and president of NCBA, mused, "It's truly amazing. A lot of lawyers didn't even know that GPs still existed, and now, I guess they don't. We'll miss you Harvey."

By the time Harvey Witsworth heads for the hills, lawyers will have stopped being jacks and jills of all trades, and become a variety of very specific subspecies in the genus *advocatus*. They will have traded the mantle of GP for the labels of Tax Lawyer, Divorce Lawyer, Real Estate Lawyer and every other imaginable substantive field of law. They will identify themselves as Civil Trial Lawyers, Criminal Defense Lawyers, Appellate Lawyers and Transactional Lawyers as well.

Even in 2010, while Harvey is still a young lawyer learning his craft, people do not look for just a lawyer; they want a Tax Lawyer or a Divorce Lawyer or Real Estate Lawyer. And practitioners oblige them, by telling potential clients what cases they do (and do not) handle. The lawyer who cannot describe what kind of work she does simply cannot attract clients seeking counsel expert in specific fields of practice. The lawyer who does not have a practice concentration cannot concentrate on becoming really good in any field of law. The lawyer who takes whatever cases come her way will lose the good cases to other lawyers who are more focused.

It might prove useful to try to understand why practice concentration leads to more successful outcomes than generalization, because more efficient economic models will supplant less efficient ones in the marketplace. Assume that there are two practice models and one of them produces better services at a lower cost to clients with a higher return for the lawyers than the other. In such a situation, over time, lawyers will gravitate to the more efficient model. In the practice of law, niche practices win out over general practices, and eventually, through a process of natural selection, the Harvey Witsworths of the world will decline and eventually disappear, as the Ada Rondacks proliferate and prosper.

One stumbling block in this economic Darwinian scenario is that inefficient economic systems can be perpetuated by government policy and/or regulation. Remember the old socialist economies of Eastern Europe? Although these systems proved economically unsustainable, they were held in place for years by repressive governments that blocked reform. Some would say that the British royal family represents such an anachronistic system, as it lumbers on, supported by the will of the British people, long after most of the old European monarchies were swept away by reform or revolution.

In the case of the legal profession, the GP model is kept alive by a system of licensure and discipline, which perpetuates the myth that lawyers in America practice law the way Atticus Finch practiced in *To Kill a Mockingbird*.[1] The truth is that even in small towns in rural county seats, lawyers like Atticus are a dying breed. Why is our allegiance to the Atticus myth so strong? Perhaps we admire the Finch values of honesty, integrity, loyalty and fairness that underscore the Atticus figure in the book. We want to be like Atticus, and we have ensconced these core professional values in our ethics rules. Atticus would take on a just cause, no matter what the odds against him and no matter how unpopular his

---

1. Harper Lee, TO KILL A MOCKINGBIRD, (J.B. Lippincott 1960).

client. Atticus was a pillar of the community and a beloved parent at the same time. Atticus could handle any case that came along, because, well, because he was Atticus.

Furthermore, in the world of Atticus Finch, clients came to see him because he had a reputation as a good lawyer, and he earned this reputation by being all things Atticus for so long. Atticus did not have billboards along the highway, or an ad in the Yellow Pages. Despite his many fine qualities, he was not listed as a SuperLawyer, and we like to believe that if Atticus were alive today, he would reject such tawdry efforts to attract new clients. Atticus would bristle at the thought that practicing law was a business.

Most commentators point to Bates v. State Bar of Arizona[2] watershed moment when law became a business. In Bates, the U.S. Supreme Court held that lawyers had a constitutional right to truthfully communicate their availability to potential clients. A year earlier, the Court, in Goldfarb v. Virginia Bar Association,[3] struck down a minimum fee schedule that was imposed on all lawyers in the state. Together, these decisions had the effect of partially deregulating the practice of law, at least with respect to fees and advertising, because firms were free to compete in an open market for legal services. In more than three decades since these cases were decided, the world of Atticus Finch was turned upside down. We might debate whether these changes have been good for the profession, but whether we like them or not, lawyers in 2010 compete fiercely to get and keep good clients, and price sensitivity is a major component of the marketplace for legal services.

What does this have to do with generalists and specialists? It is noteworthy that the legal marketplace is not a totally free market, because it remains regulated in a number of ways. One of these ways is that ethics rules continue to restrict the use of specialty status by lawyers. In Peel v. Attorney Grievance Committee,[4] the Supreme Court permitted lawyers to call themselves specialists, but permitted ethics rules to require additional restrictions to prevent the term "specialist" from being misleading. The effect of this retained regulatory component creates a chilling effect on the growth of legal specialties in the United States. Although the legal profession will probably never follow the path of the medical profession and limit practice in specialty areas to certified specialists, lawyers are moving inexorably in the direction of specialization. Despite the regulatory system propping up a mythical world of generalists, the marketplace favors specialists, and just as the Berlin Wall fell, Harvey Witsworth will retire.

The primary reason that practice concentration prevails over general practice is that lawyers who limit their services to narrow fields of practice can master the legal knowledge and skill necessary to practice in their

---

2. Bates v. State Bar of Arizona, 433 U.S. 350 (1977).
3. Goldfarb v. Virginia Bar Association, 421 U.S. 733 (1975).
4. Peel v. Attorney Grievance Committee, 496 U.S. 91 (1990).

field at a high level of competence. A general practitioner may have some knowledge about many things, but a specialist is likely to have a great deal of knowledge about a small number of things. Despite the appeal of a renaissance legal mind, the truth is that greater is better, and renaissance minds may be ideal for conversation over a bottle of wine, but they come up short in legal services.

Lawyers who concentrate on limited types of cases can build efficiency into their delivery systems, by leveraging the knowledge they amass. If Ada Rondack handles 100 tax cases per year for 15 years, she will have 1,500 cases under her belt. Based on her volume of cases, she can create systems, re-cycle forms, retrieve content and reduce throughput of legal work. She can purchase sophisticated software tools to support her system, because the cost of the technology can be amortized across all her cases. If Harvey Witsworth, the GP, takes on 3 or 4 tax cases during his career, which arguably he shouldn't, it will take him more time to get up to speed, produce the work, and deliver it to the client. Not just for tax cases, but throughout his practice, Harvey is consistently reinventing the wheel. The appeal of such a practice is that the work is always new and interesting, compared to work of the dull specialist, who sees the same basic cases over and over. The GP cannot pay for software systems to support his ever-changing caseload, because he does not do enough work in any one area to justify the expense.

Lawyers who possess greater knowledge of a practice area and implement systems to assure quality output are less likely to be sued for malpractice than lawyers who lack such knowledge or systems. Let's say that another way: experts are less likely to make professional errors than non-experts. Malpractice carriers are helping to drive the move to specialty practice by requiring lawyers to state their areas of practice, and not insure against malpractice resulting from the insured taking on a case outside the areas listed. If Harvey does not do any municipal bond work, he will not list it as a field of practice on his malpractice policy, and if he takes on a municipal bond case, his carrier will not protect him if he makes a mistake.

Lawyer specialists can communicate their availability more efficiently than generalists, because they target a narrower audience. If the lawyer's target audience is "people with legal problems," then the marketing objective is to reach the entire population; whereas, the lawyer who concentrates her practice in a narrow field, can target a smaller audience of potential clients defined by the services she intends to provide. The simple economics of marketing dictate that it is cheaper to reach fewer people than more people, but beyond the general proposition, it is also true that the more finely tailored the target audience, the more surgical the marketing message can be. So not only does the specialist spend less money on marketing than the generalist, but the money is better spent.

Collectively, these advantages mean that concentrated lawyers can deliver better services at a lower price and still earn a greater return than generalists who cannot leverage their intellectual work product. This does not mean that generalists cannot be excellent lawyers or that specialists always deliver a faster, better, cheaper product. It does mean, however, that on the whole specialists trump generalists when it comes to providing the best service at the best price with the best return for the lawyer. It follows that over time lawyers will choose the more efficient model and become specialists and that the ranks of generalists will decline.

If generalists have an advantage in the marketplace, it may be their adaptability. Because they have some exposure to many areas of law, they may be better equipped to shift professional gears with economic change. A lawyer who has invested in a narrow practice concentration may wake up to find that a once booming practice area has withered almost overnight, and a lucrative business has become a worthless pit. This may be a legitimate concern, but in actuality the generalist's slight knowledge advantage may not be all that great if the level of the GPs knowledge is so basic that the specialist can reach the same level of expertise quickly or transfer skills from the old specialty area to a new one.

What will it mean for solo and small firm lawyers if they can no longer make a living as general practitioners? First, it will mean that solo/small firm lawyers will be forced to develop a cognizable expertise, by associating with a senior lawyer experienced in a chosen field, pursuing education and training in a specialty at the JD, LLM or CLE level, or by spending time in a larger firm mastering a field of practice before going out on their own. It will be more difficult for someone to simply hang out a shingle and start practicing law taking whatever cases happen along. It will place greater pressure on law students and recent graduates to make specific career choices at an earlier time than they have in the past.

Second, specialization will manifest itself in virtual practice. For example, a lawyer who concentrates her practice in the area of patent law may not have enough patent work in the small town where she lives to sustain a practice. As a GP, she could have done a little of this, a little of that, and gotten by. As a specialist she will need to have an on line presence to draw clients from a larger pool to maintain sufficient volume to keep her practice afloat. More on line practitioners providing similar services will drive down the price of services, and challenge practitioners to distinguish themselves in the eyes of potential clients. On line lists, referral systems, social media and peer networks will become commonplace tools to connect with clients. Other forms of electronic marketing will become commonplace, and on line practices will predominate the legal marketplace.

Third, not all lawyers will provide services directly to clients; many solo and small firm lawyers will work with other organizations, both inside and outside the private practice of law, to complete discrete legal tasks. These contract lawyers will perform outsourced work from law firms, law departments on a project-by-project basis.[5] They will compete

---

5. *See* Tina Brown, "The Gig Economy: Now That Everyone Has a Project-to-Project Career, Everyone is a Hustler," The Daily Beast Blogs & Stories (Jan. 12, 2009, 5:34 a.m.), *available at*

with off-shore outsourcers for this work. The model for the future solo lawyer will be someone who has a specific legal expertise and skill set, works virtually from home, rents conference space as necessary to meet clients or others, and handles projects for clients and/or other lawyers.

Fourth, as lawyers go virtual, they will in turn rely upon virtual staff. Although many functions once handled by paralegals and secretaries will be assumed by technology applications, when a human touch is needed, lawyers will hire support on line for specific projects. In this sense, the cost of running a practice will be significantly reduced, because the two largest overhead expenses in the bricks-and-mortar practice world are staff and space. Virtual lawyers will have to spend more money on technology than their precursors, but the cost of this technology will be amortized across all the work they do.

Finally, the more routine the work in the virtual marketplace, the more price sensitive it will be. Generic services will provide the narrowest profit margins, and many solo and small firm lawyers will have to compete in this environment. As services move away from generic in the direction of unique, they become less price-sensitive. Lawyers will be challenged to add value to the work the do, communicate this value to clients, and gain recognition as experts in their fields of practice. The generalists, like Harvey Witsworth and Atticus Finch, endangered species in 2010, will become extinct in the not so distant future.

Perhaps there is a window of opportunity for the generalists. Just as the medical profession has created the primary care physician, who serves a the first point of contact for patients, and a referral source for medical specialists, there may be room for a primary care lawyer, who sees clients when they are legally injured and refers them to a legal specialist who can serve their needs. Such a lawyer could be funded by referral fees from the specialists, because we do not have an insurance system that pays the primary care professional as medicine does. The primary care lawyer would have to be trusted by people in the community, possess a broad general knowledge of legal problems, and maintain contacts with a wide variety of specialists in order to make the right referral in the right circumstances. Just imagine:

	Atticus Finch **Primary Care Lawyer** **Case Evaluation and Referrals**	

Much has been written about the transformation of large firms from big, to bigger, to colossal, but much less about the future of solo and small firm practice. Yet it should be clear from this article that the changes that have transformed BigLaw, have not left LittleLaw unscathed. In order to

---

http://www.thedailybeast.com/blogs-and-stories/2009–01–12/the-gig-economy. The "Age of Gigonomics" is discussed in the first part of Rachel Littman's article "Training Lawyers for the Real World," in the September 2010 issue of the *Journal*.

survive in these times, lawyers have to develop a cognizable expertise. Whether we call this expertise a concentration, a niche, or a specialty, the shift away from general practice is changing the way that solo practitioners and small firm lawyers work, including the way they connect with clients, deliver their services and charge fees.

The implications of this transformation are affecting the timing and process for making career choices, as well as the ways that young lawyers gain experience and training. Technology contributes to this paradigm shift by making information available in more places and in greater quantity, forcing small firms and solos to focus on the qualitative aspects of the advice they give, and to compete with virtual service providers in the marketplace.

Problems and Questions

1. What factors favor specialization in the legal services marketplace? Economics? Efficiency? Marketability?

2. What are the negative considerations of becoming a specialist? Are generalists more adaptable in a shifting marketplace than specialists? Is the variety of work more interesting?

3. Will GPs ever disappear entirely, or will they evolve? What will general practice of the future be like?

4. Will the legal profession ever become rigidly specialized like the medical profession? Why or why not? Do state specialty certification programs move us in the direction of the medical model?

CHAPTER 4

THE TRUTH ABOUT LAW FIRMS

■ ■ ■

A. WHAT IS A LAW FIRM?

In this chapter, you should learn the basics of how law firms are organized. You will look at the most common form of business organization for lawyers—the partnership, as well as other business entities, which lawyers are increasingly choosing. An understanding of the basic partnership law is necessary, because a law partnership is no different from any other partnership except that its business is practicing law. You will have a chance to compare the advantages and disadvantages of the partnership form compared to other forms of doing business. In the process of examining law firm formation documents, you will develop legal drafting skills as well.

1. GENERALLY

There are more than 50,000 law firms in the United States. At least 650,000 lawyers engage in private practice of law, more than 60% of them in law firms, including partnerships or other forms of group practice. Since 1970, the growth of large law firms has been dramatic, including considerable consolidation of formerly separate practices into unified, multi-city branch offices, the acquisition of smaller offices by larger ones, and the spinoff of practice groups from some firms to join others.

Multi-lawyer law practices—those that are not individually owned and operated—are generally referred to as law firms. In 2000, 76% of law firms were small, with 2 to 5 partners; 19% of law firms are considered medium-size, with more than 5 up to 20 partners; and large firms with 20 to 100 partners comprise 5% of the law firms. In recent decades, a new classification of very large firms has emerged, including organizations with several hundred partners; these firms represent only 1% of the number of law firms, but an amazing 14% of the lawyers in private practice. Law firms may also include two to four times as many employed lawyers as partners, and a non-legal support staff as large or larger than the legal staff. This means that several thousand individuals may work in one organization in offices scattered around the world.

The largest law firms exceed one thousand lawyers, including partners, associates and other salaried lawyers. These numbers may seem large, but the largest firms are small in comparison to many non-legal businesses, even professional service firms. These mega-firms, however, are still immense when compared to small firms and solo practitioners that make up the majority of private practitioners.

Despite a decline since 1950 in the percentage of lawyers who practice alone, solo practice is still the most common organizational form in the legal profession. The percentage of lawyers who call themselves solos has declined steadily since 1950, although the actual number of solos has increased. *See* Barbara Curran and Clara Carson, 2000 LAWYER STATISTICAL REPORT, Am. Bar Found., 2004. *See* AMERICAN BAR ASSOCIATION, *Lawyer Demographics* (2002), *available at* http://www.americanbar.org/content/dam/aba/migrated/marketresearch/PublicDocuments/ lawyer_demographics_2012_revised.pdf-3k-2012-06-23demographics2012.authcheckdam.pdf.

There are two kinds of individual practice. One is the true solo practice—the lawyer practicing by herself, providing legal services, perhaps with a single secretary, but at most supported by a small staff of paralegals, investigators and secretaries. The second type includes the individual practitioners who hire one or more associates, and often employs a fairly large support staff. Looking at the total number of people who work at the second solo model, it should be apparent that such a practice can be a fairly large organization. In any event, it is worth noting that solo practices in the United States represent 38,000 business organizations (76% of 50,000) providing legal services, i.e., law firms.

It may help if we think about all organizations that provide legal services to clients as law firms. These group practices may be organized as traditional partnerships, limited liability partnerships, professional corporations, professional associations, informal partnerships, and sole proprietorships. Other office sharing arrangements, where lawyers do not establish the legal equivalent of partnership, may have many of the characteristics of true law firms. Branch offices of large firms may fall under the structural arrangements of a larger organization, but still operate day-to-day like a small firm.

For example, suppose a large firm in Denver acquires an eight-lawyer firm in Colorado Springs. Although the Colorado Springs partners are incorporated into the Denver partnership and the Denver base provides a variety of support services to the Colorado Springs outpost, the lawyers and staff in Colorado Springs continue to practice and relate to each other as they did before they became part of the larger firm.

Within law firms, it is helpful to distinguish two classes of people—those who are partners or shareholders, and those who are not. Most firms operate on a leverage principle: salaried non-partners do work that brings in money for the partners. If law firms could not generate a profit from the work of employed lawyers, partners would derive no return on their investment. Partners are the owners of the legal business. Those who are not owners of the business are employees, whether they are referred to as associates, of counsel, non-equity partners, or some other name. Employed lawyers do not take the same risks that the owners do, and it follows that they do not reap the same rewards.

The ratio of employed lawyers to partners in law firms is between 0:1 (in practices where there are no associates at all) and 4:1 (in the most highly leveraged practices). In smaller firms the employed lawyer to partner ratio is typically in the range of 1:1, whereas the ratio tends to increase as firms get larger, to 2:1, and higher. In the largest firms, the ratio often exceeds 3:1, in part because of the turnover that occurs in large firm practice, but also because the largest firms can provide a stream of legal work to keep a larger number of associates busy generating profits for the partners.

This has not always been the framework. Traditionally, law firms drew a distinction between junior and senior partners. An individual's ownership interest increased over time, so that senior partners with greater longevity held more of the firm's equity, earned more money, and wielded greater clout than partners with lesser tenure in the firm. Over the years, partnership compensation shifted to more performance-based formulas, with the result that being older did not necessarily mean being more powerful in many firms. Today, it is common for new equity partners to purchase their interest in the firm over time, financing the purchase over an extended period. Senior associates who are not invited to become equity partners (owners), often remain employees as non-equity partners, of counsel, staff lawyers, and permanent associates.

2. THE LAW FIRM PYRAMID

Organizationally, the law firm is sometimes pictured as a pyramid, because there is limited leadership at the top with a broad base of employees. Chart 4–1 depicts the traditional view of this pyramid. The partners sit at the top of the pyramid, overseeing a larger number of associate lawyers, who sit atop an even larger number of non-legal support staff at the base. Senior partners outnumber junior partners; senior associates outnumber junior associates; and senior staff outnumber junior staff. In order to add more partners at the top, a firm had to grow the entire pyramid. Associates followed an up-or-out path: if they did not "make partner," they left the firm. If the firm did not constantly grow in order to create new partnership opportunities, it risked the loss of associates to provide financial leverage.

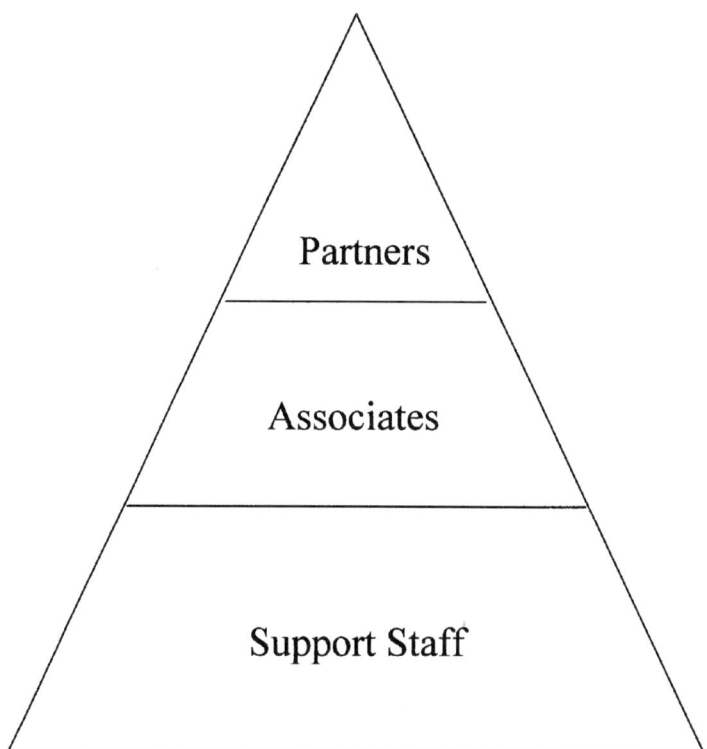

Chart 4–1 Traditional Law Firm Pyramid

The emergence of senior-level non-partner attorneys is altering some basic aspects of the relationships between lawyers and clients, lawyers to each other, and lawyers within the legal profession. In order to maintain or increase compensation among equity partners, many firms have made it more difficult to become a true partner. These firms have developed terms, e.g., non-equity partner, contract partner, income partner, of counsel, staff lawyer, to describe these senior-level lawyers. This approach not only protects the compensation of the equity partners, but it also reverses one of the major drawbacks of the so-called "up or out" model for associates by retaining experienced lawyers who do not make partner at the firm.

The depiction of this new version of the law firm pyramid appears in Chart 4–2. Notice how a new group of lawyers has emerged between the partners and associates in Chart 4–1. Notice also how a class of professional managers has appeared between the lawyers and the support staff. This trend had its origins in large firm practice, but has trickled down to smaller organizations, as all firms seek to overcome the limitations of the traditional pyramid.

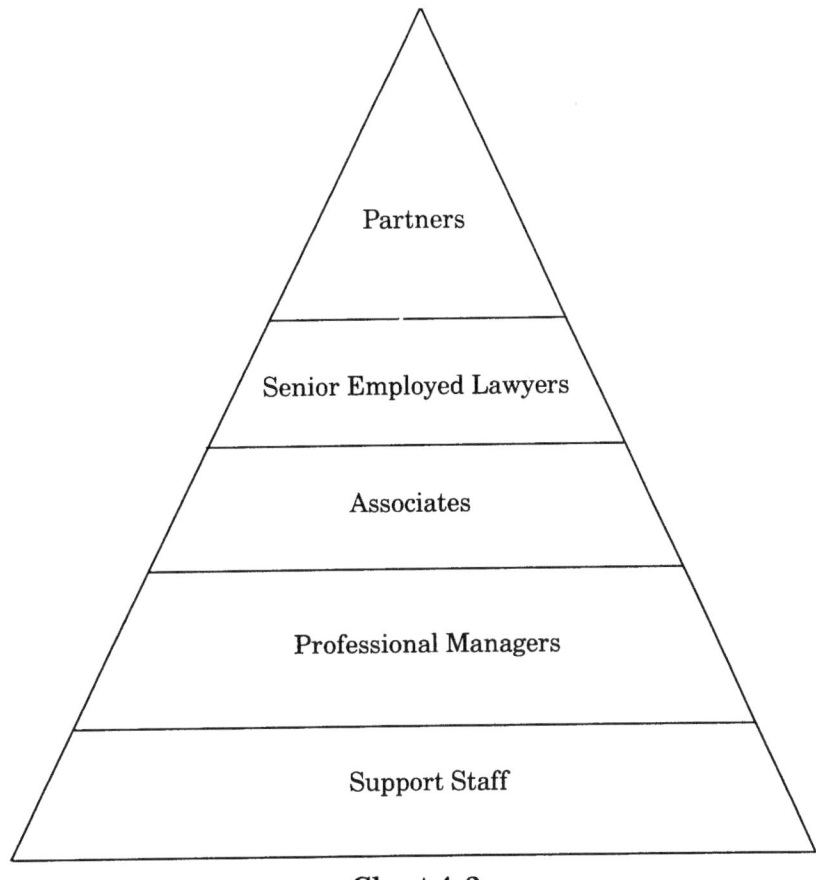

Chart 4–2
The New Law Firm Pyramid

The emergence of new tiers in the partnership pyramid has significant implications for compensation plans. First, the firm can permanently leverage these employees; although they will continue to receive annual salary increases, the firm will continue to earn a profit on their work. Second, the firm will not need to hire as many new associates, assuming that there is lower turnover at the mid-level (6–8 years) in the firm. Third, it will be easier to hire upper-echelon specialists laterally without the constraints of having to offer a partnership with the job. Fourth, many firms will offer a second non-partnership track for associates. Thus, permanent associates would include lawyers never considered, as well as those passed over for partnership.

With the evolution of equity and non-equity partners, law firm ownership has taken an interesting twist. Equity partners invest the capital needed to finance the legal business. In return, they are compensated in the form of net profits; they make management decisions for the organization; and they retain equity in the value of the business, which they can take with them when they leave. In contrast, non-equity partners (and other employed lawyers) are compensated through salary, even if they share indirectly in profits through bonuses and incentive arrangements. It should come as no surprise that the true equity partners receive the lion's share of the net income, make most of the management decisions, and own a piece of the net worth of the firm itself.

Two interesting recent developments regarding equity ownership of law firms deserve mention here. The first involves the de-equitization of partners. In a number of large law firms, the interest of some partners has been changed from equity to non-equity status, i.e., from ownership to employee status. Although this practice is not new—it has been common for retiring partners to become "of counsel" to the firm—the contemporary twist is that the partnership votes out members that a majority consider less-productive (and hence less-deserving of profit-sharing) partners for the benefit of the remaining productive partners. This phenomenon came to light in 2002 when a group of de-equitized partners at Sidley & Austin, sued the firm for age discrimination. They were all within the ages protected by the federal Age Discrimination Act (ADA). The de-equitized partners argued that Sidley's management structure made them nominal partners anyway, so it was appropriate for them to seek redress as employees under the ADA. Although the case was eventually settled, settlement was reached only after a federal district court denied Sidley's motion for summary judgment, holding the plaintiffs had established a claim upon which relief could be granted. *See, EEOC v. Sidley & Austin*, 315 F.3d 696 (7th Cir. 2002).

A second trend that is at least indirectly influencing equity in American law firms involves law firms outside the United States raising capital through public financing, i.e., the sale of stock. The 2007 Legal Services Act in the United Kingdom allowed law firms to raise capital by offering publicly-traded stock. Australia followed the UK lead, and today several law firms in both countries have taken advantage of the new laws. Previously, law firms in those countries were limited in the same way that U.S. firms are; Model Rule 5.4 prohibits non-lawyer ownership of law firms. The American Bar Association Ethics 20/20 Commission investigated whether Rule 5.4 should be liberalized to allow nonlawyer ownership, but in early 2012, the Commission concluded that the American rule should not be changed.

Although the tendency to create multiple classes of lawyers occurs most often in large law firms, the phenomenon has taken hold in smaller firms as well. While the focus of this course remains on small law firms, because that is where most students eventually practice, patterns of practice in larger organizations may shed light on emerging trends in small firm practice.

One evolving fact of life in law practice is that an increasing number of associate lawyers will never become equity partners in the firms where they work. Consolidation of ownership interests may be attributed to greed, to a decline in the growth of the legal industry, to competition in the marketplace, or some combination of these factors, but it is a very real phenomenon. Whether a lawyer employee is called a permanent associate, a non-equity partner, of counsel or something else, the reality is that this individual is never going to be a true partner, in the traditional sense of the word, as they understood it when they entered law school.

Before 1980, when an associate joined a firm, she generally assumed that if she did a good job, put in her time for five to ten years (depending on the firm), she would be elevated to partnership. Certainly, some lawyers would not make the grade and would be quietly let go, while others might find they did not like the firm and leave on their own, but the associate who performed competently and did not ruffle too many feathers, could expect to become a partner.

More recently, law firms have recognized that some lawyer employees bring value to the firm as practitioners, but that they can work for the firm without becoming partners. They are not forced to leave the firm; instead, they are encouraged to maintain a long-term relationship with the firm as employees. In part, firms have recognized the economic idiocy of firing experienced professionals after seven or eight years because they do not meet partnership criteria unrelated to competence as a lawyer. In part, firms have had to deal with the economic reality that partnership opportunities are limited.

For example, if a firm has a ratio of associates to partners of 2:1, where each associate generates a profit of $200,000, and one of the current crop of associates becomes a partner, the firm will need to hire three associates (two to maintain the leverage for the new partner and one to replace the associate who became a partner) to maintain its 2:1 ratio, and profitability. Viewed another way, the firm will have to have enough new work to keep three associates busy in order to elevate one associate to partnership.

In the current practice environment, because the utilization of employed lawyers has become increasingly common, being denied partnership is no longer a badge of dishonor. An associate may do all the right things and develop into an excellent attorney, but for economic reasons, the firm simply may not be able to offer a partnership to every candidate. Such a lawyer may continue to work at the same firm, move laterally to another firm, find other lawyers with whom to form a partnership, or move in-house with a firm client.

Some firms even establish two tracks for associates; one typically culminating in partnership consideration (the partnership track), and the second track for associates who will never be considered for partnership (the non-partnership track). In such firms, the associates know at the outset where they stand and what they can expect long term.

Some firms also allow women who come in under the partnership track to elect a non-partnership track if they do not want to put in the hours necessary to be considered for partnership while they are raising children. This so-called "Mommy Track" has been subject to considerable criticism that it can be used as a tool for denying partnership opportunities to women lawyers, that it reinforces the glass ceiling in many firms, and that it forces women to choose between motherhood and partnership. In response to this criticism, some firms have taken pains to make clear that women may return to the partnership track with proportional credit for their work during their child-raising years, in other words, extending the opportunity to be considered for partnership.

A variation on the non-partnership track is part-time lawyering. A lawyer who has family or other commitments may not want to put in the number of hours required of a full-time employee, and the firm may agree to pay a reduced salary and benefits for lawyers who assume this status. Firms have been slow to acknowledge that part-time lawyers could be considered for partnership on the basis of total experience, not just chronological tenure at the firm.

The danger is that in a firm where the full-time lawyers work sixty to eighty hours per week, part-time is more likely to translate into 35–40 hours rather than 20–25 hours. Depending on the circumstances, it may be feasible for two lawyers to share a single job, each carrying one-half the load (and receiving half the pay) of a full-time lawyer in the same position. Such job sharing arrangements, popular in other industries, have been slow to gain acceptance in the legal employment arena. See also the section of the New York State Bar Association Task Force on the Future of the Legal Profession Report (2011) on "Work–Life Integration and the Practice of Law."

Many firms employ lawyers with a designation "of counsel." These lawyers may be retired or semi-retired partners, or experienced lawyers hired to handle specific kinds of cases, but who are not offered a partnership in the firm. It is increasingly common for firms to retain experienced lawyers, who possess a cognizable expertise the firm can tap or a specialized clientele. These "of counsel" lawyers may have retired from another firm, or may have been left out in the cold when a former firm merged, split or downsized.

Some firms hire lawyers on a contract or consulting basis, either for temporary or short-term projects. These contract lawyers often possess specific expertise that the firm can utilize, although they may also be junior level lawyers with experience comparable to that of an associate. By hiring these lawyers on a piecemeal basis, the firm can save money, because it is not economically feasible to employ an associate full-time. Some lawyers are even developing contract lawyer businesses where they actually sell their services—from legal research to litigation—to other lawyers. Because of the flexibility afforded to legal employers and elimination of benefits paid to full-time employees, contract lawyering is becoming increasingly popular in the legal workplace. Some young lawyers sustain themselves completely working "gigs" with a variety of firms instead of working for one firm on a full-time basis. *See,* Barbara Durkin,

A Whole New World Gigonomics, Human Resource Development and the Brave New Lawyer, New York State Bar Association Journal (September 2011).

What all these developments mean is that the notion of what it means to be a law firm, and what it means to work in a law firm have changed considerably over the course of recent years. We might want to speculate about what these changes mean for the practice of law as well as for individual lawyers. We might also want to consider whether the practice of law is at the beginning, middle, or end of a period of change, and whether or how practice may continue to change in the future. The topic of employed lawyers will be taken up again in Chapter 8, where we will address issues involving the employment relationship more fully.

PROBLEMS AND QUESTIONS

1. Do arrangements such as non-equity partnerships and of counsel arrangements serve only the interests of the firms' owners, or can they benefit employed lawyers' career objectives as well? What are your reasons?

2. Why do firms need to raise capital? Is it just to increase the partners' equity, or is it to address other economic issues? How are de-equitization practices similar to and different from public financing efforts for the financial health and market competitiveness of law firms?

3. Might some firms misuse a non-partnership employment track for associates to funnel women who choose to have children into a "mommy ghetto?" Will a two-track system segregate candidates according to law school? Will long-term employment of a cadre of non-partner attorneys alter some basic aspects of the relationships between lawyers and clients, lawyers to each other, and lawyers within the legal profession?

4. Do contract and part-time lawyering arrangements serve only the interests of law firms, or can they benefit individual lawyers' career objectives as well? What are the benefits to law firms that use contract lawyers? Are there any negative considerations or risks? Under what circumstances might you elect to work as a contract lawyer?

5. Would you consider using permanent associates, non-equity partners, and other long term employment relationships, or would you strive to offer partnership to all associates who join your firm? What are the pros and cons of each approach? Are there other alternatives worth considering for your law firm's long term stability?

6. If you started your own firm, would it be oriented toward growth, or would you want to build a stable but successful small firm? If you see your objective as being a 100–lawyer firm fifteen years down the road, what kind of organizational framework would facilitate moving easily through continuing periods of transition? If you want to stay small, how do you build in ways to make it more difficult to change, add partners or expand? What are the advantages and disadvantages of just remaining a solo practitioner without the aggravation of having to consult with peers before making decisions?

B. THE RELATIONSHIP AMONG PARTNERS

Preliminarily, it is important to clarify the usage of one particular term in this book: partner (and its cousin, partnership). Strictly speaking, a partner is a member of a partnership, which involves a business relationship involving two or more individuals, discussed later in this Section. Many lawyers also use the term partner loosely to refer to any individual with shared ownership interest in an organization that provides legal services. Thus, the shareholders in a professional corporation may refer to themselves as partners, even though they are not technically partners. Increasingly, the term partner is used to denote a level of experience and independence in handling client matters, regardless of ownership status in the firm. Thus, an equity partner referring a case to her non-equity partner, may say to the client, "I'm going to ask my partner Smith to handle your matter." As used in this chapter and elsewhere in the book, the terms partner and shareholder may be used interchangeably to refer to law firm owners, whereas, employed lawyers will only be referred to as partners when they are described as non-equity partners.

There are many reasons for lawyers to form partnerships. Every organization must have some operational framework, and a partnership provides such a framework while allowing flexibility. How detailed the agreement should be will depend on how well the partners know each other, how long they have worked together, how much mutual trust they share, and how complicated their financial arrangements are.

There is no single formula and no one "correct" way to structure a partnership agreement. The agreement ought to somehow embody the philosophy of the organization. For instance, the terms of the agreement are likely to be quite different, depending on whether the organization is governed by democratic principles or functions as a dictatorship. The structure might be influenced by such matters as the services lawyers in the firm will provide, the age of the partners themselves and the law of the jurisdiction(s) where they choose to practice. Regardless of what considerations influence the business form of the organization, the individuals who create the organization will have to make some decisions. Even where the owners fail to make affirmative decisions, they will find that they have made choices about the form of their law firm by default.

In the broadest sense, aspiring partners need to reach some general consensus about the direction they want the firm to go. If they do not share a common vision for the practice, the demise of the firm, at some point down the road, is virtually inevitable. This vision, or practice philosophy, may be stated explicitly as a mission statement, or implicitly between the lines in the agreement itself.

It may be easy to overlook long-term goals and objectives when drafting specific terms in a partnership or other formation agreement, but in fact the words of the agreement define the relationship among the partners. Putative partners should ask themselves; "When we put these words into the agreement, what does this mean to us as people working together? What does it mean to our relationship with each other?" Insofar as a law partnership or other business form includes a group of people who agree to practice law together, their agreement establishes the ground rules.

Although a law practice is a business enterprise, it is also a family; this is particularly true of smaller firms. A partnership is a family with a pre-nuptial agreement, but a family nonetheless. While the business of law practice is important, the personal side of the organization is equally important and cannot be neglected.

Prospective partners may choose to address many issues when they draft a partnership agreement, but some matters such as office rules and internal policies are best left to decision making in the course of business or inclusion in the office policy manual. Many details can be left out of the agreement, but if something is critical to the philosophy of the firm it should be incorporated in the partnership agreement. Many considerations that influence the content of the agreement may not be apparent at first glance, but require extended discussions among the prospective partners before they reach agreement on the form of the partnership.

1. PARTNERSHIP PRINCIPLES

The concept of partnership is an old one in Anglo–American law. In order to promote some uniformity among the states, the Commissioners on Uniform State Laws drafted the Uniform Partnership Act in 1914 ("UPA"). The UPA, one of the first of many uniform state laws, has been adopted by four-fifths of the states. In recent years, a number of jurisdictions have adopted the Revised Uniform Partnership Act ("RUPA"), which treats partnerships more like corporations in certain situations than the UPA did. In addition, a number of states also have passed laws authorizing limited liability partnerships ("LLPs"), limited liability companies ("LLCs"), professional associations ("PAs"), professional corporations ("PCs"), and other organizational forms.

There are two types of partnerships: general and limited. General partnerships include relationships where the partners have roughly the same authority and risk, unless altered by the terms of their agreement. Limited partnerships have reduced responsibility and liability for certain partners and greater responsibility for others. In addition, there are commercial or "trading" partnerships and professional or "non-trading" partnerships. Most law firms could be characterized as general non-trading partnerships.

In order to form a partnership, an express or implied agreement is essential. However, no particular formalities are required in order to effectuate this agreement. Thus, both written and oral agreements may be equally valid. This is important to lawyers who share office space with other lawyers. These sorts of arrangements may result in an implied oral agreement and partnership status may be imputed to them for purposes of legal and professional liability.

In order to establish the basis for understanding among the partners, written partnership agreements must include the following elements:

- date of agreement
- names and addresses of partners
- nature or purpose of business
- name of partnership
- duration of the partnership
- place where business will be carried on
- signatures of the partners

Partnership agreements may contain a number of other terms as well. These terms, although not necessary for the agreement to be valid, are often the most important elements in the agreement. The UPA provides defaults for a number of aspects of the relationship among partners. If the individual partners desire terms different from the UPA defaults, they need to include such terms in the agreement, including:

- capital contributions
- duties of partners
- method for settling disputes
- rules for withdrawal of partnership funds
- formula for distribution of profits
- provisions for dissolution of the firm or termination of a partner's interest
- adding new partners
- modifying the terms of the agreement

Each state has its own statutory requirements for written partnership agreements, and these vary from state to state. For instance, some states have fictitious name statutes that must be observed. In most states, partnership agreements do not need to be filed with the state in order to become effective, but other forms of business, such as LLPs do.

The UPA defines a partnership as an agreement by two or more persons to carry on business for a profit. As long as there is a business purpose, an informal agreement is sufficient. The partnership may or may not own property, but generally, partnership property is a broad term embracing everything owned by the partnership including:

- capital
- furniture and other fixtures
- title to real property

- retirement plans
- cash
- accounts receivable
- goodwill (although law firms traditionally could not claim goodwill, the adoption of Model Rule 1.17 permitting the sale of a practice, specifically recognizes good will in a law practice).

The question of property frequently becomes a significant issue during dissolution or termination discussions. Departing partners will want to take out their equity (assets less liabilities) in the practice, and the value of partnership property is of critical importance in calculating equity. Remaining partners have an interest in assuring that the exodus of value associated with a partner's withdrawal from the partnership is not so burdensome on the remaining partners that it forces a *de facto* dissolution of the firm.

All partners are liable for the debts and obligations of the firm. Debts are considered liabilities of both the individual partners and the firm itself; thus, the property of each individual as well as property of the firm may be used to satisfy the debt. However, if the partner acted outside the scope of his authority as a partner, the partnership may be able to escape liability. In addition, most states now permit lawyers to organize as limited liability partnerships, which (like corporations) limit the liability of individual partners to their investment in the business.

The UPA provisions for dissolution also may be relevant to law firms. Under the UPA, the departure of any partner causes the dissolution of the partnership; the remaining partners may reform into a new partnership, but the old entity ceases to exist. The UPA's default rule may be overcome by the express terms of the agreement. The partners may choose to address dissolution and termination of partnership interests by express terms in the agreement. A partnership may also be dissolved in contravention of the agreement, which may give rise to a cause of action for breach of the agreement. The Revised UPA presumes continuity of partnerships, just as for corporations, so under RUPA, the departure of one partner will not effect a dissolution of the partnership. Under both UPA and RUPA, the partners should define the circumstances and terms under which the agreement will terminate.

2. THE WRITTEN AGREEMENT

Although a written partnership agreement is not necessary, and a surprisingly large number of law firms operate without one, a written partnership agreement is the best defense possible against misunderstandings among the partners about the scope and meaning of the partners' relationship. A written agreement is almost always preferable to an oral one. A written agreement will clarify rights and duties, establish procedures for making decisions, and decide in advance financial questions that could generate litigation if not resolved. The form a written partnership agreement takes depends on many factors that will vary from firm to firm:

- The philosophy and goals of the organization;
- The partners' personalities;
- The amount of detail the partners desire to incorporate into the agreement;
- Matters the partners agree to resolve as they arise;
- The effect of capital contribution, income production and client generation on the division of profits; and
- Provision for what will happen if the agreement goes sour.

The partnership agreement should be a unique statement created by the particular individual parties to the agreement, rather than some standard document. The partnership agreement is like a pre-nuptial agreement in a marriage: it is easier to reach agreement on terms at the outset when everyone is in love than at the end when things are falling apart. Appendix D–1 (page 443) contains a model limited liability partnership agreement. Appendix D–2 (page 455) provides a partnership agreement checklist, showing how the elements of the agreement can be drafted into a written document. Remember: no single form of agreement is correct for all firms; the lawyers who create the law firm should create a document that articulates the terms of their particular agreement.

3. IMPLIED PARTNERSHIPS

Many lawyers do not formalize their arrangements to practice together. Office sharing, work for space, and other innovative non-partnership arrangements are becoming common. In some cities professional management firms offer turn-key law offices for lawyers. These offices provide space, support services, library facilities and basic management systems for tenants at a fixed rate. Such ventures present an array of pitfalls for the unwary. In addition to practical management considerations, the specter of malpractice actions hangs over these alternative business arrangements, just as it would for traditional practice forms. It is not enough to practice with ordinary professional care; since you can be held vicariously liable for the acts of others, you must take care to protect yourself from their negligence as well.

In *Myers v. Aragona, et al.*, 21 Md.App. 45, 318 A.2d 263 (1974), the Maryland Court of Appeals held that a lawyer who shared office space with another lawyer who client funds, was estopped from claiming that the two were not partners if they acted as partners in their dealings with the clients and the public. In that case, lawyer Gordon misappropriated funds from clients, who obtained a judgment against both Gordon and Myers. Myers argued that although the two used the name "Law Offices of Gordon and Myers," they were not partners. In its holding in favor of the clients, the Court found Myers liable for the misappropriation, by his partner, of funds entrusted to the partnership. Even if no actual partnership existed between Gordon and Myers, Myers is nonetheless, by virtue of his using or allowing the use of the name "Gordon & Myers, Attorneys at Law" on the "Settlement Statement[s]" and "Law Offices Gordon & Myers" on letterheads estopped from denying the existence of the partnership. He may not now be heard to say that he was not, in fact, a partner, but that he and Gordon merely had a "relationship." In the eyes of the law, that "relationship" is as much a partnership, insofar as third parties are concerned, as if there had been formal Articles of Partnership subscribed to by both Myers and Gordon. The Court cited the Maryland's version of the Uniform Partnership Act as the basis for liability.

In another case, Lansky approached another lawyer named Komisarow with a proposition for Lansky to move into Komisarow's office and do work for space. This was agreed to by both lawyers. After a time, the parties began to handle a few legal matters together and fees were shared. On one occasion Komisarow asked Lansky to assist on a case in return for a fifty-fifty split of the fee. After doing the work, Komisarow kept the entire fee, and Lansky sued. The oral "space for services" agreement between Komisarow and Lansky was treated as an implied partnership, so Lansky was entitled to his share of the fee. *See Komisarow v. Lansky*, 139 Ind.App. 351, 219 N.E.2d 913 (1966).

The California Court, in *Redman v. Walters*, 88 Cal.App.3d 448, 152 Cal.Rptr. 42 (1979), ruled that even the termination of an apparent partnership by an innocent partner did not relieve the innocent partner from liability based upon the malpractice of the other partner during the time that the purported law firm represented the client-plaintiff. Although such decisions seem harsh, they are consistent with general partnership law, both in recognizing that partners are jointly and severally liable for each others' torts, and that client has a right to rely on the apparent authority of a partner to act on behalf of the partnership.

More recent cases are consistent with the approach taken in *Myers*, *Komisarow*, and *Redman*. The more plebian observation, "If looks like a duck, swims like a duck and quacks like a duck, it's a duck," is probably an apt description of the situation. Whether lawyers who work together in common offices need to go as far as to disclaim partnership status is not clear, but at the very least they should not act in ways that communicate, even inadvertently, to clients and others that they are partners.

4. OTHER FORMS OF ORGANIZATION

Although most law practices are organized as either partnerships or sole proprietorships, many lawyers are experimenting with a variety of different organizational schemes. The motivations for these creative arrangements are as varied as the structures themselves: reducing taxes, reducing exposure to liability for malpractice, cutting operating costs, expanding the client base, and improving services to name a few. It should not be surprising to see more innovative approaches to lawyering in less stable economic times.

Some of the "new" organizational forms include professional associations and corporations, associations of individual corporations, limited liability companies and partnerships, office sharing and space for services arrangements, regional networks, in-house ancillary non-legal services and external business subsidiaries.

Professional corporations and professional associations are not novel concepts. It has always been possible for a group of lawyers to incorporate, providing that they meet the statutory requirements of the state of incorporation. The evolution of Subchapter "S" corporations, individual corporations, and increasing flexibility of organizational requirements in many states have encouraged more small businesses to adopt the corporate form. Many states have specific legislation that allows professional groups to form professional corporations or associations.

Careful tax and estate planning on the part of attorneys in a firm could lead them to select one form over another. Some firms use the corporate form to shield assets of the individual attorneys from the risk of professional liability. Other lawyers, for similar reasons, have created individual corporations that participate in a professional association. In the future, it is likely that the relative advantages of incorporation will shift as tax, labor, corporation and malpractice laws change. Lawyers, often slow to respond to some changes in practice, such as technology, for example, tend to react quickly to changes in the law, which might affect their financial well-being.

In many jurisdictions, legislatures have passed laws that permit the creation of limited liability companies ("LLCs") and limited liability partnerships ("LLPs"). These business forms permit the partners or owners of closely-held businesses to enjoy the benefits of corporate or partnership status while shielding the owners from personal liability by capping liability at the level of individual investment. Although it is not clear yet whether courts will pierce the organizational veil to hold shareholders and partners personally liable for malpractice awards against themselves, other lawyers or the firm itself, many professional firms have reorganized as LLCs and LLPs in order to shield the owners from professional liabilities.

It might also be useful to some readers to think about legal service organizations outside the private practice of law. If private law firms deliver services to clients on the open market for profit, a variety of other organizations deliver legal services outside this environment. In such offices the lawyers work in an organization where the legal activities are funded from other sources or where the law office is a cost center in an organization engaged in some other form of business for a profit. Nearly 40% of all lawyers work outside the realm of private practice, so these institutional law offices represent a significant segment of the attorney population. Some (but not all) of these offices are listed below:

- Corporate law departments, including tax, intellectual property, contracts, litigation support, labor and securities;
- Trust departments;
- Insurance adjustment offices;
- Government law offices, including federal, state and local agency counsel and law departments;
- Prosecutors, including U.S. Attorneys, district attorneys, county attorneys and others;
- Public defenders;
- Publicly and privately funded legal action and law reform organizations;
- Political Action Committees (PACs);
- Military law offices;
- Judicial and court administration offices;
- Educational institutions, including law schools;
- Bar and other professional associations.

What all these institutional law offices have in common is that they provide services to a clearly defined clientele, in many cases a single client, and a funding source other than legal fees. Just as in private practice, there are costs associated with delivering legal services, so are there costs associated with the operation of an institutional law department or other law offices not funded through client fees.

PROBLEMS AND QUESTIONS

1. What elements are indispensable to a written partnership agreement? Can you think of other matters that should be included? What language could be employed to effectuate the desired results? Should lawyers hire lawyers to prepare a partnership agreement? Is the partnership agreement more like a pre-nuptial agreement or a set of by-laws for a business?

2. Are the problems described in the questions above common to all law partnerships or only to larger firms? Are the solutions suggested appropriate for all firms or just to larger ones? In what ways are the problems of small firms unique? When does a firm cease to be small?

3. What do the *Myers*, *Komisarow* and *Redman* cases suggest to lawyers contemplating non-partnership group practices? What should lawyers Myers and Lansky have done differently? Must lawyers anticipate unethical, illegal, or dishonest conduct from other lawyers?

4. How does law firm growth affect the partnership compensation system? What is wrong with simply splitting the profits equally? Should the terms of the profit distribution plan be incorporated in the partnership agreement, a separate document, or decided each year? What are the advantages/disadvantages of each approach?

5. How should a law firm address the problem of aging partners? Is mandatory retirement the answer? If so, at what age should lawyers be retired? If firms do not have a mandatory retirement age, how do they decide when a lawyer is no longer productive or capable of practicing law competently?

6. In light of the partnership issues involved in creating ancillary or subsidiary businesses, are lawyer/nonlawyer ventures dangerous? Is the opposition from the organized bar, to law firm diversification into non-legal business, well founded? Are there rational arguments for and against business ventures with nonlawyers in any of these areas: business? Ethical? constitutional? What are the implications for the practice of law?

7. Could a public interest law firm organize itself as a not-for-profit organization under I.R.C. § 501(c)(3)? How would such an arrangement affect partner compensation and other organizational matters?

8. Can you think of circumstances where your firm would find it advantageous to create some form of business affiliation with nonlegal service providers? What are the advantages and disadvantages or pursuing innovative service delivery models? How would you structure these relationships in order to avoid possible disciplinary charges?

C. COMPENSATING THE OWNERS

One of the toughest tasks for any law firm is setting policies for compensating the partners. Under the UPA, partners share profits as well as the risk of loss equally. Although this concept appeals to the democratic instincts in all of us, in the real world, an equal distribution of profits rarely works over the long term. Because partners are compensated through the division of profits, resentment may develop. It is human nature for individuals to believe that they work harder, bring in more clients, or make other more valuable contributions than other partners. Like the pigs in George Orwell's *Animal Farm*, lawyers frequently believe that some animals should be more equal than others. In fact, many law firm breakups are triggered by disputes over money.

Compensation systems attempt to establish in advance the factors to be used in distributing profits in an equitable manner. It should be noted that no system is right for every firm, and every firm must develop its own plan for compensating the owners in light of its members, practice, goals and philosophy.

The following article provides a flavor of the considerations that go into making compensation decisions. For law students this seems like a fairly simple question: fairness demands that everyone share equally, but when the question plays out in real life, partners often peg their comparative self-worth, status in the firm, and personal self-image to how much they are paid.

TEN TERRIBLE TRUTHS ABOUT LAW FIRM PARTNER COMPENSATION

From *Edge International*, by H. Edward Wesemann.
(http://www.edge.ai).

Just about the only law firms where a significant amount of time and effort is not spent determining partner compensation are solo practitioners. It seems that in every other firm, regardless of whether it has 5 lawyers or 500, more time is spent talking about each other's compensation than any other management or practice topic. In fact, it is rare that any meeting or retreat of a law firm partnership doesn't dissolve into a discussion of the inadequacies of the compensation system. Law firm partners love nothing more than fretting and talking about how they compensate each other.

Given the per partner profits many firms enjoy, it would not seem that dividing the spoils would be such a demanding task. Yet in some firms committees devote hundreds of hours delving through reams of computer reports in search of the perfect allocation of the firm's net income. I believe there are 10 inescapable truths about law firms' approach to compensating their partners that make the process harder and less successful than it should be.

1. Lawyers Often Equate Compensation With Management

It is not surprising that the public views lawyers as people who are only motivated by money, because that is precisely the way lawyers view themselves and their partners. You get what you pay for is the mantra of most law firm managers and, as a result, there is the belief that if you just set the reward high enough, lawyers will do whatever is asked of them. If it really is all about money, a firm shouldn't be surprised when its biggest rainmaker moves to the firm across the street for more money.

2. Law Firms Believe in Theory X

Management theorists suggest that there are two schools of management. Theory X postulates that everyone is naturally lazy and, if given the chance, will be indolent. Theory Y proposes that people actually want to work hard and do a good job; it is simply management's responsibility to motivate and train them. Law firms are hard line *Theory X* so most partner compensation systems are designed to assure that no one is overpaid.

3. Management is Divorced From Compensation

Even the largest law firms with hundreds of millions of dollars in revenues are run by part time managers whose compensation is based more on the clients they originate or their billable hours than on the success of their management efforts. Conversely, if the principle means of providing an incentive for partners is compensation, shouldn't the managers, who are responsible for getting things done, control the compensation?

4. Partners Are Constantly Afraid of Being Cheated

Unlike virtually every other business, most law firms have open compensation systems where every partner knows the compensation of every other partner. As a result, partners are more concerned about how they are being paid in relation to their fellow partners than the actual amount of their compensation.

5. There Are No Ties Between Compensation and the Performance it is Designed to Incent

In many firms the compensation list is published in a memo with no mention of why individual partners' pay is being increased or decreased. Firms rarely announce their expectations of partners, either as a group or individually. Instead, they give out vague signals on what is the expected behavior or level of performance.

6. Committees Avoid Responsibility for Compensation Actions

Typically, partner compensation is set by the management committee or a compensation committee so individual members can deflect responsibility for the results. In many firms, the compensation procedures keep the proceedings of the committee secret to assure that no partner can fully understand or question the message transmitted by compensation actions.

7. Compensation Systems Ignore Motivation

Psychologists tell us that recognition is, for most people, one of the greatest motivational tools that managers have. Most businesses that want their people to be successful look for every opportunity to hand out awards, send the best people on trips or give dinners in their honor. Lawyers are generally thought of as having high ego needs, yet law firms usually seem to strive to avoid singling anyone out for praise.

8. Law Firms Drive Partners to Be More Interested in the Size of Their Slice Rather Than the Size of the Pie

Increasing a partner's share of profits is a zero sum game. For one partner's share to go up, another's must go down. But many firms spent more time *dividing* than *creating*. It would seem to make more sense to focus partners' interest on increasing the total profits of the firm.

9. There Are Not Enough Dollars to Reward Some Things That Really Matter

By becoming meritocracies, law firms have embarked along a system of devoting a disproportionately large share of profits to the superstars who control business. As a result, there is little left to differentiate the rewards to those partners whose contributions (mentor associates, per-

10. Many of the Most Profitable Law Firms Have Lockstep Compensation Systems

Since compensation systems are highly confidential aspects of law firm governance, it is difficult to be definitive, however, there is at least anecdotal evidence to suggest that there is a correlation between profitability and compensation systems. Firms with the highest per partner profits seem to have more subjective ways of determining partner compensation including lockstep or modified lockstep systems (systems where increases in compensation is heavily determined by seniority). Less profitable firms seem to depend more on formulas and other objective statistics.

The real truth for law firms is that *three years of law school doesn't supercede five million years of evolution.* Nothing about being a lawyer causes a partner to be motivated by anything different than doctors, business executives, plumbers or bus drivers. Therefore, law firms should look outside their profession when designing compensation and recognition systems. It could have amazing results.

The next article examines some of the common systems used by law firms to make partner compensation decisions. There are basically three ways to handle these decisions, 1) fix the split in the operating agreement, 2) decide on the split as a business decision each year, or 3) create a formula that determines the split based on agreed upon criteria.

COMPENSATION SYSTEMS: FOR THE LOVE OF MONEY OR THE MISSION OF THE FIRM

From *Law Practice* Magazine, by David Bilinsky and Laura Calloway
(http://www.americanbar.org/publications/law_practice_home/law_practice_archive/lpm_magazine_articles_v32_is7_an9.htm).

"The love of money is the root of all evil"—or so the saying goes. At the very least, the words assuredly strike a chord with anyone who has ever faced the task of developing or modifying a law firm's compensation system. That is a project that all too often seems like a "mission impossible."

Developing a compensation system can be a weighty task. And that is especially true if you set out to do it *right*—which means establishing a system that reflects the new realities of practicing law while preserving the principles on which the firm was founded.

How can you accomplish the goal? To guide you, let's explore the different components, issues and other things you need to think about when developing or modifying your firm's compensation system in a way that will best suit the firm and its members.

The Firm's Business Objectives

What gets measured gets done. What gets compensated gets measured *and* done. When looking at your firm's mission statement, do you see objectives that are laudable but more often observed in the breach than in the performance? Perhaps the root cause is a misalignment between your firm's compensation formula and your mission statement.

There are many items that can be taken into account when deciding how to slice the profit pie (several of which are covered in the following sections). However, if the reward for performance is felt to be less than the effort required, or if the performance is not explicitly rewarded, then certain activities will be given only lip service—or ignored entirely. A notorious example is the "eat what you kill" system, which, in its simplest form, solely rewards collected fees. Under this system, it is hardly surprising that no partner or associate in the firm wishes to spend *any* time on *any* task that does not result in billable hours—especially ones with a high probability of being collected.

Even under other compensation systems, activities such as time spent converting an agreement into a firm precedent or time spent on firm administration usually fall into the compensation gap. Accordingly, if something is important enough to be included in your mission statement or stated to be a firm goal, then it should be recognized in the way the firm rewards performance.

The Formula Approach: Allocations at a Set Percentage

There are many methods used to divvy up the profit pie. The formula system has an explicit list of items that are rewarded, with each item weighted at a specific percentage to determine final compensation. As an example, let's assume the following:

- A small firm has a basic formula system under which 50 percent credit is given to collected fee revenues and 50 percent credit is given to fee origination.
- There are two partners—partner A, who bills $350,000 in a given year, and partner B, who bills $200,000 in the same year.
- Partner A originated 0 percent of the work, and partner B originated 100 percent of the work for the firm.

The compensation formula for the firm is:

$$\frac{(\text{partner fees collected}) + (\text{partner fees generated})}{(\text{total fees collected}) + (\text{total fees originated})} \times 100 = \% \text{ partner's share}$$

In this example, the result for partner A is:

$$\frac{(\$350,000) + (0) = \$350,000}{(\$550,000) + (\$550,000) = \$1,100,000} \times 100 = \% \ 32$$

The result for partner B is:

$$\frac{(\$200{,}000) + (550{,}000) = \$750{,}000}{(\$550{,}000) + (550{,}000) = \$1{,}100{,}000} \times 100 = \%\,68$$

So, while Partner A bills more, he is only entitled to 32 percent of the firm's profit because of the weight given to the fee origination credit. Partner B, although she bills less, is nevertheless entitled to 68 percent of the profits owing to her rainmaking efforts.

As you can see, both the inclusion (or exclusion) and the weights assigned to the different factors in the compensation agreement can have a profound impact on the final distribution of the firm's profit pie.

The Subjective Approach: Distribution by Committee

Other law firms use a purely subjective distribution system. In this approach, there is no precise formula used to determine the profit distribution among the partners. Instead, the firm's compensation committee decides the profit allocation from year to year based on purely subjective grounds.

This system, of course, allows for great latitude in how profits get distributed each year—and it can also allow for the factoring in of different items from year to year as conditions change. However, it can quickly result in the breakup of the firm unless a great deal of trust is placed in the ability of the compensation committee members to reward each of the firm's lawyers fairly and equitably.

The Blended Approach: Adjustable Criteria

Then there are the blended compensation systems, which combine a formula with the subjective system. They do so by taking into account an explicit number of factors—which account for, say, 80 percent of a lawyer's compensation—together with a pure subjective factor for the remaining 20 percent. This allows for an adjustment of the overall compensation along subjective criteria. Thus, the firm rewards its explicit goals through the formula but also allows for the reward of criteria that may not be specifically taken into account in a true formula approach.

For example, the firm's formula could recognize items such as the following:

- Fees collected
- Fees generated
- Time spent on firm administration
- Time spent mentoring younger associates

At the same time, the subjective criteria could take into account items like these:

- Pro bono work that generated high publicity for the firm

- Bar association activities
- Time spent on continuing legal education and the like

Note that in both the blended system and the straight formula system, another issue to consider is whether to use the compensation formula to determine the division of next year's profits (prospective) or the year just ended (retrospective). There are firms that follow each method, and there are pros and cons to each.

Other Things to Think About

Along with deciding which approach to gear your system toward, there are (as you might guess) a host of other issues to consider when developing a law firm compensation system. Here are some essential ones for savvy firms.

Metrics: Remember, what gets measured gets done. That is why it's smart to development some quantitative answers to questions such as the following:

- What is the ratio of the highest paid partner to the lowest?
- How does the compensation of different practice groups or practice areas compare?
- What about the compensation paid to different offices?
- How important are these perceived differences, and what effect do they have on performance and culture in the firm?
- To what degree are certain partners able to influence the compensation division?

You should consider these questions in the context of your own compensation system—at least to acknowledge that there are many levels on which compensation will influence behavior in the firm.

Communication: Almost as important as the split of profits is the method used to communicate the compensation decisions to the members of the firm. Most firms would want to share only the criteria used to determine compensation. After all, how do you use the compensation system to change behavior unless the compensation criteria and their importance are known? Others will go further and distribute to all partners a list of what each partner receives in compensation.

In either instance, the firm wants to ensure that the criteria for rewarding extraordinary effort (but not necessarily the resulting bonuses) is made known to all partners and associates, in order to communicate that there are rewards for going beyond ordinary expectations.

Full faith: Almost all firms will use a compensation committee in determining how to slice up the pie—even if that "committee" is composed solely of a beneficent despot. In any case, to make compensation decisions on a fair and equitable basis, the compensation committee must have the trust and respect of the firm's partners. Otherwise, the compensation dialogue will degenerate and (as indicated earlier) may even result in the breakup of the firm.

Input from others in the firm: If your compensation system employs subjective criteria, to what extent are the opinions of various partners, practice group chairs and important staff members sought? Unless yours is a pure eat-what-you-kill firm, the importance of teamwork cannot be underestimated. And, as such, the opinion of team members is vital in determining compensation so that teamwork and effort are properly rewarded.

So, Did It Work?

The final criteria for judging the appropriateness of any compensation system gets assessed after you have given the particular system "a try." Specifically, after allocating a year's profits, you need to ask whether your system did, indeed, promote the goals that you set out in your business plan. Here you have to determine the tools used to measure your progress (or lack thereof) and whether your compensation system needs to be modified as a result.

Given the importance of retaining talented partners and associates in today's competitive and more mobile society, the compensation system should not be a reason to lose talent to the competition around the corner. The goal of any compensation system is to recognize extraordinary performance and reward it, while motivating everyone to perform above their current comfort zone.

PROBLEMS AND QUESTIONS

1. How are the terms compensation, income, profit, and equity related as they apply to partner compensation? How does the meaning of these words affect the approach a firm should take to rewarding partners?

2. Are problems involving the allocation of profits common to all law partnerships or only to larger firms? Are the solutions suggested in the readings appropriate for all firms or just to larger ones? In what ways are the problems of small firms unique? When does a firm cease to be small? How does law firm growth affect the partnership compensation system?

3. What is wrong with simply splitting the profits equally? Should the terms of the profit distribution plan be incorporated in the partnership agreement, a separate document, or decided each year? What are the advantages/disadvantages of each approach?

D. THE LIFE CYCLE OF A LAW FIRM
1. FROM GROWTH TO MATURITY

Successful law firms tend to grow. Although many small firms stay small, and many lawyers never take on partners, most large law firms started small and grew. In part, they grew because they served their clients well, because they were run well, and because they planned well. This last element, planning for growth, is important in the long-term practice development of a law firm.

As firms grow, they frequently seek to serve larger clients and handle larger matters. There are, however, a limited number of opportunities for this high-end business, and the more exclusive the clientele the greater the competition. Thus, expansion is more than numerical growth. Hiring lawyers to do more work will be a futile exercise if there is no more work to give them. The firm must plan for growth in conjunction with its efforts to develop a marketing plan.

Not all growth is generated internally. When a firm hires a lateral partner, it is doing more than acquiring an employee. It is merging its practice with the new partner's practice. In fact, it has become fairly commonplace for distinct law firms, sometimes very large firms from different cities, to merge their practices.

It is also not unusual for law firms to develop branch offices in different cities, sometimes by merger and sometimes not. As law practice has become less local, law firms have expanded their practices beyond the towns and cities where they were founded. Some firms have established affiliations with non-legal organizations, hired nonlawyer professionals and created non-legal subsidiaries that expand not only the geographic coverage of the firm but also the scope of services themselves.

The following article discusses some of the phenomena associated with the life cycle of a law firm. We sometimes think of businesses restructuring themselves in difficult economic times in order to survive, but businesses also reinvent themselves as they evolve. Law firms are no exception.

PLCs SPUR STRATEGIES FOR SUCCESS
From *New Jersey Law Journal*, by Marian L. Matthaey (July 26, 1990).

Evidence of an increasingly competitive legal marketplace confronts attorneys on a daily basis. More and more, we hear of the escalating price of hiring new attorneys from top-name law schools—and its impact on firm profits. There is news of law firm mergers across the United States and Canada practically every week. Just what this all means would be unclear, were it not for the experience of other service industries that have traveled this road before. Students of marketing theory know that every product-or service goes through a "product life cycle" which consists of four stages introduction, growth, maturity and decline. The graphical representation of a service's product life cycle (PLC) is generally a bell-like curve that depicts its revenue performance over time.

PLC curves can and should be used to plan a law firm's marketing strategy. They can also be used to predict competitive marketing activities at other law practices. PLC curves of different law firms will vary according to a number of factors including how long a firm has been in business; the location of the practice; legal services provided; the number and fee levels of attorneys employed there; and the number and type of clients served.

There is, however, a PLC curve which represents the "average" American law firm. This curve can be used to identify the life-cycle stage of the law firm and its competitors, and most importantly, to plan its marketing strategy. The traits that characterize each stage of the "average" law firm's life cycle are explained below.

Start–Up

- Slow growth in revenues and the number of new clients.
- Highs overhead and administrative costs.
- Negative profits as the firm struggles to break even.
- Firm concludes that the best way to market the firm is simply to be good lawyers.

Growth

- Rapid growth in revenues and the number of new clients.
- The addition of practice areas to serve the needs of existing clients.
- Fee levels and profits rise.
- Additional attorneys and support staff are hired to service growing demand.
- Administrative chaos.
- Competitors begin to enter specific market niches in increasing numbers (local markets and specific industries).
- Firm continues to believe that the best way to market the firm is simply to be good lawyers.

Maturity

- Revenue growth slows.
- Compaction increases as the supply of law firms lawyers catches up with demand.
- The number of law firm mergers increases.
- Law firms look for ways to protect their client base from erosion in order to maintain historical growth trends.
- The firm begins employing innovative approaches to market and price its services.

- Marketing/recruiting expenditures rise, and sophisticated marketing personnel are hired.
- Profits begin to erode due to falling revenues. As a result, more money needs to be spent on marketing and recruiting.

Decline

- Revenues and profits decline rapidly.
- Fee schedules become more flexible.
- The notion of the "institutional" client dies.
- Law firms specialize to stay competitive, and employ fewer attorneys.
- Weak firms are acquired by stronger firms or go out of business.

While it is apparent that the American legal industry is in the maturity stage, this should in no way be seen, as its death knell, for maturity is the longest stage of the PLC and can last from less than five years to many centuries. A number of innovative marketing strategies can be employed by law firms operating in a mature industry, whether they themselves are young or well-established. Some of them are described below.

Law firms can distinguish themselves by catering to the unique needs of specific market segments. A law firm can divide its clients into market segments by grouping them according to industry groups (insurance companies, manufacturers, health-care institutions, service businesses), legal practice areas (litigation, corporate/commercial, environmental), or geographic location (local, statewide, national or international). The legal services offered can than be streamlined according to the specific needs of one or more segments.

For example, some firms have created special practice groups that cater to the insurance industry, health care sector, environmental clients or local companies. They have developed news letters and brochures that provide meaningful information targeted at the specific audiences they want to address. Still other firms have attorneys routinely speak to association groups where members of targeted segments tend to congregate, or write by-lined articles for publications that they regularly read.

Protecting Existing Client Base

One of the best ways for law firms to protect their existing client base is to be aware of changes in clients' needs or wants—and to respond to them. This can be as simple as telephoning important clients regularly, scheduling informal breakfast meetings or lunches, or inviting them out socially.

Many law firms opt to have outside consultants independently interview their own clients. This helps the firm identify potential trouble spots early, such as billing or pricing problems, personality conflicts, unmet client expectations, and attempts by other law firms to steal the business away. A law firm can also conduct this type of survey itself, either in person or over the telephone.

Another, way to increase the loyalty of existing clients is to introduce them to other lawyers at the firm, thereby cross-selling the firm's services. This will reinforce the idea to these clients that they are important and that you want their business. It will also strengthen the link between the client and your law firm if new business is actually consummated.

Create Additional Practice Areas

There are several ways to create additional practice areas and increase the law firm's appeal to both existing and potential clients. The first is to recruit experienced attorneys with relatively modest compensation requirements and existing clients. This can be accomplished by hiring lawyers who have been out on their own, law professors or attorneys seeking part-time employment (they probably have another source of income), or former public servants (they may have worked for government or social-service agencies in the past). In the case of these new hires, it is important to specify quotas for bringing in new business immediately or over a specific short-term period.

A second approach involves sharing office space with attorneys in another city. Such space need not be expensive or plush; its sole purpose lies in giving the firm access to clients and prospects located in the distant city.

A third tactic is to merge with another law firm. This approach has its advantages as well as its disadvantages. Its benefits include sharing the experience and reputation of an established law firm that is familiar with the local market, of different clients and practice areas in your own market.

Leveraging expenses is another advantage of this approach. The downside includes struggling to apportion expenses between the law firms and adjusting to the firm culture of an unknown entity.

. . .

The problems encountered by lawyers who leave existing law firms to start new firms are no different than those faced by two or more independent practitioners who decide to merge their practices. Chances are very good that you will be merging your practice with the practice of one or more other lawyers at some time during your career as a lawyer. In addition to all the issues that confront any entrepreneurial activity, mergers introduce other complications from managing egos to conflicts of interest.

2. DEATH AND RETIREMENT

Traditionally, lawyers were presumed to be responsible for putting away enough cash to be able to live comfortably in retirement and protect their families in case of death. The practice of law generally provided an income sufficient to allow attorneys to do this. As law firms gradually replaced individual practices, and the legal business became less profitable in terms of earnings compared to gross revenues, law firms have been forced to assume greater responsibility for retirement planning of members.

In many firms, the founding partners have assumed that younger lawyers they brought into the firm *were* the retirement plan. These lawyers often resent carrying the load of an older partner who does not work as much as when he was young. This situation creates an unfortunate clash, which neither side can win. The materials in this section address some of the basic questions involving retirement and death.

If it seems to you that this area is incredibly complex, you are correct. If you are not a tax specialist, you may find retirement planning to be confusing and arcane. Unfortunately, every lawyer must learn the basics in order to make sound decisions about retirement. You may turn to a tax lawyer, accountant, or sales representatives for help, but if you are a decision-maker in the firm, you cannot decline to develop some sophistication about your options.

The next article addresses a subject that is difficult to confront in real life: death. Unfortunately, many lawyers die before they retire, so firms must plan for such a possibility as well.

A LOSS IN THE FIRM

From *Pennsylvania Lawyer*, by Christine L. Arnold (October 15, 1985).

This is a story about someone who died.

In particular it is a story about a lawyer who died.

He wasn't a corporate counsel or an international businessman, and the daily crises he solved weren't as dramatic as the ... price of steel in Japan. But ... those who depended on him found him no less conscientious because of it. He spent a lot of time tying up the loose ends in their lives and he was very good at it. It wasn't because it was his job. It was because he enjoyed it.

He was a modest, sympathetic, small-town lawyer who loved the law.

He was my father.

My father was an old-fashioned lawyer with Main Street in his blood. He wore conservative business suits and those black wingtips that lawyers of his generation wear even in their dreams. He kept his hair cut very short and his expression smooth and even.

He greeted friends and strangers alike with a non-partisan, gentlemanly good-nature, and because of this and because he was a homegrown boy, he was well-liked in our small, insular, middle-class town. He would do almost anything for almost anyone. James K. Arnold was the kind of a man other men call a good guy.

Late last summer a nameless pain crept into his spine. The cancer, as yet unrecognized, had spread quietly from his lung. He was incapacitated almost immediately. He never walked again and the pain never subsided; instead, perversely, it flourished as he grew weaker. He wore a good front for his friends and his colleagues, spoke a lot about beating the disease and convinced those who wanted to be convinced that he'd be back running their lives in no time.

You've probably heard time after time how vicious cancer gets. You may know that sometimes it gets particularly vicious. As January drew to a close his cancer finally consumed him.

He was a plan-maker and a good lawyer, but I don't think he ever made the kind of plans he might have made for someone else with a terminal disease, because in the end I'm not sure he knew he was going to die. I know he didn't want to.

[A]fter graduation from law school and stints in the armed services, two young lawyers formed a partnership. Its make-up was simple enough—my father and one of his high school friends, both hometown boys, both graduates of the same college and law school, both alike in the ways young men from the same town will be, yet as different from each other as two peas from different pods. It was a comfortable partnership; each complemented the other. Over the years it grew, until at its largest it consisted of three partners and two secretaries.

In the year before my father became ill, the third partner in the firm left to become a common pleas judge, and an assistant district attorney came into the office part time to absorb some of the work. About nine months later, my father became stricken with cancer. With these two developments, the firm went from three full-time partners to one full-time partner and one part-time associate in a little less than a year.

It was a drastic reduction in income and manpower, and while health and accident insurance took care of some of the firm's earnings, and while the legal agreement between my father and his partner, John Slike, had some contingencies for illness or injury, the business suffered. There was a severe loss of income, but bills and salaries still had to be paid. Reports and work that my father singularly performed as office manager, ranging from payroll to quarterly reports, had to be picked up by the firm's chief secretary and it increased substantially her workload.

. . .

Thelma McCauslin, the firm's secretary and a seasoned legal assistant who had been with the firm almost from the start, was surprised by the volume of work my father had handled that now had to be turned over to others.

In dealing with clients, my father tried as well as he could to do some work from his hospital bed, but because of the effects both of the disease and its treatments, it soon became apparent he wouldn't be able to do what he had planned. In addition, the strict timing of tax season was approaching, and the bulk of his work in those early months of the year normally involved processing tax records and returns. But this year, as he slid closer to death, he would be unable even to begin to read the voluminous amount of tax law updates or to study the changes in his Computax forms.

John Slike saw clients who had to be seen and put in extra time to try to tackle the most immediate problems, such as property settlements that had to be handled, litigation with time requirements or marital matters.

"If people called," says Thelma, "the squeaky wheel effect took place."

But there was work that didn't get done simply because there just wasn't anyone to do it. All of the preparation and research that normally went into a seemingly endless flow of tax returns did not get done, so all the tax work had to be "shipped out completely" to accountants, says Thelma. Wills and trusts were put aside, she says, "if the people were under 85 and looked pretty good. We did little medical examinations," to see if "we could hold off for a month or so." Corporate matters such as minutes for meetings were also put on the back burner.

My father rebelled against the mere suggestion of death and while it seemed to bolster him against his disease, this posture only made it harder for his co-workers and regular clients to prepare for the inevitable. "There was always a glimmer of hope," says John, "but nothing more than a glimmer." A lot of people who didn't see my father regularly or only spoke with him on the phone believed from his upbeat demeanor that he would be back in a matter of months and were shocked soon after to find him on his deathbed.

Books containing tax law information and new tax forms arrived and there was no one to read or work on them, but it was out of the question, out of deference to his battle, to cancel orders. As the firm's bookkeeper and office manager he had always handled payroll, quarterly reports, bill-paying, bank-account balancing and had developed systems peculiar to his way of doing things that he followed without interruption for years. There was no one who knew his system as well as he did, and the practice began to mire down in paperwork. He had always taken care of it; you could count on him to do it, Thelma says, and it was far more time consuming than anyone suspected.

The disease took its course in five months, perhaps kind in its cruel brevity. There was a little more time to prepare for the inevitable than if he had died from a heart attack or in an accident. But five months is not a long time, and he was not as realistic about the effect of his absence, understandably, as he might have been. So it was harder than it might have been to prepare for the aftermath. Non-acceptance is a particularly common occurrence when someone finds himself dying, and lawyers, despite their preoccupation with the future, are no different from bricklayers or college professors when the inevitable becomes personal.

Partnership agreements have contingencies for illness and death, but John says, "it's difficult to draft something to fit all the given situations." He says he knows now that an important factor to consider when preparing for such situations is not just the cost of buying out the other partner's interest in the firm, but also the cost of the time spent reassuring clients and adjusting office management following a severe disability or death. Covering that cost in contingency planning would help "to fund the firm until it is reestablished," he says.

Also, John thinks more now about what would happen should he be stricken by an illness or suffer injury from an accident. He admits he never thought much about what would happen to the firm in the past, because he knew he could depend on my father and their former partner to keep things going for him. Now he says, "If I get hit by a car, what would happen to the firm?"

... ["Key person"] insurance paying a partner's share directly to the firm or other kinds of income coverage could help lessen the financial stress. "Larger law firms have the edge," she says, in long range planning, since "seniors" often bring "juniors" into their areas of practice in preparation for lessening their workloads and retiring, and the quantity of able bodies makes it easier to pick up the lost partner's workload.

Early after my father's death, John and Thelma found themselves caught up in work that wasn't "income-producing." For a while, John spent his normal working day just talking to people, reassuring them, familiarizing himself with their problems and their personalities. Evenings and weekends were used for dictation and his own work.

Thelma, because of her good-natured familiarity with clients over the years, suddenly became the principal liaison between the firm and its dependents, "particularly with the older ones," she says. They had called her during my father's illness for updates on his progress and later just to express their sadness and sympathy. Now it was incumbent upon her to answer their everyday questions and let them know "the firm is still here." In many ways, she was directly responsible for protecting the client base after my father's death. She was the first line and without her friendly persuasion and patience, many clients might have moved immediately to other lawyers, feeling forgotten.

[I]t is important to develop a "we relationship" with clients instead of an "I relationship" as a way of protecting the firm from client loss after the death of a partner.... [K]eep communication broader and not reliant on one individual.

Thelma says many clients responded as though the world had been inexorably changed for them, or as if they had been cheated in some way by my father's death. "What am I going to do?" she says most remarked, "I relied on him." ... [M]y father dealt with a great many of his clients and he was almost overprotective in his way. It has been hard for those who grew comfortable with his manner to find another in quite the same mold.

. . .

Many clients will stay with the firm, growing accustomed to new faces and new ways of doing things (the part-time associate has now left the district attorney's office and is with the firm full-time). But some will go elsewhere in search of a new advisor, because my father's relationship with clients was almost always on the "I" level. It was his way of dealing with people, and while it may have harmed the firm's future, it endeared him to his clients and helped to fortify the aura of friendliness the firm continues to enjoy.

The months have passed since my father's death earlier this year, and as with all such things, the world has continued to spin and adjustments that once seemed enormous have begun to become habit.

The bookkeeping is now falling into place, and accountants are being consulted for financial advice. Time spent on reassuring clients and catching up on work is tapering off. While the financial transition is not yet complete, "the bills are going out on time," says John, and the flow of paper is re-approaching its normal speed. The re-evaluation of the nature of the practice, now no longer a partnership, has taken place and plans for the future have been considered.

But in a small firm, where partners and co-workers are old friends, where annual parties are held and vacations are shared, the loss is never really mitigated. There are daily reminders of my father—a key carefully hidden for emergencies, a light-hearted contest over the yearly growth of two sapling trees...." Letters and phone calls from those still unaware of my father's death require explanations.

"You spend a lot of nights," says Thelma, "wondering what to do and how to do it. A small firm like this gets to be family."

"A partnership is sort of like a marriage," says John. "You don't know whether you can find someone" again.

According to demographic studies, large number of lawyers from the Baby Boomer Generation will reach retirement age in the next two decades. Some firms have already confronted the myriad problems associated with retirement for lawyers who remain active and productive, as well as those who face expenses related to debilitating health problems. Succession planning is not something that firms will have to get around to someday, but a very real issue for partners today. ABA President Karen Mathis created a Second Season of Service Commission in 2006 to help aging lawyers to find new ways of serving the public in their golden years.

PROBLEMS AND QUESTIONS

1. What is your reaction to the various forms of law firm restructuring? Are they good for the practice of law? The legal profession? What problems do these approaches create?
2. Why do the Rules of Professional Conduct prohibit lawyers from using restrictive covenants as other businesses do? Is this a good or a bad idea? Why?
3. How much must be put aside for retirement? How should such retirement plans be funded? Who should decide? Who should administer the plan?
4. Are the psychological aspects of retirement as important as financial questions? Is the assumption that an attorney's skills eventually diminish a valid one? Does the answer depend on the type of practice? If some lawyers become less competent to practice law with advancing age while others do not, how should a firm decide if and when some can no longer practice?
5. What is the cost to a firm when a partner retires, if the retiring lawyer earned $150,000 annually and has at the age of retirement a life expectancy of 15 years? What if a retired lawyer outlives the actuarial projections for his demise? What is the potential cost? What is the cost to the firm to continue to provide support such as secretarial assistance and office space? What alternatives are available to a law firm?
6. Rule 5.4(a)(1) of the *Model Rules of Professional Conduct* provides for payment to a deceased lawyer's spouse for income derived from the lawyer's work in progress. Why is there a specific rule to cover this contingency? How are such payments different from payments under a pension plan?

3. METAMORPHOSIS

Although many solo and small firm lawyers simply close their offices when they retire, or their offices close when they die unexpectedly, the more common practice is for law firms to transition to different membership and leadership over time. In a small firm or solo practice, this might involve bringing in a younger lawyer to take over the practice. Although the ABA Model Rules of Professional Conduct provide in Rule 1.17 for the Sale of a Law Practice, including all the assets of the practice, including goodwill, the problem in selling a law practice finding an appropriate value for the practice.

Because law firms are not bought and sold on an open market, there is no fair market value for the ongoing business. The buyer and seller have to determine a value based on the net worth of the business, and traditionally, goodwill was not included in the computation of value. In other words, a buyer could acquire the building, furniture, computers and files of the seller, but no expectation of continued work. Rule 1.17 allowed lawyers to place a value on the anticipated future business of the practice, understanding that clients have no legal commitment to continue to be represented by the successor lawyer or firm.

In the case of solo practices and many small firms the reputation of individual lawyers may be more important to clients than the brand name of the firm, so even if a lawyer Bob Smith buys the practice of Larry Jones, clients will soon learn that Jones has retired, even if Smith retains the name of Jones & Smith, or Larry Jones and Associates.

In the case of boutique firms that have developed an institutional identity, as well as larger firms that establish historical continuity, the question is less vexing, but firms generally survive such transitions. However, the departure of individual lawyers may lead to the loss of key clients, and the loss of clients can undermine the stability of the original firm.

Larger firms may be able to survive partner defections, and in some cases entire practice groups have seceded to start their own firms or join other firms, and the original firm survives. A continuing exodus of lawyers and clients, however, may make the bleeding firm, or parts of it, a takeover target. If a firm fails to find a partner for merger or acquisition, it may collapse or simply be forced into bankruptcy. This was evident in the collapse of storied New York law firm Dewey LeBoeuf in 2012. In that case, economic consideration triggered reduced partner compensation, which in turn led a few partners to leave the firm. Over a period of months more lawyers, perhaps reading the handwriting on the walls, headed for the exit, until the meltdown of the entire organization ensued. When it was all over, the lawyers were gone and Dewey was no more, leaving only a bankruptcy court filing in its wake.

From a broader perspective, law firms are a little like the people who work in them: they are born, grow to maturity, carry out their business objectives, slow down, and come to an end. The end may come in the form of retirement, dissolution, metamorphosis into a new organization with new lawyers, or merger into some other organization(s). A continuing challenge for law firm leaders remains how to transfer power to successor leadership, sustain the firm when its founding members move on and find ways for the firm to evolve organically and competitively in the legal marketplace.

PROBLEMS AND QUESTIONS

1. If businesses can live forever how can the lawyers who practice in legal businesses assure the immortality of their organizations? Is this all about ego, or are there important reasons to keep organizations alive and well over time?

2. If you wanted to buy a practice, how would you place a dollar value on the expectation that clients of the lawyer selling the practice would follow you when you take over?

3. If a firm is in decline, what can the leaders do to turn around its economic fortunes? When things start to go bad is dissolution inevitable?

CHAPTER 5

MANAGING THE PRACTICE OF LAW

■ ■ ■

A. MANAGEMENT AND LAWYERS

The practice of law in the United States is a multibillion-dollar industry (see annual reports produced by the U.S. Bureau of Labor Statistics, http://bls.gov/ooh/Legal/Lawyers.htm), indispensable to the functioning of modern society. The delivery of legal services by lawyers to the people they represent is fundamental to the process of dispute resolution, and ultimately to the legitimacy of the justice system in this country. Although the law itself is constantly changing, a truth that all lawyers and law students implicitly understand, the fact that the practice of law is constantly evolving may be under-appreciated by those in the business of delivering legal services. Certainly, longtime practitioners will readily admit that practice has changed over the course of their careers, but most have not stopped practicing long enough to examine the implications of change on their day-to-day work. If anything, most practicing lawyers are reactive rather than proactive.

Actually, most lawyers are ill-equipped to run a business organization efficiently and profitably. Some of this is due to self-selection. If most of us had wanted to go into business, we would have gone to business school. Instead, we made a conscious decision to practice law, only to find out when we graduate that we have to run a business in order to pursue our chosen career.

Some critics charge that lawyers are greedy, and that money clouds lawyers' professional judgment. In reality, most lawyers work hard and expect a fair return on their investment, but very few get rich practicing law, and fewer still are outright crooks. If a law firm can provide legal services more efficiently, both clients and lawyers will benefit through lower costs for the services and a better return to the providers.

Disciplinary authorities confirm that lawyers who get into trouble over financial matters often are experiencing economic difficulties that tempt them to cut corners or take other inappropriate actions. Thus, it should not be too much of a stretch to say that a well-run legal business is also likely to be a professional practice.

One of the reasons that lawyers are not prepared for the business aspects of practicing law, in addition to self-selection and misconceptions about professionalism, is that their legal education does not adequately prepare them for the business of practicing law. The law school curriculum is heavily weighted in favor of teaching a vast amount of substantive information and developing a narrow range of legal skills through a traditional pedagogical framework based upon the so-called Socratic method, euphemistically referred to as "learning to think like a lawyer." This approach would have been unrecognizable to Socrates, but more importantly, it has very little in common with the actual work of lawyers. It is sometimes said that recent bar examinees know more law and less about what to do with it than anyone in the profession.

Many legal educators are re-examining the structural approaches to legal education and the preparation of lawyers for the practice of law. The traditional framework of legal education remained relatively unchanged for generations, but the changing realities of law practice and society have forced legal educators to re-think some of their basic assumptions. Law schools today universally offer clinical and lawyering skills courses, and individual professors are experimenting with different teaching methods in traditional courses.

PROBLEMS AND QUESTIONS

1. Is it accurate to say that lawyers management skills are wanting? What can lawyers do to get up to speed?
2. What is the role of law school in preparing lawyers as practice managers? What do you expect to get out of this course to help you be a better manager?

B. MANAGEMENT THEORY AND PRACTICE

Management theory is not new to many fields of business and industry, where thinking about how to improve efficiency and productivity is a central concern. Managers and executives in most large companies and many small ones study business in college, and those who did not receive business degrees during their undergraduate education often return to graduate business programs for MBAs or other advanced degrees. Over the years, academics in business schools have provided an intellectual framework for management by conducting research and writing on how organizations work. Competing theories attempt to describe how business leaders can best direct a work force and produce a profit for the company.

Many of the ideas and principles of business management fail to filter down to professional service firms generally, and law firms in particular, perhaps because lawyers are inherently stubborn about incorporating business and managerial principles into their work. Lawyers could learn something from their counterparts in the business world, and from business school writers who attempt to articulate management theory and define business practice. Although a review of this literature is beyond the scope of this casebook, several articles are included below to give law students an insight into B-school thinking.

1. B–SCHOOL THINKING

Business schools have explored the management of professional services firms for generations. The literature, both academic and popular, surrounding the science of management is both extensive and sophisticated, yet ignored by most lawyers. Publications such as the *Harvard Business Review*, and other academic journals are replete with case studies of professional service firms in general and law firms in particular.

Authors like Peter Drucker, one of the pre-eminent management voices of the twentieth century, as well as numerous other business school authors, have examined such issues as quality, leadership, vision, and innovation, to name a few, and yet, this scholarship is often lost on lawyers. Business schools offer courses dealing specifically with the management of professional service firms, and business school academic literature is replete with scholarship that could arguably benefit lawyers. Drucker, mentioned above, has this to say about management in the entrepreneurial age:

THE COMING OF THE NEW ORGANIZATION
From *Harvard Business Review*, by Peter F. Drucker (January/February 1988).

The typical large business 20 years hence will have fewer than half the levels of management than its counterpart today, and no more than a third the managers. In its structure, and in its management problems and concerns, it will bear little resemblance to the typical manufacturing company, circa 1950, which our textbooks still consider the norm. Instead it is far more likely to resemble organizations that neither the practicing manager nor the manager scholar pays much attention to today: the hospital, the university, the symphony orchestra. For like them, the typical business will be knowledge-based, an organization composed largely of specialists who direct and discipline their own performance through organized feedback from colleagues, customers, and headquarters. For this reason, it will be what I call an information-based organization.

Businesses, especially large ones, have little choice but to become information-based. Demographics, for one, demand the shift. The center of gravity in employment is moving fast from manual and clerical workers to knowledge workers who resist the command-and-control model that business took from the military 100 years ago. Economics also dictates change, especially the needs for large businesses to innovate and to be entrepreneurs. But above all, information technology demands the shift.

Drucker's observations concerning the shape of knowledge-based organizations seem uncanny in light of the information revolution that has swept through business and industry over the past two decades. Although the multi-layered hierarchical organization that typified 1950s era businesses has not disappeared from the landscape, many corporations have acted dramatically to streamline their operations. This drama is played out through reorganization, downsizing, acquisition, and merger. Drucker also notes that information technology is a central component of this paradigm shift, and although Drucker is speaking about business enterprises generally, the application of his concepts to the practice of law is undeniable.

Law firms and other professional service organizations traditionally have operated with much less hierarchy, management and structure than many other forms of business. Some commentators from the business school arena have focused particularly on the management of these small professional service firms. From the outside looking in, but drawn from the wider experience of business research and theory, they see things about the management of law firms that we lawyers may not. David Maister, presently a management consultant, but formerly a business professor specializing in professional services organizations, is typical of this insightful breed:

LEGAL STRATEGY 101: IT'S TIME FOR LAW FIRMS TO RE-THINK THEIR BUSINESS MODEL

From Knowledge@Wharton, April 29, 2009.

The global financial crisis is reshaping many businesses—and tradition-bound, top-drawer law firms are no exception. While the legal industry had begun to face the need for change before the current economic downturn, the crisis is accelerating trends that will alter the structure and operations of law firms going forward.

The sudden lack of liquidity has led to a dearth of transactions, killing demand for many legal services. At the same time, clients facing their own financial pressures are increasingly scrutinizing budgets and demanding more value for their legal expenses.

In the short term, firms are laying off lawyers and support staff, delaying new hires and, in come cases, closing their doors. Fundamental characteristics of the industry are also being called into question, including fees based on billable hours and the partnership structure of law firms. "There were signs before the crisis that the business model had to evolve. The crisis is just making it more urgent," says Wharton management professor Olivier Chatain.

The sudden and steep drop in business has been particularly hard on law firms because of their structure, according to Chatain. A typical law firm is owned by its partners, who are supported by the work of many associates. Law firms refer to the ratio of partners to associates as "leverage." In good times, the arrangement produces strong profits, but when revenues fall, highly leveraged firms can find it particularly difficult to sustain all those associates. As a result, if revenues at a law firm decline 10%, profits can fall 30%, Chatain says. "These firms are very sensitive to downturns. [Because] the partners have to break even every year, they have to do immediate cost-cutting to make sure they adapt their overhead and expenses."

In response, firms have been forced to take harsh measures, says Robert J. Borghese, a Wharton lecturer and principle of the Borghese Law Firm with offices in New York and Philadelphia. "Most large firms are leveraged up for big deals. With no big deals coming through the door, there's not a lot of work for associates so firms have to delever [cut] employees. There's definitely going to be a sea change in the law industry as a result of the credit crisis."

Beyond staffing, Borghese says firms face pressure from clients to move away from a payment model based on hourly rates. "Billable hours will always be here, but you will see more of a movement toward retainers and fixed fees."

More clients these days are trying to negotiate flat fees for services so they have a better sense of what their legal expenses will be upfront, says Chastain, adding that the industry has not always relied on charging by the hour. Prior to World War II, a fee based on hourly rates was the exception in legal pricing. Clients "want to have more value for their money, and that means the hourly rate may not be the best way to set prices. This is something law firms are not comfortable with. The whole model with many associates working for the partners is predicated on associates billing a lot of hours."

While the financial pressure on law firms is now acute, Chatain says the industry faces more challenges over the long term as clients begin to pay more attention to the value they receive from their lawyers. Some clients have become more aggressive in pitting firms against one another. For example, in the United Kingdom, General Electric staged an online auction process to select legal representation.

In the United States, the Association of Corporate Counsel (ACC), which represents in-house lawyers, who typically hire outside law firms for specialty work, has introduced a new set of guidelines for law firms and corporate counsel. The guidelines are designed to make both sides work to keep costs in line with the value of the legal services provided, while assuring a fair return to law firms. The arrangement is similar to the types of agreements made famous by Japanese automakers and their suppliers that create value throughout the supply chain. The suppliers, in this case law firms, agree to provide their services at a fair cost, though perhaps not necessarily the lowest cost, and client companies agree to provide a steady stream of business.

The ACC also has drafted a sample covenant for companies to share with their legal providers that outlines specific steps the two sides could agree to take. For example, the covenant calls for clients to define objectives in the engagement, pay bills promptly and understand that budgets may need to be revised for unforeseen events. Law firms would agree to learn the client's business and strategic objectives, give honest feedback on whether the client's objectives in a matter are realistic and attainable, and use appropriate staffing to pursue a case.

Susan Hackett, [former] general counsel of the ACC, says the new approach to value is necessary because law firms had become so expensive that their fees often outstripped the value of the problem they were brought in to resolve. "You can have many lawyers and paralegals all billing on a matter worth $50,000 of exposure adding up to a grand total of $250,000. That's crazy."

According to Chatain, the traditional model was designed to provide clients with top legal advice because of the brutal winnowing out of associates along the path to partner. Anyone who made it to partner was likely to be extremely talented and hard-working. In recent years, however, he says younger lawyers have been less interested in the traditional route because of the long odds and personal hardships of becoming a partner, diminishing the likelihood of getting the best and brightest at every step of the process. "There's a concern that maybe it's getting harder to keep the best employees within the firm. These trends were there before the crisis; the crisis is only making it worse."

According to Stephen Burbank, a law professor and former general counsel at the University of Pennsylvania, the legal profession has been slow to innovate, but is now beginning to explore new business models.

In recent years firms have experimented with outsourcing legal work to India and other low-cost countries, but that strategy has not been very successful, Burbank says, adding that companies are turning to "in-sourcing"—or building up their own in-house legal departments—to do work that had been done by expensive outside firms. He points to Cisco and the Ace insurance group as examples of companies that have created large, multidisciplinary legal departments handling everything from regulatory matters to environmental issues.

In-house departments, adds Hackett, can use less expensive employees to do some routine work, such as creating files or managing documents that do not require the specialized skills of a high-priced lawyer.

Chatain says another emerging model is the "virtual" firm, which acts as an intermediary between clients and lawyers who have left big firms in order to work on a freelance basis. An example is Axiom Legal, a New York based company that hires lawyers for temporary assignments. Axiom clients include Google, Dow Jones, NBC and General Electric.

Axiom lawyers used to work in big firms and are well-trained, but didn't want to join the "whole rat race," according to Chatain. The clients receive service similar to a major law firm at less cost. "Almost everyone is happy," says Chatain, except for the traditional law firm, "which is unhappy because it actually trained the lawyers."

Burbank says law firms are hampered from creating innovative business structures by their own regulations that prohibit anyone who is not a lawyer from owning shares in a firm. He argues that this rule, supported by the American Bar Association and state supreme courts, which oversee the regulation of law firms, has protected firms from competition, but also stifles innovation by denying firms a way to offer more flexible services at lower cost. This prohibition has kept law firms from being able to tap the venture capital or equity markets, leaving them dependent on debt financing, which has been difficult to attain in the current environment.

Meanwhile, law firms in Europe and the United Kingdom are now undergoing a period of rapid deregulation following passage of Britain's Legal Services Act of 2007, which allows for alternative business structures and non-lawyer ownership of firms, Burbank notes. "It is quite conceivable that within 10 years, you will have a largely deregulated legal profession in the U.K. and Europe. Given the phenomena of globalization, it's hard to imagine this won't put incredible competitive pressure on large American law firms."

. . .

Aside from plaintiff's lawyers, Burbank says, most lawyers are not entrepreneurial by nature and have long been shielded from competition. "They have a monopoly, and that is how they have survived."

He points out that the regulation, in part, protects individuals from dishonest or unprofessional lawyers. However, he argues that the regulations should be tailored to the type of client being served. "Individuals need more protection against their lawyers than a sophisticated corporation," Burbank states. "We don't have that flexibility and every time you make a proposal for fundamental change in the regulation of the legal profession some lawyers come out waving the flag of the individual. They may have the best motives in the world, but the result is that law firms have little incentive to innovate."

Joseph Ryan, an adjunct professor of management at Wharton who teaches in a specialized management program tailored for Reed Smith, the international law firm headquartered in Pittsburgh, says law firms need to learn to think strategically. Partly because of the nature of their work, law firms tend to be focused on the problem at hand, rather than larger strategic goals, he suggests. "The way a lawyer sees things is more analytical than synthetic. They don't connect the dots."

Ryan says that with today's new financial pressures, law firm managers must think beyond individual transactions and build deep relationships with clients to anticipate their needs rather than reacting simply to cases that arise. He suggests that other service firms, such as advertising agencies and consultants, have done a better job of relating to their clients in this way.

Law firms also tend to celebrate individual rainmaking partners, but no one individual can supply the kind of comprehensive service today's clients demand, Ryan adds. While "rainmaking is virtuous," he says, "strategic account management is a team game. The question is how do you let the rainmaker continue to grow the business and discover the needs of the client, but integrate other people from the firm into the team?"

Ryan cites three levers to building strategic thinking into a law firm. The first is defining a process for allocating resources which could result in more effective collaboration across practice and geographic areas. A second lever is clearly articulating the firm's competitive advantage and value proposition. The third is developing an honest assessment of talent within the firm and making the most of that talent.

Mark Dembovsky, a London-based partner at Reed Smith and the firm's chief strategist, worries that the current crisis and its drastic staff reductions may prevent firms from building practices that will be sustainable into the future. "I see the lemming principle [at work]. There is a lot of panic and, to me, that's a big worry because what happens in a year's time when the market turns around and firms must recruit? It takes a while to build up your practice. Those law firms that have the guts to do it are using this opportunity to build up certain practices that they might not have otherwise done because of the competition for lawyers."

Despite his concern that firms may be overreacting now, he agrees there is no question that law firm management must learn to think and act more like corporate business leaders. He says part of the problem is that in the current law firm structure, most partners serve many functions, in addition to providing legal expertise to clients.

The partnership structure is a plus for firms because it creates a collegial environment, Dembovsky suggests. But unlike a corporation with professional managers, a law firm's shareholders—its partners—are also expected to run the business day-to-day. "Therefore, they have great difficulty letting go and allowing other people to take on responsibility for finance or strategy or human relations." In many firms, he notes, the highest fee producing lawyer is viewed as a good lawyer and is automatically chosen to run the practice group, whether or not he or she is an effective manager.

Only in the past 10 years have law firms begun to think about bringing professional managers into parts of the firm which are often run by committee—without an individual responsible for directing any part of the business. The challenge for law firms, he says, is to find a new way to introduce professional lines of responsibility and management without destroying the firm's collegial and consensual nature—which inspires trust and, in the end, benefits clients.

"One mustn't knock the partnership structure," he says, "but one needs to see how to build on top of that structure to maintain the positive elements of a partnership with the positive elements of a well-run corporation."

Similar books and articles on professional service firm management abound in the business literature, although most of these are ignored by practicing lawyers. Lawyers could learn a great deal from the business literature, including popular non-fiction works, if they would take the time to look. See the Resources Section (Appendix A) of this book, or peruse the Business Section of almost any bookstore (or book website, e.g., http://www.amazon.com).

2. THE LEGAL PERSPECTIVE

Despite the myriad changes facing the legal profession, the basic principles of effective office management are not new. Law practice management, strategic planning and organizational systems are not novel. Dwight McCarthy and Reginald Heber Smith articulated many ideas, which recur in present day literature on law practice management, long before most living lawyers were born. Despite the rapid changes in technology and other aspects of practice, many of the basic principles of sound management have not changed over the years. McCarthy was telling lawyers how to practice law on the verge of the Great Depression, and Smith was writing just after America entered World War II, in times that were both different and similar to our world today.

THE FUNCTION OF MANAGEMENT
From *Law Office Management*, by Dwight G. McCarthy (1927).

The changing law practice—It is well to recognize that the lawyer of to-day occupies a different position from that of his predecessors of fifty years ago. His relations to the social structure have changed. He is operating in a different environment. He is functioning in an entirely new way.

The romance of advocacy, and the glamour of the courtroom, still cast their spell over the profession of law, and the public conception of legal procedure is gained mainly from a few exploited cases, or the morbid details of much advertised criminal trials. But the real fact is that the bulk of the lawyer's work is done in his office. There is no blare of trumpets, nor widespread publicity as he sits at his desk. Nevertheless it is the backbone of his practice.

The conditions surrounding the practice of law are changing. Competition is becoming keener. The rapid increase in the number of lawyers tends to divide up the business. Banks, trust companies, and title companies are encroaching on the lawyer's preserves in spite of the laws prohibiting the practice of law by corporations. Collections agencies are absorbing the collection business and keeping the bulk of the fees. Hostile legislation such as workmen's compensation acts for the purposes of reducing personal injury suits, ... acts for simplifying titles and abstracts, arbitration laws and conciliation statutes, and many others too numerous to mention, are curtailing the practice of law. Moreover, the demands upon the lawyer's time are multiplied ... and routine office work steadily encroaches upon valuable time that should be devoted to more important matters.

These changing conditions must be met by a readjustment of the methods of practice. He must know the methods and process by which business functions. His design must change to meet each new demand.

AN OVERVIEW

From *Law Office Management*, by Reginald Heber Smith (1942).

Our legal periodicals and bar association reports are full of articles about the proper organization of the courts and the efficient administration of justice, but for some strange reason they are virtually barren of articles about the organization of law offices and the efficient practice of the law. Certainly it is essential that citizens should have their day in court as promptly and as cheaply as possible, but it is just as important that a person who wishes to consult a lawyer about a matter of litigation or needs legal advice or legal instruments drawn should be able to obtain expert service without delay and at a minimum cost. These desirable ends are much more likely to be produced by a well-organized office than by one in which there is no real system and the organization is haphazard.

By temperament most lawyers are strong individualists, and instinctively they shy away from the idea of a "system," fearing that it implies a lot of rules, rigmarole, and restraints. We are apt to take refuge in the thought that after all we are engaged in a profession, not a business. But does it follow that we are entitled to practice our profession in an unbusinesslike manner? The statement that a law office needs an accurate cost accounting system seems revolutionary, but if every business concern has to know its costs, why should the law office be immune? Finally, there is a widely held idea that carefully planned organization is an expensive luxury, which only the very large firms can afford. I should put it the other way around; I think it is the smaller firms handling the average legal business of average people, which are most in need of efficient organization. I believe that the basic principles of organization are just as applicable to a two-member firm as to one of ten partners or to one having fifty lawyers on its staff.

. . .

The extinction of the dinosaur proves that mere size is no guarantee of survival in the competitive struggle for existence. Neither is mere smallness a guarantee.... In the practice of law, the growth of the firm organization to a reasonable size in harmony with its community environment enables its members, to a greater or lesser degree, to specialize in their work. Specialization is the first key to maximum efficiency and minimum cost.

The service lawyers render is their professional knowledge and skill, but the commodity they sell is *time,* and each lawyer has only a limited amount of that. Efficiency and economy are a race against time. The great aim of all organization is to get a given legal job properly done with the expenditure of the fewest possible hours.

A brief analysis lays bare the root problem that confronts every person who tries to earn a living by practicing law. The law is so vast that no one person can know it all, and no one pretends to. A client's case (let us say an income tax matter) involves a point with which the lawyer is not familiar. Probably any lawyer can find the law, but it may take a non-specialist ten hours, whereas the specialist in tax law should be able to answer the same question in half an hour. The general practitioner either must spend the ten hours or fail to give the client fully competent advice. The client may be able to pay for one hour of time but not for ten. The nature of the case and the amount involved may not warrant the expenditure of more than five hours. The logical solution then would seem to be to have lawyers specialize in the great fields of the law and along functional lines—one to be devoted to real property law, a second to corporation law, a third to taxes, a fourth to the trial of cases in court, and so on.

But most clients do not go to lawyers because they are specialists in a given field; they generally are not even aware of it. They go to a given lawyer because they know, like, and trust that person. The client with a tax case is just as likely to go to the real estate expert and the client with a land problem to go to the tax expert. Each lawyer who has received a case is hesitant about referring it to the appropriate expert. Perhaps he or she ought to and, if very busy, may, but it is human nature not to want to lose a case and possibly a client. Self-preservation is here at cross-purposes with efficiency.

It is in the public interest and in the lawyer's own interest that this problem should be resolved. It is plainly in the public interest that all its essential services shall be performed as efficiently as possible. This applies to legal services. If new lay agencies, being less hampered by tradition and custom, discover or invent ways of getting things done more efficiently and more cheaply, they will constantly encroach on what have been regarded as the prerogatives of the legal profession. Committees on Unauthorized Practice of the Law have done splendid work, but they will ultimately be in the position of King Canute if the organized Bar lets them down. There is no reason for the Bar to default. The Bar can do anything lay agencies can do and, because of education, discipline, and standards, can do it better, provided only that the Bar will adopt and utilize modern principles of systematic organization, which the lay agencies do use but on which they need have no monopoly.

. . .

The partnership form permits a group of members of the Bar who are specialists to associate themselves together in one organization. Then, to continue our analogy, the client with the tax case who comes to the partner who happens to be a real estate expert need not be sent out of the office; the attorney can either get the advice from the partner who is a tax expert or can introduce the client to that partner. There will be just one fee and that must somehow be shared by the two partners.... They will need to have certain records, but the system can be built up from a very few original entries which the lawyers must make themselves; everything else can be done for them by clerical assistants.

. . .

The incidence of legal business, furthermore, is very uneven and is not always correlated to pure legal ability. Some lawyers by a virtue of reputation, personality, friendships, connections, and similar factors have more work than they can handle; some lawyers have too little. Also, it is a common experience that work tends to "come in bunches." In a partnership of reasonable size these inequalities can be evened out to a considerable extent, provided the people in the organization will freely avail themselves of each other's time and skill. The system must encourage them to do precisely that; in fact it must reward them for so doing. When all members feel that the system is fair to them and that they can work happily together as a team, maximum output is achieved, the work is accomplished in the minimum amount of time, and the clients are well served.

If we fast-forward from the eras in which McCarthy and Smith wrote, and examine some of the modern literature on law practice management, we see many of the same issues. As the French say, *Toujours le change; toujours le même.* Lawyers have always had a need to know how to manage the business side of the practice, and probably have always been as uncomfortable with the demands of that side of their work as they are today.

In more recent times, lawyers have considered the need for effective law firm management in today's evolving practice environment. Paul Sullivan, in a September, 1998 article in the *Illinois Bar Journal*, entitled *Management Is Not a Noun*, divides practice management into five broad categories: Human Resources, Systems, Facilities, Finances, and Marketing. Aside from the quibble that the word "management" *is* a noun, Sullivan's point in the article is that "Management in a successful organization ... means action." The following article from the *Wall Street Journal* urges law firms to embrace business management principles:

LAW FIRMS EMBRACE BUSINESS SCHOOL 101: AS RECESSION BITES, MORE ATTORNEYS ATTEND MANAGEMENT TRAINING AND TAKE MINI–M.B.A. COURSES

From Wall Street Journal, by Alina Dizik, May 20, 2009.

Bankers, consultants and marketers aren't the only professionals looking to beef up their business skills for competitive advantage these days. At a growing number of law firms, top attorneys are being trained like business people, using executive education courses designed to strengthen management and business skills.

Some firms have been actively teaching lawyers business skills for the past half-decade. But this year's shrinking client lists—and profits—have encouraged more law firms to invest in management education. "Law firms are still run the way they were in the 17th century," says James Bailey, a leadership professor at the George Washington School of Business who studies law firms and helps run a program for managing partners. "They never really had to worry about [management skills] because every law firm in the country made money every year."

More firms are turning to short, executive education programs at business schools. Responding to the demand and eager to shore up losses from corporate training budget cuts, business schools are creating new programs for lawyers. The courses are often tailored for individual firms or geared toward partners and high-potential attorneys. The classes aim to prepare attorneys to either take top management positions at firms or help them better understand their business—and their clients' businesses.

"When you have the kind of challenges we have right now, (you need) really well-trained, smart managers talking the same language," says Kevin Fitzgerald, a partner at Nixon Peabody LLP who was one of the first in his firm to attend an executive education program at Harvard University in 2007. The program is designed for employees of professional service firms, and includes training on how lawyer-managers can lead firms successfully. Despite a tighter budget this year, Nixon Peabody still plans to send about six participants to the program.

Meanwhile, some firms are using business training to give their attorneys a better understanding of clients. At Wilmer Cutler Pickering Hale and Dorr LLP in Boston, Jane Eiselein, director of professional development, says the firm last September piloted an executive education business program for second-year associates taught by Northeastern University. "We realized our associates don't have an inside view of how our clients work," says Ms. Eiselein, who said the program was successful and will be offered at other locations this year.

Jim Hever, head of the Client Development Centre at Addleshaw Goddard LLP in London, attended Harvard's program last year, and said that the program helps the firm's partners learn about the needs of their clients. "Lawyers are business solutions and to be able to be that, you must have an understanding of business dynamics," says Mr. Hever.

In September, the executive education program at Georgetown University McDonough School of Business will offer a custom program tailored to a large global firm with several thousand attorneys. The three four-day modules will focus on each of the firm's key practice areas, says the business school dean, George Daly, and revolve around topics including new regulatory issues, client development and leadership training.

In other cases, schools are partnering with legal organizations to build their offerings. In early 2008, Boston University School of Management partnered with the Association of Corporate Counsel, a trade organization for in-house counsel based in Washington D.C., for a mini-M.B.A. program for its members. The $1,940, intensive course lasts three days and focuses on the skills traditionally taught in business schools—organizational behavior, finance, accounting, risk analysis, marketing and strategy.

This year, Boston University added a fourth session, including one hosted at its executive education facility in Los Angeles, in an effort to meet the growing demand for the program. So far, more than 300 attorneys have passed through the program.

Recent attendees say the course has boosted their business acumen. Renee Benjamin, a senior counsel at CalPortland Company, attended the program in Los Angeles last month. Ms. Benjamin says that not only did the program improve her finance skills, but it also helped her get a better understanding of how business decisions are made. Boston University is also planning a comprehensive follow-up program for attorneys who have completed the program, says the business school's director of executive education Elizabeth Nassar.

George Washington University launched a degree program in law firm management with executive training provider Hildebrandt Institute in 2005. The two-year program targets firm managers and combines residencies with online learning. The main goal: To teach participants how to apply general management skills to law firms. George Washington's Mr. Bailey says business acumen for law professionals is critical nowadays. "(Firms have) gotten big; they've gotten complex and don't have the management talent to run the large convoluted organization," says Mr. Bailey.

European business schools are also getting into the game. IMD, a business school in Lausanne, Switzerland is in talks to offer a custom executive M.B.A. program to a global law firm with offices in more than 50 countries next year and about 4,000 employees, says professor Sean Meehan, dean of external relations at the school.

The firm and the school are in the process of developing modules for the degree, which will be designed to help the organization grow globally.

And in the last few years, IE Business School in Madrid has added law firms to its client roster, including Cuatrecasas and Uria Menendez, says Dean Santiago Iniguez. The school was approached by the firms to develop offerings for attorneys three years ago. Participants delve into workshops on topics including working across borders, and market segmentation, both of which are relevant to firms with an international growth strategy. "Managing partners at law firms resemble CEOs of conventional corporations and they need to practice similar managerial skills," says Mr. Iniguez.

Problems and Questions

1. What common themes do you see in the articles about law practice management from the Business School literature, the popular legal press and legal writers?
2. Peter Drucker notes that demographics, economics and information technology all demand a shift in the way businesses are organized and operated. *See* also Gary Hamel and C.K. Prahahalad, *Competing for the Future* (Harvard Business School Press, 1994). What does he mean by using the word "demand," and what are the implications for legal practitioners?
3. Writings by Tom Peters, *see e.g., Circle of Innovation* (1998), suggest that the transformation of business is occurring at such a rapid rate that the old virtues of organization and planning no longer serve businesses very well? Are the views of Peters at odds with those of contemporary law office management consultants? If the old virtues no longer work, what are the new virtues that do?
4. Dwight McCarthy and Reginald Heber Smith were giants of law practice management in their respective eras. McCarthy talks about competition, including competition with nonlawyers, while Smith makes a poignant plea for greater efficiency. Are these issues relevant to practitioners today? How has law practice changed since then? How has it stayed the same?
5. Should lawyers turn over management to people trained in business? Should law firms look more readily to other businesses to learn how to resolve business problems? What are the consequences of failing to address these issues?

C. MANAGEMENT AND PROFESSIONAL FAILURE

Lest we are left with the impression that management problems dwell completely within the realm of theoretical inquiry, it might be useful to take a look at a law firm where mismanagement produced consequences beyond imagination. See, for example the problems that one firm encountered, at http://www.iht.com/articles/2006/02/14/bloomberg/bxlaw.php.

If concepts such as quality, excellence and competence are desirable goals for lawyers and law firms, then malpractice, disbarment and incompetence are the opposite. It should come as no surprise that the same behaviors are related to both excellence and failure in professional services. Professional failure, however, represents an inability to achieve quality services. The following discussion looks at the problem of professional failure through the lens of risk management as a tool for reducing the incidence of professional error.

Professional failure is what happens when lawyers and law firms make mistakes that reflect upon their professional competence to deliver services satisfactorily. The circumstances under which professional standards may be breached are varied, but the systems for sanctioning professional failure are few. Clients may have an action for legal malpractice or other civil remedy. Complainants may seek disciplinary action against lawyers who violate professional rules of conduct. Judges may be able to penalize certain behavior associated with cases over which they preside. Lawyers themselves can sanction colleagues informally in the legal community. Finally, market forces may work to eliminate inefficient or ineffective providers, arguably at some cost to individual consumers.

The concept of professional failure recognizes that not all lawyers live up to their professional obligations. Despite educational and admission requirements, a certain percentage of practitioners will make mistakes that cause harm to clients or bring discredit to the profession. When such instances occur, the system of justice breaks down. Two sanctioning systems deserve special attention, because they provide primary enforcement for standards for lawyer conduct. These systems are the civil malpractice and the lawyer disciplinary systems.

1. THE CONCEPT OF RISK

Even the best law firms make mistakes; the best systems break down. Managing the probability of professional error is what risk management is all about. The term "risk management" is often used in connection with professional liability insurance, but the concept is much broader in its application.

Assuming that there is some risk associated with all legal work, risk management involves planning for the possibility that a lawyer's error will result in an actionable harm to a client. One way to deal with risk is to assume it: assumption of the risk in tort law is basically the notion that someone with a duty to act with reasonable care entertains a known risk. A lawyer who undertakes to make her services available to clients is presumed to know that there is some likelihood she will commit a professional error that harms the client. When someone assumes a risk, and causes harm, that person may be charged with liability.

Under principles of vicarious liability, partners can be held responsible for each other's malpractice, as well as for the conduct of subordinate lawyers and support staff. If the firm or individual lawyer does not insure against the risk, it is often said that the risk is retained. A firm may choose to retain certain risks because the potential liability is so low or the likelihood of harm occurring so slight that it is willing to retain the potential liability. If a firm ignores the possibility of professional error causing harm, it in effect retains the risk by default. The alternative to retaining a risk is to insure against it.

In his book, *Risk Management for Lawyers* (ABA 2007), Anthony Davis, a lawyer who advises law firms on how to avoid malpractice, underscores the importance of management in malpractice avoidance, because many of the matters mentioned in the self-audits go directly to management practices. Davis leads law firms through a series of risk management audits designed to assess particular management issues that carry a degree of risk. If the firm can identify its problems, Davis contends, it will be able to take steps to change its behavior and reduce the risk. Ignorance may be bliss in some matters, but in law practice management it is better to be forewarned of potential future problems and conflicts.

2. MALPRACTICE

The first method through which attorney conduct is regulated is the action for legal malpractice based upon breach of the professional standard of care. Malpractice actions do not necessarily coincide with grievance proceedings, although a disgruntled client could file both a grievance and a lawsuit against his attorney.

Because clients today are more willing to sue their lawyers than in the past, every lawyer must consider the potential malpractice risks when she takes a case. The following case is one of the most cited cases in legal malpractice law, but it illustrates not only the basic elements of legal malpractice, but also the practical dilemma that lawyers encounter every day when potential clients seek representation.

TOGSTAD v. VESELEY, OTTO, MILLER & KEEFE
Supreme Court of Minnesota, 1980.
291 N.W.2d 686.

PER CURIAM. This is an appeal by the defendants from a judgment of the Hennepin County District Court involving an action for legal malpractice. The jury found that the defendant attorney Jerre Miller was negligent and that, as a direct result of such negligence, plaintiff John Togstad sustained damages in the amount of $610,500 and his wife, plaintiff Joan Togstad, in the amount of $39,000. Defendants (Miller and his law firm) appeal to this court from the denial of their motion for judgment notwithstanding the verdict or, alternatively, for a new trial. We affirm.

[In August 1971, John Togstad was treated by Dr. Paul Blake, a neurological surgeon, for an aneurism, but surgery left Togstad severely paralyzed in his right arm and leg, and to speak Joan Togstad met with attorney Jerre Miller regarding her husband's condition after Mrs. Togstad became suspicious of the circumstances surrounding her husband's tragic condition. Mrs. Togstad told Miller what happened at the hospital, although she brought no records with her. Miller took notes and asked questions during the meeting, which lasted 45 minutes to an hour. At its conclusion, according to Mrs. Togstad, Miller said that "he did not think we had a legal case, however, he was going to discuss this with his partner." She understood that if Miller changed his mind after talking to his partner, he would call her. When Mrs. Togstad did not hear from Miller, she decided "that they had come to the conclusion that there wasn't a case." No fee arrangements were discussed, no medical authorizations were requested, nor was Mrs. Togstad billed for the interview. Mrs. Togstad denied that Miller had told her his firm did not have expertise in the medical malpractice field, urged her to see another attorney, or related to her that the statute of limitations for medical malpractice actions was two years. She did not consult another attorney until one year after she talked to Miller. Mrs. Togstad indicated that she did not confer with another attorney earlier because of her reliance on Miller's "legal advice" that they "did not have a case." Miller testified that "there was nothing related in her factual circumstances that told me that she had a case that our firm would be interested in undertaking." Miller also claimed he related to Mrs. Togstad "that this was only my opinion and she was encouraged to ask another attorney if she wished for another opinion" and "she ought to do so promptly." He testified that he informed Mrs. Togstad that his firm "was not engaged as experts" in the area of medical malpractice, and that they associated with the Charles Hvass firm in cases of that nature. Miller stated that he told Mrs. Togstad that he would consult with Hvass. that he called Hvass, and that Hvass thought there was no liability for malpractice in the case. Consequently, Miller did not communicate with Mrs. Togstad further.]

This case was submitted to the jury by way of a special verdict form. The jury found that Dr. Blake and the hospital were negligent and that Dr. Blake's negligence (but not the hospital's) was a direct cause of the injuries sustained by John Togstad; that there was an attorney-client contractual relationship between Mrs. Togstad and Miller; that Miller was negligent in rendering advice regarding the possible claims of Mr. and Mrs. Togstad; that, but for Miller's negligence, plaintiffs would have been successful in the prosecution of a legal action against Dr. Blake; and that neither Mr. nor Mrs. Togstad was negligent in pursuing their claims against Dr. Blake. The jury awarded damages to Mr. Togstad of $610,500 and to Mrs. Togstad of $39,000.

. . .

1. In a legal malpractice action of the type involved here, four elements must be shown: (1) that an attorney-client relationship existed; (2) that defendant acted negligently or in breach of contract; (3) that such acts were the proximate cause of the plaintiffs' damages; (4) that but for

defendant's conduct the plaintiffs would have been successful in the prosecution of their medical malpractice claim.

. . .

We ... conclude that ... the evidence shows that a lawyer-client relationship is present here. The thrust of Mrs. Togstad's testimony is that she went to Miller for legal advice, was told there wasn't a case, and relied upon this advice in failing to pursue the claim for medical malpractice. In addition, according to Mrs. Togstad, Miller did not qualify his legal opinion by urging her to seek advice from another attorney, nor did Miller inform her that he lacked expertise in the medical malpractice area. Assuming this testimony is true, as this court must do, we believe a jury could properly find that Mrs. Togstad sought and received legal advice from Miller under circumstances, which made it reasonably foreseeable to Miller that Mrs. Togstad would be injured if the advice were negligently given. . . .

Defendants argue that even if an attorney-client relationship was established the evidence fails to show that Miller acted negligently in assessing the merits of the Togstads' case. They appear to contend that, at most, Miller was guilty of an error in judgment which does not give rise to legal malpractice. However, this case does not involve a mere error of judgment. The gist of plaintiffs' claim is that Miller failed to perform the minimal research that an ordinarily prudent attorney would do before rendering legal advice in a case of this nature. The record, through the testimony of Kenneth Green and John McNulty, contains sufficient evidence to support plaintiffs' position.

. . .

There is also sufficient evidence in the record establishing that, but for Miller's negligence, plaintiffs would have been successful in prosecuting their medical malpractice claim. Dr. Woods, in no uncertain terms, concluded that Mr. Togstad's injuries were caused by the medical malpractice of Dr. Blake. Defendants' expert testimony to the contrary was obviously not believed by the jury. Thus, the jury reasonably found that had plaintiff's medical malpractice action been properly brought, plaintiffs would have recovered.

Based on the foregoing, we hold that the jury's findings are adequately supported by the record. Accordingly we uphold the trial court's denial of defendants' motion for judgment notwithstanding the jury verdict.

. . .

Affirmed.

Togstad offers several lessons for practitioners. Perhaps the most important lesson is to avoid getting into a swearing match with a client. Although the court does not come right out and say it, when Mrs.

Togstad's version of the facts differs from lawyer Miller's, the court believes Mrs. Togstad. The case also illustrates the need for non-engagement letters to establish the fact that no attorney-client relationship exists. As for the malpractice itself, the court opines that at a bare minimum, a lawyer owes a duty to mention the relevant statutes of limitation when advising someone in a professional setting, even if the lawyer does not ultimately undertake the representation. When a client relies on a lawyer's advice resulting in the loss of a cause of action against another, the client is very likely to go after the lawyer in an effort to obtain compensation for the loss.

Malpractice can happen to almost any firm. Seyfarth Shaw, a highly respected labor and employment firm in Chicago, was hired by fitness guru Billy Blanks, known for introducing the Tae Bo exercise program. Blanks had paid $11 million in fees to his former agent before discovering that the agent was unlicensed. He then paid over $400,000 in legal fees to Seyfarth, only to learn that the firm had filed the case in the wrong venue and ultimately missed the statute of limitations in the correct venue. The firm was also charged with fraudulent concealment for not alerting Blanks to the missed deadline. The firm was hit with a $35 million malpractice verdict, including punitive damages (not covered by malpractice insurance). The moral of the story: even the best firms can make misstates, so all firms need to be constantly vigilant.

3. MALPRACTICE INSURANCE

The topic of legal malpractice insurance may seem daunting at first blush. Law students who have never had to buy malpractice insurance before may have a number of questions about what it is, how it works, and what it costs. Even experienced attorneys who are reviewing their malpractice coverage may find the variety of options and companies confusing. A few brief comments may help to put the subject into perspective.

Malpractice insurance is like any other form of casualty insurance, where an insured pays premiums to an insurer to protect against certain risks. A risk can involve any event that imposes liability on the insured. In the case of malpractice insurance, risk is the possibility of professional error, whether that person is a doctor, lawyer, accountant, or other professional. Premiums go into a fund that is used to pay out liability if an insured risk comes to pass. This pool of funds, now owned by the insurance company, is then used to pay for judgments or settlements against a liable individual, essentially passing the element of risk to the insurer. The assumption is that not all insured policy holders will require payment from the fund at the same time.

The cost of legal malpractice insurance (the premium) is based upon the amount of risk that the insurance company assumes, as well as the amount of risk the lawyer retains. Premium rates are then determined by using actuarial calculations that assess the scope of liability, as well as the likelihood, extent and limits of the company's coverage. The extent of the risk to be insured is influenced by the area of legal practice, attorney experience, the size of firm, the geographic location of the firm, the attorney's prior record, risk prevention activities of the insured, the amount of time since an active malpractice occurred, and other factors.

Liability depends upon the size of cases the lawyer or law firm is handling. A lawyer handling a $100,000 low-end real estate transfers is not on the line for as much liability as a lawyer who routinely handles multi-million dollar commercial transfers. The limits of liability are governed by the amount of risk retained by the insured and the exclusions from coverage in the policy.

The framework for legal malpractice insurance is no different from that of your car insurance You pay premiums based upon the type of car you drive, your age, driving record, and the history of claims in your specific geographic locale. You can reduce your premiums by increasing your deductible, not taking some of the coverage, reducing the policy limits, or even just by the fact that you have moved to another location. Whatever you do not insure is your responsibility, because if this risk comes to pass, you, not the insurance company, will be responsible for any liability. A policy will often say that the insurance company does not have to pay if you fail to pay your premiums, or lie to them about the facts in a claim. You may also be able to reduce your premiums by demonstrating that you have never gotten a ticket or taken a defensive driving class, or purchased special safety equipment for your vehicle.

In the case of legal malpractice insurance, your policy will have both a deductible and policy limits; so, if a claim is less than the deductible or more than the policy limit, the insurance company will not cover the damages. Your policy will require you to report to the insurance company in a timely way that you think you may have committed an act involving malpractice. You cannot lie to the insurance company about the facts. Your policy probably only covers negligent acts (malpractice) and not intentional torts; if you punched your client in a fit of rage, your malpractice carrier will not help you. You may get a break on your premium rates if your claims record is clean, if you take steps to reduce the risk of professional error with a calendar system, or you limit your practice area to specific fields.

Most legal malpractice insurance in force today is written using a "claims made policy". This means that when you buy insurance for a particular year, you are covered for all the claims that occur during that year. This approach contrasts to an "occurrence policy", which protects against all of the malpractice that occurred in a particular year. Occurrence policies lost favor with both insurers and lawyers because of the uncertainty of coverage (when did the malpractice occur?), keeping up with the old policies, and the effect of inflation on coverage (the limits on older policies were often insufficient to cover the extent of liability and inflated dollars).

A claims-made policy premium increases with each year of coverage. Assume that you graduate from law school and take out a malpractice insurance policy. In the first year you are only buying insurance to cover the claims from one year; the second year your insurance covers two years; the third year, three; and so on. At some point in time, usually after ten to thirteen years in practice, the number of new potential claims will roughly equal the number of claims being extinguished due to the passing of time, statutes of limitation or the unlikelihood of discovery. In the case of a lawyer who changes firms, the new firm may need to purchase additional insurance to cover claims against the new attorney during the policy year.

4. DISCIPLINE

The other primary mechanism of lawyer regulation—the disciplinary system—is utilized for the purpose of maintaining the integrity of the legal profession. Lawyers, as members of a self-regulating profession, have promulgated rules governing professional conduct. These rules are enforced by a system of local committees that hear grievances and prosecute them. The discipline may range from a private reprimand to disbarment.

Most law students think of professional responsibility as a body of information contained in a law school course. They do not think of the rules as guidelines for competent practice, even though most jurisdictions are willing to accept violation of a disciplinary rule as evidence of professional negligence in legal malpractice cases. It may be helpful to think of the ethics rules as practice standards and the disciplinary process as a system for maintaining the quality of law practice and enhancing the professional image of all lawyers. The *Model Rules of Professional Conduct*, have been adopted in almost all of the states. It cannot be stressed enough the importance of an attorney becoming an expert in professional responsibility, particularly if they will be working in a smaller work environment where supervision might at times be lacking: Your professional life may depend on your being well versed in the rules of professional conduct (or maybe something a bit less dramatic; the point is that law students look at PR as a course instead of a way of life).

PREAMBLE, MODEL RULES OF PROFESSIONAL CONDUCT

American Bar Association (1983).

The Rules of Professional Conduct are rules of reason. They should be interpreted with reference to the purposes of legal representation and of the law itself. Some of the Rules are imperatives, cast in the terms "shall" or "shall not." These define proper conduct for purposes of professional discipline. Others, generally cast in the term "may," are permissive and define areas under the Rules in which the lawyer has professional discretion. No disciplinary action should be taken when the lawyer chooses not to act or acts within the bounds of such discretion. Other Rules define the nature of relationships between the lawyer and others. The Rules are thus partly obligatory and disciplinary and partly constitutive and descriptive in that they define a lawyer's professional role. Many of the Comments use the term "should." Comments do not add obligations to the Rules but provide guidance for practicing in compliance with the Rules.

The Rules presuppose a larger legal context shaping the lawyer's role. That context includes court rules and statutes relating to matters of licensure, laws defining specific obligations of lawyers and substantive and procedural law in general.... The Rules do not, however, exhaust the moral and ethical considerations that should inform a lawyer, for no worthwhile human activity can be completely defined by legal rules. The Rules simply provide a framework for the ethical practice of law.

Furthermore, for purposes of determining the lawyer's authority and responsibility, principles of substantive law external to these Rules determine whether a client-lawyer relationship exists. Most of the duties flowing from the client-lawyer relationship attach only after the client has requested the lawyer to render legal services and the lawyer has agreed to do so. But there are some duties, such as that of confidentiality under Rule 1.6, which may attach when the lawyer agrees to consider whether a client-lawyer relationship shall be established. Whether a client-lawyer relationship exists for any specific purpose can depend on the circumstances and may be a question of fact.

. . .

Failure to comply with an obligation or prohibition imposed by a Rule is a basis for invoking the disciplinary process. The Rules presuppose that disciplinary assessment of a lawyer's conduct will be made on the basis of the facts and circumstances as they existed at the time of the conduct in question and in recognition of the fact that a lawyer often has to act upon uncertain or incomplete evidence of the situation. Moreover, the Rules presuppose that whether or not discipline should be imposed for a violation, and the severity of a sanction, depend on all the circumstances, such as the willfulness and seriousness of the violation, extenuating factors and whether there have been previous violations.

Appendix C, pages 429–442, includes several specific Rules of Professional Conduct that are relevant to Law Practice Management. The Rules themselves do not mention the disciplinary system, which they support. In every jurisdiction, however, there exists a grievance system for imposing discipline on lawyers who violate the Rules. Although these systems differ slightly from state to state, there are some common elements:
- A code of professional conduct, usually promulgated by the state supreme court in consultation with the state bar;

- A grievance committee system (usually a local committee) empowered to receive and investigate complaints that lawyers have violated the rules;

- Power for the committee to dismiss or act informally on a complaint, or refer the matter to a formal hearing;

- Procedural rights to due process, representation and appeal;

- A burden of proof less than the criminal "beyond a reasonable doubt," but greater than the civil preponderance of the evidence;

- In some states, issuance of advisory ethics opinions (which eliminate the need for lawyers to test rules by violating them).

Each year, hundreds of lawyers around the country are disciplined. Still, there remains a perception among the lay public that lawyers often fail to police their own members. Disciplinary records demonstrate that a small percentage of complaints actually result in discipline, and that many lawyers who are disciplined are eventually reinstated to the practice of law. Statistics also suggest a high correlation between mismanagement and misconduct leading to discipline. For example, in *In Re Castro*, 164 Ariz. 428, 793 P.2d 1095 (1990), the Arizona Supreme Court disciplined a lawyer for misuse of client funds, when the lawyer could not reconstruct transactions involving his client trust account. The concurring opinion of Justice Feldman said, in part,

> I write separately to express my views on the so-called "bookkeeping system" used by this respondent. Respondent testified that he threw away the "chits"—little pieces of paper on which he made notations about funds received—and was therefore unable to render an account of his clients' funds, as required by the former rules.
>
> As I see it, he would have been unable to render an adequate account even if he had kept the chits and claimed they had served to refresh his memory. The rule he was charged with violating [Rule 1.15] required an attorney to maintain "records" of all client funds in his possession and to render an appropriate "account" to the client regarding those funds ... Such records should comply with generally accepted accounting principles or, at least, bookkeeping standards. While lawyers need not be skilled accountants, they are charged with the responsibility of maintaining records that will enable them to account for client funds in a businesslike manner. Attorneys lacking knowledge in bookkeeping or accounting should retain a bookkeeper or accountant to set up a proper system of accounting for their office.
>
> Slips of paper on which notations are made that may serve to refresh the recollection of the lawyer some years after the event do not qualify as records or books of account. In the future, I will take the position that lawyers who cannot produce acceptable ledgers, journals, or other recognized books of account will have failed to comply with the current requirements of [Rule] 1.15, ... Not having acceptable

records of clients' funds is, without more, grounds for summary suspension under the present rules.

Thus, even though the lawyer may not have intended to misuse client funds, the failure to manage funds entrusted to him is sufficient to prompt discipline. Throughout this course, you will see examples demonstrating that good management can avoid mistakes that can get you into trouble.

PROBLEMS AND QUESTIONS

1. Are the actual ethical issues facing practicing lawyers different from the problems you discussed in Professional Responsibility class? What issues are more likely to concern a practicing lawyer than a law student or professor? What would *you* do if your client:

   - Makes sexual advances towards you?

   - Commits perjury on the witness stand?

   - Advises you that she intends to defraud the company she works for?

   - Asks you to file suit against her neighbor who you have represented off and on for over a decade?

   - Gives you several pieces of expensive jewelry to hold while she is away on an extended trip around the world?

2. How might money problems get you into trouble (e.g., mismanaging client funds, getting into billing disputes)? What settlement and negotiation problems might you encounter? What does a lawyer do when a client wants to sue merely out of spite or when she refuses to settle a suit that has dragged on too long?

3. Are lawyers today "under siege?" Are clients expecting better services from professionals now than in the past, or are client expectations unreasonable today?

4. What should a lawyer like Miller in the *Togstad* case do? If he decides that he cannot or does not want to represent someone who has come to his office for an initial consultation, what steps can he take to protect himself? What minimal advice must he provide in such situations?

5. Should lawyers be required to carry legal malpractice insurance, or should they be allowed to self-insure as is the case in most jurisdictions today? When might it make sense to retain the risk and in effect self-insure against harm to clients?

6. What happens when a law firm is rendered insolvent by a legal malpractice award? What if the award exceeds the coverage limits of the firm's malpractice policy?

7. Can lawyers reduce the risk of malpractice through effective management practices? If so, which ones? Should insurance companies reward well-managed law firms with lower rates the way that auto insurance companies reward "good" drivers?

8. Describe the risk points in law firm practice. For each one, what can the law firm as an institution, and individual lawyers as regulated professionals do to protect themselves?

9. What do you do when a client sues you or files a complaint with a Grievance Committee? To what extent is effective practice management related to the risk of professional error that could lead to discipline or malpractice? What skills, including management skills, must a lawyer possess in order to practice competently?

10. Do you think the public impression that lawyers do not police themselves is justified? Do lawyers need more vigorous prosecution of ethical violations, or a better image? Is the problem one of discipline or of public relations? What can the law firm do in order to avoid client grievances? What can individual lawyers do?

D. PARADIGM FOR STUDYING LAW PRACTICE MANAGEMENT

Law Practice Management can be divided (like Gaul) into three parts: management of the organization, management of the legal work product, and management of the individual as a professional person. Law students sometimes smugly argue that they will not have to manage the firms, agencies and legal departments where they will work, but in truth survival in any organization requires a working knowledge of how the organization operates. Moreover, all lawyers are managers of the legal work for which they are responsible, and they must become proficient in the skills they need to carry out these activities.

Some of the topics addressed in this book are relevant to all three aspects of law practice management. For example, the law firm may have a marketing plan to attract and retain clients. Marketing may be a component of the delivery of legal services. Personal marketing skills may help individual lawyers to become rainmakers. It is easy to appreciate the fact that the law firm has to manage its finances, or the practice will not thrive. It may be less apparent, however, that the legal services delivery team must bill clients for work and manage client funds, or there will be no finances to manage. It follows that the individual lawyer must have some degree of knowledge of financial matters in order to survive in either of the other two arenas.

Whether it is this year, or next year, or ten years from now, almost all lawyers will at some point in time assume management responsibilities in their law offices. As for the legal work product, every lawyer who is responsible for legal work is responsible for the quality of that work, even if she works under the direction of another lawyer. She is responsible for the timeliness of the work, the performance of support staff in getting the work done, and the satisfaction of clients to whom the work is delivered. In this sense, *all* lawyers are managers. In the broadest sense, some management skills, such as time, financial and technology management, are not limited in their application to legal settings. Even lawyers who never practice law need these skills in order to succeed.

These are two obvious examples of the overlap created by the organization of this book, but there are many others. In the final analysis, although the study of law practice management may focus at different times on managing the firm, managing the practice, and managing the individual, it is impossible to avoid the synergies among these three approaches.

Although these aspects of law practice management are distinct, there is considerable overlap. For instance, management obviously entails organizing and operating the law firm itself, although many new lawyers become involved with management in a number of ways, such as recruiting or marketing. Some of them may be running their own firms, or assume management responsibilities the partners do not want. These management responsibilities may reflect on their individual management skills and impact upon their ability to deliver legal work to clients.

This casebook has been prepared with the hope that students will learn what they need to do to be effective as practitioners at all levels of practice management. The goal of the course is to give people the tools they will need to succeed in the practice of law. Despite the fact that law school graduates enter a highly competitive marketplace for legal services, those who take this course will graduate armed with practical information that will give them an edge in the real world.

Law practice management is valuable, even necessary to practitioners seeking to meet their professional obligations to clients ethically, competently, and efficiently. Substantive legal knowledge in a number of areas is necessary in order to be an effective manager of legal work, and, in fact, a substantial body of law is developing which deals with law firm operations. Thus, the topic of law practice management involves not only a discrete set of lawyering skills, but also a body of substantive legal knowledge.

This book includes articles, cases and commentary on a variety of issues relevant to the broad topic of law practice management. Accompanying each chapter are practical questions and problems, which may be completed individually or in small groups. Students may form "law firms" in which each firm is responsible for its work product, or they may discuss the problems in class. These problems are taken from the real life experiences of practicing lawyers, and represent the challenges that will face new lawyers sooner or later.

The materials are divided into sixteen chapters in four parts:

- Part I (Chapters 1–4) "The Business of Law" contains an introduction to the subject of law practice management with a discussion of some of the underlying themes incorporated in the course.
- Part II (Chapters 5–11) "Managing the Legal Organization" looks at the law firm as an organization, and addresses both the business form and marketing of the law firm.

- Part III (Chapters 12–14) "Managing Legal Work" addresses management of the legal work product using law office systems.
- Part IV (Chapters 15–16) "Managing Your Professional Life" explores management of the individual lawyer as a professional person and addresses the skills you will need to succeed in the practice of law. A final Epilogue takes a look the future of law practice in light of what you have learned in this course.

Your particular class may emphasize some of this material to the exclusion of other material, or it may cover the entire contents of this book. In addition to the chapters themselves, a number of appendices have been included to supplement the readings and provide additional resources for you to use.

This class should be a practical learning-by-doing skills course. Some of the problems require you to work in small groups or law firms to complete various projects. In one sense the skill of collaboration is often overlooked in law school, although in the real world lawyers learn that law is not a solitary enterprise and that cooperation, collaboration and teamwork are essential to effective practice management.

Finally, during the course of this semester, you should take the time to look at the firm, law department or agency where you work or have worked during law school. Although a few of you may have limited exposure to real world law practices, most of you will have seen one or more law offices in action. As a class you have collectively seen the good, the bad and the ugly. As the class progresses continue to observe what goes on in these organizations in light of what you are learning. Think of yourself as a management consultant who has been brought in to evaluate these organizations. Share your observations with your professor, classmates and group members.

PROBLEMS AND QUESTIONS

1. How do you see the three main aspects of law practice management playing out in your career as a lawyer? In a law firm, can some individuals possess strengths in areas that others do not?

2. What management skills do you presently have as a result of pre-law school education and work experience? What skills do you still need to master in order to be an effective manager?

3. Identify no less than three or more than five members of your Law Practice Management class who will be your law partners for the duration of the course. Look for people with whom you think will complement your management skills and work style, not necessarily your social acquaintances.

   For purposes of maintaining a degree of common ground in completing the projects, it will help to make certain assumptions about the fictitious law firms that you will be creating. Students or the professor may wish to modify these assumptions, but for those who elect to go by the book, what follows is a portrait of your model law firm:

Firm Description

You and your former law school classmates are planning to open a new law firm. You will all be partners in this firm, located in _____ (select a city or county where you plan to practice unless assigned by the professor). The firm's practice will consist of one or more substantive fields that you will identify in a later chapter. The firm hopes to grow its practice slowly, and in time establish itself as a leading firm in its core practice area(s).

Your firm should have four or five partners. You are all less than three years out of law school and have some experience in other firms. You will need to capitalize your venture, but you should assume that none of you has more than $20,000 in savings to put into the firm. You may draw upon the real life skills, experience, and talents of your personnel to complete the various assignments in this course.

Your firm will be given various assignments during the course, which should be completed by the firm as a group. As in real life, the allocation of responsibility is up to you. You must decide whether one or more partners or associates or a committee is involved. However, the entire firm is responsible for the work product.

In addition to the foregoing, you must operate under the rules governing your firm in your partnership agreement (see Chapter 3). You may amend the agreement by filing amendments with your professor. You may remove a non-productive partner or associate provided you follow the procedures set forth in your agreement. An expelled lawyer will become a solo practitioner for the remainder of the course, completing all assignments individually. Your work product is cumulative in that what you spend or do each week affects what you can do in future weeks.

---

4. Take some time to learn about your new partners. What personal experiences and skills do they bring to the table? What traits will help to create a positive attitude in your firm? Are these the same things you would look for in partners out in the real world?

5. After you have gotten to know your partners, designate one person to serve as the managing partner, who will be responsible for taking the lead in organizing the work of your group. What qualities should you look for in a managing partner? How are these different from the qualities you might seek in any other partner in your law firm?

6. Looking at the law firm you have formed, can you take a snapshot of the practice of law in your community? What practitioners are delivering what services to what clients? Which clients are well-served and which are poorly served? What organizations, both law firms and nonlegal organizations are likely to be your competitors for business?.

7. In the firm that you have formed, attempt to articulate the forces that will affect the way you practice law. What threats and challenges do these forces present for the firm? What opportunities will arise out of the changes brought about by these forces? This is sometimes called a SWOT Analysis (for Strengths/Weaknesses/Opportunities/Threats). How does your firm fare in such an analysis? See Appendix E, page 459.

8. Looking back to the material on partnership agreements in Chapter 4, prepare a law firm partnership (or other organization) agreement, which incorporates those elements you consider important to your firm's goals and objectives. You should apply the assumptions described in Question 3, above. You may also want to consult the sample agreements in Appendix D, which contains a Model Limited Liability Partnership Agreement, D-1, page 443, and Appendix D-2, page 455, a checklist showing how the elements of the agreement can be drafted into a written document. You should also look at the "Law Firm Questionnaire," Appendix E to get a sense of what your law firm will look like.

Part 2

Managing the Legal Organization

■ ■ ■

CHAPTER 6

STRATEGIC PLANNING AND MARKETING LEGAL SERVICES

■ ■ ■

A. BACKGROUND

Strategic planning is a term used to describe an organization's long-term goals and objectives in order to maximize its impact in the marketplace. Marketing is the process by which businesses, including law firms, seek and obtain clients or customers. These two activities are synergistic if not synonymous, so they will be addressed together in this chapter. Before examining strategic marketing and planning; however, it is important to understand the historical context within which lawyers operate, because lawyers do not operate in an unregulated free market when it comes to marketing their services.

Lawyers have always engaged in marketing, insofar as they sought to attract new clients and offer new services to existing clients, even though advertising of legal services was prohibited by the Canons of Ethics and later the Code of Professional Responsibility from 1908 until 1977. The ban covered direct advertising, in-person solicitation, and many indirect forms of marketing. Lawyers were expected to develop a reputation over an extended period of time, and to obtain new business through referrals from former (satisfied) clients. Any organized campaign by an attorney to attract clients or suggest that known or unknown persons needed legal services violated the ethical rules.

The pervasiveness of these regulations produced a chilling effect on the active marketing of legal services. In 1977, the U.S. Supreme Court in *Bates and O'Steen v. State Bar of Arizona,* 433 U.S. 350, 97 S.Ct. 2691, 53 L.Ed.2d 810, held that advertising of routine legal services by lawyers was constitutionally protected commercial speech. The Arizona Bar, unsuccessfully argued that the ban on advertising was an appropriate exercise of regulatory power, notwithstanding the interest in fostering the free exercise of commercial speech, for a number of reasons: 1) the adverse effect on professionalism; 2) the inherently misleading nature of attorney advertising; 3) the adverse effect on the administration of justice; 4) the undesirable economic effects of advertising; 5) the adverse effect of advertising on the quality of service; and 6) the difficulties of enforcement. *Bates* recognized the right of the Bar Association to impose reasonable regulations on advertising, but refused to permit a complete ban on truthful advertising by lawyers.

In the decades since *Bates*, lawyers have slowly emerged from their restrictive cocoons to test their wings in an environment far different from the one they had experienced previously. One of the earliest observers of this emergence was Lori B. Andrews, a research lawyer for the American Bar Foundation. Her 1980 book, *Legal Advertising: The Birth of a Salesman,* pointed out that *Bates* not only opened the door to newspaper ads for legal services, but to a whole different attitude toward seeking new clients. The term "law firm marketing" described by Andrews, soon became a buzzword for a plethora of activities much broader than contemplated by the Court in *Bates*.

Since Andrews' observations in 1980, additional court cases, amendments to the ethical rules, and extensive experimentation have continued to push the limits of legal marketing, reflecting wide differences among lawyers concerning the limits of this fledgling industry. Although media advertising by law firms has not become as prevalent as some observers predicted in the years immediately following *Bates*, marketing has had an impact on virtually every law firm in the United States. It is hard to imagine a law firm that does not apply marketing principles and practices to client development. Some firms retain full-time marketing directors; others utilize public relations firms on retainer; many firms have hired consultants to help them develop marketing plans. Although lawyers are novices at marketing compared to those engaged in many other business fields, they are catching up fast.

The underlying ideas are simple: an organization must determine what services it intends to deliver; who will buy the services; who will compete with the organization; and how it will communicate with potential buyers to convince them to retain the organization. The implementation of these principles is much more complicated. Not only must law firms spend considerable time developing and carrying out marketing plans, but planning these activities also can encroach upon the ongoing legal work of the firm. Furthermore, a marketing study may upset long-held assumptions about clientele, services, profitability, and the roles of individuals in the firm. The uncertainties of the regulatory framework, coupled with the relative lack of sophistication among lawyers about marketing, lead many firms either to ignore the need to deal with marketing or to hire outside professional services.

A new law firm really has no choice but to develop a marketing plan before committing financing to the business. A firm that starts out with a plan can more easily review and revise the plan, than can existing firm creating a plan from scratch.

Before considering the issue of marketing, it may be useful to look at the legal background of advertising and solicitation. It becomes apparent in the cases since *Bates* that bar associations continue to cast their nets as broadly as possible in order to prohibit the greatest amount of advertising. At the same time, individual lawyers have continued to challenge restrictions that interfere with their efforts to attract clients. Conceptually, these efforts can be viewed as a continuum from word-of-mouth advertising to hard-sell face-to-face solicitation. The former approach was permissible before *Bates*; the latter is still prohibited. Ironically, the more direct the communication, the more effective the results are likely to be. Any salesman will tell you that their best shot is a face-to-face meeting with a motivated buyer. The more practical problem for a lawyer or law firm is deciding whether to risk professional discipline to engage in an arguably acceptable but technically impermissible method of securing clients.

The following case illustrates the tension that exists between advertising lawyers and bar regulatory authorities regarding what and how lawyers can communicate their availability to prospective clients:

ALEXANDER v. CAHILL
U.S. Court of Appeals, Second Circuit, 2010.
598 F.3d 79.

CALABRESI, CIRCUIT JUDGE: New York's Appellate Division adopted new rules prohibiting certain types of attorney advertising and solicitation, which were to take effect February 1, 2007. The new rules barred ... testimonials from clients relating to pending matters, portrayals of judges or fictitious law firms, attention-getting techniques unrelated to attorney competence, and trade names or nicknames that imply an ability to get results. The amendments also established a thirty-day moratorium for targeted solicitation following a specific incident, including targeted ads on television or in other media. Plaintiffs, a New York attorney, along with his law firm and a not-for-profit public interest organization, challenged these provisions as violating the First Amendment. The District Court agreed in part—it declared most of the content-based rules unconstitutional, while upholding the thirty-day moratorium. Both Plaintiffs and Defendants ... appealed from portions of the District Court's decision.... [W]e conclude that the District Court properly granted summary judgment to Plaintiffs with respect to the content-based advertising restrictions, with the exception of the prohibition on portrayals of fictitious law firms. We likewise conclude that the District Court properly granted summary judgment to Defendants with respect to the thirty-day moratorium. Accordingly, we affirm the District Court's opinion in large part, and reverse in part.

BACKGROUND

A. The Parties ...

[The Plaintiffs are an individual (James Alexander), a personal injury law firm that Alexander is a managing partner at (Alexander & Catalano), and a not-for-profit consumer rights organization (Public Citizen). The firm used various broadcast and print media to advertise including commercials that contain special effects of smoke and electrical currents surrounding the firm's name; effects that depict Alexander and his partner as giants towering above local buildings, running to a client's house so quickly they appear as blurs, and providing legal assistance to space aliens; depicting a judge in the courtroom that the judge is there "to make sure [the trial] is fair; "comical scenes; slogans such as "heavy hitters;" and phrases like "think big" and "we'll give you a big helping hand." No disciplinary actions have been brought against the firm or its lawyers based on firm advertising. Fearing such action, the firm halted its advertisements. Defendants, four presiding judges, were appointed as part of the disciplinary committee by the four Judicial Departments of the New York Supreme Court, Appellate Division, and responsible for adopting the New York disciplinary rules.]

Rules . . .

C. The Present Action and District Court Decision . . .

[Plaintiffs filed their complaint on February 1, 2007, the date the new rules were to take effect seeking declaratory and injunctive relief against enforcement of the rules and arguing infringement of their First Amendment rights. On July 23, 2007, the District Court granted partial summary judgment to both the Plaintiffs and the Defendants. Applying the test for commercial speech set forth in *Central Hudson*, the District Court found the disputed provisions of § 1200.50(c) unconstitutional but concluded that the thirty-day moratorium provisions survived constitutional scrutiny. The District Court held that a ban on irrelevant, unverifiable and non-informational advertising needed legal support, must be analyzed under by the *Central Hudson* test, and needed legal support.]

DISCUSSION

This case calls on us . . . to assess the scope of First Amendment protection accorded to commercial speech, and the measure of evidence a state must present in regulating such speech. . . . The Supreme Court has established a four-part inquiry for determining whether regulations of commercial speech are consistent with the First Amendment: [1] whether the expression is protected by the First Amendment. For commercial speech to come within that provision, it at least must concern lawful activity and not be misleading. Next, we ask [2] whether the asserted governmental interest is substantial. If both inquiries yield positive answers, we must determine [3] whether the regulation directly advances the governmental interest asserted, and [4] whether it is not more extensive than is necessary to serve that interest. *Central Hudson Gas & Elec. Corp. v. Pub. Serv. Comm'n of N.Y.*, 447 U.S. 557, 566 (1980).

A. The Disputed Provisions Regulate Commercial Speech Protected by the First Amendment . . .

[Defendants' appeal the District Court's threshold conclusion that the First Amendment protects advertising that is irrelevant, unverifiable, and non-informational.] The Supreme Court first recognized attorney advertising as within the scope of protected speech in *Bates v. State Bar of Arizona*, 433 U.S. 350 (1977), in which the Court invalidated a ban on price advertising for what the Court deemed "routine" legal services. In so doing, the Court reserved the question of whether similar protection would extend to "advertising claims as to the quality of services [that] are not susceptible of measurement or verification." *Id.* at 383. . . .

[The Supreme Court has held that states may impose regulations to ensure that the stream of commercial information flows clean and free. However, since *Bates*, the Supreme Court has not offered fully consistent descriptions as to what constitutes protected commercial speech with respect to attorney advertising and has left uncertainty to the level of protection for advertisements that lack precise informational content.]

In the end, we agree with the District Court that, with one exception discussed below, the content-based restrictions in the disputed provisions of § 1200.50(c) regulate commercial speech protected by the First Amendment. In almost every instance, descriptions of the first prong of the *Central Hudson* test are phrased in the negative, and the only categories that *Central Hudson*, and its sequellae, clearly exclude from protection are speech that is false, deceptive, or misleading, and speech that concerns unlawful activities. *See, e.g., Florida Bar v. Went For It, Inc.*, 515 U.S. at 623–24 ("[T]he government may freely regulate commercial speech that concerns unlawful activity or is misleading. Commercial speech that falls into neither of those categories . . . may be regulated if the government satisfies [Central Hudson's remaining three prongs]." (citation omitted)); *Ibanez v. Fl. Dep't of Bus. & Prof'l Regulation, Bd. of Accountancy*, 512 U.S. 136, 142 (1994) ("[O]nly false, deceptive, or misleading commercial speech may be banned."). The Supreme Court has also emphasized that "States may not place an absolute prohibition on certain types of potentially misleading information . . . if the information also may be presented in a way that is not deceptive." *In re R.M.J.*, 455 U.S. 191, 203 (1982); *see also*, e.g., *Peel v. Attorney Registration & Disciplinary Comm'n of Ill.*, 496 U.S. 91, 100–01 (1990); *Shapero v. Ky. Bar Ass'n*, 486 U.S. 466, 479 (1988); *Zauderer v. Office of Disciplinary Counsel of the Supreme Court of Ohio*, 471 U.S. 626, 644 (1985). We conclude from these precedents that the Central Hudson analysis applies to regulations of commercial speech that is only potentially misleading.

The speech that Defendants' content-based restrictions seek to regulate—that which is irrelevant, unverifiable, and non-informational—is not inherently false, deceptive, or misleading. . . . This is insufficient to place these restrictions beyond the scope of First Amendment scrutiny.

There is one exception to this conclusion. Subsection 1200.50(c)(3) prohibits "the portrayal of a fictitious law firm, the use of a fictitious name to refer to lawyers not associated together in a law firm, or otherwise imply that lawyers are associated in a law firm if that is not the case." N.Y. Comp. Codes R. & Regs., tit. 22, § 1200.50(c)(3). The District Court invalidated § 1200.50(c)(3) in its entirety. *Alexander*, 634 F.Supp.2d at 249. Plaintiffs acknowledge, however, that they intended to challenge only the first clause of this subsection—prohibiting portrayals of judges—and they do not oppose Defendants' appeal seeking reinstatement of the prohibition on fictitious firms.... This portion of § 1200.50(c)(3) addresses only attorney advertising techniques that are actually misleading (as to the existence or membership of a firm), and such advertising is not entitled to First Amendment protection. *See Florida Bar*, 515 U.S. at 623–24. Accordingly, and subject to the above-mentioned construction, we reverse the District Court's invalidation of that portion of § 1200.50(c)(3) that prohibits advertisements that include fictitious firms.

Having concluded that the remainder of the disputed regulations falls within the zone of protected commercial speech, we turn to the rest of the *Central Hudson* test. The Supreme Court has explained that "[c]ommercial speech that is not false or deceptive and does not concern unlawful activities may be restricted only in the service of a substantial governmental interest, and only through means that directly advance that interest." *Shapero*, 486 U.S. at 472 (quotation marks and alteration omitted). "The party seeking to uphold a restriction on commercial speech carries the burden of justifying it." *Edenfield v. Fane*, 507 U.S. 761, 770 (1993) (quotation marks and alteration omitted). We apply the three remaining prongs of *Central Hudson*, in turn, to each of the two categories of regulations set forth above.

B. *Central Hudson* and the Content–Based Regulations

1. Substantial Interest

Under the second prong of *Central Hudson*, the State must identify "a substantial interest in support of its regulation[s]." *Florida Bar*, 515 U.S. at 624. *"[T]he Central Hudson* standard does not permit us to supplant the precise interests put forward by the State with other suppositions." Id. at 624 (quotation marks omitted). [The state interest is to prohibit advertisements that are deceptive and misleading, and this is supported by the report by the New York State Bar Association's Task Force on Lawyer Advertising] This state interest is substantial—indeed, states have a generally unfettered right to prohibit inherently or actually misleading commercial speech. *See, e.g., Edenfield*, 507 U.S. at 769 ("[T]here is no question that [the State's] interest in ensuring the accuracy of commercial information in the marketplace is substantial."); *In re R.M.J.*, 455 U.S. at 207 ("States retain the authority to regulate advertising that is inherently misleading or that has proved to be misleading in practice."). The disputed regulations codified at § 1200.50(c) therefore survive the second prong of the *Central Hudson* analysis.

Defendants also assert an interest in "protecting the legal profession's image and reputation." (Appellants' Reply 30) In *Florida Bar*, the Supreme Court recognized a substantial interest "in preventing the erosion of confidence in the [legal] profession." *Florida Bar*, 515 U.S. at 635. Defendants explain that their interest in preventing misleading attorney advertising is "inextricably linked to its overarching interest" in maintaining attorney professionalism and respect for the bar. (Appellants' Reply 30) This interest also supports the disputed regulations.

2. Materially Advanced

"The penultimate prong of the *Central Hudson* test requires that a regulation impinging upon commercial expression 'directly advance the state interest involved; the regulation may not be sustained if it provides only ineffective or remote support for the government's purpose.' " *Edenfield*, 507 U.S. at 770 (quoting *Central Hudson*, 447 U.S. at 564). The state's burden with respect to this prong "is not satisfied by mere speculation or conjecture; rather, a governmental body seeking to sustain a restriction on commercial speech must demonstrate that the harms it recites are real and that its restrictions will in fact alleviate them to a material degree." *Florida Bar*, 515 U.S. at 626 (quotation marks omitted).... [The Supreme Court in *Ibanez* held that a party does not meet its burden if the words are 'potentially misleading.']

.... Defendants have not submitted any statistical or anecdotal evidence of consumer problems with or complaints of the sort they seek to prohibit. Nor have they specifically identified any studies from other jurisdictions on which the state relied in implementing the amendments. *See Alexander*, 634 F.Supp.2d at 248. Against this background, we test each of the disputed § 1200.50(c) provisions.

a. Subsection 1200.50(c)(1): Client Testimonials

This subsection prohibits advertisements that include "an endorsement of, or testimonial about, a lawyer or law firm from a client with respect to a matter that is still pending." N.Y. Comp. Codes R. & Regs., tit. 22, § 1200.50(c)(1). The Task Force Report observed that testimonials can be misleading because they may suggest that past results indicate future performance. (Task Force Report 26–27) ... The Task Force noted ... that "it would be an improper restriction on a client's free speech rights to prohibit client testimonials outright." (Id.) The Task Force Report therefore does not support Defendants' assertion that prohibiting testimonials from current clients will materially advance an interest in preventing misleading advertising. Indeed, the Report "contradicts, rather than strengthens, the Board's submissions." *Edenfield*, 507 U.S. at 772.

Nor does consensus or common sense support the conclusion that client testimonials are inherently misleading. Testimonials may, for example, mislead if they suggest that past results indicate future performance—but not all testimonials will do so, especially if they include a disclaimer. The District Court properly concluded that Defendants failed to satisfy this prong of Central Hudson with respect to client testimonials.

b. Subsection 1200.50(c)(3): Portrayal of a Judge

This subsection prohibits "the portrayal of a judge." N.Y. Comp. Codes R. & Regs., tit. 22, § 1200.50(c)(3).10 The Task Force Report observes that "a communication that states or implies that the lawyer has the ability to influence improperly a court" is "likely to be false, deceptive, or misleading." (Task Force Report, App. I, 11) . . . The advertisement in which Alexander & Catalano use the portrayal of a judge, for instance, depicts a judge in the courtroom and states that the judge is there "to make sure [the trial] is fair." This sort of advertisement does not imply an ability to influence a court improperly. It is not misleading; an advertisement of this sort may, instead, be informative ..... Defendants have not met their burden with respect to the wholesale prohibition of portrayals of judges. This prohibition consequently must fall.

c. Subsection 1200.50(c)(5): Irrelevant Techniques

This subsection prohibits advertisements that "rely on techniques to obtain attention that demonstrate a clear and intentional lack of relevance to the selection of counsel, including the portrayal of lawyers exhibiting characteristics clearly unrelated to legal competence." N.Y. Comp. Codes R. & Regs., tit. 22, § 1200.50(c)(5). . . .

A rule barring irrelevant advertising components certainly advances an interest in keeping attorney advertising factual and relevant. But this interest is quite different from an interest in preventing misleading advertising. Like Defendants' claim that the First Amendment does not protect irrelevant and unverifiable components in advertising, Defendants here appear to conflate irrelevant components of advertising with misleading advertising. These are not one and the same. Questions of taste or effectiveness in advertising are generally matters of subjective judgment. Moreover, as the Task Force Report acknowledged, "Limiting the information that may be advertised ... assumes that the bar can accurately forecast the kind of information that the public would regard as relevant." (Task Force Report, App. I, 8)

Defendants have introduced no evidence that the sorts of irrelevant advertising components proscribed by subsection 1200.50(c)(5) are, in fact, misleading and so subject to proscription. . . . Moreover, the sorts of gimmicks that this rule appears designed to reach—such as Alexander & Catalano's wisps of smoke, blue electrical currents, and special effects—do not actually seem likely to mislead. It is true that Alexander and his partner are not giants towering above local buildings; they cannot run to a client's house so quickly that they appear as blurs; and they do not actually provide legal assistance to space aliens. But given the prevalence of these and other kinds of special effects in advertising and entertainment, we cannot seriously believe—purely as a matter of "common sense"—that ordinary individuals are likely to be misled into thinking that these advertisements depict true characteristics. Indeed, some of these gimmicks, while seemingly irrelevant, may actually serve "important communicative functions: [they] attract[] the attention of the audience to the advertiser's message, and [they] may also serve to impart information directly." *Zauderer*, 471 U.S. at 647. [Plaintiffs prove that these techniques attract viewers and the Defendant has shown any consumers who have been mislead by them. Therefore,, Defendants cannot meet their burden for sustaining subsection 1200.50(c)(5)'s prohibition under *Central Hudson*.

d. Section 1200.50(c)(7): Nicknames, Mottos, and Trade Names

This subsection bars advertisements "utiliz[ing] a nickname, moniker, motto or trade name that implies an ability to obtain results in a matter." N.Y. Comp. Codes R. & Regs., tit. 22, § 1200.50(c)(7). We conclude, once again, that the evidence on which Defendants rely fails to support this regulation.

There is a compelling, commonsense argument that, given the uncertainties of litigation, names that imply an ability to obtain results are usually misleading.... [The Task Force Report observed that terms that suggest the outcome in a case are likely to be false, deceptive or misleading but did not recommend an outright prohibition.] Defendants' rule, by contrast, goes further and prohibits such descriptors—including, according to the Attorney General, Alexander & Catalano's own "Heavy Hitters" motto—even when they are not actually misleading. The Task Force Report therefore fails to support Defendants' considerably broader rule....

[The Court was not persuaded by sole reliance on Friedman v. Rogers, 440 U.S. 1 (1979) which upheld a prohibition on optometrist trade names, since it did not employ the preceding Central Hudson's First Amendment analysis and movant in that case provided substantial evidence to support the prohibition.]

3. Narrowly Tailored

The final prong of Central Hudson asks whether the "fit" between the goals identified (the state's interests) and the means chosen to advance these goals is reasonable; the fit need not be perfect. *Florida Bar*, 515 U.S. at 632. As this Court has explained, " 'laws restricting commercial speech ... need only be tailored in a reasonable manner to serve a substantial state interest in order to survive First Amendment scrutiny.' " *N.Y. State Ass'n of Realtors v. Shaffer*, 27 F.3d 834, 842 (2d Cir. 1994) (quoting *Edenfield*, 507 U.S. at 767). Nonetheless, "restrictions upon [potentially deceptive speech] may be no broader than reasonably necessary to prevent the deception." *In re R.M.J.*, 455 U.S. at 203. "[T]he existence of numerous and obvious less-burdensome alternatives to the restriction on commercial speech is certainly a relevant consideration in determining whether the 'fit' between ends and means is reasonable." *Florida Bar*, 515 U.S. at 632 (quotation marks and alteration omitted). More precisely, the Supreme Court has emphasized that "States may not place an absolute prohibition on certain types of potentially misleading information ... if the information also may be presented in a way that is not deceptive." *In re R.M.J.*, 455 U.S. at 203. And the Supreme Court has also affirmed that a state may not impose a prophylactic ban on potentially misleading speech merely to spare itself the trouble of "distinguishing the truthful from the false, the helpful from the misleading, and the harmless from the harmful." *Zauderer*, 471 U.S. at 646.

On this basis, even if we were to find that all of the disputed Section 1200.50(c) restrictions survived scrutiny under *Central Hudson*'s third prong, each would fail the final inquiry because each wholly prohibits a category of advertising speech that is potentially misleading, but is not inherently or actually misleading in all cases.... New York's rules prohibiting ... all testimonials by current clients, all portrayals of judges, and all depictions of lawyers exhibiting characteristics unrelated to legal competence are similarly categorical. Because these advertising techniques are no more than potentially misleading, the categorical nature of New York's prohibitions would alone be enough to render the prohibitions invalid.

Moreover, "nowhere does the State cite any evidence or authority of any kind for its contention that the potential abuses associated with the [disputed provisions] cannot be combated by any means short of a blanket ban." *Zauderer*, 471 U.S. at 648; see also *Peel*, 496 U.S. at 109 (noting that the mere potential for misleading "does not satisfy the State's heavy burden of justifying a categorical prohibition"). As the District Court observed, the State could have, for example, required disclaimers similar to the one already required for fictional scenes. *Alexander*, 634 F.Supp.2d at 250; see N.Y. Comp. Codes R. & Regs., tit. 22, § 1200.50(c)(4) (fictional scenes). Nothing in the record suggests that such disclaimers would have been ineffective.... [The record shows that disclaimers were suggested and the Federal Trade Commission stated that New York could adequately protect consumers using less restrictive means.] Defendants have failed to carry their burden with respect to Central Hudson's final prong. We therefore conclude, like the District Court, that the disputed portions of subsections 1200.50(c)(1), (3), (5), and (7) are unconstitutional....

C. Central Hudson and the Moratorium Provisions

Plaintiffs' cross-appeal challenges the District Court's decision upholding New York's time-limited moratorium on solicitation of accident victims or their families. "In cases where a legal filing is required within thirty days, the moratorium is limited to a fifteen-day cooling off period." *Alexander*, 634 F.Supp.2d at 253. New York's moratorium provisions apply to all media through which an attorney might initiate communication "directed to, or targeted at, a specific recipient or group of recipients." N.Y. Comp. Codes R. & Regs., tit. 22, § 1200.52(b)....

[W]e construe the moratorium provision as inapplicable to (a) broad, generalized mailings (Oral Arg. ~12:06:18); (b) general advertisements conveying an attorney's experience in handling personal-injury suits, even when these advertisements appear near news stories in a newspaper that the attorney knows will be filled with coverage of a particular accident (Oral Arg. ~12:02:38–12:03:00)13; or (c) advertisements informing readers of an attorney's past experience with a particular product where that product has caused repeated personal-injury problems (as with the Dalkon Shield advertisement at issue in *Zauderer*). (Oral Arg.~12:04:11)

We turn now to the remaining Central Hudson inquiries relevant to the moratorium provision.

1. State Interest

In *Florida Bar*, the Supreme Court recognized as a substantial state interest "protecting the privacy and tranquility of personal injury victims and their loved ones against intrusive, unsolicited contact by lawyers." *Florida Bar*, 515 U.S. at 624. That case considered a thirty-day moratorium on direct-mail solicitation of accident victims (or their families). This case similarly involves a moratorium on contacting accident victims (and their families).... *Florida Bar* makes clear that Defendants' stated interest is substantial.... The moratorium provisions thus meet the requirements of *Central Hudson*'s substantial interest prong.

2. Materially Advanced

Florida Bar upheld Florida's moratorium rule, which is similar to the New York provisions before us. Several other states have since adopted analogous regulations prohibiting targeted solicitation of accident victims for specific periods of time.... New York's moratorium provisions seek to address the same harms that the Florida Bar Court recognized in upholding a thirty-day ban on direct-mail solicitations. And the New York provisions seek to address those harms through similar means—a time-limited moratorium on targeted solicitation of potential clients. *Florida Bar* makes clear that such means materially advance the state's interest. We conclude, therefore, that Defendants have met their burden under this prong of *Central Hudson*. See *Moore v. Morales*, 63 F.3d 358, 361–62 (5th Cir. 1995) (relying largely on *Florida Bar* in upholding a rule prohibiting attorneys, physicians, and other professionals from soliciting accident victims within thirty days following the accident).

3. Narrowly Tailored

Were New York's moratorium provisions limited to direct-mail solicitation, there would be little question as to their constitutionality. See *Falanga v. State Bar of Georgia*, 150 F.3d 1333, 1340–41 (11th Cir. 1998). But New York's moratorium is not so limited. As the District Court recognized, "The moratorium provisions in this case extend by their plain language to television, radio, newspaper, and website solicitations that are directed to or targeted at a specific recipient or group of recipients." *Alexander*, 634 F.Supp.2d at 253.

The Supreme Court has in some circumstances favored a technology-specific approach to the First Amendment. See *United States v. Playboy Entm't Group, Inc.*, 529 U.S. 803, 813 (2000) ("Cable television, like broadcast media, presents unique problems, which inform our assessment of the interests at stake, and which may justify restrictions that would be unacceptable in other contexts."); *Reno v. ACLU*, 521 U.S. 844, 868 (1997)

("[E]ach medium of expression may present its own problems." (quotation marks and alteration omitted)); *FCC v. League of Women Voters of Ca.*, 468 U.S. 367, 377 (1984) ("[W]e have recognized that 'differences in the characteristics of new media justify differences in the First Amendment standards applied to them.'" (quoting *Red Lion Broad. Co. v. FCC*, 395 U.S. 367, 386 (1969)))....

In the context before us, we eschew a technology-specific approach to the First Amendment and conclude that New York's moratorium provisions—as we construe them—survive constitutional scrutiny notwithstanding their applicability across the technological spectrum. We focus first on the potential differences among media as to the degree of affirmative action needed to be taken by the targeted recipient to receive the material Plaintiffs seek to send. For many media forms, it is about the same. Thus, to us, the affirmative act of walking to one's mailbox and tearing open a letter seems no greater than walking to one's front step and picking up the paper or turning on a knob on a television or radio....

E-mail has replaced letters; newspapers are often read online; radio streams online; television programming is broadcast on the Web; and the Internet can be connected to television. *See* Christopher S. Yoo, The Rise and Demise of the Technology–Specific Approach to the First Amendment, 91 GEO. L.J. 245, 248 (2003) ("[T]he impending shift of all networks to packet switched technologies promises to cause all of the distinctions based on the means of conveyance and the type of speech conveyed to collapse entirely."). Furthermore, Internet searches do not bring a user immediately to the desired result without distractions. Advertisements may appear with the user's search results; pop-up ads appear on web pages; and Gmail (Google's e-mail service) creates targeted advertising based on the keywords used in one's e-mail. In such a context, an accident victim who describes her experience in an e-mail might very well find an attorney advertisement targeting victims of the specific accident on her computer screen.

States are increasingly responding to these expanded and expanding roles of the Internet. Several already apply existing attorney professional responsibility rules to electronic and Internet advertisements and solicitations. *See* Amy Haywood & Melissa Jones, Navigating a Sea of Uncertainty: How Existing Ethical Guidelines Pertain to the Marketing of Legal Services over the Internet, 14 GEO. J. LEGAL ETHICS, 1099, 1113 (2001).... [Texas and Florida have added language to address Internet solicitation in their disciplinary rules. The New York Task Force Report also concluded that disciplinary rules should be enforced equally across all types media advertisements.]

Accordingly, we conclude that even acknowledging that differences among media may be significant in some First Amendment analyses, they are not so in this case....

a. Porcelain Hearts

The Supreme Court has recognized the particular sensitivity of people to targeted (plaintiff's) attorney advertisements during periods of trauma. To the extent that the attorney advertisements, regardless of the media through which they are communicated, are directed toward the same sensitive people, there is no reason to distinguish among the mode of communication. Depending on the individual recipient, the printed word may be a likely to offend as images on a screen or in newspapers.

In *Florida Bar*, the Court recognized the state's "substantial interest ... in protecting injured Floridians from invasive conduct by lawyers." *Florida Bar*, 515 U.S. at 635. As the dissent in *Florida Bar* pointed out, the primary distinction between the targeted letters at issue in *Florida Bar* and the untargeted letters at issue in *Shapero v. Kentucky Bar Association*, 486 U.S. 466 (1988), was that "victims or their families will be offended by receiving a [targeted] solicitation during their grief and trauma." *Florida Bar*, 515 U.S. at 638. The dissent argued that the majority should not "allow restrictions on speech to be justified on the ground that the expression might offend the listener." *Id*.

But the majority of the Supreme Court in *Florida Bar* held otherwise. It focused on a subset of the public in analyzing the First Amendment: essentially, a First Amendment analogue to tort law's thin-skull plaintiffs, those who have a "porcelain heart." Some accident victims and their families might welcome targeted solicitations that inform them of their legal rights immediately after the accident (particularly when insurance companies may already be knocking on their doors). Other accident victims and their families might be perturbed—but not outraged—by the targeted solicitations. The Supreme Court, however, tailored First Amendment law, in the context of attorney solicitations, to the most sensitive members of the public. It is with these porcelain hearts in mind that we must evaluate New York's moratorium.

b. Wemmick's Castle

In addition to a heightened concern for public sensitivity to potentially offensive attorney communications, the Court in *Florida Bar* upheld the moratorium in part because of its belief that people should be given more of an option to avoid offensive speech in the privacy of their homes. *See Florida Bar*, 515 U.S. at 625 ("[W]e have consistently recognized that the State's interest in protecting the well-being, tranquility, and privacy of the home is certainly of the highest order in a free and civilized society." (quotation marks and alterations omitted)).

. . .

One important aspect of residential privacy is protection of the unwilling listener. Although in many locations, we expect individuals simply to avoid speech they do not want to hear, the home is different. "That we are often 'captives' outside the sanctuary of the home and subject to objectionable speech ... does not mean we must be captives everywhere." *Rowan v.*

U.S. Post Office Dep't, 397 U.S. 728, 738, 90 S. Ct. 1484, 1491, 25 L.Ed.2d 736 (1970) ... Thus, we have repeatedly held that individuals are not required to welcome unwanted speech into their own homes and that the government may protect this freedom. *Frisby v. Schultz*, 487 U.S. 474, 484–85 (1988) (some internal citations omitted)....

Yet, a letter in a mailbox is no more intrusive than the newspaper in the mailbox, the e-mail in one's inbox, the television in the living room, the radio in the kitchen, or the Internet in the study. Arguably, mail is directly targeted at a residence, whereas television, radio, and the Internet may be viewed outside the home. But the Court has seemingly not focused on this distinction, and, instead, has held that the home should be protected from offensive language that disturbs domestic tranquility through the airwaves:

Patently offensive, indecent material presented over the airwaves confronts the citizen, not only in public, but also in the privacy of the home, where the individual's right to be left alone plainly outweighs the First Amendment rights of an intruder. Because the broadcast audience is constantly tuning in and out, prior warnings cannot completely protect the listener or viewer from unexpected program content. To say that one may avoid further offense by turning off the radio when he hears indecent language is like saying that the remedy for an assault is to run away after the first blow. One may hang up on an indecent phone call, but that option does not give the caller a constitutional immunity or avoid a harm that has already taken place. *FCC v. Pacifica Found.*, 438 U.S. 726, 748–49 (1978) (internal citation omitted) (upholding the FCC's regulation of radio broadcast); *Rowan*, 397 U.S. at 736–37 ("[A] mailer's right to communicate must stop at the mailbox of an unreceptive addressee."). Once again, we find no reason to distinguish among these media for our First Amendment analysis.

c. Lawyers' Reputations

Finally, *Florida Bar* recognized the state's "substantial interest ... in preventing the erosion of confidence in the [legal] profession that ... repeated invasions [of privacy by lawyers] have engendered." *Florida Bar*, 515 U.S. at 635.... A solicitation that offends is not likely to be any less detrimental to the reputation of lawyers when spoken aloud, displayed on a computer screen, or conveyed by television.

Accordingly, we conclude that ads targeting certain accident victims that are sent by television, radio, newspapers, or the Internet are more similar to direct-mail solicitations, which can properly be prohibited within a limited time frame, than to "an untargeted letter mailed to society at large," which "involves no willful or knowing affront to or invasion of the tranquility of bereaved or injured individuals and simply does not cause the same kind of reputational harm to the profession" as direct mail solicitations. *Florida Bar*, 515 U.S. at 630....

As with Florida Bar's "short temporal ban," New York's moratorium permits attorneys to advertise to the general public their expertise with personal injury or wrongful death claims. It thereby fosters reaching the accident victims, so long as these victims are not specifically targeted. It further allows accident victims to initiate contact with attorneys even during the thirty days following an accident. *See Florida Bar*, 515 U.S. at 633.... No doubt the statute could have been more precisely drawn, but it need not be "perfect" or "the least restrictive means" to pass constitutional muster. *Bd. of Trustees of State Univ. of N.Y. v. Fox*, 492 U.S. 469, 480 (1989).

CONCLUSION

The thorough and well-reasoned opinion of the District Court is AFFIRMED, except as to N.Y. Comp. Codes R. & Regs., tit. 22, § 1200.50(c)(3)'s ban on "the portrayal of a fictitious law firm, the use of a fictitious name to refer to lawyers not associated together in a law firm, or otherwise imply[ing] that lawyers are associated in a law firm if that is not the case." With respect to this portion of § 1200.50(c)(3) only, the judgment of the District Court is REVERSED.

Problems and Questions

1. Think about the lawyers involved in challenging the rules prohibiting lawyers from advertising their services. Would you bet your license on winning a Supreme Court case? Were attorneys like *Bates*, *Ohralik*, *Shapero* and *Zauderer* thinking about this when they violated the rules?

2. Where along the continuum of communication should we draw the line separating advertising, which is permissible, from solicitation, which is not? Compare the professionalism arguments addressed in *Bates* to the discussion of the same issue in *Florida Bar*, cited in the *Cahill* case? Does Justice O'Connor's opinion represent a doctrinal departure for the Supreme Court in lawyer advertising cases?

3. Suppose your law firm wants to create a website to promote its services. Do you have regulatory concerns about any of the elements that might be incorporated into the website?

4. What will the evolution of constitutional law doctrine mean for bar association regulators? The lawyer on the street? Clients? The public?

B. DEVELOPING A STRATEGIC MARKETING PLAN

1. GENERAL PRINCIPLES

It is one thing to understand the marketplace, appreciate the regulations governing lawyer advertising, and generate creative ideas for marketing the law firm's legal services. Without a marketing plan designed to assure that these good ideas come to fruition; however, the firm is likely to be stymied. The demands of current crises and deadlines will give lawyers a plethora of reasons for not undertaking the critical exercise of implementing a marketing plan.

The actual process of developing a marketing plan involves a number of identifiable steps. The same suggestions may apply to a group of experienced lawyers splitting off from an existing firm, or to a firm just getting started. Law firm marketing efforts are most likely to be effective if they are supported by a marketing plan. Too often, law firms approach marketing by focusing on the marketing techniques themselves rather than on the market for their services. They will eschew television ads because they think such tactics are tacky. They will develop a firm brochure because they heard that other firms had developed their own brochure. They decide to put up a Web site because it sounds so hip and cool. Marketing decisions in firms like these tend to be statements of personal preference unconnected to the potential consumers of the firm's services. The following article presents one legal consultant's views on how to approach the marketing dilemma:

IMPLEMENTATION OF A MARKETING PLAN

From *The New York Law Journal*, by Joel A. Rose (March 3, 1992).

Ed, John, and Mary founded their 26 attorney, highly rated law firm 12 years ago. Ed and John are the principal rainmakers. Together they account for about 65 percent of the firm's business. Most of the other attorneys work on client files generated by Ed and John. In December, John announced that he was leaving the firm to become a principal at one of the firm's investment clients. Ed had some health problems and decided to reduce his involvement in firm activities. The other partners were reasonably certain that they could service and retain the firm's clients. However, some uncertainty existed about their ability to retain a few of the larger and more profitable clients that remained with the firm because of the quality of work performed and the personal relationships between John and the chief executive officers of these companies.

In light of this, the partners retained a law firm management consultant to develop a marketing strategy for the firm so they could continue to fulfill their personal and professional objectives. After meeting with the partners, the consultant's initial recommendation was that a marketing committee be formed to evaluate the firm's resources and determine the potential market for those services.

To accomplish these objectives, the consultant recommended the following procedural steps:
- Assess the strengths and weaknesses of the firm, its "practice mix," competition and the potential market;
- Establish goals to be achieved;

- Agree on marketing objectives to satisfy the market related goals; and

- Develop a marketing plan by coordinating specific strategies to achieve the marketing objectives.

The partners decided that the best method of marketing to existing clients is to ensure the performance of quality work in a timely and responsive manner and be sensitive of the client's legal and non-legal needs. To accomplish this, partners were assigned responsibility for managing each of the firm's practice areas. Attorneys were instructed to ensure that their work product and/or general interaction with the client was tailored to satisfy the needs of the client as perceived by the client, not the attorney. To accomplish this, attorneys were urged to:

- Establish a good rapport with clients. Engage in social and business pleasantries (lunches, entertainment, provide unsolicited information likely to be of interest) and show concern by calling periodically to inquire how the client is faring, visiting the client's place of business to better understand it, etc.

- Find practical and economic solutions to enable the clients achieve their objectives. Attorneys were advised not to tell clients that a desired course of action is inappropriate without suggesting alternative approaches, if possible.

- Lead the client to make the proper decisions. Provide clients with the tools to make a decision, without forcing the decision.

- Meet deadlines, avoid setting unrealistic ones.

- Identify other legal needs. Identify the client's needs and interests beyond the scope of the current work and be sensitive to how the client is faring and to problems that may be anticipated. Explore the "bigger picture" to determine if other legal problems exist and how they may be resolved.

- Educate the client about the firm's capabilities. Attorneys got information about the expertise and accomplishments of other partners and were told to make certain their clients are aware of the full range of firm services. They were also encouraged to introduce clients to other members of the firm at every opportunity.

- Share information. Inform clients by phone, letter or photocopy of an article of interest, etc. of specific developments in the law of which they should be aware.

- Be sensitive to broader needs, especially to the position of the contact person at the client and in advancing that individual's personal needs and goals to the extent such activities do not conflict with the client's representation.

- Be a team player by assisting one another in marketing existing and potential clients.

A former client is one for whom the firm performed services in the past. Depending on the relationship and results of prior service, some of the techniques for current and potential clients were used. An organized strategy for attracting clients was developed, including:

Continued individual initiative combined with a marketing team. Attorneys were encouraged to take the initiative that may include a team marketing effort. Each attorney was expected to identify and approach at least 10 potential clients each year. On a team basis, two or more partners were responsible for identifying potential clients and enlisting appropriate attorneys and other referral sources to approach these clients.

- Proper preparation. Whether proceeding individually or as member of a marketing team, recommendations were provided on how attorneys may:
  - Identify potential new clients.
  - Identify the "decision makers" whose responsibility is to assign legal work to law firms or who approves such referrals.
  - Evaluate the legal and non-legal needs and objectives of the potential client and the chief decision makers.
  - Evaluate the firm's ability to meet those needs.
  - Identify the contacts that the partners, the firm's existing clients or other friendly third parties may have with the potential client and the chief decision makers.
  - Review available information about the potential client and the decision makers.
  - Select an appropriate method of approach that would be properly received and permit education of the potential client about the firm, i.e., (lunch, seminar, entertainment, direct mail, friendly third party, etc.).
  - Insure that the marketing committee coordinates the efforts of attorneys in soliciting and/or servicing potential client.
- Receptive environment. Attorneys were taught how to create a receptive atmosphere that helps attract potential clients by implementing various general marketing strategies and recommendations.

General strategies to increase marketing success include:

- Promotion of a firm image. Create a universally accepted image of what and who the firm is, what the firm stands for, what it has to offer and the manner in which its services will be performed. This image must be appropriately communicated to the legal community and the marketplace. Since many of the firm's partners were not as well known as the founding partners, it was important that the firm try to achieve this goal by:

- Developing an expanded mission statement to help the firm differentiate itself from the crowd, beyond the credo of "quality legal services, on time at a favorable price."
- Preparing a two-page resume listing specific skills, accomplishments, honors, etc. to be circulated among attorneys and staff and made available, with the mission statement, in an attractive binder and placed in the reception area, so that all could better appreciate the qualities that the firm has to offer. Attorneys are responsible for informing the firm of any significant new experiences, honors, positions, etc., as they occur to update resumes.
- Maintaining appearances of individual offices and common areas.

• Name identification and creation of a message of expertise and stability. The names of the attorneys in the firm were placed before the public in as many favorable forms as possible, including:
- Identification of the firm name and that the firm is a "full service" law firm.
- Publication of articles in legal and trade magazines.
- Participation by attorneys in positions of authority and leadership in civic, social and religious organizations and bar associations.
- Developing firm stability, public concern and a sense of paying "civic rent" by financially supporting, or offering pro bono services to, worthy community activities as a firm, where appropriate.
- Each member of the firm was sensitized to use of the media.
- Institutionalizing the name of the firm by use of stationery that increases the emphasis on the name and changes the emphasis of listing individual attorney's names by seniority. Recognition of admission to more than one bar was noted. The message communicated by these changes is one of a firm that acts as a team having far-reaching capabilities.

• Marketing Committee. The role of the marketing committee was upgraded to implement and assess the results of the marketing plan, to recommend changes to it and to collect and maintain useful information on potential clients, contacts and marketing tools.

• Marketing efforts should receive regular attention. Marketing became a permanent agenda item for the partnership meeting and the firm meeting.

• Increased budget for marketing. The marketing plan was enhanced by modest additional financial commitment, i.e., a business development expense account was increased to a minimum of $500 for partners and $200 for associates. Business development activities were budgeted at 1.5 percent of gross revenue.

- Improve product mix. Certain areas of practice within the firm were upgraded through inside and outside CLE training; two lateral hires were employed so that the firm may be perceived as "a full service firm."
- Commitment to excellence. Each attorney was expected to attain a level of expertise in an area of firm practice that will enable that attorney to be "marketed" as a leader in the field.
- Advance planning. Annually every attorney was accountable to identify his or her own goals and objectives for client development for review with the marketing committee.
- Proper staff attitudes are a positive marketing force. Each member of the professional and administrative staff was interviewed by a member of the marketing committee and told that what they communicate to others professionally and non-professionally about their jobs and the people they work for spreads a message about the firm.
- Seminars. Attorneys were encouraged to participate in the presentation of seminars sponsored by the firm or others targeted at specific groups of existing, former and/or potential clients or sources of referral.

The implementation of this marketing plan required a significant amount of time, effort, cooperation and enthusiasm on everyone's part. Given the competitive pressures and the likelihood that they will increase, the implementation of and adherence to a coordinated marketing plan was perceived to be the key to the firm's growth and survival.

The concept of a marketing plan is simple: create a message that will reach the clients you want to represent. Craft your message so that recipients will respond positively. Invest sufficient resources in developing and delivering the message to get the job done. Measure the effectiveness of the plan, and revise it regularly over time.

Despite the simplicity of planning, most law firms do not think about marketing in a strategic way. It may be useful to examine some of the big marketing mistakes that law firms typically make. These mistakes are also simple, but they are fundamental. The following basic principles address these fundamental mistakes:

- **Give the clients what they want and need to hear, not what you want to hear.** This is one of the most common advertising errors, and it is not limited to law firms. The advertiser may respond to very different appeals than the targeted audience. If you do not know what your prospective clients would like, ask them. Informal surveys, focus groups, client feedback ("What brought you to our office?") and other forms of market research can be conducted inexpensively and effectively. If you do not do your homework, it is unlikely you will create a successful marketing plan.

- **Invest in your marketing plan.** Marketing activities must be budgeted and funded. Lawyers are very good at coming up with ideas, but not so proficient at implementation. It is easy to say, "I'll take a prospective client to lunch once a week," and quite another thing to do it. It is easy to say, "What this firm needs is a website," and another thing to get the site up and running. Remember that every task in the marketing plan requires an investment of time and energy, and many tactics also require an investment of money. Lawyers and staff must realize that while they are working on marketing, they are not working on cases. Marketing work must be given priority, or it will be relegated to the back burner. Marketing activities must be given credit, not just for client origination, but also for actual time expended.

- **Develop a message platform: a short statement that capitalizes what it is you do for clients.** Too many firms never develop a clear message, and they never develop an identity within their markets. You should have a ready answer if someone comes up to you and asks, "What does your firm do?" "We represent people who are injured in automobile accidents, and we are willing to go to court to make them whole." Compare that to this answer: "Well, we like to litigate, but we handle some other stuff too. A lot of our work is plaintiff's personal injury, mostly automobile accidents, because, well, that's where most of the P.I. work comes from. A lot of firms just try to settle out of court with the insurance companies but we're all experienced trial lawyers, so we like to go to court. We've been doing this for 25 years, and did I mention that we do other cases besides P.I.?" Straightforward. Succinct. Focused. Clear. These are adjectives that describe a good message platform.

- **Marketing is an on-going activity.** Many law firms seem to think that if they discuss marketing at a partners' meeting every few months, they do not have to do anything else. Or they think that if they delegate marketing tasks like writing letters and designing ads to secretaries, they have done enough. Such discussion may make the partners feel good, but it will do little to bring clients in the door. In truth, marketing is not the exclusive domain of one or two rainmakers, or even the partners. Every lawyer needs to be involved in marketing the firm and its services to clients every day. Just as the firm needs to develop a marketing plan, each individual lawyer needs to have a personal marketing plan as well.

- **Involve everyone in the firm.** Marketing is not something that one or two rainmakers do, or that should be restricted to the partners. Associates, legal assistants, secretaries, and other employees support the marketing program in many ways, whether it is through their own contacts with clients, preparing written materials, or assisting other lawyers to carry out marketing responsibilities. Staff should understand the message platform, the importance of marketing to the future of the firm, the firm's marketing strategies, and the roles they will play in marketing efforts.

- **Once you get clients, strive to keep them.** For one thing, it costs less to keep a current client than it does to attract a new one. More significantly; however, the best advertising you can get will come from satisfied clients. They will sing your praises in the community, and bring new clients to your door. Conversely, dissatisfied clients will tell the world how unhappy they were with your services. An effective marketing plan should make sure that every client is a satisfied client. Satisfaction is not determined so much by whether the client won or lost their case, but more on the way he was treated by the lawyers and their staff, whether they feel you've represented them conscientiously. Another benefit of keeping your clients happy is the decreased likelihood that they will sue you for malpractice.

- **Know the rules that govern legal advertising and solicitation.** The limitations on how lawyers are permitted to market their services inevitably affect the content of the firm's marketing plan. An understanding of what the ethical rules permit or do not permit (see Section A above) is likely to influence many aspects of the marketing plan.

2. CREATE A PLAN

With these general considerations in mind, let us turn to the marketing plan itself. A marketing plan can be developed when the firm is first created, or after it is already in business. The plan can be composed at an extended retreat, or through a series of meetings. The process can be led by an outside consultant/facilitator, or directed by the firm's leadership. The plan should be reduced to writing, and someone should be given the responsibilities for its implementations. The plan should be reviewed periodically to reflect not only changes in the marketplace, but also to assess its effectiveness. The marketing plan may be a part of the firm's larger business plan (see Chapter 11). Although there are different ways a marketing plan could be structured, the following model is simple enough for a small firm to use, yet comprehensive enough to be effective.

a. Analyze the Marketplace

The objective of this first stage of the marketing plan is to get an accurate picture of the legal needs of the public in the area where the firm intends to practice law, including how people will utilize the legal services that the lawyers in the firm want to provide. Take a close look at the demographics of the geographical area in which the firm will practice. Look at the characteristics of the population in that area. Identify what kinds of legal problems the people in this area have. Every community has its own unique mix of people, industry, government, and practice concentrations. Sometimes these observations are intuitive (e.g., there is very little admiralty work in Denver; there is considerable agricultural law in western Iowa). Sometimes insights may require some digging.

Much of the demographic information you will need to conduct this market assessment is available in public documents, or private research that can be purchased. Census information, Bureau of Labor Statistics reports, business school research, court records of filings and settlements, Internet databases, bar association economic surveys, and private studies offer a wealth of information for those willing to look for it. Bookstores also sell publications that digest demographic information from a variety of sources, e.g., titles such as *Places Rated Almanac*. Anecdotal information from clients, lawyers, judges, business people, and newspapers can provide subjective, but often valid perceptions about the marketplace.

The key for law firms of all sizes is to recognize that it is difficult if not impossible to produce a good marketing plan without understanding the marketplace. It is not necessary to have a Ph.D. in Economics to collect and assess demographic and other information, but it is critical to complete this step.

b. Assess the Competition

Competition is the essence of a free market system. Providers of goods and services compete for clients and customers, and the most efficient will prevail over the least efficient. In law, this means that wherever you practice and whatever type of law you choose, other legal service providers will operate in the same arena that you do. If you start a new firm, there will already be competing firms in the marketplace. If you have an existing firm, there will always be upstarts intent on taking your market share.

In addition to facing competition from within the traditional members of the legal industry, the new lawyer faces increasingly stronger forces from "diversified" legal professions, who are really members of other industries entering the legal industry as a side business. Whatever your position, you will face competition, and in today's world, competition does not always come in the form of other lawyers. A variety of professional providers may seek to handle problems that traditionally have been considered to be within the domain of the legal profession. The only true way to overcome competitive forces is to provide a unique service, a service like no other, or distinguishing the services you provide from others in your vicinity in some other way. Realize that it is probably not in your best interest to reinvent the wheel, so really look to the weaknesses of the competition Once you establish yourself as unique and separate from others in the industry, you are still the target of entering youngsters whose sole objective it to take hold of your market share and make it their own.

Arguably, the most important aspect of developing a marketing plan is identifying the competitive forces. It is critical to truly understand why your competitors are successful, or not. It is important to identify these competitors, not only who they are as lawyers, but also what clients they represent. Find out what services they perform and how well they perform them. Look at the things these other providers do not do or do not do well. Attempt to draw a comprehensive picture of your competitors and how you can exploit their weaknesses.

c. Evaluate Yourself

At this point in the process, you have looked outward to get a clear, objective picture of your potential clients, and you have taken stock of your competition. The next step is to take a snapshot of your firm, to identify your strengths and weaknesses. This step is ultimately subjective and introspective, but it needs to be a candid, hard look at what you bring to the table. This assessment should look at the skills and experience of the lawyers and staff members, the practice interests of the lawyers, their contacts in the marketplace, and the resources available to the firm to reach and service potential clients.

In a law firm retreat, this assessment is sometimes conducted through what is called a SWOT exercise (standing for Strengths, Weaknesses, Opportunities, Threats). The SWOT process can serve as a useful tool in assessing your situation. In lieu of a structured retreat, the self-assessment can be completed over time through careful research, analysis, and discussion. For an excellent guide to strategic planning, see *The Lawyer's Guide to Strategic Planning*, by Thomas C. Grella and Michael L. Hudkins (ABA, 2005).

d. Identify a Niche

Analysis and synthesis of the information gathered in the three previous steps should lead to the identification of a market niche: that segment of the marketplace that you intend to claim as your own. The key to any effective marketing plan is to clearly define this niche, because it identifies both the clients your firm will seek to represent and the services your firm will seek to provide.

The idea of a market niche is difficult for many practitioners to grasp. They intuitively think that in a competitive environment they should cast their nets as widely as possible, taking in whatever cases they can. This is the mentality of the general practitioner, and we live in an environment where the general practitioner is dead. Whether we call it specialization, practice concentration, boutique practice or niche practice, it means limiting the types of substantive legal work the firm is willing to handle. In today's world, no firm can be everything to all clients. Not only is it impossible for lawyers to attain confidence in all areas of the law, it is much more difficult to reach a general population than a targeted audience.

Law is not unlike many other fields, in which specialists prove to be more efficient than generalists. Both in terms of marketing and service delivery, law firms with an identifiable focus win out over firms that try to be everything to everybody. This concept has made giants out of beginners. Henry Ford was able to provide a product, the automobile, to a greater number of people at a lower cost, because he was able to increase the internal efficiency of the factory. His analysis of the economy holds true for all businesses, even those providing service, and yes, even law firms.

For instance, a law firm that limits its practice to real estate transactions can focus on developing a real estate clientele and implementing systems that deliver the legal work product efficiently and profitably, because it does not need to spend resources on learning other areas of law, subscribing to other journals, attending a greater variety of CLE courses, and appeal to yet another community of potential clients—instead it can concentrate on expanding its knowledge of a narrow area of law—real estate. Consequently, most of the forms are already part of the system hence no one will have to draw a new one up, once you conduct market research, you merely need to update, rather than begin from scratch. These mechanisms add up, and in totality decrease the cost of running the business per customer. Not surprisingly, surveys show that specialist lawyers make more money than generalists, a phenomenon common with many other professional fields.

The identification of a niche requires making some tough decisions. The firm has to examine the client environment, understand the strengths and weaknesses of competitors, and possess a strategic vision for itself. Individual lawyers may have to make compromises in order to build a practice that complements the firm's vision. For start-up firms, an initial niche may not be where the firm wants to find itself over the long term.

An established firm may need to eliminate practice areas that do not fit within the scope of its niche. Some firms may develop a family of practice areas, while others choose to limit their practice to a very narrow range of cases. The bottom line is that you have to bite the bullet, decide what you want to be, and build your practice with a sense of direction and purpose.

e. Develop a Plan

Once you have established a niche, the rest should be easy. If you know who your clients are and what services they will need, you should be able to describe how you will deliver those services, and how you will communicate your availability. The identity of the clientele and services will in many cases dictate the media and the message of marketing strategies. One definition of marketing is that it is the process of identifying what business you are engaged in and communicating your availability to those who need what you offer.

The major pitfall for the unwary is to begin the marketing process without developing a marketing plan. Just because the firm down the street used Yellow Pages ads effectively does not mean that your firm will be able to do so. The big city mega-firm is not likely to find its clients using late night television ads during infomercials, although for some types of firms this might prove to be an effective marketing approach.

In the same way, it is not enough to have a plan without allocating resources (time and money) to the plan, assigning responsibility (both for the overall plan and for individual tasks), creating a timetable, and assessing the effectiveness of marketing strategies. All the firm's research, planning and creativity can be wasted if the implementation phase of the plan does not work. Given the tendency of lawyers to focus on immediate crises, marketing plans can easily be set aside if there is not a genuine commitment to follow through.

In the next section, you will explore the mechanics of creating a marketing plan for your firm. As you proceed, consider what combination of activities will support your efforts to exploit your market niche. Think about ways that specific marketing tactics might be crafted into an integrated and successful marketing plan. The marketing activities described are by no means all the approaches that law firms can and do utilize. Nor do they represent a list of activities that every law firm should try. The preceding discussion on how to create a marketing plan should have made clear the importance of molding the plan to the practice.

PROBLEMS AND QUESTIONS

1. If you were starting a new firm, how would you produce a marketing plan? How would you evaluate the marketplace and the need for legal services in the community where you intend to practice? Who would you view as your competition, and what services do these providers handle well or poorly? What special skills and contacts do you have? What do you see as your market niche? What strategies will you implement to attract the clients you hope to serve? See Appendix F, page 461, for a checklist of steps involved in creating a marketing plan.

2. In developing a marketing plan, what information might experienced lawyers have access to or need that recent graduates might not?

C. IMPLEMENTING A MARKETING PLAN
1. MARKETING MECHANICS

Perhaps because lawyers are relative newcomers to the marketing business, and perhaps because of the residual antipathy within the profession to marketing generally, lawyers are typically unsophisticated marketers. They often follow in the footsteps of other lawyers and law firms, a strategy that is almost anathema to real marketers. Lawyers frequently give lip service to marketing principles without committing the resources and energy to marketing to do it effectively. There is something to be said for following the pack: you are not likely to find yourself in hot water with disciplinary authorities if you do not try anything out of the ordinary. A conservative marketing philosophy, however, is not likely to set the firm apart from its competitors, who are all doing the same things.

Additionally, thinking outside the box has never been a forté of the legal mind. Lawyers tend to be conservative, unimaginative and uninspired when it comes to marketing. Several factors contribute to the creative vacuum. Most lawyers do not have training or experience in marketing, so they are just not very good at it. When they attend seminars on marketing lawyers usually learn from other lawyers who are little better than they are. Having just gotten into the marketing business in 1977, lawyers do not have much experience with marketing. Even today, ethical rules place limitations on lawyers that most business organizations do not face. Lawyers who aspire to spend their time practicing law are no more enamored of marketing tasks than they are of other management responsibilities. In short, it should not come as a surprise that lawyers do not understand how to market their services effectively or achieve a marketing success.

In reality, marketing is always changing. What worked for one generation of lawyers may not work for another. What worked for one lawyer last year may not work for the same lawyer this year. Consumers by nature become saturated with older and timeworn messages; they respond to new messages at least in part because they are new. Think about the times you have seen an innovative television commercial for the first time. It catches your eye. But when you have seen the same commercial dozens of times, you just tune it out, or run to the refrigerator for a snack.

This also holds true for law firm marketing campaigns. If you go to your lawyer and see a new brochure in the reception area, you might read it. When you come back again, you will be less inclined to re-read the brochure. After several visits you ignore it completely. Or your lawyer may send out a newsletter on "Developments in Real Estate Law." You might find the newsletter interesting and useful, especially if you are involved in real estate. But if every lawyer in town sends you a real estate newsletter, you might place them all on a "to be read" pile that never is.

Changes in how people respond to marketing campaigns also reflect changes in the demographics, social attitudes and needs of the community itself. For instance, a community characterized by young parents may over time evolve into a community of empty-nesters. Their problems and needs would have changed over the years. Hence, the legal services they would require would have changed also.

A final reason that marketing continually changes is that the competition changes. Other firms may respond to your successful efforts. They may come up with a new twist on their own (e.g., hiring a well-known lateral partner). Satchel Paige, the famous baseball pitcher, once remarked, "Don't look back. Someone might be gaining on you." For lawyers, this means that the competition is always close at your heels, ready to take your business.

Lawyers, to be successful marketers, must be innovative. They must discover approaches that no one else has used. They must be willing to experiment. They must form the cutting edge. They need to balance their conservative traditional inclinations with the need to be innovative. Most lawyers join the trailing edge of marketing instead. They do not take chances. They do not exercise creativity. They do not attempt methods they have not seen other lawyers employ. This is unfortunate, because one legacy of *Bates* has been the opportunity to innovate in the marketing of legal services.

2. THE ECONOMICS OF MARKETING

The simple economics of marketing require organizations to spend money to attract customers who will generate revenue, sufficient to cover the marketing and other operational expenses, and generate a profit. If the organization buys an ad in the newspaper, it is not enough that the ad generates enough money to pay for itself. Of course, this means learning the origin of all new business, whether a referral from another lawyer or response to a Yellow Pages ad. Assuming the firm can obtain this information, it is not too great a step to ascertain the fees collected for the work involved, and the amount of profit generated by the marketing effort.

Marketing involves more than cash outlays; it almost always involves opportunity costs—time spent on the marketing effort that would otherwise be spent delivering billable work to clients. Firms that ignore the human costs are often frustrated, because they do not account for revenue lost to time spent on marketing, or because they do not follow through on marketing activities due to the time demands of clients for legal work.

One other factor is important to remember: the more targeted marketing is, the more efficient it is. If a brochure is sent to the entire population of the city where a law firm is located, it will be very costly. If, however, the firm can identify the target audience—the potential clients the firm wants to reach with its message—the cost is much less.

Suppose the brochure cost one dollar per recipient to deliver. If the brochure is delivered by mail to 50,000 residents of the county, it will cost the firm $50,000. If the firm can deliver 1,000 brochures to a trade show for potential clients in an industry the firm represents, the cost is $1,000. Assuming the firm attracts the same ten clients either way, and the clients generate $50,000 of legal work, the mailing is not an effective way to generate clients, whereas the trade show is. Thus, firms that have a clear, narrow vision of who they want to represent and where to reach these prospects will fare much better in the marketing arena than a firm with a general focus or ill-defined marketing plan.

3. REACHING THE MARKETPLACE

Law firms employ a variety of different techniques to market their services. Some are very traditional, and existed even before the ban on advertising was lifted, while others are more creative and *avant garde*. In the final analysis, a firm cannot develop its marketing plan from a laundry list, but must tailor the marketing strategies to its particular clientele, market and culture. The essence of marketing is to know, first, what services you want to deliver, second, to whom, and, third, the marketing methods that will attract those prospective clients to the firm.

PROBLEMS AND QUESTIONS

1. Think about organizations outside the law that have successful marketing strategies: Disney, Nike, McDonald's, Walmart. What do these companies have in common with respect to their marketing message? In what ways are they different, and why? Can law firms learn anything from these companies, or is law simply too different?

2. Now consider the magazine industry. What happened to national weekly magazines like *Life, Look*, and *Saturday Evening Post*? Why have these general circulation journals been supplanted by specialty magazines like *People, Smithsonian*, and *Popular Mechanics*? Again, are there lessons to be learned by law firms?

3. How much does it cost a law firm to attract one new client? How much does it cost to bring in enough new clients to sustain and grow the practice? How do we know such things?

4. Look at the following list of marketing techniques. Which ones do you think will be effective? Does it matter who the firm is? Who it hopes to represent? What caveats would you offer to a firm about these approaches:

    - A law firm brochure?
    - Client seminars on legal topics?
    - Pro bono handling of a highly publicized case for a popular cause?
    - Briefing lunches for key clients?
    - Videotapes on legal services in the firm's waiting room?
    - Speaking at community functions?
    - Running for political office?
    - Hosting an informational interview talk show on legal issues of public interest on local radio or television?
    - Notices of availability on a computer network bulletin board or web site?
    - A newspaper column or article?
    - A holiday open house for current and prospective clients?
    - Press releases concerning law firm successes (e.g., settled cases)?
    - Regular attendance at country or social club events?

5. What other approaches to law firm marketing would you recommend? What is the cost in both dollars and time to implement each? How would you measure the effectiveness of these marketing efforts?

6. What would the marketing director at a large corporation have to say about the way lawyers market their practices? What about a public relations or advertising agency executive? Or a business school marketing professor? In what ways is the legal services industry unique? In what ways is it the same as nonlegal organizations? What could we learn from these other industries?

7. In a small firm without a larger administrative staff, how does the planning and implementation of a marketing plan take place? Who is responsible? Who does the work? Who pays if it doesn't get done?

8. In the law firm you have created for this class, using the model presented on pages 149–156, develop a marketing that will attract and keep the clients you want to represent.

Chapter 7

Managing Clients

■ ■ ■

A. CLIENTS AND LAWYERS

At a basic level, there is no law practice without clients. Legal work does not exist in the abstract, apart from real people with real problems. Practice development is ultimately client development. In this chapter, you will consider how client service contributes to the development of a law practice. Later in the course, you will learn more about the mechanics of delivering legal services to clients, but at this point you should consider how providing good service builds clientele, and conversely how the treatment of clients impacts their perceptions of the quality of the services they receive.

Individual practice development and law firm practice development are inextricably related, and that the owners of law firms are most often the lawyers whose individual practice is portable, because they have built trust and loyalty among their clients. The materials begin with a discussion of the philosophical approach to services called client-centered lawyering, followed by a section on legal fees and billing practices. The materials then conclude with some of the problems that arise involving fee disputes between lawyers and their clients.

1. CLIENT–CENTERED LAWYERING

Just as the legal profession has evolved over the past century, so has the lawyer-client relationship. Certainly, the practice of law has changed, but so have clients. The educational level and business acumen of the average individual has risen since the days when Lincoln practiced law in rural Illinois during the 1840s. Legal problems have multiplied; the growth of big government and big business has produced whole fields of legal problems that did not exist before. Mass communication media have placed vast amounts of information in the hands of anyone who wants it, focusing people's attention on legal rights and remedies, but concurrently erecting barriers to understanding the legal system.

One thing has not changed, however. When an individual comes to a lawyer for help, that person needs assistance to solve a problem. Generally, if the client could have solved the problem without calling in a lawyer, he would have done so. The lawyer's role as problem-solver is often overlooked in this era of adversarial tactics, but it is central to the concept of client service. On a human level, the needs of Lincoln's clients and our clients today are not all that different.

An entire school of legal educators advocate a revolutionary "client-centered" approach to lawyering. One of the earliest books on this subject, *Lawyer and Client: Who's in Charge,* by Arnold Rosenthal, analyzes the fundamentals of the lawyer-client relationship. The following materials build upon this basic proposition. Rosenthal suggests that because the legal problem belongs to the client, the lawyer's primary responsibility in the relationship is to carry out the objectives of the client. Basic agency principles underlie the client-centered lawyering theory. The lawyer is agent for the client/principal. The lawyer is empowered to act on behalf of the client, but at the client's direction. At the same time, the lawyer exercises considerable discretion in strategy and tactics on account of the lawyer's special knowledge and skill. The client is "in charge" of the representation, but the lawyer is more than a hired gun.

The ambiguity surrounding the limits of the authority of lawyer and client are demonstrated in the ethical rules of the legal profession. The 1969 ABA Model Code of Professional Responsibility, in DR 7–101(A)(1), stated that "A lawyer shall not ... [f]ail to seek the lawful objectives of his client through reasonably available means...." This objective-means dichotomy may reflect the reality of the relationship, but it provides precious little guidance to the lawyer as to when she should or should not assume control of decision making. The present ABA Model Rules of Professional Conduct attempt to overcome the vagueness of the Model Code language. Model Rule 1.2 states, in part:

> (a) A lawyer shall abide by a client's decisions concerning the objectives of representation, and, as required by Rule 1.4, shall consult with the client as to the means by which they are to be pursued. A lawyer may take such action on behalf of the client as is impliedly authorized to carry out the representation. A lawyer shall abide by a client's decision whether to settle a matter. In a criminal case, the lawyer shall abide by the client's decision, after consultation with the lawyer, as to a plea to be entered, whether to waive jury trial and whether the client will testify.
>
> . . .
>
> (c) A lawyer may limit the objectives of the representation if the limitation is reasonable under the circumstances and the client gives informed consent.

Model Rule 1.2 must be read in tandem with Model Rule 1.4, which establishes an informed consent standard for communications with clients, including clients' decisions regarding the scope of representation. Rule 1.4 states:

(a) A lawyer shall:

    (1) promptly inform the client of any decision or circumstance with respect to which the client's informed consent ... is required ...;

    (2) reasonably consult with the client about the means by which the client's objectives are to be accomplished;

    (3) keep a client reasonably informed about the status of a matter;

    (4) promptly comply with reasonable requests for information; and

    (5) consult with the client about any relevant limitations on the lawyer's conduct when the lawyer knows that the client expects assistance not permitted by the Rules of Professional Conduct or other law.

(b) A lawyer shall explain a matter to the extent reasonably necessary to permit the client to make informed decisions regarding the representation.

One might ask what the relevance of client-centered lawyering is to a course on law practice management. The simple answer is that the relationship between lawyer and client defines many approaches to management. On another level, however, client-centered lawyering implies that if lawyers carry out their clients' objectives, clients will be more satisfied with the services they receive. Satisfied clients will return the next time they need a lawyer, and they will refer others. The client-centered approach, based upon two-way communication, offers the best opportunity to resolve client problems within the bounds of the law, and consistently with the lawyer's professional responsibilities. Moreover, open communication allows the client to appreciate the lawyer's effort on the client's behalf, by billing regularly and in detail, focusing on action items rather than time spent, and communicating value in the overall bill.

2. MANAGING CLIENT RELATIONS

In the book, THROUGH THE CLIENT'S EYES: NEW APPROACHES TO GET CLIENTS TO HIRE YOU AGAIN AND AGAIN (ABA 3rd ed. 2008), Henry Ewalt and Andrew W. Ewalt, the authors talk about what lawyers should do to build positive relationships with clients. The authors ask how well lawyers would do if their clients filled out "client satisfaction" cards. The Ewalts reject the notion that clients are inevitably disposed to dislike their lawyers because law is such an adversarial activity, or that half the clients will be unhappy with their lawyers, because someone has to lose every case. Clients want someone with whom they can talk about their problem, someone who will listen to them, and someone whom they can trust. Successful lawyers know how to build relationships with clients, and these relationships bring clients back again and again. Just saying that strong client relationships are important is not enough; lawyers must take affirmative steps to improve client relations skills or they will never build a lasting base of loyal clients. In an era when consumers are notoriously fickle, relationship skills are at a premium.

PROBLEMS AND QUESTIONS

1. Is the standard for allocating decision making authority between lawyer and client clear? Are there still areas where power is not delineated in the legal representation? How would you as a lawyer resolve this conflict?

2. What do you think about the idea of a client satisfaction card? How well do you think most clients would rate their lawyers? Why? Do you think that client satisfaction is impacted by the adversarial nature of legal disputes? If so, how can lawyers overcome negative client reactions?

B. FEES AND BILLING

In their book, *How to Draft Bills that Clients Rush to Pay*, J. Harris Morgan and Jay Foonberg cite research going back to the early 1960s by the Missouri Bar on what clients want from their lawyers. The study, which has been replicated in more recent years, concludes that the number one factor in client satisfaction is the client's perception of the lawyer's effort on behalf of the client. This being the case, it is critical for the lawyer to demonstrate effort in a way the client understands and appreciates. If the lawyer is working hard, but the client does not know it, the lawyer's effort is like the proverbial tree falling in the forest that no one hears. Morgan and Foonberg suggest that lawyers can demonstrate effort through the billing process, by incorporating clear descriptions of their work, using action verbs rather than columns of numbers to show what they have done.

Lawyers must make money in order to survive. There are very few practitioners whose independent wealth permits them to provide their services *pro bono publico*. Not only must they earn enough to pay themselves, they must earn sufficient income to cover the costs of operating the law office. Due to the historical anomaly codified in Model Rule 5.4 that lawyers may not "practice with or in the form of a professional corporation or association ... if a nonlawyer owns any interest therein," law firms do not have the option of "going public" in order to raise capital. Thus, law firms are generally undercapitalized as business organizations. This means that the money to run the legal business must derive substantially from legal fees. Partnership contributors and bank loans may infuse some cash into the organization, but the bulk of financing for most law firms depends upon fee income.

Sometimes the rhetoric of professionalism suggests that law cannot be a "money-getting trade." Ironically, a great deal of unprofessional conduct by lawyers, including invasion of client trust accounts and conversion of client property, may be motivated by insufficient cash flow for the offending lawyer. Conversely, a prosperous lawyer is less likely to be tempted to engage in misconduct of a financial nature.

1. LEGAL FEES

The ABA Model Rules of Professional Conduct require that all fees must be reasonable. Model Rule 1.5 (a) defines reasonableness in terms of eight factors:

(1) the time and labor involved, the novelty and difficulty of the question involved, and the skill requisite to perform the legal service properly;

(2) the likelihood, if apparent to the client, that the acceptance of the particular employment will preclude other employment by the lawyer;

(3) the fee customarily charged in the locality for similar legal services;

(4) the amount involved and the results obtained;

(5) the time limitations imposed by the client or by the circumstances;

(6) the nature and length of the professional relationship with the client;

(7) the experience, reputation, and ability of the lawyer or lawyers performing the services; and

(8) whether the fee is fixed or contingent.

Rule 1.5 also places limitations on contingent fee arrangements, suggests that fee agreements should be in writing, and provides for the division of fees by lawyers who are not in the same firm.

In one sense the rules governing fees are intended to protect clients from the avarice of some lawyers and to protect the reputation of the profession as a whole. In another sense, however, the rules make clear the right of lawyers to earn a living from the practice of law. The term "reasonable" appears to protect the lawyer as much as it does the client. Pragmatically, legal fees are always connected in some way with profitability, and the business side of the practice of law.

Ever since the Missouri Bar economic study, mentioned by Foonberg and Morgan, reported that lawyers who kept time records made more money than lawyers who did not, lawyers have been obsessed with the billable hour. The trend toward hourly billing has diverted the attention of lawyers, clients and the courts away from the idea that lawyers provide a service that has a value to the client. Although time expended is one measure of that value, it is not the only one. In recent years, many lawyers have begun to talk in terms of "value billing." So entrenched is hourly billing that many clients and some courts have resisted value billing, despite the fact that the Model Rules of Professional Conduct envision a reasonable fee as encompassing much more than time expended by the lawyer.

It does not follow from the utilization of non-time based fees that timekeeping is irrelevant. Whether you bill by the hour, by contingent fee, or by some other method, your work can be translated into an hourly rate. You received $X for Y hours of work; therefore your hourly rate is $X/Y. For instance, if you charge a flat $300 for a will and spend two hours on the matter, your rate is $150/hour. If you receive one-third of a $15,000 jury award in a PI case that required 250 hours of work, your rate is $20/hour. Assuming that you know the cost of running your office and the total number of billable hours expended on client matters, you can calculate your cost per billable hour. If your overhead costs were $75/hour in the above PI case, a net loss of $55/hour would result.

Suppose the cost of operating a law office for a solo practitioner amounted to $150,000 per year. In order to earn $150,000, the solo would have to generate gross revenue of $300,000 (overhead equaling 50% of revenue). If this lawyer bills and collects for 1,500 hours at $200 per hour, she would generate the necessary revenue to cover her expenses and reach her compensation goal. Regardless of whether she bills her work on an hourly basis, as flat fees (300 $1,000 fees), or contingent fees (one-third of ten cases generating $900,000) hours, she needs to generate $300,000 revenue. Notably, if she produces $300,000 revenue, regardless of her billing method, if she divides gross revenue by the number of hours devoted to client work during the year, she can calculate an effective hourly rate. Thus, the effective hourly rate for 1,500 hours is $200, but for 2,000 hours, it is only $150, and for 1,000 hours, it is $300. Furthermore, if overhead is $150,000 and the lawyer bills 1,500 hours, it costs our hypothetical solo practitioner $100 per hour to operate her office, and if her effective billing rate is less than that, she is losing money.

It is possible through careful financial planning and efficient management of the timekeeping/billing system to make sound economic decisions about staffing, compensation, fee structure, clientele and other matters. Many firms do not manage their fees in this way. As a result, they are reduced to making pure guesses about critical issues involving their finances. Since overhead costs have increased in recent years as a percentage of gross receipts (from 30–40% to 50–70% by some estimates), law firms can no longer afford to neglect income and cost analysis. In order to collect the data to conduct such an analysis, careful records must be kept.

The following article discusses another area of fee management: fee agreements. The ABA Rules of Professional Conduct, in Rule 1.5, suggest, but do not require (except for contingency fee cases) that fee arrangements should be in writing. Proposed 2001 amendments to the Model Rules would have required written fee agreements in virtually all representations. Anecdotally, it can be observed that most fee disputes arise because there is no clear understanding between lawyer and prospective client as to what services will be performed, how much such services will cost and how they will be billed. It is ironic that lawyers, who advise clients to always "get the agreement in writing," will tell clients, "We'll work it out later," when it comes to legal fees.

2. ENGAGEMENT LETTERS

USING ENGAGEMENT LETTERS

From *The Essential Formbook*, by Gary A. Munneke and Anthony E. Davis (1999).

A very eminent lawyer, in a very eminent New York City law firm, once told Anthony Davis; "We at (very eminent law firm) don't believe in engagement letters; our principal clients have been clients for more than 50 years, and would be *embarrassed* if we presented them with an engagement letter." That immediately brought to mind the summer camp director's announcement to the campers' parents on visitors day: "Please do not offer gratuities or gifts to the counselors; they will be *embarrassed....*" Since there remains considerable opposition to the idea of engagement letters among some lawyers, and misunderstanding about their uses and scope among many more, this chapter is designed to demonstrate why the first of these quotations is as ridiculous as the second.

Engagement letters perform several essential functions in the client intake process. They help establish the trust that forms the basis of the attorney-client relationship. They help eliminate misunderstandings and reconcile differing perceptions and expectations critical factor in client satisfaction and referrals over time. Good engagement letters define the many aspects of the attorney-client relationship. Much of their value lies in the way they compel both the client and the lawyer to focus, at the very beginning of the relationship, on what each side expects to accomplish, the ways in which both will work toward the desired goal, and the timetable by which they will arrive at the desired result.

For greatest effectiveness, the engagement letter should reflect extensive prior discussions with the client. It should summarize the mutual agreement of both sides regarding the scope, limitations and terms of representation. In short, the engagement letter should be the culmination of a thorough client intake process conducted by the lawyer, during which both sides have thoroughly explored and agreed to the parameters of the relationship, and the engagement in great detail. The process as a whole, by recording both sides' understanding, should create the foundation for the trust that should develop between lawyer and client as the engagement proceeds.

Beyond their trust-building role, engagement letters are also good business. The process of discussing and preparing engagement letters can help resolve and avoid differences that, left unaddressed, will hinder effective client relationships and lead to misunderstandings or disputes. A recently completed ABA study points to inadequate or improper communication with clients as a major factor in malpractice claims. The engagement letter—perhaps the most important of all client communications—can head off potential liability disputes by formalizing and documenting the intentions and expectations of both the client and the firm. It is no accident that some states' ethics rules actually require engagement letters or, at least, written fee agreements.

In today's litigious climate, maintaining good client relations is more challenging than ever. The ABA study identified three key client relations problems driving claims against attorneys: failure to obtain client consent; failure to follow client instructions; and improper withdrawal or representation. To avoid such failures, you should establish standard procedures to earn your clients' confidence—by making all parties' expectations and obligations explicit; by clarifying the scope, cost, and likely effects of your services; and by demonstrating your understanding of the legal and factual issues involved. Good engagement letters take time, but they are never a waste of time, as some lawyers claim. Establishing a positive relationship with a client is the best investment you can make, as well as a vital risk management tool.

Benefits of the Engagement Letter

- The engagement letter establishes the scope and limitations of the firm's services and states the basis on which fees will be computed. Engagement letters can play a critical role in establishing good client relations and reducing the frequency and severity of malpractice claims over time.

- The engagement letter provides a necessary foundation for the conduct and management by the firm of the whole client relationship. Unlike oral agreements, a letter can provide written evidence of the parties' actual intentions if a dispute arises.

- Engagement letters also play a vital part in the firm's conflict of interest avoidance system. Clear identification of the client serves as the initial phase in determining that all conflict of interest issues have been resolved.

- For new clients, the engagement letter establishes an initial framework for bilateral agreement and confirmation. A sample engagement letter can be used to set the opening agenda for lawyer-client discussions.

- For existing clients opening new matters, a brief note referring to the original engagement letter can help avoid misunderstanding and create an appropriate record. Some attorneys avoid the use of engagement letters for existing clients of long standing. This is a mistake—even long-time clients have sued for malpractice. Clients typically respect firms for demonstrating businesslike management of their affairs.

- Clear delineation of the parties' responsibilities and obligations is especially important to limit liability exposure in joint representations and in contingent fee and *pro bono* matters. Even if, ultimately, no fee is paid, you are still vulnerable to liability claims and should take steps to head them off.

Establishing Effective Client Communication Procedures

Effective client communications begin with a comprehensive discussion and preparation of a carefully drafted engagement letter for each client. Engagement letters are appropriate for all new clients, including *pro bono* clients. Existing clients can be given engagement letters following a review of the matters for which the firm is presently engaged; all new matters should be the subject of a separate letter, although these may refer to the terms of the original engagement letter.

A good engagement letter can be brief, but it should address all relevant issues to help you build constructive, team-oriented relationships with your clients. . . .

The courts have frequently become involved in the question of legal fees. Many fee disputes end up in litigation despite the remonstrations of the ethical codes against suits by lawyers to collect fees from their clients. In addition, because court approval is usually required when cases are settled before trial, judges are in the position to approve attorney fees agreed to as part of the settlement. Thus, much judicial verbiage has been expended on this topic, in cases involving discipline, breach of contract, and petitions to reduce fees.

For example, in *Bushman v. State Bar*, 11 Cal.3d 558, 522 P.2d 312, 113 Cal.Rptr. 904 (1974), a lawyer was disciplined for charging a fee that the court described as "so exorbitant and wholly disproportionate to the services rendered as to shock the conscience." The lawyer billed his clients, who had limited resources, $2,800 for legal services in a simple divorce. The client signed a retainer agreement and a $5,000 note to secure payment of the fee, payable $300 in advance and $50 per month. The lawyer claimed to have spent over 100 hours on the case, but was unable to document this time, and the record indicated that the matter had been dispatched rather quickly. The Court said, in part, "Although Bushman performed legal services for Barbara, he was unable or unwilling to document the 100 hours he assertedly spent on the matter. The $2,800 charge was based on far less time than the 100 hours Bushman claims to have spent on the case, and even if he had actually worked a sufficient number of hours at $60 an hour to justify a fee of $2,800, it was so high in this situation as to shock the conscience. . . . An examination of the file in the Cox matter reveals that only a simple, almost routine set of documents was filed by Bushman on Barbara's behalf. Although he asserts that the case was 'quite involved,' he is unable to articulate any complex issues, which required extensive research or specialized skills. The only documentation in the file indicating any research whatsoever is a one-page 'Points and Authorities' filed in support of an order to show cause, which cites the text of five statutes and one case, without any argument. Aside from interviews with the defendants and a doctor, the only additional services performed by Bushman were two appearances in court for hearings on orders to show cause.... It is of some significance in this connection that Cox's attorney spent slightly more than five hours on the case."

Not all fee disputes arise out of a disagreement about the amount of the bill. If the bill does not clearly describe the basis for the charges, a client may believe that the lawyer is overcharging for services. For example, suppose a lawyer sends a bill to the client for the lawyer's work at $200 per hour, the charge typically incorporates overhead expenses, such as support staff, as well as the value of the lawyer's time. If, on the other hand, the lawyer charges separately for her time (at $200 per hour), the secretary's ($20/hour), the paralegal's ($25/hour), and other administrative costs, the total fee may be the same, but the uninformed client may think that this unbundled bill is an attempt to charge more money for the same service, even though the lawyer is trying to give the client a more accurate bill. The client may think that the lawyer's regular hourly fee should cover everything, and that breaking out charges is akin to a restaurant that decides to use an a la carte menu after offering complete dinners in the past.

In the end, lawyers need to remember the sensitivity involved in the billing process. Almost any aspect of the fee setting and billing processes can deteriorate into a dispute if the lawyer and client do not reach an understanding about the basis for the fee, and if the lawyer does not regularly and accurately communicate the basis for the bill during the course of the representation. Most fee disputes can be avoided, but it is not always easy to do so, given the fact that clients may not fully understand how to place a value on the services that lawyers provide.

3. BILLING FOR SERVICES

The topic of billing is addressed further in Chapter 11, dealing with Financial Management. It is introduced here, because the way the bill is handled can be critical to the lawyer-client relationship. The billing process is much more than a simple means for the lawyer to get paid; it is a tool for improving the way the client views the lawyer and values the lawyer's services. The following passage illustrates a positive approach to billing that many lawyers fail to consider.

EXCERPT

From *How to Draft Bills Clients Rush to Pay*, by
J. Harris Morgan and Jay Foonberg (2005).

The First Meeting

As you begin the first conversation with the potential client, show that you really care. Start by expressing concern for the client, not by discussing fees. For instance, if someone tells you they have been injured take care to show you really care about the client first as a human being. The effort projected in the bill is part of an overall approach of demonstrating concern for the client's well-being and needs, which begins at the initial intake and carries through to the final bill.

Demonstrate a high level of integrity in the way you handle cases. This will indicate to clients that there also is integrity in the billing process. Before you discuss money at the first interview, project integrity and build trust. For example, give clients some understanding about conflicts by checking for problems while clients are in your office. Then talk about their case and give an honest assessment of it before you decide whether to handle the matter. Clients should know what the lawyer's expectations are, and the lawyer must know how to manage client expectations regarding services, outcome, and billing.

Communicate competence by using the appropriate terminology, citing relevant cases you have handled or reviewed and their outcomes, and acknowledging up front some of the obstacles that you may encounter and how they can be handled. Demonstrate concern and honesty by referring the client to another lawyer when you lack competence in the subject matter to handle the case.

. . .

Discuss the Fee

Most clients want to have at least a ballpark idea of the fee—of what it will cost them to be represented until the matter's completion. Clients, however, are afraid to raise the issue of fees with lawyers. Therefore, lawyers must initiate discussion about the cost of their services. To do so, lawyers must first assess the case, determine the time that will likely be involved, apply the rate for their time per hour, charge for staff time, and shift a pro rata share of technology costs for the case. Only then can the lawyer offer a reasonably reliable fee estimate to the client. Lawyers should overestimate the charge rather than underestimate it, as many lawyers are tempted to do to get the client's business. Remember if you give the clients an estimate that you can do the job for $5,000 and you complete it for $4,300, you're a hero. However, if you estimate a fee range of $250 to $750 and the final bill is $800, the client will be reluctant to pay.

You must have a rule that you will never let a client leave the first interview without discussing fees. Give a ballpark determination of the fee, such as, "I believe the fee will be about $500," or, "My experience is that this type of matter can normally be handled here for about $6,000." Because you will have talked about money, it means that you will keep adequate records, through which you can keep track of what your overhead is and what you ought to be charging. The client will be happy to pay you.

. . .

Present a Written Estimate

Always present the fee estimate in writing. If you seem to be getting close to exceeding the estimate you should update the estimate for the client as it changes or you will be less likely to get paid. Telling someone it will cost $500 and then trying to charge them $2,000 does not show respect.

You might say, "John, remember I told you that this would cost $500. I am sorry, but I have to tell you it will cost closer to $2,000 because of . . . which I could never have foreseen." Keeping the client informed of fee changes is an integral part of any successful billing process. Of course, all costs exceeding a predetermined amount will require the client's approval.

After the services have been rendered, the lawyer should submit a written bill as soon as possible. Morgan and Foonberg suggest using a form that focuses on demonstrating effort, rather than time. Because the client is interested in the lawyer's "concern," a bill that reflects actual effort is much more effective than one reflecting how many hours the lawyer has put into the case. For some legal services (e.g., wills), the lawyer can expect payment at the point of service, while for others the lawyer must send the bill out later. For continuing relationships and lengthy cases, lawyers should bill their clients on a regular basis. Morgan and Foonberg point out that most clients are likely to find twelve monthly bills of $1,000 more palatable than one bill at the end of the year or six months after the representation for $12,000.

4. FEE DISPUTES

Billing should be much more than collecting money efficiently; it should be an important part of maintaining strong client relationships. Interestingly, when lawyer-client relationships turn sour, one of the most common results of the conflict is a fee dispute. Although the evidence is anecdotal, fee disputes undoubtedly linger in the background of many disciplinary complaints and lawsuits against lawyers. A noted risk management advisor to law firms, Anthony Davis, argues that lawyers should never sue their clients to collect a fee, because the client will often counterclaim for legal malpractice. Davis' view is that if the client is already unhappy about the services already, a lawsuit can escalate the fee dispute to an adversarial level. Although lawyers may legally exercise their legal rights to collect fees from clients, it is almost always desirable to resolve disputes without going to court.

If the lawyer and client do not have a clear mutual understanding about what the lawyer will do for the client and what fee the lawyer will charge, the client is likely to be disappointed when the fee is higher than he anticipated. Especially if the client is not satisfied with the services or the outcome of the representation, the client may resent a higher than expected bill. In short, if the client does not believe that he has received value for the money he has paid, he may expect the lawyer to make things right, by doing more work, reducing the fee, or explaining the bill in greater detail. If the client is not satisfied with the outcome of these efforts he may pursue other avenues of redress:

- Refusing to pay (self-help);
- Filing a disciplinary complaint against the lawyer;
- Seeking arbitration or mediation, if provided in the jurisdiction;
- Exploring legal action against the lawyer;
- Badmouthing the lawyer in the community.

Because all of these outcomes are less than satisfactory, the lawyer needs to do everything possible to avoid getting into fee disputes in the first place. Although it is usually not advisable to accept a reduced fee for services, candid conversations between lawyer and client, in which both sides are willing to listen and compromise, may avoid more serious problems.

PROBLEMS AND QUESTIONS

1. Suppose Donald Trump calls his lawyer on the phone and asks for advice on whether to accept an offer of $50,000,000 to sell an office building he owns, and the lawyer advises him to accept the offer. Suppose also that the next week Trump receives a bill from his lawyer for $1,000,000, which he pays. Is a $1,000,000 fee for a one-minute phone call reasonable? Can $60,000,000 per hour ever be reasonable? Does it make any difference that the client is a sophisticated consumer of legal services and paid the bill? Does it matter that Trump is satisfied with the service rendered?

2. Legal fees may be based upon both hourly charges and a variety of other factors. Hourly billing, based on some kind of timekeeping system, remains the most common fee structure, despite the repeated suggestion that fees must be based on more than time. Are lawyers to be forever fettered to the billable hour? What alternatives exist to hourly billing?

3. What can a lawyer do when a client refuses to pay a bill? What are the limits on an attorney's efforts to fee collection?

4. What could the lawyer in the *Bushman* case have done differently to avoid the problems that landed him in court? What lessons do these cases teach us about how lawyers should deal with clients in fee disputes? Is there a difference between how the attorney's conduct should be treated in a civil action to recover fees and a disciplinary proceeding?

5. Why are fee arrangements so problematical for lawyers? Is it because at this point in the attorney-client relationship the attorney and client stand on conflicting and potentially adversarial footing? Is the difficulty simply fallout from the hackneyed image of the "shyster lawyer"? Is the problem one of poor business practices by lawyers?

6. Are you comfortable with the advice to use a written fee agreement in conjunction with an oral explanation? What else could you do to make sure you collect your fees and avoid fee disputes with your clients?

7. Does it make any difference if the ultimate fee is reasonable and if the client agrees to the method by which the fee is determined?

8. Do the requirements of professionalism clash with the demands of earning a living? Can both professionalism and economics find accommodation in an effective system of setting fees and billing clients for services?

C. PHONE CALLS

In almost every jurisdiction, disciplinary counsel report that the number one complaint they receive is that lawyers do not return their phone calls. Although lawyers are not usually disciplined for failing to return calls, unless some other problem ensues, like missing a court deadline as a result of missing a call, it does reflect a communication gap. The failure to respond may be perceived by clients as a lack of interest in the client's case. Of course, lawyers argue that some clients call all the time, and that they want free advice over the phone. Lawyers complain that they are not babysitters for clients who need their hands held.

Problems and Questions

1. To what do you attribute the failure of lawyers to return phone calls? With secretaries, answering services, voice mail and cellular phone service, how could this continue to be a problem?

2. Does the reluctance of lawyers to respond to clients' calls reflect a deeper problem in the way lawyers manage client expectations, information about cases and service?

3. With the advent of smartphones, where lawyers can be accessible by voice, e-mail and text, is there a risk that lawyers and clients might be too connected? How should lawyers handle 24–7–365 connectivity?

CHAPTER 8

MANAGING LAWYERS AND SUPPORT STAFF

■ ■ ■

A. HUMAN RESOURCES MANAGEMENT

This chapter examines human resources management. Because of the scope of the subject matter, it might be useful to consider the organization of the material. The first section of the chapter addresses principles associated with human resources management generally. The second looks specifically at professional, paralegal and clerical staff support. Some writers refer to this as the nonlegal staff, but for reasons that will be discussed later, we will avoid the pejorative label. A third section looks at the elements of human resource management in law firms. The next section addresses particular issues involved when the employees are lawyers, including associates, contract lawyers, and senior salaried lawyers in the firm. The final section examines how to get the most out of staff employees.

1. THE VALUE OF EMPLOYED LAWYERS AND SUPPORT STAFF

No aspect of practice management is as critical to the long term success of a law firm as building and keeping a strong staff. Law firms should think of the people who work in the office as human resources, to be grown and nurtured, rather than as fungible commodities, to be exploited and discarded. Enlightened law firms recognize that long term stability is critical to the financial viability of every law firm. There are several keys to managing human resources effectively (discussed more fully in Section C of this Chapter):

- Recruiting capable, qualified individuals
- Hiring the best and the brightest talent
- Training employees to do their jobs proficiently
- Evaluating the progress of firm employees over time
- Compensating employees to reward excellence
- Terminating those who do not measure up to firm standards

- Motivating employees to work enthusiastically and grow professionally.

Law firms do not make these decisions in a vacuum; a web of labor and equal employment laws influence every aspect of human resources management. Competition for qualified employees may make it challenging to attract and keep the best people. Changes in life situations among employees may produce turnover that is totally unrelated to job satisfaction or performance.

The term support staff could be used to refer to all employees in the law office, although in practice, lawyers, whether they are owners or employees, provide the core business function of delivering legal services to clients. All lawyers, in the sense that they are personally responsible for the legal work they handle, oversee not only their own work product, but also the work of employees who are not licensed to practice law. See Model Rule 5.3. Thus, in the law firm context, and consistently in this casebook, the use of the term "support staff" refers to those employees who are not lawyers, including secretaries, legal assistants, administrators, professional staff, and clerical assistants. These individuals often outnumber the legal staff in many firms.

When you graduate from law school, you may not be asked to administer your law firm's budget or develop the firm's marketing plan, but there is little doubt that you will work as a supervisor of support staff, and therefore should think of yourself as a human resources manager. It follows that you should develop supervisory skills in order to be effective. Additionally, you should gain an understanding of the roles of the various support staff members and their relationship to the legal staff.

2. LAWYERS AS MANAGERS

Anyone who has served as a manager or supervisor of other people in a work environment knows that it is important to get the most out of those who work for you. By maximizing productivity, business organizations hope to maximize profits. Law firms are no exception. Unfortunately for many law firms, productivity translates into working long hours and institutional myopia. At too many firms, the bottom line has dictated human resources policy. Both lawyers and support staff can suffer from this mentality.

Another consideration is that most lawyers have never taken a course on how to manage people. Many have little or no experience as supervisors, and many learn how to manage by observing other lawyers. Law firms have their share of supervisors with anger management issues, as well as, passive-aggressive, anal-retentive and borderline personality disorders. Most of the problem managers fall into the category of inept, rather than sociopathic, however. At the same time, many law firms have skilled and effective managers. The one salient difference between human resources management in a law firm and in any other type of business is that the HR Manager at the company probably has an MBA with a concentration in HR, as well as years of experience; most lawyers, even the good managers, lack this training and experience.

Responsible law firms need to create a working environment conducive to the professional development and personal growth of the lawyers and support staff that they employ. Someday, a law firm will discover that happy employees are productive employees, and that satisfied employees do not quit in order to pursue other opportunities. This firm will figure out that it can make more money in this way than by burning out successive crops of new hires. And when this happens, the applicants will wear down the path to this law firm's door.

Responsive law firms need to create an environment that is conducive to professional development, personal growth and institutional loyalty amongst its lawyers and staff. This stems from a fundamental truth that happy/satisfied employees are more productive, but perhaps the most significant aspect of a happy work force, given the unique characteristics of the legal services industry, is the manner in which clients come to rely on their lawyer and his firm for the duration of their lives; and the tremendous force that word-of-mouth plays in the industry. Word-of-mouth is the single most important influence on the success of a law firm.

We've already spoken about the importance of maintaining happy clientele, but maintaining happy workers is even more important from a structural perspective, if not from an external viewpoint. How does it look to an outsider when a successful attorney leaves a firm to go elsewhere? Such behavior is probably indicative of dissatisfaction, never a good sign. If the attorney or staff leaves and the firm is lucky enough in that the client remains with the firm, how many hours will the firm lose in yet another employee familiarizing him/herself with the case? The bottom line is that law firms need to be very aware of necessity to keep the turnover rate as low as possible and reward its employees sufficiently/accordingly.

3. LAW FIRMS AS EMPLOYERS

Legal employers are covered by a variety of labor and employment laws. The influence of these laws extends to lawyer and support staff employees alike. The workplace is covered by a wide variety of laws that protect employees in many different ways. Law firms that employ people must abide by these rules and regulations like any other employer. Sometimes lawyers forget that they are not exempt from the demands placed upon them by labor law. And although very small firms may be exempt from applying certain laws limited to employers with a certain number of employees, such firms still must be aware of which laws apply to them. The following article provides a brief overview of this legal framework.

LEGAL CONSIDERATIONS

From *The Essential Formbook*, by Gary A. Munneke and Anthony E. Davis (2001).

Law firms are governed by a plethora of laws and regulations. Although relationships among the partners is governed by partnership law and partnership or other formation agreement, and many of the employer-employee relationships can be characterized as at will, law firms cannot turn a blind eye to employment laws. Some law firms behave as though they were immune from the rules that govern other types of business, but there are no "lawyer exemptions" in the coverage of federal or state statutes and regulations. The problem is compounded by the fact that legal obligations of employers vary from state to state, and sometimes city to city within a state. The legal considerations include, but are not necessarily limited to equal employment opportunity (EEO), sexual harassment, Americans with Disabilities Act (ADA), and the Fair Labor Standards Act.

. . .

The ADA protects individuals with disabilities from workplace discrimination. The law does not compel employers to hire workers who cannot perform a job because of their disabilities, but rather requires employers to make reasonable accommodation for disabled persons. Thus, a law firm would not be expected to retain a blind person to chauffeur the firm limousine, but would be expected to provide a reader for a blind attorney.

The Fair Labor Standards Act deserves mention, because many firms misunderstand its coverage. They think that they do not have to pay overtime to any salaried employee; whereas the FLSA guarantees overtime and other benefits to all employees who are not exempted from its coverage. Exempted (non-covered) employees generally include professional staff and highly trained legal assistants, while clerical and less qualified paraprofessional staff are non-exempt. Whether one is exempt or not is based upon the nature of the job itself—education, independence, responsibility, and pay level—not whether pay is characterized as hourly wages or salary.

Traditionally, law firm employment relationships were treated as employment at will, meaning that either side may terminate the relationship at any time for any reason or no reason. The terms of employment are seldom reduced to writing, because an employment contract may give the parties rights and obligations they would not have under employment at will. The common law doctrine of employment at will has been modified by both statute and judicial decision. The Fair Labor Standards Act has the effect of removing protected employees from the sometimes harsh operation of the employment at will doctrine.

Finally, employee staff manuals may also impute requirements to both employers and employees. If the manual provides that employees get two weeks vacation per year, the employer probably cannot deny vacation to an employee or penalize someone for taking it. If the manual says that hours of work are from 9:00 a.m. through 5:00 p.m., the employee is on notice that he or she can be disciplined for habitually failing to show up to work on time. The American Bar Association Law Practice Management Section publishes two excellent model manuals for small and large firms respectively. Both these titles are too large to be incorporated in this book, but they should be considered an important part of any human resources management program.

There are other laws that impact the law firm's human resources management program, but the ones listed above are the most likely to create problems for the typical firm. For instance, law firms are not exempt from laws governing organized labor, and although most law offices are not unionized, there are some exceptional cases, and the prospect of staff seeking to form a collective bargaining unit remains a possibility.

Equal employment laws cover law firms from the federal to the local level. Court decisions can have a significant impact on the hiring process. Law firms are not immune from laws prohibiting discrimination. Lawyers and professional staff may be exempt from a number of labor laws, such as the Fair Labor Standards Act, and employed lawyers are with few exceptions not unionized. However, equal employment laws apply in the arena of lawyer hiring and promotion to partnership, as the following case illustrates.

Traditionally, lawyer and other professional employees were considered to be at-will, meaning that either the employer or employee could end the relationship at any time with or without cause. The at-will relationship could be modified by an employment contract, but the custom in legal employment did not include such contracts, and the employment at will arrangement remained the dominant employment relationship. The employment-at-will doctrine has been limited in recent years by both legislation and court decisions.

Although many law firms are under the jurisdictional minimum number of employees (15) to be covered by Title VII of the Civil Rights Act of 1963 (as amended), prohibiting employment discrimination based on race, sex, religion, national origin, or ethnicity (see, e.g., Collins v. Rizkana, 73 Ohio St.3d 65, 652 N.E.2d 653 (1995)), they may be covered by state and/or local non-discrimination regulations, and they may encounter difficulties in recruiting new lawyers if they are perceived to engage in discriminatory practices.

The following cases illustrate some of the problems law firms face in the equal employment field:

In *Foley, Hoag & Eliot and United File Room Clerks and Messengers of Foley, Hoag & Eliot,* 229 N.L.R.B. No. 80, 1977–78 NLRB Dec. (CCH) ¶ 18,116 (1977), the NLRB held that "since law firms as a class . . . have a substantial impact on interstate commerce, [the Board will] assert jurisdiction over them [if they meet an] appropriate jurisdictional standard." Earlier case law to the contrary was "overruled in light of the U.S. Supreme Court's finding in *Goldfarb v. Virginia State Bar,* 421 U.S. 773 (1975), that the practice of law is 'trade or commerce' within the meaning of the federal antitrust laws. That holding [was declared] equally applicable to 'commerce' within the meaning of the National Labor Relations Act."

In *EEOC v. Dowd & Dowd, Ltd.,* 736 F.2d 1177, 34 FEP Cases 1815 (7th Cir. 1984) the court ruled that the Dowd firm was not covered by Title VII because it had less than fifteen employees. For the purposes of Title VII an employer is a "person engaged in an industry affecting commerce who has fifteen or more employees for each working day in each of twenty or more calendar weeks in the current or preceding year." See 42 U.S.C. § 2000e(b) (1976 & Supp. II 1978). Although courts have counted part-time employees in computing the number of employees for Subsection 701(k) purposes, partners have been treated as employers, not employees. [O]n appeal, the Seventh Circuit held that "shareholders in professional corporations that [are] engaged in practice of law are not employees of that corporation for purpose of Section 701(b) of Civil Rights Act of 1964; the role of shareholder in professional corporation is far more analogous to partner in partnership than it is to shareholder of a general corporation, and partners are not employees of partnership." Id.

In Hishon v. King & Spalding, 467 U.S. 69, 104 S.Ct. 2229, 81 L.Ed.2d 59 (1984), the U.S. Supreme Court considered a situation in which a law firm recruited a law student with literature and promises that she would be provided an equal opportunity with men considered for partnership in the firm. The Court held that even if the partnership offer itself was not covered by Title VII, the employment relationship with the associate was, so Hishon was protected under the law.

More recently, former partners of Sidley & Austin brought suit against their former law firm alleging that Sidley's changes to the retirement plan discriminated against them on the basis of their age. Under the amended plan, Sidley & Austin demoted 32 partners to counsel or senior counsel status. Of the 32 partners, 30 of them were over 40 years old. The case was settled after the judge held that the plaintiffs had stated a claim upon which relief could be granted. See *EEOC v. Sidley Austin LLP,* 437 F.3d 695 (7th Cir. 2006).

The implications of these decisions are far reaching for the legal profession, because they affect what firms promise candidates when they make an initial offer, what associates' expectations are when they are considered for partnership, and how firms evaluate and record their progress. Many law firms do not consider the impact of labor law decisions on their personnel policies. Cases like these illustrate, however, that firm employees are often willing to go to court to vindicate their rights. It follows that law firms should recognize their employees, rights, and should treat them fairly and equitably.

PROBLEMS AND QUESTIONS

1. The hiring partner of a major Texas law firm once said that "people are the meat and potatoes of our firm." What did he mean by this statement? Does the principle have relevance outside the state of Texas?

2. Imagine two law firms that are similar in every way, except that one firm experiences regular turnover, from partners down to secretaries. Suppose you are a client of this firm, and every time you visit the firm, there is a new receptionist. Your file has been turned over to a succession of associates. At the other firm, all the lawyers and the staff have worked at the firm for years. You see the same faces every time you come in, and you know who is handling your case. Which firm inspires more confidence in you as a client? What concerns do you have about the "revolving door" firm? Why?

3. Have you done any of the following as a supervisor:

    - Assigned work to a subordinate?
    - Interviewed candidates for a job and made hiring decisions?
    - Conducted a performance evaluation?
    - Fired someone?

    Describe the experience.

4. If you have not had these experiences as a supervisor, can you think of work experiences where someone else has had to do the things described in question 3, above. What was your impression of how well the supervisor handled these sensitive tasks? Would you have done anything differently?

5. Can you think of general management concepts that could help lawyers to manage staff more effectively? Do rules for managing a non-law business always apply in a law firm setting? Why or why not?

6. Should law firms have a policy objective to avoid being sued or to create a non-discriminatory work environment? Do professional standards impose on lawyers a duty to treat fellow lawyers fairly in employment? What can a firm do to create a positive work environment for lawyers of color? Women lawyers? Disabled lawyers? LGBT lawyers?

7. What should a firm do to address sexist attitudes among lawyers? Or an unreconstructed racist? What would you do if one of your partners during a campus interview asked an African American applicant personal questions about her ability to "fit in" at an established predominantly white law firm?

8. What problems do law firms presently face in dealing with this array of law? Are there other areas of discrimination that firms should address in

addition to those described in this chapter? How should firms, especially small ones, keep up with this complex and evolving area of law?

9. Could paralegals join with associates to form a separate bargaining unit within the firm? How would this alter the underlying management philosophy of the unionized firm? Do you think law firms are likely to unionize in the near future? Why or why not? Will the emergence of permanent associates and staff attorneys change this?

10. Many small firms fall below the minimum number of employees (15) to be covered by Title VII of the Civil Rights Act of 1964, which prohibits employment discrimination on the basis of race, creed, sex or national origin. Are these firms free to discriminate against associate candidates? Are there other mechanisms that govern the hiring process? If so, what are they, and are they effective?

11. Some women and students of color argue that EEO laws have just pushed discrimination underground. Instead of a blatantly sexist or racist interviewer, a firm might say all the right things but behave quite differently. Do you see evidence of this kind of subtle, unspoken discrimination? Are there ways to combat it?

12. Since 1964, other forms of discrimination have come under scrutiny, leading to legislation to extend protection to new classes of protected employees, including age (the *Sidley* case), disability, and sexual orientation. Have the hiring prospects for older, disabled and gay lawyers improved as a result of this expanded coverage? Are there other forms of discrimination that deserve protection in addition to those described in this section?

B. ADMINISTRATIVE AND SUPPORT STAFF

1. WHO MAKES UP THE SUPPORT STAFF?

Law office support staff are sometimes referred to as "nonlegal personnel," including secretaries and other support staff, paralegals or legal assistants, and professional staff. Although the ratio of nonlawyers to lawyers in law offices is normally between 1:1 to 2:1, it may be more or less. The effective management of this support team can make or break a law firm. Good lawyering can only go part way in providing legal services competently and efficiently. In an era of high overhead and diminishing profitability, the nonlawyer staff is more important to the firm than at any time in the past.

Although professional staff positions are more prevalent in large firms, many small firms elect to employ professionals in areas where lawyers do not possess the expertise or want to handle management responsibilities. These professional positions include: law firm administrators, personnel directors, recruitment administrators, marketing directors, librarians, and management information systems administrators.

A firm that delegates responsibilities to employees who have not attended law school or been licensed to practice law must be sensitive to a number of issues. Delegation to nonlawyers shifts power away from the partners. Some partnerships may find this difficult to do. The decision should not be made lightly. Such delegation, however, raises ethical issues, because of the prohibitions against entering into a partnership, splitting fees with nonlawyers, and allowing a nonlawyer to influence a lawyer's independent professional judgment (See Model Rules, Rule 5.4 (a-c)).

Firms hiring professionals must take steps to avoid giving an interest in the partnership itself to those not licensed to practice law or giving nonlawyer managers the power to direct the outcome of particular legal services. Do you see how a law firm administrator might say to a lawyer that the firm has put enough time into a particular case, and that the case needs to settle right away, even if the lawyer thinks the case should go to trial?

Ultimately, the question is: who is best qualified and positioned to perform a given task? Some work can only be performed by lawyers. Other work may be completed by nonlawyers under supervision. Still other work may be performed without direct supervision. Some work is typically done by either lawyers or nonlawyers. Regardless of who actually handles specific tasks, all work is ultimately the responsibility of the lawyer, and the supervisor lawyer may be vicariously liable for the acts of subordinates (See *Model Rules*, Rule 5.3).

Generally, work should be handled at the lowest level where it can be done competently. It makes no sense to have a $300/hour lawyer doing work that can be done by a $7/hour file clerk. Deciding when to hire support staff to handle routine functions is an important question. Salary and benefits often represent the largest item in a law firm's budget, and in an overstaffed firm payroll costs can eat away the profits. On the other hand, in an inadequately staffed firm, the lawyers may find themselves doing all their own clerical work instead of billable legal work, a practice that can have just as deleterious an effect on profitability as overstaffing.

In smaller firms, many jobs do not justify a full-time employee, but the work must be handled by someone nevertheless. In such cases it is common to combine two or more functional positions in the job description of one employee, e.g., the secretary who also serves as bookkeeper and receptionist, or to outsource tasks to contract services as discussed in Section B6 of this Chapter (page 185).

2. LAW FIRM ADMINISTRATORS

As law practice has developed from a cottage industry into an institutionalized industry, the use of law firm administrators has proliferated. Today, when the business aspects of practice are so demanding, many lawyers welcome professional managers to help them direct the day-to-day operations of the firm.

Large firms today cannot exist without legal administrators. The back office administrative staff (not including the support staff for legal work) runs the business of the law firm. In addition to a Chief Executive Officer, Chief Operating Officer and Chief Financial Officer (just like major corporations), large firms employ directors for Human Resources, Information Technology, and other business operations. With a goal of supporting the lawyer management, i.e, the managing partner or committee, and freeing the lawyers to practice law, these employees have grown in influence and number.

Small firms increasingly discover that delegating administrative tasks to administrators can free them to spend more time on legal work. Although the Firm Administrator may wear many hats, and the lawyers may be more directly involved in day-to-day decision making, the trend is also in the direction of allocating more and more responsibility to managers who do not practice law.

Legal administrators come in many shapes and sizes. Despite wide differences in background, pay, authority, and duties, these individuals share one attribute: they are exercising control over the operation of organizations that were run exclusively by lawyers in the recent past. As the ensuing materials suggest, the advent of nonlawyer administrators has produced new problems for law firms as well as numerous advantages.

WHY HIRE PROFESSIONAL MANAGERS?

From *The ABA Guide to Professional Managers in the Law Office*,
by Joel A. Rose, edited by Carolyn Thornlow (1996).

There is no question that professional law office managers make important contributions to the financial and operating success of the legal organizations in which they are employed. The value of these legal managers can only increase as they continue to apply business principals to legal organizations and to enhance productivity by developing automation and maintaining and analyzing financial data and management information to ensure the delivery of high-quality legal services, in a timely manner, at fees clients are willing and able to pay. Increasingly, astute managers are exercising influence on virtually all decisions affecting the "business of law" and are providing management support to those lawyers who are responsible for managing and coordinating substantive practice areas.

A wise managing partner of a major New York City law firm [said] ..., "the continued growth and profitability of this law firm depends on two factors: The first is the people in it. This is the single most important element. The second is the ability of the firm's lawyer management to exercise good judgment and continue to make sound business decisions that will contribute positively to the firm's financial growth and to the healthy interpersonal relationships among and between the partners, the partners and the associates, and between the lawyers and the administrative support personnel. I hope the future lawyer managers of this firm are as fortunate as I was to work with as able an administrator as I have.

Without a competent administrative legal executive who possesses the financial acumen, business insights and management skills, my job as a managing partner would be considerably more difficult and stressful, if not impossible to perform."

These higher-level support staff members are part of a law firm's administrative team. In larger firms, the positions described above may be subdivided into many more jobs, while in smaller firms they may be combined into one or two individuals who wear many hats. Functionally, they engage in activities critical to management of the firm and the delivery of legal services to clients. Viewed in another light, the work has to be done by someone, and if the firm does not hire support staff, the lawyers must do the work themselves. If the organization does not have a firm administrator, a managing partner will have to do the administrative tasks. To the extent that lawyers assume administrative responsibilities, they are unable to devote their energy to client matters.

3. PARALEGALS

As the legal services industry has grown, so has the legal assistant industry. At one time, secretaries functioned at different times as administrators, typists and paralegals. Over the years the roles of secretary, paralegal and administrator became increasingly differentiated.

Some firms use the term legal assistants when they refer to paralegals, but in practice the two terms are essentially indistinguishable. Firms began to utilize paralegals for a host of routine tasks in the delivery of legal services. Over the years, paralegals have become common, and much of the routine work previously handled by the lawyers is now regularly delegated to paralegals.

Many colleges offer paralegal training programs, which prepare students for careers in law firms doing work that does not require a JD degree. A paralegal typically handles very specific tasks, such as calendar management or document preparation that can be done the same way each time. A paralegal works under the direction of a lawyer, and does not exercise legal judgment in the same way that a lawyer does.

A good analogy might be an assembly line worker at a manufacturing plant, whose job involves completing the same tasks for each unit that comes down the assembly line. In the case of legal services, cases might be viewed as projects, and to the extent that each project is the same (routine), the delivery of the service is like an assembly line. The lawyers might design the product or the assembly line, or make modifications along the way, but the paralegals work the line and assemble the legal product.

Law firms can reduce costs by developing paralegal employees with a high level of skill performing specified tasks at a level of pay less than they would have to pay lawyers. In firms that do not use paralegals, the lawyers themselves often have to handle these recurring tasks. It may seem counter-intuitive to say that firms can become more profitable by spending more money, but it is true. Of course, the firm has to have enough work to keep the assembly line running, but that is a different issue.

4. LEGAL SECRETARIES

Next to the lawyers themselves, legal secretaries are the most indispensable employees in a law firm (in some cases they may be more valuable than the associates). The lawyer-secretary dyad probably evolved after typewriters came into common use in law offices, supplanting the quill pen and hand-drawn documents.

The role of the legal secretary has changed in recent years, not only in response to changes in the practice of law, but also in response to changes in the role of women in the workplace. During much of the 20th century women comprised virtually the entire secretarial work force. The women's movement of the turn of the last century may have given women a hollow victory: low status, low pay jobs in a male-dominated world. In law, where most lawyers practiced alone or in small firms, the secretary, armed with her trusty typewriter, became the lawyer's "girl Friday," performing any and all tasks the lawyer felt were beneath his station. She was the receptionist, typist, filing clerk, paralegal, administrator, cook, confidante, and cheerleader. "Get my coffee, Alice," and "Give it to my girl to type up," were the orders of the day.

The role of women has changed since the 1960s. Not only are more men joining the secretarial ranks, but employers are recognizing the need to focus on the professional side of secretarial work. Word processing and other aspects of computerization have created a new set of skills for secretaries. In many offices, word processing specialists have replaced generic secretaries. Other secretarial functions have evolved into discrete positions: administrative assistant, office manager, bookkeeper, and file clerk.

There is probably no single consensus job description for the legal secretary today. In many small firms, the office manager is often the most experienced secretary. In some organizations, word processing pools staffed by word processing secretaries have reduced the amount of typing that personal secretaries of lawyers must do. Thinkers opened the door to new areas of responsibility. Based on the nature of their work, many secretaries are actually legal assistants.

With the growth of large law firms, secretarial positions have become increasingly specialized. This topic is considered again in Chapter 12, but it may help here to view secretarial functions in terms of four broad categories:

- producers,

- gatekeepers,
- supervisors,
- assemblers.

These functional positions are described below:

Producers include those secretaries whose jobs consist of the production of the work product that goes out of the law office: letters, forms, documents and reports. The category may include either word processors or individual secretaries. These secretaries may even know desktop publishing. As times have changed, so have the tools of the trade. Just as shorthand gave way to dictation, dictation is giving way to voice recognition software in the production process.

Gatekeepers, on the other hand, control information coming into the law office. The most basic embodiment of the gatekeeper is the receptionist who answers the phone and greets visitors to the office. In many law offices this person is the least experienced and least skilled member of the secretarial staff. A different view of the receptionist's position would involve assigning the job to a higher-level employee with broad discretionary authority to make decisions about where to direct incoming calls, mail, clients, and visitors. Such an individual would be more intimately involved with the coordination of attorneys' individual calendars as well as the calendar of the law firm as a whole. The lawyer's individual secretary often performs the gatekeeping functions of handling mail, screening calls, maintaining the lawyer's tickler and calendar systems, making arrangements for travel and other activities, and troubleshooting in a variety of areas.

The supervisory functions of legal secretaries may involve the supervision and direction of less senior secretarial staff, and oversight for administrative functions either personally or in a supervisory capacity. It is not uncommon for an experienced secretary to give direction to law clerks, paralegals and even some wet-behind-the-ears associates. Firms should recognize, however, that when they give management responsibilities to secretaries they are at some point creating managers. Since the secretarial profession remains predominantly female, lawyers should be sensitive to work assignments that are recognized as secretarial when performed by women, but would be described as managerial (and compensated accordingly) if performed by a man.

The assembler function entails putting together documents, and assisting the attorney in the development of cases. In truth, the assembler secretary is a legal assistant. Before legal assistants were common, experienced legal secretaries ordinarily performed these functions. Today, many firms have never changed the terminology, or redefined jobs. Thus it is often the case that the assembler is also the producer and gatekeeper.

5. OTHER CLERICAL EMPLOYEES

It would be difficult to make a list of all of the conceivable non-legal employees in a law firm. Particularly in large law firms, the support staff can be large and diverse. The smaller the organization the more likely it is that different functions will be combined in the job description of individuals. Other functions will be contracted out, or not dealt with at all except on an as needed basis (e.g., catering). Assuming that services are always more expensive when purchased on the open market, a simple rule of thumb for a firm is to hire someone when the cost of buying the service on a contract basis is greater than the cost of employing someone to do the job. A firm that spends $50,000 annually on editorial services may want to consider hiring an in-house editor. Firms should monitor the cost of contract services to avoid paying too much for what they receive.

There is no one formula that would identify the staffing needs for any given law firm, because these decisions depend on the needs and resources of the particular firm involved. If the firm builds its staff around the tasks that must be performed rather than arbitrary job titles, it is more likely to succeed in developing an effective staff.

6. CONSULTANTS, CONTRACT AND OUTSOURCED SERVICES

One of the real revolutions in the legal service industry has been the grass roots development of support services for law firms. These cottage industries blossomed during the decade of the 1980s, as new technologies evolved, law practice became more complex, and business considerations became increasingly relevant to firms.

The traditional firm was almost self-contained. The lawyers, secretaries, legal assistants and other staff employees performed all of the work of the firm. Equipment was purchased or leased, space rented or bought, and management directed by one or more partners. Law firms were generally insular. They might retain an accountant, an investigator, a private cleaning service; they might occasionally hire expert witnesses for trials.

Today, law firms are much more likely to seek outside help for specific needs; they are also able to find professionals who can satisfy those needs. The choice is frequently an economic one; can an outside service perform the needed work for less expense? The choice may also be one of expertise or competence; can the outside individual or group provide a level of service or expertise not possessed by anyone in the law firm? For many organizations, the volume of work involved does not justify hiring a full-time or even part-time staff person, so paying for certain services as they are needed makes business sense.

Law firms commonly utilize two specific types of services: consultants and contract support services. Consultants are individuals who come into the firm on a project basis to evaluate a problem, conduct a program, or to advise the firm about any number of matters. Consultants may assist the firm with anything from litigation support to technology, from support of substantive legal matters (e.g., jury consultants) to management issues. A contract support service is one that performs a specific function for the law firm on an ongoing basis. A few examples of areas where contract services are typically used include: cleaning, photocopying, decorating, secretarial, legal research, computer or management information, libraries, in-house training, and investigation. Some firms are even utilizing contract services for paralegals and lawyers to handle temporary or short-term legal work.

It is important for law firms, particularly small firms, to appreciate that there are options to hiring new staff. In order to compete in today's legal market, lawyers must deliver their product—legal service—to clients as efficiently as possible. The growth of organizations that accept farmed-out work suggests that this development is a realistic one for many law firms. Although consulting and contract services may not be the best solution for the human resources needs of all firms, these approaches do make sense as an alternative to the expensive proposition of hiring full-time staff for many organizations.

Problems and Questions

1. How does a law firm manage paralegal programs? Who is in charge? What should the program accomplish? Can every law firm benefit from using paralegals successfully?
2. How often do law firms neglect the professional development of the legal staff? Do most law offices provide a sound basis for training new associates? What is the objective of training? To assure quality of the firm's work product? To improve efficiency and firm profitability? To develop well-rounded proficient practitioners? Do any of these objectives work at cross-purposes?
3. What are the advantages and disadvantages of hiring a professional staff to manage a law firm? Can small firms afford professional managers?
4. Try to think of all the *possible* positions of employment that a law firm might create. Can you separate these positions into legal, professional, paraprofessional and clerical categories? Can you break the job titles on your list into functional activities?

C. EMPLOYED LAWYERS
1. ASSOCIATE LAWYERS

Legal personnel are the core of every law firm: the people who bring in the business, do the legal work, and represent the clients. A law firm is nothing but an association of individual lawyers who provide services to people. The lawyers in a law firm are not only its present, but its future.

We have already discussed lawyers as owners of law firms in Chapter 4, but a great many lawyers, as well as most law graduates, work as employees of some organization. Like the nonlegal support staff, they draw a paycheck and do not share directly in the profits of the organization. Some firms may offer bonuses or other profit-sharing plan, but they are still employees. In fact, a significant percentage of private practitioners are not partners or shareholders in the firm where they work. These lawyers are employees of the organization, just as legal assistants, secretaries and administrators are employees. Although employed lawyers, in theory, are eligible to become partners, whereas nonlawyer employees are not, both lawyers and nonlawyers should be viewed as human resources by the owners.

If law firms do not use employed lawyers, the owners must earn a living based their own legal work. For example, suppose the partners in a law firm earn an average of $150,000 per year, based on their own billings. Suppose also that the firm employs associates at a 1:1 ratio of associates to partners, who generate a profit (gross revenue less expenses, including salary) of $100,000 per partner. The partners then will take home $250,000 per year.

Unfortunately, many employed lawyers do not think of themselves as the future of the firm. They find themselves bogged down in legal work to support the partners' future, but not their own. Many employed lawyers live and die by the billable hour. If they do not bill enough hours, they may be thought of as slackers with little hope of making partner. The fear of failing to produce sufficient billable hours and the prospect of increasing the chances of reaching partnership by exceeding production expectations often provide both stick and carrot for motivating younger lawyers. Aside from the philosophical issues involving the exploitation of labor, law firms face fundamental questions about how to best utilize legal staff.

It is no secret that many associates are not happy with their positions. Experienced lawyers seem to take the attitude that if they survived this period many years ago, so can present associates. Many lawyers appear to go further, however, and suggest that the experience somehow builds character. This macho approach to learning may be a variation of the old dad's tale, "You kids have it so easy. When I was your age we walked seven miles through the snow to get to school and no one ever picked us up." Or it may be a variation on the old puritan theme that anything really worth having requires pain in its attainment. Or perhaps lawyers simply view this as a rite of passage, like a protracted hell week in college.

The most charitable explanation for the status quo suggests that the answer may rest more upon benign neglect than any sort of malevolence. Since lawyers are lawyers by choice and managers by necessity, they frequently lack the training, skills or motivation to deal with personnel issues effectively. It is easier to do what everyone else does than to explore alternatives. This attitude gets lawyers and the legal services industry into trouble frequently—we are not proactive and innovative; we are reactive, and hence always lagging behind.

This does not mean that the first few years of practice will not be difficult. New lawyers expect to be frustrated as they learn to become competent. When they learn their craft, they are likely to be less dissatisfied with their work. Likewise, no one said that law is a nine-to-five job. Clients can have emergencies at any time. Opponents and judges can scuttle weekend plans. But when associates work from eight in the morning until midnight, and bill clients over 250 hours per month for services, something is amiss. The answer to the economic woes of law firms cannot be simply to require people to work more hours. There is something wrong with an attitude toward associates that is reminiscent of the popular television commercial for toasted chips, "Crunch all you want. We'll make more."

2. SENIOR EMPLOYED LAWYERS

Lawyer employees may be referred to by any number of names, depending on the circumstances and organization of the law firm (see also the earlier discussion of "The Law Firm Pyramid," pages 61–67:

- Associates (the most common label), but also including—
  - Senior associates,
  - permanent associates,
- Of counsel,
- Staff lawyers,
- Non-equity partners (who, despite the use of the word "partner," are essentially paid employees),
- Contract lawyers.

Many of the largest law firms operate under a corporate structure rather than a traditional partnership model. In these firms the number of lawyer-owners is typically smaller, and the number of employed lawyers greater. The expectation for new lawyers hired by these firm is not that they will become partners, but rather that they can become long-term employees in a stable professional organization. This does not mean that some new lawyers do not become partners or shareholders, or that there is no lawyer attrition. It does represent a shift in focus within the legal community. This trend is expanding into smaller law firms and shows now signs of retreating.

3. ADMINISTRATIVE LAWYERS

An increasing number of lawyers serve in administrative positions in law firms, particularly large firms, as well. Although these lawyers do not for the most part practice law—i.e., deliver services to clients—they represent a growing career path for individuals who want to remain a part of the practice of law without practicing law. Many of these administrative positions are discussed earlier in this chapter. See also Gary Munneke,

William Henslee and Ellen Wayne, *Nonlegal Careers for Lawyers* (ABA 2006):

- Law Firm Administrator,
  - Chief Executive Officer (CEO),
  - Chief Operating Officer (COO),
  - Chief Financial Officer (CFO),
  - Compliance Officer,
- Director of Human Resources,
  - Director of Recruiting,
  - Affirmative Action Officer,
  - Pro Bono Director,
  - Continuing Legal Education Director,
- Director of Information Technology,
  - Law Librarian,
  - Litigation Support Manager,
  - Research Director,
- General Counsel.

Employed lawyers—whether they work in administrative capacities or deliver legal services—do not take the same risks that the owners do, and it follows that they do not reap the same rewards. Recent law school graduates, who lack experience, client contacts or capital to start their own practice often find it attractive to accept a salary in exchange for the experience, opportunity for partnership, and access to clients. More senior lawyers may conclude that employee status suits them as well, because they do not want the pressures of marketing to clients, the responsibilities and risks of managing a law firm, or the hours required to compete for partnership.

PROBLEMS AND QUESTIONS

1. What do you think about the "we'll make more" approach to managing associates? What is the down side risk of treating human resources as fungible? Is there something to be said for creating a "sustainable law firm," which hires, trains and uses legal talent over the long term to meet the needs of a renewable client base?

2. The problem of associate dissatisfaction is not new. Beginning in the 1980s, studies showed that law firm associates in their first three years of practice were most dissatisfied, but that their satisfaction level increased as they developed greater competency and control of their personal lives. Yet some associates never feel satisfied, and many leave the practice of law, while many others labor on through unrewarding careers. Is it possible to distinguish those lawyers who will eventually find satisfaction

in the practice of law from those who will not? What can you do at this stage of your career to help yourself to be in the former group and not the latter?

3. How often do law firms neglect the professional development of their legal staffs? Do most law offices provide a sound basis for training new associates? What is the objective of training? To assure quality of the firm's work product? To improve efficiency and firm profitability? To develop well-rounded proficient practitioners? Do any of these objectives work at cross-purposes?

4. Based on your firsthand knowledge, is lawyer training satisfactory? If not, why not? Do small firms encounter special problems in training associates? If so, how can such firms mount an effective training program?

5. Whose responsibility is it to train lawyers for the practice of law? Do bar sponsored programs solve the training problem? Do they help? Do the law schools have a role to play, or should legal education eschew teaching lawyering skills in favor of theory and analysis?

6. What other benefits should lawyers expect? Can you think of some (e.g., bar review tuition for recent graduates, sabbaticals for partners)? In recent years, questions of parental leave policies have increased dramatically. How much time should be allowed? Should men *and* women be covered? May attorneys return to the firm post-leave at a reduced level of work? Will this extend the time to partnership? Some companies use a "cafeteria" approach to benefits; each employee may allocate a benefit allowance for whichever benefits meet his or her needs. Can this concept work in law firms? Why or why not?

7. Look again at the description of Winters & Sommers, LLP, a "typical" large firm, in Appendix P (page 505). What human resources issues does the management of this firm face regarding its legal staff? What issues confront the employed lawyers? How are these different from or similar to lawyer HR problems faced by small firms?

D. ELEMENTS OF HUMAN RESOURCES MANAGEMENT

Human resources management can be thought of as a cycle that begins with the recruitment and hiring of new employees, to their orientation and training, then to evaluation and feedback, then to compensation and benefits, then to growth and promotion (and occasionally to discipline), and eventually to termination or retirement. When an employee leaves the firm (or ceases being an employees), the cycle begins anew. The materials that follow provide a brief overview of this human resources cycle.

1. RECRUITMENT AND HIRING

HOW TO HIRE, RETAIN, AND MOTIVATE YOUR STAFF

From *Family Advocate,* by Larry Rice (Winter, 2000).

Have you ever noticed how lawyers with staff problems sound like clients with marriage problems? The ones with the worst problems have no idea why they have them. As domestic relations lawyers, we deal with relationships on a daily basis and we think we understand them. The relationship that you have with your staff can be as happy as a honeymoon or as dysfunctional as any bad marriage. We hope we learn from the relationship disasters we see.

The following observations are based on more than 20 years' experience in law-office-management relations. Some were successful, some were disastrous, but all led to my current state of law office bliss.

Just as you probably didn't live happily ever after with your first date, you may not want to hang on forever to your first paralegal. The "best" employer and the "best" employee will not necessarily be the "best" for each other. Every lawyer and every staff person are unique. Matching personalities and work styles leads to a successful long-term commitment.

My paralegal and I find that her early-morning work patterns mesh well with my preference for working late. Between us we cover the office 10 to 12 hours per day. You will not work well together if your paralegal is a laugh a minute, but you have no sense of humor. (If you didn't have a sense of humor, however, you probably wouldn't be practicing family law.)

Hire for intelligence and initiative; you can train for skills. Basic ability and attitude are the product of a person's life. As wonderful as you think you are, you are not likely to be a life-altering experience for any new staff person.

. . .

For the very reason that your client should have executed a prenuptial agreement before entering into this last marriage, you need a contract with your staff. It should set forth in plain English just what is expected. You may want to discharge your ethical obligation to protect your client's confidentiality by having your new employee also sign a confidentiality statement.

If you have hired a person with intelligence and initiative who is helping to develop your practice, you want to keep that person. To do so, you will need to convey your respect and appreciation. First, find out what "respect" and "appreciation" mean to that person, and then, within the boundaries of lawful conduct and the budget, deliver it.

Typically, lawyers in small firms are understaffed and underpaid. But you must be realistic about what's possible. Do not give a staff person more work than can possibly be done and then be surprised when he or she can't deliver. Likewise, if you hire an intelligent person and big firms in your area are paying more money than you are and providing better benefits, do not be surprised when that person gets smart and gets packing.

In a small firm family law practice you do have some options. You can supplement pay with occasional bonuses. A standing percentage may pose ethical problems, but a bonus every month or so based on your activity level and discretion shouldn't be a problem.

The goal is to give your office staff a sense of ownership in the practice. Nothing says "thank you for putting up with whiny clients" better than five magic words: Pay to the order of.

Don't be a jerk. It is probably true that there are more jerks per capita in the legal community than the world at-large. Unless you selected and hired a paralegal who's a masochist, don't be a jerk at the office. Your staff can respond with malicious obedience. Malicious obedience stems from your antagonizing your paralegal to the point that he or she does what you say, not what is right. Believe me, you will suffer for it. Once you have reached this stage, an office divorce is the best course.

Employees want a few things besides money, benefits, and a reasonable workload. That gets us back to respect, and that gets us to the issue of coffee. Apparently, the worst thing a lawyer can do (within the bounds of legality) is to condescendingly tell the paralegal to get the coffee. It is a universal complaint lodged against arrogant bosses. Get your own coffee and pick up a cup for your paralegal. You will be surprised at how soon your paralegal will ask if you'd like a cup of coffee, rather than complain about being a waitress.

The best return comes from minimal investments in staff happiness. Buy a bag of miniature chocolate bars and hand them out. It is hard for anyone to say "the boss is a jerk" with a mouthful of chocolate.

Although many aspects of the recruitment and hiring process apply equally to lawyers and support staff, special considerations apply to the hiring of lawyers. Not only do law firms think of new legal talent as an investment in the future of the firm, but they have to address other issues, like licensing, conflicts of interest and potential for client development as well. Although your start-up firm in this course will probably not hire associate or lateral lawyers during its first two years of operation, the prospect of hiring lawyers at some point in the future is a very real possibility. For this reason, the following article is included in this section of the chapter:

[This material has been adapted from *Your New Lawyer: The Legal Employer's Complete Guide to Recruitment Development and Management*, edited by Michael K. Magness and Carolyn Wehmann, American Bar

Association (1984, 1992), and *The Legal Employers Placement Handbook*, by Gary A. Munneke, The University of Texas School of Law (1980).]

Over 40,000 new lawyers enter the legal job market each year, and over 50,000 practicing lawyers change jobs annually. This represents nearly 100,000 new jobs every year. The average starting salary for new lawyers has been reported by the National Association for Law Placement to be over $65,000, and somewhat higher for experienced lawyers. Legal employers pay at least $7 billion dollars in annual salaries to newly hired lawyers.

Fewer than 20% of all law graduates go to work in large firms. Nearly four out of five lawyers in private practice work alone or in firms of 10 lawyers or less. Clearly, most of the hiring in this country is done by small firms. Such firms, however, generally pay very little attention to the risks associated with hiring new lawyers. The impact of a bad hiring decision is much greater in a small firm than in a large one. In a firm of 1,000 lawyers the cost of a bad investment can be spread 1,000 ways. When a five-lawyer firm makes a bad decision, the economic impact on the firm is shared by only five partners.

The hiring needs of smaller firms are not as predictable as they are in large firms. This is primarily because the natural turnover rate (every retiring attorney must be replaced with a new attorney) is practically non existent in smaller firms, and the supply of work dictates the firm's expansion. While it may appear that small firms do not need to invest in a hiring procedure or screening of some sort because of such a low need, or expectation of a need, to hire new attorneys, for reasons mentions above, the approach undertaken by the small firm should be just a sophisticated and thorough as that of a larger firm. Smaller firms may not have hiring needs all the time, and those needs may not be as predictable as they are in large firms, but they do arise. At such times the small firm must be as sophisticated in its approach to the recruitment process as the larger firm; in addition, a small firm must be more careful than a firm that can play the numbers game.

Assessing the Need to Hire a New Lawyer

When does a law firm know that it needs to add an attorney? When management looks at the backlog of work and observes that most of the lawyers work more than 60 hours a week, and when projections suggest that for the next six months to a year these workloads will not change, it is a likely indication that the firm needs some help.

Surveys suggest that the average number of billable hours for all lawyers in the United States is a little over 1700 hours per year. This is almost 33 hours per week, and one assumes that the average lawyer charges only about two-thirds of her time in the office to client work, this figure represents a 50 hour workweek. In larger firms the average number of billable hours can exceed 2000 per year. The average for partners is somewhat less than for associates, suggesting that associates have to work harder than partners. But we knew that.

A firm should be able to project at least one thousand hours of available work in order to assimilate a new associate. (From where does the work come?) There may already be a backlog. Everyone is working hard, with no end in sight. All the lawyers are billing 2400 hours per year; they have not seen their families in three years. The firm may anticipate specific new business opportunities on the horizon, sufficient to generate enough work to keep a new lawyer busy. The economy may be booming in the area where the firm practices.

Various surveys point to an average growth rate in law firms of about 5% a year. If a firm has 10 lawyers and those 10 lawyers bill 1,700 hours annually, or 17,000 hours, 5% of 17,000 is about 850 hours, which is inadequate to justify hiring another associate.

Generally, when a firm attains a size of more than ten lawyers, it reaches a critical mass, and thereafter will need to hire new lawyers on a regular basis. Firms with less than ten lawyers must make an affirmative decision to grow, while larger firms must make an affirmative decision not to. This partly explains why larger firms devote more time to problems of recruiting, training, and developing new lawyers than smaller ones.

The growth of a law office is an unavoidable issue, which must be addressed. It is inevitably intertwined with other aspects of law office economics and management. In this light, questions of growth and hiring cannot be ignored. Some employers may not have to deal with the problem annually, but periodically it will emerge to confront them.

One question every firm ought to ask is "Do we want to grow?" A firm may like its size, or the mix of people. The lawyers may not want to get involved in recruiting, training and developing new lawyers. There is something to be said for just maintaining the status quo and sending the business somewhere else because every additional member of the team *will* inevitably change the team dynamic in some manner. Despite the common perception, growth is not the only answer, and may be more of a curse than a blessing. Many sole practitioners like being sole practitioners, and decided to fly solo because they wanted to avoid having to deal with a group dynamic. Many small law offices have developed stable, harmonious and efficient relationships which change may disrupt. Some individuals have difficulty working with others, and an addition to the office may mean another potential conflict. Where previous disagreements among members have been settled or buried, bringing in a new lawyer may resurrect them. These are but a few situations in which a decision to expand may be unwise.

There are alternatives to hiring lawyers. In one sense, adding a new lawyer means not making some alternative choice: hiring additional non-legal staff, or upgrading equipment. A computer system at $5,000 may be an alternative to a new associate at $65,000. A firm should look at all these alternatives before deciding to hire another attorney.

Some law offices may decide to recruit an experienced attorney. The pool of qualified, available and experienced candidates, however, is not likely to be as large as the pool of inexperienced ones. Making the decision to hire laterally or right out of school is a difficult one. Many small firms find that it is economically feasible and desirable to hire someone with two to three years (or more when looking for a specialist) of experience, because they let somebody else do the initial training.

In order to avoid the necessary investment in a beginner, some firms turn to lateral hiring, i.e., hiring from other firms attorneys with experience. This presents a host of other problems as it raises the difficult question of money. Hiring laterals presents difficult salary questions because other associates in the firm will be affected by the lateral entrant's salary. Someone who has worked for a small firm in rural Iowa for three years is probably making less than the lateral from a big firm in New York or Houston.

And, of course, one of the problems with laterals, as well as recent graduates, is the bar exam. If the person is not licensed in the jurisdiction, the firm may have to wait several months for bar results before a new hire is able to practice law. There is a possibility that the person will fail the exam, and, despite the match the firm is back to square one.

Costs of Recruiting

The decision as to whether or not to expand a law office is of great importance to the future well-being of every law practice from the sole practitioner to the 300–lawyer office. Skyrocketing inflation in everything from law books to salaries has made efficient operation a necessity for economic survival, and growth should be given the same careful analysis that other business and management questions receive. Yet, little attention has been given to either the question of whether or not to recruit, or (the issue of) how to recruit more economically.

A new lawyer in all probability will not produce sufficient income to break even or show a profit for a firm for some time after being hired. The break-even point may occur from six months to two years after a new lawyer joins the firm. If the annual overhead costs (space, furniture, telephones, secretarial assistance, etc.) approximate the lawyer's annual salary, then an associate paid $65,000 for the first year will cost the law firm $130,000. Even discounting the time and costs of hiring and training, the investment in a new attorney is a significant one extending over a period of several years.

A solo practitioner with gross receipts of $250,000 and an overhead of 50 percent will net $125,000. Yet, if the cost of adding a new lawyer is $130,000, it must be paid from the practitioner's pocket. Consider a first year associate who bills 1,000 hours—a figure that takes into account the new lawyer's gradually increasing productivity—at $100 per hour; in the preceding example, he or she would produce a net loss of $30,000. A larger office can spread this loss among a larger group, and the loss is, therefore, less economically significant for the firm. A $30,000 loss shared by 10 lawyers amounts to $3,000 each; by 100 lawyers, only $300 each.

The employer must be able to withstand financially an initial period of loss in order for its recruitment investment to be considered successful. Otherwise, tremendous pressure is put on both the office and the new lawyer. The firm cannot rely on the new lawyer to generate any new business at first; thus the new lawyer's workload will have to be supported by business the office generated before he or she joined the firm. When a new lawyer is first added, he or she generates very little income. Gradually, over time, the associate's work begins to produce a profit, and after the profit exceeds the initial loss, he or she is usually admitted to partnership.

Chart 8–1

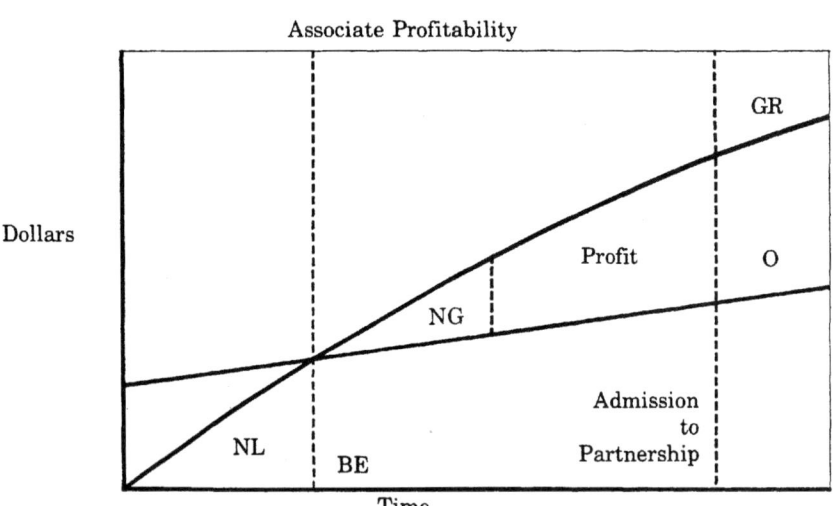

It is expected that the associate with increasing gross receipts (GR) will be economically detrimental to the firm at first, break even (BE) at a point one to three years after joining the firm, and thereafter be a profitable part of the firm's practice. The associate's overhead (O) for use of office space, secretarial help and so forth will generally increase slightly over the years, and his or her salary will be another factor of increased overhead to the firm.

There are other risks involved when considering whether to invest in the hire of a new associate—some associates never reach partnership; and some never show a profit, in other words, while investing in some associates is profitable in the long run, some never turn a profit for the firm and are a lost investment forever. Planning before hiring may considerably reduce the likelihood of a "bad investment," but it can not eliminate the inherent risk of the inability to see into the future. Lawyers and law firms can only attempt to predict the probable course of development of a potential associate through careful study of their past achievements and their compatibility with the firm's internal culture.

Hiring is costly in the immediate future. If the firm decides to hire someone, it will cost money. There are indirect as well as direct costs. The direct costs involve interviewing, whether at a law school, some other venue or the firm's office. Indirect costs include such items as lost time. When interviewing a candidate, a lawyer is not working for a client, rather the interviewer is the representative of the firm's future face, hence the investment is worthwhile, but note the immense indirect costs associated with the process of selecting a new colleague.

When attorneys meet to discuss candidates, they are spending time that could be used on client matters. Indirect costs are probably the largest expense in the recruiting process, and many lawyers have no idea how much time they spend, or how many billable hours they lose. When the large firms talk about spending $100,000 per hire, much of that is lost lawyer time. Some costs associated with hiring a new person after the individual accepts the firm's offer: increased overhead, including secretarial assistance and office space; moving expenses, bar review courses and a number of other things in addition to salaries. A careful cost-benefit analysis is desirable.

The actual cost of making the initial contact with candidates is the smallest part of the total expense of bringing someone on board. Training, overhead and salary expenditures are substantial and must be borne by the office until the new lawyer's work begins to produce income.

Rather than setting a fixed salary for new lawyers, some offices use an output-oriented formula for determining pay. The *Rule of Thirds* method sets maximum compensation at one-third the expected billings the new lawyer will accumulate. Thus, for new attorneys to earn $65,000 they must bill approximately $195,000. The rest of the money would cover overhead and training costs.

If an employer makes a bad decision, the economic consequences go far beyond the loss of recruiting costs and salary. Few employers can afford to absorb such expenses on a regular basis, if at all. If employers anticipate recruiting costs, budget necessary expenses and minimize waste, they can maximize the probability of making sound decisions, and manage the recruiting process of recruiting more successfully.

A firm considering entering the recruiting sweepstakes, should sit down and figure out what it will cost to bring in another person compared to the income the new person will be expected to generate. Although these costs are sometimes hard to see, they are predictable.

The cost to a legal employer of recruiting a new lawyer varies widely with the method used to locate and attract the prospective associate. The extent of the recruitment program should be a function of the employer's total budget. For every employer there is an outside limit, a point at which the costs become too great. Even the largest law firms can recruit at only a few of the accredited law schools, and although some firms spend hundreds of thousands of dollars on recruiting annually, they must decide where and how their dollars are best spent. The same basic economics influence the sole practitioner or small firm in deciding to take on a new lawyer.

Hiring

Interviewing and recruiting may at first glance appear to be synonyms, but they ought not be thought of in this way. Interviewing is the process of determining whether the applicant would be a beneficial addition to the legal team already in place. Interviewing can occur any place—on the street, in a law school, in the office, or elsewhere—any time two people get together to discuss employment. Interviewing an applicant for a job is not like interviewing a witness. Nor is it like interviewing a client., though some of the same skills are used.

Recruiting, on the other hand, is selling. It is convincing the candidate that *this* firm is the right place to spend his or her professional life. Firms sometimes feel that the thousands of law graduates out there must be desperate to work in their offices. It may be true that there are people looking for work, but the question is: Can they get the right person (as opposed to any person) to come to work for them? It is important to realize for both parties in this process, the prospective hire and the hiring firm, that the selection of a candidate unfit for the firm's practice will destroy the practice's equilibrium. After all, we spend more time at work than at home in any given day.

An interviewer must know what he or she is looking for *before* conducting an interview. In a large organization, a collective decision should be made. Consider the kind of work the new attorney will be doing, the academic and extracurricular background which will be required to do the job, and the intangible personality factors that may influence a close decision. If some of the selection factors are made available to students in the employer resume before interviews, a certain amount of self-selection will take place. The interviewer should have a plan for eliciting information from the interviewee.

It is in this area that the experienced interviewer has an edge over the novice. Interviewing skills, like many lawyering skills, are developed and not in-bred. Many trial lawyers, accustomed to picking jurors, perceive themselves as good judges of people. Whether this is true is subject to debate, but there can be little doubt that personal attraction, magnetism, chemistry, "good vibes," hunches, intuition or whatever one wishes to call it, plays an important part in the evaluation process and should not be ignored. A good interviewer learns to trust his feelings without being blinded by them.

Once it has been decided which qualities are important in a prospective employee, different techniques can be used to systematically evaluate the various candidates. The thrust of the entire selection process should be to analyze a person's decision-making, life-direction and problem-solving abilities. By structuring interview inquiries along those lines—and here's the key—listening very carefully to the responses, a firm can begin to form a reliable feeling for how well that person's goals and abilities mesh with those the firm considers important.

Law firms face thorny problems involving compensation for both employed lawyers and support staff. A fair, workable compensation scheme should adequately reward everyone in the firm for work done, *and* provide incentives to produce in the future. The associate, paralegal and secretary in effect, sell all of their professional services to one organization for a fixed salary. The salary is based on the fair market value for comparable employment in the market, a figure substantially less than the retail cost of the services provided by the firm to clients. For example, an associate may spend 3,000 hours per year in the office (60 hours/week x 50 weeks) for a salary of $65,000, less than $22/hour. The firm, however, may bill the associate's time at $150/hour; if the associate bills 1,800 hours to clients, 90% of which is actually collected, the firm may gross $243,000. Even assuming that the cost of supporting the associate equals the associate's salary (another $65,000), the firm still will net $113,000 on the associate's work. Thus, although it is expensive to employee associates, if the firm has enough work to keep them busy, it can earn substantial profit from the arrangement

If the associate were in private practice she might be able to bill her work at the same $150/hour, but she would also have to market her services to obtain clients and pay overhead expenses of at least $75/hour. Her profit of $75 per hour, would be multiplied by the number of hours billed to clients. If she has no clients, then $75 x 0 = $0; if she bills 1,000 hours (assuming that marketing and administrative expenses limit the amount of time she can spend on client matters), and that she also collects 90% of her bills, she would earn $67,500. slightly more than she would as an employed associate. For many young lawyers, the guarantee of a fixed salary is a better deal than the risk of earning more or less as an independent practitioner. The differential between the $150/hour market value of her services versus the $22/hour she earns as an employee represents a quid pro quo for, among other things, providing a client base, training, office space, support, and the opportunity to be considered for partnership.

Whether this is a good business deal for the parties is a question open to some debate. For instance, the associate may not bill 1,800 hours for two or three years—or never. She may take the training and then leave the firm taking some of their clients with her (See *Adler, Barish, et al. v. Epstein*, 482 Pa. 416, 393 A.2d 1175 (1978)). A firm may make a substantial investment in an associate and get absolutely no return on its investment.

The fact remains that most law school graduates choose to work for an existing organization during their early years of practice rather than open their own firms. The security of a salary and relative job security usually outweigh the risks of entrepreneurship, particularly in an era when students can graduate with $50–60,000 or more in student loans to repay. The National Association for Law Placement produces an annual salary survey for recent graduates. Portions of the survey are reproduced below:

Chart 8-2

Chart 8-2

National Association for Law Placement, 2012
http://www.nalp.org/2012_associate_salaries
Median Base Salaries by Associate Year and Firm Size (as of April 1, 2012)

Associate Year	FIRM SIZE — Number of Lawyers														
	2-25		26-50		51-100		101-250		251-500		501-700		701+		All Sizes
Median	# Rept	Median	# Rept	Median	# Rept	Median	# Rept	Median	# Rept	Median	# Rept	Median	# Rept	Median	# Rept
First	$70,750	10	$90,000	21	$100,000	38	$110,000	62	$145,000	67	$125,000	70	$145,000	83	$125,000	351
Second	75,100	7	94,500	22	103,000	37	112,500	63	160,000	64	124,000	66	155,000	85	127,000	344
Third	78,850	14	94,750	19	112,000	35	116,000	64	170,000	65	127,275	70	160,950	96	131,250	363
Fourth	80,000	12	105,600	21	115,700	36	120,000	64	180,000	68	135,600	75	167,075	97	137,700	373
Fifth	83,450	12	107,450	24	114,650	41	124,000	63	205,000	63	143,600	77	180,000	96	144,350	376
Sixth	86,000	8	118,000	19	115,000	38	130,000	62	215,000	65	145,000	75	185,000	99	150,000	366
Seventh	—	—	123,000	16	127,000	35	134,000	57	225,000	65	153,000	73	200,000	95	159,000	345
Eighth	95,000	11	118,250	16	126,150	22	135,000	44	250,000	54	160,000	71	210,975	84	169,100	302
Summer Associates ($/week)															
1st year	—	—	1,175	10	1,350	20	1,900	37	2,800	55	2,300	47	3,075	35	2,100	208
2nd year	—	—	1,450	20	1,600	29	2,000	48	2,800	64	2,300	69	3,075	87	2,300	321
3rd year	—	—	1,275	5	2,050	12	2,000	8	3,100	21	3,075	19	2,100	12	2,800	77

The "# Rept." column indicates the number of offices reporting. For purposes of this summary report, medians have been rounded to the nearest $25.

Surveys of experienced attorney salaries are produced by several legal consulting firms, various state bar associations and professional organizations (e.g., Association of Legal Administrators). Salaries for nonlegal personnel as well as lawyers may vary considerably according to size of firm, location, and job requirements. Salary information may be often available through research studies by business schools, institutes, government agencies as well. Such surveys may reflect local, state or national markets.

Most lawyers either know or can find out what the "going rate" is for employees in their geographic area. In larger organizations, it may be necessary to develop a compensation plan with salary ranges and classifications for different positions. Thus, all individuals with the same job title would be paid within the same salary range. Generally, large firms in large cities have the highest pay scales, small firms in small rural towns the lowest. (The topic of salaries and benefits is addressed again in Chapter 11, *Managing Financial Resources*).

2. ORIENTATION AND TRAINING

The most important day on any job is the first one. It sets the tone for the entire employment relationship. After the interview process, both employer and employee enter their relationship with the expectation that it will be successful. The fact that many employment relationships do not work out is testament to the fact that things can go wrong along the way.

The orientation program gives the employer an opportunity to start out on the right foot. Having a plan for the employee's first day is critical not only to integrating the individual into the organization, but also to give the new employee a sense that the new workplace is organized, competent and efficient. Perhaps most important, the first day is not too early to show the new employee the human face of the firm. A warm welcome will allay whatever trepidation the new employee may feel in the new environment.

Beyond these generalities, the orientation process ought to include several specific components:

- Meet with management for an official welcome. Whether this is the managing partner, office administrator or human resources director, an official welcome is always in order.
- Don't make the new employee wait. This day is special.
- Provide the new employee with a staff manual and other critical policies that will be necessary to function in the office. Give the employee a chance to read and ask questions about these documents.
- Take care of the paper work as soon as possible. It might make sense to send out forms that need to be completed in advance, or set aside some time during the day to fill them out.
- Introduce the new employee to his/her direct supervisor, and give the two time to meet.
- The supervisor should have an initial work assignment ready for the new employee to begin as soon as possible.
- Introduce the new employee to other staff with whom the new person will work on a regular basis, as well as peers in the office.
- Take the new employee to lunch, and if necessary acquaint the person to the area where the office is located, including restaurants, stores, services, parking, ATMs, and other points of interest.
- Have the new employee's work area ready to go and fully equipped.

- Remind the new worker that the firm is excited to have this person on the team.
- Follow up a few days later to assure that all logistical matters have been handled, that employee questions have been answered, and that work is going well.
- If there are problems, deal with them right away; the longer they fester, the worse they will become.

For many positions, a level of expertise is required that new employees may not possess when they arrive. Someone might have all the paper credentials, but lack specific experience on a software system used by the firm. It is in everyone's interest to escalate the learning curve, so the employee becomes productive at the earliest possible time. Learning by trial and error is inefficient, but it also risks mistakes that can be problematic to the firm in other ways. Either through mentoring, evaluated assignments, in-house classes, or external training programs give new workers the tools they need to do the best job possible.

3. FEEDBACK AND EVALUATION

After hiring a new employee, a firm must train and develop this person to become a productive part of the organization. At the same time, the firm must address the sometimes conflicting tasks of making the individual, from the new associate to the lowest file clerk, happy with her job while at the same time evaluating her work. It is often very difficult for small firms with limited resources to maintain effective evaluation programs.

Many law students, through their work in law firms as part-time clerks or summer associates, get a glimpse of how lawyers are trained. Law schools offer both live client clinics and practice skills courses. Many states have adopted mandatory continuing legal education requirements, and some states require or recommend attendance by new lawyers at "bridge-the-gap" programs. Delaware imposes a post-graduate internship for all bar candidates. Despite these efforts, however, preparation for the practice of law remains spotty, and some graduates actually find themselves starting to work at law firms with little or no practical training.

Evaluation of both new lawyers and staff should take place at some designated time after the individual is hired, typically six months. Prior to this initial evaluation, these new employees are often considered by their employers as probationary. Although most new employees complete this probationary period successfully, from time to time the firm will discover that it has made a mistake, or the employee will determine that the firm or job was not what she expected. A probationary evaluation interview permits the parties to sever such a relationship quickly and easily. For most employees this initial evaluation serves as a benchmarking exercise for both employer and employee to communicate the employee's progress and future expectations.

After the probationary evaluation, regular evaluations at six month or one year intervals are appropriate. Many firms tie this evaluation process to annual raises, but it is not necessary to do so. What is important is that the employer articulate clear standards of evaluation, conduct the evaluation process in a predictable, even-handed way, and communicate the results to employees in a timely and direct manner. This ensures that risk of failed expectations is minimized. The Employee is aware of what is expected from him, and the employer is able to invest in the new employee with some certainty. The evaluation interview is typically handled by the employee's direct supervisor, although if an employee has many supervisors, or has transferred positions during the year, the process might be different.

Feedback represents an informal form of evaluation that takes place on a regular basis as work assignments are completed. Rather than waiting to communicate with employees at formal evaluation periods, it is often more effective and easier to let people know whether they have met expectations on an ongoing basis. Supervisors should recognize that they cannot simply provide all positive or all negative feedback; they need to recognize successes as well as mistakes. Feedback should be specific rather than general (e.g., "you mis-cited this case on page 22," rather than "your bluebooking stinks."). Negative feedback is most efficaciously delivered in private, while praise more often than not deserves an audience.

4. COMPENSATION AND BENEFITS

Compensation of the employed staff represents not only payment for services rendered by employees, but the largest single expense item in most firms' budgets. For most law firms, salaries, benefits and other expenses related to human resources represent the largest line in the firm's budget. Some firms spend 70 cents out of every overhead dollar on personnel. Earlier sections have mentioned the costs associated with recruiting and training, but these pale in comparison to salaries and benefits. On the one hand, compensation represents payment to an individual for the value of his or her work, but compensation should be viewed as a management tool as well.

People in the world of work attach considerable importance to salary matters. Not only do they want to feel that they are being paid on par with other people who have comparable jobs, they view raises, bonuses and other financial perks as indicia of their status in the organization. Employers send messages about their satisfaction with someone's work, recognition of accomplishments and indication of an individual's long-term future with the organization through the compensation system. Employers also create incentives and disincentives for certain behaviors through financial awards and punishment.

It is virtually impossible to escape these aspects of compensation. For this reason, it is important for employees to view the compensation system as fair and equitable. If they believe that compensation decisions are based on factors other than performance, it will affect their morale, motivation and loyalty. Although an employee may feel under-paid, that person will probably not quit because of money alone, but if the same person believes that he has been treated unfairly, the firm will not be able to keep him.

Many law firms try to pay as little as possible for staff salaries. Salaries for employees not licensed as lawyers, e.g., secretaries and legal assistants, will be governed by market forces outside the legal community. The competitors in recruiting talent include organizations such as corporations, banks and the government. Increasingly, lawyers and law school graduates are looking outside the realm of private practice for career opportunities, which subject law firms to additional market pressures in the hiring arena.

Raises in most organizations are tied to annual cost of living increases reported in government statistics. Within a general range of increases, salaries may be more or less based on merit, which in turn should be linked to objective evaluations. During periods of rapid inflation, annual increases tends to be higher, but employers often find it difficult at such times to keep up with the cost of living.

Many firms supplement base salaries with a bonus system on an annual, or some other periodic basis. There are several advantages to a bonus system. The payment does not become attached to the employee's base salary, so it does not bind the firm for the future. If the financial picture is better or worse the next year, the firm can gauge bonuses accordingly. Bonuses seem more like rewards than entitlements, so the firm probably gets more mileage from a bonus than a salary increase. Because bonuses are often given at the end of the year around the holiday season, there are benefits for both employer and employee with such an arrangement.

Every law firm is in business to make money. If it does not reward its members adequately, it will not continue to exist as a business entity. The record in recent years of firms that have disintegrated because the income base failed to provide adequate compensation for its members would surprise many law students.

There is a psychological component to the notion of adequate compensation. One individual's poverty could be another's wealth. Yet, when a firm collectively addresses the issue of compensation, it must consider the individual concepts of sufficient income for work done, as well as group goals and objectives.

Although the term "compensation" means two different things from two perspectives, compensating staff for the value of their services and compensating the owners of the business as a return on their investment, this chapter addresses the former issue. Chapter 11, *Managing Financial Resources*, covers compensation of the owners through distribution of profits. Although the partners, especially in professional corporations, may pay themselves a salary, in actuality, they are really prepaying their share of the profit. If the firm loses money, the owners may have to waive their salaries, but they still have a legal obligation to pay employees.

Many firms approach compensation in a very ad hoc way, responding to the marketplace. They pay as little as they can and as much as they need. They try to solve personnel problems by throwing money at them, yet they often ignore the needs of workers until they erupt in crisis. A more enlightened approach is to develop and administer a compensation plan that rewards performance, reduces disputes, and motivates personnel at all levels.

Employee benefits are a part of virtually all jobs. Although law firm benefits are often less than those of companies in business and industry, they can be instrumental in employee satisfaction, longevity and productivity. Although this chapter does not go into a great deal of detail about benefit plans, because of the inherent complexity of the subject, the issue is one that every law firm must address. The following list describes the most common forms of employee benefits:

- Health insurance;
- Life insurance;
- Disability insurance;
- Workers compensation and unemployment insurance;
- Professional liability insurance;
- Retirement plan;
- Vacation and leave;
- Educational benefits;
- Continuing education and training;
- Parking;
- Professional memberships;
- Social memberships;
- Day care;
- Bonuses, overtime opportunities;
- Promotion, advancement;
- Special firm events.

Some of these benefits are tangible, and involve either direct payment by the employer or investment in an activity that indirectly benefits employees, e.g., an annual holiday party or picnic. Some benefits may be intangible, such as a positive work atmosphere or attractive offices. Whatever the benefits package, employees should clearly understand that their total compensation is more than just employees' salaries. Benefits typically range from as low as 10% of gross salary to over 30%, with large firms providing more benefits (at least tangible ones) than small firms.

5. DISCIPLINE AND TERMINATION

DISCIPLINE AND TERMINATION

From *The Essential Formbook,* by Gary A. Munneke and Anthony E. Davis (2001).

Despite the best efforts of all involved, not all employment relationships evolve successfully. Some employees learn that they are not satisfied with the work, surroundings, compensation or other factors in their employment. Some employers discover that the person they hired is incapable of developing the skills necessary to attain competence in the job for which he or she was hired, or is incapable of fitting into the work team in the office; in serious cases, employees may breach client confidences, misappropriate money, or engage in other improper/illegal acts. In many of these situations, the disenchantment is a mutual and interwoven pattern: attitude affects performance; performance affects evaluation; evaluation affects attitude. The downward spiral continues until the relationship is irretrievably broken.

The goal of the entire employment process is to hire and retain people who are both capable of doing the work for which they were hired, and who obtain satisfaction and reward from their jobs. No one sets out to have an employee quit or be fired. Certainly, hiring qualified and motivated individuals is critical—we cannot make a silk purse out of a sow's ear. Undoubtedly, training and mentoring are integral to transforming raw talent into productive workers—human resources in the truest sense. Clearly, firms can create an environment in which employees want to come to work, feel they are contributing significantly to the firm's mission, and look forward to continuing the relationship for a long time.

The process of growth as an employee, however, inevitably is fraught with setbacks, challenges and frustrations. The feedback and evaluation processes inherently identify negative performances that need to be improved along with positive conduct that should be replicated. Both legal and support staff require nurture and patience before they become full contributors to the legal service delivery team. A fundamental assumption of every human resources system is that employees have the potential to grow in their jobs; a corollary of this assumption is that they will make mistakes along the way.

Discipline

The discipline process is inter-related with the evaluation and training processes, in that it is always the remedy of last resort. If work problems can be resolved through other approaches, it is almost always better for the firm in the long run not to implicate the disciplinary system. Unfortunately, many employers are reluctant to sanction employees when it is appropriate or necessary, an omission that can come back to haunt them if termination becomes necessary, or in the worst case the firm is sued for wrongful discharge or other reason. For example, if an employee's performance is consistently substandard and yet performance evaluations are glowing, a subsequent decision to fire the individual may be subject to challenge.

A good disciplinary system should contain several key elements, which will contribute to the creation of a impression of fairness among all employees:

- The system should be in writing (in a staff manual or other document);
- The process and content of the system should be communicated clearly to employees from the time they are hired, and reinforced periodically;
- The system should be observed and administered equitably;
- The system should include a triggering mechanism, such as a supervisor's complaint;
- Accurate records of all transactions, including verbal reprimands, should be maintained;
- Communication of charges should be delivered in a timely manner to the employee;
- The employee should have an opportunity to respond to any criticism or charges, in writing if appropriate;
- Sanctions—reprimands, written warnings, termination—should be communicated to the employee personally by a direct supervisor;
- In the case of termination, the basis for the termination should be delivered to the employee personally and in writing, and in appropriate circumstances steps taken to protect office security; and
- Any appeal process should be explained to the employee at the time the disciplinary action is announced.

Complaints concerning employee performance may arise as a part of a regular employee review, as a result of a pattern of behavior that cannot await the next scheduled review, or following a single serious act of misconduct. Some behavior, such as embezzlement, mishandling of client trust accounts, intentional breach of client confidences, or other conduct that could subject the supervisory lawyer to discipline, malpractice or criminal charges, may justify immediate dismissal, lest the lawyer's inaction be treated as ratification of the misconduct.

As a matter of policy, the firm should have some means of delineating matters subject to the disciplinary process from those that are less serious and handled informally. The staff manual or separate disciplinary policy should articulate the conduct that will lead to discipline, e.g., theft, insubordination. Where the problem involves a pattern of conduct over time, such as regularly careless or inferior work product, tardiness or absenteeism, or failure to follow established procedures, institution of a formal complaint typically follows a period of informal attempts in feedback, evaluations or admonitions to improve performance, so the reasons for institution of the disciplinary process is seldom a total surprise to the employee. The gravity of a blot on the employee's permanent record may be enough to get a miscreant's attention. The authority to initiate formal action should be established clearly, particularly if the power to discipline is granted to an associate or staff supervisor. Typically, such a decision will be made by more than one person in consultation.

Sanctions for misconduct can include verbal warnings or reprimand, written warnings; suspensions of employee's pay, forfeiture of bonuses or raises, reimbursement, or fines. Such penalties may include firing. Some firms may also employ financial disincentives as well, such as docking pay, these need to be carefully administered, however, in order to assure that they do not violate any of the employee's legal rights to the compensation. In the case of a written warning, suspension or termination notice, the written document should clearly set forth the grounds for the action, including history if necessary and the specific terms of the punishment. It should be dated and signed by the employee and the complaining supervisor.

Termination

In the case of suspension or termination, special precautions are always desirable. The action should take place in a private setting such as an office where it will not be viewed by the entire office staff, but there should be at least one witness to the action both to confirm what was said—a disgruntled employee may fabricate statements or events, or claim ignorance of what was communicated—and to supplement any details. The terminated employee will go through a series of reactions from disbelief ("You're kidding?"), to anger ("You can't get away with this!"), to despondence ("What's going to happen to me?"), to bargaining ("Can't we work something out?"), to acceptance ("Okay, I'll go"). These are completely normal, and should not come as a surprise; it would be more of a surprise if the employee said nothing at all. Remember that this is *not* the time to negotiate; if you were not sure about the decision, you should have pursued a less extreme form of discipline.

When the firm decides to terminate someone, the actual firing should merely communicate the terms and reasons. Dismissal from a job is one of the most traumatic events that can take place in anyone's life, so the terminated employee in all likelihood will not be happy (although sometimes a frustrated person who lacked the nerve to quit may be relieved). In a small number of cases, discharged employees may engage in acts of sabotage such as deleting computer files or shredding documents. Occasionally, fired employees may become irrational enough to commit acts of violence against those they believe have wronged them. Law firms have not been immune from disturbed former employees who (to use the vernacular) "go postal." Although it is an unlikely scenario, every firing should contemplate how to handle the worst-case scenario of a terminated employee inflicting harm to himself or others. Particular sensitivity to past behavior patterns such as angry outbursts, use of violent imagery in ordinary speech, unusually aggressive posturing in confrontational situations, and a history of mental illness may provide warning signs.

In the case of lawyers, there remains one additional issue with respect to the termination of an employment relationship—actually, with respect to the termination of a partnership interest as well, and that is the prohibition against covenants not to compete, common in many industries.

Model Rule 1.8(h) prohibits lawyers from participating in a covenant not to compete. The reason for this rule is that clients have a right to hire the lawyer of their choosing, and a covenant not to compete prevents clients from doing this. Thus, law firms cannot ask lawyers who are dismissed or quit to sign a document agreeing not to practice law in a geographic location or a substantive practice area permanently or for a period of time. By extension, the rule prevents firms from requiring departing lawyers to limit their practice in ways that accomplish the same result indirectly. The firm can, however, limit the right of the departing lawyer to solicit the firm's clients for legal work after the lawyer leaves the firm.

PROBLEMS AND QUESTIONS

1. If you were the hiring partner in a small firm, how would you decide when it made sense to hire a new lawyer? What about support staff?
2. What would you do to make sure that you interview the best possible candidates? Does it make sense to hire law students as part-time law clerks, and then select associates from the ranks of clerks?
3. Where might you look to find candidates for support staff positions? Community colleges? Other firms in the area? On line job boards?
4. How would you structure an orientation that forged a bond between the firm and its new employees?
5. In law offices where you have worked, how would you rate the evaluation and feedback or staff? If it was good, what made it so, in your mind? If it was not, what was lacking and how would you have made it better?
6. In addition to the benefits described on the list in Appendix G, what other benefits should lawyers expect? Can you think of some?
7. In recent years, questions of parental leave policies have increased dramatically. How much time should be allowed for parental leave? Should men *and* women be covered? May attorneys return to the firm post-leave at a reduced level of work? Will this extend the time to partnership?
8. Some companies use a "cafeteria" approach to benefits; each employee may allocate a benefit allowance for whichever benefits meet his or her needs. Can this concept work in law firms? Why or why not?
9. Should the benefits for nonlawyer employees be the same as for lawyers? Why or why not? Should professional employees (e.g., firm administrator)

be grouped with clerical employees or with the lawyers for purposes of benefits?

E. GETTING THE MOST OUT OF STAFF

In the business world, the topic of motivation has attracted much more attention than it has in the legal marketplace. We all have experiences dealing with offices where staff went out of their way to help us, did more than was asked with a smile, and appeared highly motivated in their work. We have all been to offices where everyone seems to be waiting for the 5:00 whistle, where no one seems to care whether you (the customer) come or go, and where no one seems to be motivated to do anything.

Just as we hope to encounter energetic, motivated people as consumers in the marketplace, we should strive to build such a staff when we are owners of a business. Not only does such a staff produce more work and build better customer or client relations, it is likely that the firm will experience less employee turnover in the long run. A firm with an experienced, stable, loyal and motivated staff inevitably will be more successful than a firm with unhappy, unmotivated employees, looking for their first opportunity to get out. Moreover, a firm that is always hiring and training new employees to replace others who have quit can never be as profitable as a firm with a stable core of experienced workers. The goal for employers is to inculcate loyalty and motivation.

PROBLEMS AND QUESTIONS

1. Could it be that short-term economic objectives have interfered with the long-term goal of effective production of legal services? Can law firms continue to ignore the professional development and personal satisfaction of associates and expect to succeed over the long term? Is it in the best interest of law firms and their staffs to address "lifestyle" issues?

2. Can you think of general management concepts that could help lawyers to motivate staff more effectively? Do rules for non-law businesses always apply in a law firm setting? Why or why not?

3. Prepare a human resources plan and organizational chart for your law firm staff. Include job descriptions and supervisory relationships to lawyers and firm management. See Appendix G, pages 463–465.

Chapter 9

Managing the Law Office

■ ■ ■

A. THE LAW OFFICE AS A PLACE TO WORK

This chapter takes a look at the law office—the physical space where the lawyers work and practice law. This chapter will consider various options for office space including rental, purchase and office sharing. You will learn what factors to consider when you select an office location, and evaluate what you will need to do to create an efficient and pleasant working environment. These elements not only provide the physical resources that you will need in order to deliver legal services effectively, but they also contribute to the firm's image in the eyes of clients and the public. Finally, you will conduct a cost benefit analysis of these resource alternatives and make recommendations to the firm accordingly.

All law firms have offices. The office is a physical embodiment of the firm's identity. It is often the first thing a client or prospective client sees and the last thing the client remembers about the firm. In terms of marketing, the law office is critical to the firm's efforts to reach its clientele. Visitors' impressions are molded by the location, design, decor and atmosphere of the office. In terms of the delivery of services, the organization and layout of the office are critical.

Although pundits have predicted the advent of the virtual law office, the truth is that everybody has to be some place. Whether that place is a laptop computer that goes where you go, a traditional office in a law firm in a glass tower in some city, or a desk in your own home, you will require physical resources to support your work. Organizations need an office to sustain an institutional self-image as much as they do to provide a workplace.

For most law firms the law office represents a home base for the business enterprise. This home base should provide functionality for the people who work there, as well as make a statement about the firm's image. It is not enough for the office to be pleasing to the eye; if it is not functional, it is not a good office. Too many law firms focus more on external or superficial considerations than operational ones. Anyone who has worked in an office that was non-functional for its purposes will appreciate the need to maintain space that works.

You will probably spend more time in your office than any place else in your daily life. If this place is not pleasant and conducive to productivity, it can have a profoundly negative impact on your psychological well-being. Conversely, a positive physical environment can make even the most onerous work palatable.

Each of us can think back over our work experiences to some work place that was physically unappealing. It may have been the dank, dark, dreary décor; it may have been a dangerous location; it may have been the sheer inefficiency of the place; it may have been that your personal workspace was claustrophobic or unmanageable. You may have experienced a workplace that had all these attributes and more. If you can remember this office from hell, you can probably also recall how much you hated to get up and go to work every day. You may note that you were unable to get as much done as you would have liked because of the physical limitations, and you might even reflect that when you left that job, the work environment was at least one (if not the only) consideration in your decision to leave. If you are still working at such a place, you are probably thinking to yourself, "I can't wait to get out."

In contrast, you may have had the opportunity to work in a place that made you feel good just going in every morning. The office was clean and bright. Everyone had sufficient space to get their work done; work flowed through the office quickly and efficiently and everyone seemed to enjoy being at work. If you can capture the image of that good workplace, you should set as a goal the re-creation of that environment in future offices.

As a law student or new associate, you may not be able to control some aspects of your physical surroundings, although you probably have some control over your own workspace. At some point in your career, you may have the opportunity to design office space for an entire firm. If you keep this vision in mind, you may be able to improve the quality of life for everyone in your organization. If this place is not pleasant and conducive to productivity, it can have a profoundly negative impact on the psychological well-being of everyone. Conversely, a positive physical environment can make even the most onerous work palatable.

A by-product of creating a positive and efficient environment for work is happy workers. Happy workers are productive workers, and long-term workers. The converse of this axiom is that a negative and inefficient work environment creates unhappy workers, and unhappy workers are unproductive short-term workers. While the effects of dissatisfaction and turnover caused by poorly designed offices are hard to document, studies have shown that environmental factors are important to workers. Thus, these intangible factors may have positive or negative effect on a law firm's effectiveness in providing legal services.

Fortunately, specialists in law office design—architects, engineers, decorators, consultants, and other lawyers—can help law firms plan their space requirements. Yet, the key to the successful design of office space is careful attention to the needs of all those who will be working in the setting and a cooperative approach to allocation of space and resources. It is easy to approach space problems from a territorial/political point of view, but such an approach is unlikely create the most efficient working environment for the firm.

PROBLEMS AND QUESTIONS

1. Have you ever worked in an office or other place that was inefficient, depressing and negative? What was it like? What made it that way?
2. Have you ever worked in an office or other place that was efficient, exciting and positive? What made it that way? What elements of that workplace could be implemented in less positive environments to make them more like your positive example?
3. In designing an office, is there a tension between appearance and functionality? How does a law firm balance the countervailing considerations?

B. OFFICE DESIGN

The law office provides a number of important functions for a law firm: it is the institutional and psychological work home for the people in the firm; it is the place where they conduct their business; it is a repository for records and information; it is a place where services are delivered to clients; it is a statement to the world about the identity and image of the firm.

Many law firms design their offices with little thought or imagination. They tend to replicate what they have seen at other law firms or offices where they have worked in the past. There are two prevalent approaches to law office design for law firms. The first starts with a glass box office building placing partners, in descending order of power, in windowed offices around the perimeter (corner offices or locations go to the senior partners, less appealing venues to lower level partners, and smaller or shared offices to associates). If any glass is remaining after the lawyers are ensconced in their offices, the most important nonlegal staff (e.g., the top law firm administrators) take what is left. The remaining support staff members, again in descending order of perceived importance, are ensconced within the bowels of the office box. Private but windowless inner offices go to administrators; senior legal assistants and secretaries get cubicles in a widened hall outside the lawyers' offices; and low-level clerical workers in whatever corners and cubbyholes can be dredged up. The center core of the box contains on one side the file room, copy room, and other work areas, and on the other side near the elevators, the reception room, conference rooms, restrooms, and other public places.

The second typical model is the old house. Particularly in many small towns, lawyers have purchased older homes in what was once the city's prime residential area but is now near the heart of its bustling downtown.

These lovely 19th century Victorians or earlier 20th century art deco masterpieces can be fixed up to make a great impression. They might even earn a firm a plaque for its efforts at historic preservation. Unfortunately, these gems are usually far less efficient as working offices than they were as houses. Designed as living space, houses almost never make the transition to business space with grace. The reception area may have once been a parlor; the conference room was the dining room; the lawyer's offices were once bedrooms (but at least they have adjoining baths); staff and work areas are often cut up out of living rooms, carriage houses and other assorted spaces. Almost all of these buildings have certain inherent inefficiencies (people have to run up and down stairs to see each other, make copies or conduct business; in one office, the only way to get from the parking lot into the building without going around a city block was through the senior partner's office). The plumbing, electricity, and structure of old buildings may be of dubious habitability, and some offices can even become a money pit. Old buildings seldom are accessible to the handicapped or elderly.

Some firms design office space from scratch. They sit down and figure out their needs. They retain competent architectural and engineering assistance and they obtain input from everyone who will be working in the office. The advantage to building from the ground up is that the firm can create an environment that meets its particular needs, rather than some generic law office. The disadvantage to designing an office from beginning to end is the time, energy, frustration and costs that typically accompany any building project. As with the crab, however, moving into someone else's digs may prove to be an uncomfortable fit, at best.

Many firms avoid having to deal with extensive design considerations by moving into space being vacated by other law firms, accounting firms, or other professional businesses. These firms are like hermit crabs, seeking a shell that is generally the right size and then wriggling in.

1. CORE FUNCTIONS

In one sense, legal work creates some general parameters for office layout. It might help to think about the office as comprising two distinct areas: the front office and the back office. In terms of the front office, image is a central consideration; in the case of the back office, efficiency is the key.

The front office is the part of the office that clients and the public see. The entrance usually leads into a reception area that is the first point of contact for clients. The rest of the public part of the office usually contains one or more conference rooms (depending on the size of the firm) and public facilities. The kitchen or lunchroom may also be incorporated into this area if it is used to provide food or refreshment for the conference or reception areas.

The back office is where the work is done. The back office usually contains individual offices or work places for lawyers and support staff.

This part of the office also contains workspace, equipment, communications and storage areas. The configuration of these activities should attempt to place work groups in close proximity, provide easy access to support functions, assure private and quiet workspace, and maximize the utilization of the space itself. Often, there is tension among these various objectives.

Space planning is much more than creating a set of floor plans. Today, Internet connectivity is an important consideration, just as telephone and fax service have been in the past. As technology advances, the options for connectivity increase, and the cost of upgrading service can be substantial.

Amenities, such as window treatments, art, plants, lighting, and furniture are important for people who work in the office, as well as visitors from the outside. In urban areas, parking may be a consideration for clients as well as staff. Depending on the location, heating and air conditioning considerations may be important. A myriad of other questions must be decided in even the simplest office layout plans. When a large firm moves from one location to another, the process can take years to plan and cost millions of dollars. Given the magnitude of the investment for law firms large and small, it makes sense to do it right.

2. THE INFORMATION RESOURCES CENTER

There was a time when almost every law office had a law library. Some small law offices utilized law school, court or cooperative libraries, most allocated one or more rooms to housing books and conducting legal research. Even firms that did not have a formal library maintained some small collection of books that lawyers and staffs used on a regular basis. The cost of providing space (often reinforced and always specialized), deliver retaining staff (frequently professionals with advanced degrees in library science), and implementing policies (e.g., purchase and circulation), all added to the cost of overhead in the law firm. Library space, in particular, could be burdensome on a firm with an extensive collection of books.

With the use of electronic databases and the Internet to conduct legal research and the migration of information resources to users' desktops (see Chapter 10), many firms are asking whether they need a law library at all—and most decide that the answer is no. Not only does a library facility require shelves, computers, desks and other amenities to support research activities, a card catalog or other indexing and checkout system that needs to be maintained. If the library is large enough, the librarian will require additional office space as well.

If the firm decides to maintain a formal space to conduct research it is more likely to be called an Information Resource Center (IRC) than a library. In some firms conference rooms double as (IRCs). The IRC can also be used as work space for law clerks, meeting and conference space

These multiple functions may be facially economical but often cause friction due to use conflicts in the long run.

If the firm decides not to dedicate specific space to the library, it must have a specific plan for distributing hard copy books—and no one has suggested that printed books and materials will disappear entirely from law offices—throughout the office Firms may house books in lawyers' offices, existing conference rooms, reception areas or hallways. When books are dispersed about the office, it may be more time-consuming to track down a volume than if the collection is housed in one central place. The importance of a locator system may increase. Additionally, DVDs and other electronic materials need to be stored in a designated accessible but secure place.

If a firm does not set aside space for a formal library, it must address a number of other questions, including:

- Delivering information to users in electronic form at their desktops or other workstations;
- Maintaining such print resources as the firm decides not to use in electronic form;
- Providing alternative space for activities that may once have occurred in the library, such as—
    - Conferences,
    - Firm meetings,
    - Training.
    - Law clerks
    - News clippings and announcements;
- Disposing of books that had been part of the firm's library in the past, but are no longer needed.

Regardless of what choices firms make about information systems (a topic discussed further in Chapter 10), the choices it makes will have implications for the allocation of space. Planning for space inevitably involves planning for how lawyers and staff will access, process, and deliver information in the electronic age.

3. SECURITY

A special consideration in law office design is security. Every business has some security considerations: avoiding theft, screening those who do not help the business at the office, limiting access to information. Because of lawyers' special responsibilities for the confidentiality of client information, security takes on special significance.

Lawyers are usually very cognizant of confidentiality requirements in their direct communications with adverse parties and other non-clients. In contrast, many lawyers do not realize that the office itself creates opportunities for the breach of client confidences. One common problem involves conversations about cases in public areas where they can be overheard by unintended third parties.

Another typical situation arises when lawyers meet clients in their offices rather than a conference room, and clients must walk through the work area of the law office. Visitors can sometimes see computer screens, read information on secretary's desks, see people they should not see, and even pick up documents if they are so inclined. Lawyers are sometimes called upon to hold client's property in trust, but have no safe or other secure location for storing such property. Inadvertently sending faxes or e-mail to opposing counsel or third parties is not an uncommon occurrence. Access to computer user files can be problematic as well. Despite the availability of password protection, encryption, and cloud storage, many firms are careless about the maintenance of electronic files. Unshredded trash containing sensitive documents can also be a source of compromise.

Although many of these problems can be addressed through the office policies governing individual behavior, the risks can often be minimized by the way the physical environment is designed. If consideration is given to where and how confidential information could fall into the wrong hands, planners can design space that minimizes if not eliminates those risks.

4. GROWTH

One area that is problematic for all firms is how to plan for growth or respond to a decline in size of the firm. If it were possible to design an office for a certain number of lawyers and staff, anticipating the amount of space necessary for the firm would be fairly predictable. No firm stays the same size forever, as the number of lawyers and staff fluctuates over time. Generally, law firms tend to grow as their business develops; sometimes the growth can be dramatic. Eventually, the space in which the firm is housed will become inadequate.

On the other hand, a decline in business, the departure of practice groups, the retirement of senior lawyers and periodic downsizing may leave the firm with too much space. If the firm leases or builds extra space in contemplation of growth that does not occur, it may end up paying for space that it does not use. If the firm experiences unanticipated growth, it may be forced to move, or lease non-contiguous space; there are no simple answers to these questions. Space planning should be incorporated in the larger process for strategic planning by the firm. It may not be possible to predict precisely what the firm's needs will be, but if the firm has an idea where it is going, it may be able to make some educated guesses.

5. LEASE OR PURCHASE

A final consideration in space planning is a central one: Should the firm lease or purchase office space? A law firm can either lease office space in a building or own its own space. There are advantages and disadvantages to each option, although the costs are comparable. The lease generally costs less up front, but the firm does not build equity to offset costs. The lease does not require the firm to cover maintenance, security, utilities, and other services, but the lessee pays the lessor a premium for these services. The only way to assess the relative merits is to add up all the costs associated with each option over the projected period of time the firm will use the space. In fact, each lease or purchase option will have to be compared to each other option in order to choose the best one. Even doing this, however, some variables, such as what the market for commercial office space will be like in the future, may be calculated guesses. As it is with buying vs. leasing a house or apartment to live in, the buyer makes the best guess she can with the information at her disposal and hopes for the best. An experienced real estate broker might be able to reduce some of this risk, but it can never be eliminated.

Problems and Questions

1. Take a look at the Model Law Office Floor Plan shown in Appendix I, page 474. What changes would you make to the layout in order to improve its efficiency? What are the space requirements for the typical law office? In what ways are the these requirements of a lawyer's office similar to and different from those of a doctor's office? Or an accountant's office?

2. What functional space does a law office need in order to carry on its work? What is the best way to provide work space for lawyers and staff? Cubicles or private offices? What are the advantages and disadvantages of each? What other activities of a law firm need specific space allocated to them?

3. How much will that space cost? Are there ways to save money with regard to your space needs? Are their things that you would not be willing to cut in order to reduce costs?

4. If you had to choose between rehabbing an older historical house close to the courthouse in the downtown area of the city where your firm is located, or a build-out of space in a newly constructed Class–A office tower also in downtown, or a build-out of office space in a suburban strip mall close to where lawyers in the firm live, which would you choose, and why?

5. What are the pros and cons of leasing office space vs. buying a building or office? Can you think of other alternative office arrangements that law firms or individual lawyers might consider?

6. Develop an illustrated working plan for the layout of your office. You should allow for workspace for all personnel and provide areas for other functions necessary for the operation of the law firm. Also, prepare an estimate for the cost to rent or buy space in the geographical area in which your firm will be located. See the checklist in Appendix H–1, pages 467–468.

C. INSIDE THE WALLS

1. OFFICE EQUIPMENT

This section will focus on planning the needs of the law firm for equipment, furniture and amenities. One of the fundamental issues facing law practice today is how to leverage computer technology to maximize the benefits for clients. Another issue is how to manage the process of change as systems evolve to reflect advances in technology. This task includes analysis of various facets of technology in light of automated approaches to the delivery of legal services. The materials in this chapter will look at how technology affects the people who work in law offices and will explore the implications of technological change on the future of the legal profession.

Most law students today have grown up around computers at school, at home and at work. They may not have a clear understanding of how to use technology, but they do appreciate its importance. For those students who somehow have avoided learning basic technology skills, it will be important to develop these tools, if not for this class, then certainly for the practice of law.

Lawyers, in one sense, are slaves to their equipment. They rely on machines to effectuate the delivery of legal services to their clients. Jay Foonberg, of Beverly Hills, CA, commented that lawyers are paper salesmen. "We give our clients paper," says Foonberg, who adds that the clients sometimes seem to think that they are buying paper rather than advice. He tells the anecdote of a lawyer who is called by a client on the phone, gives the client advice, and sends out a bill for $100.00. A second lawyer is called by his client and asked the same question. The second lawyer, however, puts his advice in writing and sends it to the client with a bill for $300.00. The first lawyer's client is upset with the bill, while the second is not, suggests Foonberg. Why? The paper is a concrete embodiment of the lawyer's effort. Although in today's world, lawyers may send clients e-mail messages with attached documents, the idea has not changed.

If we dealt exclusively in oral as opposed to written communication, office equipment would not be as important as it is. A desk, chair and couch would be sufficient for any law office that utilizes just oral communication. This is not reality. And because it is not, we must harness equipment in order to manage the paper that consumes our work.

The question of whether to buy or lease equipment is an important one. Firms cannot rely simply on the direct costs and tax consequences of equipment acquisition. They must consider the technological environment in the firm as well. For equipment that is technologically volatile, leasing may be a better alternative than purchasing. If the useful life of a piece of equipment is less than the life of the contract, a lease may be preferable. Furthermore, if the vendor provides for upgrades to lease holders, a lease may be the better alternative. If the item you acquire is likely to be as good in twenty years as it is today (e.g., a couch) purchase may make more sense.

2. COMPUTER SYSTEMS

The computer network is at the heart of the modern law office. New products, such as portable scanners, thumb drives, audio and video cards, tablets and smartphones, to name just a few, have forced businesses to regularly rethink their technology needs and to reinvest in technology applications and systems on a regular basis.

The challenge when writing about technology for a casebook is that the rate of change in technology is so rapid that much of what is written today is out-of-date before the book is printed. New cases can be handed down that overturn cases included in your substantive casebooks; imagine what it would be like if 80% of the reported cases were overturned every two years!

This section attempts to present the topic of law office computing broadly, without reference to current versions of hardware and software, which will be replaced by newer releases before the ink is dry on these pages. Although technology is constantly changing, a pattern of applications for law offices has emerged over the past two decades that will support legal services delivery systems. Law students, who may be very familiar with technology generally, still may need to learn more about technology specific to the field of law.

Large firms can spread the cost of new technology. They can hire professionals to free the lawyers and staff from technical details. They can hire consultants to assist them to provide training or to organize systems. They can operate redundant systems until the bugs are worked out. In solo practices and small firms the burden of transition falls directly on those who, at the same time they try to develop and learn new systems, must continue to operate old ones, increasing the burden of implementation substantially.

Obsolescence also impacts small firms more heavily. Large law firms have the luxury of treating the investment in technology as a regular budgeted expense, whereas small firms tend to view the acquisition of technology as a capital expenditure. Small firms would do themselves a favor by recognizing that they should budget for technology the same way they do for staff and other necessary costs of operation.

Although some small firms and solos have embraced technology, many struggle with technology issues. A few basic suggestions may help:

- designate someone in the firm to become the technology guru
- don't penalize people for the time they spend learning
- know when to use consultants
- read as many books and articles as possible

- go online for information (see, e.g., http://www.americanbar.org/groups/law_practice_management.html)
- talk to other lawyers who have dealt with the same problems
- budget money for maintaining and upgrading computer systems
- amortize the cost of technology over its useful life
- make the introduction of new technology as easy as possible
- don't try to do everything at once
- know what **you** want or need (as opposed to what looks cool) for your practice
- review your decisions periodically—in this area particularly, things change

Small firms and solo practitioners are constantly challenged when it comes to technology. If they intend to practice successfully in the new millennium, they do not have an alternative. Certainly there are choices about how to utilize technology, and all firms must make decisions based on their particular needs. They will have to invest psychologically as well as monetarily in order to remain competent, to compete with other service providers, and to gain control of their personal and professional lives.

Undoubtedly, technology offers many advantages to lawyers in the practice of law, although risks are implicit in the adoption of such technology. In the play *Inherit the Wind*, a dramatization of the Scopes Monkey Trial battle between Clarence Darrow and William Jennings Bryan, the Darrow character inquires:

> "Gentlemen, progress has never been a bargain. You've got to pay for it. Sometimes I think there's a man behind a counter who says, "All right, you can have a telephone; but you'll have to give up privacy, the charm of distance. Madam, you may vote; but at a price; you lose the right to retreat behind a powder-puff or a petticoat. Mister, you may conquer the air; but the birds will lose their wonder, and the clouds will smell of gasoline!"

3. OTHER TECHNOLOGY

Law offices rely on more equipment than just computers. Along with office space and staff salaries, increases in the cost of equipment have dramatically increased the cost of doing business for law firms. Law offices today could not function without telephones, copiers and other forms of equipment. As with computers, technology is changing many of these machines in profound ways. The sections below address some of the issues involved in planning for law office equipment needs.

Telephone systems have undergone and continue to be subject to rapid technological evolution. These technological advances have produced a fragmented and confusing marketplace. A telephone system represents a major investment for every law firm. Electronic communication has transformed the way lawyers send and receive documents along with such fundamental ideas as what constitutes a legally valid signature. Just a few years ago lawyers relied on a variety of other methods to do the same job, but more and more office functions have migrated to the electronic environment.

Advances in telecommunications have spread throughout the world, revolutionizing the connectivity of individuals and businesses. Today, it is possible to e-mail potential clients over the Internet, phone them, fax them, or maintain contact by digital wireless communications. The cell phone has become ubiquitous, and to call the communicating device a "telephone" is really a misnomer. Mobile communications devices not only send and receive audio, but text and images as well. Although there are some privacy and security risks associated with wireless communications (the calls are broadcast after all), more and more lawyers use wireless devices to keep up with their mobile practice and personal lives. In addition, many firms are utilizing VOIP (Voice Over Internet Protocol) technology as an alternative to land lines and wireless technology for telephone service.

Videoconferencing is becoming more common as the cost of video technology comes down and advances in technology to permit the transmission of the greater amounts of information needed for video. Short of true videoconferencing, many lawyers now use meeting software with streaming video permit real-time face-to-face meetings. This technology is available and being used in the marketplace, not some futuristic vision from a modern-day Jules Verne.

High speed transmission lines, communications satellites and microwave towers combine with traditional landlines to increase exponentially the volume of information that can be transferred almost instantly to anywhere in the world. Lawyers are learning that they must remain connected to their clients, their offices and the courts wherever they go. This constant availability imposes a new kind of tyranny on lawyers. Houston lawyer Sam Guiberson says that we are "hunter-gatherers of the electronic plain." By this he means that our work is no longer limited to the hours of 9–5, 5 days per week. With modern technology, we are available 24/7/365. Our Paleolithic forebears on the African plain were opportunists, who took their food where they found it. When a zebra wandered by the camp, they did not say, "We're off for the weekend. We'll catch it Monday." No. they hunted when they could, gathered when they had to, and survived the best they could.

The copy machine has become ubiquitous in the modern law office. Law firms today run on paper, and copies of documents are necessary to every law practice. It is difficult to imagine law practice without copy machines. At the same time, critics argue that lawyers are too dependent on paper, that they copy and save material that they will never need, and that many documents and images are better stored electronically.

Copy machines today are not like the copiers of a generation ago. These machines contain built-in computer memory and software that permits a range of functions that were unimaginable previously. Copiers can be connected to office networks, or detached, depending on the firm's needs. They can keep track of copies by user, client, department, date or other relevant factor. They have password security and electronic troubleshooting. They not only copy, sort, collate and staple, they also print, scan and fax. There are a variety of options from desktop copiers, to large commercial machines, to outsourced services.

Scanning technology is the reverse of printing. Instead of producing a hard copy of an electronic document, scanning reduces a hard copy to an electronic document. The electronic document can either be converted into manageable text in Word or some other program, or stored as an image, in Adobe (.pdf) or some other format. Simple scanning has been around for years, and firms routinely use scanners to produce documents that can be edited by users. Creating digitized documents has also been used to generate images that cannot be changed (at least not easily).

In the case of high-volume projects, imaging has replaced copying and storing in hard copy documents that need to be indexed stored and retrieved quickly and accurately. Most firms do not have the capacity to conduct imaging in-house, and so must use outside vendors to perform imaging services. Imaging technology has grown substantially in recent years, as the document management industry has taken on the task of converting masses of paper documents into images, which can be stored, indexed, retrieved and used. Think really big cases with warehouses of discovery, court records, university and law school libraries, and law firm case files. In projects like these, the imaging process may extend over months or years, but if digitized images themselves are useless unless they are accessible to the users of the data. The implications for law practice, for legal consumers and for the judicial system are just beginning to be felt, but most observers believe that they will be significant over time.

Voice recognition software has nearly replaced dictation equipment and stenographic dictation. Although some lawyers still prepare documents long hand or use stenographers, most opt for the speed and efficiency of dictation, and many compose documents themselves.

Several technological advances have expanded the horizons of computer use by lawyers. Fax technology allows exact copies of documents to be transmitted over the phone lines. Scanning technology permits hard copies of documents to be converted into computer files compatible with word processing programs. Imaging technology gives lawyers the option of transforming pictures, diagrams or text into a (bit-mapped) file that can be retrieved. Photocopy and laser printing technologies permit the reproduction and output of documents. Voice recognition systems allow computers to understand verbal commands from users. Satellite networks allow electronic information to be transmitted worldwide.

We are witnessing a merging of several technologies involving computers, through the Internet, over telephone lines, and by television over cable into an enormous interconnected worldwide network. Experimental programs explore these limits and set new boundaries. Within the professional lives of most students graduating from law school today, technological changes unheard of now will be introduced. The legal services environment inevitably will continue to change. The only constant in this milieu may be change itself. The issues for the real people who will be required to cope with these events cannot be dismissed. For the law firm manager the risks and opportunities make this an exciting and challenging period. For the practicing lawyer, also, the need to keep up with automation will be as important as the need to stay abreast of the law.

4. FURNISHINGS

To the casual observer the office furnishings—furniture, art, window treatments, lighting, flooring, signage, and other elements of office interior, are almost an afterthought. But ask the administrator of any law firm that has moved in recent years how much thought goes into all these questions. Everything from ergonomics, to OSHA standards, to firm image, to efficiency, to worker satisfaction is on the table (pardon the pun). The expense of furnishing a new office constitutes a major investment for any law firm relocation. An enlightened approach to lawyering requires careful consideration of environmental concerns, including furniture and the way it is laid out. The following article takes this inquiry one step further.

GO WITH THE FLOW: TAPPING INTO POSITIVE ENERGY IN OFFICE DÉCOR THROUGH FENG SHUI PRINCIPLES

From *ABA Journal*, by Hope Viner Sandborn (October 2001).

Debra Morse remembers the day when she and Cathleen McCandless—a consultant in the ancient Chinese art of feng shui—went to work in Morse's office. One of McCandless' first suggestions seemed rather provocative—that Morse put a thriving plant in a certain corner, a place that feng shui principles suggest is key to generating income.

Feng shui, the practice of living harmoniously with the energy of the surrounding environment, requires the careful placement of objects within that environment. If there is a positive flow of energy, feng shui adherents say, prosperity and good health will follow.

But can a plant in a corner of the office cause an attorney's practice to thrive?

Within 24 hours, Morse says, four new cases had been referred to her by attorneys she hadn't heard from in more than a year.

Morse, a plaintiffs lawyer who recently moved into her new office at San Diego's Kalafer & Associates, thinks that some of her newfound cases may very well be the result of the plant and her recent effort to design her office according to feng shui principles.

"It has to be more than mere coincidence," says Morse, an associate who handles medical malpractice, elder abuse and catastrophic injury cases.

Alexys Kalafer, the firm's senior partner, maintains that something changed after McCandless tinkered with Morse's office. "As much as I'd like to pooh-pooh it, I think it has some reality," she says.

When McCandless and Morse first closed the door and went to work, the staff and attorneys made fun of Morse. "We really thought she was out to lunch," recalls Kalafter. "But as soon as they opened the door, it was like this room had all sorts of excitement and energy. There was such an instant difference, and it wasn't about decorating. After all, they had the same things they started with."

Kalafer thinks that Morse's office now exudes positive energy and warmth. "It sounds crazy," she says, "but it is now a happy office."

Morse says she is comfortable and more productive in her workspace now. Kalafer puts it this way: "After McCandless' visit, Debra seemed to say, 'I'm at home. OK, let's get to work.' "

The Bar Is Now Open

Slowly, attorneys nationwide have begun using feng shui to improve their offices, as doctors and dentists have done for some time now. Even some bar associations are hosting seminars on the practice. The Denver Bar Association, to name but one, has had its lobby redone in accordance with feng shui principles.

Part of the reason for the interest in feng shui, even from people who might otherwise be skeptical of such things, is that it can be quite practical, even commonsensical in its approach to design.

. . .

"The office should give an impression of beauty and success," McCandless says. "When you surround yourself with beauty, success will follow."

One key feng shui tenet well-worth considering is that your seat should face your office door—not necessarily in a direct line but so you can see people as they enter. This gives you control over the space and makes you feel more confident. It's also more inviting for guests.

Denver attorney Miles Cortez recalls how, after he made that small change, clients and colleagues noticed the difference, saying the office felt more comfortable.

Cortez also eliminated clutter from his office, to create a more pleasant and welcoming environment—another important feng shui principle. "Clutter gives the impression of confusion or of overextension," says Cortez.

"Most of us who do well in the business are overextended. But you don't want to give that impression, you want to give the impression that you are there to attend to clients' needs."

Clutter also impedes energy flow, says Kathy Zimmerman, a California feng shui consultant and instructor. "It is not peaceful to work in." She suggests placing only the project you are currently working on atop your desk. Keep others out of sight to avoid feeling overwhelmed.

Placing colorful artwork, especially pieces depicting nature, in an office is also important. Cortez already had a lot of art, but a feng shui consultant helped him place it strategically to create a better energy flow.

"Everybody should concentrate on having a glorious work area," says Cortez. "You spend a lot of time in the office and you do a lot of stressful things in it. It is important to have a comfortable, pleasant, welcoming atmosphere."

5. SUPPLIES

The preceding discussion covered the major equipment groups found in law offices. There are literally hundreds of minor pieces of equipment that a particular firm may want or need (e.g., electric pencil sharpeners, disk holders, binders, and the old, reliable postage machine). These items are usually grouped with supplies (e.g., pens, yellow pads, stationery) as an office expense. Individually, these items are inexpensive; collectively they represent a substantial fixed annual cost. At the same time, it is important for the office to have sufficient supplies and adequate small equipment on hand to carry on the work of the office smoothly and efficiently. Someone in the office needs to be responsible for ordering, maintaining and distributing supplies to users. Without controls the supply closet door can become an expensive drain on the firm's financial resources.

You may react to this litany of office products like the boy who received *The Encyclopedia of Penguins* from his grandmother as a birthday present: "It contains more than I care to know." But equipment is much more relevant to the work of lawyers than penguins are to the life of the average kid. Since lawyers subsist on equipment and the technology to drive it, they should understand this complex and growing field, which will continue to evolve in the coming decades.

PROBLEMS AND QUESTIONS

1. Prepare an inventory of all law office equipment you will need to acquire in order to operate your law firm. Make the necessary selection of vendors and turn in a summary of costs for acquisition, operation, and maintenance of all equipment. If certain functions are to be contracted out,

describe the arrangements, costs, and rationale for doing so. See the checklist in Appendix H–2, pages 469–472.

2. Recommend a computer hardware system for your office. Since you will cover the acquisition of software for office applications in other assignments, this assignment should focus on the equipment side of the equation. Explain the costs of acquisition and operation of the necessary hardware and support.

3. What price do we pay for technology? What does a firm lose when uses technology to deliver legal services? Consider the following scenarios. What are the practical, legal and ethical issues for lawyers?

- A paralegal in your firm is dismissed for absenteeism. In anger, she reformats the hard disk on her computer destroying hundreds of client files. Many documents are backed up with hard copies; many are not.

- At 4:30 on the afternoon of a 5:00 filing deadline for an appeal, a severe electrical storm knocks out the power in your building. The computer is down until after 6:00. The Clerk's office closes promptly at 5:00. Although copies of your documents are available on a flash drive, you made numerous revisions to your work during the final day. These changes were not saved, and were wiped out in the power failure.

- An associate in the firm announces his resignation, giving you one month notice. On his last day of work, he mentions that he has copied all the firm's forms, client lists, and software for his new office. The forms, while somewhat standard, have been modified over a period of years by the firm. The client lists are considered an asset of the firm, although the information could probably be pieced together from other sources. The software is all licensed by various vendors.

- The firm utilizes an electronic communications network. An adversary has anticipated nearly every recent move of the firm in a high-stakes lawsuit, leading the attorney on the case to conclude that someone is hacking into the firm's computer files surreptitiously through the network.

- On the same network the firm is served with a complaint against a longstanding client. The lawyer handling the case assumes immediately that such service is invalid. Some time later the same lawyer receives in her electronic mailbox a copy of a summary judgment order in the case.

- On the firm's internal electronic mail system, a woman who works as a receptionist receives a series of sexually suggestive anonymous messages. She threatens to sue the firm on sexual harassment grounds if the unwanted conduct does not stop.

- The firm's office manager who implemented almost all of its computer systems, and is the only person who understands how the entire system works, comes in for an annual review demanding that the firm double her salary. If not, she will quit.

4. In addition to the equipment described in this chapter, can you think of other equipment that law firms must obtain?

5. How should the firm budget for supplies and small equipment? How should the firm control these costs? Should the firm do anything to prevent the unauthorized conversion of supplies and small equipment? Why should it matter?

6. Is the task of furniture selection and placement one that can or should be delegated to a consultant with expertise in the area? Should individual lawyers and staff make decisions about their own workspace or should such questions be handled as a matter of firm policy? How much money should the firm spend on "curtains and drapes"? If you had to choose among a great computer system, higher compensation or more pleasant surroundings, what would you choose? Why?

7. What do you think about applying feng shui principles to your office design? If not feng shui, then what elements go into the ambiance of your office? What look and feel do you want to achieve and why?

D. WHAT LIES AHEAD?

Assuming that computers are here to stay and assuming further that the technology will continue to advance (or, in the minds of the cynical, at least evolve), it is fair to conclude that law practice will continue to change. It follows that the this change will alter the way we work, the places we work, and our relationships with the people with whom we work. This means that the law office as a place to work will continue to evolve as well. As is the case with other areas of practice management, wise practitioners will stay abreast of these events while the less prudent will continually struggle to catch up.

THE MOBILE LAW OFFICE—FROM LINCOLN TO THE LINCOLN LAWYER

From New York State Bar Association Journal, by Gary Munneke (September 2011).

Mickey Haller runs his practice from the back of a Lincoln Town Car, with the help of an ex-con driver, traversing the freeways and surface roads of L.A. Working from the back of his mobile office, Haller is able to interview clients and witnesses, to make required court appearances and to enjoy the other accoutrements of Angelino life. Perhaps this is author Michael Connelly's idiom for the fractured life of the 21st century lawyer.

The story of the Lincoln lawyer, however, really starts out with Lincoln, the lawyer. The other Lincoln, who practiced law in the 1830s to the 1850s in central Illinois, before going on to bigger things as an icon of American history, was then and now the quintessential trial attorney. As a boy, I lived in Decatur, the self-proclaimed "Soybean Capital of the World," an agrarian metropolis about halfway between the capital—Springfield—and the campus of the University of Illinois—"Fightin' Illini"—Urbana–Champaign. None of this would be germane to this article but for the small log cabin, which was used as a courthouse, located in

Decatur's Fairview Park, where Lincoln, the lawyer, tried several cases as a circuit-riding lawyer.

After learning the law by reading legal commentaries at night, because he couldn't quit his day job, Lincoln was admitted to the Illinois bar on September 9, 1836, after successfully passing an oral, not written, examination, and being certified as possessing good moral character. In the spring of 1837, Lincoln associated himself with J.T. Stuart, in Springfield, and later a partner, Stephen T. Logan, before taking on William Herndon as his junior partner. During this period, Lincoln customarily spent about six months of every year "riding the circuit," trying cases in local communities too small to have permanent courthouses or established local practitioners.

The elegant Greek Revival Lincoln–Herndon Law Offices in Springfield attest to Lincoln's success in the practice of law. The building is fit for a respected barrister and budding politician on the American stage. Lincoln's office would be at once familiar to visitors from our era, who would observe a receiving area, plush offices for the two partners, and back office spaces for files, supplies, and real work. To this day the Lincoln–Herndon model epitomizes law offices throughout the United States.

Lincoln the circuit rider traveled by horse following the courts from county to county in a land where the legal system was still in its infancy. Lincoln found work by traveling to the work. He built a clientele by representing real people in real disputes. When he returned to a circuit venue, so did his clients, and they recommended him to their friends and neighbors, eventually leading him to bigger clients like the Illinois Central Railroad, and the good life in the capital. In one sense, Michael Connelly's Mickey Haller is a modern-day paean to the original Lincoln Lawyer.

This leads to the question: (with apologies to the Bard) "What's in an office? A workplace by any other address would smell as sweet." What is the purpose of this brick-and-mortar edifice that most of us commute to daily to carry out our work? For many of us, in order to reach this home away from home, we sit in congested traffic or battle the mobs on commuter trains on a daily basis. A lawyer who spends 10 hours in the office, five days a week, 50 weeks each year, will spend 2,500 hours over the course of 250 days in a year at this place—and if we are honest, many of us spend many more hours and many more days than that in the office. For what?

The traditional answer is that we go to a place to do work. For lawyers, the office was the physical location where they went to carry out the multitude of tasks associated with the practice of law. It was a place where they could meet with clients, confront adversaries, conduct negotiations and confer with their partners and associates about cases; it was where the business of delivering legal services took place. The law office was the physical repository of files and records associated with client matters, a storage facility for supplies, and a home for office machines and equipment ancillary to the practice of law. The office was also a workplace for support staff, where lawyers would go to manage and supervise the people who worked for them.

For Lincoln, the office in Springfield was a base of operations from which he launched his circuit practice and political campaigns, but it was also convenient to the two courts in which he appeared most often, the United States District Court for Illinois and the Illinois Supreme Court, where his reputation as an advocate was legendary. With a partner back in Springfield, Lincoln could represent clients on the circuit while still maintaining a visible presence and servicing clients at the home base.

Arguably, electronic communication systems offer an efficient alternative to the traditional model epitomized by the Lincoln–Herndon office. Today, lawyers and staff can work at home (or wherever they might be), access files and other resources via the Internet, and handle all those contacts with clients, other lawyers and third parties without ever going to their law office. Like the movable practice of Mickey Haller and Abe Lincoln before him, the 21st century law office is not anchored to the ground. This mobility presents a number of questions and opportunities.

. . .

What is the purpose of an office? Is it just an anachronistic throwback to an era when electronic communication did not exist? . . . [P]ractitioners have a great deal invested in having an office—if it was good enough for Lincoln, it should be good enough for us. Somewhere in the back of my mind, however, a little voice keeps repeating that the future might not be the same as the past.

Law offices are the product of an era when workers had to go to a central location to do their jobs. Whether they worked in a factory or an insurance company, one had to be there or be square. The Industrial Revolution introduced the concept of aggregating a workforce that could deliver products and services on an exponentially larger scale than the cottage industries that preceded industrialization. The late J. Harris Morgan, the father of modern law practice management, often said that lawyers were like tailors, handling one case at a time, when they should be delivering their services on an assembly line. Whether or not Morgan was right about the need to automate the delivery of legal services, he assumed (in the 1970s and 1980s) that lawyers would provide these services out of a law office. The sea change that now confronts us is the notion that the physical office may be superfluous.

An office, however, provides lawyers more than a desk and chair. An office imbues its occupants with a professional identity—an ephemeral sense that they belong somewhere that they can call their work home: "If you want me, you can find me here." Arguably, this sense of connection between us and our work in a physical space is more important than many people realize. It may also be the case that for lawyers trying to strike a balance between their personal and professional lives, having an office to go to in the morning is as important as having a home to go back to in the evening.

A law office creates a visual identity for the law firm. Whether it is located in an old house on "lawyers' row," a high-rise office tower in Center City, a downtown storefront, a multi-lawyer suite, or a strip mall in the 'burbs, the setting of the office says volumes about its occupants. Inside, the furniture, art, floors and other visuals contribute to the unique identity of each and every firm, reflecting the collective personality of the organization that inhabits this environment. Whether this *je ne sais quoi* reflects an institutional culture or the particular personalities of firm leaders, the law office embodies the lifeblood of the firm. We might fairly ask whether a law firm can exist without the law office to capture its personality and culture. We might also ask whether a law firm can stay together for long if its workers are dispersed to the four winds and they have no core, no hive, to which they can return.

Perhaps the most important aspect of the law office is the human contact among the people who work there and the visitors who pass through. In a workplace, we get to know our fellow workers. We laugh and cry with them; we fight with them; we face mutual challenges with them. We get to know them as individuals, and we share with them the camaraderie of a common enterprise. Sometimes, face time matters. It might be possible to restructure the office to eliminate the extraneous influences, to improve efficiency, and to support flexibility, but these improvements have to be weighed against what is lost, which may be the *esprit de corps* that translates into loyalty to the organization and its leaders. Maybe the physical law office has a value organizationally, which cannot be quantified, which many of us take for granted, but which we dispense with at our peril.

The answer may be that we need our law offices more for our own self-image and professional peace of mind than as a necessary element in the legal service delivery process. To the extent that a law firm develops an institutional identity, the law office might be the glue that holds the firm together. Will employees have the same loyalty to the institution if it does not exist anywhere in the temporal world? Will the next generation of lawyers, raised on computer games and social networking, find the current crop of lawyers' need for face-to-face contact as strange as they would find riding a horse around the circuit to represent their clients? The answers to these questions are less than clear.

There is little doubt that the physical law office is changing. Libraries, which, not too long ago, took up considerable space in most law firms, are ancient history for many firms that do their legal research electronically. File rooms in many firms have shrunk as paper records have been digitized and stored electronically. Secretarial pools have disappeared as the role of legal secretaries has evolved. And if predictions hold true that many firms will be hiring fewer associates in the years ahead, the footprint of the law firm will continue to shrink. Given the facts that law firms spend more on office space than any overhead expense except salaries, and that the cost of office space has risen dramatically in recent years, this is not a bad thing. To the extent that economic considerations drive the way law offices use physical space, it will not be surprising to see firms choose alternatives that cost less money and further reduce the brick-and-mortar workplace.

. . .

Many law firms are experimenting with office alternatives. Given that more than a few law firm dissolutions have been triggered at least in part by rent and other occupancy expenses, there are powerful incentives to build a better mousetrap. Technology provides the tools to innovate change, but the risk of getting it wrong is formidable as well. Will lawyers in the next generation work from home, a Lincoln Town Car, a professional hive, an office hotel, or just practice wherever they happen to be? Will law firms in office buildings and Lincoln–Herndon offices be recognizable to lawyers of the next generation? Will we all be chauffeured around in Lincoln Town Cars to ply our trade? Will lawyers exist only in cyberspace, delivering e-services to clients they never see, assisted by staff they never meet? Will the brick-and-mortar law office survive, and if so, will it need to evolve to do so? Only time will tell.

THE 21st CENTURY LAW OFFICE ... IT'S NOT YOUR FATHER'S OFFICE ANY MORE

From *Probate and Property* (February, 2000).
By Dennis L. Greenwald.

One of the challenges for the real estate industry in the new millennium will be determining how ongoing technological advances will affect the development and use of real estate. With technological advances occurring at an accelerating pace, making well-founded predictions about the development and use of real property very far into the 21st century is daunting, to say the least. As that great philosopher and former New York Yankee Yogi Berra, once said, "prediction is really difficult ... especially when it's about the future!"

Nevertheless, certain themes of how individuals and businesses will use the office workplace are emerging. For example, high speed telecommunications, telecommuting and other "live-work" models, the "paperless workplace" and the personal computer as the "virtual office" seem permanent fixtures of tomorrow's workplace. There is little doubt, then, that technological change will necessitate new models for developing, sizing, configuring and using office space and, correspondingly, new ways of dealing with the leasing process, lease terms and conditions and the lawyer's role in negotiating leases.

Changes in Physical Space: Technology, Technology, Technology

If "location, location, location" has historically been the catch phrase for real estate, a future motto might well be "technology, technology,

technology." Technology will have such an enormous impact on the workplace that new and old buildings will need technological amenities to be competitive. Being technologically advanced, however, will mean more than just having so-called cutting edge or state of the art technological capabilities, because today's technology can easily be obsolete tomorrow.

To be competitive, office buildings will need to be what is sometimes called "techno-ready"—that is, capable of accommodating new (and perhaps not yet created) technologies. For example, some developers are creating vertical conduits for future technologies, whether it be fiber optic technology or something not yet invented. As a more complicated example, building designers are increasingly trying to make building systems "application independent." In other words, the building wiring will be able to accommodate different software architecture instead of a single software architecture. Unfortunately, because technological applications outgrew the technological hardware of what were called "smart buildings," those buildings now seem like dunces. Thus, forward thinking developers are focusing as much on technological *flexibility* as they are on being state of the art.

Mobility

Technological advances in the office environment have resulted in changes in both the speed with which information is transmitted and the method for transmitting information. Until very late in the 20th century, information was transmitted manually and, consequently, relatively slowly. Overnight mail couriers and fax machines, both of which are of relatively recent vintage, changed the model for transmitting certain kinds of information. Until the use of the personal computer became pervasive, however, the typical way of accessing a piece of information was the same during the 1980s as it was for most of this century—namely, by having the file folder in one's hand.

Beginning in the 1980s, information could be sent via overnight mail with efficiency. Even then, written information was still fundamentally anchored to a particular location until someone could manually retrieve it. Cyberspace, with its laptop computers and wireless e-mail devices, has brought the method for transmitting information to an entirely new dimension. The result has been that information formerly housed in one specific location, available only during office hours, by only one person at a time, is now available to an unlimited number of people, all at the same time, 24 hours a day, every day. As a consequence, employees need not have access to a specific office to access information or to communicate with one another, their customers or clients.

Thus, instead of retrieving information by driving to an office, picking up a file and driving to a meeting at another location (and thereby precluding anyone else from accessing that information while an employee is absent with the file), all an employee needs is a laptop to access the same information. This is one of the reasons why the computer is sometimes called the "virtual office."

The net effect of this change in communications and information technology is that employees need not necessarily have one specific office every day, less space is required per employee and employees can effectuate live-work or other telecommuting models, spending less time at the office. Depending on the particular kind of business, employees also might be able to work staggered hours, because information can be accessed, modified and transmitted to others independently of whether other employees are available.

Architectural and Design Reconfiguration

These trends will affect future changes in the physical space of offices, such as smaller individual offices, diminished requirements for filing, copying and other office services, increased telecommuting, fewer on-site employees, larger mechanical closets and computer and other technological equipment rooms. It is therefore reasonable to conclude that the size and configuration of floor plates will change. One change likely to occur first will be the conversion of internal, windowless space (which in high rise buildings has traditionally been used for office services such as filing, copying and mailroom functions) into work stations. Another significant change will be the shrinkage, if not the complete elimination, of libraries and other areas containing written reference materials. Hard copies of those materials will be taken off of shelves and loaded into the computer. There might even be a reduction in the size of parking areas as a result of increased telecommuting and fewer full-time, on-site personnel.

Not all technological changes, however, will result in a reduction in office space requirements. Increased technology usually requires larger computer rooms and other mechanical closets to house the larger hardware for a business's computer needs.

If offices become more portable and office space therefore becomes more utilitarian, tenants may be unwilling to pay for certain architectural amenities such as more elegant building lobbies and other common areas. Indeed, as technology increasingly becomes important, developers might redirect dollars that they have historically devoted to design elements to pay for technological infrastructures.

Technological advancements might change the way commercial developments are built and configured in countless ways. Consider the following as a small representative sampling. With the growth of online shopping, will certain kinds of retail stores disappear or require less space? What will video stores have to offer when viewers can rent movies by means of satellite transmission? Will the number of libraries and other reference and information centers decrease or at least diminish in size as their materials become readily available via the Internet? Will the demand for branch banks decrease as consumers increasingly conduct banking transactions by electronic means?

. . .

Office? ... What Office?

With the proliferation of increasingly inexpensive communication devices such as mobile phones, voice mail, car fax machines, laptop computers, home computers, home printers, home faxes, hand-held e-mail devices (that require neither electrical current nor a phone line), as well as new devices constantly coming on the market, who needs an office? That question is, of course, an exaggeration; but parties should consider how office technology is already beginning to change dramatically the size and use of office space.

- **Voice mail**. Voice mail and automated phone operation have reduced, and in some cases eliminated, the need for telephone receptionists. The potential result is not only fewer employees but also reduced space requirements.

- **Mailrooms**. Remember the mailroom? A number of employees performed numerous tasks, including copying, sending and receiving faxes, distributing mail, faxes and interoffice memoranda; delivering documents downstairs, across the street or across town; taking baskets of mail to the post office twice a day; moving boxes of files around the office and to and from off-site storage; and a variety of other tasks principally directed at moving paper manually. With the introduction of the computer and e-mail, these jobs are either eliminated or drastically reduced. Thus, office services areas, including file rooms, will diminish in size. Who needs all those copiers, fax machines, messengers and filing clerks when they can transmit so many documents via e-mail and download them onto disks instead of hard copies? Also, there is less need for all of those employees.

- **Office as dataport**. In the future, a telephone and a dataport may be all a number of office workers need to perform most of their job functions. This is particularly true for employees who travel or otherwise have jobs that demand a great deal of mobility. Indeed, files and other paperwork will be an encumbrance rather than a necessity. As a result, there will be less need for file space, secretaries and other traditional office amenities.

- **Telecommuting**. Employees can telecommute and leave the driving to someone else. If a paperless office can largely be accomplished, then telecommuting or other live-work arrangements (that is, working part-time or full-time from home or other off-site locations) becomes a fact of office life for certain kinds of employees. There will be less need for office space; more flex time for certain employees (because information is available 24 hours a day on the computer and access to that information is not necessarily dependent on the presence of other employees); fewer office amenities; and perhaps a reduced need for parking.

- **Conference rooms**. With the advent of videoconferencing and other Internet-based meetings, there is some debate as to whether businesses will require more or fewer conference rooms. On the one hand, Internet-based meetings can be handled on a single computer screen and there is no need to congregate in a conference room. On the other hand, with increased telecommuting and smaller office size, in-person meetings might increasingly occur in conference rooms instead of individual offices.

- **Voice recognition technology**. Technology is being developed so that text can be input through voice recognition. As a result, there will be less need for secretaries and certain other staff. Again, fewer employees may mean diminished space and parking requirements.
- **Proximity**. As we move closer to having paperless offices, various departments within a business can communicate with each other without transmitting information manually. The effect of this will be that various departments will no longer need to be geographically centralized. There will be more "satellite" offices and perhaps less need for tenants to require options to expand into contiguous space.

There is, of course, no blueprint for dealing with ongoing technological changes in the workplace. We can be certain, however, that technological changes will continue to occur with increasing speed. This process will necessitate flexibility and adaptability for landlords, tenants and their counsel if they are to remain efficient and competitive. No doubt, offices and office buildings in the 21st century will look increasingly different and function differently as technologies are designed and implemented.

Some specific trends are clear, such as smaller and less paper-intensive offices, increased dependence on communication technologies, more telecommuting and other live-work arrangements and geographic decentralization. Longer range trends are more difficult to predict, but the business community is wisely developing a "be flexible or die" mentality toward technological change. The business community seems keenly aware of another Yogi Berra aphorism: "The future, there's just no stopping it!"

PROBLEMS AND QUESTIONS

1. What are the implications generally for organizations that downsize their physical office space in favor of work arrangements where employees work from home or mobile locations? Will this trend impact service industries like law more than it will manufacturing or direct sales industries?
2. Can lawyers reap the benefits of combining a physical office with virtual work environments? How? Will the need for less physical space reduce the cost of doing business for law firms, or will other expenses arise to replace those of maintaining an office?
3. Will the "virtualization" of law firms impose challenges to the institutional cohesiveness of law firms; in other words, can you have a law firm

when, as Gertrude Stein said about Los Angeles, "There is no there there."?

4. What would a virtual law firm look like? Where would lawyers and staff work? Where would lawyers meet clients? What would happen to paper records law firms traditionally keep?

CHAPTER 10

MANAGING INFORMATION AND TECHNOLOGY RESOURCES

■ ■ ■

A. THE INFORMATION BUSINESS

In this chapter, we will discuss how to organize, manage, and develop law office information resources, including print and electronic resources and databases. You will assess the needs and costs for acquiring and maintaining these resources. You will consider various alternatives to traditional libraries including DVDs and on line services. You will also explore the avenues for managing the information available to you through technology.

It should be readily apparent to anyone who thinks about it: Lawyers are in the information business. Much of what we refer to as "legal advice" is, in fact, information about the rights and responsibilities of our clients under the law, or communications with others—opposing parties, courts, and administrative agencies, and public media—on a variety of levels. Lawyers who cannot find, process, analyze, and disseminate information cannot fulfill their responsibilities adequately. With respect to clients, Model Rule 1.4, states: "A lawyer shall keep his client reasonably informed about the representation," but the lawyer's duty to inform does not end there.

It is not news that we are in the midst of an international information revolution. Much as the printing press in the 15th century transformed medieval society, computer and communication technologies have transformed our world into a new Information Age. In some ways, this Information Age promotes universal egalitarianism: information is equally accessible to everyone. Once the private domain of scholars, religious leaders, and political powerbrokers, the average person on the street with the wherewithal to look can gain access to almost any information. The impact of this phenomenon has been analyzed by futurists (see e.g., Marshall MacLuhan in *The Gutenburg Galaxy*; Alvin Toffler in *Future Shock,* Tom Friedman, *The World Is Flat*), and the media (see e.g., *The Matrix,* a film in which machines subjugate the human race).

The relationship between information provider and end user of information is changing as well. While information tends to be more accessible, there is so much information that many people find themselves overwhelmed—awash in a sea of information. This disconnect challenges the ability of information users to find and exploit information efficiently in the electronic environment. It should not be surprising that individuals with specialized skills are helping those who need information to manage it more productively. In the world of electronic information, the process of disintermediation (sometimes referred to as "cutting out the middleman") eliminates the information wholesaler, who merely passes on information that consumers could obtain directly. At the same time, purveyors who can add value to transactions for consumers become more helpful.

The travel business provides a good example of this phenomenon. Travel agents suffered greatly when consumers learned that they could go to on line travel Web sites to book flights, hotels and cars, and to access other travel-related information. Travel agents who developed special value-added expertise (e.g., what are the best hotels in China?) succeeded because they improved the efficiency of information delivery. In short, travel agents who learned to add value to consumer transactions have thrived, and those who failed to add value have found themselves at a competitive disadvantage.

Lawyers have to figure out how to add value to legal transactions. Lawyers serve as cyber-guides to clients with respect to legally-related information. Yet, huge amounts of legal information is accessible through electronic databases—laws, court decisions, legal analysis, forms, and guidance. Lawyers who simply give clients what they can easily find on line (and probably more cheaply) will find it hard to stay afloat. Conversely, lawyers who use the raw information to make sense of legal information, and thereby add value to legal transactions will become invaluable to clients.

The information revolution raises some troubling questions, to be sure. It is now possible to collect vast amounts of personal information, to invade the privacy of others, and to commit criminal acts on a level never before imagined in history. Information is the proverbial double-edged sword, with the potential for both good and evil. Lawyers and other inhabitants of cyberspace must now address a new set of ethical issues.

If technology is revolutionizing legal services to clients, it should not come as a surprise to learn that it is revolutionizing the business of law as well. Fortunately, from the beginning of the computer era, some lawyers have pushed the limits of technology, and stayed on the cutting edge of developments in the computer industry. A number of tech companies have focused on creating applications for law and other professional offices. As succeeding generations of technological advancement have entered the legal marketplace (a generation representing one to two years), new products have been more powerful and user-friendly than the ones they replaced. Today, almost all law offices are wired, and although some have embraced technology with greater enthusiasm than others, most lawyers recognize that they need to add value to clients by managing legal information in ways that clients cannot, and by delivering services more economically than clients could obtain them through self-help or nonlegal competitors.

B. COMPUTER APPLICATIONS IN THE LAW OFFICE

This section highlights the primary computer applications designed for law offices (See Chapter 9 for a discussion of hardware products.) Computer applications are programs for the computer, written for a particular purpose. The "software" tells the "hardware" what to do. Before the widespread availability of commercial software, computer programs were either written for a specific user or installed in dedicated equipment (e.g., a standalone word processor). Generally, there are three types of application software: generic, industry specific, and customized. Generic software is designed to handle a particular type of task regardless of the industry (e.g., word processing). Industry specific software is designed to handle a type of task unique to an industry (e.g., legal timekeeping/billing). Customized software is programmed for a specific user and application. Increasingly, generic and industry-specific commercial software programs are flexible enough to allow modification to meet the needs of specialized users, thereby reducing the demand for customized programs.

Most small law firms will require many, if not all, of the following technology practice applications:

- high level work processing
- document assembly
- project management
- calendaring
- personal information management
- time and billing
- financial management
- knowledge management
- spreadsheet
- presentation
- practice system management
- conflicts checking
- case management
- client relationship management
- access to the Internet

- e-mail
- data and file transfer
- encryption and security
- electronic research
- shopping
- document scanning/copying/faxing
- video conferencing
- continuing legal education

Many of these applications are available commercially, but some are proprietary. A generic commercial solution might not suit all firms, but many will find that most of their computing needs are met with the software they bought with their computers. In order to make good decisions, lawyers should compare *all* the associated costs and benefits of the alternatives they are considering:

- purchase price
- hardware purchases and upgrades
- installation costs (including lawyer/staff time)
- consultant costs
- conversion expenses (conversion from manual or older computer systems)
- learning costs
- lost time due to unfamiliarity or working out the bug
- value of time saved (hours x billing rate)
- the number of hours the program will be used

An application that is used two hours per day 250 days per year for three years would be in actual use for 1,500 hours during this period. Another application might only be used once a month for four hours over the three year period—less than 150 hours. If both products cost $1,500, the first one would cost $1/hour and the second $10/hour. This provides a much more accurate picture of the cost than by looking at the purchase price alone.

More law firms are investing in cloud technology, which involves a subscription price for application software, which is updated on an ongoing basis, rather than by periodic upgrades. Cloud computing can also reduce the requirements for office servers and document storage space, and allow users to access technology from wherever they can connect to the Internet.

Small law firms and solo practices that elect to use generic software may find that it is sufficient to meet most of their law office computing needs, and that acquisition of more expensive products designed for law offices specifically is unnecessary. The following list of programs illustrates how an office can accommodate many of its needs using off-the-shelf products, many of which come pre-loaded on new computers. Although this example uses Microsoft Office Professional, WordPerfect Office would provide the same coverage.

- MS Word: word processing
- MS Access: client database including conflicts checking and a file numbering system
- MS Outlook: personal calendars, mailing and to do lists, as well as for intra-office communications (the receptionist maintains an Outlook file containing a firm-wide calendar with appearances, statutes of limitation, meetings, conference room bookings, and other important firm-wide dates)
- MS Excel: real estate settlement sheets and other financial calculations
- MS PowerPoint: trial and other presentations
- MS Internet Explorer: internet access and communications
- Timeslips: timekeeping and billing
- QuickBooks: budget and financial matters; trust accounting; payroll
- HotDocs: document assembly
- Amicus Attorney: Case Management

A 2011 Report of the New York State Bar Association Task Force on the Future of the Legal Profession addressed the question of technology in the practice of law in some detail. The section of the report addressing those issues is included below:

TECHNOLOGY AND THE PRACTICE OF LAW

New York State Bar Association Task Force on
the Future of the Legal Profession (2011).

The practice of law has been through a period of rapid technological innovation during the last twenty-five years. Although the basic nature of legal services generally remains the same, the way we practice has changed dramatically. One of the clearest examples of this change is in the realm of technology and knowledge management....

Given the many, varied, and increasing technological changes in recent years, it is difficult to predict what will come in the next three to five years. Bill Gates famously observed that "we always overestimate the change that will occur in the next two years and underestimate the change that will occur in the next ten." ... [M]most lawyers have a "herd" mentality when it comes to such technology—they neither want to lead nor be left behind.

We take this approach in light of what we see as the failure of many law firms to evaluate periodically and redesign their work flow to assure that their entire system operates efficiently and effectively. Instead, many firms focus only on portions of the system, adopting particular technologies to address specific problems, thereby potentially winning incremental improvements in one area while complicating other areas and burdening the overall system. What begins with good intentions often results in diminished efficiency. The Task Force believes the primary challenge of technology in the coming years is to redesign the way we work so that technology is fully integrated into our work flow in an efficient and effective manner.

Finally, this section of the Report is addressed to lawyers rather than technology specialists because it is important that lawyers be involved in the selection and implementation of the technology and knowledge management methodologies used in their practice. Practicing lawyers need a basic understanding of these tools and methodologies so that they can guide their technology advisers to select tools that support, rather than distort, their practice.

PRACTICAL APPROACHES TO THE ADOPTION OF TECHNOLOGICAL SOLUTIONS

There is an instinctive tendency to be enthralled by the latest technological tool, whether it is a web-platform that promises more efficient project-based communication with colleagues, or a new piece of hardware that promises to automate functions previously performed by hand, or a new "app" that brings a wealth of information to a hand-held device. Software and gadgets, however, should never be adopted unless they make sense within the larger context of how a firm operates and should rarely be the starting point for an evaluation of how to harness technology....

I. Employ a Systems–Based Approach

A systems-based approach to the use of technology begins with an assessment of the functions the firm performs and the related flow of information and work amongst its personnel. This process often reveals duplicated efforts and a need to streamline access to information.

As a first example of an area that can benefit from a systems-based approach, consider the new matter intake process. In the natural rush to begin work on a new client engagement, a lawyer checks for conflicts and then opens a new matter in the time and billing system as quickly as possible, often with little thought to providing a comprehensive description of the matter or categorizing the engagement by matter type, industry, or the lawyers involved. As the matter progresses, the client's goals may change, but they are not likely to be reflected in the firm's recorded matter information.

After the matter closes, there is no system in place to assist the lawyer or others when seeking new business or building a team with relevant experience. There is no way to look for internal precedents from similar matters and no way to analyze the firm's business to better understand the types of matters it tends to take and its record with respect to those matters. In each case, an initial matter description that is accurate and thorough, and systemically updated, could be very helpful. It would eliminate the need to query multiple systems or to track down information from the lawyers involved in the matter when seeking relevant experience for other matters or when preparing marketing materials.

In a truly systematic approach to the new business process, the lawyer opening the matter provides a basic description, including the matter type and client industry. This information, along with information relating to the lawyers involved, is then periodically updated either automatically or through updates from the lawyers on the client team. The updated information is then shared automatically across all relevant systems (time and billing, conflicts, document management, expertise location, staffing database, and marketing database). Now, when the business need arises, the firm has current matter information readily available.

In the systems-based scenario, (1) each piece of information has a single home and a custodian charged with its upkeep; (2) information is entered once in the host system and provided to other systems as necessary to avoid the double entry of that information; (3) information is kept in a particular silo (e.g., the database supporting a time and billing system or a document management system) that is easily accessible for use across silos; and (4) the streamlined information search does not interrupt the billable work of the firm.

Electronic billing is a second example of an area that can benefit from a systems-based approach. The legal profession has come a long way from submitting legal bills that simply stated, "For Services Rendered." Today, most hourly billing requirements involve Uniform Task Based Billing Codes in increments with explanations broken down by ten or fifteen minutes. With this granularity, however, come bills that can be hundreds of pages long and difficult to understand.

As electronic billing, or e-billing, has become more sophisticated, it has allowed the bill reviewer to understand the level of work and hourly charges over time, and it has made the task of reviewing large bills much simpler. Today, e-billing allows clients and insurance companies to aggregate bills, organize charges by type of work performed, and customize the process to "flag" or highlight certain types of billing errors or concerns. Thus, the client can take a monthly bill and understand it in relationship to the total costs, compare the charges to the budget, and pinpoint any questionable charges.

Because e-billing affords a greater understanding of the time and cost involved, the conversations can focus more readily on the "value" of the work performed. In litigation, for example, the number of hours spent on a typical motion to dismiss can be determined, compared across like cases, and more accurately budgeted up front. Thus, instead of a discussion after the work has been performed, the client and lawyer can discuss together the cost/benefit of work before agreeing to a particular course of action.

Mutual dialogue about risk versus cost, based on real data from past cases, has the potential to change the way law is practiced and improve the lawyer/client dynamic.

Although e-billing has been driven mostly by large clients wanting more consistent and detailed information about work done on their behalf, law firms, too, can employ e-billing internally for more efficient case management. A firm can develop the data necessary to see how efficient it is, or is not, at doing certain kinds of work. Over time, the firm can use this data to analyze how well it handles various tasks and to budget legal expenses for the client.

II. Define the Goals for Applying Technology to a Legal Practice

Adopting technological solutions without considering the goals to be achieved by that technology has led many firms down the path of spending large sums of money to acquire computer hardware and software that are underutilized, or worse, that result in increased frustration and reduced productivity. Typically, the most important goals to consider when adopting new technologies are: (1) improving work product quality while reducing costs; (2) increasing the satisfaction of the firm's clients and lawyers; (3) enhancing efficiency, (4) minimizing risk exposure; (5) maintaining confidentiality and security; (6) supporting mobile and flexible work arrangements; and (7) achieving high levels of knowledge capture and sharing. Unless investment in technology addresses these factors in a comprehensive manner, that technology is unlikely to be durable.

Although substantial investments in technology may not be possible or appropriate for everyone, and particularly not for smaller firms, a law firm that takes a minimalist approach to technology and these goals may find itself at a disadvantage with respect to clients. Clients are often ahead of their lawyers when it comes to technology. They often expect their lawyers to have access to the same technologies they use and become frustrated when their lawyers lag behind. Having common platforms allows firms to strengthen their relationships with their clients while better managing costs. For example, some clients have moved law firms toward common platforms for e-billing. Law firms should look for other common platforms that they can leverage to enhance client relationships.

III. Understand and Embrace the Concept of "Knowledge Management"

Lawyers have always understood the value of the information and experience gleaned from client engagements, *i.e.*, "knowledge management." The goal of knowledge management is to ensure that the right information is in the right hands at the right time, leading to better decisions about legal strategy and the business direction of the firm.

As a practical matter, knowledge management within a firm may involve systematic efforts to capture work product and learning as well as methods to retrieve and share that knowledge. Knowledge management principles can also be used to streamline support functions and enhance information sharing across administrative departments, reducing wasted time spent in fruitless searching or duplication of effort. Finally, as one commentator has suggested, too many lawyers are torn between not wanting to be early adopters and dreading being left behind. The result is that some lawyers fail to optimize the tools they have, let alone take advantage of the most appropriate tools available.

IV. Educate and Train Lawyers ...

Given the importance of technology to the practice of law, the legal profession shares the burden of finding a way to help lawyers understand and use technology more effectively. The Task Force recommends that law schools and firms increase (or begin) the education and training of lawyers about practical ways to use technology in their practices.

. . .

Similarly, law firms should invest in, and require, the training of both new and established lawyers to understand and adopt the efficiencies that technology can provide. If senior attorneys do not take a lead role in implementing a firm's strategic investments in technology, the firm is unlikely to develop a culture that will allow technological innovation to succeed.

CURRENT TRENDS AND TOOLS

Although the Task Force cautions against a "tools-first" approach, a survey of some applications and technologies that are finding their way into law firm practice provides some insights into how firms are using new technology. This section considers some of the technological solutions with which lawyers are experimenting and some of the issues related to their adoption. Some of these solutions (such as Web sites and e-filing) are already widely used, while others (such as cloud computing, iPads, and social networking) are just beginning to venture into the legal landscape.

I. Cloud Computing

In many areas of commerce, "cloud computing"—loosely defined as the use of Internet-based shared servers or applications hosted by third parties—promises to be a major technological step forward in collaboration, mobility, and infrastructure. For more than two decades, internal law firm technology infrastructure has been centered around data storage, servers, and telecommunication. Flexible cloud platforms, however, have the ability to assume this responsibility externally, allowing many users to access the information in a fully mobile manner. Cloud computing has the potential to connect lawyers and clients seamlessly to the same data and software, even when working remotely.

For small firms, cloud computing may inexpensively serve all of their computer software needs by allowing them to outsource their IT infrastructure, maintenance, and support. A single service provider may, for one price, provide online all of the tools a lawyer needs to practice law and manage his or her practice, including case management, billing, calendaring, creating documents, storing and organizing those documents, and providing the tools to search and retrieve them, along with fully mobile communications functionality (e-mail, phone, and videoconferencing). Users no longer need to worry about hardware for storage and back-up, licensing software upgrades, or virus protection. Although many of these services are available to some extent today, users may need different devices for each operation and may pay separately for access to each service. As the market consolidates, cloud computing will provide all of this in one bundle.

Larger firms may be less trusting of third-party hosts. They may be more inclined to invest in private cloud computing where applications and data are hosted by a central, secure source, and made accessible to other attorneys, clients, and vendors. Although potentially more costly, the establishment of private clouds offers some presumptive advantages in terms of security and customizability, which may be necessary given the proprietary and confidential nature of much of the material handled by lawyers. However, confidential data are not necessarily inherently safer, merely because they are hosted locally. Any data storage device can be compromised, including data stored on a "local" law firm network, particularly a network that is insufficiently staffed with professionals untrained in threat detection and into which many people have password-based access. Sophisticated third-party cloud platforms—both public and private—use secure locations for their servers with trained staff on-site to deal with threats.

. . .

II. Mobile Computing

With mobile computing, a waiting lawyer can be a working lawyer. Mobile devices allow for uninterrupted Internet connectivity and access to electronic files and other resources available at the office. This level of information access allows attorneys to adapt to situations as they unfold, gather last-minute research that could prove decisive, and quickly address a client's concerns from anywhere in the world.

A new generation of tablet computers has entered and may soon take over the marketplace. The iPad and its competitors can be switched on almost instantaneously, have large touchscreens with solid functionality, Web access, cameras, room for software applications that perform a myriad of duties, and an on-screen keyboard. Tablets can give lawyers access to large amounts of information—such as briefs, cases, and Web sites. Tablets certainly have the potential, at least in the near term, to become the primary mobile work machine for many and to become a "game changer" in the world of legal technology.

Law firms must recognize that mobile computing also has disadvantages and that, in some situations, it can make practice more, rather than less, burdensome. Professional demands tether attorneys to the array of devices so they maintain an unbroken connection with work long after the office is locked. Many lawyers find themselves unable to disconnect from their clients' needs. Law firms should establish guidelines that address this issue, identifying conditions under which attorneys are, and are not, responsible for maintaining a connection with the workplace, and recognizing that for the sake of the profession, it may not always be necessary or wise to have an instant response to every issue....

Finally, firms must recognize that perhaps no technology has transformed the daily practice of law more than e-mail, particularly now that it has become an ever-present feature of a myriad of mobile devices. Communications that were once accomplished by traditional letters or telephone now occur in seconds, with neither the time provided by letters nor the personal interaction provided by a telephone call. Clients often expect instant responses and instant analyses. Further, many lawyers find that, despite their best efforts to the contrary, their days are largely driven by what has been called the tyranny of e-mail. Firms should work to develop tools that will assist their attorneys in prioritizing and organizing the ever-increasing flood of e-mails.

III. Virtual Law Firms

Developments in technology have created the opportunity to form new kinds of law firms and legal enterprises. Brick-and-mortar law offices are competing with—and in some cases being joined by—overhead-saving small firms that exist "virtually," meaning they exist and work almost exclusively online. Using the latest technology, virtual law firms can gather and share information online through secure sites or platforms that reside on the Internet. Improved encryption systems, pervasive web usage, and the ease of digital document and information transmissions have allowed the "virtual law firm" to become a viable option.

In some of these arrangements, communications are transmitted online through a portal, perhaps with enhanced voice or videoconferencing capabilities. Clients and potential clients may register with a law firm site, log in, fill out questionnaires, check work, and make payments. Firm Web sites may have third-party servers located in a secure facility, regimented and redundant back-up systems, and file encryption. If work is primarily transactional in nature, clients may receive a finished document, reviewed by an attorney at a price point that meets their budget requirements—and provided only upon final payment. Clients that require litigation or other services that are difficult to handle remotely may be referred to an appropriate legal practitioner.

Marketing a virtual legal practice requires a level of professionalism and web marketing expertise that can be daunting to new attorneys or attorneys contemplating such a transition. Without a branded, traditional brick-and-mortar practice from which to network, a virtual legal practice may use search engine optimization tools and professional marketing services, as well as alternative marketing approaches such as social networking.

Virtual law firms are representing clients across a broad range of practice areas, including transactional services, intellectual property, tax, commercial law, energy, and employment. Multijurisdictional virtual law firms with multiple attorneys are currently in operation, and compliance with different states' laws will be an important issue for these entities, as it is for multijurisdictional brick-and-mortar firms.

IV. Online Advertising and Social Media

A law firm Web site is a window into the firm and may be the first impression a prospective client has of the firm. A firm's Web site often highlights news about recent victories and awards received, describes its practice areas, provides biographies of attorneys and staff, and showcases the firm's strengths. Often the site contains alert memos on current legal issues, as well as downloadable intake forms. Increasingly, clients are coming to expect "push-out" alerts from firms about cutting edge legal developments.

Law firms that wish to use their Web sites to develop business should carefully select keywords that reflect the terms for which potential clients would be expected to search and that match both the law firm's practice areas and geographic location. By understanding the intricacies of Web site keyword optimization, a firm can increase its visibility in search engine results.

Lawyers must always be mindful of permissible advertising when creating and maintaining a Web site. The same caution applies to other Internet postings on services such as Facebook, Twitter, and LinkedIn that may also be subject to rules of professional responsibility for advertising.

Social networking is another area in which lawyers communicate and advertise. The 2010 ABA Legal Technology Survey reports that 56% of its respondents maintain a presence in an online social network such as Facebook or LinkedIn. Among large firm respondents, 63% maintain a presence in an online social network. The following reasons were given for participating in social networking: professional networking (76%); socializing (62%); client development (42%); career development (17%); and case investigation (6%).

Social networking allows a lawyer to create and maintain relationships with current and potential clients and to share his or her expertise on the subjects discussed in public forums. It also provides the opportunity for search engines to index the material so that the search engine can return the postings in its search results. Confidentiality and ethical cautions apply to social networking as they do to other forms of communication, but perhaps more so with "social" communications that some may forget are permanently and publicly recorded.

Lawyers using social networking sites should become knowledgeable about the potential implications of such use. Given that these tools are still sufficiently new that their impact is not yet fully understood, and the rules governing how lawyers should use them are still not settled, lawyers should be cautious about their use. Confidentiality of lawyer-client communications easily could be breached when posting inquiries or comments online. A public list of an attorney's contacts or "friends" on a site or a link to a Web site belonging to a client may cause a breach of a confidential relationship. Also, providing "casual advice" online may lead to a claim that an attorney-client relationship has developed, which could lead to the lawyer's being disqualified from representing a client adverse to the person to whom he or she provided the advice—or potentially worse, a breached duty to a present or former client not to act in a manner adverse to the client's interests. It is important that lawyers know how to limit access to information they provide on such sites.

Web sites, blogging, and social networking do not respect state boundaries, potentially leading to issues relating to the unauthorized practice of law in jurisdictions outside of the states where the lawyer is licensed to practice. At a minimum, when using any of these tools, lawyers should use disclaimers to indicate clearly the state in which the attorney is licensed. Moreover, social networking media could be construed as advertising, and, depending on the communication, could be considered a solicitation.

Within the past few months, NYSBA and the New York City Bar Association have issued guidelines on when it is appropriate for a lawyer to gather information about an opposing party on Facebook. The guidelines address when it may be inappropriate to contact an opposing party or witness to view private profiles. The Task Force recommends that NYSBA's Committee on Standards of Attorney Conduct pay continued attention to ethical issues created by the use of new media in practice.

V. Extranets

An extranet allows a firm to provide electronic documents, billing information, and interactive forums with clients or other parties outside of the firm. Extranets generally control who has access to documents and information on an individual basis. For example, the general counsel of a client and his or her key staff might be given access to legal documents that others at the client might not have permission to see or an extranet may provide a means for co-counsel to share information.

One promising area for extranets is the client library. A client library is an extranet into which a firm can post work that was done on behalf of the client, including historic documents, closing sets, real time or past billing information, client alerts drafted by the firm that relate specifically to work that is being done for the client, and other material that might be of interest to that client. A library can also contain model documents, access to automated forms, and expertise systems to provide advice to a client without the client having to speak directly with a lawyer.

Some large corporations have started to mandate that their outside counsel use a common system for housing and sharing their work product, not only with the client, but with the client's other outside counsel. Client control over the library allows the client to maintain and neatly organize the work product from various sources. Such control means that a client can easily facilitate cooperation among its outside counsel and no longer needs to search multiple sites to locate its work product.

VI. Enterprise Search

Most of the useful information in a law office is no longer stored in tabbed paper folders located in file cabinets, but is instead stored on hard drives and file servers. Finding such files at a later date can be time consuming, if not impossible, if the files are poorly organized. With ever growing pools of digital information, it is critical that lawyers have the tools necessary to find documents and other relevant information they need quickly and efficiently. Enterprise search provides the ability to search for and locate documents across all of the firm's systems, including document management systems, e-mail systems, and financial systems.

As these sources of knowledge grow and spread out across different systems, it is essential that the search results be both comprehensive and relevant. Traditional keyword searches, while helpful, tend to be either underinclusive or overinclusive. Recently, there have been improvements in search technology in the area of concept searching. Concept searching uses mathematical and statistical models to find related concepts, as opposed to merely finding matching words, and it can often provide more relevant and comprehensive results than traditional methods.

Large firms and corporate counsel have the means to purchase search tools and document management systems that include concept searching tools, but small firms without the financial or technical resources may forgo the expense of such tools, possibly putting them at a competitive and technological disadvantage. To help make these tools available to small firms, NYSBA should consider working with its new concept search engine provider to have the vendor develop a service for the benefit of its membership.

VII. E–Filing

Electronic filing (or e-filing), already mandatory in federal courts, is rapidly becoming a required filing standard throughout New York State courts. Given that almost every legal document is created on a computer, and that most attorneys and parties are using electronic mail to communicate, integrating these methods into the court system has improved efficiency by removing the need to print and store paper versions of the documents or to visit courthouses to retrieve them. Depending on the e-filing method, the filed documents may be searched and indexed in a database for ease of access, retrieval, and review. E-filing significantly reduces the amount of space needed by courts and attorneys for storage of filings, and the use of off-site backups can protect against loss of files due to natural or man-made disasters. For attorneys and litigants, e-filing reduces production and transmission costs for papers and related documents, and it lowers travel and service costs for attorneys located far from the courthouse or from their adversaries.

. . .

Since this article was written, legal applications have proliferated. Many of these tools make it easier for lawyers to work from multiple platforms, using the same programs and information with different devices at multiple locations. Cloud computing, supposedly named for the clouds in the sky on the Microsoft home screen, allows lawyers to access data and applications stored on host servers from anywhere with an Internet connection. The availability of all this technology, however, does not diminish the need for individual lawyers and law firms to decide which applications they need to deliver services to their clients, and to implement the technology so that everyone in the organization can use it. One thing that has not changed in recent years is that you can throw money at the latest technology, but if people cannot or do not use it, you might as well work with pens and yellow pads.

Problems and Questions

1. Now that law offices universally have computer networks, application software, and access to the Internet, what are the new frontiers? Will Apple's iPad replace the Blackberry as the indispensable tool for lawyers? What other developments on the horizon will have an impact on the practice of law?

2. The majority of lawyers were born before 1980, and many entered the practice of law, before the advent of the personal computer, and this generation of lawyers was slow to adapt technology in the practice of law. Today, law school graduates have been around computers since they started kindergarten, and the technophobic generation is gradually retiring. Will a generation of tech-savvy younger lawyers propel the practice of law into a new wave of law office applications? If so, what?

3. Do you agree with the assessments of the New York State Bar Task Force? What does this mean in terms of technology planning for law firms? Should clients have a role in the technology decisions lawyers make?

C. KNOWLEDGE MANAGEMENT

In the past, a discussion of legal research tools and information resources would fall under the general topic of the law library. The library was a place in the law firm, where books were stored and lawyers or their assistants could go to do research on legal questions. Small firms that did not have the money to underwrite a full library often used law school, bar association, or other firm libraries. Some creative groups even created co-op or shared libraries. The costs associated with such a law library were significant: space, shelves, tables and chairs, books, staffing and oversight. Even today, many law firms retain their collection of printed law books, because they view it as an important investment. Chapter 9 includes a discussion of the physical requirements for a law library in the context of planning for office space. This chapter addresses how to manage legal information itself.

The availability of electronic resources—both electronic versions of printed material and new resources such as online databases—and desk-top access to information have revolutionized the way lawyers conduct legal research. In many firms, print materials have been replaced by electronic counterparts, which are available either on line or on DVD. The need for separate space to house books and conduct research has diminished, and firms have shifted the support that once went to libraries to technology. The law librarian has been transformed from curator of a book museum to an information specialist, adept at assisting users to take advantage of the vast information at their fingertips.

1. RESEARCH

Lawyers are in the business of doing legal research and reporting the results of that research to the courts, to their clients, and to each other. From your first year of law school, you learn that it is more important to know how to find something than to remember it. Those lawyers who have developed the skill of effective research generally have the edge over those who are less proficient. In deciding whether to use print or electronic media, law firms have to consider a number of factors. There is no single right or wrong answer for every firm, other than to say that the information resources should be chosen to meet the research needs of the law firm's users.

- *Costs:* Books are expensive, and they are not getting cheaper. DVDs, e-books, and printed books generally are priced comparably by publishers, i.e., the same information costs about the same in either format. DVDs save money in terms of storage, although they require their own infrastructure to work effectively. Online services are regarded by many lawyers as too expensive, although in reality expenses are often run up by inefficient users. Westlaw and Lexis both offer low-cost programs for small firms, and Internet alternatives such as http://www.findlaw.com, and various non-commercial Web sites provide inexpensive access with less sophisticated search tools than commercial engines. In many cases, the cost of acquiring or accessing information can be passed on to clients, provided the lawyer keeps accurate records for billing purposes. Where it is not possible to bill clients for research, law firms might prefer free sites, but even when the firm must absorb research costs, it may still be worthwhile if the information is added to the firm's knowledge base. As a final note, the more efficient the research, the lower the cost of information, so training and practice for all staff members who access electronic information is always important.

- *Needs:* The firm must think about what books it absolutely, positively, must have. It is important to assess needs from the beginning because not every firm requires the same books. Some areas of practice are more book-dependent than others. If you have a tax practice, you may want the Tax Code and Regs in hard copy. In other areas of practice, you might need to keep other critical titles. You must assess the type of business you expect to get—whether generalized or specialized—and the main books needed to support such a practice. Consider the geographic location of your offices. It may make more sense to go electronic to retrieve materials that are used less frequently. Some subject matter may be in a constant state of flux (e.g., regulatory rules), while other materials remain static (e.g., case law—*Marbury v. Madison* has not changed since it was penned by Justice John Marshall two hundred years ago.).

- *Alternatives:* It is important to note that today lawyers have alternatives to maintaining large, full-service in-house libraries. Even large firms are now taking a hard look at what works for them. The idea of the electronic library is emerging as a realistic possibility for modern law firms. In the future, more and more firms will turn increasingly to electronic media as the central source of legal information. On the other hand, a law firm that already has a substantial traditional library may want to maintain those resources, while investing in new information resources in electronic versions.

In short, if you think about how you will be using the information you need, you may find questions about what medium to choose answer themselves. The solution is certainly not a one-size-fits-all approach. Given the significant expenditures law firms must make for information resources, the investment of time and energy to make good decisions in this are well spent.

2. INFORMATION RESOURCES

The concept of information resources is evolving as the relationship of the legal profession to information evolves. Lawyers are required to access, retrieve and digest not only cases and other traditional information resources, but also non-legal information from external databases. This has forced many law firms to rethink their ideas about what resources they will need in order to serve their clients. Law firms must consider how they can act as information providers in order to deliver services directly to clients electronically. This concept, sometimes described as e-lawyering, offers lawyers the opportunity to reach entirely new audiences, but it may fundamentally transform the nature of what lawyers do and the relationship between lawyers and clients.

One aspect of technology that has received considerable attention in the legal community involves how small firms and solo practitioners can take advantage of technology to level the playing field in their dealings with larger firms. Although large firms typically can invest more money in more sophisticated technology, smaller firms derive benefits from being able to compete effectively with larger organizations. The following article, first published in 1999, remains accurate in 2012, because it captures the sense that the gains for small firms are definitely worth the investment:

IMPLEMENTING TECHNOLOGY IN THE SMALL LAW FIRM: HOW TO GET BEYOND AN UNFULFILLED PROMISE

From *Law Technology News*, by Professor Gary A. Munneke (March, 1999).

Depending on who is talking, technology is either the boon or bane of small law firm practice. Technophiles describe computers as the great equalizer between small firms and large ones, because they put into the hands of skilled practitioners the tools they need to compete effectively against larger adversaries. Others suggest that technology simply widens the gap between large and small firms, because computers cost money and large firms can spend more money on technology solutions than small firms.

Let's be clear about one thing: the debate about whether law firms, regardless of size, should automate is over—the computers have won. Virtually every law office today is equipped with some sort of computer equipment. Even if pocket resistance remains of lawyers who still refuse to put hands to keyboard, the war is over. Lawyers may cling to the old ways, but legal staffs at least have made the change.

The problem now for the majority of law firms large and small is how to utilize technology. It is apparent from visiting law offices and talking to average lawyers that they do not take advantage of all the technology they have, much less possess a clue as to what technology they need. Many of the benefits of technology do not accrue to law offices, because the inhabitants fail to understand what different applications can do for them. Some lawyers may appreciate what technology can bring, but they just don't have the time to learn it. To them, the learning curve is so time consuming that it is easier to do things the way they have always done them. A client database would be nice, but who is going to learn *MS Access*, set it up and input the data. A computer time and billing system would be helpful, but who is going to practice law while we set it up.

Arguably, the cost of implementing new technology is more easily borne by larger firms. They can spread the cost of development more widely; they can hire in-house IS professionals to free the lawyers and staff from the technical details; they can bring in outside consultants to provide training or to organize systems; they can operate redundant systems until the bugs are worked out. In solo practices and small firms the burden of transition falls directly on those who, at the same time they try to develop and learn new systems, must continue to operate old ones. If something doesn't work in a small law office, it isn't a glitch, it's a catastrophe.

The burden of obsolescence also impacts small firms more heavily. Whereas larger law firms tend to view investment in technology as a regular budgeted expense that just like staff and space will recur every year. Small firms tend to view the acquisition of technology as a capital expenditure, like buying furniture or a phone system. They finally ... [bought] some new-fangled PC's (best on the market!) about two years ago. What do you mean by saying that these "new" machines are no good?

Finally, in many small offices there is simply no leadership on technology. In most organizations, someone has to catch the technology bug. Whether that person is a staff member or a lawyer, if someone in the firm is not an advocate for technology, then technology will flounder. In large firms, there are simply greater numbers—if you have 100 lawyers in your firm and an equal number of support staff, you are more likely to find a few techies from the 200 candidates than in the small firm with two lawyers and five staff members.

What is a law firm to do? It is plain to see that some small firms have embraced technology, and there are plenty of examples of individual lawyers who have used computers to transform the way they practice law. Here are a few simple prescriptions to make it easier to enhance the utilization of technology tools in the small law practice:

Designate someone in the firm to become the technology guru. Accept that this assignment will take some time and energy; don't penalize the person or no one will take the assignment. In a small office, the person may be a staff member, who finds the challenge of technology to be energizing. The person might be a new associate or law clerk who has grown up with computers. It might be one of the lawyers who recognizes the need, and is willing to assume the mantle of leadership.

Know when to use consultants. Many small firms feel that consultants represent a luxury they just cannot afford, especially when the consultant's work consists of looking at your watch and telling you what time it is. In many situations, reading books and articles, or going on line (check out http://www.americanbar.org/groups/law_practice_management.html, for instance), or talking to other lawyers who have dealt with the same issues will be preferable to paying someone to do your thinking for you. On the other hand, do not be afraid to use consultants when it makes sense to accelerate the learning curve, for system engineering or training. A solo practitioner from Washington, DC, known for his fiscal conservatism in the office, commented recently that the $2,000 he spent on a consultant to implement his time and billing system was the best $2,000 he ever spent.

Budget money for maintaining and upgrading computer systems every year. Whatever you spent to buy your system, you will need to spend half that much each year thereafter to keep it running. Remember that even if you buy the latest technology, the average life of both hardware and software is 12–18 months, before it is obsolete. You may be able to squeeze a little more time out of an old engine, but eventually you will have to replace it. Whatever you do, don't think that you will find any deals on the trailing edge.... If it helps psychologically, amortize the cost of technology over its useful life. If you spend $2,500 for a new laptop, and you figure it will be used five hours a day for two years (250 days per year), before you junk it, the cost is just $1 per hour. The bottom line is that you just have to bite the bullet and spend the money.

Make the introduction of new technology as easy as possible. Give potential users books; send them for training; bring in a trainer. Let lawyers and staff play with new technology and learn to like it. Technology applications are like those people whom it takes a while to get to know. Don't try to do everything at once. If you get a new time and billing system, don't tell the staff that they have to start using *MS Excel* the same day. Encourage people to discover the power of the programs they have. Even with generic products like word processors, most law office personnel use only a fraction of the potential tools.

Lastly, know what you want for your practice. Don't buy a scanner because Gates & Neukom down the street has one; buy a scanner because your practice needs one. This is not an idle distinction. It is possible to buy a lot of technology you don't need if you fail to assess what you do need. If you look at your office operations, particularly systems that are still handled manually, and ask yourself if the technology exists to improve performance, making decisions about what to buy becomes much easier.

Most law firms at a minimum need high-level word processing, document assembly, calendaring, time and billing, and financial management programs. For many firms, database, spreadsheet and presentation programs are integral to their practice environment. For some firms, substantive practice systems, conflicts checking, case management and client contact programs can improve the efficiency of service delivery. Increasingly, electronic communications are becoming common for e-mail, data and file transfer, research, and product information. It is beyond the scope of this article to suggest specific vendors, but there are a variety of products and services tailored to the small firm ... For more information, see http://www.techshow.com, ... [as well as] a number of other regional shows are periodically sponsored by bar associations and other companies.

It is not always easy for the small firm practitioner to stay abreast in the ever-changing world of law firm automation. Despite the challenge, it is not an impossible chore. In the end, however, it is not really an option. You have to keep up with technology to practice competently; you will have to get the most out of your computers if you are going to survive in the coming decade.

The Internet and Resources sections, which appear in Appendices A (pages 417–421) and B (pages 423–427), include a number of specific listings for technology resources, but given the rapid evolution and volatility of the technology marketplace, it often makes more sense to go to current periodicals, Web sites and blogs to stay abreast of the latest developments.

PROBLEMS AND QUESTIONS

1. Is the duty to keep clients reasonably informed about their cases helped or hindered by technology? How can lawyers communicate legal information to those who need it electronically? How do they deal with clients and prospective clients who do not understand computer technology?

2. Do lawyers and law firms ever provide general legal information to consumers, which is then used by those consumers fashioning self-help remedies for legal problems? Is this a specialized niche practice or something that all firms need to do? How does e-lawyering help to deliver legal information services effectively? Is there a nexus between providing informational services and traditional legal services?

3. Does it make sense to describe the law library as the firm's Information Resource Center? Is it the function of a library to collect books and other materials, or to provide an information management service for the firm? What are the implications of such an approach? Financially? Organizationally? Functionally? Practically?

4. Given the trend toward electronic resources, does the twenty-first century library need books at all? If it does, which ones? And if it needs fewer books, does it even need a dedicated room called a library? Does it make more sense to say that every lawyer and legal assistant has a library on her desktop?

5. What is the role of the law librarian in the information age? Would a better term be Information Management Specialist? Are such individuals more likely to be found as law firm employees or as consulting services utilized by the firm as needed? Are information services involving legal research related to information services involving management of the firm's technology infrastructure?

6. If the technology exists to locate previously obscure technical data, at what point does a lawyer commit malpractice when her research fails to locate such information?

7. If the rate of obsolescence for new technology is twelve to eighteen months, how can law firms ever keep up? What does it mean for the

economics of law practice that law firms must constantly invest in new and upgraded technology in order to remain competitive?

8. Develop an information resources plan for your firm, including an assessment of electronic versus print products. How will the firm manage these resources for the benefit of clients? Should clients pay for research services? See Appendix J, page 475.

CHAPTER 11

MANAGING FINANCIAL RESOURCES

■ ■ ■

A. UNDERSTANDING THE BASICS

Financial management is perhaps the most singularly critical function to the success of any business, because it determines whether the business will thrive, or wither and die. Law firms are not immune from this economic determinism. Having a financial plan, which governs the operations of the firm, is a necessary part of financial management. The corollary of this principle is that financial mismanagement characterized by the absence of a disciplined financial plan is a shortcut to economic disaster for the organization.

In this chapter you will learn how to develop financial plans for your law firm. You do not need to be an accountant to be able to understand the basic principles of financial planning. In a firm, undoubtedly you will use an independent accountant to assist you with your financial planning, even if one of the partners is a CPA. All firms must manage their financial resources; some do a better job than others. Whether yours is a solo practice or a firm of several hundred lawyers, someone has to collect fees, pay bills, and balance the checkbook. In addition, virtually all firms anticipate generating a profit for the partners, so money management is central to the practice of law. Although some law offices may be funded from sources other than fees, the challenge of managing costs and living within a budget can be just as critical as it is in a firm funded through client fees.

This chapter is divided into three parts. The first covers basic financial terms and principles. This material may seem very simplistic to you, if you possess an extensive background in business, finance, or accounting (e.g., a CPA license, MBA degree, or practical experience in business before law school). Hopefully, you will gain a different perspective, when you apply your knowledge to the legal field. If you are one of those people who have never taken an accounting or business course, the concepts, language and processes may all seem new. Just as in discussions involving technology and other subjects in this course, some students will face a steeper learning curve than others. The second part addresses financial management in the private law firm setting. The third examines the process of financing a new start-up law practice. Notably, although most law students do not start their own firms immediately after law school (although some do), a great many will do so at some point in their legal career.

Imagine a law firm that does not have to worry about money. The lawyers work reasonable hours and charge fees that clients consider fair. The lawyers pay the bills, and whatever is left, they take home. There is always plenty to go around and no one ever complains about being short-changed. As business grows, the firm adds associates, who will be paid a comfortable salary and know that if they work hard they will someday be partners. A small but dedicated support staff receives salaries, which may be much less than any of the lawyers, but most likely are better than they could make doing almost anything else in town.

The popular myth persists in many quarters that there was a time in the not too distant past when this idyllic picture was reality for most lawyers, and that the financial opportunities for lawyers were much better than today. Many practitioners who look back on the "good old days" tend to romanticize the past and demonize the present. In truth, although the formula for success has changed, the need for lawyers to practice in a business-like way has not. Lawyers in past generations, who could not generate enough fees to pay the bills, went out of business. Lawyers, who did not compete successfully in the marketplace, found themselves at the bottom of the legal food chain, even in the days when no one would speak openly about marketing. This basic tenet of the practice of law is as true today as it ever was.

The need for lawyers to understand how law firms operate financially remains a constant for the practice of law. Keep in mind that some aspects of financial management for law firms are unique to the practice of law, especially in the areas of trust accounting (Model Rule 1.15), capitalization (Model Rule 5.4 (d)), and selling the practice (Model Rule 1.17). An understanding of the financial foundations of law practice should be an integral part of every future lawyer's education, even though many law schools do not address this topic in any coherent way. Regardless of your background, consider yourself lucky to participate in this discussion.

Students who are less comfortable with finances, never having had the responsibility for managing a business, or in some cases, never even having their own personal checking account, may find that these materials present a challenge. The skills of financial management, however, are utilized in managing your law firm, in the work you do for clients, and in your personal life every day. Practicing law without a sound grounding in financial management should be unthinkable, so it will be well worth your time to develop your skills in this area.

This theme is pursued further in Chapter 15, which deals with professional development. In addition, if you need more help getting up to speed in this area, *see* Robert Hamilton & Richard Booth, BASIC BUSINESS

CONCEPTS FOR LAWYERS, (3rd ed. 2002), Charles H. Meyer, ACCOUNTING AND FINANCE FOR LAWYERS, (1995), or other comparable guide.

The economic realities of present day law practice place a premium on effective financial management, and are clearly seen when one looks at the profit or loss statement of the law office. Think about this basic equation: The differences between the revenue (fees earned or income) by a law firm minus the expenses incurred from operating the office will equal the net profit or loss for the period covered, i.e., I–E = P(L). Since profit can be increased only if the spread between income and expenses increases, firms are often under pressure to reduce expenses or increase revenue. Further, if expense exceeds income, generating an operating loss, most firms cannot stay in business for long.

Let's say that a law firm decides that the partners need to earn more money. They can increase their profit in several ways:

- charging higher fees (but the location of the practice and competitive market forces place a natural limit on how much firms can charge);
- working longer hours (but the reality of time places a limit on how many hours an attorney can bill);
- securing new and better clients (but there is a finite amount of legal business available);
- reducing expenses (although expenses may be reduced through sound financial management, there are limits as to how much money a firm can save before financial cuts affect productivity); or
- borrowing more money to finance the firm's expansion (but overextending borrowing should be a concern as revenue is needed to repay loans).

Financial management involves both financial planning (budgeting) and financial control (administration). Financial planning, as the term suggests, requires those charged with managing the firm's finances to look forward and project income, expense and profitability in the future. It involves marketing, financial decisions, personnel changes and other strategic decisions, which will insure the future viability of the firm. Over time, the firm may be able to improve the predictability of future projections by reviewing past performance and correctly assessing such factors as the economy and the firm's own growth potential. Financial planning is an inexact science, but an inescapable activity for every firm. Financial control involves not only accounting for the daily cash flow and the reporting of monthly financial results, including current income and expenses, but also the internal procedures for everything from maximizing income and controlling expenses, to basic activities like processing invoices. A law firm that cannot plan and control its finances cannot hope to become or remain economically viable.

Too often, law firms ignore financial planning and abdicate their responsibilities for financial control. Some firms appear to think that bookkeeping is a clerical task left to a staff member and accounting is an annual ritual delegated to the firm's accountant. Many lawyers are not trained in accounting, and are therefore uncomfortable dealing with financial matters. Lawyers and law firms, however, must understand some basic accounting principles (if not for themselves, at least for their clients), and should actively participate in administration of the firm's financial operations. Certainly, in larger firms, individual lawyers, especially associates, do not have to get involved in money matters on a daily basis, but if all lawyers were aware of the importance of maintaining financial control in such matters as printing, photocopying, process server's fees, or even telephone costs, the firm will benefit as it would have lower expenses and more profit at year end.

As for financial planning, it is no longer enough to take last year's revenue and expenses, and increase them by the rate of inflation to get next year's budget. Before the firm sets its budget, it must look at its goals and establish what it expects the financial picture to look like next year. Once the goal is solidified, the firm must evaluate where the revenue will be generated—how to attract new business and increase fees. Some of these decisions will arise from marketing efforts, or establishing new practice niches (See Chapter 6). On the expense side, planning must examine all expenses, including both variable (those which are based on usage), and fixed (those based on predetermined rates such as rent, loans or leasing of equipment). Once the budget is set for the following year, the allocation of funds over the course of the year becomes a major consideration. Budgeting as a part of the broader long range planning process is more time-consuming, but inherently more meaningful, than straight line projections.

Financial planning in one sense involves rolling up your sleeves and diving in. Often one or more of the lawyers involved will have some degree of financial acumen, but whether the lawyers are sophisticated or not, it is always wise to engage the services of a CPA to create and monitor the financial plan. All lawyers should have at least a rudimentary understanding of Microsoft Excel, QuickBooks, or other financial software, and a basic understanding of accounting terminology and principles. Before proceeding with the financial planning process, law firm owners should keep several broad considerations in mind.:

- First, start-up firms do not have a financial history to review when they create their first budget. They have only their own estimates of revenue and expenses tempered by information obtained concerning comparable firms.

- Second, it is easy for a new firm to overestimate income by ignoring the realities of client development, cash flow (i.e., the delay between doing the work and getting paid), and administrative non-billable time. In other words, a new firm that plans to require each lawyer to bill 2,000 hours worth of fees in its first year of operation may be making an unwarranted assumption about its ability to acquire the number of clients to achieve this revenue expectation.

- Third, in the event that the revenue expectation appears to be falling short of anticipated growth, be aware that cutting expenses is seldom an effective way to manage profitability. Since many costs are fixed, budget trimming is seldom a meaningful exercise. Look at how Congress struggles with the federal budget, tinkering with small line items while failing to reduce major expenditures (e.g., pensions or debt service). Furthermore, be aware that some customers may notice you "cutting back" and may be a bit leery as to whether you will be here tomorrow.

Law students are sometimes daunted by the prospect of financial administration, and would prefer to ignore money questions or delegate them to someone else. Unfortunately, in the final analysis, the law firm profitability may depend on how well its financial resources are managed. Not only does this affect the compensation of the owners of the firm, but also the livelihood of everyone employed by the association. Although technology-based tools, from spreadsheets to accounting software, can help make financial administration more palatable, and professional assistance from CPAs is readily available to law firms, the lawyer-owners in the final analysis must roll up their sleeves and learn to be effective financial managers.

PROBLEMS AND QUESTIONS

1. Do you think the idyllic model for law firm economics, described on page 261, is a realistic one? Why or why not?

2. Have the economics of law practice changed over the years, creating greater financial pressures for law firms? What are your reasons? Are these changes merely a part of the economic cycle or do they portend a fundamental shift in the way law firms operate?

3. What types of legal organization do not rely on income from legal fees to cover their costs and generate profit? How does elimination of the profit motive change the dynamics of budgeting in these organizations? Why is money still important?

4. If income less expenses equals profit or loss, what is the best way to maximize profit? What happens in the real world when a profit-based firm generates an operating loss?

5. Is a law firm more likely to improve its financial picture through planning or control? What tools are available to help the firm manage these two processes?

B. LAW FIRM FINANCIAL MANAGEMENT

In the following sections, you can refer to Appendix L (pages 484–498,) to view a set of Model Law Firm Financial Reports. You might also use financial management software or a spreadsheet to create a law firm budget following the checklist provided in Appendix K (pages 477–482). Either way, you will find it helpful to shift your focus from the conceptual to the practical as you come to terms with this material.

1. CAPITAL

Capital was not an always an important consideration in law firm financial planning, because law offices were very inexpensive to open and operate. Most of the firm's income appeared on the bottom line as profit. The modern law office, however, contains a variety of sophisticated equipment, from computers to cellular phones. It is housed in a "smart" building with a host of amenities. It employs a staff of paraprofessionals and clerical workers to support the work of the lawyers. In such an environment, capital is much more important than it was in earlier times. In order to start a law firm today, lawyers have many complex financial decisions to make, including how much money they will have to invest in the business—a concept called capitalization.

Capital refers to the individual partner's actual investment in the firm. Equity is the present value of that investment. Capital can come in the form of tangible assets (e.g., cash, securities), personal property (e.g., furniture, equipment) or real property (e.g., land, a building), or intangible (e.g., clients) assets. The value of clientele or goodwill may also be treated as an asset (See Chapter 4, pages 93–94). For example, when a lawyer moves from one firm to a new one, she often brings her clients with her, and the expected income those clients will generate may be treated as goodwill.

The first step in capitalizing a new law firm involves determining how much money will be required to cover start-up expenses and reserves necessary for potential negative cash flow during the first year of operation. The range of capital investment may run between several thousand dollars to more than $1 million. As part of the start-up planning process, the future partners must make accurate projections regarding all anticipated expenses and revenues. A tendency may exist to be overly optimistic about revenue, which can cause serious problems when cash reserves are depleted. Some of the factors to be considered are:

- the number of lawyers and staff members in the organization,
- the location and type of practice,
- the tastes of partners, and
- the ability of individuals to negotiate good deals on leases, equipment salaries, etc.

Each partner is required to deposit funds representing a predetermined interest in the business into a capital account. In a basic partnership agreement, all members will contribute equal amounts, but partnership agreements vary considerably as to the terms of partner contribution.

If there is no partnership agreement, the Uniform Partnership Act contemplates that all partners will contribute shares equally to the partnership.

In many firms, different partners make different contributions, and if this happens the firm will have to decide whether variable investments will lead to variable voting, compensation and power. As a general proposition, the golden rule applies: "Those who have the gold make the rules." It is important that non-cash contributions be credited to the contributing partner in such a way that the partner receives a fair value for those contributions. In a situation like this, the partners must either assume that all contributions are equal, or they must place a value on non-cash contributions and require cash supplementation if the non-cash contribution does not match the cash contributions of others. If the partners with the non-cash contributions do match the difference in cash, then the partnership, through agreement, can alter the percent of profits, voting and control each partner can receive.

If the firm is organized as a corporation, the partners are referred to as shareholders, and their capital contributions purchase shares in the company. In the same way that all of the partners in a law partnership must be lawyers, a law corporation may not sell shares to nonlawyers or passive institutional investors (See Model Rule 5.4(d)). In the District of Columbia, law firms may include nonlawyer partners under certain circumstances. Recently, the United Kingdom and Australia have opened the door to public financing of law firms, i.e, where a law firm can raise capital by selling stock either through a stock market or private investors. Whether this trend will impact the financing of law firms in the U.S. remains to be seen, but there are clear advantages to raising capital from outside sources.

Law firms treat capital in two ways. In many firms, the capital contributions are merged into the net worth of the firm. Capital contributions convert to cash on hand, which is an asset. The net worth (also expressed as equity or value) of the firm is determined by subtracting liabilities from assets (A–L = V). When a lawyer leaves the firm, he should receive his proportional share of the firm's net worth. Thus, suppose someone invested $50,000 to become a partner in a firm. After ten years this lawyer leaves the firm, and there are now five equal partners. Suppose also that the net worth of the firm is presently $500,000. In this scenario, the present value of the departing partner's interest would be $100,000. If a new partner joins the firm, she should be expected to buy in based on the present value of the firm. Suppose the two original partners invested $20,000 each fifteen years ago to start the firm; there are now five partners and the firm is worth $500,000. The new partner should be expected to contribute $100,000 to purchase an equal interest in the firm.

Other firms treat the capital contribution of partners like loans to the partnership, and maintain the original contribution on the books, at least, in the partner's capital account. Here, the firm is obligated to pay the departing partner the value of his or her capital contribution and a proportionate share of the net worth after treating the capital investment of the other remaining partners as liabilities. Some firms may allow partners to borrow from the capital account—in effect, giving themselves loans—provided that they pay back amounts that reduce the balance in their capital account. A partner who leaves the firm with a reduced capital account should be required to reimburse the loans through a reduction in the payment of the value of the partner's share.

From time to time it may be necessary for an ongoing law firm to ask partners for supplemental capital contributions. For instance, the firm may decide to upgrade the computer system for $50,000. If there is not enough cash on hand to cover the proposed expense, one alternative to borrowing is to ask the partners to contribute to the firm through supplemental capital.

In summary, capitalization encompasses the investment of the partners in the law firm. This can take whatever form is necessary to get the firm started. Once the partnership is established, the distribution of their investments is determined by the partnership agreement, or if none exists, by the Uniform Partnership Act. Once the investments are made, financial planning takes over to preserve the funds, while trying to increase the investment made by each partner.

2. EXPENSES

a. Start-up Expenses

Start-up expenses refer to funds you will need to pay out in order to open the doors of the office for business. When lawyers contemplate opening a law practice, they inevitably incur certain expenses before they can serve any clients. Whether the office is in your home or in a commercial setting, whether it is a solo or group practice, these expenses cannot be avoided, although the lawyers may consider, "what are the bare essentials to make the operation work?" Examples of these expenses would be:

- telephones,
- a computer,
- printer/fax/copier,
- a place to do business,
- advance advertising,
- malpractice insurance,
- supplies, and
- any standard day-to-day operations necessary to plan the opening.

Once the office is functional and ready to serve clients, the start-up expenses can be pre-paid or rolled over to regular operating expenses. If there is cash available, and it is expected that there would be some from the capital invested by the partners, it is appropriate to use it to cover start-up expenses. Alternatively, some or all of these expenses might be paid over time through accounts or loans.

For example, computer equipment may be purchased outright with cash, or expensed over time. Let's say the firm purchases a computer system for $15,000. It can either write a check for $15,000 to Dell, reducing the capital available for other purposes, or pay approximately $460 per month for three years at 5% interest (or other terms), increasing the monthly overhead. Expenses paid over a period of time are said to be amortized, essentially expensed on a monthly basis. This type of accounting is one reason why a certified public accountant is strongly recommended to help plan your treatment of the day-to-day operations.

The important thing to remember about start-up costs is that they are necessary before any business can be transacted. The lawyer must always be aware that success is not guaranteed, and even the most elegant or elaborate law office cannot guarantee it. But the bill collector will guarantee that he will come knocking if the debts are not paid. So be conservative with your initial office surroundings, and once clients start knocking, upgrade your investments as appropriate.

b. Operating Expenses

Operating expenses involve outlays needed to run a law firm on an ongoing basis. Expenses may be either fixed or variable. Fixed expenses are those, which cannot be negotiated after agreement. These may take the form of loans, which are paid in the same amount every month, or rent, which is constant every month. Variable expenses fluctuate with usage, such as telephones, electricity, and postage.

A major consideration in any business is to realize what one can do when in financial difficulty. A firm that anticipates financial problems down the road can cut back on some basic expenses. For instance, it may be able to stop Federal Express and use US Postal Service for package delivery. Variable expenses can usually be reduced, but fixed expenses cannot. Rent is rent, and if you do not pay the lease on your copier, Kodak may come and take it away.

It is important to appreciate the problems that can arise with fixed costs. If the firm borrows to raise needed cash, and it already has fixed costs to pay, the burden of payments may be unmanageable. One must be aware that when a loan is negotiated, there will be more cash on hand—but if the firm does not generate additional revenue to cover the increased cost, it will not be able to survive.

In summary, the partners should be aware of the amount of control they have over expenses, and, when planning, consider the pros and cons of each expense item, as well as how each might be curtailed, if need be, to save money. Although it is false economy to cut essential operations, start-up firms may think twice about what is essential. It might make sense to forego some of the "bells and whistles" until after the firm has established its economic viability. When the firm has established that it can pay its bills and compensate the partners as well, it can begin to think about increasing spending levels in non-critical areas.

3. INCOME

Income represents the value of cash or other assets received by an individual or organization during a period of time 1) in exchange for services, 2) from the sale of goods or property, or 3) as profit from investments. Although law firms earn income in any of these ways, most firms generate the vast majority of their income from the sale of legal services. It is axiomatic to say that if a firm does not earn sufficient income to pay its bills, it cannot generate a profit for the partners/owners. Because partners are compensated through the distribution of profits, it should be obvious that fee income is the linchpin of the law firm economic model. In fact, firms typically have less flexibility in their ability to reduce expenses than they do to increase income.

The term revenue is sometimes used as a synonym of income, although technically revenue may be defined as income received from normal business activities, usually from the sale of goods and services. For law firms, revenue is primary the sale of legal services, and since almost all firm income is legal fees, for purposes of this discussion the two terms are almost if not precisely interchangeable.

4. PROFITABILITY

In a law practice, fees paid by clients generate revenue. This is the most crucial component of the profit equation—no revenue, no profit. A more complete discussion of fees and billing in the context of client relations appears in Chapter 7, while systems to track time and billing are discussed in Chapter 14. In this chapter, we look at fees as a component of financial management.

Fees represent what the lawyer earns from performing services for clients, and fees usually indicate how well the firm is performing in the marketplace. Fee revenue also reflects how well the firm has forecasted its expectations during the budgeting process. When the firm targets certain clients, based upon a lawyer's expertise, revenue projections reflect an expectation that a predictable number of clients will seek the lawyer's services. If the firm has created a good marketing plan, there should be a high correlation between fee projections and actual revenue. Conversely, an overly optimistic plan can result in fees that do not reach projections. If this happens, the firm must determine the reasons why fee projections were not met, and take steps to remedy the problem. It may be due to a number of causes:

- poor service,
- bad publicity,

- the timing of fees earned, such as a delay in recovering settlement proceeds in personal injury cases,
- a slowdown in a particular practice area,
- a broad economic downturn,
- a failure to bill clients regularly,
- slow collections, or
- some other unanticipated reason.

Sometimes, the cost of delivering the service is greater than the price the firm can charge for the service in the marketplace. When the firm analyzes its fee income, all these variables must be considered.

The most common billing system is based on hourly fees, where a law firm sets an hourly rate (R) for billing its work. Multiplying the numbers of hours worked (H) by R equals fees earned (F), so $R \times H = F$. Overhead (O) can also be calculated on an hourly basis by dividing total overhead by total hours billed. For example, if a firm has overhead of $1,000,000 and bills 10,000 hours to clients the overhead rate = $100 per hour billed. So, if the billing rate R = $300, the firm's profit would be $200 for each hour billed.

As more firms explore alternatives to hourly billing, the delivery cost becomes an important consideration. One of the benefits of hourly billing is the fact that when the billing rate is tied to time, the firm can set a billing rate that generates a profit for each hour of work, based on the rough costs of running the office. In a flat fee system, some cases will take more and less than the average amount of time and resources, so the flat rate must be set at a level that generates a profit based on the average of all cases of that time. This in turn means that the firm needs to know the delivery costs for the cases upon which the flat fee will be based. For example, if a firm handles 100 real estate matters, it needs to know that these cases will collectively cost an average of $5,000 per case before setting the price of the service at $10,000.

Profit refers to the income (fees and other revenue generated) less the expenses (fixed and variable) incurred in the operation of the business. Every business owner aspires to make a profit, and will probably not stay in business without it. Profitability may be elusive for the first year of operation for any business, including a law firm. At some point in the life of the firm or business, however, the owners should see a return for their investment and effort. The firm must anticipate that the revenue from fees will exceed the expenses incurred, not only for all matters, but also for each individual matter, or else income will not exceed expenses for the budget as a whole.

If a firm does not achieve its revenue goals, it must take a close look at what went wrong. If the firm is not attracting clients, or is attracting clients, but they are the wrong kind, firm leaders need to find out why, and make changes accordingly. If there is not enough income to cover overhead (even if revenue is higher than budgeted), the firm may need to trim expenses. An independent accountant and consultant may be in a better position than the lawyers in the firm to assess the situation, because they can look objectively at the whole financial picture and can make objective recommendations. What the lawyers cannot do is ignore the signs of trouble and wait until the problems have become too large to fix.

5. BILLING, COLLECTIONS AND REALIZATION

Billing and collecting fees for legal work are integral parts of the financial management process. The topic of billing is discussed elsewhere in this book in Chapters 7 and 14. In Chapter 7, you learned about the timekeeping and billing processes in relation to managing clients. In Chapter 14, you will focus on timekeeping and billing systems as a part of the delivery of legal services. In this Chapter, however, billing is viewed in its fundamental state, as a device to collect money from clients, to fund the firm's operations, and to generate profit to compensate the owners of the legal business.

When a lawyer completes work for a client, that work has value. We measure this value by the amount of money the client is willing to pay the lawyer for the service. The goal of the billing process is to capture as much of the value of the service rendered as possible. In most cases, lawyers do not realize the full value of their services. To understand this phenomenon, think of the value of the lawyer's service in terms of percentages. At the moment the lawyer does the work, the service is worth 100% of its value. Over time, however, this value declines. The reasons for this decline are several:

- We live in a world of perpetual economic inflation; the dollar you hold today will be worth 99.x cents tomorrow and less as time passes.

- If the lawyer holds the money, it will increase in value, because she could invest it at current market rates; when the client holds the money, the client earns the interest, and the lawyer does not benefit from this added value.

- The lawyer may not be able to bill for all of her work. She may forget to record some of her time. She may conclude that she (or her associate) spent too much time on the matter and that she cannot in good conscience bill the client for her inefficiency. This is sometimes called writing down the bill.

- The lawyer may have to share fees with another lawyer, or pay credit card processing costs.

- The lawyer will incur costs associated with the billing process. If sending out a bill has an attached cost, sending out three bills will cost three times as much. If more draconian measures are required (e.g., bringing in a collection agency or suing the client), these costs further reduce the value of what the lawyer ultimately collects.

- The lawyer may not be able to collect some or all of the charges in the bill. The longer the time after the work is completed, the less likely it is that the lawyer will be able to collect the value of her work. She may, at some point, write off the bill as uncollectible.

In short, the longer the wait between the time the work is done and the fee is collected, the less the value of the lawyer's work. You can see the loss of value in Chart 11–1. It should be apparent that ideally the lawyer should collect her fees in advance (retainers) or at the point of service (e.g., a real estate lawyer takes a fee at settlement when funds are disbursed).

Chart 11–1 Value of Work over Time

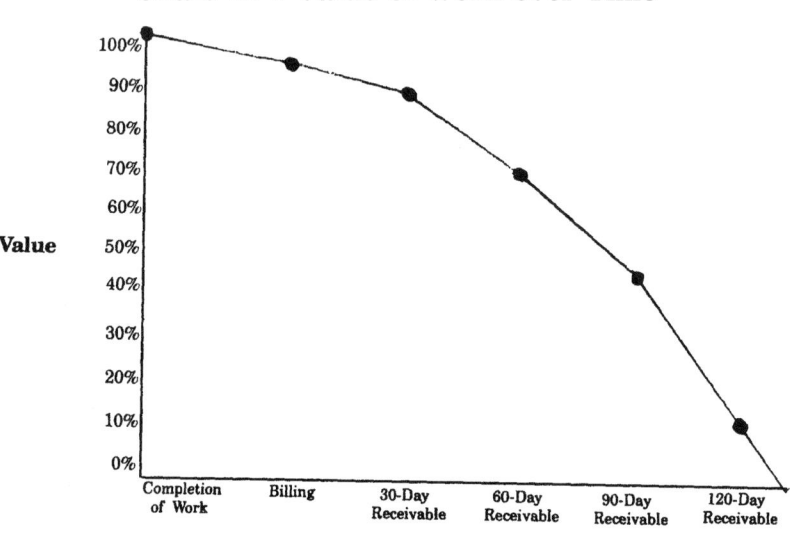

When it is necessary to bill for work after the fact, the lawyer will only collect some percentage of the total value. This percentage is called realization. Thus, if the value of a lawyer's work is $100,000, but at the end of the day she collects $80,000, her realization is 80%. Although realization rates can vary according to the type of practice and local custom, the important question here is how to maximize realization. As a general rule realization above 90% is good, and realization below 80% leaves something to be desired. In order to collect the greatest percentage of the value of the lawyer's services possible, the lawyer should take a number of steps:

- At the outset, use a written fee agreement that clearly sets forth the scope of the representation and the basis for the fee. Not only does a written agreement establish in the client's mind the value of the lawyer's service, but also the act of signing the written agreement formalizes the client's commitment to pay.

- During the course of the representation keep records of time spent on the matter, whether you are billing by the hour or not. If you do not record your time, you *will* lose some of it. Keep the client informed through interim billings of the progress of your work.
- Bill promptly, regularly and in detail. Make sure the bill clearly reflects your effort.
- Have a collection policy. If the client fails to pay, follow up in 30, 60 and 90 days, with follow up letters of increasing stringency.
- If the client does not pay, call the client directly to determine the reasons for non-payment. Do not delegate this task to a secretary, billing clerk or legal assistant. The lawyer has the most clout with the client.
- Produce reports of aged receivables (unpaid bills). Most financial systems will generate charts showing 30, 60, 90 and 120–day receivables in descending order of amount owed. Spend most of your energy on the largest, most recent debts. The older the debt the less likely you are to collect, and the smaller debts may not justify your extra effort. Invest in the big-ticket items.
- Know when to walk away (and know when to cut a deal). At some point you may simply abandon your efforts to collect unpaid fees. You can sue or turn the debts over to a collection agency, but such actions have their own hidden costs in fees, lost goodwill, time and energy.

If you imagine that the value of a solo practitioner's work is $500,000 with an overhead of 50%, at a realization rate of 70% the solo collects $350,000 and takes home $175,000. At 80%, the same lawyer collects $400,000 and takes home $200,000; at 90%, the lawyer takes home $225,000 (twice as much as the 70% lawyer). Thus, the lawyer or law firm that manages receivables effectively can produce profound results for the bottom line.

6. COMPENSATION

A second problem in many firms is deciding how to divide the profit. If we imagine the firm's net profit as a pie, the question becomes: how big of a piece does each partner get? The choices that a firm makes about how to allocate compensation will be a major factor in determining the partners' and employees' satisfaction level. Hardly a week goes by without reading in the national legal tabloids that some firm has split up or lost a contingent of lawyers over who gets the money.

A great deal has been written about partnership compensation plans. As far back as 1942, Reginald Heber Smith, in his classic monograph *Law Office Organization*, suggested a plan for allocating a firm's profits (see pages 105–107). Over a half-century later firms are still struggling with the same issues. Like marriages ending in divorce, many law firm breakups will be able to trace the roots of their conflict to differences about the allocation of money. On the other hand, some firms have managed to establish compensation plans that are systematic, orderly and equitable. These firms have enjoyed stability and growth in part because they have learned how to deal with compensation issues.

The financial management equation is significantly affected by compensation. On the one hand, the largest item of overhead in most firms is personnel. Salaries and benefits may represent from 50–70% of all overhead expenses. In the scenario above with $250,000 overhead, this would mean that staff could cost from $125,000 to $175,000. Not only have the costs of staffing increased dramatically over the past several decades, they continue to escalate, and law firms are often at a disadvantage competing against large companies for talent. Further, in large part due to spiraling health care charges, the cost of benefits has risen significantly as well. The topic of staffing is covered in Chapter 8, but it is worth noting here that law firms pay dearly to retain the employees they need to operate efficiently.

The owners of the legal business are paid in the form of profit. In some organizational models, the firm may hire the lawyer-owners as employees and pay them a salary, but this is in a sense illusory. If the firm cannot make payroll, it undoubtedly will be the partners who do not take home a paycheck. Many firms place undistributed profits in individual drawing accounts, from which partners can withdraw funds as needed. Either way, if there is no profit, there is nothing left for the partners. Chapter 4 addressed compensation of the owners. In terms of financial management, however, it is important to remember that the owners get paid after all the expenses (including staff) are paid out of the fees that are actually collected.

Traditionally, because law firms were relatively inexpensive to operate, partners took virtually all the profits out of the firm as draws. The concept of retained earnings was foreign to many firms. As operating costs, capital expenditures, and risks have increased, law firms have been increasingly pressed to reinvest some of the profits. A rule of thumb in the business world is that companies should keep six months of operating expenses in reserve at all times. In the example of a firm with $250,000 annual overhead, this would mean keeping a reserve account of at least $125,000. Although many lawyers continue to operate from hand to mouth, an increasing number are creating reserve funds and allocating some portion of profits to those accounts.

Those lawyers who do not wish to deal with the trials and tribulations that come with dividing the pie may avoid the problem by pursuing a sole proprietorship. Remember, however, that profit derived from an individual practice is strictly related to your own efforts. Many solos come to realize that there are often not enough hours in the day to do earn enough for a comfortable living. The individual practitioner takes home whatever is left after the bills are paid—a fairly simple income distribution system.

7. BUDGETING AND REPORTING

Implicit in any financial structure is the notion that financial data, once collected can be reported to management and used as a tool in making decisions not only about day-to-day operations, but long term. A number of financial management software tools are available to law firms, including the most popular program for smaller firms: Quick Books. Although there a number of other commercial software financial management products on the market, some firms utilize financial software that is a part of an integrated practice management software, such as Juris, TABS3, Practice Master or Abacus. Recently, cloud computing systems have begun to replace desktop systems in the law office environment. In some cases vendors are offering a cloud-based alternative to their earlier systems; in other cases, new vendors, such as CLIO have entered the market. Other firms use their own proprietary software developed either in-house or by the firm's financial advisors. Recently, cloud computing options have become increasingly popular. With such systems, both application software and data are stored on distant servers, rather than locally on servers in the firm's offices. The advantages include the ability to continually upgrade software, the increased security that a cloud-based system can provide, and the reduction in cost associated with not having to maintain local storage space for programs and data.

Given the multiplicity of options, the firm should select a system that is right for its size, type of practice, financial situation, and partner sophistication. It always makes sense to determine whether the firm's financial package will be compatible with the system used by the firm's accountant or CPA. Thus, the accountant should be a participant in discussions about financial software.

Financial planning begins with assumptions. For example, the firm might assume that inflation in the coming year will be approximately the same as in the current year, or that the size of the firm will remain constant over the course of the year. If the assumptions underlying a budget change, the budget numbers will change. It is useful, therefore, to articulate the assumptions at the beginning of the budget planning process. Additionally, if any aspects of the reports need to be explained, they should be. Sometimes, just looking at spreadsheets or even pie charts generated by the software can be overwhelming, if the numbers are not explained.

All software contains income and expense categories to which transactions can be posted. Most software starts with a template that the firm can customize to meet its unique needs. Software should also have levels of security governing who can access financial data and under what circumstances. All software will permit reports of financial activity over the course of designated time periods. At a minimum, the financial reports should include:

- Projected budget—anticipated income and expense over the course of the coming year, usually capable of being broken down by month and quarter. The projected budget typically also reports how the current year (month, quarter) compares to the same period in the prior or former years. Most software can also compare budgeted results to actual results.

- Actual budget—this report shows the actual income and expense for a given year, including reports by month and quarter.

- Cash flow—this report shows the actual cash deposited in the firm's operating account and the expenses debited to the account. Generally speaking, the firm must always have enough money in its operating account to pay its bills.

- Balance sheet—also referred to as a statement of assets and liabilities, the balance sheet reports the current net worth of the firm, but software should be able to generate comparisons to prior years as well.

- Many software programs permit users to develop more sophisticated or detailed reports to answer special questions about the source and allocation of financial resources.

Having the capability to generate financial reports is not helpful if the partners do not take the time to study the reports, to meet about financial questions and to participate in financial decisions over time. As lawyers delegate more financial decisions to non-lawyer managers, this has the potential to become a problem.

Note that the firm's client trust accounts should be maintained completely separately from its operating accounts. The topic of trust accounts is covered in more detail in Chapter 14, but it is worth noting at this point that although the trust account(s) may use the same financial software as the firm's financial management accounts, the two must always be kept totally separate. See Model Rule 1.15.

Finally, in many firms, a CPA will conduct an independent audit of the firm's books. This audit will employ Generally Accepted Accounting Principles (GAAP) to ascertain the reliability of the firm's financial records. Although it is unusual, law firms are not immune to financial misconduct by partners or employees. The certified accounting will typically generate a balance sheet, an audited budget and a review of cash flow. These audited reports should mirror the unofficial reports produced by the firm during the course of the year.

8. FINANCIAL PLANNING

As mentioned at the beginning of this chapter, sound financial planning is a critical component of any law firm's long-term success. Working with numbers may not be the most exciting activity for many lawyers, but it is at best a necessary evil. Any comprehensive long-range plan that ignores financing will be inadequate at best, or disastrous at worst. Other financial questions have an important effect on the success of the firm:

IT'S THAT TIME OF YEAR: SOME TIPS TO HELP MANAGE YOUR FIRM'S BUDGETING PROCESS

From *Accounting for Law Firms*, by John G. Iezzi (December 2001).

The end of one year and the beginning of another is sometimes a stressful time for law firm managers. It is the time they must answer the question constantly being raised by their partners: How much are we going to make next year? With compensation time approaching, each partner becomes overly consumed with the potential income that the firm can achieve in the coming year and the share of that income that will be allocated to them.

Fortunately, this doesn't have to be a stressful time if the managers approach the budgeting or financial planning process with the correct mind set, and more importantly, with an understanding of the process. This process permits managers to more easily and accurately project profitability and put them in a better position to answer questions raised by the owners. Following are some suggestions to help managers through this process:

First of all, contrary to popular belief, expenses are the easiest to project. Compensation, related fringe benefits, occupancy costs and perhaps the insurances such as malpractice make up 85 percent to 90 percent of the expense budget and are relatively easy to predict with a high degree of certainty. Don't get hung up on how much the firm is going to spend on office supplies and postage; just add some percent to last year's number and go on with life. Within a short period of time, your expense budget can be fairly complete. It can be fine tuned as the prior year closes and the final numbers are determined against which comparisons can be made. Obviously, unusual items that did occur or will occur need to be considered.

The income side is the most important part of the budget and it, too, is fairly easy to predict, assuming you are capable of manipulating the ingredients that go into projecting revenues on the basis of the firm's overall capacity to produce profits or net income. Remember, owner compensation equates to net income. It is not an expense but rather is placed "below the line" after expenses are subtracted from gross receipts.

To determine the firm's capacity to generate net income, the manager must be aware of the factors that must be considered in the budgeting process. These factors are affected by the culture of the firm as it relates to billable hour production; to the financial management effectiveness of the attorneys as it relates to billing and collection efficiency, and to the client base as it relates to billing rates, rate discounting and billing

realization. Thus, before getting started, the law firm manager must have the following information:
- Number of timekeepers at each level, i.e., partners, associates and legal assistants,
- Average billable hours at each level,
- Average billing rates at each level,
- Beginning work in process and accounts receivable levels,
- Timing of billing and collections,
- Rate variance percentage,
- Billing variance percentage,
- Estimated accounts receivable write-offs.

Most of this information will come from various firm records, either historical or otherwise, that have been kept on the firm. A five-year average would be most appropriate for determining these factors, which will even out the years that may have been exceptionally high or exceptionally low.

Once accumulated, this information is then placed in one of the many financial planning models that exist and the net income levels are calculated. What-if scenarios can be prepared to alter the assumptions in the event that the end result is not in keeping with what the owners believe should be the income expectations for the ensuing year.

Keep in mind that it is difficult to go against history for the sole purpose of elevating net income to a number that the partners want to achieve. For example, if it is the culture of the firm for the associates over a period of time to average 1,750 hours per year, it would be silly to assume 1,900, simply to inflate net income to a more acceptable level. The fact remains that a firm with a stagnant number of attorneys over a three- or four-year period will find it difficult to materially affect net income levels without major changes in those areas that affect the budget in the most significant manner. This would include increased billable hours, or increased rates or perhaps a change in the method by which clients are billed and collections are monitored.

Regardless of the methodology of preparing the budget, at the end of the day the firm still must determine its overall capacity to produce revenues. To do that, it must examine those factors identified above. Unless this is done, it will not be possible to accurately project net profits or to monitor results during the year in the event income levels are not being achieved. As a result, the owners get unreasonable expectations that cannot be met and that create internal strife throughout the year, particularly when draw checks cannot be distributed.

In addition, keep in mind that net income does not necessarily equate to cash available for distribution. This can only be calculated through the cash flow analysis that starts with net income from the budget but then takes into account the sources and uses of cash that do not go through the income statement, such as client advances, debt reduction and fixed-asset acquisition, or those with no cash effect such as depreciation.

PROBLEMS AND QUESTIONS

1. Can you imagine a legal services organization that would not need to generate a profit in order to survive? Why would the bottom line be relevant to such a "firm" anyway?

2. What income is actually realized from the work expended by the lawyers in a firm? What percentage of fees billed are collected and when? If unbilled and uncollected fees represent a depreciating asset, how can firms maximize collections?

3. What law firm expenses, if any, can be controlled? Can a firm cut costs without cutting services? How?

4. Can money problems be eliminated or alleviated? Do you agree with the authors of the readings in this chapter as to how firms should address financial issues?

5. What is capital? Why is it important to a law firm's financial health? How do firms acquire initial capital? How do they obtain later infusions of capital?

6. What are the pros and cons of borrowing to finance a law practice as opposed to investing in the practice? What limits on outside investment do lawyers face that other types of businesses do not?

7. What do we mean by the term cash flow? Why is cash flow important? Why is it critical in the start-up phase of the business?

8. What are the start-up expenses of a law firm? What expenses can be deferred and what expenses must be front-loaded? Why would a firm defer start-up expenses rather than pay them up front?

9. What income is actually realized from the work expended? What percentage of fees billed are collected, and when? If unbilled and uncollected fees represent a depreciating asset, how can firms maximize collections? What expenses, if any, can be controlled?

10. Using a financial software program, develop a two-year financial plan for your firm, showing the following:
    - Assumptions in your budget plan
    - Initial capitalization, including partner contributions and loans;
    - start-up expenses;
    - Cash flow analysis on a quarterly basis;
    - A budget reflecting anticipated profit (loss)
    - A balance sheet showing the firm's net worth—
        - On opening day,
        - At the end of one year,

- At the end of two years.
- You should utilize income and expense projections developed in prior assignments.

C. FINANCING A LAW PRACTICE

1. INTRODUCTION

When a law firm opens its doors for the first time, it must have in place financing to support start-up costs and contingent resources to provide for possible negative cash flow, which is most likely to occur in the early months of practice. Law firms face special problems in the area of financing that other organizations do not in that they are not unique in selling a particular product that consumers demand. A law firm is unlike a corporation in that a corporation can sell stock when it needs capital. When a law firm needs additional cash, however, it can't sell shares or ask rich relatives to invest in the firm by promising them an equity interest.

New businesses require investment, which can come in the form of capital contributions or loans. For a law firm, capital must come from the partners/owners, since lawyers are prohibited by Model Rule 5.4(d) (or its state counterpart) from financing a law firm with capital investment from nonlawyers. Although the rules to not prohibit lawyers from borrowing money from nonlawyers, whether it be the local bank or your rich Uncle Bob, they do prohibit nonlawyers from securing an equity position in the firm for their investment. For example, when you buy stock in a company, you own a share of that company and you hope to receive dividends representing a portion of the profits in the business.

You also anticipate that the value of the company (the equity) will increase, as well. The price of the stock represents its value, and a good stock investment should increase in value over time. Since Model Rule 5.4(d) does not allow nonlawyers to have an equity interest in the law firm, as a lawyer you must be very careful about what type of investment you should accept.

Despite limitations in the Model Rules on non-lawyer equity investment, there are many options for structuring initial financing. Although a law firm cannot go public with an Initial Purchase Offering (IPO), as allowed in the U.K. and Australia, it still has a number of options worth considering. While passive investment is not allowed, there are no restrictions on law firms seeking commercial or proprietary loans, which must be repaid. Ironically, lenders may exert the same kinds of pressures on law firm decision making that investors would, but law firm borrowing has never been a suspect form of financing. A law firm may obtain financing from one or more "sugar daddy" partners, but such arrangements are likely to involve the investing lawyers getting something for their largesse. There is no one option that is right for all firms. Finding a solution to a firm's capitalization problems depends on the firm's unique circumstances.

In a law firm, the partners invest in the business. Their compensation is based on the net profit of the business. As owners of the law firm, partners or shareholders hope that their initial capital investment, like the value of stock in a company, will increase over time. It is this type of capital investment that Model Rule 5.4 prohibits permits.

Other types of investment present similar problems. One of the other ideas for a possible infusion of cash may come from passive investments. A passive investment may involve a limited partner, who owns a share of the business, but is not active in its operation. If the passive investor is not a licensed lawyer this type of investment is also prohibited under Model Rule 5.4(d). Although pension plans represent an exception to the general rule against profit sharing with nonlawyers, if the pension plan is merely a vehicle for otherwise impermissible passive investment, it may be improper. Rule 5.4(a) provides for the estate or spouse of a lawyer in the firm to participate in a pension or profit-sharing arrangement, but prohibits others from doing so.

For instance, suppose a law firm hired a nonlegal consulting firm to handle its administration for an agreed upon fee (which would be an appropriate action), but then permitted the consulting firm to contribute capital through "voluntary" contributions to and to take profit through the profit-sharing provisions of the pension plan. Such a scheme might come under scrutiny.

The same might be true for an elaborate lease arrangement permitting the infusion of capital and the allocation of profit by a passive investor. It is not clear whether or not it is possible to circumvent the strictures of Rule 5.4 through innovative structuring of the business relationship, or whether bar associations are even willing to prosecute lawyers whose only ethical sin is to seek creative financing. It is clear that as the costs of starting and operating a law business escalate, more legal practitioners will be forced to find novel forms of financing in order to operate successfully.

The only acceptable method for financial investment in the law firm, if it does not have enough capital drawn from the initial partners, is to seek supplemental financing through loans, lines of credit and other forms of financing that require scheduled repayment. In unusual circumstances, funding may come from private grants or federal programs that do not require repayment.

2. PARTNER CAPITAL CONTRIBUTIONS

The concept of capitalization, discussed above (see pages 265–267) is integral to the financing of law firms. Regardless of how capitalization by the partners is structured, every new firm has initial cash requirements. In its simplest form, the capital investment of a new partner should be E/P, where E = total equity, and P = the number of partners. In many firms, however, different partners have different equity; typically the initial equity of new partners is less than the equity position of senior partners. In some cases, the firm may finance a new partner's equity, with repayment of the "loan" over time. Some firms may include partners chosen for their ability to infuse cash into the business. Such cash cows, if they do not otherwise stack up as partner material, are not usually wise choices simply because they have money. Cash-poor rainmakers should be scrutinized carefully as well to make sure they can deliver the clients.

Remember, the law firm needs cash, but it also needs partners who can bring in the clients and can deliver on the services. The field of law is, at its very essence, a service industry, and if the service is anything less than good, there are other competitors down the street ready and able to take the business away.

3. BORROWING

One important question for every new firm to ask is, "How should we allocate financing between cash contributions and loans?" If you do not have much cash, the answer to that question may be easy. In many cases, however, the answer is not so simple. You may be able to take your savings, sell some stock, collect your graduation present and come up with a nice little nest egg for starting your firm. Such a plan may leave you cash poor, with all of your assets tied up in the equity of this new law firm.

Loans, on the other hand, do not require partner investment up front, but defer payment until such time as the loans become due. Usually, loans are paid off as fixed expenses over time in the ordinary course of the business. The terms and conditions of lending arrangements are varied and depend on the circumstances and objectives of the borrower and the repayments terms set by the lender.

The negative aspect to borrowing is interest. One way to look at interest is that it is how much you have to pay to borrow money. In the lending business, the loan principal is an asset that the lender lets you use. Interest, on the other hand, is the lender's way of making a profit. By giving the borrower use of the bank's money, the bank hopes to get its principal back, plus interest, which is in effect the bank's fee for using the money. In the lending business, there is always some risk that the borrower will not be able to repay the loan. The anticipated risk determines the rate of interest the lender charges for the use of its funds. Not surprisingly, the riskier the loan, the more expensive it will be for the borrower, which is manifested in higher interest rates. When borrowing, consider these general rules:

- secured loans are cheaper than unsecured loans;
- variable interest rates are riskier than fixed rates;
- borrowers with good credit histories are less risky than borrowers with poor credit;

- lenders are also likely to charge a lower rate over a longer period of time and a higher rate for a shorter duration;
- lenders will favor loans for fixed amounts over lines of credit that can be activated or not at the borrower's discretion; and finally,
- the cost of money is influenced by the prime interest rate, which is the rate charged by the Federal Reserve to its best bank customers when they borrow money. The banks in turn will make loans to businesses and individuals at a number of points above the prime rate. The prime rate fluctuates over time and economic conditions; thus, the borrower should be aware that borrowing during certain times will be more expensive than others.

One disadvantage of loans is that they increase fixed operating costs, because a payment is due each month, whether or not the firm has made any money. When a firm takes out a fixed loan, it should be aware, that even during periods of negative cash flow, the loan repayment is still due. It follows that if borrowing is excessive and the cash flow is low, the ability to repay the loan may be jeopardized. If fees fail to generate sufficient revenue, financial difficulties are certainly foreseeable. If times are tough and there is no possibility of an infusion of cash, an investor's only way of getting any return on his investment may be through the dissolution of the business or a termination of the ownership interest, assuming there are any assets remaining after the creditors have been paid.

Loans come in many forms ranging from short-term business loans to lines of credit. Repayment of them may be fixed, subject to variable rates or balloon payments near maturity dates. Borrowers often have options about how to structure their debt. For the start-up firm, this often means reducing payments during the critical first year of the business. Law firms, like other start-up businesses, typically go through a period during which expenses exceed income. When a firm opens its doors, it has no clients and no revenue. Expenses, on the other hand, begin to accrue from the first day. Additionally, even if clients retain the firm when it first begins operations, the firm must do the work, bill the client, and collect the fee before the money is deposited in the bank.

A delay in fee collections may create a problem if payment for the expenses is due but the clients' checks are in the proverbial mail. This can be a major concern during the first few months of a law firm's existence, especially because it may take ninety days or more to attract the first clients, complete the necessary work, bill for services and receive payment for the work. If cash flow becomes a problem, the firm may need to ask the lender for more generous terms, borrow additional funds, or return to the partners for another infusion of capital.

In reality, clients will not simply appear at the firm's doorstep the day it opens. A well-orchestrated marketing plan will attract clients in increasing numbers over time. All firms will have client problems when they open, including firms consisting of lawyers from other established offices. Clients of any professional are always reluctant to move to a new practice when there was a comfort level at the old one, even if it was your trusted professional that moved.

Law firms may be able to avoid some of these foreseeable financial problems by requiring advance retainers, handling work involving point of delivery payment (wills or property closings) and avoiding cases with high up-front costs and a long or risky payout such as plaintiff's personal injury work. For example, PI work is problematic for start-up firms, because cases often require up-front investment by the firm at a time when it has little or no free cash. Notwithstanding these efforts and careful planning, most firms will experience a period of negative cash flow during the early months of practice.

A standard in the business world is to break-even after the first year. Break-even is accomplished when the firm's revenue for the year equals expenses. In the first few months of the law firm operations, expenses are expected to exceed revenue, as there is a delay in client billing and the client base is usually not reached immediately. At some point, revenues should exceed expenses, but true break-even occurs only after the losses from negative cash flow in the early months of operation are recouped. In order to break even during the first year, the total revenue must equal the total expenses during that period.

Jay Foonberg, author of *How to Start and Build a Law Practice*, advises start-up lawyers to have two years-worth of living expenses in the bank before they open their practice. Thus, even in a worst-case scenario, the owner(s) will not have to take anything out of the business for a two-year period. A riskier approach would be to set aside one year's living expenses, but anything less would be foolhardy. There is always a chance that in the first weeks the office is opened for business, a client will walk in and leave a one million dollar retainer, but that is very unlikely.

Most practitioners can expect some tough times in the early months, with minimal increases in fee revenue, reaching equilibrium between revenue and expenses sometime towards the end or just after a year in business. The second year should produce some profitability and result in compensation for the owner(s). As a rule of thumb, you should not anticipate taking profit from the business during the first year, but for the second year you should anticipate that your income (profit) will be equal to what you would have earned in a salaried position doing the same work in the same community. Hopefully, in subsequent years, you will earn more than you would earn on salary. In short, opening a law firm is not a get-rich-quick scheme, but for those willing to persevere it can be financially rewarding.

Before opening for business, the firm must attempt to forecast the early months' negative cash flow. Expenses, including loan repayment, can be budgeted with some degree of accuracy. Start-up expenses, including prepayments (e.g., deposits for rent, utilities, etc.) and capital expenditures (e.g., purchased equipment such as desks, chairs and computers) can be projected as well. Revenue is the uncertain element in the equation (Will paying clients actually show up?)

One conservative way to estimate revenue is to assume, for year one, that revenue will equal expenses. Next, plot the expenses for the first year on a monthly basis. Then, plot the revenue over the twelve months of the year as follows: assume no collections for ninety days (three months), then project revenue over the next nine months using a straight-line increase, with the total revenue for the year equal to the total expense. This approach will generate a projected negative cash flow for the early months (the sum of the monthly differences between revenue and expense).

By adding the negative cash flow to the projected start-up expenses and subtracting the partner(s)' capital contributions, you will have calculated a number representing the amount of outside financing you will require. Even if the firm's break-even occurs early enough in the first year of operation to minimize negative operating cash flow, if the start-up expenses exceed the available capital, financing will still be necessary.

**Chart 11-2
Cash Flow Projections**

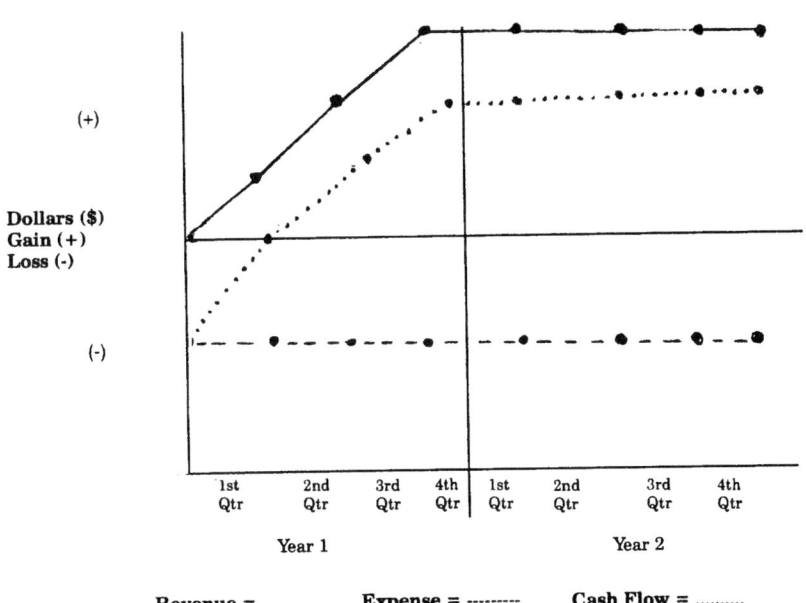

**Chart 11-3
Profit (Loss) Projection**

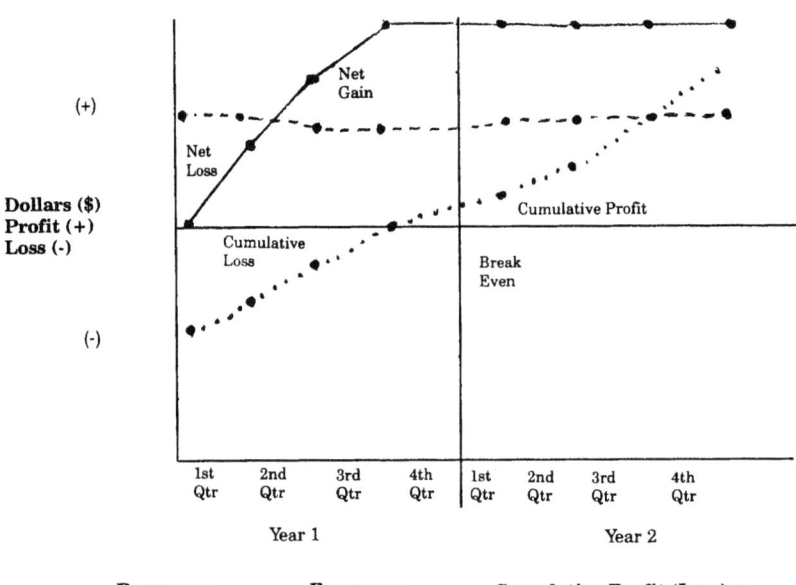

Stated another way, you have to have enough money in the bank to pay all the bills until the business brings in enough money to cover expenses on an ongoing basis. New firms must consider whether it is possible to defer payment of some start-up expenses. Generally, in law firms, as in most businesses, the firm may amortize certain expenses by paying them over a period of time. Amortization of expenses (e.g., paying for equipment on an installment plan) has the effect of lowering fixed costs during the critical start-up phase of the business and extending repayment into a period where a revenue stream exists

Assuming that the partners make capital cash contributions, some or all of the cash requirements may be covered. Any projected loss not covered through capital, must be underwritten by outside financing. Even if the firm achieves positive cash flow before the end of the first year, it still needs cash to pay the bills at the beginning of the year. The firm may want to borrow money, in advance, to cover anticipated negative cash flow it is reasonably certain will occur, or a line of credit for unanticipated operating losses.

Perhaps the worst example of law firm financing is described in the book *A Civil Action,* by Jonathon Harr in which a law firm financed its operations through credit cards and obtaining new credit cards to pay off old ones, a strategy that eventually bankrupted the firm:

> Gordon kept in his desk drawer a large collection of credit cards bound with a rubber band. These cards were all charged to the hilt

and useless. He had used them to get cash advances to pay operating expenses and salaries. Woburn had turned him into a prodigious consumer of credit and he often received invitations to apply for new credit cards. These came from banks he never heard of—in Nevada, Arizona, North Dakota, and California. Gordon called them "shyster cards." The banks would charge 22.9 percent interest, but Gordon didn't mind that. He liked the cards because they required him to pay only 1 to 2 percent of the principal each month. He'd fill out the application forms and send them back by Federal Express. Within a month, each new credit card would be laden with thousand dollars of debt. *A Civil Action,* Vintage Books, New York, p. 347 (1995).

A few simple rules may provide guidance to the start-up firm regarding financing. Consideration of these principles may avoid a lot of grief and will maximize the prospects for financial stability in the firm at the earliest possible time.

- Do not be afraid to borrow money when you need it, but do not borrow more than you need. Always anticipate financial problems and be aware that debt must be paid back. This may seem like a simple admonition, but this is not always easy to accomplish.

- If you must err, err by estimating expenses on the high side and income on the low side. It is always better for the actual profit to come out better than projections, than it is to come out worse.

- Be brutally honest. Too often, new businesses deceive themselves about how much they will make and when, as well as how much it will cost to get started and run the business.

- Get help. A certified public accountant, a lawyer experienced in small business start-ups, a banker or a consultant will be able to offer objective advice on budget planning and financing. The Small Business Administration offers a service called SCORE (Senior Core of Retired Executives) who can help to advise entrepreneurs. Your own counsel is often not the best advice in such situations.

- Give yourself plenty of lead-time. If you are in law school, you can begin to develop your financial plan while you are still in school, while you study for the bar and while you wait for the bar results. If you are in a firm, develop your plan to open a practice over a period of time. Remember: even if you are in school or planning to join a law firm, the chances are very good that some time during your career, you will be opening an office alone or with other lawyers. It makes sense to always have a contingency plan in the back of your mind.

No set of guidelines can guarantee success. On the other hand, there is a great deal that you can do to reduce the risk and maximize the likelihood that your law firm will be financially viable. A word about risk-taking: you cannot be risk-averse and be a successful entrepreneur. This means that you must be willing to undertake a venture and assume debt and expenses without knowing if or when you will see a dime in your pocket. You must be willing to lie awake at night wondering how you will possibly be able to pay the bills. You must be willing to put in whatever hours it takes to become productive. You must be confident enough in your own skills both as a lawyer and a businessperson to make your vision a reality.

Starting a business may not be for everyone. If you grew up in an environment where you always had an allowance and where your parents always had a paycheck from an employer, the uncertainties of being an entrepreneur may be more than you are able to undertake. If, on the other hand, you grew up in an entrepreneurial family, and from an early age appreciated the uncertainties of self-employment, you might be better equipped to deal with the pressures that come with starting a business. If you have always worked for someone else, you might be more comfortable where you have a boss, subordinates and a place in some corporate structure than you would being the boss yourself. Conversely, if you have opened your own non-legal business before law school, you may be better equipped to start a law business after graduation. There are exceptions to this rule, but very often one's comfort level with the risks of entrepreneurial ventures is highly correlated to the likelihood of success in such ventures.

4. CREATING A BUSINESS PLAN

Assuming that you will need to obtain financing for your new law firm, you should anticipate the process and take steps leading to the likelihood of a favorable decision. A key component of the financing process is the development of a business plan. Although it makes sense to develop a solid business plan for any start-up business, a banker or other lender will, undoubtedly, want to see a business plan before making a decision to lend you money. A business plan is a good indicator of whether you have done your homework and whether you are the kind of risk the lender wants to take.

The business plan should contain four components: an overview, a marketing plan, a resources plan, and a financial plan. These should be consolidated into a single, attractive and easy to read document.

a. Overview

The overview or summary of the business plan should state concisely what business you plan to undertake, how you will attract a clientele, what resources will support you in your endeavor, and a summary of your financial projections, including a specific statement as to how much money you will need. A business lender with experience reviewing many loan applications will be able to get a good idea about the merits of your plan from this overview. The overview should, ideally, be one page in length, but in no case longer than two pages. It should summarize what the rest of the plan will say in greater detail. It should be positive and honest in its appraisal. Most importantly, it must be persuasive.

b. Marketing Plan

The marketing plan was discussed in Chapter 6. This plan should be incorporated into the business plan. The importance of the marketing plan cannot be underestimated: it will demonstrate that you have identified a targeted customer base for your services and developed a feasible plan to reach that audience. If you do not have prospects or a methodology of how to bring in clients, no lender will be willing to go out on a limb to finance your business. The marketing plan will also need to ring true with the lender's own assessment of the marketplace and the firm's projections.

c. Resources Plan

The material covered in Chapters 8–10, represents the heart of the resources plan. This part of the business plan should describe who will be the players on your team, including both lawyers and support staff and consultants and advisors. The plan should describe the skills and background of the key players, and summarize the costs of obtaining their services. This section of the plan should contain an organizational chart showing lines of authority and decision-making responsibilities as was outlined in any partnership agreement.

The resources plan should describe the physical and information resources available to the new organization, including: office space, equipment, furniture, and books/electronic information resources. These physical and information resources should be designed to support the human resources' arm of the organization. There should be some overarching philosophy and a clear relationship with both the marketing and financial plans. This section should clearly identify the names of an accountant, legal representative, banker, consultants and other advisers who have been or will be working with the firm during the start-up phase.

d. Financial Plan

The last, but perhaps most critical element of the business plan, is the financial plan. The financial plan should include the following elements, along with an explanatory text and appropriate charts:

- A pro forma (projected) budget showing profit or loss for the first two years of operations;
- A start-up plan, including—
    - Capital contributions of the partners;
    - Projected start-up expenses (incurred before operations begin);
    - Anticipated loans;

- A cash flow analysis demonstrating both the need for financing through negative cash flow in the early months and the prospect for positive cash flow thereafter;
- A statement of net worth showing assets and liabilities. Although the net worth of many start-up firms is not great, this chart is useful because it establishes the business' equity position, including both investment and physical assets, and debts and other liabilities.

These three reports are discussed more fully earlier in this chapter. They should be included in the business plan along with descriptive notes to explain figures that may, otherwise, be confusing.

5. SELLING THE PLAN

After preparing the business plan, you will need to present it to a lender, and make a case for financing your firm. It is worth noting that lawyers are trained to be persuasive, so in one sense, this presentation involves nothing more than doing what law school has prepared you to do. At the same time, there are things you can do to improve the likelihood you will obtain financing:

- Develop a relationship with the lender before you go in for a loan. You can start, now, to build a banking relationship in the geographic area in which you plan to practice. Meet the banker, personally, so he or she is not a stranger when you go in to ask for money.
- Establish credit. Borrow money at this institution or others, and pay it back. A good credit rating is one of the best attributes that any prospective borrower can have.
- Be willing to pledge assets as security. If you have a home or other tangible assets, the lender will be more comfortable making a loan knowing that it can turn to a security interest in case of default. A willingness to pledge personal assets, also, has the positive affect of demonstrating your commitment to the project to the lender.
- Be professional. Set up an appointment to meet concerning your loan application. Be on time. Dress like you were going to argue a case before the Supreme Court.
- Relax. Shake off the butterflies. Prepare what you plan to say. Anticipate the difficult questions. Be friendly but not familiar. Make your case succinctly and clearly.
- Know your plan. Be prepared to answer questions about the business plan or to refer to parts of the plan as necessary.
- Do a dress rehearsal. Get someone who is familiar with financials to prep you for the actual presentation.

All of these suggestions make it more likely that your proposal will gain favorable consideration. Do not be disheartened, however, if you have to go to several lenders in order to get a favorable decision. Although the track record for start-up law firms is considerably better than for most other start-up businesses, you should not assume that all lenders understand the economics of the legal profession or the prospects for your firm. They may have read stories about an oversupply of lawyers or had bad experiences with lawyers in the past and you will have to persuade them that you are a good risk.

PROBLEMS AND QUESTIONS

1. What impediments to financial stability is a start-up law firm likely to encounter? Does the 50% failure rate for new businesses generally apply to law firms? Why or why not?

2. Combine your firms marketing, resources and financial plans into a coherent document with a 1–2 page overview.

PART 3

MANAGING THE LEGAL WORK PRODUCT

■ ■ ■

Chapter 12

Providing Excellent Services

■ ■ ■

A. THE YIN AND YANG OF EXCELLENCE

This chapter addresses the duality of achieving excellence in the practice of law. When law firms take affirmative steps to practice law prudently, they also avoid the mistakes that get them into trouble. Actually, success and failure, competence and incompetence, excellence and ineptitude are all related. The same activities contribute to the achievement or non-achievement of professional standards. Yet, it is generally preferable to think in terms of striving for excellence in the practice of law rather than avoiding trouble sliding by with minimal effort. A major theme of this book is that excellent management produces excellent lawyers and conversely poor management produces professional failure. It takes work to practice competently, but a commitment to quality can be the best defense against the twin risks of professional malpractice and discipline.

The Eastern religious concept of yin and yang has some application to the question of competence in the Western practice of law. Like the interlocking circles of the symbol, we need to understand that excellence and failure are two faces of the same coin.

The behavior that produces quality legal services is often the same behavior that is lacking when lawyers fail to meet the professional standard of care. Thus, maintaining a good calendar system can ensure that a lawyer does not miss deadlines, and failing to maintain a calendar can be the cause of overlooking a critical date.

Problems and Questions

1. Can you think of particular ways that lawyers behave that reflect the yin and yang of excellence illustrated above?

2. Why is it preferable to strive for excellence rather than to just avoid mistakes? Are there times when it is necessary to keep minimum standards of behavior and/or liability in mind?

3. Apart from malpractice and discipline, what are the consequences of delivering an inferior work product? What are the benefits of producing an excellent product?

B. MANAGING QUALITY

Quality is illusive. We often observe it as much by its absence or failure as by its presence. We don't notice that our electric lights go on every day but we do react quickly when there is a blackout and the power system fails. Like other businesses, law firms must understand that the quality of their product is integral to their long-term success. Individual lawyers must understand that their professional reputation rests on the quality of their work. Quality is about excellence: creating the highest standards and then living up to those standards. Quality runs from top to bottom in an organization. Quality means delivering excellent service to every client. The best lawyers can be betrayed by incompetent filing clerks, a defective fax machine, or an inappropriate comment made by a receptionist during an incoming phone call from a client.

Quality control means inspecting the work before it goes out the door. Quality assurance means building quality into the product at every step along the way. In the end, quality assurance trumps quality control as an approach to receiving excellence. Quality improvement is a philosophy that products and processes can always get better.

Excellence, which may be described as a measurement of quality, is a constantly receding goal. As a process gets better, the room for incremental improvement becomes smaller, but it is still present. A commitment to quality starts with the leadership of an organization, but implementation of quality must be internalized throughout the work force. The old adage "If it ain't broke don't fix it" should be replaced with "If it ain't perfect, improve it." A final note: in the end, quality wins out, over hype, over window dressing, over luck, and over BS. In short, unless all the people who work in an organization strive every day to fulfill these lofty ideals, these statements become nothing more than platitudes,

1. DEFINING QUALITY LEGAL SERVICES

In his book *Zen and the Art of Motorcycle Maintenance*, Robert Pirsig explores the elusive concept of quality through the prism of a motorcycle road trip. The central question Pirsig poses is whether quality is extrinsic or intrinsic. In other words, does a product or service possess quality because of its inherent characteristics or because it is perceived to possess quality by the world. In the context of legal services, the dichotomy may be rephrased by asking whether quality legal services are determined by the integrity of the internal delivery system or by the perception of clients that they have received excellent services.

Pirsig concludes that quality is both intrinsic and extrinsic. In the case of legal services, this means that lawyers have to strive to produce the best possible work product, but that they must also demonstrate to clients that the services they receive are excellent. We have discussed the client service aspect of this dual focus in Chapter 7; the delivery aspect will be addressed in Chapter 13.

One thing is clear: quality, however it is defined, is not just the responsibility of the lawyer or the law firm partners. A commitment to quality must filter down to every person who works in the office. For this reason, it is useful to talk about a legal services delivery team. This team concept makes several assumptions about the nature of legal work: Let's take a look at these:

- First, legal work can be subdivided into several different functional areas;

- Second, legal work can and should be assigned to different individuals based on their particular skills and education;
- Third, less complex work should be delegated to the lowest level where it can be performed competently;
- Fourth, the size and the makeup of the team will vary with the complexity and substance of the legal work;
- Fifth, legal work can be separated into discrete tasks assigned to particular members of the team; and
- Sixth, lawyers are the team leaders of work involved in the delivery of legal services.

This last point deserves amplification. With respect to legal work, a lawyer must retain responsibility for the quality of the legal work product. Model Rule 1.1 requires the lawyer to provide legal services competently, and Model Rules 5.1 through 5.3 establish the responsibilities of supervisory and subordinate lawyers, as well as non-legal staff. Collectively, these rules imply that the lawyer must act competently within the context of group practice and supervise subordinates within the team. In a multidisciplinary context, a lawyer who provides the legal component of a larger nonlegal service may be subordinate to a non-lawyer professional, but with respect to the legal service itself, the lawyer is ultimately responsible for the quality of the legal portion of the overall service.

The supervising lawyer in a legal matter is often a partner, but not necessarily. Although associates frequently serve in subordinate roles, they may assume responsibility for a case, which makes them the supervisory lawyer. Moreover, whether subordinate or supervisor, the associate is still responsible for the quality of her legal work, even though there is a lead attorney on the case. Every lawyer is charged with a duty to use the ordinary care and prudence of a reasonable lawyer in the jurisdiction. Every lawyer with a license to practice in that jurisdiction in effect holds herself out as possessing the requisite skill and competence to handle the work she undertakes, and can be sued for malpractice if she fails to exercise such care.

The ethical conduct of any lawyer in a firm can be imputed to other lawyers who worked on or were responsible for the case. The malpractice of an associate can be imputed to a supervisory lawyer, and the liability of one partner can be imputed to the other partners. Additionally, the mistakes of nonlegal support staff may be charged to their supervising attorney either directly or on a failure to supervise theory. What this means for the new lawyer is that her license to practice law raises a presumption of competence, and all lawyers are charged with possessing the skill and knowledge of the proverbial reasonable lawyer.

2. MEASURING QUALITY

If defining quality is not easy, measuring quality can be downright difficult. It may be like Justice Potter Stewart's definition of obscenity ("I know it when I see it."); it may be like the consumer protection test from product liability law (consumers know it when they see it), or it may be quantifiable through objective standards. All three of these approaches have some merit.

The Potter Stewart experiential approach reminds us that we can sometimes see great lawyering. Johnny Cochran's closing argument in the O.J. Simpson murder trial is a classic ("If the glove don't fit, you must acquit!"). And the reverse is often true. In *Wagenmann v. Adams,* 829 F.2d 196 (1st Cir. 1987), a lawyer assigned by a judge to represent a client charged with disorderly conduct did not oppose a prosecutor's request for overnight psychiatric observation of the client. As the facts unfolded, it turned out that the client had become agitated because of his daughter's impending marriage to a young man (á la the movie *Father of the Bride*). In a malpractice suit filed by the client against the lawyer the court held that expert testimony was not necessary to establish that the lawyer's conduct fell below the requisite standard of care. Yet, *post hoc* anecdotal evidence of professional failure lacks the certitude and predictability necessary to guide our behavior.

Consumer expectations are illuminating as well. A client may not know whether his lawyer is brilliant, mediocre or two steps ahead of the grievance committee. What the client does know, however, is whether he received value in the transaction. On the practical side, satisfied clients are not likely to sue their lawyers for malpractice or file grievances against them. On the other hand, dissatisfied clients often articulate their dissatisfaction by filing lawsuits or grievances.

Internal quality standards are often implemented through systems, manuals, checklists, feedback, evaluation and case reviews. Law firms may borrow from published standards to create their own measurement tools. Assuming that a standard captures a desired behavior, it is not difficult to determine whether a person in the organization attained a requisite level of performance. Once identified, substandard performance can be dealt with in a number of ways: training, job reassignment, or sanction. If systems are not performing, they can be improved.

Objective standards, sometimes referred to as metrics, provide benchmarks against which a lawyer's or law firm's performance can be measured. Such benchmarks may be established through internal measurement systems, or they can be found in independent sources. See Section 5 on "Professional Standards," below, for specific tools designed to create and measure practice standards in law offices.

Consultants, bar association practice management advisors, malpractice insurance carriers, and other independent auditors may also contribute to the evolution of practice standards. Objective standards allow a lawyer or law firm to measure performance based upon criteria developed by experts, quantifiable by research, and verifiable by testing. The difficulty with any set of standards is that it takes time and resources to develop the standards. Individuals and firms may resist the intrusive nature of standards review. Sometimes the individuals and organizations most in need of review eschew placing themselves under a microscope, while those least in need of examination welcome the opportunity. In the end, however, all professionals are judged under the microscopes of their clients, so it is always preferable to plan for quality than to wait to hear from clients that quality standards have broken down.

3. TECHNOLOGY AND QUALITY

Technology gives lawyers powerful tools to increase proficiency. The ability to store and retrieve excellent work products, to maintain information databases, to search for crucial information, to communicate quickly and accurately with clients, opponents, courts, and third parties, to organize and manage legal work, and to reduce or eliminate error-generating manual tasks. It could be argued that it is a breach of the professional standard of care in today's practice environment not to use these tools that are available to all lawyers.

In the final analysis, technology is a fundamental tool for building and maintaining an efficient business system, but just as importantly as a tool for improving the quality of services delivered to a court or one's clients. Lawyers often think of technology solely in terms of improving efficiency or increasing profitability. Although technology can do those things, it provides lawyers with much more. Technology gives lawyers tools to practice more carefully, research more thoroughly, record more accurately, and work more predictably than they could using manual systems. Technology helps the lawyers to produce a high-quality work product and to reduce the risk of professional error at the same time. Technology enhances service in a number of ways:

- Leveraging the intellectual work product of the firm—instead of starting from scratch with each new case, technology permits lawyers to store and retrieve their prior work product in a form that can be modified and used again and again. Assuming that a firm produces a legally sufficient document in one case, the same document can be utilized as the foundation for sound legal documents in other similar cases. If a firm improves upon a form, it is easy to change the form for future use. The collective knowledge of all the lawyers in the firm can be pooled, organized and used by anyone in the office.

- Instructing and training—technology makes it easy to explain how to do something, whether the explanation is in the form of instructions for handling a particular activity or a part of office training generally. The descriptions of processes can be recorded, saved and retrieved by individuals charged with completing assigned tasks. Unlike oral explanations, where the instructor always wonders whether she covered all the points, written directives are thorough and do not change unless the process itself is modified. Information stored in electronic files can be easily accessed by someone who needs help.

- Assuring accuracy—data input into a database, spreadsheet or word processing file is reliable because once it is recorded it does not change. Once information is input correctly, it can generally be used in a variety of different ways. With respect to spelling, grammar, and formatting, word processing programs help to avoid errors. With respect to numeric data, spreadsheets and calculators assure the accuracy of computations. Technology helps to avoid mistakes in scheduling, managing files and cases, and a variety of other activities.

- Leaving no stone unturned—legal research, once hit–or–miss, and hopelessly tied to the availability of printed materials, is now virtually unlimited. Not only does the smallest firm have access to the same resources as the largest law library, lawyers can tap non-legal resources and databases related to their cases. Technology also provides a variety of tools to manipulate research and incorporate it into the legal work product.

- Communicating instantly—Technology has dramatically reduced the amount of time it takes to deliver and respond to messages. Lawyers, clients, courts, and agencies can collaborate to resolve problems from almost anywhere in the world. Lawyers can get information into their client's hands without delay. Expressions like "the check's in the mail" and "I tried to reach you but you weren't in" are loosing strategic value.

- Creating a picture—a picture can be worth a thousand words, and graphic images supplementing or even replacing text may be able to convey a message more powerfully than the written word ever could. From charts, to video depositions, to computer animations of events, to document packaging, computers improve quality by making the legal work product more comprehensible.

- Time to think—to the extent that technology saves lawyers time, they may have greater freedom to think about new theories or arguments, more feasible alternatives for solving problems, improved methods for doing things, and document review.

Technology, however, is a double-edged sword. Although computers can improve the quality of practice, technology has unleashed a number of problems as well. Some of these include the following:

- GIGO ("garbage in—garbage out") is particularly apt in law. Data entry errors may become imbedded in documents and databases, and passed on to future generations of work product. Bad research does not improve in quality, just because a lawyer used WESTLAW instead of books to do it.

- Lawyers still need to proofread documents. Even if the document is computer generated and proofed by a senior paralegal, there is no guarantee that it is free of errors. Careless cutting and pasting of information can create total non-sequiturs that only a legal eye might catch.

- Lawyers still need to edit. There is a tendency in modern drafting to append more and more verbiage to documents without taking anything out. Such practices often do little to improve the quality of documents, and in fact may make them more cumbersome and less comprehensible.
- Backup your files. Maintain and utilize backup systems for all office files that are stored electronically. One server crash or computer virus can destroy as much as an office fire.
- Metadata—software programs record an electronic history of documents, and this history can have evidentiary or other strategic value for adversaries.
- Know what your technology can do. Having technological capability, whether in the form of hardware, software, or Internet resources, has little value if it is not utilized. Many law firms use only a fraction of the technological tools at their disposal.

The next system covers practice systems, and you should consider how the systems described can improve the quality of services, and then how technology applications can contribute to the improvement of these systems. Without specific tools, quality improvement is just empty rhetoric. Everybody wants to do a better job; how we accomplish that objective is the real challenge. The following article demonstrates one example of how technology can be subverted within a law firm.

THERE'S JUST SOMETHING ABOUT LARRY

From *Law Technology Product News,* by Gary A. Munneke (December 1999).

LARRY. Everyone in the firm knows it. The lawyers know it. Members of the staff know it. The clients know it. Only Larry doesn't know it. Larry either missed the technology revolution or else he just does not know what to do with it.

The irony is that Larry believes that he is on the technology train. He fails to understand that the train has left the station without him. How can this be?

To understand Larry, one has to understand how Larry practices law. For the last 25 years Larry has engaged in what is euphemistically referred to as a general practice—not the kind of full-service practice many large firms would describe as a general practice, but the kind of practice where Larry built his practice around clients who walked through the door.

When Larry started to practice law, lawyers were not allowed to market their services to prospective clients. Although he understands that marketing is okay today, he still considers it a little unseemly to rely on anything other than word of mouth to get new clients.

When Larry got out of law school, he did not know much about how to run a practice, but the senior partner in the first firm where he worked showed him the ropes. Larry learned that there was a certain way to organize files, prepare for a case, bill for his services. Back when Larry was starting out there were no computers in law offices, so the key to success in the practice of law was to follow these tried and true manual systems religiously.

Inherent in the practice model Larry was taught was the notion that lawyers should spend their time practicing law and delegate the non-legal work to support staff. To Larry, delegation meant that the roles of the lawyers and support staff were clearly delineated. Practicing law meant preparing cases, drafting documents, advising clients and going to court. Everything else—typing, filing, calendaring, billing, answering the phone, making copies, and answering to his every demand—was the work of staff.

Larry felt like he was a hands-on boss because he often dictated directly to his subordinates the content of documents, pleadings, bills, correspondence and other work.

At the same time, however, he offered precious little direction as to how they should handle their end of the practice. After all, how could he know any more about calendaring or filing than they could know about the law? Anyone who worked for Larry often felt that they were usually left to their own devices, except for Larry's bouts of dictation and occasional directives.

This is the way lawyers practiced law in Larry's first firm, and it worked. The lawyers made a decent living and the work generally got done. Being a generalist was interesting because lawyers and staff were always learning how to handle new cases. After a few years, Larry opened his own firm, which he administered the same way his mentor had taught him.

Over the years, Larry did not notice how his practice was slowly losing its edge. He lost a lot of staff to other firms and businesses in the community. His income was flat. In the early '90s, he attributed the situation to the recession, later to the glut of new lawyers in town. He lost a few really good clients to a handful of practitioners who concentrated on narrow fields of law. He found that he no longer enjoyed the work he had once loved.

Larry tried to keep up with the changing practice of law. He reluctantly took out an ad in the Yellow Pages. When other firms in town invested in technology, Larry invested in technology. He was one of the first on lawyers' row to get word processors. When PCs came along, ... Larry tried to keep up by acquiring faster processors, Windows, a networked environment, and Internet access. Larry even learned how to spout the computer jargon ("We need better thruput on these docs.")

The dirty little truth was that Larry didn't know squat about technology. He bought when someone he knew in another firm bought first, or when the staff complained that the secretaries down the street could do something with technology they couldn't. He spent his money uncritically and ultimately unwisely. A local computer consultant was more than glad to advise Larry on what to do, because Larry didn't have a clue what the consultant was talking about. Moreover, Larry would never let on that he was ignorant by asking a question. The consultant knew.

Larry barked to the staff that they needed to use the technology at their disposal to work more efficiently. When they asked him how they should implement new automated systems, however, he replied that it reflected poorly on them if they were not willing to show some initiative and learn to use technology. The staff knew who was unwilling to learn.

Larry asked the office manager to set up an internal e-mail system, but Larry never used it. He continued to hand deliver communications to staff members, and if e-mail came up, he pretended to have read their missives. The firm also had a computer calendar system, but staff members were required to write all appointments into his desk calendar as well as to record them electronically.

Despite the exhortations of the office manager, Larry insisted on writing out all his time records, and having a secretary transcribe them in the computer system. As for the drafting of documents, Larry insisted on dictating legal documents to secretaries to make sure they were correct. In short, although he surrounded himself with the trappings of technology, Larry continued to practice law the way he had in 1975. His concept of role differentiation drove him to view computers as tools to help the support staff. In Larry's mind, computers were just faster, more expensive typewriters. Like answering the phone, working with computers was just not in a lawyer's job description.

There are more than a few Larrys in the practice of law. They act like they embrace technology; they believe they embrace technology. They just do not get it....

The Larrys of the world undermine the viability of technology in the office by giving lip service to change, while in reality digging in their heels against it. They frustrate those who work with them and around them. They find themselves in stagnant or declining practices, but do not understand that they are the major impediment to change in their office. If you or someone you know is a Larry, you cannot continue with business as usual. Larry has to change.

The first step is for Larry to admit that he is in denial—he is getting in the way of progress.

Second, Larry needs to change some assumptions. Computers are tools to help practice more effectively; lawyers have as much use for computers as support staff do. Lawyers cannot survive in the practice of law without exercising personal leadership in using computers.

Third, Larry needs to stop trying to keep up with the Joneses in making technology decisions, and do his own homework. He needs to learn enough about his office applications and hardware to be able to teach his staff how use the systems personally. Larry also needs to know what questions to ask his consultant to get the right answers for his firm.

Fourth, Larry has to understand that redundant systems are ultimately inefficient and that he needs to get rid of the old manual systems when the two overlap.

Finally, Larry must recognize that technology has changed the practice of law. He cannot practice law the way his mentor did in the '60s and '70s. The logic and configurations of computer-based systems are often different than manual systems.

The first step—recognizing the problem—is the most difficult one for Larry. Some people think that you can't teach an old dog new tricks; but they are wrong. It is not easy to change but it is not impossible. Read about technology; talk to others about technology; go on line; practice technology; admit that you are a dunce.

The alternative is not a pretty one. If you do not change your ways, you will probably be out of business in five years. Even if you keep your practice alive, you will continue to struggle, make less money and feel more burned out. In this light, there really isn't any choice. Change or else. You can't let them whisper, "There's something about Larry," anymore.

4. THE SEARCH FOR EXCELLENCE

Many books and articles attempt to describe the elusive characteristic we call excellence. Sometimes it seems like these theories *du jour* come and go like weather patterns. It seems difficult to recognize lasting concepts, when nothing appears certain or permanent. Yet, the constant striving for excellence helps the lawyer-manager sort out guiding principles to apply in the daily grind of the practice of law. See Pirsig, Zen and the Art of Motorcycle Maintenance, p. 62, and accompanying text.

Law firms constantly strive to improve the quality of their services, because quality is an essential ingredient in excellence. A firm might be well-organized, market itself effectively and provide its services efficiently, but if the quality of the work product is substandard, the clients will not return, and they will tell others about their bad experience. From another perspective, inferior work invites civil liability. This is true whether the business is manufacturing a product or providing a service. Shoddy work not only disappoints consumer expectations; it also carries a greater risk of harm to the consumer.

Management expert W. Edwards Deming explored the dimensions of quality improvement over half a century in his research and writing.

Beginning in the 1930s, Deming championed an approach to quality that he called Total Quality Management. (TQM). Rebuffed by American industry and management theorists of the time, Deming was able to sell his ideas in post-World War II Japan, where he helped rebuild Japan's bombed out industries into new economic powerhouses, based on his management principles. The success of Japanese industries, particularly the automobile industry, led to the gradual acceptance of TQM by American and Western European business. In 1950, Dr. Deming gave a lecture to 80% of the top management people in Japan. What follows is an English translation of the original Japanese transcript.

DR. DEMING'S 1950 LECTURE TO JAPANESE TOP MANAGEMENT

http://hclectures.blogspot.com/1970/08/demings-1950-lecture-to-japanese.html.

Statistical product quality administration is a splendid new tool. It is being applied in every industry, beginning in modern Japan and America as well as England, New Zealand, and various other countries. Whether it be on a large scale or a small scale, it is being researched and executed in an extremely large number of manufacturing plants. Some results of this are:

1. Costs go down
2. Producers can economize on raw materials
3. Production levels increase, and waste decreases
4. Product quality becomes more uniform
5. Producers and consumers gain the ability to agree on product quality
6. Quality is improved, so inspections may be reduced
7. Appliances and techniques can be used to a higher degree

It is already twenty-five years since statistical product quality administration was implemented in America, but it was not developed much until 1942, and the extent of its use was narrow.

In modern Japan many technicians, mathematicians, and statisticians are researching statistical product quality administration. Furthermore, since coming to Japan I have learned that the splendid achievement these people have made in statistical product quality administration is already apparent. The results from all these countries is surprising. They have demonstrated superb ability in the statistical sphere.

The knowledge and brains applied to statistics by the Japanese are an essential national resource; it is important in the same way as water power, forests, and railroads. And that statistical knowledge, much like water power, is not useful at all unless it has an impact on work opportunity and work. With water power, if one were to get rid of turbines and generator machines, no power would emerge.

Similarly it may be recognized that without effective use, all of modern Japanese statistical knowledge would not be helpful to the advance of products, product quality, or product uniformity. You all must look for people who have both statistical knowledge and excellent experience with technical knowledge and employ them in factories. In addition, to aid your technicians you must seek mathematical statisticians as consultants.

However, no matter how excellent your technicians, you who are leaders, must strive for advances in the improvement of product quality and uniformity if your technicians are to be able to make improvements. The first step, therefore, belongs with management. First, your company technicians and your factories must know that you have a fervor for advancing product quality and uniformity and a sense of responsibility for product quality.

Nothing will come of this if you only speak about it. Action is important. If you demonstrate enthusiasm for the improvement of product quality, your product quality administration will certainly advance. Responsibility for product quality means guaranteeing one's own factory's products to the utmost degree possible. The greatest guarantee of product quality is not words, but executing product quality administration. When you effect product quality administration, show administrative charts or methods as an indicator, as there is no better way to guarantee product quality to the consumer.

By showing enthusiasm toward product quality and uniformity and responsibility to product quality, you will gain the opportunity for your technicians to put product quality administration into effect.

However, product quality administration at the factory cannot be implemented in a single day. It requires a long time. At first do it on a small scale, and once you think that has value, then expand. The process of product quality administration, consisting of the combination of statistical and manufacturing techniques is long and tiring.

Well, I think you must share an interest in how I define statistical product quality administration. Product quality administration is most useful, and moreover it illustrates the methods by which producers can economically produce the goods that buyers indicate they want.

All of the words in this definition have their respective meanings. "Economic production" means low price production: in other words, elimination of waste; faster production; fewer defects in products, raw materials or machines; the practical use of techniques; improved uniformity in product quality; and the opportunity for producers and purchasers to agree on product quality.

"Most useful" means the design and product quality must suit the purpose of the good; raw materials, mechanical manufacturing techniques, transport, and products must be the best as we consider them from the viewpoint of the marketplace. If you do not conduct market surveys about what quality or what design will be in demand, your products will not succeed in being "most useful."

The product must match the market. The product quality must be adapted to that market. If product quality is too high, or too low, it will not be right. If product quality is too good, the price is very high, and only a quite limited group of people can afford to purchase it. Even so, if product quality is too low, despite low prices, people will not repeat the purchase, and before long the business will slow down. Therefore, in order to make the most useful product, you must conduct market surveys about what kind or product quality and what kind of design are required. Additionally, through market surveys, you must make sure of the price buyers can pay for the product.

On this subject, there are other reasons why continuing market surveys [are] useful to economical production. Every month you must make roughly the right amount of product, or you cannot achieve economical production. If you are left with 10%, or 25%, of your goods unsold, your profits will disappear. Further, if you cannot respond to a large number of orders, you will not maximize your profit. As a result, in order to achieve economical production, it is necessary to conduct market surveys. Based on market surveys, you will he able to stand on a stable foundation of monthly product sales. Then you can find out what kind of people (e.g., wage workers, farmers, businessmen) demand that product; or whether, having bought the product once, they will not buy it again; or whether the people who bought it are satisfied with the product; or again if they are unsatisfied, why they are not satisfied. Thus by means of market surveys, you can effect administration of advertising, product design changes pricing, and production.

No matter what kind of manufacturer you are, if you have long-term plans, you must work to implement product quality administration in the wider meaning, as in the definition which I laid out a moment ago.

In the last ten years there has been no scientific method which has experienced such rapid expansion as has statistical theory. In the context of today's Japan, the most useful thing for manufacturers could be nothing but the appropriate application of statistical techniques.

At the end of my discussion of market surveys, I would like to explain my thoughts on the problem of statistical product quality administration with a diagram. This diagram not only makes clear my thoughts on product quality administration and market surveys, but I think it is extremely easy to understand. Below I have drawn a pie graph "wheel" divided into four sections:

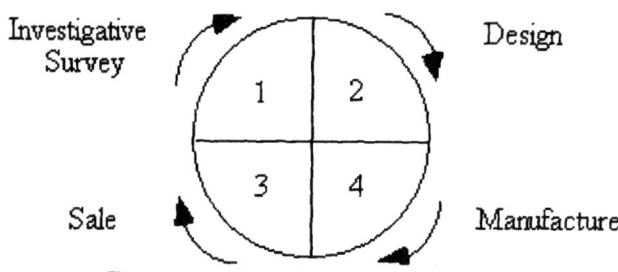

Concepts regarding product quality
Sense of responsibility for product quality

This wheel rolls along the line of "concepts regarding product quality" and "sense of responsibility for product quality." The fact that the four stages of the wheel are connected one to the other with no beginning and no end is very important. This is the reason why I drew a circle. You must not stop product design or testing. When your products emerge into the real market, after having inquired into how the product is useful to people, and what they think of it, you redesign it. There is no end to product quality administration. Using product quality administration, producing goods continually being improved, I want you to make more and more adapted items that buyers will want, designing, redesigning, and then finding cheap, better ways to make them. While this certainly benefits the purchasers, it benefits you as well.

. . .

To conclude, I want to offer you one or two things I have realized about the statistical techniques that are currently being used. Number one: at the first stage, design, you must conduct market surveys and inspections, applying the statistical techniques for experimental and planning methods and inspection of samples. Furthermore, you must perfect the manufacturing process, using the technical skills of factory workers and machines, and utilizing these techniques to conduct inspections of raw materials.

Number two: in manufacturing in the second stage good product quality and uniformity of product quality are important. This means that by the time of shipping, you can transport quality products through the use of statistical techniques of inspection of samples, experimental planning methods and marketing surveys.

Number three: at the third stage, sales, the statistical technique of the market survey is used.

Number four: at the fourth stage of service research the techniques of sample inspections, experimental planning methods, and market surveys are used.

After you have reached the fourth stage, you return once again to the beginning stage in wheel. Here, then, putting together thoughts from your previous results, you may begin to implement product design changes.

I repeat myself, but the necessity of statistical techniques must not be ignored. Without them I deeply believe that businessmen cannot long sustain their prosperity. What I just spoke about now is true not only in Japan, but equally in Chicago, Manchester, or Amsterdam. Every businessman around the world is now facing these same problems.

Late in life, Deming achieved recognition as father of the quality movement. By the 1980s, businesses of all kinds were caught up on the Deming approach to quality improvement. Even law firms jumped on the bandwagon (see e.g., Robert Greene, *The Quality Pursuit*, ABA; Walker and Ciamentaro, *TQM in Action: One Firm's Journey*, ABA, 1999).

Many law firms, however, resisted the notion of total quality management as a comprehensive system. They could accept the idea of quality improvement in the abstract, but found it burdensome to implement such a system. For many firms, short-term deadlines and immediate client demands always took precedence over long-term aspirations and incremental improvement.

The fundamental principles of TQM are not difficult to understand. Quality can either be controlled by inspection and review (as is the case when an attorney reviews documents for mistakes before they go out the door), or assured by eliminating defects from products or services during the production process. Deming assumed that all product manufacturing processes and complex professional service delivery systems would contain both flaws in the system and some risk of production mistakes. If the system could gradually improve the design and reduce mistakes, the total quality of the product-service would improve. Deming's concept of quality was always consumer-driven: the purchaser of a product or service knew whether the product or service did what was expected at a price that was reasonable and fair. Deming believed in constantly measuring satisfaction of consumers as a tool to improve quality.

Deming subjected every segment of a business organization to a cycle of benchmarking in which three things occur: 1) performance is measured; 2) reasonable goals established for improving processes are based on feedback from consumers and workers; and 3) periodic assessment takes place as to whether goals were attained. In this way, the underlying processes would constantly improve. A corollary of this proposition would suggest that no system is perfect, and that there is always some room for incremental improvement.

In many industries, benchmarks could be developed on an industry-wide basis (see e.g., ISO 9000 Standards). To assure quality, manufacturers and others suppliers of component parts would need to require their own suppliers to apply TQM practices in order to assure the quality of the component. For example, a real estate law firm that subcontracts the work of abstracting titles to someone outside the firm might still rely on the quality of the abstractor's work product in order to assure the quality of the law firm's work product.

Perhaps the most controversial aspect of Deming's theory was the idea that quality was best managed on the front line by the team of workers that assembled the product or service. Deming rejected hierarchy in favor of individual empowerment of team members to spot problems and act to resolve them. For Deming, the people closest to the action were most likely to be able to identify and resolve the problem. If responsibility for decision-making was removed several steps up a long chain of command, there would be little incentive among workers to find mistakes and fix them. These team concepts flew in the face of the great weight of management theory, and many businesses found it difficult to change traditional ways of doing business. For example, General Motors had to create an entirely new division, called Saturn, when it wanted to implement an automobile production model based on the Japanese team approach.

Although law tends to be practiced in teams, it has proven difficult for many law firms to abandon hierarchy and to disperse decision making power among team members. Part of this may be due to the ethical requirements for lawyers to maintain responsibility for their work product (see Model Rule, Rule 5.2), but part of the problem may derive from lawyers' inability to relinquish control of anything in their offices.

5. PROFESSIONAL STANDARDS

Some of the flavor of the quality practice movement is carried over in the quest to establish law practice standards. If lawyers only knew what these standards of performance should be they would be able to mold their behavior and perform in accordance with those standards. The concept of standards is not new to law. The bar exam and character review associated with licensure, as well as the educational requirements of law school, impose professional standards. The Rules of Professional Conduct, and their application to standards of care in legal malpractice, constitute standards for ethical behavior. Court rules also establish standards of behavior for representation of clients before tribunals, as well as informal mechanisms represented by professional customs.

Internal practice standards have been the subject of considerable debate, and lawyers have resisted any form of outside auditing of their procedures. The American Law Institute–American Bar Association Committee on Continuing Professional Education has been the most aggressive group in the legal profession in attempting to tackle the question of professional standards. As early as 1988, ALI–ABA promulgated *An Appraisal for Peer Review and Other Measures to Enhance Professional Performance* (ALI–ABA 1988), which was designed to allow lawyers within a firm to review each other. More recently, *Achieving Excellence in the Practice of Law*, Second Edition (ALI–ABA 2000), addressed the practical side of achieving excellence, by providing checklists, examples, references, and discussion of those critical elements of lawyering that combine to assure excellence in practice.

Nancy Byerley Jones, a former practice management advisor with the North Carolina Bar Association, and now a private consultant, has written a book, *Self–Audits for the Busy Lawyer* (ABA 1998), that walks lawyers through a self-evaluation process in a number of key management areas. Law firms must decide whether quality is important to them, and if it is, they should invest in creating and maintaining quality just as they invest in technology, human resources, and other elements of the law firm infrastructure.

In Britain, the Law Society of England and Wales (The English Bar Association) developed *Lexcel*, a voluntary program to foster practice standards, based on ISO 9000 Standards. Law firms that successfully submitted their practices to the *Lexcel* standards review process received a certificate (not unlike the Good Housekeeping Seal of Approval for products in the United States). A number of other bar associations outside the United States have begun to develop professional standards for lawyers in those countries.

Whether or not the American legal profession can establish performance standards for lawyers in this country remains to be seen. Professional standards often address minimal competencies, i.e., a level of competency below which an individual may be sanctioned. Books on the subject assume a voluntary process, in which those firms desiring to enhance quality can utilize standards as a tool in that effort.

Problems and Questions

1. After reading this section on quality, do you have any better sense of what quality means? Must one understand underlying management theories in order to apply quality principles to the practice of law? Or is quality something that everyone can achieve through hard work and dedication?

2. In Robert Pirsig's book, *Zen and the Art of Motorcycle Maintenance*, the author asks whether quality is inherent in an object, or whether it is something that is perceived from the outside. Is quality craftsmanship built into a product or service, or is quality determined by the consumer expectations? Pirsig concludes that quality is both intrinsic and extrinsic simultaneously. Is he right? How might Pirsig's point of view be applied to the delivery of legal services?

3. Have you encountered anyone like Larry, the law firm partner who knows just enough about technology to be dangerous? Have you met older lawyers who absolutely refuse to use computers at all? How about lawyers who believe that computers are just fancy typewriters that should only be used by secretaries? How should law firms deal with technophobic lawyers who do not want to get with the program? Will this problem just disappear as older lawyers retire from the practice of law?

4. How can technology improve the quality of legal services delivery? To be more specific, what does technology add to the arsenal of tools at the

lawyer's disposal that is not available with manual systems? Do you agree that lawyers can apply these approaches to management? Are there aspects of the practice of law that make it unique?

5. In your law firm group, make a list of steps that you would implement in carrying out a policy of "zero defects." How would you communicate this policy to staff and assure that it is followed?

CHAPTER 13

MANAGING SUBSTANTIVE LAW PRACTICE SYSTEMS

■ ■ ■

Lawyers deliver legal work to clients through substantive practice systems. In order to manage legal work you need to understand what activities constitute legal work. You will also need to understand the management of legal work through the lens of substantive practice systems. In this section, you will learn some of the basics of law office systems, including what a system is in the context of a law office, and fundamental ideas for managing these systems.

It will help you to appreciate these underlying concepts as a fundamental element of working in a real law office. Many students struggle with the material on systems, because it seems new and foreign to them, never having practiced law, even though they have used organizational systems all their lives. Mastery of these important principles, however, will provide law students with tools that they will use throughout their professional lives.

A. WHAT IS LEGAL WORK?

Lawyers perform a variety of problem-solving functions for their clients. Given the presence of legal issues in a multitude of complex modern transactions, lawyers deal with clients and professionals from areas outside the law. Some work such as litigation and preparation of legal documents is easily described as legal work. Other activities such as business planning or mediation may be performed by professionals outside the law as well as by lawyers. This dichotomy raises the question as to whether such work is legal work.

It is probably futile to attempt to delineate legal and non-legal work. There is certainly not a bright line or statutory definition for such a demarcation. Although scholars and Unauthorized Practice of Law Committees may debate the questions, it is safe to say that both lawyers and consumers of legal services have a rough sense of what constitutes legal work. For purposes of this course, it makes sense to use define legal work operationally, based on what lawyers actually do, specifically, the work that may subject them to professional liability, i.e., work performed by lawyers for clients where the lawyer is expected to exercise reasonable professional care.

This definition excludes transactions in which lawyers may exercise business judgment as a participant in the transaction, not as a lawyer. In a world where lawyers and law firms operate ancillary businesses, practice in multidisciplinary settings, and develop equity relationships and other affiliations with their clients, the distinction between the legal and nonlegal work becomes almost meaningless. In the end, the individual lawyer must exercise all professional judgment, comply with ethical rules, and pursue excellence in practice.

PROBLEMS AND QUESTIONS

1. How would you define legal work? Going to court? Drafting legal documents? Negotiating terms of an agreement on behalf of a client? What else? Is it work that lawyers do; i.e., if it is done by a lawyer it is legal work? Is it work that involves the exercise of legal analysis and judgment? What makes such work uniquely legal? What do lawyers bring to their work that sets it apart from similar work performed by nonlawyers?

2. Are there certain transactions, like drafting wills or contracts that are fundamentally legal? Are some legal transactions performed by people who are not lawyers? Should the state restrict the delivery of legal work to lawyers through laws prohibiting the unauthorized practice of law?

3. It is sometimes said that lawyers have a professional monopoly on the delivery of legal work. Apart from representing individuals and organizations in court, what activities are covered by this monopoly?

B. LEGAL SERVICES DELIVERY TEAM

Legal services are typically delivered by a team—a topic introduced in Chapter 7. Although some lawyers practice alone without a support staff, most—even those we describe as *solo* practitioners—utilize a secretary and other legal assistants to help them practice more efficiently and profitably. As we think about the delivery of legal services to clients, it is not hard to recognize the fact that a number of different people in a law office may be involved with the client or the client's work during the course of the representation. If we assume that these individuals function best when they work together, then we are talking about a team—a legal services delivery team.

In law school, the practice of law is sometimes presented as a solitary endeavor—a service performed by a lawyer for a client. In the real world, the lawyer almost always relies on the support of one or more support staff, including junior lawyers, paralegals, secretaries, and others. This collective enterprise functions like a team, in the sense that every member plays a role and contributes to a successful outcome. The lawyer may be the focal point of this delivery team, but she is seldom its only member.

Law firms are professional services organizations, which means that they produce high-level, complex work for individuals and entities through the lawyers and staff who work at the firm. The organization, as an institution, is responsible for the quality of all of the work performed by everyone who works there. The firm's name is on every document and communication that goes out the door; the firm's reputation and success depends upon its ability to consistently produce excellent work.

Within the firm, lawyers work with professionals, paraprofessionals and support staff to deliver client services. Each individual is responsible for a particular job, a subset of the total work product. Practicing law is a corporate, as opposed to a solitary activity. In the real world, the effective delivery of legal services requires competence at all levels of the delivery team.

Even in a solo practice, the lawyer is typically dependent on the work of a secretary or legal assistant, or contract services. The concept of the solo practitioner, working alone without any assistance is a popular myth that has little basis in reality. Even the ubiquitous "road warrior" whose secretary is his trusty laptop, must purchase support services from time to time, work with co-counsel, experts, various kinds of advisors, and of course clients. In reality, legal services are much more likely to be produced as a product of group activity, including the lawyer and his staff, as well as the client.

In times past, many lawyers did practice law without the assistance of others. On the American frontier, where the land was sparsely populated, and the lawyers few in number, it was not uncommon for a lawyer to ride the circuit, following the court to various stops within the jurisdiction where cases were held. The image of a young Abe Lincoln is sometimes evoked, traveling through rural Illinois during the first half of the nineteenth century. A vestige of the circuit-riding lawyer lives on today, in the form of the individual practitioner, who plies his trade with the help of no more than a personal laptop computer.

The invention of the typewriter in the 19th century transformed the practice of law at the end of that era, just as the personal computer has revolutionized the practice of law today. The typewriter allowed the lawyer to dictate or write out drafts of letters, documents, pleadings and briefs for transcription, editing and final presentation. Freed from the mundane demands of spelling, penmanship, and the time required to produce such documents, the lawyer could focus his attention on the more cerebral legal issues. A typewriter, however, did not produce documents by itself. It required an operator, a typist or secretary, who possessed the skills to operate the typewriting machine quickly and efficiently. In time, the solitary lawyer gave way to the lawyer-secretary team.

Through most of the 20th century, this lawyer-secretary model was the predominant form of providing legal services. Even in law firms of many lawyers, the individual lawyers had personal secretaries who managed every aspect of their professional lives. It was not uncommon for a lawyer to keep one secretary throughout his professional career. The use of the pronoun "he" is deliberate here; in the earlier part of the 20th century, almost all the lawyers were men (while the secretaries were not). An experienced legal secretary was much more than a typist. She handled administrative matters, bookkeeping, and routine legal drafting. Many lawyers today cling tenaciously to the lawyer-secretary team model, although other more flexible models are emerging.

The legal services delivery team has undergone further metamorphosis, due largely to the development of the personal computer. To understand this transition, it is important to recognize the fundamental quality of computers that makes them essential to the practice of law—the power to save, store, and retrieve prior work product so that it may be used again, and manipulated or modified to produce a new work product modeled to the circumstances of new cases.

J. Harris Morgan, of Greenville, Texas, one of the fathers of the contemporary law practice management movement, as far back as 1975, recognized the potential that automation offered to the legal profession. Since Morgan began preaching the need to automate legal services, computers have evolved from cumbersome automatic typewriters (one of the first popular forms was the IBM MTST, which relied on magnetic tape to store information until it was needed; the power of these machines was such that whole pages could be stored for later use). As both computer hardware and software became more powerful, more law firms took the leap from manual to computerized systems. Today, although law firms universally use computers to help them deliver services, there remains a wide gulf between the least and most sophisticated users in the marketplace.

The work of both the traditional lawyer and secretary have adapted to the availability of computers. The processes and activities associated with systems are ideally handled by computer software, because of the capacity of technology to organize, sort, store and retrieve information. Where the lawyer, secretary, and other team members can produce and manipulate text or data, the many possibilities for streamlining office work increase dramatically. The traditional lawyer-secretary model gives way to a team with more players and more specialized roles.

The lawyer is still the captain and the leader of the team. It is the lawyer who provides legal services to the client, and who is ultimately responsible for the quality of the legal services rendered. In this sense, every lawyer who does legal work for others is a leader of a legal services delivery team. One does not have to be the managing partner of the firm to be a manager in this context. In addition to managing the delivery of the legal work product, the lawyer is also responsible for solving complex legal problems, drafting complicated language for documents, and offering high-level advice to clients. See Model Rules, Rules 5.1 and 5.3.

There is a level of legal work that can be described as "routine," and such work in the past was often handled by the lawyer personally, or delegated to the secretary. Preparing standardized documents, filling out repetitive forms, and answering simple questions requires legal training, but not the level of expertise of a legally-educated individual. Such work may be delegated to someone who possesses legal training or experience, but not a J.D. We typically call these people legal assistants or paralegals. They can be assigned routine legal work, thereby freeing the lawyer to perform complex legal tasks and permitting the secretary to handle purely secretarial work. Today, paralegals are an integral part of the legal services delivery team in many law offices, whereas in other offices, secretaries perform the work of legal assistants without the title.

The role of the secretary has evolved as well. Functionally, secretarial work has bifurcated into two distinct areas: administrative work and word processing. In some firms, these two distinct types of work have led to a splitting of jobs into administrative secretaries and word processors. The administrative secretary, or "gatekeeper," handles the flow of paper, phone messages, and mail through the office. This individual is often responsible for scheduling, billing, and other administrative support activities.

In the old days, every lawyer was assigned a secretary. As other jobs have been created, and lawyers themselves have gone online, law firms have found that one secretary can handle the administrative work of three to four lawyers. The word processing secretary is a specialist in generating high volume, high quality written work. The person who fills this job must not only be an excellent keyboardist, but also must be able to design documents that look good. Ideally, the word processing secretary is a skilled professional who can generate a high volume of work delegated by the lawyer, legal assistant or administrative secretary.

Practically speaking, each legal services delivery team is headed by a supervising lawyer. In many firms, this means that specialized support staff often work as members of more than one team. This does not mean that the volume of work generated by a particular attorney would not require a dedicated support staff for that delivery team, or even that multiple lawyers, legal assistants or secretaries might not be needed for some teams.

The modern team concept permits the flexibility to create service teams that meet the demands of the work. In the one lawyer-one secretary model, it was not unusual to see one secretary struggling to finish a product while another, whose supervisor was out of town, read a book. The key to the modern approach is the creation of specialists who can perform a narrow set of responsibilities very efficiently, and that these specialists are utilized flexibly and effectively.

The chart below illustrates several variations of the legal services delivery team. There is no magic or correct approach for every law firm or every situation. Even the old model of the lawyer working alone has resurfaced as the lawyer working with a computer and no staff. In that situation, the lawyer performs all four of the functional responsibilities in the delivery of legal services.

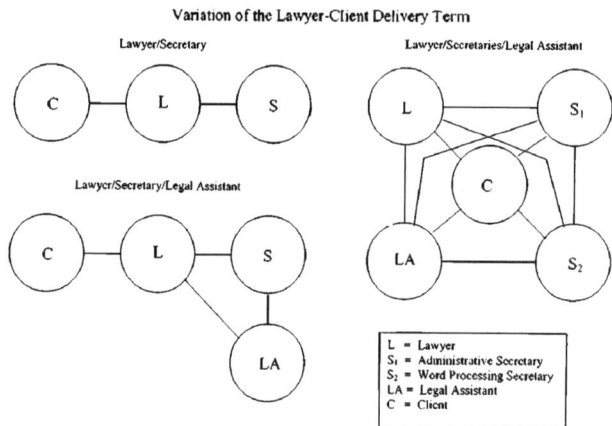

Chart 12-1

The thing to remember is that in every legal service, somone must perform the leadership and complex legal tasks, someone must handle the routine legal tasks, someone must serve as a gatekeeper to distribute the administrative work, and someone must function as a word processor. Whether these functions are performed by one person, two, four, or more will depend upon the circumstances and the need of the lawyers providing the services.

In some firms, other individuals may be utilized as a part of the legal service delivery team. Many practice areas utilize investigators, experts, jury consultants, animation professionals, technical support, economists, financial analysts, and others too numerous to name. Every substantive practice area is different, and to the extent that additional players are required to make the teamwork, those individuals are integral to the delivery team in those areas.

Law firms can hire these additional team members as employees, if the volume of work is sufficient, or on a contract or consulting basis if there is not enough work to support a staff position. In fact, many firms today actually contract out for lawyers, legal assistants, and secretaries in lieu of adding permanent employees. It is almost axiomatic to say that work purchased on the open market is more expensive than discounted in-house work. One would not, for example, hire a $25,000.00 per year secretary if there was only enough work to keep that person busy 40% of the time, even if it costs $20,000.00 to farm out the work to a secretarial service.

Despite the fact that much of lawyer's work takes place in service teams, almost nothing in law school prepares students for group work. You might have had a partner for moot court arguments, or a study group first year, but law school for the most part involves you being called on by the professor, you briefing the cases, you taking the exams, and you doing all the other things you have to do in law school. It comes as a shock to some people when they graduate that they have to work with a partner, a legal assistant, a secretary, and the clients. Many students are uncomfortable with group projects, where their grades depend on the contributions of other students. In the real world, your grade as a practitioner depends upon the performance of all the members of your team.

1. Is the concept of the legal services delivery team mere theory—impractical for real lawyers—or is it capable of implementation in the average law office?
2. The discussion of support staff in Chapter 8 includes descriptions of the legal and nonlegal support staff employed in law firms today. How do these various individuals fit into the legal services delivery team as described above?
3. Why has the legal services delivery team evolved over the past generation? The past one hundred years? How do you think it will continue to evolve in the coming decades?
4. As a future lawyer, how do you develop the collaboration, cooperation, leadership and other skills you will need to succeed in this team-driven practice model?

C. CLIENT FOCUS

Who is missing from this "legal services delivery team" equation? Who is the indispensable part of the legal services delivery team? The answer is simple: the client. Although the client is integral to the legal representation, the principal in the lawyer-client agency relationship, many lawyers adopt a paternalistic view towards clients generally, and exclude them as much as possible from the decision-making process and other aspects of the representation (see chapter 7).

Not only does this paternalistic approach violate the lawyer's duty to keep clients reasonably informed about the status of their case, it also reduces the flow of important information that the lawyer needs in order to give competent legal advice. The client should be viewed as an important member of the legal services delivery team. The client provides important information, serves as an investigator for important facts, and even acts as an assistant who delivers papers or performs other functions necessary for the representation. Thus, the client as a participant can often help the lawyer and other members of the delivery team to do their work more efficiently.

This approach allows the client see first-hand what efforts are being made on the client's behalf, and to help the client to become invested in the lawyer's work to resolve the problem. If the lawyer takes the problem away from the client ("this is my case"), when things go badly, the client may conclude that the lawyer did not get the job done; on the other hand, if the client and lawyer are working together to resolve the problem ("it is our case"), when things go badly, the client is more likely to conclude that things went badly.

This approach to the delivery of legal services is often referred to as "client-centered" lawyering. Theoretically, client-centered lawyering is supported by a body of legal scholarship, embodied in the Model Rules of Professional Conduct (*see* Model Rules 1.2, 1.4) and is taught through courses in client interviewing and counseling. The skills of effective client interviewing and counseling are critical to effective lawyering (See Chapter 7), and integral to the delivery of legal services through the team approach.

Problems and Questions

1. The general topic of client-centered lawyering has already been discussed in Chapter 7, but how should this play out in the actual delivery of legal services? What do authors like Pirsig and Deming tell us about the relationship between client perceptions of quality and the efforts of the firm to focus on the client's needs?

2. In agency terms, the client as principal owns the case; the lawyer as agent exercises judgment to carry out the representation. Does the fact that lawyers exercise considerable discretion in carrying out their clients' objectives place special demands on them to manage both the work product and the client expectations at the same time?

D. PRACTICE SYSTEMS

1. WHAT IS A SYSTEM?

Legal services are delivered to clients through systems. Fundamentally, a system is an organized method of completing a recurring set of tasks. A system helps us to solve problems by providing a method for resolving the problem the same way every time. A system gives life to institutional memory. We all use systems all the time to manage the things we do in our lives, so it should not come as a surprise that law firms use systems to manage legal work. If we understand the basic principles of how systems work, especially law office systems, we can be better lawyers.

At its most basic level, a system is like a habit, a personal way of doing things. When I wake up every morning, I roll out of bed on the same side, lumber to the bathroom, where I use the toilet, brush my teeth, shave, shower, and dry off, in that order. I put on my clothes in the same order, underwear, shirt, pants, socks, and shoes (I know I could put on the pants before the shirt or one sock and one shoe before the other sock and shoe, but I put on the shirt and then the pants, and both socks before both shoes). That is a habit. When I get to work, I have a cup of coffee, read the mail on my desk, return phone calls and check e-mail, before starting any other work. This, too, is a habit.

If I teach my son to get dressed the same way I do, or ask everyone in my office to start their day the same way I do, then the habit takes on a life that transcends my idiosyncrasies. I have created a system. A system can be communicated to others, replicated for others to use, taught, reviewed, analyzed, and modified. Although systems can be oral, written systems have a degree of permanency and certainty that verbal ones do not. Anyone who recalls the old parlor game "Telephone," where one person tells a story to the next person in a circle, and the story goes around the circle until the last person repeats a story that is often totally different from the one that started around the circle. So it is with oral systems—detail is lost; elements are modified; and predictability disappears.

A good system should be simple enough for people to understand and complex enough to get the job done. (In the technology context, systems are sometimes described as user-friendly, or intuitive.) It should eliminate redundancy by leveraging knowledge, and reducing errors. It should ensure a consistent result.

If a Client A comes to your firm for a will, she should get essentially the same document as Client B with the same profile of needs. If your firm has developed work product that it considers high quality, you will want to replicate that quality again and again in similar transactions by re-using your prior work, but modifying it to fit the facts of subsequent transactions.

Perhaps most importantly, good systems allocate work to the person best suited to do that work. As noted in Chapter 7, work should be delegated to the lowest level where it can be performed competently, although you do not want people in over their heads, trying to do work they have neither the training nor experience to handle. Every member of the legal service delivery teams is a specialist, who contributes to the collective output of the team to produce a quality work product efficiently and predictably. Such an arrangement should preserve professional time, or, stated another way, permit the lawyer to engage in the high-level legal work that she went to law school to learn to handle.

A good system should build quality into the process. In many situations, we use quality control in the form of inspection, to make sure that the work product meets or exceeds standards. For example, when we proofread a document or review a subordinate's work, we are engaging in quality control through inspection. Given the vicarious liability of lawyers for the acts of subordinates, such inspection is not only beneficial, but also necessary to the practice of law. The failure to exercise supervision itself might be viewed as a breach of the professional standard of care. In contrast to quality control, quality assurance involves building steps into the system to make sure that the work product meets standards before it gets to the inspection stage. Significantly, if quality assurance measures are in place, the supervisor will spend less time looking for mistakes (because there are fewer mistakes), and will not have to send work back to be corrected nearly as often.

A good system is logical, in that it has decision points and alternative paths. Critical dates and times can be identified and flagged. Reminders can be generated, to make sure that deadlines are met. The process can often be described using a flow chart, reflecting a decision tree analysis of the steps. Such de-construction into component steps not only helps to assure that the system works, but also it provides a visual tool to help users understand the big picture.

2. CREATING THE SYSTEM

In 1975, Roberta Cooper Ramo, who later became the first woman President of the American Bar Association, wrote a book called *How to Create a System for the Law Office*. Ramo noted that systems have three components: forms, instructions and information. Forms include all the information and document templates that can be retrieved and re-used in similar cases. Instructions are the directions to system users about how to access the system to achieve a particular result. Instructions may include:

- narrative text, charts
- examples of forms or prior work product
- checklists
- bibliographic resources
- legal authorities
- glossaries of terms or definitions
- other directions about where to go for help

Instructions also permit the firm to pass on information to new employees, and to protect the organization against employees who hoard information to sustain their personal power. This is the "drop-dead" rule: if your employee dropped dead one evening, would your firm be able to survive the next day? Information is the variable data that makes each case different. It includes not only the personal information collected about the client, the facts in the case and other parties, but also the research on legal questions necessary to make professional judgments.

Law office systems can be formal or informal, written or oral, complex or simple. Ramo posits a "ninety percent" rule, which holds that a good system should contemplate ninety percent of the situations it encounters. When a system covers less than ninety percent, it is inefficient, requiring users to 're-invent the wheel' with many transactions. Above ninety percent, efficiency drops, because the cost of incorporating the rare or unusual scenario exceeds the cost of handling the situation on an ad hoc basis. Viewed in another light, ninety percent of the work is routine and can often be delegated by the lawyer to other members of the legal services delivery team, leaving the ten percent of new and challenging work for the lawyer.

The process of creating a system begins with the recognition that the firm is handling repetitive tasks. If an activity is unique—you will only do it once and will never do it again—you do not need to create a system. On the other hand, certain work is repetitive, or certain tasks are done over and over again, it is reasonable to systematize the work.

New firms have the luxury of creating their systems from scratch; they might examine what other firms do, read books or articles on the subject, or simply brainstorm about what they need to do to get the work done in a systematic way. Existing firms, on the other hand, usually start by disassembling the processes they already use; these may have evolved from informal systems, or worse, no regular system at all. In either case, the process involves several steps:

- The lawyers should start by deconstructing the work process; this may involve examining the present process, breaking it down into its basic components, or studying processes in other firms.
- Ask each worker to write down what she does when she engages in an activity.
- Collect information as to how the process should be structured.
- Analyze the data with an eye toward eliminating redundancy, removing unnecessary steps, allocating responsibilities, and achieving desired results.
- Build (or re-build) your system to reflect your analysis of the process.
- This building process should focus on task responsibilities, and give each person a clear statement of the scope of task responsibility.
- Describe reporting and supervisory responsibility, as well as overall system responsibility. By defining a chain of responsibility and reporting relationships, the system builds in checks and balances for quality assurance. By designating task responsibility, the system encourages quality assurance by giving individuals ownership of their work.

- Test the system to see if the process works as envisioned. This is obviously more difficult for a start-up firm than an ongoing one, but each situation has its challenges.

3. IMPLEMENTING THE SYSTEM

Once the system is in place, implementation becomes a priority. It is important not to roll out a system before it is ready. Firm leaders will need to prepare and review written instructions. The decision to adopt the new system needs to be clearly communicated to staff, clients and anyone else who may be affected by the system. People are often fearful of and resistant to change, so any modification of "the way we have always done things" is likely to be met with some resistance.

In order to gain commitment to change, people should have an opportunity to provide input during the planning stage. Secretaries may not have veto power over the final decisions, but if they feel that someone is listening to them, they will be much more amenable to change. Buy-in at every level of the organization is critical: The implementation will either fail or breed resentment and low morale if staff members do not change their habits (a form of civil disobedience). Again, a new firm has an advantage, in that there is nothing to change, so there can be little resistance to it, although some staff members may opine, "where I used to work, we did it *this* way."

Firm leadership should introduce the new system in a positive way. Schedule meetings to explain how the system, or at least the changes, will work. Explain the rationale for system changes; describe how the system will make people's lives better, not more difficult. Create opportunities for individuals to practice, ask questions, and study the system. Provide training as necessary to give workers the tools they will need to apply the system. This is particularly true for technology. Thus, if you acquire a new calendar or billing system, make sure that you provide the training necessary for users to scale the learning curve quickly. Training may involve:

- providing documentation
- explaining procedures
- conducting or arranging educational classes
- permitting practice
- giving feedback
- conducting review

Some firms may be able to incorporate training into case meetings, staff meetings or other on-going activities. Others may want to conduct training at specially scheduled meetings, or even go off-site. Either way, it is important to build training into the implementation phase.

Be patient—new processes often produce a short-term drop in efficiency as everyone learns their new responsibilities. If you recognize that such a drop in efficiency is likely, you can plan for it and more importantly avoid frustration during the transition period.

4. IMPROVING THE SYSTEM

Systems are dynamic, which means that they change. If systems do not have the capacity to change over time, they inevitably become encrusted with history, out of touch with reality, incapable of incorporating improvements, and increasingly inefficient. For these reasons, every system should include a built in process of continuous improvement. Sometimes improvements can be incorporated into the process, such as when a firm drafts a new document and then decides to add that document to the firm's document library for later retrieval. The system should have some mechanism for eliciting and obtaining user feedback. Users often know the flaws in a system long before the bosses do. Those responsible for maintaining the system should schedule periodic review.

Perhaps the calendar system should have an annual review, just like the human employees. Where systems are allowed to grow, to learn, to capture quality work and knowledge, they can and will improve. As systems get better, they typically need fewer modifications, so change becomes increasingly incremental. In the end, however, quality is never totally achieved, and improvement is always possible.

PROBLEMS AND QUESTIONS

1. Think about systems that you have encountered in the world outside law. Can you describe any that you would characterize as particularly good? Or bad? What characteristics made them so?

2. Now think about law office systems that you have seen, either as a client or an employee. Can you describe any that you would characterize as particularly good? Or bad? What characteristics made them so?

3. Is it possible to generalize from these examples about why systems are good or bad? Can you list those elements that you would want to incorporate into your law firm's practice system to make sure it is the best possible system, and that you would want to exclude from the system to make sure it did not fail?

E. MACRO–SYSTEM OVERVIEW

Law offices employ a number of different systems. Not all of these are directly connected to the delivery of legal work. The bulk of this section will focus on law practice systems, which are designed to deliver legal services to clients. These systems include:

- Substantive systems (how our firm handles a _____ matter);

- Document assembly systems (how our firm prepares a _____ document);

- Litigation support systems (how our firm tries a _____ case).

The substantive system involves the process by which the actual substantive legal work is handled. The document assembly and litigation support systems may be thought of as sub-parts of each substantive system. In other words, every substantive system produces documents, and every case could at least in theory end up in litigation.

In addition, every substantive system is supported by several administrative systems. The administrative systems may operate differently in different substantive areas, but in a larger sense, the administrative support systems cut across all of the firm's substantive practice systems. These administrative support systems are:

- Filing and retrieval systems;
- Timekeeping and billing systems;
- Calendar and docket control systems;
- Conflict management systems;
- Client trust account systems.

The firm may use other management systems as well. The management systems help the firm to manage its operations more efficiently, but these systems are not tied directly to the delivery of legal work. Some of these might include:

- Financial management systems
- Human resources management systems
- Physical resource management systems
- Information management systems

The sheer magnitude of developing practice and/or management systems can pose a huge disincentive for many law firms to organize their work. Many lawyers find it easier to handle work on an ad hoc basis, relying on personal experience and knowledge, than to try to create more efficient office systems. Some firms continue to utilize tried and true manual approaches to service delivery, or to practice law by the seats of their pants, notwithstanding the fact that modern technology creates opportunities to acquire systems at relatively low transaction and implementation costs.

For example, suppose the purchase price of software containing a substantive practice system was $5,000, and the cost of training and implementation another $5,000. Also, suppose that the software will be used by five staff members, four hours per day, 250 days per year, over a period of a year. The net transaction cost of using this software product would be $1/hour. If we further assume that the software will reduce the time required to complete transactions in half, so that the firm could do

$500 of work in an hour instead of $250, the firm would earn $250 for an investment of one dollar.

Organizing the substantive side of the practice of law saves lawyers from continually reinventing the wheel. It ultimately means greater income to the firm and savings to the client. It represents a way to keep the challenge in law practice by focusing on the new and exciting, while routinizing the mundane. Where matters can be handled routinely, they should be. Where tasks can be completed competently and efficiently by non-lawyers, they should be. Where lawyers can devote their time to those matters requiring the exercise of professional judgment, they should do so.

Malpractice is a pragmatic consideration that militates sharply in favor of systems utilization. A system assures the firm that it will produce a product of consistent quality. Furthermore, if a client is not happy with the service, a substantive system enables the firm to defend what it has done.

For a law student who has never practiced law, substantive systems may seem difficult because students do not know all the steps to take or all the law to include. Although it may be necessary to the practice of law to truly understand how to put together a comprehensive substantive system, it is possible to learn and apply the basic principles to create a basic system.

Many law students do not know what steps must be taken to produce a piece of legal work. They do not contemplate the decision points, alternatives or allocation of work. By brainstorming with other students, after reviewing the applicable law, you may be able to anticipate many of the steps in a basic substantive system. By conferring with practitioners or your professor you may be able to expand your knowledge of substantive systems. By studying existing systems—both manual and computerized—you may be able to evaluate your creation. Remember: even the most sophisticated operational system in a law firm does not contemplate every possibility. The basics are easy enough:

- What has to be done?
- Who is responsible for doing it?
- What decisions must be made?
- Who makes them?
- When are matters done?
- How are they done?

If you prepare a flow chart of the substantive system, it will help you to visualize the decision tree and the flow of work through the system. A checklist will help you to make sure your system is comprehensive. Both the flow chart and the checklist isolate individual work assignments within the context of the larger project. Case management or project management software can also help manage the flow of work through the substantive system. See Chart 12–1, on the next page.

Chart 12-1
Practice System Overview

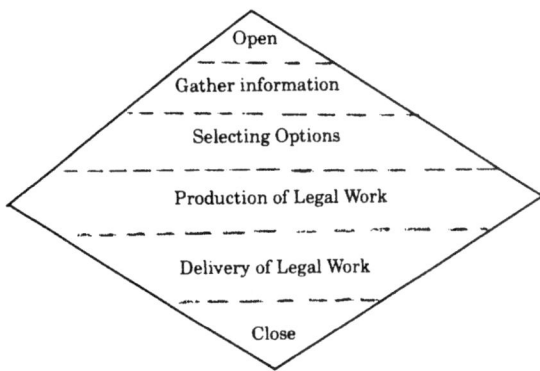

PROBLEMS AND QUESTIONS

1. Go back to the marketing plan that your firm developed in Chapter 6. You should have identified one or more practice areas that the firm seeks to pursue in establishing its market niche. Take one of the substantive practice areas and develop a chart showing the flow of activities and decision points from the time a client first contacts your firm until the client's case is closed. Try to include as many steps and alternatives as possible. You may want to brainstorm with your fellow firm members or talk to practitioners to see what they do.

2. Who will be responsible for completing the various tasks that will need to be completed at each step along the way? Who will have oversight responsibility for these tasks? How will supervisors know when employees tasked with certain responsibilities have completed their work, and how will supervisors assess the quality of work without having to re-do it?

3. How will the system allocate the non-human resources necessary to deliver the legal service to clients?

4. How will the system manage the delivery timeline in order to assure that services are delivered on schedule?

5. Do you know of software or cloudware that law firms can use to implement substantive practice systems for the area of practice that you have chosen, or other practice areas? What does such technology cost? Is it a good investment? How would you measure this?

Chapter 14

Practice System Components

■ ■ ■

A. ADMINISTRATIVE SUPPORT SYSTEMS

In the previous Chapter, we looked at practice systems in terms of the big picture, how to handle a _____ matter. The last section of the Chapter noted that the macro-system has components, micro-systems or sub-systems, which operate within the larger delivery system. If you think about it every substantive practice area is different. A family law matter is very different from a patent application or a real estate settlement. It is difficult to speak generically about the delivery of legal services. As practice areas grow increasingly specialized the systemic differences increase. Yet, at the same time, the components of legal service delivery systems are remarkably similar. It might be useful to think of these system components as administrative support systems: they support the substantive system operationally utilizing the firm's administrative functionality rather than the exercise of legal knowledge and lawyering skills. Many of these administrative activities can be handled by paralegals, secretaries and other support personnel.

This material is divided into several parts. The first part involves document assembly, or the preparation of documents delivered as part of a substantive practice system. The second part covers a number of sub-systems that can be described as administrative support systems:

- Calendar and Tickler Systems
- Filing and Retrieval Systems
- Conflict Checking Systems
- Timekeeping and Billing Systems
- Client Trust Account Systems

The final section looks at litigation support. Some practice areas are litigation-driven, e.g., personal injury practice, but even in transactional work, there is always some possibility that the matter could end up in litigation if parties cannot work out their differences. For this reason, it is useful to think of litigation as one of the components of every substantive system.

PROBLEMS AND QUESTIONS

1. Why do law firms need to think about these system components? Is it to improve efficiency by making sure that the final product is consistent every time it is delivered? Is it to make sure that there were no mistakes in the creation of the product or service? Is it to reduce the unit cost of the legal service.

2. What technology applications can that law firms use to manage these system components? Will a commercial practice system include these subsystems, or will law firms have to use proprietary or generic software? Where would you look to find the answers to these questions

B. DOCUMENT ASSEMBLY SYSTEMS

The question implicit in creating a document assembly systems is: "How does our firm prepare a _____ document?" A document is the written embodiment of system content, whether it is a written piece of paper or electronic file, documents have a physical embodiment that makes them more like products than services. Think about how the written papers developed by a lawyer in a particular case are referred to as the work product.

The process through which legal documents are prepared differs slightly with each document, but the process is always the same. Whether the document is simple or complex, routine or unique, original or retrieved, the steps that go into creating a document are similar. Even though every substantive practice system utilizes its own special universe of documents, if you understand these simple steps, you will know how to create documents in any substantive practice area.

The alternative to creating a document assembly system is to draft every document from scratch. The system in such a situation is the lawyer's memory. In contrast, a document assembly system allows a law firm to leverage its intellectual work product by retrieving documents that have already been used and modifying them in new situations. The document assembly concept assumes that the firm will use variations of a document many times. If the firm creates unique documents that are used one time only, there is little need to create a system. As the volume of work in a practice area increases, the benefits of work product leverage become more apparent. A document assembly system will also reduce the cost of document preparation, which can be translated into price breaks for the client or greater profitability for the firm.

In practice, many document assembly systems today are software or Internet-based. Computer technology is well suited to store and retrieve legal information, to utilize templates to create individualized documents and to apply a "decision tree" analysis to document production. Although the principles of document assembly apply with equal force to manual systems, technology-based systems have a number of advantages.

All document assembly systems contain the three basic components mentioned earlier in this chapter: forms, instructions and information. Forms are the underlying templates from which documents are built. Instructions tell users how to create documents. Information is the variable data inserted into each document that makes it case specific.

Some firms and software products talk about a library of forms. Before the days of computers, many lawyers used formbooks that contained all of the basic forms for a substantive practice area. Software programs often include electronic form files, but a lawyer can develop an internal set of forms for a practice area.

Language that is incorporated into every iteration of a document is sometimes called boilerplate. Boilerplate usually does not have to be rewritten because it accomplished a specific purpose, and has been accepted by the courts to mean what it says. Standard clauses include information that is the same in every version of that particular clause, although the clause itself is not used in every form of the document. Unique clauses are those drafted by the attorney to meet the requirements of specific cases. Unique clauses can be modified from boilerplate or standard clauses, or they may be drafted from scratch. Ideally, the lawyer concentrates her time on the high-end, complex drafting work, which represents the best use of the lawyer's skill.

Variable information is extrinsic to the form, and changes with each case. During the course of the representation, from the initial client interview through independent fact-gathering activities, the lawyer will have produced a considerable body of information relevant to the matter. Some of the information, such as the client name, will be incorporated directly into the document, while other information, such as the sex of the parties mentioned in the document, will operate in the background, in this example to change the gender of pronouns in the document. Client information will also have a bearing on the content of the document, for example, in a will, a married couple with children would typically require different clauses than an elderly widow with no heirs.

Without accurate information it is impossible to produce documents that accomplish their intended goal. Many firms utilize a client intake form or a document specific questionnaire to elicit information from clients necessary to the preparation of documents. Such information may be collected by having the client fill out the questionnaires in advance or in the waiting room, by an attorney or paralegal in the course of a client interview, or electronically. The advantage of on line questionnaires is that specific answers to questions will automatically trigger changes in the content of the document.

The firm will want to save this client information for possible future use. If the client comes back to revise or change the document at a later date, the information from the prior representation can be updated more quickly than collecting the information anew. It may also be useful to track changes in the status of client information over time. In some cases, it may be necessary for the lawyer to defend her work in a civil action or disciplinary complaint arising from the representation.

Client information can also be incorporated into a database containing information about all the firm's clients. A relational database would allow the firm to develop tables with information relevant to particular documents, related to a general client information database used for mailings, billings, and other purposes. Although the creation of a database structure is a fairly labor intensive activity, firms can capture much client information through other software programs, including substantive systems, time and billing systems, and financial systems. Where document specific client information is stored in a database table, the lawyer can compare the client situation to that of other clients in the table.

Instructions are the key to consistency in document assembly. The more clearly and accurately that instructions describe what steps need to be followed in what order, the more likely it is that the document will reflect the meaning of the drafter. Although a good document assembly system allows lawyers to produce documents efficiently without assistance, the real benefits of the system emerge in team practice. When two or more people are involved in the preparation of documents, it is important for everyone to be on the same page, figuratively and literally. Not only is it critical for all the players to understand the objectives of the document assembly practice, but also it is also necessary for each team member to appreciate her role, and to know the specific task assigned to her.

Just as a basketball team has a center, guards and forwards, the legal services delivery team has lawyers, legal assistants and secretaries. The lawyer is the driving force behind the document assembly team; the lawyer is ultimately responsible for the work product, will make major choices about the content of the document, and will draft complex or unique clauses for the document. The lawyer is also the primary contact point for the client in most situations. The legal assistant may be responsible for the collection of some of the information, producing standard or routine documents for review by the lawyer, and assembling documents from various clauses, boilerplate and client information. The secretary may be involved in producing a polished version of the final document, scheduling meetings relating to document preparation, and carrying other ministerial functions in the document assembly process.

Different firms may allocate responsibility for different tasks in the document assembly process differently. The key is to clearly delineate responsibility. If no particular person is assigned to a task, everyone will believe that someone else will do it. If instructions do not specify how to do something, individuals will make things up as they go along. If team members find steps incomprehensible or unduly burdensome, they will take short cuts that compromise the system.

Good instructions answer the old newspaper reporter's key questions:
- Who?

- What?
- When?
- Where?
- How? And
- Why?

The last question (Why?) is included, because team members need to appreciate the importance of their contribution to the overall process. By explaining why each step is necessary, everyone involved understands the value of their contributions.

It is not difficult to set up a simple spreadsheet with the various steps listed, and generate a list of tasks for each individual on the team, a timetable, or a checklist. A checklist can be an effective tool to make sure that every necessary step in the preparation of the document has taken place. For some simple documents, this may not be necessary, but for long, complex ones, it may be useful to the supervising lawyer to ascertain that every necessary step has been followed. In addition to responsibilities and a checklist, the instructions often contain exhibits of the form, and resources we go to for additional help.

Traditionally, systems were maintained in three-ring binders in the office, so that anyone could refer to the system master for help. In the world of substantive systems, the document assembly process may be guided by drop-down menus, dialog boxes, help features, wizards, and manuals. The intuitiveness of many of these systems makes it easy to be intellectually lazy about the content. It is important to remember that it is no defense in a malpractice suit that a lawyer relied upon bad information in a purchased substantive system. Thus, even where the firm uses a computerized document assembly system, it makes sense to maintain a separate set of firm-specific instructions on how to use the system.

Many law firms use document assembly programs, like Hot Docs or Ghostfil. These programs not only facilitate the drafting of documents in specific matters, they provide document libraries, and permit the creation of new templates from existing documents. The user goes through the old document, strips out client specific information and designates blanks to be filled in document preparation. The software will even create a questionnaire for collection of the information that goes in the blank.

The document assembly process itself is fairly straightforward. At some point in the representation, when a decision point is reached, the lawyer will conclude that a particular document is necessary. This will trigger the following steps:

- Select the appropriate document. Whether it comes from a document library, a form book, prior work product or even the client, the firm will need to start with a template or boilerplate. If the original document is not in electronic form, it may need to be scanned into a text-readable format and stripped of information not relevant to the current case.

- Collect all variable information necessary to complete the document. The information that may have been gathered earlier in the representation, or may need to be collected at the time of document preparation. In either case, the information that will go into the document needs to be assembled in a way that will permit it to be used easily.

- Select standard clauses to be incorporated into the document. Draft unique or non-standard clauses for inclusion in the document.

- Assemble all clauses and variable information into the template document, creating a draft.

- Review the draft. Certainly the lawyer and client must review the draft, but if a legal assistant or secretary is involved in the process of document preparation, they may need to do a preliminary review before the document gets to the lawyer's desk. The review process may create a loop, in which changes in the document are required, and the assembly process returns to earlier steps. Thus, a document may go through several drafts before it is acceptable to the lawyer and the client.

- The final form of the document is then used as it was intended: executed, filed, mailed, delivered, or presented.

- Save the work product. If original work has gone into the preparation of a particular document, the firm might want to incorporate new clauses into the list of standard clauses in the system. Such additions should not be made indiscriminately, or the system will become unwieldy. If, however, the lawyer believes that the fact patterns underlying the new language are likely to recur with any frequency, it makes sense to add the clause to the system.

Beyond these steps, the lawyer and team members should always be conscious of the overall integrity of the system. Review the system periodically to determine whether it is still functional. Systems are dynamic, which means that they change over time, and the system will deteriorate if its owners do not work to improve it. The ultimate test is whether the document assembly system produces high-quality documents consistently and efficiently. The concept of incremental quality improvement applies to document assembly systems, which often can be tweaked to run better and produce better results.

On another level, the law is constantly changing, and judicial decisions or legislative enactments may render document language obsolete, unenforceable or legally incorrect. For this reason, lawyers need to remain current with the law in jurisdictions where they practice, and make sure that changes in the law are incorporated into the documents they use. The more automated the system, the greater the temptation will be to rely on the system for content and to ignore changes that make the system ineffective.

AUTOMATING DOCUMENT SYSTEMS SAVES TIME AND MONEY

From *The Connecticut Law Tribune*, by Alan Schoolcraft (March 27, 2000).

Like every other business, law offices must find ways to produce more at a lower cost. A quick review of any law firm's general ledger will easily show that the largest single expense item is staff salaries and benefits. And a little analysis of how the staff spends its time will reveal that the most time consuming daily tasks involve producing paper documents.

As firms look for ways to relieve the pressure to lower costs they are increasingly turning to document automation software. Yet few attorneys are actually willing and able to learn how to program their own document automation systems, and even fewer can take the time to maintain a system once it has been developed. Instead, many attorneys who realize the value of using document automation technology rely on outside sources to develop and maintain their systems.

As they consider which product to rely on for their document automation needs, they need to make sure their choice:

- Will let them easily edit the master forms/templates. Most lawyers will never be completely satisfied with somebody else's wording, so they need to make sure they can adapt the system to their specific tastes.

- Will continue working when their word processor is upgraded. Some systems use features belonging to a specific word processor or even a specific version of a word processor. There are few things more upsetting than to upgrade a word processor only to find that it broke the document assembly software.

- Will work with all versions of WordPerfect and Microsoft Word. Many offices today have a mix of word processors in use and have found that they must have multiple versions of their document assembly software. That is particularly troubling when multiple sets of templates have to be edited every time the system is customized.

- Provides tools to help locate the form you want. A complete system may provide thousands of automated forms. If the system doesn't provide the right tools, an attorney may spend more time looking for a form that is saved with automated assembly.

- Will save and reuse data. Reusing data in the same case from one document to another is as important as automating the process of cutting and pasting the form. If a system won't store that data for use next week or next month, one of the most important aspects of document automation will be missing.

- Will track completed documents. While only a few small-and medium-sized firms can afford high-end dedicated document management systems, they should at least be able to rely on their document assembly software to begin the process of organizing their work. Since the system knows which documents were produced for which clients and where they are stored, this information should be retained and made available.

- Will establish default answers for all questions. While most systems today set up basic law firm information, there are literally hundreds of pieces of information used every day that are generally the same from one case to another. A good system will allow defaults for items such as "county where suit is filed," "Sheriff's mailing address," etc.

- Will generate both word processor and graphic type forms. Document assembly has traditionally meant cutting and pasting forms together in a word processor. In many jurisdictions and many practice areas, there is a trend toward using preprinted fill-in-the-blank forms. In those situations, a user is faced with the frustrating and archaic situation of manually filling-in a typewritten form when all of the information needed is already entered in the document assembly system.

- Will be updated and maintained on a regular basis. Keep in mind the costs and malpractice exposure that will occur if a vendor fails to keep your system updated for changes in the law or goes out of business. Above all else, before you make a decision, check out the company's history, reputation and financial strength.

Today there is a wide range of document automation software available to the legal profession. The levels of sophistication range from simple mail merge/macro-based systems to sophisticated expert systems that come close to automating the practice of law. They also range in price from less than one hundred dollars to many thousands of dollars.

PROBLEMS AND QUESTIONS

1. Look at the substantive practice system you created in the last Chapter. Consider what documents are likely to be produced as a part of that system. Now create a document assembly system for one of those documents, including the boilerplate, alternative clauses and integration of variable client information. Provide the necessary instructions so that a new employee of your firm could create a documents using your system.

2. When you retrieve language that you have saved from old documents to incorporate into new documents, is there a danger that you will use the wrong language in the new documents? How do you make sure this does not happen?

C. ADMINISTRATIVE SUPPORT SYSTEMS

Administrative support systems relate to the business of delivering legal services: calendaring, filing retrieval, conflicts of interest, time-keeping and billing, and client trust accounts. Every substantive practice system must be supported administratively, and although the systems may operate differently in different substantive areas, their fundamental components are the same.

These systems are especially important in avoiding the most common forms of professional error that lead to disciplinary complaints and malpractice claims. Although the firm may have other administrative systems, such as a human resources system, a general financial management system, an information management system, or a security system, the systems described below address the administrative support for the delivery systems specifically.

Administrative support systems operate to direct the flow of paper and work relating to client matters through the law office. Knowledge of the substantive law means little if the law office cannot deliver its product, and do so in a timely manner. Administrative support systems should run unobtrusively in the background, and integrate seamlessly with the substantive practice systems.

All practice systems require administrative support. A firm's administrative support systems cut across all the substantive practice systems. Although a firm may have a number of general administrative systems, e.g., human resources management, information management, finance and accounting, the systems discussed in this section are related to the delivery of the legal services. They include calendaring, filing/retrieval, time keeping/billing, conflict checking and client trust accounts. Each system may operate somewhat differently in each substantive practice system, but each administrative support system is really part of an integrated step of procedures for handling these recurring administrative tasks in the delivery process. See Chart 12–2, on the next page.

Chart 12-2
Practice System Integration

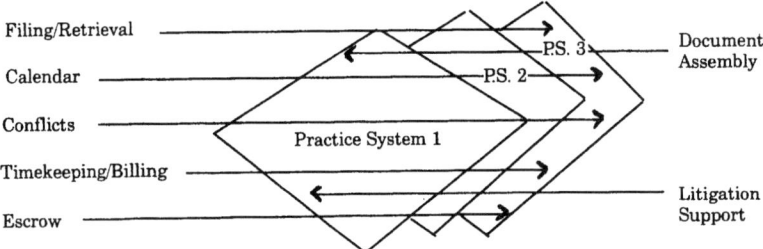

Administrative support systems are utilized by members of the legal services delivery team, although computers have streamlined many of the administrative tasks. As is the case with other systems, it is critical to assign tasks to specific individuals, and to clarify lines of reporting and decision making. Because many of the administrative functions are clearly routine, many of the tasks associated with administrative support systems can be delegated to support personnel. Such delegation requires sufficient training, comprehensive instructions and appropriate oversight. Some tasks should appropriately remain in the lawyer's hands, although many are technically non-delegable, which means that the attorney is still responsible for mistakes even if the task was assigned to a non-lawyer assistant.

Although the workings of the administrative support systems are often invisible to the client's these "back office" functions are more likely to cause professional error than the "front office" substantive legal advice to clients. Much of the inefficiency in service delivery can be traced to administrative matters, such as not being able to locate a file or creating scheduling conflicts. Well-run practice systems require reliable, accessible and functional support systems in order to operate optimally.

The following sections deal with these systems. The ideas expressed here do not represent final solutions, correct for all firms and all times; they are rather examples of how such systems operate. In practice, all systems must, to some degree, be individualized for their users. No two law offices will do all things the same way. The only true test of any system is whether it works. If you understand the basic concepts as to how these systems work, you will be able to adapt the basic principles in a variety of different circumstances.

1. CALENDAR AND TICKLER SYSTEMS

The calendar system is perhaps the most critical administrative support system for every firm. Even a solo practitioner needs to be able to manage her schedule of meetings and appearances, keep up with deadlines, and organize her time. As the number of individuals who work in a firm increases, schedule issues become more complex, and the calendar becomes a tool for managing the allocations of personnel to work assignments.

A calendar system is essentially a database with fields of information associated with scheduling events and other critical dates. The calendar should be easy to use, provide security for information, and eliminate duplications of effort. For example, an attorney might keep calendar information on a desk blotter and a pocket calendar, while the secretary keeps a separate schedule and the firm receptionist a master calendar. With dates being logged into all these places, it should not be surprising that mistakes would occur, e.g., double bookings, neglecting to write something down, writing something down incorrectly, and forgetting to tell one of the other calendar keepers to add something to their calendar. A major advantage of computerized calendar systems is that events can be scheduled one time and used in a variety of different ways.

Although it would be possible to create a calendar system from a powerful relational database program, the development costs of a home-grown system are unlikely to be justifiable, in light of the cost of available commercial products. Whether using a generic program such as Microsoft Outlook or a more industry-specific tool such as Amicus Attorney, almost all practices can find a product that meets their needs. Vendors market their products at technology shows, on Internet web sites, and in bar journal ads. Firms can usually obtain demonstration disks to look at the product directly

Products may be designed for solos and small firms, or for larger organizations; firms should find a product that meets the needs for the size of their organization. Products vary as to the degree to which they can be modified, and firms that like to tinker with the technology may be more comfortable with such products. Products also may contain a variety of other components, such as a conflict checking module or other administrative support functions. Firms must decide whether they want a turnkey system, or several separate systems. If they use more than one system, they should investigate how well the separate systems may be integrated, e.g., whether time slips will work with Amicus.

The calendar system should keep track of a number of important types of information. First, it should record the name of the individual to be scheduled. The calendar should show a date, time and location for each recorded event. Events may include appointments, conferences, appearances in court, and other activities related to the delivery of legal services.

The calendar may also show personal activities such as working out at the gym, lunches, and days off.

Furthermore, the calendar can record management activities, marketing, continuing legal education and other activities that fill the workday. For those activities associated with clients, the calendar should reflect the client name, file number, and contact information. For appearances, the calendar should include the court and docket number. The information should state where the activity will take place, and include an address if the place is away from the office.

Because many legal malpractice cases are related to missed deadlines, appearances and other scheduling errors, the importance of these systems cannot be minimized. In larger organizations, the burden of coordinating the activities of large numbers of personnel and tracking numerous cases becomes increasingly problematic.

A word about the relationship between personal scheduling and firm scheduling may be in order. The topic of individual scheduling is addressed more fully in Chapter 13 (Time Management, pages 367–370. Sophisticated law firm calendar systems permit individuals to maintain private sections of their calendars; times are blocked on the firm's master calendar, but the details are not accessible or visible to anyone but the individual and such other people (e.g., secretary) designated by that individual. Personal desktop assistants (PDAs) permit the individual to sync her personal calendar and other personal data with the firm calendar. A surprising number of lawyers maintain redundant schedules on several different calendars, thereby recreating the inefficiencies of duplicated schedules in manual systems.

Personal information managers (PIMs, sometimes referred to as tickler systems) are the individual lawyer's tool for keeping appointments and reminding her about critical dates. Traditionally, lawyers or their secretaries kept a daily calendar or a perpetual calendar on index cards. Often the lawyer and the secretary both kept a calendar, and if the firm maintained its own master calendar, the chances of miscommunication were considerable. Computers have made this process much simpler.

A number of programs allow users to create and maintain a perpetual tickler system for the individual's schedule and to integrate the PIM with the firm's overall calendar system. The typical PIM allows users not only to schedule appointments, but also directory information, expenses, reminder notes and other useful information. Personal desktop assistants (PDAs—Palms, Blackberries, and similar devices) have revolutionized calendaring by not only permitting the owner of a PDA to keep a schedule and personal database on a portable device, but also to record new information while out of the office, and to exchange data (sync) with the user's desktop system back at the office.

HANDHELD COMPUTERS KEEP USERS ENTHUSIASTIC

From *The Indiana Lawyer*, by Stephen Bour (August 29, 2001).

Lately I have been noticing a lot more people from all fields of business using handheld ... PDAs (Personal Digital Assistants). It gets my curiosity up when I see people carefully scribbling and poking away at these little devices that are about the size of a pocket calculator. Until recently I had successfully resisted the temptation to buy one of these techno-gadgets for myself. After all, I had been happily using my notebook computer for most of my mobile chores, and I was perfectly content with my conventional day planner for logging appointments and taking notes. One thing I couldn't help but notice was the almost universal enthusiasm most users had for their handheld computers. It made me wonder what I was missing.... The main applications that come with this handheld (and most others) are an address book, an appointment calendar, a to do list, a memo pad, an alarm clock and a calculator.

. . .

[C]an a PDA replace my bulky paper day planner, and ... reduce my paper clutter, especially the sticky notes that tend to accumulate everywhere around the office? ...

The learning curve for the [PDA] is not too steep. When it is first turned on, it walks you through a series of tutorials to familiarize you to the functions and operating characteristics; it takes about one hour. The most unusual new things to learn are the special pen stroke conventions that are necessary in order to input text data....

I have found the handheld to be particularly useful in reducing the clutter of notes that I previously scribbled onto whatever scrap of paper was at hand. I call the handheld my sticky-note reduction device, and it is working. Every time I pick up a random note and refer to it, I commit that information to the little computer and throw away the paper. Now I can quickly find a piece of information by using the search feature on the [PDA]. This is just one example where I find the handheld more useful than my day planner. It is much more interactive, dynamic and adaptable to changes than my paper day planner. I also like using the alarm feature to remind me of upcoming appointments. That is something the paper planner could never do. I have quit entering information in my old day planner and so far I am getting along pretty well.

A word of caution: I don't recommend switching over to the handheld computer as your primary appointment-recording tool unless you also have a desktop or notebook computer. It is essential that you regularly synchronize the data in the handheld and save a current copy of it on a computer. The handheld may be easier to lose since it is much smaller than a day planner, and it has the added risk of failure or breakage....

We have barely scratched the surface on the subject of handheld computers. There is so much more to the story. For example, there are literally hundreds of useful programs available for the Palm operating system. Many of them are available free on the Internet. Also, you can download news, weather, maps, stock quotes and much more directly to your handheld from specialized web sites.

Internet-based systems allow access to users' home e-mail and records wherever an Internet connection is available (a virtual private network, or VPN). Within the office, intranets allow exchange of data easily between lawyers and administrative staff. Even in offices with multiple offices, powerful network platforms permit integrated calendaring from distant sites.

The firm's calendar is sometimes referred to as the docket control system, because it is a tool for tracking the firm's litigation caseload. If you imagine a giant blackboard containing all critical dates for all of the firm's cases, including who must make appearances, sign off on documents and perform specific tasks, you get the idea of a calendar system. You also appreciate how daunting such a system can be. Yet, if a firm has five lawyers scheduled for seven appearances in different courts on Tuesday the 1st, at 2:00 in the afternoon, something has to give. The calendar system should be thought of as a means of managing all scheduling matters in the firm, transactional cases and administrative activities as well as court appearances and other litigation-related functions as well.

Just as with personal information management, computerized systems have been a boon to firm-wide calendaring. It is possible to track and manage an infinitely larger number of cases, as well as lawyers and staff, than could be contemplated manually. Even so, in large firms, several paralegals, top-line administrators and key lawyers may be involved in managing the system. Even in a small firm there is a need for some clearly defined individual to assume responsibility for the calendar system. The key to any computer based calendar system is that information can be input one time and then manipulated in a variety of ways, creating useful management reports.

All calendar systems should at a minimum track each active case by attorney, critical dates, and tasks to be completed. A good system should incorporate checkpoints, supervisory responsibilities and support staff assignments. The system should make appointments and communicate to attendees that their attendance is needed. The calendar should identify double bookings over-scheduling and other potential problems. It should permit both public and private (personal) calendars.

SKILLS AND SYSTEMS: THE SECRETS TO BETTER LAW OFFICE MANAGEMENT

From *The Compleat Lawyer*, by Phil J. Shuey (Winter 1998).

Many of the problems associated with malpractice claims or exposure are associated with poor law office management techniques and procedures. Fortunately, creation of good systems and regular use of them can minimize malpractice exposure.

No tasks are more important than these law office management procedures. The cost to a firm for assertions of malpractice, or even a grievance procedure, is so substantial that it should be avoided by all means possible.

. . .

Docket/Calendar

There are many reasons to have effective docket and calendar systems in your office, including to meet any statute of limitations imposed in the case, and to meet good time requirements to accomplish the work, even if a statute of limitations does not apply.

It is important to meet the expectations of the client for conclusion of the engagement, if those are reasonable. A docket/calendar system can assure that your milestones are met in a timely fashion and that the client has work product when promised. If the same system is used for calendar items as well as deadlines, make sure that there is a mechanism to separate the critical dates from important, but not essential, dates. A missed appointment is troubling; a missed deadline is threatening.

A docket/calendar system can help promote good public/client relations by assuring that work is delivered when promised, and that the firm does not always have to labor under an "eleventh hour" rush. Crisis work production provides more opportunity for errors and causes additional and unnecessary stress for lawyers and staff. While procrastination is common in the profession, commit to minimizing it. Procrastination can be offset by assuring that everyone associated with a case or matter receives copies of the reminders or ticklers to guarantee that important dates are not missed.

It is helpful to use realistic reminder dates. If set too far in advance of the deadline, reminders tend to be ignored as premature; if too close to the deadline, everyone will be placed under undesirable pressure. Assume that the worst possible thing will happen—will the system in place protect the client and the firm?

Naturally, there is a financial component to good docket/calendar management. The sooner work is completed, the sooner a final statement of account can be generated and payment received. Most lawyers make poor bankers—get the work, and then the bill, out the door!

Centralized responsibility for docket/calendar control is essential, because it avoids the possibility of critical deadlines being missed. A system or process, uniformly followed, is the safest procedure to avoid missed dates.

There is also an element of peace of mind that comes from the knowledge that critical dates will not be lost, overlooked, or misplaced because of a reliance on any one person's memory. Make sure that you have both a primary and a backup system for all docket/calendar matters. A standard form should be used for entry of information into the system to assure that essential dates and information such as responsible parties are not overlooked.

It is not enough to have a backup system; periodically, the dates in the primary and secondary systems have to be compared for completeness and accuracy. The best computerized system is worthless if it is "down," and it is prudent to have both an automated and a manual system.

For the computerized system, select a docket/calendar system that provides a "docket rule" feature. The docket rule feature allows a critical event in any substantive area to have predefined reminder dates set by the initial posting of the critical date. Hence, if a task needs to be accomplished 30 days before the critical date, the system will automatically calculate the date 30 days prior to the critical date and generate a reminder for that contingent date, as well as all other related tasks. It is helpful if the system generates past due reports on demand, and "nags" with reminders that do not go away after the due date until marked as completed.

. . .

It is impossible to effectively use time and staff, or to avoid the possibility of critical malpractice errors, if everyone in the legal services delivery team does not have access to the same information. The firm must assure that the date(s) selected are clear for all involved. Because docketed matters are of concern to everyone in the firm, it is a typical, firm-wide information need.

The calendar is a variation of the docket system, but the primary motivation is the general efficiency of having the entire firm know that appointments and reminders have been set. Additionally, because firm resources are involved, everyone must know what commitments have been made for the selected date(s). The firm as a whole has to have some sense of the type and timing of obligations.

2. FILING AND RETRIEVAL SYSTEMS

Until the advent of the paperless office, law firms will need to file papers. The filing system is important not only for purposes of storage but also retrieval. If we never needed to retrieve papers, there would be no need to save them. It follows that a good filing system should permit easy retrieval of materials from storage. In today's law office, files mean electronic files as well as paper files. The filing system must cover a number of specific matters:

- How the filing system is initiated;
- How the system is structured;
- How files are recorded and numbered;
- Who has custodial authority over the files;
- How files are checked out and used;.
- Where files are stored;
- How files are closed when the case is completed.

If lawyers saved everything from every case, the files would expand geometrically. Even the most logical filing system would soon be overwhelmed. As the following material suggests, selective destruction of the contents of closed files is integral to the efficiency of any system.

A 21st CENTURY LAW OFFICE

From *Probate & Property*, by Thomas C. Baird (July/August 2001).

... All law firms suffer headaches related to the constant costs, shuffling and storage of mounds and mounds of paper.... [Our] firm's answer was to find a way for current technology to eliminate the mounds of paper and make each office more orderly and productive. This process began by reviewing the flow of each stack of paper and the difficulties of knowing where the stacks were at different stages of the process and then determining what solutions were available. Everyone needed a way to be able to find files faster and to improve the time spent in the movement of these stacks of paper. A key element of this process was getting those stacks and boxes of papers into the computer and making them available at each desktop automatically. Since the firm had each workstation networked, it already had a central server location available for storage of files. Scanning provided a way to transfer those files to that central location, thereby eliminating the need for the files, folders and boxes of files to be moved from place to place or even to off-site storage.

The firm decided to update its copying equipment by acquiring a scanner/copier combination. From the many different brands and models offered and the wide range of prices and options, the firm chose to go with two networked units offering large capacity scanning and copying. Some units allow faxing out directly from the scanner, but the firm decided to use a fax program that was integrated with the e-mail server.

To facilitate scanning even further, small sheet scanners were placed on each desktop to handle individual letters or attachments that need to be scanned into the computer. The sheet scanners assist in the transformation of items to digital format without the necessity of going to another part of the office, where stacks of papers for scanning at some point in the future tend to stockpile. Since smaller groups of paper could be processed more efficiently, desktop scanners for lawyers and staff alike were deemed important.

Although equipment plays a part, it will not matter what type of equipment is used if the procedures are not effective. Each firm member constantly evaluates scanning versus copying. If a copy is made now, will that copy have to be scanned later? If so, don't make the copy. Scan it instead, thereby reducing steps and costs for copies. Any copy needed later can be printed from the digital image with a stroke of the finger. Scanning also eliminates the per page cost for paper or toner. The digital machines used for this type of work have very few moving parts; therefore, repairs and downtime have been reduced dramatically. Noise and lost time are also reduced.

With scanners/copiers, the firm is able to scan documents directly after they have been signed. The "copies" of the documents, which are now in digital format, can be stored, and any additional paper copies the client wants can be made from the image. This one action has made a major difference in the flow of the firm's work product and reduced time tremendously. In the past, clerks would literally spend their days copying binders upon binders so that the firm could give clients their boxes of copies. Many clients are thrilled to be handed a CD that contains scanned copies of all their signed documents instead of binders of legal documents. The CD can be provided at substantially less cost and much less time. The CPAs also prefer the CD, because it means they have less paper to store, and they too have the whole client's file at the touch of a finger.

The firm wanted to be able to complete a project without generating any paper or, at the very least, generating paper only at the very end of the process, so it has gone to "digital files." Digital files have great benefits over traditional paper files. The digital file is much easier to attach to e-mails, store on a CD or hard drive or duplicate, and keeping up with the file is much more effective and takes much less time.

When setting up a new client, the client's data is entered into the firm's accounting program. That data is automatically dumped into the firm's document management program without requiring retyping. As documents or images are "filed away" in the client's digital file, a wealth of additional information can be placed into that document's profile, which is like an electronic card file. The profile stays with the document and is viewable, allowing conflict data, legal descriptions, entity formations and other information to be easily cross-referenced or searched.

With the aid of a document management program, one is able to profile, track and index the files and their contents. The firm tried carefully to improve its use of the assets in the software applications that it had already been using. Since only small portions of software applications were being used, an effort is being made to improve that percentage.

Focusing on improving use of these applications allows the firm to greatly increase its productivity and therefore its profitability.

Through profiling, the document management program provides quick access to needed documents, whether first drafts or final signed copies. It is great to be able to access the document that was just done last week. Or the document done several years ago that took hours to create and contains that special paragraph—only no one can remember the client or when the document was done. All that anyone remembers is a portion of one of the phrases. With this system, however, within a matter of seconds, the document is on the computer screen and is being used.

It has also become common practice to produce quality digital documents for electronic distribution and collaboration with others. E-mailing documents has become more than just the transmittal of words. It is actually the transmittal of the whole work product, including the original document, revisions and so much more. If the transmitter is not familiar with the software application being used, the transmitter can actually be telling the recipient more about the work product than was desired. If care is not taken, transmitted data can reveal information that was not intended to be revealed. It is critical that the user become familiar with a program's features and turn off those features that might reveal private or sensitive information.

The firm's change to digital files applied not only to new files but also to old files. The firm began a process of emptying its off-site storage locations by culling old files of unnecessary paper and scanning certain necessary parts of the paper files for quick recall. The firm is retaining only very small portions of the paper in the files. Having instantaneous access to the contents of a client's 10-year old file is very satisfying and impresses the client. The firm has already seen the enormous benefits of scanning in documents and indexing important data from these files. Being able to find the scanned, signed copies of a set of five year old wills for Mr. and Mrs. Jones, or the legal description of the property sold to them eight years earlier, within a few seconds is invaluable and much faster than the previous alternative. In addition, the cost for storage of boxes upon boxes of paper files can run into thousands of dollars, as opposed to the minimal cost of CDs and other digital media storage. Document imaging technology allows for duplication of documents or files very quickly and is much more reliable.

Digital images can be formatted and manipulated easily, resulting in enhanced quality that with time can be lost on paper. Another aspect of storing paper files is the problem of deterioration of boxes, paper, folders, rubber bands and other items from heat or water damage. With proper backups and maintenance of a disaster plan, this is not a problem with digital files.

Working toward paperless files may not mean no paper or no files. It means that when a digital file is created, and if a paper file is necessary, the paper file has less paper in it. Surprisingly, the firm has found a large number of its paper files are no longer even created. Whenever possible, that piece of paper the client hands the firm's staff is scanned and handed right back. For the times that the firm actually needs to retain that piece of paper, each staff member maintains individual 1–31 folders and A–Z folders to temporarily hold those transition documents.

When a document, file or special paragraph needs to be located, it is accomplished much faster. Another very important point is that anyone can find the document, file or special paragraph from anywhere, whether that access is achieved on site or off site. More than one person can obtain files and information 24 hours a day simultaneously from different locations. The forced structure and text indexing of digital files allow for consistency, regardless of staff turnover, and allow retrieval of text and documents on the fly.

3. CONFLICT CHECKING SYSTEMS

Because of the ethical requirements involving conflicts of interest, law firms must anticipate conflicts in order to make decisions about new clients. Concurrent conflicts probably do not pose a serious problem in any but the largest multi-department or multi-office law firms. Since a firm cannot sue a current client (see Model Rule 1.7), the case approval process will normally recognize such conflicts. In the case of former clients, where the two matters are substantially related or where confidential information may be used against the former client, it becomes necessary to identify both the former client and the subject matter of the representation (see Model Rule 1.9). The longer a firm has been in business, and the more cases it handles, the more hazy is the institutional memory of the firm. Thus, a system designed to identify potential conflicts in a timely way is a valuable tool.

In the past, conflicts of interest arose most often as motions to disqualify counsel in litigation matters; in recent years, conflicts are increasingly the subject of disciplinary complaints (see, e.g., *Asam v. Alabama State Bar*, 675 So.2d 866 (Ala. 1996)) and malpractice actions (See e.g., *Spera v. Fleming, Hovenkamp & Grayson*, 25 S.W.3d 863 (Tex. App. 2000)). Lawyers also need some means of tracking personal conflicts, based on their own personal, financial and business interests, which would interfere with their ability to exercise independent judgment on behalf of a client.

It should be a part of the standard procedure when opening a new file to record the pertinent names and subject matter of the case. When appropriate, the names of adverse parties should be noted. These records should then be stored in a computer database, so that subsequent new clients can be checked for conflicts. It is possible to create a manual conflicts checking system, but such a system is inevitably more cumbersome and less accurate than an automated system.

CONFLICT MANAGEMENT: USING TECHNOLOGY TO NAVIGATE THE MINEFIELD

From *GPSolo*, by J. Anthony Vittal (June, 2000).

. . .

Information to Be Developed by a Conflicts–Checking System

These rules provide guidance for the development of any conflicts-checking system. Clearly, any such system requires thoughtfully designed forms for client intake and for personal attorney data, as well as a system for developing the necessary database information for lawyers joining the firm.

Client intake form. The client intake form must elicit the following information about the client and the client's matter:

- The name and address of the client, and for entities the nature of the entity and state in which it was formed, together with the name and contact information of the principal client representative if applicable;
- If the charges for the engagement are to be paid by a third party (someone other than the client), the name and address of the payer, together with the name and contact information of the principal payer representative if applicable;
- A detailed description of the nature and scope of the engagement;
- If the client is an entity, the identity of all persons affiliated with the client, including parents, subsidiaries, affiliates, partners, members of the governing board (e.g., board of directors of a corporation or management committee of an LLC), and significant shareholders;
- If the client is an individual, the identity of all persons related to the client by blood or marriage who have used the services of the firm or are potential clients of the firm;
- The case name and docket number of, and a description of all parties and issues involved in, any litigation in which the client, and any affiliate or family member of the client, is involved. This section of the form also should provide for identification of the judge to which the case is assigned (if a direct calendar matter) or the judges who are likely to hear the case (if a master calendar matter);
- The identity of all potential witnesses in the matter, including the identity of the employer of each such witness;
- If the client is a business enterprise (sole proprietorship or otherwise), the identity of the market segment in which the business operates and a description of the specific business in which the enterprise is engaged;

- For individuals, a description of the nature of any personal relationship between the client and any lawyer in the firm. For entities, a description of the nature of any personal relationship between the person in charge of the engagement for the client and any lawyer in the firm.

Historical dataset. If some or all of this data is missing from your database for current and previous engagements of your firm, you will need to develop the information for inclusion in your conflicts-checking database. Without it, you will be unable to screen for conflicts involving prior clients of your firm.

For every person who has moved or is moving to your firm from another firm, you also will need to develop as much of the same information as possible for engagements handled by each firm or agency with which the person has been associated. Acquisition of this information can be particularly difficult, as many firms refuse to release this information. Indeed, some firms will go so far as to sue to enjoin any use of their client/matter lists by personnel leaving the firm. If a complete dataset has not been brought to your firm by the person joining your firm, you should make every effort to have that person recreate the dataset from information in his or her personal files, personal information manager, and memory.

Attorney data form. The attorney data form must elicit the following information about every lawyer in the firm and must be updated at regular intervals, as well as every time the information changes:

- Every entity in which the lawyer, or a member of the lawyer's immediate family, owns an interest;
- If the lawyer is an officer or director of any corporation other than the law firm, the identity of that corporation;
- If the lawyer is the executor of an estate, the name of the decedent, the name(s) of the beneficiaries, the name of the court in which any probate proceeding is pending, and the docket number of that proceeding;
- If the lawyer is a trustee of any trust, the identity of the settlor(s) and beneficiaries of the trust;
- If the lawyer is a trustee of any non-profit corporation or foundation, the identity of the entity, the identity of all other trustees, and the identity of the employer of each other trustee;
- If any (1) parent, child, sibling, or spouse of the lawyer; or (2) person in a cohabitating relationship closely approximating marriage to the lawyer; or (3) person who has an intimate personal relationship with the lawyer; or (4) client of the lawyer also is a lawyer, the identity of the firm in which that "related" lawyer practices;

- If the lawyer has a close personal relationship with a court reporter or bailiff, the identity of that person and the judge to whose courtroom the person is assigned.

Creation of Database Management System

This information, once collected, must be incorporated into a searchable database, preferably one using an SQL (structured query language) application to access the data. The creation of this database must be handled with exquisite care to avoid your becoming a victim of GIGO [garbage in-garbage out]. Unfortunately, there is no turnkey application currently on the market that will effortlessly enable you to fully automate your conflicts-screening system. Existing conflicts-screening applications typically are relatively primitive modules appended to a time-and-billing or case management system, none of which permits the inclusion of all relevant data. This means you will have to create one from scratch if you want effective automation.

Ideally, your SQL application should be able to access and search not only the conflicts-screening database you will be creating, but also every PIM (personal information manager) on every desktop or other computer on your network. After all, to be thorough, you want to be over-inclusive when checking names against available data. If your office is not yet networked, you should consider doing so now to facilitate automation of your conflicts-screening system.

. . .

Effective Use of SQL Reports

Once you have the system designed and implemented, including the SQL scripts to search for the information needed to generate conflicts-screening reports, you may be only part of the way toward your goal. If a report shows any potential conflicts, you still will need to contact the lawyer(s) who handled or are handling the conflicting engagement(s) or who have the conflicting relationships to ascertain the nature and scope of the conflict(s).

To protect yourself against the unintended consequences of utter reliance on your technology tool, you also will need to poll all firm personnel by circulating a *Prospective New Matter Report*, setting forth the relevant conflicts-checking information. Experience teaches us that staff memories often reveal conflicts information that even the most sophisticated conflicts-checking software will not unearth and that we lawyers have long since forgotten.

With a properly designed and implemented firm-wide relational DBMS [Database Management System] as your automated conflicts-checking system, combined with a scheme that mines the memories and records of all firm personnel, you should be able to identify all potential conflicts of interest not immediately apparent from the nature or terms of the proposed engagement. If you do so, you should be able to safely negotiate the conflicts minefield, while demonstrating to your clients at the inception of their engagements that you are committed to the core values of our profession

4. TIMEKEEPING AND BILLING SYSTEMS

Although the topics of timekeeping and billing are dealt with elsewhere in this book (See Chapters 5, 11 and 13), the specifics of how to maintain an effective administrative time and billing system, deserve additional mention. The timekeeping and billing processes are integral parts of the delivery of legal services, and like the other administrative systems discussed in this chapter, these systems support the overall substantive practice systems of every firm.

TECHNOLOGY FOR TIGHTWADS: LAW OFFICE ESSENTIALS ON A BUDGET

From *GPSolo*, by Tim Mellitz (June, 2000).

. . .

You'll need to answer many questions before choosing a time & billing package.

- Does the practice require or insist on an "integrated" accounting package that includes a time & billing component?
- Does the firm issue a "substantial number" of checks for client-related expenses and advances?
- Does the firm use a single, fixed-billing format where the content and appearance of the bills do not vary to any great extent?
- Does the firm have a wide variety of different types of bills, either at the insistence of clients or senior attorneys?
- Are the firm's bills subject to audit by a third-party legal bill auditing service, . . . ?
- Is the firm's staff receptive to, and capable of learning, a given time & billing system?

No single time & billing system can meet the needs of a firm. The best that can be expected is enough "give" or understanding on the parts of both lawyers and clients to arrive at a consensus as to which system comes closest to meeting the demands of the practice.

Costs. What are your gross annual billings? If your billing system either picks up or drops just 1 percent of those gross billings it will have proven itself (for better or for worse).

Training. If the software itself can have a 1 percent positive effect on your gross income, then good, ample training (in almost *any* sophisticated program) can result in additional revenues that may well dwarf any savings or losses generated by the software *without* training.

. . .

5. CLIENT TRUST ACCOUNT SYSTEMS

Although it makes some sense to incorporate client trust accounts conceptually within the general accounting system of the firm (a subject dealt with more fully in Chapter 11), the importance of the topic to the attorney's ethical duty to segregate her funds from the client's funds lends itself to coverage as a separate administrative system. Model Rule 1.15 is clear in its requirement that attorneys must maintain separate bank accounts and keep separate records. Some states require attorneys to submit reports of trust account activities annually. See, e.g., Delaware Rules of Professional Conduct, Rule 1.15, Interpretive Guideline.

Despite the fact that it should not be difficult to keep client funds out of law firm operating accounts, violations of these rules continue to produce one of the most common bases for attorney discipline; and grievance committees tend to be less sympathetic to attorneys brought up on commingling or conversion charges than any other class of violation.

EXCERPT FROM THE ABA GUIDE TO LAWYER TRUST ACCOUNTS,

by Jay G. Foonberg (1996).

A lawyer can't deposit money to a trust account if the lawyer doesn't have a trust account. Open a trust account under your control as soon as you get your license to practice law even if you don't see an immediate need for a trust account and even if you are with a firm that has one (unless you can sign on the firm's trust account and are willing to be responsible for what other signatories on the account do with the money you deposit).

The need for a trust account may be sudden and unanticipated. You may receive a large amount of cash and need to deposit it immediately for safekeeping. A client or relative may give you a large retainer in advance or costs in advance that must be deposited immediately. If you don't have a trust account, you might be tempted to deposit the funds to a personal account or leave them totally unprotected, either of which could leave your license and assets exposed.

If you don't need the account, you'll have wasted a few dollars in check-printing charges. If you do need it, you'll be glad you have it.

Every law firm should have a client trust account in addition to the usual general office bank account, the client costs advanced bank account, and the payroll bank account. Individuals should have their own personal bank account.

If you are in a firm, consider opening your own client trust account for those cases and clients for which you are responsible. Law firms go under without prior notice to clients or junior partners and sometimes without prior notice to senior partners. You may be left with a personal trust account responsibility to a specific client. If the firm objects to you having your own client trust account, offer the firm a joint signature control on the account. Your personal assets and your license to practice law may be involved if the firm goes under or if there is a trust account problem on the matters for which you are responsible. The author has personally represented "innocent" law firm partners in state bar and malpractice proceedings, where an errant partner mismanaged the firm trust account. Alcohol, drugs, and material problems can and do cause partners to take trust account money, leaving "innocent" partners with serious problems. Trust account disciplinary rules apply equally to lawyers in megafirms and lawyers in sole practice.

In most jurisdictions the local rules or the IOLTA rules require that a trust account be in a bank or other state or federally insured institution located in the state. The account must normally be in the lawyer's state so IOLTA can get the interest under its banking agreements and so the account is under the subpoena jurisdiction of the state bar disciplinary system.

Multistate law firms must normally maintain the client's trust account in the state where the client is located, if the law firm has an office in the state, or in the state where the responsible lawyer is located. This is to protect the client. Since trust account responsibility is the primary responsibility of the individual lawyer in charge of the matter, the trust account must be in the state where that lawyer has his or her office, regardless of where the headquarters of the law firm might be.

In some cases the client may direct that funds are to be deposited and withdrawn from a bank outside the state or indeed outside the United States. The client may require this for asset protection or for any number of bona fide business or tax reasons. The lawyer will have to determine if an out-of-state or out-of-country trust account is permissible under the applicable rules. If the client wants an offshore trust account, the lawyer should get the instructions in writing and remind the client that there won't be any insurance protection. In some states, an out-of-state account is allowed if the client has some bona fide relationship to that jurisdiction and if the rules concerning insurance are satisfied. In some states, an "approved list" is maintained and only institutions or individuals on the list may be used. An out-of-state trust account may be permissible for a specific client in a specific matter, but it would be extremely unlikely that a lawyer could establish and maintain a normal trust account outside the lawyer's state.

In some cases the rules permit an IOLTA account to be in a savings and loan, a credit union, or brokerage account or other type of thrift institution insured by the state or federal government but require a non-IOLTA trust account to be in a bank. The lawyer must read the rules of the applicable state.

It may be necessary or even preferable to keep trust funds in an institution other than one regularly used by the firm or its partners for their own purposes.

PROBLEMS AND QUESTIONS

1. Describe the administrative support systems your firms will incorporate into its substantive practice system, including:

   - a document assembly system for one key document in the practice area
   - timekeeping and billing,
   - filing (including client files and other records) and retrieval (locating material already filed such as memos on substantive topics, client records, etc.),
   - calendar (for cases, hearings, etc.) and tickler (to remind personnel of critical dates such as statutes of limitation, appearances, etc.),
   - conflicts of interest, and
   - client trust accounts.

   How will these administrative support systems work? Indicate who will be responsible to see that these systems work. See Appendix M, pages 499–502.

2. Maintain time records of your activities for a period of two weeks, including the hours of 8:00 a.m. until 10:00 p.m., Monday–Friday, and any other hours spent on law-related activities at night and during weekends. Maintain records for the amount of time, type of activity, and date. Analyze your time sheets to determine how you allocate your time, and how you could more effectively utilize it.

3. When it comes time to clean a file when a case closes, who should be responsible for deciding what to throw out? Why?

4. Why do lawyers violate the sanctity of their clients' trust accounts so often? Is it ignorance? Is it poor management practice? Is it economic pressure (i.e., cash flow)? Or is it fundamental dishonesty? What can the law firm do as an institution to eliminate the possible indiscretions of individual attorneys? What should the firm do when an attorney violates these rules? What is the liability of partners for a lawyer who abuses client trust accounts?

D. LITIGATION MANAGEMENT SYSTEMS

The idea of litigation as support may seem alien to some law students, for whom the centrality of litigation to the dispute resolution process has been hammered into them since the first day of orientation in law school. The law school experience mirrors the legal process both before and during law school. Students are bombarded with subtle messages that "real lawyers go to court." In truth, most lawyers do not go to court on a regular basis, and transactional legal work is far more prevalent than litigation work in the real world. In fact, many clients seek to resolve their disputes without going to court, and litigation is a process that is triggered when everything else fails.

If we think of litigation as a process to be invoked in cases where less adversary forms of dispute resolution fail, it may be easier to think about litigation support as a component of substantive practice systems. As noted previously, every legal case includes some risk that the matter cannot be resolved without resort to litigation. Some areas of practice tend to be more litigation-driven than others; for example, criminal work is more likely to end up in court than real estate work, but both involve courtroom and non-courtroom elements.

This course does not dwell on the litigation support process, in part because law students have the opportunity to learn about litigation in Trial Advocacy classes and clinics, and in part because litigation is addressed pervasively in almost every law school course. On the other hand, other aspects of substantive practice systems are covered superficially or not at all.

Just as every substantive practice system includes documents, every substantive system also should anticipate the prospect of litigation. Even in the situations where parties seek to find legal right and resolve problems with resort to the judicial system, and even in matters where there are technically no adverse parties, the likelihood exists that legal issues cannot be resolved without recourse to the judicial system. In one sense, litigation is a process that takes place when other approaches to reach resolution have failed. Some areas of practice, such as personal injury work, may focus more on litigation as a tool in the defeat resolution process, where as other areas may view litigation as a last resort. Some firms, and certain lawyers may view trial-work as their primary occupational interest; some firms and lawyers may view litigation as a component of the substantive practice area in which they work; some lawyers eschew litigation entirely, focusing instead on transactional matters and referring cases to litigation specialists when necessary.

Litigation support involves the activities associated with trial practice within a substantive area of law. The litigation support system, like administrative support systems, may have some common elements across a range of practice areas, although each substantive area will have unique aspects to it. A litigation support system typically includes a number of components:

- Variations on the firm's filing system, including case numbering/identification, placement of documents within files, and screening of information within files.
- Pleadings.
- Discovery.
- Settlement negotiations.
- Variations on the firm's calendar system to accommodate both appearances, deadlines, and adverse parties.
- Legal research.
- Trial preparation.
- Pre-trial process.
- Brief preparation.
- Appeals.
- Document management.

As with other systems, the litigation support system seeks to standardize routine procedures, allocate responsibilities, assure the quality and timeliness of work, and improve efficiency. The litigation support system utilizes forms with constructions to manipulate information and make it easier for litigators to manage the trial process. The litigation support system endeavors to leverage the firm's intellectual work product by saving and retrieving forms and information in an organized way. As with other systems, litigation support relies heavily on technology tools. A single lawyer or small firm adept at utilizing technology applications may be able to compete effectively against work organizations that do not take advantage of available technology.

As the court systems become more automated, judges, clerks, court reporters, and parties of litigation will find themselves increasingly unable to participate in trials without technology. As this evolution takes place, law firms will need to constantly review their litigation support systems to assure that they remain up to date.

CASE MANAGEMENT FOR THE LITIGATOR
Prepared by ABA Section on Litigation,
Committee on Litigation Management & Economics (Summer, 2001).

Case management software provides attorneys with a convenient method of effectively managing client and case information, including contacts, calendars, and documents. It can be used to share information with other attorneys in the firm and can reduce the need to enter duplicate data in conjunction with billing programs and word processors. Many programs link with personal digital assistants (PDAs) so that calendars and schedules are available remotely. Some case management packages are Web-based, with more on the way, allowing any-time access to all features.

With the number of available case management software packages on the market today, it is no wonder litigators may need some assistance in selecting a program that will best suit the needs of their firm. Case management programs vary in their compatibility by firm size and features. Some programs may not be suitable for larger firms, but may contain features that effectively service a solo practitioner or small firm. When selecting a case management program, determine the case management needs first. Pick a program that enhances the practice seamlessly and effortlessly, which is not necessarily a program with every available function to implement. When uncertainty is a factor, "try before you buy." Most case management vendors allow a free trial period, where a version of the program can be downloaded from the vendor's Website (or a disk can be mailed) and used for a limited time. If additional assistance is needed in assessing the firm's needs, consider a consultant. Consultants can be found by referral, on e-mail lists, in the yellow pages, or on line. Educate yourself by reading e-mail discussion lists and products' reviews, and seek input from colleagues to find out what programs are being used and whether or not they are satisfied.

Some Features and Functions of Case Management Software

Calendaring & Docketing. Most case management offerings will perform some calendaring and docketing, but calendar layout and available functions will differ from program to program. Case management programs that are not equipped with calendars may link to separate calendaring programs.... The purpose of the calendaring and docketing feature is to allow lawyers and staff the ability to view individual or group tasks, deadlines, appointments, and meetings by day, week, or month. Some programs display icons for specific appointments, the ability to drag-and-drop a scheduled calendar appointment from one date to another, rules-based calendaring, and calculated calendar dates and deadlines. Case management programs also possess the ability to print calendars by attorney, client, or due date, and with some programs, scheduled appointments and meetings will automatically be generated onto a to-do list.

Case Management. The heart of these programs is the actual case or matter management. Time Matters—with some customizing, allows accessibility to every stitch of information about a case or contact in one location. Amicus Attorney provides a library module that allows firms to integrate legal research with case information. For example, by using the library module, research done for a case can be stored, organized, and reused in the future. Information from on line legal research vendors, such as Lexis and Westlaw, and anything on the Internet, can be stored in the library as well.

Case management programs allow conflict of interest checking, to-do list management, and provide alerts, alarms, and reminders of appointments and other critical dates. Some case management programs maintain areas of practice in separate data-bases, so attorneys can practice more than one area of law in the same case management program.

Document Assembly. All case management programs may not have the ability to generate complex documents. Some programs will interact with word processing or document assembly programs.... Some case management programs allow you to create documents and then copy and paste them into your word processor. Several case management programs support the ability to scan documents.

Time & Billing. Time and billing functionality tends not to be extensive in most case management programs. They often link, however, to a stand alone time and billing software program such as Timeslips or Tabs III. Various case management programs can perform simple features such as creating an invoice generated by tracking the length of a telephone call.

Case management software allows users to effectively manage contacts. Some contact databases provide fields for multiple addresses, telephone numbers, e-mail addresses, and Web pages. Contact searching and sorting is simple, and each contact record can be linked to multiple matters and events. Phone call details are easily logged and stored, and there are callback reminder functions.

PROBLEMS AND QUESTIONS

1. Some might argue that litigation is a substantive practice area of its own. Certainly many lawyers call themselves litigators? But isn't litigation defined by substantive practice areas, just like the other component systems?

2. In areas where litigation is not the primary focus of the legal services, for example, in much transactional work, does it make more sense for every lawyer to be able to go to court when necessary, or to farm out litigation work to litigators?

Part 4

Managing Yourself as a Professional

■ ■ ■

Chapter 15

Managing Your Professional Life

■ ■ ■

In this chapter you will look at a number of skills that underlie effective practice management. While earlier chapters of this book have addressed management from the perspective of managing the firm or the legal work product, this chapter provides an overview of the critical skills necessary to manage yourself as a professional person. You will learn how to develop these skills and use them as a tool to make you a better lawyer and to manage a professional practice. In this regard you will observe that individual practice development and law firm practice development are inextricably related. Moreover, you will note that the owners of the law practice are most often the lawyers whose individual practice is portable.

A. PERSONAL MANAGEMENT GENERALLY

Law practice management has assumed an increasingly important role in the operation of every law practice, from sole practitioners to one thousand lawyer multi-city firms. In the past, many offices used a "trough" approach to management. Imagine a pipe leading to a trough with a drain at the other end. Imagine also that money from clients comes into the trough through the pipe. A managing attorney scoops out of the trough any cash needed to pay the bills, and whatever is not removed goes out the drain and into a bucket for distribution. As long as enough money flowed into the trough to fill the bucket at the other end, no one worried much about how much was scooped out along the way, how to keep the apparatus in good repair, or how to increase the flow of dollars into the system. As operational costs have increased, more efficient systems have been created, and competition has escalated; it is no longer sufficient to rely on the old trough to fill the income bucket. Lawyers must manage the system effectively if they hope to derive a comfortable return on their work.

Large firms can hire people to handle various aspects of the management side of the practice. Directing such an administrative staff presents an entirely new set of practical problems such as ceding authority to nonlawyers, as well as ethical problems, such as supervision (see Model Rule 5.3), allowing nonlawyers to direct the lawyers' independent professional judgement (Model Rule 5.4(c)), and splitting fees with non-lawyers (Rule 5.4(a)). In a small firm or individual practice the lawyers themselves inevitably must exercise management responsibilities. Too frequently, lawyers abdicate these duties to untrained support staff or neglect management issues unless forced by circumstances to address them. Such a crisis management approach may thrill the type-A personality of the lawyer, but it courts disaster for the long-term financial stability of the firm. Small offices must accept the fact that in today's world a substantial amount of time must be devoted to administrative tasks.

PROBLEMS AND QUESTIONS

1. What is wrong with the "trough" approach to the practice of law? What have you learned about practice management that will help you to do a better job of running your practice than your predecessors?

2. If crisis management is the rule, what are the alternatives?

3. Think about good and bad supervisors that you have encountered. What were some of the characteristics that made good supervisors effective? What characteristics cause ineffective supervisors to lose the confidence of their subordinates? What aspects of your own personality are likely to be assets and liabilities in supervising staff?

B. PROFESSIONAL SKILLS

In 1991, the *Report of the American Bar Association Task Force on Legal Education and the Profession: Narrowing the Gap* (also known as the MacCrate Report), described a set of fundamental lawyering skills and values necessary to professional success. These skills and values are acquired over a continuum of experience beginning long before law school and continuing throughout one's professional career. Although reasonable minds might differ over what skills should be included in this list, or the relative importance of certain skills compared to others, the basic idea that practicing law requires the application of some set of professional skills is hard to escape.

STATEMENT OF FUNDAMENTAL LAWYERING SKILLS AND PROFESSIONAL VALUES

American Bar Association Section of Legal Education and Admission to the Bar
Task Force on Law Schools and the Profession: Narrowing the Gap (1991).

Throughout the course of extensive decades-long debates about what law schools should do to educate students for the practice of law, there has been no in-depth study of the full range of skills and values that are necessary in order for a lawyer to assume the professional responsibility of handling a legal matter. Recognizing that such a study is the necessary predicate for determining the extent to which law schools and the practicing bar should assume the responsibility for the development of these skills and values, the Task Force prepared a Statement of Fundamental Lawyering Skills and Professional Values.

. . .

Fundamental Lawyering Skills

Skill § 9: *Operation and Management of Legal Work*

In order to practice effectively, a lawyer should be familiar with the skills and concepts required for efficient management, including:

9.1 Formulating Goals and Principles for Effective Practice Management;

9.2 Developing Systems and Procedures to Ensure that Time, Effort, and Resources Are Allocated Efficiently;

9.3 Developing Systems and Procedures to Ensure that Work is Performed and Completed at the Appropriate Time;

9.4 Developing Systems and Procedures for Effectively Working with Other People;

9.5 Developing Systems and Procedures for Efficiently Administering a Law Office.

. . .

Fundamental Values of the Profession

Value § 1: *Provision of Competent Representation*

As a member of a profession dedicated to the service of clients, a lawyer should be committed to the values of:

1.1 Attaining a Level of Competence in One's Own Field of Practice;

1.2 Maintaining a Level of Competence in One's Own Field of Practice;

1.3 Representing Clients in a Competent Manner.

. . .

In the years since the MacCrate Report was released, other organizations have weighed in on the importance of professional skills. The American Bar Association–American Law Institute (ALI–ABA) produced an extensive text, called *Achieving Excellence in the Practice of* Law, which described how lawyers could develop the critical skills described in the MacCrate Report. The Clinical Legal Education Association (CLEA) developed a guide, *Best Practices in Legal Education: A Vision and a Road Map* (2007), aimed at helping legal educators seeking to integrate professional skills into the law school curriculum.

Many bar associations have instituted "bridge-the-gap programs, designed to teach new lawyers the skills they did not learn in law school, and some states have incorporated a professional skills testing in their bar examinations. Numerous conferences and articles have tackled the question of preparing law students for the practice of law; *see, e.g.*, Report of the Task Force of the Future of the Legal Profession, New York State Bar Association, 2011 (mentioned earlier in Chapter 1). This report led to passage of a resolution by the American Bar Association House of Delegates calling on law schools to better prepare law students for the practice of law.

One of the most influential publications on the subject of professional skills has been a 2007 study commissioned by the Carnegie Foundation for the Advance, *Educating Lawyers: Preparation for the Profession of Law*, by William Sullivan, Anne Colby, Judith Wegner, Lloyd Bod and Les Shulman. The Carnegie Report, as it is called, reaffirmed and updated the skills described in the MacCrate Report, but added a focus on identifying and measuring the outcomes that legal education should produce. With all these voices making the point that professional skills are integral to the practice of law, and learning such skills at the heart of legal education and practice training. It should not come as a surprise that things are changing.

Recently, the ABA amended its *Standards for the Approval of Law Schools* to incorporate a requirement that all law schools provide all students substantial training in professional skills. The standards, which are adopted by the ABA House of Delegates upon recommendation of the Section of Legal Education and Admissions to the Bar, include the following statements:

STANDARDS FOR THE APPROVAL OF LAW SCHOOLS

American Bar Association (2005).

Standard 302. CURRICULUM.

(a) A law school shall require that each student receive substantial instruction in:

. . .

4) other professional skills generally regarded as necessary for effective and responsible participation in the legal profession

. . .

Interpretation 302–2:

Each law school is encouraged to be creative in developing programs of instruction in professional skills related to the various responsibilities which lawyers are called upon to meet, using the strengths and resources available to the school. Trial and appellate advocacy, alternative methods of dispute resolution, counseling, interviewing, negotiating, problem solving, factual investigation, *organization and management of legal work*

[Emphasis added], and drafting are among the areas of instruction in professional skills that fulfill Standard 302(a)(4).

Knowledge, without the skill to apply it, is a hollow quality. The Model Rules of Professional Conduct define competence in Rule 1.1 as "legal knowledge, skill, thoroughness and preparation reasonably necessary for the representation." This Rule clearly demonstrates that professional competence requires more than knowledge of the law. In more practical terms, if practicing lawyers cannot skillfully use their knowledge for the benefit of clients, they bring little value to society and will not succeed financially.

The MacCrate Report, the Model Rules, the ABA Standards for Approval of Law Schools and the Carnegie Report all recognize that competence as a lawyer goes far beyond the ability to "think like a lawyer." Although competence is a complex concept, "organization and management of legal work" is one of the core skills of lawyering. Legal educators and practitioners sometimes point fingers at each other for not doing enough to prepare lawyers for the practice of law. In truth, the responsibility for teaching new lawyers the basic skills and knowledge necessary to practice competently is a shared obligation.

The principles enunciated in these documents establish not only that professional skills are critical to successful lawyering, but also that practice management is one of the critical skills. As lawyers, we must recognize that we are not prepared for the business side of law practice by education, experience or inclination. At the same time, in order to succeed in our chosen profession, we need to possess the business acumen to deliver the legal work product to our clients consistent with their expectations for quality service and the professional standard of care.

PROBLEMS AND QUESTIONS

1. Why all the fuss about skills? Is this what is meant by the expression that law school graduates do not know how to find the courthouse?

2. Is it possible to learn professional skills in law school, or is it necessary to learn by doing? Can legal education include both classroom training in professional skills and practical experience to hone these skills?

3. If you had to make a list of what skills you need to practice law, what would you include on your list?

4. The MacCrate Report and subsequent reports on the subject of professional skills specifically include management skills as critical skills, yet not all

law schools offer courses on law practice management. Why do you think this is?

C. CRITICAL MANAGEMENT SKILLS

The topic of professional skills was raised earlier in this chapter with a discussion of the MacCrate Task Force Statement of Fundamental Lawyering Skills and Values (see Section B, above, pages 363–364). Hopefully, this class has given you new insights into how these skills are utilized in the practice setting. The ninth skill, "organization and management of legal work," is, in reality, an umbrella for a number of specific skills, discussed below. The best lawyers are not necessarily those with the greatest intellect or the most experience, but those who possess and utilize these critical skills to maximize their performance as lawyers.

1. TIME MANAGEMENT

If there is one single skill that is most critical in practice management, it is time management. Many, perhaps most, lawyers are "Type A" personalities. They are highly competitive, thrive on pressure, and seem to enjoy the rush of adrenaline that comes with completing an assignment just before the deadline. This approach to work (and play) represents a behavior pattern that was acquired long before law school, inculcated during years in the educational system, and matured into a lifestyle after graduation. It is also a behavior pattern that can lead to thrill-seeking, addictive disorders, and physical symptoms such as hypertension and heart disease. For Type A personalities, managing time may be the most difficult skill to learn.

In the professional practice setting, effective time management is not a luxury, but a necessity. Lawyers who fail to control their schedules often discover that their practice overwhelms their lives. They find themselves regularly working twelve or more hours a day, seven days a week. They find themselves unable to devote their best efforts to any one project because they have too many other projects pressing for attention. They find themselves living from crisis to crisis, and never getting complete control of their workload. They consistently run the risk of being sued for malpractice for missing a deadline, overlooking a critical point of law, or simply failing to pursue problematic or distasteful cases they have agreed to handle. They rationalize all of this by claiming that this is just what the practice of law is like.

These lawyers are wrong. It does not have to be this way. It is never too late to take control of your professional life and change bad habits for the better. In the case of time management, not only is it possible to increase efficiency, productivity, and profitability, but also to increase satisfaction in both your professional and personal lives, while reducing the risk of professional failure that hangs like a storm cloud over so many lawyers.

Although numerous books have been written on the subject of time management, it may help to put time management into perspective. There are one hundred and sixty-eight hours in a week, no more, no less. If you subtract the hours that you spend sleeping, eating, dressing, and commuting, you are left with a number of hours representing your potential productive time. Let's say the above activities take ten hours per day, or seventy hours, you are left with ninety-eight hours. Now subtract the number of hours per week that you devote to your personal life including shopping, relaxation with friends and family, and other daily activities. It is important to set aside this time in advance, because if you don't, you will either never have a personal life, or will find that your personal life intrudes upon time that you had planned for professional activities. Let's say that you devote an average of two hours per day, or fourteen hours per week to personal matters. This leaves you eighty-four hours to spend on work.

Because of the substantial amount of non-billable time, most lawyers spend less than two-thirds of their time in the office on client matters. In our example, two-thirds of eighty-four hours would produce fifty-six billable hours of work per week. Assuming a two-week vacation, this rate of production would produce well over two thousand billable hours per year. According to numerous surveys, including a comprehensive 1997 economics survey by the New York State Bar Association, these projections are slightly higher than actual performance for practicing lawyers. Patterns of time spent on specific activities vary widely among individuals. One person might require only four or five hours of sleep per night, and, thus, have more time available for other activities. A solo practitioner may spend over half of her time on management related activities, which do not translate into billable client work. Lawyers with young children may choose to devote more hours to the care and nurture of their offspring than single lawyers or empty-nesters.

Everyone can figure out a general pattern of time utilization consistent with their own lifestyle. They can then build a schedule around realistic expectations based upon their own needs and choices. In the first instance, you must recognize that you can't do it all, and decide instead to do a limited number of things very well. A common problem for many people is that they try to cram too much into the available time. They underestimate how long everything they do will take. Their schedule becomes like a saturated sponge dripping loose ends everywhere. Give yourself enough time to do whatever you have to do. You can always bring along back-up work to fill in if you arrive or finish an activity early.

Good time management requires a good calendar system. Whether the calendar is a manual system such as a Daytimer, a computerized personal information manager (PIM), or a firm-wide calendar system (see Chapter 12), every lawyer needs to manage her schedule. Even if the lawyer's secretary oversees the schedule, there should only be *one* schedule. If the secretary and the lawyer both maintain a schedule, there is a constant risk of double booking appointments. The schedule should incorporate not only whom you will be meeting, but where the meeting will take place, and take into account travel time and other exigencies. The schedule should include a telephone number to contact someone if you get behind schedule or have to cancel an appointment.

Another excellent time management technique is the daily list. Every day, either first thing in the morning, or at the end of the day, prepare a list of the things you have to get done the next day. List them in descending order of priority with big-ticket items first; the first item would be the one thing you would accomplish during the day if you accomplished only one thing. Then, follow your list. Don't let unplanned activities intrude upon your prioritized goals. Don't undertake low priority activities in lieu of higher priority projects, even if the former is easier and more appealing than the latter. If you find that some item stays at the bottom of your daily list for more than a week, consider dropping it from the list altogether, because you will probably never get around to it.

Another suggestion is to learn to concentrate on one thing at a time. Try to schedule your time in blocks so that you can work on big projects for sustained periods. Whenever you work on a project you lose time getting started and closing up, so that the more often you go through the start-up and close down routine, the more time you waste. Additionally, you will find that the level of concentration is higher when you spend more time on a matter.

Try to avoid interruptions. Don't let telephone calls and other interruptions get in the way of productive work: Schedule your telephone calls at one particular time each day. It is simply impossible to work on multiple projects at the same time, and give each the attention it deserves.

- Deal only once with each piece of paper. Act on it, refer it to someone else, file it, or throw it away. Too often, pieces of paper become stacks on the corner of the desk, and these pieces of paper are read over and over again, and returned to the stack to be handled some other day.
- Don't procrastinate; whatever it is, do it now. Procrastination is the enemy of effective time management. When we postpone doing important work, for whatever reason, not only do we build stress, but we also create impossible time constraints that keep us from doing our best work.
- Learn to "just say no." Whether it is a new client, a bar association committee, or some other request, there are times when saying yes only creates problems. Say no when you already have too much to do, and when taking on another project means that other important projects will not get done. Know what your professional and personal priorities are, and say no when the project is not consistent with those priorities. Recognize projects that will eat up your available time with little or no tangible benefit. In the real world, doing less often means doing more.
- Take breaks on a daily, weekly, and annual basis. Find some time each day that is just yours, time when you can clear your head of all the pressures that surround you. This daily time need only be a few minutes and may involve meditation, prayer, private rumination, or just a quick catnap. After several hours of intense work peoples'

productivity tends to decrease, so, one or two short breaks in the course of the day can help you to be more productive overall.

• On a weekly basis jealously protect your relaxation time. Whether you spend that time watching football on TV, going to the symphony, or working in your garden, is not important. What is important is that you take some time for yourself each week.

• Devote time to personal relationships, or they will wither and die like plants that are not watered. It may seem strange to talk about personal relationships in a discussion about time management, but personal relationships often get scheduled out of the lives of busy professionals. Perhaps we assume that loved ones will be more understanding than bosses, perhaps we instinctively choose to devote our time to those who will help our careers most in the long run, or perhaps we use our jobs to avoid dealing with issues involving those closest to us. Whatever the reasons, if you do not nurture your personal life, you will not have to worry about having anyone to ignore.

• Take a vacation every year. Go away or stay at home, it doesn't matter; just get out of the office. Some firms have even mandated vacation time for lawyers, because many lawyers have refused to take the time on their own. They were so afraid of meeting billable hour requirements, losing an important client, or catching up on the backlog of work on their desks that they just couldn't get away. These two firms have borrowed from academia the concept of partner sabbaticals, offering partners paid sabbaticals after five to seven years of service.

All of these devices point to one thing. We all need time to break away from the demands of the workplace and to recharge our batteries. Unfortunately, the time we save over the years does not match the time we lose when our hearts stop working at the age of fifty-five.

2. FINANCIAL MANAGEMENT

Chapter 11 of this text has already presented a variety of issues related to the financial management of law firms. It should come as no surprise that financial management skills are critical to effective lawyering. Not only does the individual need to understand accounting, bookkeeping, and financial planning in order to start and operate a law firm, lawyers are also charged with fiduciary responsibility towards clients' funds that make it even more critical to understand basic financial management. In addition to handling clients' funds, many fields of law practice involve giving clients advice on matters that have financial implications. Although many lawyers do not think about this, management of one's personal finances is also important professionally, because lawyers who are in difficult financial straits are more likely to be tempted to make errors in judgment with respect to their client's or law firm's money.

The range of financial acumen among law students is considerable—from CPAs and financial planners to people who can barely balance their checkbooks. Without a basic understanding of financial concepts, practitioners are unlikely to be able to help themselves or adequately serve their clients' needs.

Because the subject matter goes far beyond the scope of this book, and because most law students possess at least fundamental accounting skills, this section does not purport to be a comprehensive instruction manual. Students who conclude that their financial skill is wanting may find that it may help to take a law school course in legal accounting (offered at some law schools), or business associations (offered almost everywhere). Some students may be able to take introductory financial courses at the college or university affiliated with their law school; others may be able to take such courses through their local community college or a continuing education program. Regardless of how such training is obtained, all law students should understand basic bookkeeping and accounting concepts.

Even though many law firms delegate the actual bookkeeping function to a support staff person, financial knowledge is necessary both for purposes of supervision and for interpreting financial reports. A lawyer who does not understand financial management will find it difficult or impossible to do either. Lawyers in large organizations may be lulled into a false sense of security by employing financial professionals to manage the books, but if the lawyers do not understand what their employees are doing, they are at the mercy of those they are supposed to supervise.

The advent of inexpensive user-friendly financial management software has made it easier for lawyers to utilize financial management tools. Access to technology, however, should not be a substitute for an understanding of the underlying principles.

3. ORGANIZATION

Organizational skills are so basic to success in life that most people do not think about them as skills at all. Unorganized people, or disorganized people, are sometimes characterized as sloppy, cluttered, flighty, and incompetent. In somewhat less critical terms, they are described as undisciplined, free-spirited, or less charitably as scatter-brained. We often think that organizational skills are somehow innate; that some of us were born anal-retentive neat-freaks and others of us were born slobs. Regardless of the answer to the age-old nature-nurture debate, it is clear that organizational skills can be taught to people who do not have them. And most of us could probably afford to be more organized than we are.

Competent lawyering requires effective file management. This includes not only client files, but law firm and personal files as well. Many law firms have a filing system that dictates filing of paperwork for client matters. If the firm does not have such a system the individual lawyer should develop one. Even if the firm utilizes a filing system, it makes sense to maintain a separate system for personal files. A filing system implies having more than just papers stuffed into manila folders and stacked in the corners of offices. A filing system should include a standard way to label files, a plan for storing files, and a method for retrieving stored information. If you cannot access information when you need it there is not much point in keeping it. We all tend to keep too much paper, oftentimes defeating our own best efforts to be able to retrieve information when we need it. In addition to the above problems, the destruction of information in files may be necessary in order to protect the confidentiality rights of clients as well as the privacy of employees and other individuals. File security may also be required to assure that only individuals who have a right to view the contents of files actually see them.

In today's professional environment, filing and retrieval apply to electronic files as well as paper. A surprising number of lawyers who are careful about the way they organize their paper files do little or nothing to protect or manage their computer files. They fail to back up their documents. They do not password protect sensitive documents. They dump everything onto a single directory or folder on their hard drive or whatever disks happen to be lying around with no structure or organization. In the paper world, this would be the equivalent of throwing all your file folders into one room when you are not using them and hunting through the piles of files when you needed one.

Another organizational skill is identifying and articulating specific tasks. Sometimes projects seem so colossal that they become overwhelming in our minds. They become so big we cannot get our hands around them. Organizational skill involves breaking down projects into manageable components. Just as a book is divided into sections, chapters and subdivisions within chapters, projects can be divided into tasks and sub-tasks. Projects and tasks often require timelines and phases for implementation. Perhaps most importantly, all tasks in a project need to be assigned to someone to do. It is almost axiomatic in the workplace that if the job is not assigned to somebody, then nobody will do it. If project management schemes have one great failing it is that they do not assign task responsibility for critical steps in a process.

Just as there exist financial management programs and calendar programs, there are project management software programs to assist lawyers to track projects, design flow charts for systems, and to chart relationships. A surprising number of lawyers do not take advantage of available technology to assist them with these basic organizational skills. Even without a computer program to assist in project management, the use of checklists can provide a simple alternative to a software solution. A checklist (discussed previously in Chapter 12) lists all of the tasks associated with a given project, and provides space for the person who completes the task to initial and date the checklist. The tasks are typically listed in chronological order, so that when the last task is completed, the project is done. The supervisor can review the checklist to see who completed each step in the process.

Another organizational skill is grouping activities. Grouping can involve placing all of a certain kind of activity in a group to handle at the same time. For example, rather than answering phone calls as they come in throughout the day, some lawyers make and return all their phone calls at a certain time. Or a lawyer might have her secretary bring all correspondence to be signed to the lawyer at the same time every day. Grouping can also involve subdividing large projects into more manageable subroutines. For instance, the case involving litigation might be divided into information gathering, investigation, pre-trial discovery, negotiation/settlement, trial, and appeals. While the specter of taking a case through all of these phases may seem formidable, taking one phase at a time is often much more manageable. The subdivisions of the project can sometimes be divided into further subsets just as an outline can be broken down into several layers of detail. By grouping activities, it is possible not only to render them less intimidating, but it is also easier to make staff assignments for responsibilities within the project.

For those lawyers who open their own practices or own and operate law firms, it is important to possess a fairly specialized set of organizational skills sometimes referred to as entrepreneurial skills. The particular talent required to give substance to a dream is not one that every aspiring business owner can claim. An example from business and industry illustrates that the skills required to sustain an ongoing business operation are often very different from those required to get it started. Entrepreneurial skill is not just one thing. It includes the ability to articulate a vision in such a way as to inspire investors, partners, and potential employees to join the venture. It requires a comfort level with risk-taking that not everyone can muster. It involves creative problem solving, where solutions are not ready-made, because the business does not already exist. It involves stamina and perseverance, which reflect a will to actualize a complex idea. It requires a strong sense of identity and self-worth, because there will always be naysayers who doubt the entrepreneur's ability to get the job done.

People who grew up in entrepreneurial families, that is, where they have seen family members start their own businesses, are most likely to be able to engage in entrepreneurial activities themselves. The fact that so many lawyers start their own practices, if not right out of law school, then at some point in their careers, suggests that lawyers are highly entrepreneurial as a group. While this may be true as a generalization, it is also worth noting that entrepreneurial activities are not for everyone. Some lawyers will be happiest working in well-established organizations, or not assuming the risks of partnership. All lawyers, however, should assess their entrepreneurial skills in making decisions concerning their career options.

Difficulties in management are not unique to law, although they may be punctuated by the fact that many lawyers do not think of themselves as businessmen or choose to devote their time to administration. As the following passage suggests, these organizational skills are utilized every day in the practice of law:

HOW TO RUN YOUR LAW PRACTICE WITHOUT LETTING IT RUN YOU

From *Legal Economics*, by Joel Altman (Jan./Feb., 1982).

Think of the lawyer's typical day consisting of eight working hours as being broken down into 80 six-minute intervals (10 per hour). Each six-minute interval can be compared to a single widget out of an inventory of 80 widgets, which a merchant has for sale. On a slow day with no sales, the merchant will go home leaving those 80 widgets in his store to be sold another day. The lawyer with "no sales" (that is, no billable time recorded) goes home leaving his store empty. By the end of the day the lawyer's "inventory" has disappeared right before his eyes.

The lawyer, therefore, must structure his affairs and organize his time so that he "sells" as close to 80 widgets per day as possible. Without becoming a fanatic, he must realize that every six-minute interval, which ticks away without being allocated for billing to a file is lost forever. To permit this to happen knowingly would be as foolish as if the merchant were to destroy one of his widgets every six minutes.

The effective lawyer recognizes that time is a valuable but depletable asset, and once it is used up, part of his inventory has been exhausted. Everything he does requires time. All work takes place in time, and consumes time. Therefore, what distinguishes the effective lawyer from the less effective lawyer is the care with which he manages his time.

I have heard dozens of lawyers say, "I cannot get organized right now because I'm too busy, but I have promised myself to get organized soon." The sad fact is that these lawyers never become organized. The best they ever achieve is a clear desk by 4 p.m. on Sunday afternoon, only to find that it is a mess again by 11 o'clock Monday morning. They continually operate from crisis to crisis, attempting to service their clients in the priority of which one yells the loudest and phones the most frequently to complain. No wonder these lawyers are under constant and increasing pressures.

The secret is not only to get organized but to adopt a system which enables you to stay organized at all times, even during those aggravating last-Friday-of-the-month afternoons with the telephone ringing off the hook, major purchase transactions blowing up, umpteen impatient clients in the waiting room, a power failure in the building, and your best client sitting across from you chatting about his golf game.

The following are practical suggestions as to how you might improve your efficiency:

- Never assume anything in your dealings with other people.
- Listen, really listen, when someone is talking to you.

- Learn from your mistakes.
- Murphy's Law operates 24 hours a day in a law firm, and states that nothing is ever as easy as it seems; everything takes longer to do than you first expected; and that if something can go wrong, it will and at the worst possible time. You should, therefore, hope for the best, but always be prepared for the worst.
- Nothing in this world is free. If you take a two-hour martini lunch, you had better be prepared to pay for it by staying late that night to get your work out.
- Try to work regular business hours, keeping your evenings and weekends free for family, friends, etc. Remember, you can only do your best, but you owe it to your clients, associates and yourself to make sure that it really is your best.

Rather than view your work as an individual task here and another individual task there, view it as a never-ending series of tasks for a number of clients, each of whom considers his or her file to be the most important and all of which must be attended to immediately. Your system must be able to cope with all these competing demands on your time, while simultaneously preserving the "personal touch" or human element. Service is the key, and you can be certain that if you do not deliver, some other lawyer will.

The object is to maximize work output, and thereby financial return, with a minimum of effort and stress on the part of the lawyer and his staff. At the same time, the lawyer wants clients to be satisfied with the financial outcome of their file. The effective lawyer quickly learns during the first interview to recognize the "bad case" and declines to act further. If it looks like a dog, barks like a dog, acts and smells like a dog, it probably is a dog, so tell the client exactly what you think and that he is probably better off not pursuing the matter. Neither party benefits from a bad case.

Procrastination deprives you of satisfaction, self-respect, success and happiness. I view it as the inability to make a decision, and the postponement of decision-making causes opportunities for profit to disappear. Recognize a problem file immediately and make a commitment to attack it head-on, and continue to do so until it is satisfactorily resolved. Putting things off to the last minute usually: 1. makes them much more difficult to do; 2. requires hasty decision-making; 3. throws the entire office into chaos and makes everyone else work harder.

Run your practice; do not let it run you. Each day *you* make the decisions, and then act on them. Don't function simply by reacting to circumstances which always appear to be beyond your control. Try to arrange your files so that you are always waiting for someone else to do something, rather than have people waiting on you. In other words, try [to] keep the ball in the other party's court. You might even find it enjoyable not having to spend time making excuses as to why you have not done things; and when asked for a status report, you simply reply, "I'm waiting for Mr. So and So."

You should implement any idea which will help save time. Invite suggestions from your staff in this regard. Believe it or not, some secretaries complain that they are not kept busy all day; you should, therefore, always ensure that there is enough work prepared for them. Also, to monitor the workflow you should have some general idea as to what your staff is working on at any given time.

Specific Suggestions You Can Implement Now:

- Everything should have a place; whenever possible, you should put things in their permanent place the first time you handle them. I suggest the use of four piles;
  - Documents requiring your attention. This would include incoming mail, outgoing mail for signatures, memoranda, etc., but not include file folders;
  - Completed dictation. When placing documents and files in this pile, they should be face down so that your secretary, by inverting the pile, can begin work from the top (the first item dictated) without having to rearrange the order of the files;
  - Material to be filed or routed to someone else. I have set aside one corner of my desk for this purpose, and if anything is placed on that spot, any staff member entering my office will remove it.
  - Material which you intend to take home for perusal. This includes such material as bar reviews, which I place in my briefcase.
- Aside from decorative and personal objects, keep nothing in your office, which is not actually being used on a daily basis. Any document, file or other article, which will not be receiving your attention within the next 48 hours ought not to be in your office if you have central filing, or on your desk if you have individual filing.
- Never have more than one file open on your desk at the same time. If a second file is needed, close the first before opening the second, and thereby avoid unnecessary aggravation searching for a misplaced document.
- The written word:
  - Write things down. Do not rely on your memory, as it is simply not good enough. Any system you adopt must provide for the accurate recording and fast retrieval of information. [Writing things] down makes it much easier for your staff [when] you are away from the office. A competent lawyer can step into my practice and look after any file without a word of instruction from me. Also, I can leave on vacation with a minimum of preparation.

- Be brief, because the fewer the words the quicker they can be dictated, typed, and proofread. Continually ask yourself if a word or phrase is essential; if not, omit it.
- While talking on the telephone or attending a meeting, get in the habit of making notes of all relevant points. Since you are a captive audience and cannot do anything else anyway, you might as well take notes. These may prove invaluable at a later date.

. . .

- Write letters that are short, clear, and concise by simply numbering each point you wish to make. These letters are not only easier to prepare, but you will usually get a reply which follows your numbered format, and, therefore, they can be dealt with faster.
- Try to answer your mail immediately upon receipt with the idea of finally disposing of each piece of paper as you initially read it. By 9:30 a.m. each day, all of my routine mail is dealt with, except those few letters requiring further consideration.
- Try to get ahead, or at least stay current, in your work. For example, upon settling a case, immediately dictate instructions for all the usual documents and letters necessary to complete the matter. Therefore, when the signed Release comes back to you, your secretary simply appends it to the next letter which is already typed, dates that letter, and sends it off. This enables you to avoid re-opening the file and familiarizing yourself with it again merely to write a single routine letter.
- Delegate work whenever possible, and ask yourself these two questions continually each day:
  - Must this task be done?
  - If so, must I be the one to do it?
    * Never forget that you still are ultimately responsible for every document that leaves your office regardless of who prepared it. By careful scrutiny, you should be able to catch any errors before it is too late.
    * Organize your day so as to see clients in blocks of time, but try to remember to remain accessible whenever possible. I find it convenient to schedule appointments every hour on Wednesday afternoon, and when that time is full, I move to another afternoon.
- Interrupt your staff as little as possible. Save up a number of matters rather than call in your secretary for each little thing. Remember that each time your secretary stops typing, it costs you money.
- Try to get many little jobs out of the way before tackling one large time-consuming job.
- Set realistic dates for completion of a client's work as you are duty and honor bound to complete it by the time promised.

- Utilize the newest and best office equipment and services you can afford.
- Use messenger services; they can usually be billed as a disbursement to your client, and there is no excuse whatsoever for you or your secretary to make deliveries.
- Precedents: documents, letters and checklists: use them. When a good precedent comes to your attention, immediately place it in a folder, with an index for the various areas of practice. That way, your precedents will be in form where they can be quickly located and used, even while they are being collected and revised.
- Know your limitations and, bearing in mind the best interests of your clients, do not take on responsibility for something you cannot do without expending far more time than would be justified or which might have an adverse effect on your health. There is nothing wrong with the judicious use of the word No. In the same way that a family doctor might refer a patient to a specialist, you should not hesitate, when necessary, to refer a client to a lawyer with more expertise.
- Never give an unqualified opinion [unless you are] absolutely certain you know what you are talking about. Always be completely candid with your clients. If you are unsure of the answer to a question, just say that this matter will require further study, then offer to look it up and call them back. Your clients will appreciate this and you will sleep better.
- Render your bill as soon as the work has been completed.

---

4. LEADERSHIP AND SUPERVISION

Leadership is an elusive quality. Countless books have tried to define it. Numerous seminars attempt to teach it. Everyone is required to exert it from time to time. Some have the mantle of leadership cast upon them through crisis; others find that it grows on them incrementally as a by-product of their experience and wisdom.

Whatever its origins, it is no exaggeration to assert that lawyers are frequently placed in positions of leadership. The very concept of representing a client entails the use of leadership skills. The history of the legal profession in the United States is full of instances in which lawyers exercise leadership in a variety of public service capacities. Even within small communities, lawyers are frequently singled out to serve on community boards, committees, and advisory panels.

The same skills that help lawyers to provide public leadership should help them to exercise leadership in the organizations where they work. Clearly the partners need to demonstrate leadership skills in giving direction to the firm. Associates can also demonstrate leadership within the firm in managing projects and taking on responsibilities. Although leadership is in many ways an intangible quality, it is likely to be one of the characteristics that partners consider when they evaluate new candidates for partnership.

An important part of leadership is supervision. Although younger lawyers are likely to be supervised during their early years of practice, they are also likely to be supervisors of the support staff. Supervisory skills include knowing how to clearly define tasks to be delegated, assigning tasks with clarity and precision, giving subordinates room to work without abdicating responsibility, providing meaningful feedback, and assuring substantive review of the quality of the subordinates' work product. Model Rule 5.3 also requires lawyers to take reasonable steps to assure that non-lawyer subordinates act within the scope of the rules of professional conduct, even though they may not be technically bound by them.

Anyone who has worked for a living can give examples of good and bad bosses. Law office support staff frequently report instances where new lawyers have been rude, arrogant, and insensitive. Ironically, the support staff at a law firm often can make or break a new associate. Remember: when you get out of law school the secretary in the firm probably knows a lot more about practicing law than you do. That person can help you to look good or can undermine your best efforts. Take time to nurture relationships with support staff; you do not need to be everyone's buddy in order to be a good supervisor, but you don't need to cop an attitude either.

5. COMMUNICATION

It should come as no surprise that lawyers are required to utilize communications skills in everything they do. The MacCrate Task Force Report identified communications as one of the fundamental lawyering skills. It is sometimes easy to forget that the same skills used to deliver legal work to clients are also used by effective managers. An uncommunicative manager is probably an ineffective manager. Some of the management-related communication skills are described below:

- *Oral communication:* Knowing how to talk to people is an asset. Whether it involves giving instructions, proving feedback, praising, criticizing, or just chatting around the coffee machine, lawyers need to be effective oral communicators. They need to recognize that arguing and pontificating are seldom effective tools in inter-personal communications. Neither is yelling and screaming likely to be productive in motivating people to work for you. If you find that you are not a natural conversationalist because you are basically shy, always on the run, or brutally straightforward, you may need to work on your technique in conveying messages to co-workers with diplomacy. Unlike clients, judges, and adversaries, you will see the people in your office every day. If you cannot get along with these people and communicate meaningfully with them verbally, you will probably not survive in that workplace. More than a few brilliant lawyers have learned this lesson the hard way.

- *Written communication:* The importance of the skill of effective writing is drummed into law students from the first year forward. It is easy to overlook the fact that good writing is important in more than legal documents; it is an essential ingredient in managing a practice, including evaluating staff, discipline, communicating among peers, billing clients, drafting instructions, sending out inter-office memos, and a host of other activities. It is important to proofread and edit drafts of internal communications, just as it is for documents that go out the door. It is not uncommon for a single word in a memorandum issued by management to the staff to become a subject of controversy, blown out of proportion, at the most inopportune time. Such gaffes can siphon off considerable energy, require hours of remedial attention, and undermine office morale. When such ill-conceived expressions become a pattern of communication, management can lose all credibility with the staff.

- *Non–Verbal Communication:* Researchers say that as much as seventy percent of the content in face-to-face communication is contained in non-verbal signals, sometimes called body language. Body language can tell when we are happy, sad, frustrated, angry, and a host of other feelings. Body language can connote where we see ourselves in the pecking order of office politics; it can let people know when we are being disingenuous or dishonest (we have all had experiences with people who say all the right things, but we know they don't mean them). On one hand, we all need to be aware of our own body language. Some people may give away very little about themselves non-verbally. These people may be perceived as distant or uncaring, even if they are not. Lawyers who have this trait may want to work on being a little more emotive. At the other end of the spectrum are people whose feelings are written all over them. They are likely to be perceived as over-emotional or possibly flighty; they may not be perceived by others as dependable, even if they are. For lawyers who suffer from this tendency it may help to work on being a little more poker-faced in dealings with others in the office. You should recognize that non-verbal communication can be modified in the same way that verbal communication can. Just as you became effective in presenting an oral argument by practicing, you can work on the way you come across to others by seeking feedback from people who will be honest with you, videotaping yourself in different situations, and just thinking about your facial expressions, body language and attitude when you talk. On the other hand, non-verbal communication involves reading the body language of others. If you just listen to the words people are saying, you will lose a great deal of useful information The senior partner might tell you that you are doing a great job, but the way she looks away from you when she says it may give you cause to wonder. Your secretary may tell you that she will be glad to take your clothes to the cleaners, while her posture tells you something completely different.

- *Electronic communications:* E-mail and other forms of electronic communication have given rise to an entire set of management problems: netiquette among e-mail users, instantaneous accessibility, the legal discoverability of messages, and Internet diversions from work. These problems did not exist for law firm managers or individual lawyers trying to practice law a generation ago. The best we can do is to understand this medium, and to use it discreetly. There may be times when the best way to send a message is to walk down the hall, close the door, and say, "let's talk." It may help to compose documents off-line, then wait before sending them. Sometimes the answer may be not to reply at all.

- *Listening:* Active listening is a skill that is just as useful to working with other people in the office as it is communicating with clients. Active listening involves maintaining eye contact with the other person, remaining attentive to what the other person is saying, providing responsive feedback, and clarifying confusing or difficult to understand messages. If lawyers would devote as much time to listening as they do to speaking, they would be substantially better managers.

- *Flirting:* Perhaps it is inappropriate to include flirting on a list of critical lawyering skills. It is here only because flirting involves oral, non-verbal, and listening communication skills. Flirting is the way people communicate physical attraction. While it might be naive to suggest that people who work together should stop being sexually attracted to each other, it would be an oversight not to acknowledge the very real dangers of office romance. Not only are there issues involving sexual discrimination and harassment that should be obvious to anyone in law school, but there are several political issues when co-workers are dating or carrying on an affair. Superiors may be viewed as showing favoritism to the sexual partner or disfavor toward a competitor. Even people who are relatively equal may polarize others in the office by their behavior. And if the problem were dicey when the people were dating, they get downright messy after the breakup. There are probably about as many tales of people who met their spouses at work, as there are horror stories about romance gone sour. Harmless flirting goes on in many offices, although in some situations even a casual wink may be inappropriate. It is important to remain sensitive to whether the conduct is unwanted, and whether it might be misconstrued by others. More serious relationships deserve considerably more thought and discussion before embarking on them at all.

In short, communication is a critical skill, not only for the aspects of lawyering that deal with client service, but also with those that impact the lawyer's relationship with staff, peers, supervisors, vendors, and others. Without this skill, a lawyer cannot hope to succeed in practice.

6. TECHNOLOGY

Understanding and using computer technology has become a necessity rather than a luxury in the practice of law. Although some law offices remain behind the curve in the use of technology, successful firms in the future will embrace it wholeheartedly. Although some senior partners continue to resist technological change, most law school graduates enter the profession with a high degree of technological acuity.

For law students, the learning curve in technology may not be so much discovering what technology can do, but learning the specific applications for the practice of law. Throughout this book, technology applications have been mentioned wherever they have the potential to assist lawyers to practice more efficiently. These applications are likely to continue to evolve for the foreseeable future, so the knowledge that one possesses at graduation from law school is unlikely to be sufficient to carry that person through a career as a lawyer. At least in this area, graduates and lawyers alike must commit to a lifetime of learning in order to maintain their competence.

7. RAINMAKING

From the dawn of history, humans have sought to cause rain to fall upon the fields and crops at the most propitious time. Without rain, there was famine. If the rainmaker could cause life-giving showers to fall upon the land, life was good. Somewhere along the line, the image of the rainmaker was applied to the modern law firm, where it came to mean a lawyer, usually a partner, whose skills in attracting new clients to the firm provided sustenance to the inhabitants of the professional service business. Rainmakers today, like their agrarian counterparts of yore, are sometimes perceived as possessing special talents, magical spells, and a connection to the gods not available to those mortals who lack their talents. Rainmakers have power and status.

Whatever mythology might have enveloped the art of rainmaking in the past, we know that rainmaking skills are more science than magic. In the case of the weather, the process of seeking clouds has replaced dancing and chanting as a main means of precipitating precipitation. In the law, enough has been written about rainmaking for clients to establish the fact that clients' acquisition and development skills can be learned.

In addition to possessing strong communications and inter-personal relations' skills, effective rainmakers are proficient marketers of themselves and their services. We have talked about marketing already, in Chapter 4, which dealt with marketing legal services from the perspective of the law firm. Marketing can also be viewed as an activity engaged in by every lawyer from newest associate to senior partner. This personal marketing skill is quite simply the ability to understand and articulate what value the individual brings to the client who uses that person's services.

Implicit in this concept is the notion that effective marketers carve out a professional niche; contact clients who need those niche services, and sell confidence in the lawyer to deliver those services. Some lawyers rankle at the mention of terms like selling, contacting, and even marketing. The rules of professional conduct and constitutional doctrine describe the circumstances within which lawyers may ethically engage in marketing activities. Nothing in the rules or the case law, however, prohibits lawyers from reaching out to new clients. It would also be inaccurate to say that marketing techniques alone are sufficient to build a practice, because unless the firm or the individual can deliver on promises made to prospective clients, they will not build and maintain a reputation for competence in their chosen field.

Law students sometimes think that they do not need to worry about rainmaking until they become partners in their firm. This overlooks the reality that without rainmaking performance these lawyers are not likely to have the opportunities to become partners in firms. It is not enough to simply assume that the partners will bring in the clients, while you turn over the work. You should work continuously on building your client base, and this is an activity that can begin now, before you enter the practice of law. In a larger sense, even if you were working as an employee in an organization, you would be well advised to view your supervisors as clients and think about the way you market your services to them. For instance, if partners in a law firm typically make substantive case assignments to associates; the associate who is able to secure the types of cases she wants is most likely to position herself favorably in the firm to develop a client base and to make partner.

The following elements are important for lawyers who desire to become rainmakers through their own personal marketing efforts (as opposed to inheriting a client base from senior partners or family ties): Have a plan; develop a network; take regular steps; establish a cognizable expertise, and review your progress regularly.

- *Have a Plan*: It is crucial that you have some idea where you are going in your professional life if you are to have any hope of getting there. Too many people are either incapable of making decisions about their careers, or unable to figure out what they want to be. While career planning is certainly not a precise science, and the future is always uncertain, there are many things that we can know about ourselves, our skills, experiences, values, interests, and all the other attributes that make us unique. On some level, we know what satisfies us personally and professionally. We know what we need to be happy and we know what stands in the way. Professionally, having a plan is essentially understanding what it is you do and want to do, figuring out where the clients are, who can use the unique help that you provide, and creating a strategy for reaching those people.

- *Develop a Network*: We all have networks, friends, family, classmates, professional contacts, and former clients who will follow our professional development, have confidence in our work, and in the end hire us or refer people to us. This network does not begin to develop sometime in the middle years of practicing law; it is built and nurtured from an early age. Although we all have networked, many of us do not organize the people we meet in any efficient way. A contact manager or personal information manager can help to begin the process of organizing your contacts over time. As you collect data about people you know and have known, you are building a valuable resource. It is not enough, however, to simply have a contact list, if you do not take time to stay in touch with the people on it. Whether you send out a newsletter, Christmas card, e-mail blast, or find some other way to stay in touch, if you do not renew your contacts regularly, the network will not help you. But if you do, a strong network will help your rainmaking immeasurably.

- *Take Regular Steps*: Learn to think about and engage in marketing activities daily. Marketing is an activity that is incredibly easy to procrastinate, as there are always short-term crises to resolve. If you are not already engaging in personal marketing activities, you may need to plan to take specific steps on a regular basis until such time as these activities become a habit.

- *Develop a Cognizable Expertise*: What sets rainmakers apart from the rest of the world? They are the "go to" people. The ones you would trust to help you out of a jam. They are not just generic lawyers, rather they are perceived as people who have special insights and can be trusted to help. In the end, your goal should be to become the world's greatest expert at something.

- *Review Periodically*: Rules are made to change. Whatever you decided last week or last month is probably subject to review today. So, your personal marketing plan needs to be updated periodically. Nothing's gone the way you anticipated? Have new elements entered the picture? Are there other new opportunities or threats on the horizon? Will different strategies get you more effectively where you want to go? Find the time to reflect on your plans.

8. SUBSTANTIVE LEGAL SKILLS

The practice of law requires substantive legal knowledge for competent representation in any given practice area. A legal generalist may have some knowledge about a variety of different fields of law, but no lawyer can know enough to practice competently in every imaginable field of concentration. Ironically, when we pass the bar exam, we are licensed to give legal advice involving a matter in any substantive area in the jurisdiction where we are licensed. In reality, two real estate lawyers in neighboring states would be more likely to handle each others' cases competently than a real estate lawyer and a securities lawyer from the same state.

A brief word about specialization may be in order here. The legal profession has never had formal specialties like the medical or engineering professions. In recent decades, however, *de facto* specialization has become the norm. Most practitioners today describe themselves as real estate lawyers, or securities lawyers or insurance defense lawyers, than as simply lawyers. Model Rule 7.4 covers communication of a legal specialty to prospective clients, and permits lawyers to communicate their specialty status as long as they meet state requirements for certification of specialties and do not mislead clients about the basis for their specialty claim. Many lawyers who find the definitional questions involving specialization murky, choose instead to talk about practice concentration, limiting their practice to certain fields, or simply stating simply what fields of law they practice.

Those lawyers who concentrate their practices in a particular substantive area inevitably learn substantially more law in that area than generalists who may be acquainted with a few general principals. Some fields of law may be less complex, and therefore more accessible to practitioners who are not specialists in those fields. These commodity practice areas do not require the same level of expertise or experience. Some areas may be practiced competently at a basic level, but require greater knowledge for more complex transactions. An example of such an area is estate planning. Most lawyers take a course in wills during law school, study wills for the bar exam, and know how to draft simple wills for individuals with small, uncomplicated estates. Clients with large estates complicated personal lives, and unusual testamentary objectives need to work with a lawyer who knows more.

Sometimes lost in conversations about legal knowledge is the skills component of each practice area. Discussions of lawyering skills often focus on the skills that all lawyers should possess, by virtue of their education and experience. The application of substantive legal knowledge in a practice area requires the utilization of different skills in different ways. Some practice areas may require skill or knowledge from fields totally outside the law. Thus, it may be helpful to think of substantive legal skills in terms of a special skill set necessary to apply substantive legal knowledge to particular problems. When someone handles cases using skills in substantive areas, we describe the product of these transactions as experience. Greater experience implies that the lawyer has honed the skills to a higher level of competence. No client wants to be a lawyer's first will, first trial, or first criminal defense anymore than a patient wants to be a surgeon's first heart transplant.

Getting the first case may not be easy, but lawyers often discover that after they have handled a substantive legal matter, they continue to get similar cases. The clients tell other people (the partners begin to recognize an associate as the expert in a particular field) and the lawyer herself seeks these cases because she can handle them more efficiently than cases she has never handled. This can be a problem when a novice lawyer finds herself getting referrals in a practice area she doesn't enjoy or want to pursue.

The reality, however, is that choices open doors to gain experience and expertise, and at the same time close doors to other practice areas that require specialized substantive legal skills. You can't do everything and you shouldn't even try. You need to decide what you want to do well and focus on developing the skills necessary to practice in that area at the highest level of competence.

Problems and Questions

1. As you look at your personal management skills, which ones will help you to be an effective manager in the delivery of legal work to clients? Do you have any traits that could get in the way? What can you do about these shortcomings? See Appendix N, pages 501–502.

2. This section enumerated several specific skill to flesh out the fundamental lawyering skill of "organization and management of legal work," described by the MacCrate Task Force. Can you think of other skills that will help you as a professional manager?

3. Are some of these skills more germane to managing the law office, as opposed to managing legal work? As a new lawyer in practice, can you ignore firm management skills and concentrate on practice management skills alone? What is wrong with this approach?

4. Think about your own communications style. Are you an effective communicator? Are you better in some areas than others? Which ones and why? Considering the different types of communication described in this section, are your messages consistent across different forms of communication? Are your non-verbal cues consistent with the verbal and written messages?

5. Do you have a personal marketing plan to sell yourself to clients, whether they are the recipients of legal services or the partners in your firm? How do you communicate your value as a lawyer to those who are in a position to retain your services?

6. Although it was written in 1982, the article by Joel Altman includes a number of very specific management suggestions for lawyers. Do you think his advice holds up today? Why or why not? What advice, if any, would you change?

D. LAW SCHOOL, CLE AND THE REAL WORLD

The MacCrate Task Force mentioned in Section B, above, also postulated an educational continuum, which begin long before we enter law school and extends throughout our professional lives. The idea is that professionals are always learning. The third year lawyer should know more than the third year law student, and the thirty year lawyer ought to know more than the third year associate. This principle applies to professional skills as well as to legal knowledge. The fact that not all lawyers continue on an upward trajectory is unfortunate but not necessarily inevitable. There are opportunities to make professional growth a lifelong process, including the following:

1. MANDATORY CONTINUING LEGAL EDUCATION

After you graduate from law school and finish the bar exam, you will break a cycle that has governed much of your life. Certainly, some law graduates go back for an LL.M. or other advanced degree, and some law students worked in the real world before coming to law school. For most law students, however, much of their lives, and certainly the last three or four years have been spent as a student. The cycle of signing up for classes, preparing for classes, taking exams unwinding after exams, and waiting for the results is a pattern that is imprinted on your brain. The necessity of getting up at 8:00 a.m. for a class in something you are not interested in at all but had to take, because it was the only thing available on the schedule, is not new to you. When you go to work after you graduate and get a job, someone will be paying you to get up at 8:00 a.m. to get to work early enough to handle cases for clients you may or may not like, because the senior partner knew you were available. Most law graduates welcome the transition to the world of practice. Although practicing law has its own set of frustrations, most graduates are ready to put away their casebooks and join the real world.

Not so fast. Law school may be over, but continuing legal education never ends. Many states impose continuing legal education requirements, which mandate attendance at a certain number of hours of courses each year. Some states require all new lawyers to attend formal bridge-the-gap programs. Some larger law firms even incorporate in-house training programs for their associates. The ABA's MacCrate Task Force in 1992 described the acquisition of legal skill and knowledge as something that occurred along a continuum. A person begins to acquire information and develop skills that will be used in the practice of law long before law school, and should continue to develop professionally long after law school is finished.

Ideally, learning should be a lifelong activity for lawyers. This does not always happen. Some lawyers are satisfied to attain a level of competence necessary to perform certain works adequately at this plateau, but not push to become better. A few lawyers make no pretense about continued learning; they practice just to get by. In states that do not have a mandatory continuing legal education program, it is possible for a lawyer who graduated from law school fifty years ago to never have taken a single continuing legal education course after graduation, and still hold himself out as a qualified lawyer to the public. Because lawyers do not require re-certification for continued licensure, disbarment may be the only remedy for lawyers who do not take steps to stay abreast of changes in the law or groom their skills periodically.

As you embark upon your career, you should make a commitment to continued lifelong learning in the law. Take continuing legal education courses in your area of practice, whether you are required to or not. Take a little time each day to read up on development in your area of practice. Talk to other lawyers about issues that affect your practice. Develop a plan for professional growth that includes short-term, intermediate-term, and long-term objectives.

The pressures of practicing law, including the demands of clients, the pressures of administrative chores, and the need to maintain a personal life all have a tendency to get in the way of professional development. If you do not make it a point to pursue your own professional growth, you can easily lose your commitment to excellence along the way.

2. PROFESSIONAL COMPETENCE

One objective for every new lawyer is the attainment of competence. The concept of professional competence is an elusive one. Bar conferences and committees have attempted to define the term and these efforts have met with limited success. It is sometimes easier to define competence by what it is not, when lawyers engage in conduct that leads to discipline or malpractice, or when they simply do not serve their clients well.

Although the licensing process seems to suggest that when a new lawyer passes the bar exam, she is competent to represent clients, just about every entry level attorney will attest to the overwhelming feelings of inadequacy that accompany advising their first client. Sometimes competence is demonstrated in an exemplary way, when an individual lawyer's handling of a matter is so impressive that it is held up as an example for others.

In practice the road to competence is an ongoing journey. A new lawyer may pass through several stages in the first few years of practice from a stage where she at least avoids embarrassing herself with her ignorance, to a level of comfort with handling matters, to a point where she truly masters her craft. Thereafter, some lawyers continue to grow to become the leaders in their fields, to excel in their work.

Earlier in this Chapter, we discussed how lawyering skills contribute to competence and the role of continuing education in developing and sustaining competence. It is important, however, to consider competence in the larger picture of professional growth over time and the interrelationship between competence and the achievement of long term career goals. A fundamental theory of careers holds that people will be successful if they are doing what they like to do, and that they usually like to do things they are good at doing. For lawyers, this means that becoming consummately good in your practice is the best way to achieve success and satisfaction.

PROBLEMS AND QUESTIONS

1. Once you are out of school, how do you maintain your competence? Or maybe the question is: how do you become increasingly more competent over the years? Is it enough to attend CLE programs? What else should you do to keep your professional edge?

2. Review the various projects you have undertaken in this course and report on your findings. What insights have you had? What have you learned that has changed your perception about the practice of law and how you will fit into it? What specifically have you learned that will help you to be a more competent lawyer?

Chapter 16

Building a Successful Career

■ ■ ■

A. MANAGING YOUR CAREER

The average law school graduate is just under thirty years old. Those who went straight through school may finish at twenty-four or twenty-five, but many law students today have worked for at least a couple of years after undergraduate school before starting law school. Others have pursued graduate programs or started families. Some law students, particularly those in part-time or evening programs may be pursuing law as a second career, after finding out that they were unhappy in the first, or even retiring from a business or occupation after twenty years or more.

Whatever your age at graduation, it is probable that you will be pursuing your legal career for a considerable length of time. Lawyers have traditionally worked beyond normal retirement ages, and in an era when people are generally living and working longer, it is not conjecture to say that at least some of today's graduates will be practicing for fifty to sixty years, well past the midpoint of the twenty-first century.

If you are just getting out of law school, unsure about where your first job will be, and uncertain about whether you will want to practice law at all, talk about long-term career objectives may seem fruitless. The choices you make now, however, can help you to get to where you want to be in your career, can help you to enhance your satisfaction over time, and can even assist you to weather the inevitable crises in your professional and personal life. Fatalism may have a certain appeal in the movies and literature, but in real life career choices are made using a set of skills that can make a difference in the quality of your life. No discussion of law practice management would be complete without exploring these career skills.

PATHS WITHIN THE LEGAL PROFESSION

From *Careers in Law*, by Gary A. Munneke (2d ed. 1997).

Lawyers practice in a variety of different settings. In all these settings, the work may be categorized as unsupervised, supervisory, and supervised. This characterization may be more meaningful than a simple partner-associate or owner-employee dichotomy. In corporate, government, and other sectors general counsels, managing attorneys, assistant general counsels, and staff attorneys replace partners and associates. Even in law firms, new categories of lawyers have been created to reflect the changing nature of the law firm pyramid: non-equity partners, permanent associates, and of counsel lawyers.

It may help to describe lawyers' work in three categories: unsupervised, supervisory, and supervised. It is possible for a single lawyer, at different times, to work under each of these circumstances. Unsupervised lawyers work directly for their clients. There is a direct attorney-client relationship. The lawyer's loyalty to the client, promise of confidence, and duty to act zealously flow differently from the relationship. The lawyer personally handles the client's work, offers advice, and represents the client's interests. These elements exist whether or not the lawyer works in a private firm, and whether or not the attorney is compensated.

Supervisory attorneys may maintain a direct relationship with the client, may handle parts of the work personally, and may be supervised by other attorneys. They may also delegate some or all of the clients' work to other attorneys. Supervisory attorneys are responsible for the quality of supervised work, the ethical behavior of the attorneys they supervise, and the timeliness of the legal product. In all but routine or simple legal work some supervision is required. Different skills are required in order to be a good supervisor as opposed to handling legal work with help. In addition to supervising other attorneys, the supervisory function also entails supervising the work of nonlegal support staff.

Supervised attorneys work under the direction of more senior lawyers. They may or may not have direct client contact but, in any event, their authority is derivative of the lawyer with whom the client relationship exists. This distinction is sometimes blurred where the law firm itself as an institution represents the clients. The distinction is also difficult in large or complex cases where some lawyers are both supervisors and supervised. This arrangement is common in corporate law departments. Remember that no matter how many lawyers are involved in the case, some lawyer at the top must be in charge of the representation and responsible directly to the client. The supervised attorney must complete the work according to the directions provided. The degree of independent work may vary widely from representation to representation. One significant aspect of the supervised attorney's work is the ethical obligation under the *Model Rules of Professional Conduct* to exercise independent judgment regarding ethical conduct. If the ethical question is one over which reasonable minds could differ, the supervised attorney should follow the course recommended by the supervisor, but if the supervising attorney is clearly requesting the subordinate to carry out conduct that would be improper ethically, the subordinate must refuse to comply. In other words, the junior lawyer must disobey his boss if the boss asks him to do anything unethical.

In general, supervisory and unsupervised work is handled by more experienced attorneys, while those with less experience are supervised. Many new lawyers may be required to handle unsupervised work. Someone who hangs out a shingle after law school may not have the benefit of senior lawyers to oversee her work. One lawyer known by the author started work at a large urban district attorney's office after passing the bar. When he arrived for his first day on the job, he found a stack of files on his desk and learned that he would be in court at 10:00 that morning. Such a scenario is not uncommon. The question is properly raised whether these lawyers can competently handle unsupervised work at that point in their careers. Unfortunately, this sink or swim approach, has permeated post-law school legal training. It is also not uncommon for very experienced lawyers to work in supervised situations, particularly in complex cases. In fact, a single lawyer may be involved as a subordinate, unsupervised, and supervisory lawyer in different cases at the same time.

The normal progression of work is to handle supervised work, move on to unsupervised work (because cases small enough for one lawyer to handle are inevitably simpler than multi-lawyer matters), and then to assume supervisory positions in bigger cases. Partners, associates, and other classes of lawyers may engage in any of these three tracks of work.

A small percentage of lawyers who work inside the formal legal profession do not practice law. These lawyers serve as administrators, teachers, judges, librarians, and technical advisors. They may or may not have moved from positions that involved delivering legal services to positions supporting the delivery of legal services. For example, the managing partner of a firm may not have time to practice law any more while the firm's librarian (also a lawyer) has never practiced law.

Problems and Questions

1. If the normal developmental path for a new lawyer is to work in a supervised setting, gradually becoming more independent, and then overseeing the work of others, how does one obtain the supervisory skills necessary to advance one's career?
2. How does someone who becomes a solo practitioner immediately after law school advance her career?
3. What activities outside of work, like public service, writing, teaching and participating in professional organizations will complement your growth as a practitioner?
4. What post-graduate educational programs are likely to enhance your career in the future:
    - Continuing Legal Education?
    - A post-graduate legal education, such as an LLM or SJD?
    - A non-legal degree program, such as an MBA, CPA or PhD?

- Professional training workshopes

B. THE LEGAL JOB MARKET

The article "Race to the Finish Line," which you read in Chapter 2, talks about the changing marketplace for legal services. Other material in that chapter paints a picture of the competitive legal marketplace where not all firms, individuals and service providers prevail. Chapter 2 also establishes that the market for legal services is both large and pervasive in our society. Not all legal services are delivered by lawyers in private practice, or necessarily by lawyers.

Beginning in 2008, stories in the legal press and blogs began to talk about a toxic mix of declining jobs opportunities and increasing student loan debt at graduation. Although fluctuations in the job market were not new, many commentators used terms like "crisis" to describe the situation. Although the economy began to improve after 2010, students, graduates and practitioners entering the job market viewed their opportunities warily. In one sense, whether the economy is strong or weak, good career planning requires constant vigilance as to market forces and opportunities.

It may be true that the job market for recent law school graduates has been not been good. The legal press has documented the travails of recent graduates who have not been able to find jobs in the practice of law or who have had job offers rescinded. Experienced associates and even partners have been laid off, and many law firms have downsized or closed their doors. And some law schools have been criticized for misrepresenting the employment picture for their graduates.

The focus of this chapter is not to re-hash the debate about how bad the job market really is, but helping individual law students to maximize their opportunities in the job market they face. Whether the economy is good or bad, whether jobs are plentiful or scarce, in every job market some job seekers are more successful than others. The following article examines the availability of careers outside the practice of law, not just a response to the dearth of legal jobs, but as an alternative path for many students with the skills to use their legal talent in different ways.

WHAT YOU CAN DO WITH A LAW DEGREE (BESIDES PRACTICE LAW)

From *From Student Lawyer*, by Gary A. Munneke (January 2012).

As a graduating law student with a couple of law firm job offers in hand, I was walking down the hall past the dean's office at my law school when the dean's secretary called to me to say that the dean wanted to see me. Ushered into his office, I was surprised to hear the dean offer me a job on the spot—as assistant dean of the law school. Among my responsibilities, he wanted me to take over the struggling career services (in those days, placement) office. For reasons I cannot readily explain, I accepted the job immediately without discussing it with family, friends, or advisors. Thus, as a newly minted lawyer I began my own personal exploration of what you can do with a law degree . . . besides practice law.

. . .

My early ABA activities included work with a group called the Standing Committee on Professional Utilization and Career Development, which was studying the problem of "too many law schools" spewing out "too many lawyers" (sound familiar?). The theory was that an oversupply of lawyers would create masses of unemployed and underemployed lawyers, who would either fill welfare lines or practice law marginally. These lawyers, it was surmised, would be tempted to cut corners ethically, provide inferior services, and drive down the income for "real" practitioners.

When the Standing Committee studied the oversupply problem, however, some amazing results came to light. Instead of hoards of bottom-feeding underemployed practitioners, lawyers who did not find legal jobs were taking positions in business and industry, supplanting applicants with degrees in business, economics, accounting, and liberal arts. The JD credential had caché in the business world, and if anyone ended up unemployed it would not be the lawyers.

The purpose of recounting this history is not to highlight the role of serendipity in our lives, but to illustrate how a decision to follow, as Robert Frost said, the road less traveled, has made all the difference for me. Although the numbers are not clear, it is beyond challenge that a significant percentage of law graduates do not practice law. According to the latest American Bar Foundation's Lawyer Statistical Report, just over 60 percent of the 1.2 million lawyers in America engage in the private practice of law. Another 10 to 20 percent work full-time as lawyers for organizations. Reports often do not distinguish in-house lawyers for the entity from lawyers who engage in management, administration, or other non-practice activities. A lawyer in private practice sells her time to a law firm, which in turn sells services to clients on the open market; or if she opens her own practice, she sells those services directly to consumers. An in-house practitioner sells *all* her time to the organization that employs her.

The universe of nonlegal careers includes positions that do not involve delivering legal services to clients—either on the open market or to a particular entity. It can be argued that almost every imaginable endeavor has legal implications, and that legal skills can enhance the effectiveness of a person in any field. Tommy Lasorda, a baseball manager who has a law degree, may use a variety of legal skills (persuasion, negotiation, analysis) to be a better manager, but it is his knowledge of baseball that defines his job. On the other hand, someone who leaves the practice of law to open a wine bar uses legal skills every day (choice of business entity, creating and interpreting contracts, overseeing human resources, licensing, and taxes, for example). There is no bright line that can define an official list of nonlegal careers, although the vast majority of lawyers who pursue nonlegal careers follow a number of identifiable paths.

People choose to pursue careers outside the practice of law at different points in time: Some come to law school with no intention of ever practicing law. While this was more common when employers routinely paid employees for pursuing graduate education, it is still true that a few first-year students in every class already know they do not want to practice law. Those in a second group decide during the course of their law school years that law is not their calling. It may be that they do not care for law school itself or that they worked in a law firm during school and found the work stifling and unsatisfying. A third group may finish law school but choose a nonlegal job because the opportunities are better outside the legal profession. During the economic downturn of 2008–09, when many law firms cut back on hiring, many law students explored nonlegal options; conversely, during the boom years of the early 2000s, many law graduates eschewed private practice to pursue what they perceived as lucrative careers in investment banking. A final group of lawyers who pursue nonlegal careers includes those who start out in private practice, but leave because they are lured away to work for clients they represented as lawyers, because they discovered that practicing law was not all it was cracked up to be, or more recently, because they were victims of law firm downsizing and layoffs.

Before embarking on a nonlegal job search, it is useful to reset your mental compass to accommodate a career that does not involve practicing law, because much of what you think about a legal career points you in the direction of practicing law for a living. For anyone considering a nonlegal career, there are several impediments.

Ladder mentality. If we perceive jobs for lawyers in a hierarchical way, we might imagine a clerkship with the US Supreme Court on the very top step, and then on the next rung a job as an associate with a large prestigious law firm, and then a fortune 100 legal department, and then a medium-sized firm, then a small firm, and then after hanging out your own shingle, on the very last rung, a nonlegal career. On some level, we know that this paradigm does not make sense; we are not fungible commodities who perform equally well in all work settings. We are unique individuals who need to find unique career opportunities that complement our personal skills, interests, and aspirations. In order to get to the point where we perceive career options as legitimate alternatives, we need to turn the ladder on its side, so that the Supreme Court clerkship, the nonlegal career, as well as the other possibilities, are different choices of relatively equal value.

Advice from loved ones. Although well-meaning, a second impediment can be the advice of loved ones. They may not understand why you would spend three years and a considerable sum of money to go to law school if you did not want to be a lawyer. The simple response is that when you graduate from law school you are a lawyer, even if you decide not to practice law. Some might quibble that you are only a law school graduate until you pass the bar. But assuming you take and pass the bar—which you will want to do if you think you might someday want to work in a setting where a law license is required—you will be a nonpracticing lawyer. Family and friends need to know that you are making a choice that is right for you and that you will use your skills as a lawyer whether you work in a law firm or not.

The universe of nonlegal career opportunities. The term "universe" implies a vast expanse of space, galaxies, and black holes; it is more than we can wrap our minds around. The legal job market is miniscule compared to the macro-employment market worldwide. In order to find a nonlegal job in a nonlegal field, we need focus and direction. The decision to pursue a nonlegal career is only the tip of the iceberg. We need to identify fields where our skills give us an advantage. We must choose areas that interest us. We may have to rely on contacts or networking to break into another field, because the law school career services office concentrates on jobs in law. Your decision to go to law school involved an assessment of what you wanted to do with your life, just as your decision to pursue a traditional legal career does; but if you decide to opt out of a legal career, you will need to engage in serious introspection and exploration of your options again.

The culture of the nonlegal field you choose. You can expect a different professional culture than law. Different fields have different educational and licensing requirements. They have their own language. They have their own hiring practices and calendars. They have their own publications and professional issues. If you want to succeed in a business outside of law, you must learn to fit into what is in many ways a foreign culture. One of the biggest hurdles may be the stereotypes that people in other professions have about lawyers. The burden will be on you to dispel their negative expectations and demonstrate that you will bring value to their organization. This may not be easy; for example, in the last sentence, is the reference to "burden" too legalistic? In any event, you may need to read professional journals in the area you want to work, gain additional credentials to be taken seriously, develop contacts and references from their world, and purge your vocabulary of legal jargon. You will also want to have answers to questions that employers might have about why a lawyer does not want to practice law.

As suggested above, the universe is infinite. However, some fields stand out, because lawyers gravitate to particular fields where they can use their legal skills. Some of these positions can be found in organizations that perform work ancillary to the practice of law, such as legal technology consulting, jury selection, accounting, or compliance. Often referred to as law-related positions, these encompass the people who provide support to law firms, but do not actually deliver legal services. Jobs in fields unconnected to the practice of law, however, may still incorporate a variety of legal issues and require the application of legal training.

The largest nonlegal employment category is business and industry. Within a typical company, lawyers outside the law department may work in human resources, compliance, communications, contract administration, purchasing, taxation, licensing, transportation, and a variety of other departments. It is worth noting that holders of the JD are second only to MBAs in terms of the number of corporate CEOs in the United States. Even a general counsel who moves from the legal department to corporate management migrates from a legal to a nonlegal position. Financial institutions, insurance companies, securities and investment firms, and real estate brokerages are the largest employers of lawyers, but almost any large company in any industry is likely to employ lawyers.

Small companies and entrepreneurial ventures are also attractive to lawyers. A legally trained investor can offer a variety of help to a new business entity. Although the lawyer may have to decide whether her role is one of counsel or participant, for some lawyers creating the business is more exciting than advising the business. A lawyer who is employed by a small company may find that she has to wear many hats. The company may not be large enough to have an in-house general counsel, yet may want to avoid the expense of outside counsel, leaving the lawyer manager to serve as informal counsel to the company.

Education is the nonlegal career field that has experienced the most growth over the course of the last quarter century. In addition to positions in law school teaching and administration, many lawyers work in college and university teaching and administration. Some of these individuals may move laterally from law school to university positions, but many others begin their careers outside the law school. Among the administrative areas where lawyers find jobs are the following: career services, financial aid, admissions, development, public relations, lobbying, library administration, and student services. Additionally, the number of lawyers working in primary and secondary education is also increasing.

A third nonlegal area that attracts large numbers of lawyers is government. At all levels—federal, state and local—lawyers work in virtually all agencies and departments. Lawyers who begin their careers doing legal work in government agencies often find that as they move up the ladder in an agency, they do more and more administrative work, and less and less law. You might start out as an assistant DA who tries cases, but by the time you are elected DA, you are more of a manager than a trial lawyer. In addition, thousands of lawyers at every level of government work in positions that are not technically legal positions. It may be the case that lawyers "legalize" their work by addressing legal aspects of their responsibilities or discovering that legal questions gravitate to them, but in the end they are managers with legal skills rather than lawyers with management skills. Within government, the largest number of lawyers can be found in the military, and many of these work in a military occupational specialty outside of the JAG Corps.

The political process has been a magnet for lawyers from time immemorial. Politics and political action are the siren song to lawyers' ears. Statistics show that more lawyers have served as presidents, governors, senators, and representatives than any other occupation. Lawyers are also well-represented on the staffs of elected officials. Take a look at any political campaign and you will find lawyers involved in every aspect of the election process.

Another growth area for JDs is communications. Some of the most obvious examples are writers like John Grisham, or television personalities like Geraldo Rivera, but less prominent figures like producer David E. Kelley (*The Practice*) fall into this category as well. Many on-air newscasters and reporters, screenwriters, actors, and studio executives are lawyers as well. Lawyers work in public relations as media consultants and marketing professionals. Sometimes writers or bloggers focus on legal subjects, but very often their legal backgrounds are unknown to their audiences.

Technology is an attractive option for lawyers, especially tech-savvy lawyers who understand both law and technology. From Internet-based application businesses, to law firm IT support, to website design, many lawyers have chosen the technology path. One area in particular deserves mention: online legal information sites. These sites, often created and managed jointly by nonlawyer professionals and lawyers, provide online services to clients who wish to represent themselves or obtain low-cost generic services that do not require the expertise or high price of a practicing lawyer. These legal sites often compete directly with bricks and mortar law firms and may walk perilously close to unauthorized practice, but they are an entrenched element of the legal services landscape in today's world, and an alternative path for at least some lawyers.

A final nonlegal career worth mentioning is public accounting. Because both lawyers and CPAs deal with taxation issues, it should not be surprising that legal and accounting services sometimes overlap. In a CPA firm, lawyers may be more involved with the consulting and compliance side, as opposed to the bookkeeping and auditing side, but it is a demonstrable fact that CPA firms regularly hire law school graduates as well as practitioners. Because partners in CPA firms must possess a CPA certification, many lawyers who go to work for accounting firms eventually become CPAs themselves.

The point should be clear: If you choose not to practice law, you will not want for opportunities. Before you decide to follow the same path that most of your classmates take, give some serious thought to what you can really do with a law degree. This advice is doubly true if you have reservations about whether practicing law is the right career for you. If you think that you might find happiness outside the legal field, take some time to look in the mirror; think about your personal and professional skills, what you like to do, what contacts and experience you have in other fields, and where you want your career to lead you. Take a chance, expand your horizons, and be ready to seize the opportunity to do something different.

Problems and Questions

1. What is the likelihood that you will practice law for the next forty years (the average length of time that recent law school graduates will work before retirement)? Is that something you would like to do, or do you see your career evolving differently?

2. Why is it so difficult for law students who have reservations about practicing law to act on finding rewarding alternatives? What *can* you do with a law degree besides practice law?

C. CREATING A CAREER PLAN

FROM THE LEGAL CAREER GUIDE: FROM LAW STUDENT TO LAWYER, 3D EDITION

by Gary A. Munneke, Ellen Wayne and William D. Henslee,
American Bar Association (2007), pages 16–23.

The serendipity of opportunity is always interwoven with aspirations and plans for the future. You may not be able to exercise control over many aspects of your life but where it is possible to make choices, you should. In the face of the obstacles thrown by fate, [you must maintain] a sense of direction and positioned themselves to make sound choices for themselves. This should be your objective as well.

. . .

The career choice process pictured in Chart 16–1 may help you to visualize the process you will follow to find a job. The entire model is basically a continued narrowing of alternatives until a final decision is reached, from a starting point where the individual has no idea what the final decision will be.

Chart 1
Munneke's Pyramid—Overview of the Process

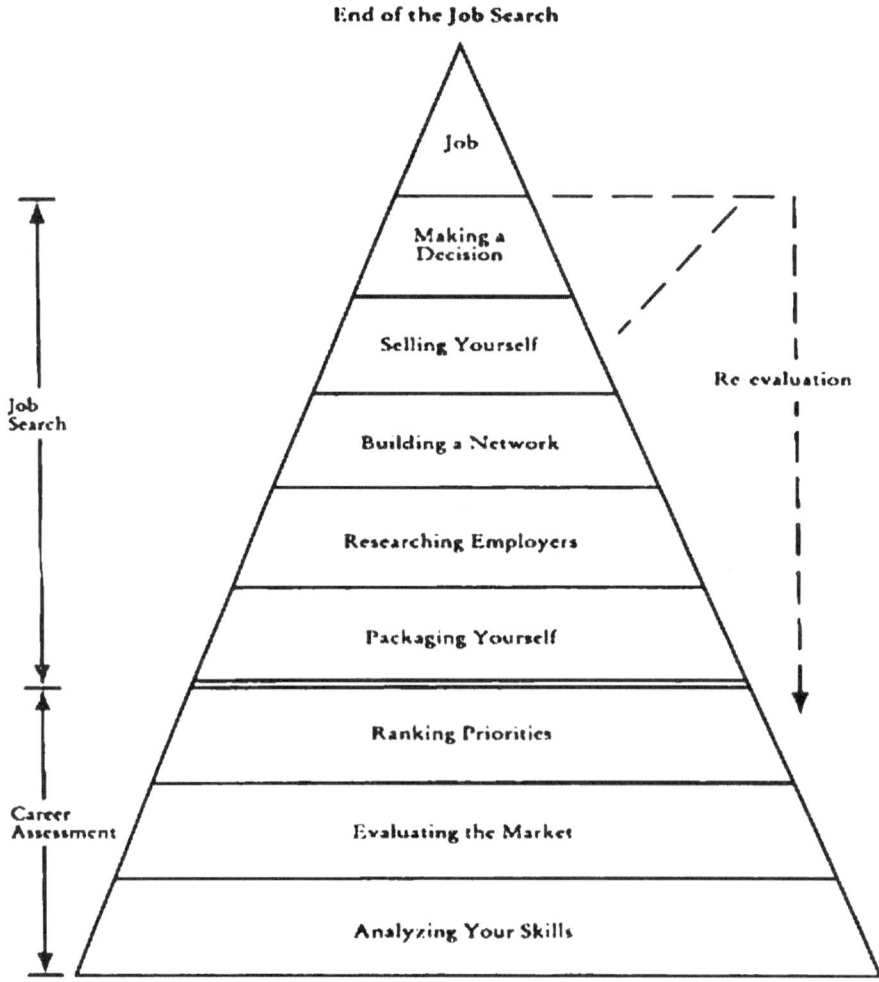

The time frame is flexible. One person may reach the third level by the beginning of the second year in law school. Another may not begin the first level until after graduation. You should allow whatever time is necessary to work through the possibilities, although ideally career assessment should begin during the first year of law school and the job search process no later than the beginning of your last year of law school.

... We avoid the term *planning*, which may infer that some magic formula will allow a person to map out his or her future with a degree of certainty. For most of us, this is simply not possible; much of our fate lies beyond our control. Factors such as economic conditions, luck, and personal handicaps will affect our goals. Career choice, on the other hand, implies ferreting out the best information, making rational decisions based on the best information available, and maximizing opportunities by acting in a timely way.

If you are not sure about which direction your professional life should take, you should allow the time to organize your thoughts. It is undoubtedly better to go through the trauma of uncertainty while you are in law school than to go to work in a position you later discover you do not like, where you have not foreseen what was foreseeable.

There are two distinct parts to the career choice process: career assessment and job search. A fundamental rule is that throughout this book, you will see the terms *career assessment* and *job search*. The first must precede the second. In other words, you have to know what you are looking for if you expect to find it. This sequence may seem obvious, but many people skip the first step, fail to find a satisfying job, and then do not understand why.

From the time you first decide to attend law school until you finally choose a job, you are evaluating, either consciously or unconsciously, the opportunities. That there are so many opportunities is fortunate, yet it is unfortunate that many people either do not investigate or are not aware of the full range of possibilities is unfortunate.

Career assessment . . . involves analyzing your personal and professional skills, which you should think of as interesting and challenging, rather than painful. Only by beginning with a perfectly honest appraisal of yourself can you make this a valid evaluation.

Every law student is unique, and a key to selling yourself is to tap into your own uniqueness. This involves your work and personal experiences, the education and training you have completed, and the skills that you have amassed before and during law school. If you try to market yourself as a commodity, your task will be immeasurably more difficult than if you define yourself as an individual. Knowing yourself will also help you to make choices about job opportunities that are best suited to your special qualities.

After you have undertaken this self-analysis, which is essentially subjective, you should begin evaluating the job market, . . . which is more objective. This step, no less than self-evaluation, requires scrupulous honesty. Here, however, you are required to look outward, to view your environment, and to see things the way they are. You must be able to confront the facts honestly and determine the relative importance of them.

Once again, for this analysis to be most effective and helpful, you must consider the positive as well as the negative. Try to balance your weaknesses against your strengths to get an entirely accurate picture. You may find yourself both expanding and narrowing alternatives by obtaining more options while limiting the areas from which you will eventually make your choice. Your market analysis is going to involve not only research on the facts, but the interpretation of those facts, which leads to the next step: ranking priorities.

By synthesizing the self-analysis and the evaluation, you should be able to generate some options.... If this does not work, you have either not done your research homework or you are not being realistic. Your goal here should be to develop a list of options, ranging from the most desirable situation you could imagine to the bottom line; i.e., what you would find acceptable if worse came to worst. At this point, we are talking about broad categories as opposed to specific positions.

Your job search will involve the pursuit of these options in the order of their priority. In other words, you will focus on the first option first, the second option second, and so forth, through your list. Moreover, as you eliminate options you will need to add new options to the end of the list. Never expend all of your options; there should always be an alternative.

If you have a hard time making up your mind about the appropriate direction for your career, you might need to work on developing decision-making skills. Uncertainty is the element that makes any decision difficult. Even though you can control the decision, you are probably aware that the element of chance influencing the outcome makes it impossible for you to have ultimate control. There will always be a certain amount of risk or chance, but you should try to minimize the degree to which chance affects the outcome.

You should chart a middle course between leaving everything to chance, which could be disastrous, and expecting to eliminate it, which is impossible. In other words, you should know what you want, be well informed of the facts, and be alert for opportunities.

[The next steps involve finding a job], including preparing a good resume, sell[ing] yourself, ... developing good interviewing techniques, securing references, and creating impressive writing samples. How many students would take a final exam cold, with no preparation? Very few. But many students fail to give adequate attention to details prior to beginning the job search, and this is often costly in the long run.

Researching employers ... is hard work for which there is no shortcut. To make a sound decision, you must take affirmative steps to gather relevant information about employers. When your inaction or indecision forecloses an opportunity (for example, letting an application deadline pass), you have forfeited your control of your destiny. Research should be easy for law students, but many forget the same skills they have developed to research a legal problem can be transferred to research on legal employers.

[N]etworking ... is aimed at expanding your opportunities by increasing your contacts with individuals, who may know about career opportunities that would interest you, help you to open doors, and provide support for you. These contacts are your eyes and ears in the world of work. They are your allies in the war against unemployment. Many students claim that they do not have "contacts" in the legal profession. Networking involves developing new contacts, as well as tapping old ones. It requires work to build a network and effort to maintain it. Yet informal channels of information represent a major source of legal jobs that you should not ignore.

.... As you start to apply for specific jobs, begin with your first priority. Either you get a job, or you do not. If not, you turn to the next possibility, and so forth through your list. When you exhaust the employers in your highest priority group, then you move on to the second group, and so on.

The final (and often overlooked) step in the process is making a decision.... If you have only one choice, the decision is easy-yes or no. If you have several choices, then you must sort out the factors to reach a final decision that is best for you in the long run. This is easily said, but not so easily accomplished.

The final [question involves] what to do when even your best-laid plans do not yield the expected results. You might discover in midstream that new skills are required for the position you want. Can you realistically obtain them, or would it be wiser to consider another field? Do the latest statistics show that competition in your chosen area is so fierce as to render it an unrealistic choice for you? What happens when the student (or graduate) goes through the whole job search with no results?

Careful analysis and thorough preparation should help you avoid this situation. However, if it does happen, it is probably best to go back to the beginning and start anew. At this point, you will probably need the help available through the law school career services office. It can be very helpful to talk about your situation with someone who has a broader view of law careers and the current job market.

. . .

Movies often use the devices of flashback and flash-forward to strengthen the plot. A flashback takes the viewer back to a time before the linear clock of the film began, to give the viewer more background or develop a character. The flash-forward lets the audience in on events that have not occurred on-screen, which are unknown to the characters in the film. Much of this section has provided a flashback to help you assess your goals with greater clarity. It might also make sense to flash-forward to look into the crystal ball to glimpse where you want your career to take you.

In the end, you can flash-forward to a job that is personally and professionally rewarding. But that is seldom the end of the story. Your career is an unfolding process, rather than a product, and career patterns evolve over time. The average lawyer will make at least five job changes in a legal career, and many lawyers even more. So the flash-forward you seem to see with clarity may have little to do with the flashback on your career fifty years from now. If you understand this model, the skills and self-awareness you have developed for the job search will help you to make career decisions throughout life, to provide for continued professional development, and to prepare for those unpredictable turns of fate the future may hold for you.

PROBLEMS AND QUESTIONS

1. Why does it make sense to formulate a career plan instead of just letting things happen? How much time does it take to engage in career planning?

2. If you have a career plan and things do not go the way you want or hope, how do you make changes in the plan in order to change directions? What would you do if nothing in your life turned out the way you planned? What new elements could enter the picture that could alter your career plans? Have new opportunities or threats appeared on the horizon since you last spent time thinking about your career? Will new and different strategies be needed to get you where you want to go?

3. What are your personal career goals? What do you want to accomplish as a lawyer? How will you achieve your objectives? Are there things you can do to increase the likelihood of career satisfaction?

4. Do you have a long term career plan? A five year plan? A one year plan? Can you articulate a vision of what you want to accomplish in the legal profession and how you are going to accomplish that vision? Describe your career goals with as great a specificity as you can, following the format provided in Appendix O, page 503, including:
   - where and how you want to practice, who you want to represent,
   - how you will attract and retain those clients,
   - what financial expectations you have, and
   - what skills you possess or develop over the years to reach these goals.

5. You probably have a law school or other professional résumé. Take a look at the résumé in light of what you have learned in this class, and revise it to reflect the professional skill set that make you unique.

6. What insights into your career objectives have you gained over the course of the semester in this class? What management skills will help you advance your professional career?

D. BALANCING LIFE AND WORK

No discussion of professional development would be complete without raising the question of balancing life and work. As a law student, you have worked hard getting through school; you will work hard to pass the bar exam; and you will continue to work hard if you go to work in a law firm or some other legal employer. In a sense, hard work is one of the rites of passage to professional status. Looking at older lawyers, however, one might wonder if it is possible to slow down. Experienced lawyers often find themselves on a treadmill that isolates them from family, friends, community, and simple relaxation. The incidence of divorce, alcoholism, burnout, heart attack, and other products of long-term stress is noticeably prevalent among the population of lawyers. Surveys of lawyers' work habits suggest that many are working harder and enjoying it less than in past decades. In the face of these developments, a number of voices have called out for lawyers to seek to achieve balanced lives. Every law school graduate should contemplate the priorities implicit in achieving personal happiness as well as professional success.

The following excerpt from a New York State Bar Association Task Force reflects the stakes for lawyers in finding balance—or if not balance at least a degree of integration in the personal and work lives. The NYSBA Report offers a variety of suggestions to law firms regarding how they can support efforts of their lawyers, especially younger practitioners, to achieve this elusive goal.

WORK LIFE INTEGRATION AND THE PRACTICE OF LAW

From the Report of the Task Force on the Future of the Legal Profession
New York State Bar Association (2011).

Over the past decade, numerous studies have concluded that organizations that implement policies and programs to support integrating an employee's professional and personal life have directly improved their profitability. There should no longer be a question that a commitment to work-life integration, or work-life balance (which terms are used interchangeably in this Report), is the right thing to do and one that makes economic sense.

The number of lawyers seeking better integration of their work and personal lives has increased in recent years. This is due, in part, to the "sandwich generation" phenomenon—as people live longer, many Generation X (those born between 1965 and 1976) and Baby Boomer lawyers (those born between 1944 and 1964) have responsibility to care for aging parents as well as for their own children.[1] Moreover, although work-life balance began as a women's issue, the increasing number of dual-earner families has made it an issue that impacts both men and women alike. Men are increasingly taking responsibility for the care of their children and elderly parents as well as for other family-related tasks and, in so doing, report dramatically increased work/life conflict.[2] In addition, technology is giving clients and other lawyers increasing access to attorneys

---

1. More than 25% of American families are involved in some way with elder/parent care. Carol Abaya, *The Sandwich Generation*, http://www.thesandwichgeneration.com (last accessed February 14, 2011).

2. Joan Williams, *Reshaping the Work–Family Debate: Why Men and Class Matter.* (Harvard University Press Oct. 1, 2010), see also Galinsky, et al., *Times Are Changing: Gender and Generation at Work and at Home*, 2008 National Study of the Changing Workforce, Family and Work Institute, 2009.

during offhours decreasing truly personal time and making it more difficult to leave the office behind.

It is important to understand that attorneys who seek work-life balance are not necessarily less committed to the practice of law or their clients. Although some attorneys do want to work fewer hours, many are often simply trying to attain more flexibility or predictability in their work responsibilities.

. . .

The lack of a sustainable work-life balance has a negative impact on the attorneys themselves. In recent decades, a plethora of literature has emerged, documenting the emotional toll visited upon significant numbers of practitioners as a result of the current training methods and the present culture of legal work environments. Organizations and employers that fail to adopt and adapt policies to ameliorate these effects, or that do not have written policies in place to do so, may bear the consequences of individuals' declining work product and potential health problems, as well as the associated business costs of attrition. At least thirty years ago, anecdotal evidence began to appear in scholarly articles and bar journals describing the toxic effects of the present physically and emotionally demanding method of educating young lawyers and its carryover into the practice of law.

Two seminal studies address this issue. The first, conducted in 1986, tracked University of Arizona Law School students in the first two years of legal practice.[3] That study was replicated and expanded among Washington lawyers in 1990. Interestingly, there was a high correlation between the Arizona study and the Washington study. Both studies' findings were disturbing.

The 1986 Arizona study found:

As the results indicate, before law school, subjects develop symptom responses similar to the normal population. This comparison suggests that prospective law students have not acquired unique or excessive symptoms that set them apart from people in general. During law school, however, symptom levels are elevated significantly when compared with the normal population. These symptoms include obsessive-compulsive behavior, interpersonal sensitivity, depression, anxiety, hostility, phobic anxiety, paranoid ideation, and psychoticism (social alienation and isolation). Elevations of symptom levels significantly increase for law students during the first to third years of law school. Depending on the symptom, 20–40% of any given class reports significant symptom elevations. Finally, further longitudinal analysis showed that symptom elevations do not significantly decrease between the spring of the third year and the next two years of law practice as alumni.... Specifically, on the basis of epidemiological data, only 3–

---

3. G. Andrew Benjamin, Alfred Kaszniak, Bruce Sales, & Andrew H. Benjamin, et al. *The Role of Legal Education in Producing Psychological Distress Amongst Law Students and Lawyers.* AM. B. FOUND. RES. J. 1986.

> 9% of individuals in industrial nations suffer from depression; pre-law subject group means did not differ from normative expectations. Yet, 17–40% of law students and alumni in our studies suffered from depression, while 20–40% of the same subjects suffered from other elevated symptoms.[4]

These findings were repeated in the Washington study:

> Compared with the 3–9% of individuals in westernized, industrialized countries who suffer from depression, 19% of Washington lawyers suffered from statistically significant elevated levels of depression. Of these individuals, most were experiencing suicidal ideation....
>
> Eighteen percent of the lawyers were problem drinkers. This percentage is almost twice the approximately 10% alcohol abuse and/or dependency prevalence rates estimated for adults in the United States....
>
> While approximately 18% of the lawyers who practiced 2 to 20 years had developed problem drinking, 25% of those lawyers who practiced 20 years or more were problem drinkers.... Alcohol abuse and dependency is a chronic and progressive disease.[5]

Finally, the authors noted that, "it appears from comparing the new Arizona alumni with the similar group of Washington lawyers that the presence of depression, problem drinking, and cocaine abuse is likely to affect lawyers at similar rates, regardless of jurisdiction within the United States."[6]

During the last thirty years, programs to ameliorate depression and alcohol and drug abuse within the legal profession have increased exponentially. Virtually every state in the nation maintains a Lawyer Assistance Program with different organizational structures and levels of support....

Although significant progress has been made in the numbers of attorneys who have benefited from these educational programs and the provision of services through the Lawyer Assistance Program, legal employers have done little to educate attorneys and staff within their organizations as to the prevalence of these diseases. Nor have they structured work environments in such a way as to foster early recognition and treatment of these diseases.

A 2009 NYSBA survey discovered that 80% of the responding law firms had no specific written policies concerning impairment due to depression or alcohol and drug addiction and 20% of the law firms surveyed would not allow leave time for treatment of these diseases.[7] As a

---

4. *Id.*, 246–247

5. G. Andrew H. Benjamin, et al., *The Prevalence of Depression, Alcohol Abuse, and Cocaine Abuse Among United States Lawyers*, 13 INT'L J.L. & PSYCHIATRY 233, 240–241 (1990).

6. *Id.* at 242

7. *See* "Survey Results & Analysis for 2009 HOD Lawyer Assistance Program Law Firm Policy Survey," New York State Bar Association, at 2, 3, Oct. 14, 2009.

result of this survey, the Lawyer Assistance Committee drafted a Model Policy on Impairment intended to be adapted and adopted by law firms or other legal employers[8], which was approved by NYSBA's House of Delegates.[9]

... Work settings that do not address stressors of the modern practice of law will continue to produce a significant number of lawyers who are depressed, dissatisfied with the quality of their lives, spend too little time with their families and communities, continue to be isolated and show increased levels of depression and addictive behaviors.

Stress is always in the background and often in the foreground of work, life and balance issues. Everyone experiences stress, so it is important to remember that stress itself is not debilitating. Too much stress at the wrong time, however, can cause a variety of negative outcomes. Former practitioner George Kaufman offers practical advice to lawyers, whose lives are often filled with stress.

REDUCING STRESS: UNDERSTANDING AND MANAGING THE TIGERS IN OUR HEADS

From *Law Practice Management*, by George W. Kaufman, (October, 2001).

... In our field, we consider the pressures of practice something to be lived with, like a birthmark, rather than something to excise from our lives, like a boil. We are told that the pressures come with the territory and that if we can't stand the heat, we should get out of the kitchen.

Where would we go? Into the arms of another firm or corporate practice? Perhaps the bench or nonprofit law? Maybe public service? The problem is that wherever we might travel, we take ourselves. And if we haven't altered our perspective around the work we do, the stresses of lawyering follow us around like an afternoon shadow.

The primary source of stress derives from the way we practice. Our system encourages adversarial behavior. In the June 21 issue of New York magazine, the cover story, titled "Law Is Hell," says that "life at the city's top firms has become a state of war." Money and power appear to be the aphrodisiacs that lawyers and firms crave. Unfortunately, these short-term fixes offer little stability to lawyers or the law firms where they work. We have only to look at public trials or watch late-night talk shows to hear the way that lawyers interact. We are constantly struggling to get or keep clients, meet unreasonable deadlines, juggle multiple matters and still keep a life. Since we are trained in this process, we perform well.

---

8. *See* "New York State Bar Association Lawyer Assistance Committee Model Policy," New York State Bar Association, Apr. 9, 2010.

9. *See* "New York State Bar Association Resolution Adopted by House of Delegates," New York State Bar Association, Apr. 10, 2010.

Unfortunately, in the very act of our performing, we are unaware of what that performance costs us.

Stress carries a high price tag. Too high. We need to understand what stress is, what stress does and what practical steps we can take to dilute it. Stress is something to be managed, not eviscerated. Simply put, a stressor is anything that throws the body out of balance. It can be a sudden event or just something we anticipate happening. Our response to stress is the way that our body tries to restore balance. When physical danger suddenly appears, several automatic body responses occur. When Cro–Magnon man encountered a saber-toothed tiger in the forest, his body responses were remarkably similar to your own when you encounter what seems a life-threatening situation.

Here's a summary of body changes:

- Adrenaline is released into the body.
- Pupils dilate to let in more light.
- Blood flow to extremities is reduced to minimize bleeding.
- Heart rate increases, carrying oxygen to cells.
- The liver releases stored sugar to meet increased energy needs.
- Digestive organs receive less blood.
- Perspiration increases to cool the body.
- Chemicals release to make the blood clot more rapidly.

Each of these changes is designed to prepare us either to fight or flee from the danger that has caused our body to react. Without these body changes, our chances of survival against external danger would be seriously reduced.

In modern society, of course, most tigers live in our heads. While we still need to deal with external threats when they occur, we have developed our consciousness so that stress responses can be triggered by our thoughts. Since our body doesn't distinguish between real dangers and the dangers we create by thought, it goes through the same physical changes in either case.

In times of danger, the body's response to stress can be a weapon that saves your life. When the danger passes, your body returns to equilibrium. The surges of energy you experienced subside and your metabolism slows. However, when you are feeling anxious on a continual basis, the body keeps trying to arm itself against danger and remain on alert. This type of stress is known as chronic. The body maintains a constant presence of stress hormones. Suddenly, the weapon the body forged to thwart danger has become a weapon turned against itself.

The most unfortunate expression of chronic stress is the wearing down of the body's immunological system. The weakest part of the body becomes the most susceptible to disease. As the body tries to adapt to physiological changes resulting from chronic stress, its resistance is diminished. Here are other by-products of chronic stress:

- Depression
- Insomnia
- Memory loss
- Greater rate of impotence
- More miscarriages
- Elevated blood pressure
- Rapid wearing out of the cardiovascular system

Even though the dangers are obvious, we resist making changes in our behavior until illness strikes us with the swat power of a 2–by–4 block of wood. By then the damage from chronic stress has already occurred. We are too late for prevention and must instead work on repairing the body.

Work can produce an inexhaustible supply of new stressors that keep our body in a state of constant alert. Life goes out of balance as work demands more and more of our waking time. We lose touch with our relationships, our feelings, our ability for self-care and our creativity.

In the long run, we need to find ways of reprioritizing our values and acting in concert with the values we espouse. Those life changes address stress at its source. Perhaps no other endeavor we undertake will be as important—or as hard. Yet when accomplished, no other endeavor will be as life affirming.

That's in the long run. But what can be done today? There are a host of relaxation techniques that chip away at the harmful effects of stress and give us pockets of relief. They are not substitutes for change—just useful palliatives until change happens.

Most of us breathe too rapidly. Our breathing is shallow and primarily takes place in the upper lungs. When we're angry or emotional, we often hold our breath. When we're fearful, we tighten our stomach muscles. This action doesn't let the diaphragm expand into the stomach. Instead, it forces us to breathe from our chests.

Learn to breathe from your diaphragm. Lie down. If you can't lie down, find a place where you can lean back in a chair. By keeping the body straight, the diaphragm has room to expand. Place your left hand on your abdomen and your right hand on your chest. Breathe so that your left hand rises and falls instead of your right hand. If you take deep breaths, your right hand will also begin to rise and fall, but it will do so later and in a less pronounced way.

Breathe in slowly and take deep breaths. After you inhale, hold your breath for a few seconds before exhaling. When you exhale, allow a soft sigh (the sigh of relief) to escape as a way of releasing tension.

Do this for two minutes. If it feels difficult, stop. The object is not to push yourself, but to relax yourself. Find a comfortable way to introduce this type of breathing into your routine. You can catch yourself at moments in the day when you've lost the connection to diaphragmatic breathing. Just take a few deep, slow breaths from the abdomen as a way of remembering this type of breathing. It will slow you down.

When things get busy, we give up pieces of ourselves in favor of work. It takes a catastrophe to surrender even a small part of our workload. While we all need a break in our daily schedules, when we look at our appointments, we find that there's no time.

Try scheduling an appointment with yourself. Consider taking three hours a week—during the workday—just for you. Look at your calendar and find some open spots. You can take the three hours in one shot or spread them out in half-hour modules. (No 10–minute billing cycles, please.) Mark the time in your calendar and let it have the same gravity as a work appointment. If you have to cancel (as you might with business appointments), schedule it at another time.

Plan what you're going to do with your self-appointment when the time comes. It could be going to the gym, reading or taking a walk. You decide. But it can't be work. Finding time is a personal reminder to care for yourself and the beginning step to putting more balance into your daily routine.

Most of the toys we accumulate are expensive. If it's golf or tennis, we trade up as technology and advertising entice us into believing we can be better players by improving our equipment. Meditation is a self-improvement toy that needs no equipment, takes 20 minutes to play and doesn't require a partner or an opponent. Meditation is a space game. When we play, we are finding ways to create space in our lives. We are uncomfortable with empty time and no activity to occupy us. The beauty of meditation is that it provides a way of stepping out of the fast lane.

As a kid, I used to be fascinated with one amusement park ride. You stood in a silo-shaped space and leaned against the wall as the silo turned faster and faster. At a certain speed, you were pinned against the wall and couldn't move. The floor dropped out, but you were stuck in place as though crazy glue was attached to your clothes. Centrifugal force. When we practice law in the fast-forward mode, we are stuck against the walls of work with no way to move. Meditation slows the speed of the moving silo and puts the floor back under us. That practice slows us down and increases relaxation. It facilitates our efforts to take our bodies away from living in a state of chronic stress.

Stress is so common in our culture that the era in which we live has been referred to as the Age of Anxiety and the Century of Stress. It is critical that we find a way to lighten up. The suggestions offered here are just an introduction to a world of relaxation techniques. There are many other ways to practice relaxation—yoga, massage, exercise, saunas, vacations and biofeedback, to name a few. The more experiences you have with these practices, the more tools you will have to offset stress and rebalance how you allocate time.

Multitasking is one of those words that sounds great and feels rotten. Instead of doing several tasks well, we rob a little from each one to avoid failure. Instead of raising the bar of excellence, we see how far it can drop without collapsing.

The anonymity of the telephone, for example, encourages multitasking. We can be speaking to a client while rummaging through our desk, sorting mail, organizing papers and reading e-mails. Don't succumb to this temptation. When you're on the telephone, give your attention to the person at the other end. Your real attention. When the phone rings, take two deep breaths before you answer it. If your secretary transfers your calls, say you'll be on in 15 seconds. Use the time to focus on breathing in deeply and exhaling slowly. Do it twice. The breathing will move you away from the six other things you were doing and bring your attention to the one task now before you. The breathing will ground you in the here and now. When you answer the phone, the caller will have your attention.

When you finish, take two more deep breaths. Don't rush them—or your effort will be wasted. The deep breaths are a way of ending your involvement with the conversation before beginning something else.

Problems and Questions

1. To what extent has the tendency of lawyers to work longer and longer hours affected the following:
   - Credibility with the public as a result of withdrawing from community life?
   - Quality of practice as a result of burnout, substance abuse, and addiction?
   - Balanced lives of lawyers, who sacrifice relationships, families and peace of mind to meet billable hour requirements?
2. How important is it to you to find balance in life and work? If friends, family and relaxation are important to you, what steps will you take to assure that you find time to balance personal considerations with the demands of work?
3. Can effective practice management provide a window of opportunity for lawyers to engage in community leadership and service? How?

E. EPILOGUE

As this course draws to a close, you should think back to the various topics covered in this book. One of the first subjects raised at the outset was how the legal profession generally and the practice of law specifically are changing. If you graduate from law school in 2013 at the age of 25, and you practice law for 40+ years, you will retire in 2053, or later. Of course, some of you will retire sooner, and some considerably later, but the point is that this is a long time. Given the pace of change over the past 40 years, it is reasonable to assume that the profession will continue to change over the course of the next four decades. Succeeding in the practice of law, or whatever career you choose, will require you to effectively manage change.

The late Robert B. McKay, former Dean and Professor at New York University School of Law and a leader in the American Bar Association, once quipped that lawyers tend to face the future by looking consistently at the past. He was alluding not only to our propensity to ignore (and perhaps escape) the future, but also to our particular approach to solving problems by looking at precedent.

As a law student, you are entering a world in flux. Advances in technology, transportation, medicine, and a host of other fields have produced unprecedented in human history. In many ways, these advances have made life more satisfying than in earlier ages. Not everything has changed for the better, however. War and social upheaval are prevalent. The environment is at risk. Complexity has spawned disputes, and the justice system created for an agrarian economy often seems ill equipped to cope with the problems of a technological world.

The legal profession has not avoided problems that face other parts of society. In fact, legal problems permeate virtually every area of business and human relationships. The legal system, and ultimately lawyers, is called upon the help to resolve these myriad problems. Frequently, lawyers are viewed as the cause of the problem, rather than as part of the solution.

The practice of law has changed dramatically as well. The costs of starting and maintaining a law practice, from capital investment to operating expenses have risen dramatically. Competition, from other lawyers, non-legal professional service providers, and electronic resources, has squeezed the average lawyer's ability to generate income. Commodity practices especially face a profitability squeeze. Lawyers have been pushed inexorably toward specialization and boutique practice. This movement has been fueled by increased willingness by clients to see lawyers when they are not satisfied with the results of the service.

Many lawyers report a disatisfaction with life and career over the past several decades. This decline is not a question of money, because over the years most layers have managed to keep up with inflation. Rather, many lawyers claim that they are working more and enjoying it less. The number of hours lawyers put in at the office has increased steadily in recent years. The demands of clients have become more strident and contacts with adverse parties have become less civil. Many lawyers find that they have less time for family, friends, personal interests, community service and pro bono work. Law students are often forced to work to pay the bills, and still emerge from law school with a heavy debt load, which impacts post-graduate quality of life.

This course has been structured to serve as an antidote to the ills of modern law practice. Although a law school class cannot change many of the forces at work in the world that impact on professional and personal life, an examination of how to manage a law practice can provide tools that students can use after they leave school to avoid the pitfalls and exploit the opportunities. Hopefully, you have learned enough about the nature and economics of the practice of law, the skills required to succeed as a lawyer, and insights into your own particular talents to make sound choices about your future options.

One of the most fascinating things about periods of change is the plethora of opportunities. In times of stability, inertia, legacy, tradition and the past dictate who we are and what we can become. In times of change, innovation, creativity, adaptability and novelty, are more likely to assure survival. In such an environment, lawyers who resist change and ostrich-like stick their heads in the sand will find themselves out of touch, out of date and out of work. Lawyers who study and embrace change will find a niche for themselves in the evolving world.

You enter the practice of law with a clean slate. You do not carry the baggage of history like many experienced lawyers do. You are most likely to understand and appreciate the technological tools at your disposal, and to be able to communicate with the clients of tomorrow.

One thing has not changed: there is no substitute for hard work and commitment. You cannot expect good fortune to fall into your lap, or to develop a practice without effort. Whether you choose to practice alone, in a law firm, in a corporation or government agency, in a professional services organization, in a non-profit association, or in a totally non-legal business endeavor, the tools you have gained in this class will help you. They will help you to run your business, or if you are working for someone else to understand how the business is run, they will help you be a manager of the work for which you are responsible, whether legal work for clients, or some other professional service or product. They will help you to perform more effectively and competently in all areas of your life. These skills will help you to forge a personal life as well as a successful career.

Fortunately, you are equipped to enter this brave new world. Unfortunately, thousands of your classmates and hundreds of thousands of former law school graduates are not. In a competitive world, small advantages sometimes produce big differences. The object of this course has been more than to teach you how to run a law firm; the real purpose has been to help you to compete successfully, to get ahead and to achieve satisfaction in life. The end of this class should represent not a conclusion, but a beginning of a process of life long learning. Most pundits suggest that the changes we have witnessed in our lifetimes are just a glimmer of what is yet to come.

Given the diversity of the legal profession, perhaps it is an overgeneralization to speak of lawyers as a group. More likely, some will face the future while others ignore it and hope that it goes away. Hopefully, after taking this course, you will be among the lawyers who look ahead, identify the trends, implement wise choices based on the best information, and achieve success in your practice, whatever form it may take.

Problems and Questions

1. Do you agree with Dean McKay's assessment of lawyers' view of the world? If he is right, will this problem-solving paradigm serve us well in the future or drag us down? Will it keep lawyers from dealing with the future or will it become one of many tools we use to cope with change? If you think he is wrong, how would you describe the way lawyers approach the future?

2. As society becomes more diverse, as the economy becomes more globalized, and as new industries emerge, how will the makeup of the profession evolve? How will law firms accommodate a growing diversity of ethnicity, culture, religion, customs, and laws?

3. What has this course taught you about what lawyers need to do to succeed in a complex and ever-changing world? If you could list the three most important things you have learned, what would they be?

4. Is it time to re-think the economic foundations upon which the practice of law is built? Can precedent-obsessed lawyers ever be forward-thinking enough to reform their own institutions before change forces them to respond?

APPENDIX A

RESOURCES ON LAW PRACTICE MANAGEMENT

■ ■ ■

ABA Center for Professional Responsibility, *Annotated Model Rules of Professional Conduct*, ABA 7th Edition (2011)

*Bilinsky, David J., *Amicus Attorney in One Hour for Lawyers*, ABA (2003)

*Brendan, Ann E. and John D. Goodhue, *Persuasive Computer Presentations: The Essential Guide for Lawyers*, ABA (2003)

Bukics, Rose Marie and Cynthia M. Urbani, *Accounting and Finance for Lawyers: Basic Understandings and Practices*, ABA (1998)

*Cobb, William C., *A Planning Workbook for Law Firm Management*, ABA–LPMS (1985)

*Coleman, Francis T. and Douglas E. Rosenfeld, *Handling Personnel Issues in the Law Office: Your Legal Responsibilities as an Employer*, ABA (1996)

*Coolidge, Daniel S. and J. Michael Jimmerson, *A Survival Guide for Road Warriors: Essentials for the Mobile Lawyer*, ABA (1996)

Cotterman, James D. (Altman Weil, Inc.) ed., *Compensation Plans for Law Firms* 5th Edition, ABA (2010)

Davis, Anthony E., Risk Management: *Survival Tools for Law Firms*, 2nd Edition, ABA (2007)

*Denny, Robert W., Carol Jordan and Sandra Yost, *Keeping Happier Clients: How to Build and Improve Client Relations*, ABA (1991)

Dimitriou, Demetrios, *Law Office Procedures Manual for Solos and Small Firms*, 3rd Edition, ABA (2005).

*Durham, James A., and Deborah McMurray, *The Lawyer's Guide to Marketing Your Practice*, 2nd Edition, ABA (2003)

*Evans, Daniel B., *Wills, Trusts, and Technology: An Estate Lawyer's Guide to Automation*, ABA (2004)

Everett, Pamela I., *Fundamentals of Law Office Management*, West 3rd Edition (2003)

Ewalt, Henry W., *Through the Client's Eyes: New Approaches to Get Clients to Hire You Again and Again*, 3rd Edition, ABA (2008)

Foonberg, Jay G., *How to Get and Keep Good Clients*, 3rd Edition, ABA (2007)

Foonberg, Jay G., *How to Start and Build a Law Practice*, 5th Edition, ABA (2004)

Foonberg, Jay G., *The ABA Guide to Lawyer Trust Accounts*, ABA (2007)

*Freund, James C., *Lawyering: A Realistic Approach to Legal Practice*, Law Journal Seminars—Press (1979)

Gibson, K. William., ed., *Flying Solo*, 4th ed., ABA (2005)

*Giuliani, Peter A. and Duane E. Watts, *Financial Management of Law Firms*, ABA–ELPS (1979)

*Goluboff, Nicole Belson, *Telecommuting for Lawyers*, ABA (1998)

Green, Lawrence G., Managing *Partner 101: A Guide to Successful Law Firm Leadership*, ABA (2001)

*Greenberg, Gary, *How to Build and Manage an Entertainment Law Practice*, ABA (2001)

*Greene, Arthur G. ed., *Getting Started: Basics for a Successful Law Firm*, ABA (1996)

*Greene, Arthur G. ed., *Strengthening Your Firm: Strategies for Success*, ABA (1997)

*Greene, Arthur G., *The Lawyer's Guide to Increasing Revenue: Unlocking the Profit Potential in Your Firm*, ABA (2011)

Greene, Arthur G., and Thomas A. Cannon, *Paralegals, Profitability, and the Future of Your Practice*, ABA (2003)

*John G. Iezzi, *Results Oriented Financial Management*, 2nd ed., ABA (2003)

*Greene, Robert Michael, ed., *The Quality Pursuit*, ABA (1989)

Grella, Thomas C., and Michael L. Hudkins, *The Lawyer's Guide to Strategic Planning: Defining, Setting, and Achieving Your Firm's Goals*, ABA (2004)

*Hamilton, Robert and Richard Booth, Business Concepts for Lawyers, Foundation Press (2002)

*Haserot, Phyllis Weiss, *The Rainmaking Machine*, Shepard–McGraw Hill (2011)

*Hatoff, Howard I., ed., *The Art of Managing Your Support Staff*, ABA (1986)

Hazard, Geoffrey C. and W. William Hodes, *The Law of Lawyering*, 3rd ed., Vol 1 & 2, Prentiss Hall—Law and Business (2011)

Hildebrandt International, *Anatomy of a Law Firm Merger: How to Make or Break the Deal*, 3rd Edition, ABA (2004)

*Hornsby, William E. Jr., *Marketing and Legal Ethics: The boundaries of Promoting Legal Services,* 3rd Edition: The Boundaries of Promoting Legal Services, ABA (2000)

*Jones, Nancy Byerly, *Easy Self-Audits for the Busy Law Office*, ABA (1999)

Kaufman, George W., *The Lawyer's Guide to Balancing Life and Work: Taking the Stress Out of Success*, 2nd Edition, ABA (2006)

*Killoughey, Donna M., *Breaking Traditions: Work Alternatives for Lawyers*, ABA (1993)

Levitt, Carole A., and Mark E. Rosch, *The Lawyer's Guide to Fact Finding on the Internes*, 3rd Edition, ABA (2006)

*Magness, Michael K. and Carolyn Wehmann, eds., *Your New Lawyer*, 2d ed., ABA–LPMS (1992)

Mallen, Ronald L. and Jeffrey Smith, *Legal Malpractice*, 6th ed., Thomson Reuters (2012)

Miller, Bruce W., *HotDocs in One Hour*, 2nd Edition, ABA (2001)

Morgan, J. Harris and Jay Foonberg, *How to Draft Bills Clients Rush to Pay*, 2nd Edition, ABA (2003)

Mosten, Forrest S., *Unbundling Legal Services: A Guide to Delivering Legal Services a la Carte*, ABA (2000)

*Munneke, Gary A., *Seize the Future: Forecasting and Influencing the Future of the Legal Profession*, ABA (2000)

Munneke, Gary A., and Ellen Wayne, *The Legal Career Guide: From Law Student to Lawyer*, 5th Edition, ABA (2007)

*Munneke, Gary A. and Ann L. MacNaughton, *Multidisciplinary Practice: Staying Competitive and Adapting to Change*, ABA (2001)

Munneke, Gary A. and Anthony E. Davis, *The Essential Formbook: Comprehensive Management Tools for Lawyers*, Volumes I–V (with annual supplements) ABA (1999–2007)

Munneke, Gary A., William D. Henslee and Ellen Wayne, *Nonlegal Careers for Lawyers*, 5th Edition, ABA (2006)

Nischwitz, Jeffrey, *Think Again: Innovative Approaches to the Business of Law*, ABA (2007)

Pinson, Linda, *The Lawyer's Guide to Creating a Business Plan: A Step-by-Step Software Package*, ABA (2005)

*Poll, Edward, *Attorney and Law Firm Guide to the Business of Law*, ABA (2002)

*Poll, Edward, *Collecting Your Fee: Getting Paid from Intake to Invoice*, ABA (2002)

*Ramo, Roberta Cooper, *How To Create a System for the Law Office*, ABA (1978)

*Randall, Kerry, *Effective Yellow Pages Advertising for Lawyers: The Complete Guide to Creating Winning Ads*, ABA (2002)

*Reed, Richard, *Beyond the Billable Hour*, ABA (1990)

*Reed, Richard C., *Billing Innovations: New Win–Win Ways to End Hourly Billing*, ABA (1996)

*Reed, Richard C., ed., *Win–Win Billing Strategies: Alternatives That Satisfy Your Clients and You*, ABA (1992)

Riskin, Gerald A., *The Successful Lawyer: Powerful Strategies for Transforming Your Practice* (available in print and audio CD), ABA (2005)

Robertson, Mark, and James A. Calloway, *Winning Alternatives to the Billable Hour: Strategies That Work*, 2nd Edition, ABA (2002)

Roper, Brent D., *Practical Law Office Management*, West 3rd Edition (2006)

Sapp, John R., *Making Partner: A Guide for Law Firm Associates*, ABA 3rd Edition (2006)

Schultz, Jon and Marjorie., *Designing Your Law Office*, ABA (2006)

Shannon, Marcia Pennington and Susan G. Manch, *Recruiting Lawyers: How to Hire the Best Talent*, ABA (2000)

Silkenat, James R. and Jeffrey M. Aresty eds., *The ABA Guide to International Business Negotiations: A Comparison of Cross–Cultural Issues and Successful Approaches*, 3rd Edition, ABA (2009)

Siskind, Gregory H. with Richard P. Klau and Deborah McMurray, *The Lawyer's Guide to Marketing on the Internet*, 3rd Edition, ABA (2007)

Snyder, Theda C., *Women Rainmakers' Best Marketing Tips*, 3d Ed., ABA (2010)

*Somach, Stuart L., *How to Build and Manage an Environmental Law Practice*, ABA (2000)

*Staudenmaier, Heidi McNeil in cooperation with the Maricopa County Bar Association eds., *Changing Jobs: A Handbook for Lawyers in the New Millennium*, 3rd Edition, ABA (2003)

*Stein, Jacob A., *The Law of Law Firms*, Clerk Boardman (1995)

Susskind, Richard, *The End of Lawyers?: Rethinking the Nature of Legal Services* (2009)

*Thornlow, Carolyn, *The ABA Guide to Professional Managers in the Law Office*, ABA (1996)

*Vogt, M. Diane and Lori-Ann Rickard, *Keeping Good Lawyers: Best Practices to Create Career Satisfaction*, ABA (2000)

*Weishar, Hollis Hatfield and James A. Durham, *Marketing Success Stories: Conversations with Leading Lawyers*, 2nd Edition, ABA (2004)

Wert, Robert C. and Howard I. Hatoff eds., *Law Office Policy and Procedures Manual*, 6th Edition, ABA (2011)

*Zwicker, Milton, *Successful Client Newsletters: The Complete Guide to Creating Powerful Newsletters*, ABA (1998)

*Classic Books: Titles marked with an asterisk represent older books that either remain useful or were in their day significant influences on the field of law practice management.

APPENDIX B

SELECTED INTERNET RESOURCES

■ ■ ■

This Appendix includes a number of Internet sites that provide information about law practice management. The list is not intended to be exhaustive, and like everything else on the Internet, law practice management resources are always in flux. The book by Carole A. Levitt and Mark E. Rosch, *The Lawyer's Guide to Fact Finding on the Internet, 3d Edition*, published by the American Bar Association, includes a wide variety of on line resources that lawyers can use, along with guidance on how to navigate the sites.

Association Sites

http://www.americanbar.org (American Bar Association) This is the main site for the ABA, and is probably the largest and most robust legal site in the world. It is possible to drill down through literally hundreds of pages for specialized entities, legal issues, and other information.

http://www.americanbar.org/groups/law_practice_management.html (ABA Practice Management Section) books, periodicals, and law practice management resources, as well as links to events such as the legal technology show, Techshow (see also http://www.techshow.com).

http://www.americanbar.org/groups/gpsolo.html (ABA General Practice Solo and Small Firm Division) This ABA link takes browsers to special resources for small firms and solo practitioners, to help them practice more effectively.

http://www.lexisone.com/practicemanagement/index.html (Lexisone)—This resource targets start-up small firms, with links to management sites and a technology corner.

http://www.americanlawyer.com (American Lawyer Media) ALM is the largest publisher of legal periodicals in the United States, including *American Lawyer*, *The National Law Journal*, and a number of state newspapers for lawyers. ALM also provides many other ancillary products and services for lawyers, including news, newsletters, and conferences, such as the annual *Legal Tech* show in New York.

http://www.alanet.org (Association of Legal Administrators) ALA is an organization comprised of individuals who serve as law firm administrators and other law office professionals. Like the ABA–LPM site, it provides a wealth of information about conferences, periodicals, products and vendors related to law firm management. The site also contains information about local ALA chapters, and career paths in the field.

http://www.law.com/jsp/lawtechnologynews/index.jsp (Law Tech News) This site provides information on the latest products, services and events to help shape a law practice.

http://soholawoffice.com (Small Office Home Attorney) An interesting site on how to get out of the rat race and battle big firms right from your own home.

http://blog.technolawyer.com/technolawyer/index.html (Technolawyer Community) Technolawyer is a free online community legal for technology and business leaders. It provides users the opportunity to share knowledge and experiences about a large collection of products.

http://www.findlaw.com/19lawpractice/lpm.html (Business.com) This interesting search site helps identify law practice management resources from a variety of categories.

http://www.findlaw.com/19lawpractice/lpm.html (Findlaw.com) Findlaw is a large site with a great many resources on legal subjects. The law practice page focuses on legal practice information and material, such as marketing guide and case management guides.

http://www.colpm.org/ (College of law Practice Management) The College of Law Practice Management honors and recognizes distinguished law practice management professionals, sets standards of achievement for others in the profession, and funds and assists projects that enhance the highest quality of law practice management.

(Megalaw.com) This website is devotedto law practice management and legal service resources.

http://www.catalaw.com (Catalaw) Catalaw, as the name evokes, is an on line catalog for legal sites, providing links by means of an on line catalog to a varied group of law related sites.

Various state and local bar associations provide materials on law practice management, and have links to other resources and conferences in this field. These sites may prove helpful to people in the area served by the association. Here are some of the larger bar sites:

- http://www.abcny.org (Association of the Bar Association of the City of New York)
- http://www.nysba.org (New York State Bar Association)
- http://www.texasbar.com (State Bar of Texas)
- http://www.floridabar.org. (Florida Bar Association)
- http://www.calbar.ca.gov. (California State Bar Association)

- http://www.njsba.com. (New Jersey State Bar Association)
- http://www.isba.org. (Illinois State Bar Association)

Software

http://www.adobe.com (Adobe Software) This software allows you to create forms and to alter forms that are found on a lot of web sites, such as court documents that you can prepare for submission.

http://www.microsoft.com (Microsoft Corporation) The basic site for all Microsoft products. This includes all parts of the office suites, as well as the windows update program. Customer support is also provided.

http://www.dell.com (Dell Computers) The website for the most popular providers of computer hardware, is included here not as a recommendation, but as recognition of the volume of business the company handles.

http://www.tigerdirect.com (Tiger Direct) Tiger Direct provides a comprehensive site for anything you would need regarding technology, from built-from-scratch computers to scanners to web cameras.

http://www.critical.com (Critical) This website specializes in computer memory. The site is easy to use to isolate the specifications of particular computer models, which can be very helpful.

http://www.2b1inc.com/timeslips.html (Timeslips) This software allows users to schedule and bill clients for different tasks by assigning them matter numbers.

http://www.worlddox.com (World Dox) World Dox has created indexing software, which allows firms to assign matter numbers to each client and subsequently file all documents created under a particular client.

http://www.abacuslaw.com (Abacus Law) This practice management software helps lawyers organize and simplify their law practice. Abacus can track court dates, statutes of limitation, avoid scheduling conflicts and also has features like Court Rules. Again, inclusion of this site is not an endorsement of the product, but a recognition of its strong position in the marketplace.

http://lawofficesoftware.org (Law Office Software)–Makes customized software tailored to a particular practice.

http://thomsonreuters.com/products_services/legal/legal_products/a-z/ (Pro Law) A site through Thomson–West with special integrated software that unites a lot of different programs to provide communication between different parts of running a law office.

http://www.capterra.com/law-practice-management-solutions (Capterra)— Capterra lists software websites useful for legal office management.

http://www.my.reallegal.com (Real Legal) These discovery and case management tools, and other products seek to make everything in the law office work together.

(Affinity) Affinity is an easy-to-use system that manages billing, invoices, cases, calendaring, contacts, events, notes, research and documents in a single system.

http://www.casewizard.com (Case Wizard) A practice support to that lets lawyers keep documents they create handy, track of other parties in the matter, and records dates and expenses.

(Esq. Ware) This software is designed to be easy to use. It has a case management program, personal case law library, document maker, validity checker, and a program so you can take your info on the road with you too.

http://www.pclaw.com (PClaw.com) PC Law provides products for a number of management functions a law practice needs to function effectively.

General Law Sites and Blogs

http://www.findlaw.com (Findlaw) Mentioned above for its LPM links, Findlaw is a robust site containing resources for students, lawyers, educators, job listings, law reviews. Pretty much everything law related is somewhere on Findlaw.

http://www.westlaw.com (Thomson West) The leading legal search engine for research on cases, codes and other legal information.

https://pm.lexisnexis.com/store/home/?l=1&e=1 (LexisNexis) A competitor of Westlaw.

http://www.martindale.com (Martindale–Hubell) This directory allows users to search for lawyers by location, name, size and practice area; it is useful for job searches as well. See also http://www.lawyers.com.

http://www.nolo.com (Nolo) Nolo provides legal information to consumers who want represent themselves pro se and undertake other self-help legal action. The site itself is rich in general information and frequently asked question sections, as well as products for purchase.

http://www.ilrg.com (Internet Legal Research Group)-This site was established in 1995 to serve as a comprehensive resource of the information available on the Internet concerning law and the legal profession, with an emphasis on the United States of America.

http://www.law.com (Law.com)–A part of the American Lawyer Media empire, law.com lists blogs, legal technology, newsletters, CLE opportunities, products and advertisements. See also http://dictionary.law.com, an online directory of legal terms.

http://www.lawguru.com (Lawguru) Law library, legal search tools, legal forums, legal frequently asked questions, and employment ads.

http://www.legalethics.com (Internet Legal Services) A select group of searchable articles focused on ethics, but at different levels, such as federal, states and courts.

http://www.uslegalforms.com (USLF) Over 36,000 legal documents, as well as form packages, office products, and a bookstore are contained in this site.

http://www.alllaw.com (All Law) All Law provides information about research lawyers, legal organizations, schools, forums, and federal and state resources.

http://www.lectlaw.com ('lectric Law Library) Here is some helpful information on legal topics, geared towards those not in the law business.

http://www.law.net (Law.net) This site has legal forums on web hosting, legal directories, and newsletters.

APPENDIX C

SELECTED MODEL RULES OF PROFESSIONAL CONDUCT

■ ■ ■

As adopted by the American Bar Association House of Delegates, February, 2002

ABA Center for Professional Responsibility http://www.americanbar.org/cpr

[Although in one sense all the Rules of Professional Conduct are relevant to the management of a law practice, those reprinted here represent requirements that lawyers and law firms must address in management systems and policies. Because actual state Rules of Professional Conduct may differ from the ABA Model Rules, readers should consult with the Rules applicable in their jurisdiction. Ed.]

Rule 1.1 Competence

A lawyer shall provide competent representation to a client. Competent representation requires the legal knowledge, skill, thoroughness and preparation reasonably necessary for the representation.

Rule 1.2 Scope of Representation and Allocation of Authority Between Client and Lawyer

(a) Subject to paragraphs (c) and (d), a lawyer shall abide by a client's decisions concerning the objectives of representation and, as required by Rule 1.4, shall consult with the client as to the means by which they are to be pursued. A lawyer may take such action on behalf of the client as is impliedly authorized to carry out the representation. A lawyer shall abide by a client's decision whether to settle a matter. In a criminal case, the lawyer shall abide by the client's decision, after consultation with the lawyer, as to a plea to be entered, whether to waive jury trial and whether the client will testify.

(b) A lawyer's representation of a client, including representation by appointment, does not constitute an endorsement of the client's political, economic, social or moral views or activities.

(c) A lawyer may limit the scope of the representation if the limitation is reasonable under the circumstances and the client gives informed consent.

(d) A lawyer shall not counsel a client to engage, or assist a client, in conduct that the lawyer knows is criminal or fraudulent, but a lawyer may discuss the legal consequences of any proposed course of conduct with a client and may counsel or assist a client to make a good faith effort to determine the validity, scope, meaning or application of the law.

Rule 1.4 Communication

(a) A lawyer shall:

(1) promptly inform the client of any decision or circumstance with respect to which the client's informed consent, as defined in Rule 1.0(e), is required by these Rules;

(2) reasonably consult with the client about the means by which the client's objectives are to be accomplished;

(3) keep the client reasonably informed about the status of the matter;

(4) promptly comply with reasonable requests for information; and

(5) consult with the client about any relevant limitation on the lawyer's conduct when the lawyer knows that the client expects assistance not permitted by the Rules of Professional Conduct or other law.

(b) A lawyer shall explain a matter to the extent reasonably necessary to permit the client to make informed decisions regarding the representation.

Rule 1.5 Fees

(a) A lawyer shall not make an agreement for, charge, or collect an unreasonable fee or an unreasonable amount for expenses. The factors to be considered in determining the reasonableness of a fee include the following:

(1) the time and labor required, the novelty and difficulty of the questions involved, and the skill requisite to perform the legal service properly;

(2) the likelihood, if apparent to the client, that the acceptance of the particular employment will preclude other employment by the lawyer;

(3) the fee customarily charged in the locality for similar legal services;

(4) the amount involved and the results obtained;

(5) the time limitations imposed by the client or by the circumstances;

(6) the nature and length of the professional relationship with the client;

(7) the experience, reputation, and ability of the lawyer or lawyers performing the services; and

(8) whether the fee is fixed or contingent.

(b) The scope of the representation and the basis or rate of the fee and expenses for which the client will be responsible shall be communicated to the client, preferably in writing, before or within a reasonable time after commencing the representation, except when the lawyer will charge a regularly represented client on the same basis or rate. Any changes in the basis or rate of the fee or expenses shall also be communicated to the client.

(c) A fee may be contingent on the outcome of the matter for which the service is rendered, except in a matter in which a contingent fee is prohibited by paragraph (d) or other law. A contingent fee agreement shall be in a writing signed by the client and shall state the method by which the fee is to be determined, including the percentage or percentages that shall accrue to the lawyer in the event of settlement, trial or appeal; litigation and other expenses to be deducted from the recovery; and whether such expenses are to be deducted before or after the contingent fee is calculated. The agreement must clearly notify the client of any expenses for which the client will be liable whether or not the client is the prevailing party. Upon conclusion of a contingent fee matter, the lawyer shall provide the client with a written statement stating the outcome of the matter and, if there is a recovery, showing the remittance to the client and the method of its determination.

(d) A lawyer shall not enter into an arrangement for, charge, or collect:

(1) any fee in a domestic relations matter, the payment or amount of which is contingent upon the securing of a divorce or upon the amount of alimony or support, or property settlement in lieu thereof; or

(2) a contingent fee for representing a defendant in a criminal case.

(e) A division of a fee between lawyers who are not in the same firm may be made only if:

(1) the division is in proportion to the services performed by each lawyer or each lawyer assumes joint responsibility for the representation;

(2) the client agrees to the arrangement, including the share each lawyer will receive, and the agreement is confirmed in writing; and

(3) the total fee is reasonable.

Rule 1.6 Confidentiality of Information

(a) A lawyer shall not reveal information relating to the representation of a client unless the client gives informed consent, the disclosure is impliedly authorized in order to carry out the representation or the disclosure is permitted by paragraph (b).

(b) A lawyer may reveal information relating to the representation of a client to the extent the lawyer reasonably believes necessary:

(1) to prevent reasonably certain death or substantial bodily harm;

(2) to prevent the client from committing a crime or fraud that is reasonably certain to result in substantial injury to the financial interests or property of another and in furtherance of which the client has used or is using the lawyer's services;

(3) to prevent, mitigate or rectify substantial injury to the financial interests or property of another that is reasonably certain to result or has resulted from the client's commission of a crime or fraud in furtherance of which the client has used the lawyer's services;

(4) to secure legal advice about the lawyer's compliance with these Rules;

(5) to establish a claim or defense on behalf of the lawyer in a controversy between the lawyer and the client, to establish a defense to a criminal charge or civil claim against the lawyer based upon conduct in which the client was involved, or to respond to allegations in any proceeding concerning the lawyer's representation of the client

(6) to comply with other law or a court order; or

(7) to detect and resolve conflicts of interest arising from the lawyer's change of employment or from changes in the composition or ownership of a firm, but only if the revealed information would not compromise the attorney-client privilege or otherwise prejudice the client.

(c) A lawyer shall make resonable efforts to prevent the inadvertent or unauthorized disclosure of, or unauthorized access to, information relating to the representation of a client. (As adopted in Resolution 105A Rule 1.6(c)).

Rule 1.7 Conflict of Interest: Current Clients

(a) Except as provided in paragraph (b), a lawyer shall not represent a client if the representation involves a concurrent conflict of interest. A concurrent conflict of interest exists if:

(1) the representation of one client will be directly adverse to another client; or

(2) there is a significant risk that the representation of one or more clients will be materially limited by the lawyer's responsibilities to another client, a former client or a third person or by a personal interest of the lawyer.

(b) Notwithstanding the existence of a concurrent conflict of interest under paragraph (a), a lawyer may represent a client if:

(1) the lawyer reasonably believes that the lawyer will be able to provide competent and diligent representation to each affected client;

(2) the representation is not prohibited by law;

(3) the representation does not involve the assertion of a claim by one client against another client represented by the lawyer in the same litigation or other proceeding before a tribunal; and

(4) each affected client gives informed consent, confirmed in writing.

Rule 1.8 Conflict of Interest: Current Clients: Specific Rules

(a) A lawyer shall not enter into a business transaction with a client or knowingly acquire an ownership, possessory, security or other pecuniary interest adverse to a client unless:

(1) the transaction and terms on which the lawyer acquires the interest are fair and reasonable to the client and are fully disclosed and transmitted in writing in a manner that can be reasonably understood by the client;

(2) the client is advised in writing of the desirability of seeking and is given a reasonable opportunity to seek the advice of independent legal counsel on the transaction; and

(3) the client gives informed consent, in a writing signed by the client, to the essential terms of the transaction and the lawyer's role in the transaction, including whether the lawyer is representing the client in the transaction.

(b) A lawyer shall not use information relating to representation of a client to the disadvantage of the client unless the client gives informed consent, except as permitted or required by these Rules.

(c) A lawyer shall not solicit any substantial gift from a client, including a testamentary gift, or prepare on behalf of a client an instrument giving the lawyer or a person related to the lawyer any substantial gift unless the lawyer or other recipient of the gift is related to the client. For purposes of this paragraph, related persons include a spouse, child, grandchild, parent, grandparent or other relative or individual with whom the lawyer or the client maintains a close, familial relationship.

(d) Prior to the conclusion of representation of a client, a lawyer shall not make or negotiate an agreement giving the lawyer literary or media rights to a portrayal or account based in substantial part on information relating to the representation.

(e) A lawyer shall not provide financial assistance to a client in connection with pending or contemplated litigation, except that:

(1) a lawyer may advance court costs and expenses of litigation, the repayment of which may be contingent on the outcome of the matter; and

(2) a lawyer representing an indigent client may pay court costs and expenses of litigation on behalf of the client.

(f) A lawyer shall not accept compensation for representing a client from one other than the client unless:

(1) the client gives informed consent;

(2) there is no interference with the lawyer's independence of professional judgment or with the client-lawyer relationship; and

(3) information relating to representation of a client is protected as required by Rule 1.6.

(g) A lawyer who represents two or more clients shall not participate in making an aggregate settlement of the claims of or against the clients, or in a criminal case an aggregated agreement as to guilty or nolo contendere pleas, unless each client gives informed consent, in a writing signed by the client. The lawyer's disclosure shall include the existence and nature of all the claims or pleas involved and of the participation of each person in the settlement.

(h) A lawyer shall not:

(1) make an agreement prospectively limiting the lawyer's liability to a client for malpractice unless the client is independently represented in making the agreement; or

(2) settle a claim or potential claim for such liability with an unrepresented client or former client unless that person is advised in writing of the desirability of seeking and is given a reasonable opportunity to seek the advice of independent legal counsel in connection therewith.

(i) A lawyer shall not acquire a proprietary interest in the cause of action or subject matter of litigation the lawyer is conducting for a client, except that the lawyer may:

(1) acquire a lien authorized by law to secure the lawyer's fee or expenses; and

(2) contract with a client for a reasonable contingent fee in a civil case.

(j) A lawyer shall not have sexual relations with a client unless a consensual sexual relationship existed between them when the client-lawyer relationship commenced.

(k) While lawyers are associated in a firm, a prohibition in the foregoing paragraphs (a) through (i) that applies to any one of them shall apply to all of them.

Rule 1.9 Duties to Former Clients

(a) A lawyer who has formerly represented a client in a matter shall not thereafter represent another person in the same or a substantially related matter in which that person's interests are materially adverse to the interests of the former client unless the former client gives informed consent, confirmed in writing.

(b) A lawyer shall not knowingly represent a person in the same or a substantially related matter in which a firm with which the lawyer formerly was associated had previously represented a client

(1) whose interests are materially adverse to that person; and

(2) about whom the lawyer had acquired information protected by Rules 1.6 and 1.9(c) that is material to the matter;

unless the former client gives informed consent, confirmed in writing.

(c) A lawyer who has formerly represented a client in a matter or whose present or former firm has formerly represented a client in a matter shall not thereafter:

(1) use information relating to the representation to the disadvantage of the former client except as these Rules would permit or require with respect to a client, or when the information has become generally known; or

(2) reveal information relating to the representation except as these Rules would permit or require with respect to a client.

Rule 1.10 Imputation of Conflicts of Interest: General Rule

(a) While lawyers are associated in a firm, none of them shall knowingly represent a client when any one of them practicing alone would be prohibited from doing so by Rules 1.7 or 1.9, unless the prohibition is based on a personal interest of the prohibited lawyer and does not present a significant risk of materially limiting the representation of the client by the remaining lawyers in the firm.

(b) When a lawyer has terminated an association with a firm, the firm is not prohibited from thereafter representing a person with interests materially adverse to those of a client represented by the formerly associated lawyer and not currently represented by the firm, unless:

(1) the matter is the same or substantially related to that in which the formerly associated lawyer represented the client; and

(2) any lawyer remaining in the firm has information protected by Rules 1.6 and 1.9(c) that is material to the matter.

(c) A disqualification prescribed by this rule may be waived by the affected client under the conditions stated in Rule 1.7.

Rule 1.15 Safekeeping Property

(a) A lawyer shall hold property of clients or third persons that is in a lawyer's possession in connection with a representation separate from the lawyer's own property. Funds shall be kept in a separate account maintained in the state where the lawyer's office is situated, or elsewhere with the consent of the client or third person. Other property shall be identified as such and appropriately safeguarded. Complete records of such account funds and other property shall be kept by the lawyer and shall be preserved for a period of [five years] after termination of the representation.

(b) A lawyer may deposit the lawyer's own funds in a client trust account for the sole purpose of paying bank service charges on that account, but only in an amount necessary for that purpose.

(c) A lawyer shall deposit into a client trust account legal fees and expenses that have been paid in advance, to be withdrawn by the lawyer only as fees are earned or expenses incurred.

(d) Upon receiving funds or other property in which a client or third person has an interest, a lawyer shall promptly notify the client or third person. Except as stated in this rule or otherwise permitted by law or by agreement with the client, a lawyer shall promptly deliver to the client or third person any funds or other property that the client or third person is entitled to receive and, upon request by the client or third person, shall promptly render a full accounting regarding such property.

(e) When in the course of representation a lawyer is in possession of property in which two or more persons (one of whom may be the lawyer) claim interests, the property shall be kept separate by the lawyer until the dispute is resolved. The lawyer shall promptly distribute all portions of the property as to which the interests are not in dispute.

Revised Rule 1.17 Sale of Law Practice

A lawyer or a law firm may sell or purchase a law practice, or an area of law practice, including good will, if the following conditions are satisfied:

(a) The seller ceases to engage in the private practice of law, or in the area of practice that has been sold, [in the geographic area] [in the jurisdiction] (a jurisdiction may elect either version) in which the practice has been conducted;

(b) The entire practice, or the entire area of practice, is sold to one or more lawyers or law firms;

(c) The seller gives written notice to each of the seller's clients regarding:

(1) the proposed sale;

(2) the client's right to retain other counsel or to take possession of the file; and

(3) the fact that the client's consent to the transfer of the client's files will be presumed if the client does not take any action or does not otherwise object within ninety (90) days of receipt of the notice.

If a client cannot be given notice, the representation of that client may be transferred to the purchaser only upon entry of an order so authorizing by a court having jurisdiction. The seller may disclose to the court in camera information relating to the representation only to the extent necessary to obtain an order authorizing the transfer of a file.

(d) The fees charged clients shall not be increased by reason of the sale.

Rule 5.1 Responsibilities of Partners, Managers, and Supervisory Lawyers

(a) A partner in a law firm, and a lawyer who individually or together with other lawyers possesses comparable managerial authority in a law firm, shall make reasonable efforts to ensure that the firm has in effect measures giving reasonable assurance that all lawyers in the firm conform to the Rules of Professional Conduct.

(b) A lawyer having direct supervisory authority over another lawyer shall make reasonable efforts to ensure that the other lawyer conforms to the Rules of Professional Conduct.

(c) A lawyer shall be responsible for another lawyer's violation of the Rules of Professional Conduct if:

(1) the lawyer orders or, with knowledge of the specific conduct, ratifies the conduct involved; or

(2) the lawyer is a partner or has comparable managerial authority in the law firm in which the other lawyer practices, or has direct supervisory authority over the other lawyer, and knows of the conduct at a time when its consequences can be avoided or mitigated but fails to take reasonable remedial action.

Rule 5.2 Responsibilities of a Subordinate Lawyer

(a) A lawyer is bound by the Rules of Professional Conduct notwithstanding that the lawyer acted at the direction of another person.

(b) A subordinate lawyer does not violate the Rules of Professional Conduct if that lawyer acts in accordance with a supervisory lawyer's reasonable resolution of an arguable question of professional duty.

Rule 5.3 Responsibilities Regarding Nonlawyer Assistants

With respect to a nonlawyer employed or retained by or associated with a lawyer:

(a) A partner, and a lawyer who individually or together with other lawyers possesses comparable managerial authority in a law firm shall make reasonable efforts to ensure that the firm has in effect measures giving reasonable assurance that the person's conduct is compatible with the professional obligations of the lawyer;

(b) A lawyer having direct supervisory authority over the nonlawyer shall make reasonable efforts to ensure that the person's conduct is compatible with the professional obligations of the lawyer; and

(c) A lawyer shall be responsible for conduct of such a person that would be a violation of the Rules of Professional Conduct if engaged in by a lawyer if:

(1) the lawyer orders or, with the knowledge of the specific conduct, ratifies the conduct involved; or

(2) the lawyer is a partner or has comparable managerial authority in the law firm in which the person is employed, or has direct supervisory authority over the person, and knows of the conduct at a time when its consequences can be avoided or mitigated but fails to take reasonable remedial action.

Rule 5.4 Professional Independence of a Lawyer

(a) A lawyer or law firm shall not share legal fees with a nonlawyer, except that:

(1) an agreement by a lawyer with the lawyer's firm, partner, or associate may provide for the payment of money, over a reasonable period of time after the lawyer's death, to the lawyer's estate or to one or more specified persons;

(2) a lawyer who purchases the practice of a deceased, disabled, or disappeared lawyer may, pursuant to the provisions of Rule 1.17, pay to the estate or other representative of that lawyer the agreed-upon purchase price;

(3) a lawyer or law firm may include nonlawyer employees in a compensation or retirement plan, even though the plan is based in whole or in part on a profit-sharing arrangement; and

(4) a lawyer may share court-awarded legal fees with a nonprofit organization that employed, retained or recommended employment of the lawyer in the matter.

(b) A lawyer shall not form a partnership with a nonlawyer if any of the activities of the partnership consist of the practice of law.

(c) A lawyer shall not permit a person who recommends, employs, or pays the lawyer to render legal services for another to direct or regulate the lawyer's professional judgment in rendering such legal services.

(d) A lawyer shall not practice with or in the form of a professional corporation or association authorized to practice law for a profit, if:

(1) a nonlawyer owns any interest therein, except that a fiduciary representative of the estate of a lawyer may hold the stock or interest of the lawyer for a reasonable time during administration;

(2) a nonlawyer is a corporate director or officer thereof or occupies the position of similar responsibility in any form of association other than a corporation; or

(3) a nonlawyer has the right to direct or control the professional judgment of a lawyer.

Rule 5.5 Unauthorized Practice of Law; Multijurisdictional Practice of Law

(a) A lawyer shall not practice law in a jurisdiction in violation of the regulation of the legal profession in that jurisdiction, or assist another in doing so.

(b) A lawyer who is not admitted to practice in this jurisdiction shall not:

(1) except as authorized by these Rules or other law, establish an office or other systematic and continuous presence in this jurisdiction for the practice of law; or

(2) hold out to the public or otherwise represent that the lawyer is admitted to practice law in this jurisdiction.

(c) A lawyer admitted in another United States jurisdiction, and not disbarred or suspended from practice in any jurisdiction, may provide legal services on a temporary basis in this jurisdiction that:

(1) are undertaken in association with a lawyer who is admitted to practice in this jurisdiction and who actively participates in the matter;

(2) are in or reasonably related to a pending or potential proceeding before a tribunal in this or another jurisdiction, if the lawyer, or a person the lawyer is assisting, is authorized by law or order to appear in such proceeding or reasonably expects to be so authorized;

(3) are in or reasonably related to a pending or potential arbitration, mediation, or other alternative dispute resolution proceeding in this or another jurisdiction, if the services arise out of or are reasonably related to the lawyer's practice in a jurisdiction in which the lawyer is admitted to practice and are not services for which the forum requires pro hac vice admission; or

(4) are not within paragraphs (c)(2) or (c)(3) and arise out of or are reasonably related to the lawyer's practice in a jurisdiction in which the lawyer is admitted to practice.

(d) A lawyer admitted in another United States jurisdiction, and not disbarred or suspended from practice in any jurisdiction, may provide legal services through an office or other systematic and continuous presence in this jurisdiction that:

(1) are provided to the lawyer's employer or its organizational affiliates and are not services for which the forum requires pro hac vice admission; or

(2) are services that the lawyer is authorized to provide by federal law or other law or rule to provide in this jurisdiction.

Rule 5.6 Restrictions on Right to Practice

A lawyer shall not participate in offering or making:

(a) A partnership, shareholders, operating, employment, or other similar type of agreement that restricts the right of a lawyer to practice after termination of the relationship, except an agreement concerning benefits upon retirement; or

(b) An agreement in which a restriction on the lawyer's right to practice is part of the settlement of a client controversy.

Rule 5.7 Responsibilities Regarding Law–Related Services

(a) A lawyer shall be subject to the Rules of Professional Conduct with respect to the provision of law-related services, as defined in paragraph (b), if the law-related services are provided:

(1) by the lawyer in circumstances that are not distinct from the lawyer's provision of legal services to clients; or

(2) in other circumstances by an entity controlled by the lawyer individually or with others if the lawyer fails to take reasonable measures to assure that a person obtaining the law-related services knows that the services are not legal services and that the protections of the client-lawyer relationship do not exist.

(b) The term "law-related services" denotes services that might reasonably be performed in conjunction with and in substance are related to the provision of legal services, and that are not prohibited as unauthorized practice of law when provided by a nonlawyer.

Rule 7.1 Communications Concerning a Lawyer's Services

A lawyer shall not make a false or misleading communication about the lawyer or the lawyer's services. A communication is false or misleading if it contains a material misrepresentation of fact or law, or omits a fact necessary to make the statement considered as a whole not materially misleading.

Rule 7.2 Advertising

(a) Subject to the requirements of Rules 7.1 and 7.3, a lawyer may advertise services through written, recorded or electronic communication, including public media.

(b) A lawyer shall not give anything of value to a person for recommending the lawyer's services except that a lawyer may

(1) pay the reasonable costs of advertisements or communications permitted by this Rule;

(2) pay the usual charges of a legal service plan or a not-for-profit or qualified lawyer referral service. A qualified lawyer referral service is a lawyer referral service that has been approved by an appropriate regulatory authority;

(3) pay for a law practice in accordance with Rule 1.17; and

(4) refer clients to another lawyer or a nonlawyer professional pursuant to an agreement not otherwise prohibited under these Rules that provides for the other person to refer clients or customers to the lawyer, if

(i) the reciprocal referral agreement is not exclusive, and

(ii) the client is informed of the existence and nature of the agreement.

(c) Any communication made pursuant to this rule shall include the name and office address of at least one lawyer or law firm responsible for its content.

Rule 7.3 Solicitation of Clients

(a) A lawyer shall not by in-person, live telephone or real-time electronic contact solicit professional employment from a prospective client when a significant motive for the lawyer's doing so is the lawyer's pecuniary gain, unless the person contacted:

(1) is a lawyer; or

(2) has a family, close personal, or prior professional relationship with the lawyer.

(b) A lawyer shall not solicit professional employment from a prospective client by written, recorded or electronic communication or by in-person, telephone or real-time electronic contact even when not otherwise prohibited by paragraph (a), if:

(1) the target of the solicitation has made known to the lawyer a desire not to be solicited by the lawyer; or

(2) the solicitation involves coercion, duress or harassment.

(c) Every written, recorded or electronic communication from a lawyer soliciting professional employment from anyone known to be in need of legal services in a particular matter shall include the words "Advertising Material" on the outside envelope, if any, and at the beginning and ending of any recorded or electronic communication, unless the recipient of the communication is a person specified in paragraphs (a)(1) or (a)(2).

(d) Notwithstanding the prohibitions in paragraph (a), a lawyer may participate with a prepaid or group legal service plan operated by an organization not owned or directed by the lawyer that uses in-person or telephone contact to solicit memberships or subscriptions for the plan from persons who are not known to need legal services in a particular matter covered by the plan.

Rule 7.4 Communication of Fields of Practice and Specialization

(a) A lawyer may communicate the fact that the lawyer does or does not practice in particular fields of law.

(b) A lawyer admitted to engage in patent practice before the United States Patent and Trademark Office may use the designation "Patent Attorney" or a substantially similar designation.

(c) A lawyer engaged in Admiralty practice may use the designation "Admiralty," "Proctor in Admiralty" or a substantially similar designation.

(d) A lawyer shall not state or imply that a lawyer is certified as a specialist in a particular field of law, unless:

(1) the lawyer has been certified as a specialist by an organization that has been approved by an appropriate state authority or that has been accredited by the American Bar Association; and

(2) the name of the certifying organization is clearly identified in the communication.

Rule 7.5 Firm Names and Letterheads

(a) A lawyer shall not use a firm name, letterhead or other professional designation that violates Rule 7.1. A trade name may be used by a lawyer in private practice if it does not imply a connection with a government agency or with a public or charitable legal services organization and is not otherwise in violation of Rule 7.1.

(b) A law firm with offices in more than one jurisdiction may use the same name or other professional designation in each jurisdiction, but identification of the lawyers in an office of the firm shall indicate the jurisdictional limitations on those not licensed to practice in the jurisdiction where the office is located.

(c) The name of a lawyer holding a public office shall not be used in the name of a law firm, or in communications on its behalf, during any substantial period in which the lawyer is not actively and regularly practicing with the firm.

(d) Lawyers may state or imply that they practice in a partnership or other organization only when that is the fact.

APPENDIX D–1

MODEL LLP AGREEMENT

■ ■ ■

_____, L.L.P. A New York State Limited Liability Partnership

This agreement, dated as of the __ day of _____, 20__, by and between [Names of partners] is made with the purpose of forming a limited liability partnership. In consideration of the contributions to be made as provided herein and of these premises, the parties hereto agree as follows:

ARTICLE 1 DEFINITIONS

1.1. <u>Definitions</u>. The following terms shall have the meanings set forth below:

(a) "Act" shall mean the New York Limited Liability Partnership Law.

(b) "Agreement" shall mean this Operating Agreement, as originally executed and as amended from time to time in accordance herewith and with the Act.

(c) "Agreed Value of Contributed Property" means the fair market value of the property at the time of contribution as determined by the partners.

(d) "Articles of Organization" shall mean the Articles of Organization of the Partnership, as filed with the New York Secretary of State, as amended from time to time in accordance herewith and with the Act.

(e) "Bankruptcy of a Partner" shall mean (1) the entry of an order for relief with respect to that partner in a proceeding under the United States Bankruptcy Code, as amended from time to time, or (2) the partner's initiation, whether by filing a petition, beginning a proceeding or in answer to a proceeding commenced by another person, of any action for liquidation, dissolution, receivership or other similar relief, or the partner's application for, or consent to the appointment of, a trustee, receiver or custodian for its assets. For purposes of this definition, a partner's consent shall be treated as given if an order appointing a trustee, receiver or custodian is entered by a court of competent jurisdiction and is not dismissed within ninety days after its entry.

(f) "Capital Contribution" shall refer to the cash, services, property or other assets contributed by the partners to the Partnership. Capital contributions shall be attributed to the contributing partners, and valued as of the date of contribution.

(g) "Capital Interest of a Partner" shall be expressed as a percentage determined by dividing (1) the amount of the balance of the positive Capital Account associated with the partner's Partnership Interest by (2) the aggregate balances of the Capital Accounts of all Partners whose accounts have positive balances, as adjusted through such date in accordance herewith.

(h) "Code" shall mean the Internal Revenue Code of 1986, as amended, or any corresponding provision of any succeeding law.

(i) "Partnership" shall refer to the law firm of _____, L.L.P.

(j) "Fiscal Year" shall mean the Partnership's accounting, tax and fiscal year, which shall be the calendar year.

(k) "Initial Capital Contribution" of a partner shall mean its initial contribution to the capital of the partnership pursuant to this agreement.

(l) "Involuntary Withdrawal of a Partner" shall mean withdrawal as a Partner as a result of an event described in Section 1.1(u) paragraphs (i) & (ii).

(m) "Management Interest" shall mean its right to participate in the management of the business and affairs of the partnership, including any right to vote on, consent to, or otherwise participate in, any decision or action of or by the partners hereunder or under the Act.

(n) "Partner" (collectively "Partners") shall mean each person who (1) executes a counterpart of this Agreement as a Partner as of the date hereof or (2) is admitted as a partner after the date hereof in accordance herewith, provided that, in each case, a partner shall always have a management interest.

(o) "Partnership Interest" shall mean a partner's entire interest in the partnership, including its Capital Interest in the Partnership and Management Interest.

(p) Net Profits and Net Losses shall mean, for each Fiscal Year (or other period for which they are determined), the income and gain, and the losses and deductions of the Partnership, respectively, in the aggregate or separately stated as appropriate, determined in accordance with generally accepted accounting principles consistently applied.

(q) Person shall mean any individual, partnership, limited liability Partnership, corporation, joint venture, trust, association or any other entity, domestic or foreign, and its respective heirs, executors, administrators, legal representatives, successors and assigns where the context of this Agreement so permits.

(r) Transfer shall mean any sale, assignment, transfer, gift, exchange or bequest or other disposition of a Partnership Interest, in any manner, voluntary or involuntary, by operation of law or otherwise but shall not include a pledge, hypothecation or other contingent transfer of rights unless or until such contingency occurs.

(s) Treasury Regulations shall mean regulations promulgated under the Code in effect as of the date hereof or hereafter amended or adopted.

(t) Voluntary Withdrawal of a Partner shall mean its withdrawal as a Partner as a result of an event described in Section 1.1(u) paragraph (vi) or (vii).

(u) Withdrawal Event with respect to any Partner, shall mean its (i) death; (ii) voluntary retirement or withdrawal from the Partnership.

ARTICLE II FORMATION AND BUSINESS OF THE PARTNERSHIP

2.1. Formation. The Partnership was organized on _____, 20__ in accordance with and pursuant to the Act.

2.2. Name. The name of the Partnership is _____, L.L.P. Under that name, Partnership may engage in any business as permitted by applicable law, or under any other name determined from time to time by the partners and according to the New York Code of Professional Responsibility.

2.3. Purpose of the Partnership. The purpose of the Partnership is to engage in the practice of law, and activities incidental thereto, in the State of New York. The Partnership may exercise all powers necessary to or reasonably connected with the Partnership's business from time to time, and may engage in all activities necessary, customary, related or incidental to any of the foregoing. There must be a unanimous vote to change the Partnership's purpose.

2.4. Principal Office. The Partnership's principal place of business shall be located at _____, or such other place determined from time to time by the Partners.

2.5. Partners. The names, addresses and Capital Interests of the Partners are set forth on Exhibit A attached hereto, as amended from time to time.

ARTICLE III PARTNERS

3.1. <u>Liability for Partnership Debt</u>. No Partner shall be personally liable for any debts, losses or obligations of the Partnership by reason of its being a Partner, except to the extent of its Capital Contribution and any obligation to make a Capital Contribution.

3.2. <u>Management by Partners</u>. The property, business and affairs of the Partnership shall be managed by the Partners, who shall have full authority, power and discretion to make all decisions with respect to the Partnership's business, perform any and all other acts customary or incident to such management, and perform other services and activities set forth in this Agreement in accordance herewith and with the Act. Except as otherwise set forth in this Agreement or determined by the Partners, each Partner shall have authority to bind the Partnership with respect to any such act, provided that the Partners have approved it in accordance herewith or with the Act.

3.3. <u>Dealings with the Partnership; Other Business Activity</u>. Subject to the requirements of this Agreement, any Partner thereof may make loans to, borrow from and transact such other business with, the Partnership as may be approved by the Partners in accordance with this Agreement. Loans made pursuant to this Section shall comply with the provisions of Section 4.7. Nothing contained herein shall prevent a Partner from engaging in other related enterprises.

3.4. <u>Meetings of Partners</u>.

(a) The Partners shall meet annually for the purpose of transacting such business as may come before the meeting on the third Tuesday in March, or at such other time as shall be determined by the Partners, at the principal office of the Partnership.

(b) Special meetings of the Partners may be called by any Partner, for any purpose or purposes, unless otherwise prescribed by the Act or the New York Code of Professional Responsibility, and shall be held at such times and places within New York State as the Partners may from time to time determine.

(c) Notice of the time, place and purpose or purposes of each meeting of the Partners and of the first regular meeting under Section 3.4(a) shall be delivered to each Partner entitled to vote at the meeting either personally (including by courier) or by telephone, telegraph, facsimile or first class mail, postage prepaid, addressed to it at its mailing address set forth in Exhibit A attached hereto, not less than ten or more than thirty days prior to the date of the meeting. An affidavit of a Person giving such notice shall, absent fraud, be prima facie evidence that notice of such a meeting has been given. Notice of meeting need not be given to any Partner who, either before or after the meeting, executes a waiver of notice, or who attends such meeting without objecting, at its beginning, to the transaction of any business because the meeting is not lawfully called or convened.

(d) Quorum. Partners holding more than 50% of the Capital Interests shall constitute a quorum at any meeting of Partners. In the absence of a quorum at any meeting of Partners, a majority of such interests so represented may adjourn the meeting from time to time for a period not to exceed sixty days without further notice. If the period of adjournment is for more than sixty days, or if after the adjournment a new record date is fixed, a notice of the adjourned meeting shall be given to each Partner of record entitled to vote at such meeting. At an adjourned meeting at which a quorum shall be present and represented, any business may be transacted that might have been transacted at the meeting as originally noticed. The Partners present at a meeting may continue to transact business until adjournment, notwithstanding the withdrawal during the meeting of a Partner whose absence results in less than a quorum being present.

(e) Manner of Acting. If a quorum is present at any meeting, the vote or written consent of Partners holding at least two thirds of the Capital Interests shall be the act of the Partners, unless the vote of a greater or lesser proportion is otherwise required by the Act, the Articles of Organization or this Agreement.

3.5. Action without Meeting. Any action required or permitted to be taken at any meeting of the Partners may be taken without a meeting, without prior notice and without a vote, if Partners holding voting interests sufficient to authorize such action at a meeting at which all of the Partners entitled to vote thereon were present and voted consent thereto in writing. Such consents shall be delivered to the Partnership by hand or by certified or registered mail, return receipt requested, for filing in the Partnership records. Action taken under this section shall be effective when all necessary Partners have signed a consent, unless the consent specifies a different effective date.

3.6. Participation in Meetings by Telephone and Other Equipment. Partners may participate in a meeting by conference telephone or similar communications equipment, by means of which all persons participating in the meeting can hear each other and, such participation shall constitute presence in person at such meeting.

3.7. Record Dates. For the purpose of determining (a) Partners entitled to notice of, or to vote at, any meeting of Partners, or (b) the identity of Partners for any purpose, the date on which notice of the meeting is mailed, or on which the declaration of such distribution is adopted, as the case may be, shall be the record date for such determination. When a determination of Partners entitled to vote at any meeting has been made as provided in this section, the determination shall apply to any adjournment of the meeting. The record date for determining Partners entitled to take action without a meeting pursuant to Section 3.5 shall be the date the first Partner signs written consent.

3.8. No Preemptive Rights. No Partner shall have any preemptive, preferential or other right with respect to (a) making additional Capital Contributions, (b) the issuance or sale of Partnership Interests by the Partnership, (c) the issuance of any obligations, evidences of indebtedness or securities of the Partnership convertible into, exchangeable for, or accompanied by, any rights to receive, purchase, purchase or subscribe to, any Partnership Interests, or (d) the issuance of any right of, subscription to or right to receive, or any warrant or option for the purchase of, any of the foregoing.

3.9. <u>New Partners</u>. The entrance of new partners into the partnership will be governed by the New York Uniform Partnership Act § 18. In order for a potential partner to be admitted there must be a unanimous vote in favor of the new applicant by all current partners of the firm. If the candidate receives a favorable vote, the individual will be required to purchase its position by an amount to be determined by a unanimous vote by all current partners. The amount will reflect the current value of the firm, but in no case shall the amount be less than the contributions of the original partners (See Section 4.1).

ARTICLE IV CAPITAL; CAPITAL ACCOUNTS

4.1. <u>Initial Capital Contributions</u>. Upon the execution of this Agreement, the Partners shall contribute to the Partnership the cash and property as set forth in Exhibit "A."

4.2. <u>Additional Capital Contributions</u>. Partners shall be required to make the Capital Contributions as set forth in Section 4.1 of this Agreement. No Partner shall be required to make additional Capital Contributions unless required by the vote of Partners holding more than two-thirds in interest to enable the Partnership to continue its business. No Partner shall have personal liability for any obligation of the Partnership.

4.3. <u>No Interest on Capital Contributions</u>. Partners shall not be paid interest on their Capital Contributions.

4.4. <u>Return of Capital Contributions</u>. Except as otherwise provided in this Agreement, no Partner shall have the right to receive any return of any Capital Contribution.

4.5. <u>Form of Return of Capital</u>. If a Partner is entitled to receive a return of a Capital Contribution, the Partnership may distribute cash, notes, property or a combination thereof to the Partner in return of the Capital Contribution.

4.6. <u>Capital Accounts</u>. A separate Capital Account shall be maintained for each Partner. If the Partners determine that the Capital Accounts must be adjusted to comply with Section 704(b) of the Code, then the method in which Capital Accounts are maintained shall be so modified. Any such change in the maintenance of the Capital Accounts shall not materially alter the economic agreement among or between Partners.

4.7. <u>Loans</u>. Any Partner may make or cause a loan to be made to the Partnership in an amount and on such terms as are approved by the holders of two-thirds of the Partnership Interests of the Partners.

ARTICLE V PROFIT, LOSS AND DISTRIBUTIONS

5.1. <u>Distributions</u>. Cash available for distributions shall be distributed at such time and in such amounts as may be determined by the Partners in accordance with the Partnership Interest of each such Partner.

5.2. <u>Limitation on Distributions</u>. No distributions shall be declared and paid unless, after giving effect thereto, the assets of the Partnership exceed the Partnership's liabilities.

5.3. <u>Allocations of Profits and Losses</u>. After giving effect to special allocations as may be required for any taxable year of the Partnership, Profits and Losses shall be allocated to the Partners in accordance with the Capital Interest of each such Partner.

5.4. <u>Offsets</u>. The Partnership may offset all amounts owing to the Partnership by a Partner against any Distribution to be made to such Partner.

5.5. <u>Liquidation and Dissolution</u>. If the Partnership is liquidated, the assets of the Partnership shall be distributed to the Partners in accordance with the balances in their respective Capital Accounts, after taking into account the allocations of Profit or Loss, if any, and distributions if any, of cash or property.

5.6. <u>Amendment</u>. The Partners are hereby authorized, upon the advice of the Partnership's tax advisor, to amend this Article to comply with the Code and the Regulations promulgated under Code Section 704(b) and with the New York Code of Professional Responsibility; provided however, that no amendment shall materially adversely affect distributions to a Partner without the Partner's prior written consent.

ARTICLE VI TAXES

6.1. <u>Tax Status and Returns</u>. The law firm shall be considered as a partnership for purposes of its tax classification. The Partners shall cause to be prepared and filed all necessary Federal, State and local income tax returns for the Partnership. Each Partner shall furnish Partners all pertinent information in its possession relating to Partnership operations that is necessary to enable the Partnership's income tax returns to be prepared and filed.

6.2. <u>Tax Elections</u>. The Partnership shall make the following elections on the appropriate tax returns:

(a) To adopt the calendar year as the Fiscal Year;

(b) To adopt the cash method of accounting and to keep the Partnership's books and records on the income tax method;

(c) If a Distribution as described in Section 734 of the Code occurs or if the Partnership Interest of a Partner is transferred as described in Section 743 of the Code occurs, upon the written request of any Partner, to elect to adjust the basis of the property of the Partnership pursuant to Section 754 of the Code;

(d) To elect to amortize the organizational expenses of the Partnership and the start-up expenses of the Partnership under Section 195 of the Code ratably over a period of sixty months as permitted by Section 709(b) of the Code; and

(e) Any other election that the Partners deem appropriate and in the best interest of the Partnership.

Neither the Partnership nor any Partner may make an election for the Partnership to be excluded from the application of Subchapter K of Chapter 1 of Subtitle A of the Code or any similar provisions of applicable State Law, and no provisions of this Agreement shall be interpreted to authorize any such election.

6.3. Tax Matters Partners. The Partners shall designate one Partner to be the "tax matters partner" of the Partnership pursuant to Section 6213(a)(7) of the Code. Any Partner who is designated "tax matters partner" shall take any action as may be necessary to cause each other Partner to become a "notice partner" within the meaning of Section 6223 of the Code.

ARTICLE VII TRANSFERABILITY

7.1. Restrictions on Transfers. No Partner may Transfer all, or any portion of, or rights in, its Partnership Interest.

7.2. Certain Transfers of No Effect. Any Transfer or attempted Transfer of a Partnership Interest in violation of the terms of this Agreement shall be null and void and have no effect. Each Transferor hereby agrees to indemnify the Partnership and remaining Partners against any and all loss, liabilities and damages arising directly or indirectly out of any Transfer or purported Transfer in violation of this Agreement.

ARTICLE VIII WITHDRAWAL OF A PARTNER

8.1. Right to Withdraw. The Voluntary Withdrawal of a Partner shall be permitted upon three months written notice to the partnership.

8.2. Repurchase of Interest.

(a) If the business of the Partnership is continued in accordance with the provisions of this Agreement after a Withdrawal Event, the Partnership shall repurchase the withdrawn Partner's Partnership Interest at a Purchase Price determined and payable as set forth below. The closing of the purchase price shall take place within ten (10) days after the parties have agreed on the Purchase Price or it has otherwise been determined in accordance herewith.

(b) If the Partnership, acting by its Partners, and the withdrawn Partner or its successor-in-interest, as the case may be, cannot agree upon the purchase price within thirty (30) days after the Partnership receives notice of the Withdrawal Event, the Purchase Price shall be equal to the book value of the withdrawn Partner's equity in the Partnership, computed in accordance with generally accepted accounting principles, as of the end of the Fiscal Year preceding the year in which the Withdrawal Event occurred. Book value shall be determined by the Partnership's accountants, whose determination shall be binding.

(c) Where the Partnership repurchases the Partnership Interest of a Partner who has withdrawn in breach of this Agreement, the purchase price shall be reduced by any amount to be paid by the withdrawn Partner as liquidated damages pursuant to this Agreement.

8.3. <u>Damages for Breach</u>. If a Voluntary Withdrawal Event of a Partner occurs in breach of this Agreement, such withdrawing Partner shall pay to the Partnership within 90 days following the date of the Withdrawal Event the sum of fifteen thousand dollars ($15,000) as liquidated damages for such breach, and not as a penalty, the parties acknowledging that such amount is reasonable in light of the amount of damages that such breach would cause this Partnership.

ARTICLE IX DISSOLUTION AND TERMINATION

9.1. <u>Events Causing Dissolution and Winding Up</u>. The Partnership shall be dissolved and wound up upon the first to occur of the following events:

(a) the written consent of majority in Capital Interest of the Partners;

(b) a Withdrawal Event with respect to any Partner unless the business of the Partnership is continued as provided below. Notice of any Withdrawal Event shall be given to each of the other Partners by the withdrawn Partner or his or its successor-in-interest, if any, within ninety (90) days after the date thereof;

(c) the sale or disposition of all or substantially all of the business or assets of the Partnership; or

(d) the entry of a decree of a judicial dissolution under Section 702 of the Act; or

(e) the end of the stated term (if the duration is other than perpetual).

9.2. <u>Election to Continue the Business of the Partnership</u>.

(a) Notwithstanding the provisions of Section 9.1 of this Agreement, an event specified in Section 9.1(b) shall not result in the dissolution, winding-up and termination of the Partnership, if within one hundred ninety (90) days after the occurrence of any such event, a majority in Capital Interests of the remaining Partners elect in their sole discretion to continue the business of the Partnership. If the business is continued, any remaining Partner that does not vote to do so shall nevertheless continue as a Partner.

(b) If the Partners elect to continue the business of the Partnership, the Partnership shall continue as a limited liability Partnership pursuant to the Act under this Agreement until a subsequent event causing a dissolution hereunder or under the Act, in which event an election as to whether or not to continue the business of the Partnership will again be required.

9.3. Winding up of the Partnership. Upon the dissolution of the Partnership the Partners may, in the name of and on behalf of the Partnership, prosecute and defend suits, whether civil, criminal or administrative, and sell and close the Partnership's business, dispose of the Partnership's property, discharge the Partnership's liabilities and distribute to the Partners any remaining assets of the Partnership, all without affecting the liability of Partners. Upon winding up of the Partnership, the assets shall be distributed as follows:

(a) to creditors, including any Partner who is a creditor, to the extent permitted by law, in satisfaction of liabilities of the Partnership, whether by payment or by establishment of adequate reserves, other than liabilities for distributions to Partners under Section 507 or Section 509 of the Act; and

(b) to Partners and former Partners in satisfaction of liabilities for Distribution under Sections 507 and 509 of the Act; and

(c) to Partners first for the return of their Capital Contributions, to the extent not previously returned, and second respecting their Capital Interests, in the proportions in which the Partners share in Distributions in accordance with this Agreement.

9.4. Termination. Upon completion of the Dissolution, winding up, liquidation and distribution of assets of the Partnership, the Partnership shall be deemed terminated.

9.5. Articles of Dissolution. Within ninety (90) days following the dissolution and commencement of winding up of the Partnership, or at any other time when there are no Partners, Articles of Dissolution shall be prepared, executed and filed in accordance with the Act.

9.6. Nonrecourse to Other Partners. Except as provided by applicable law or as expressly provided in this Agreement, upon dissolution, each Partner shall receive a return of its Capital Account solely from the assets of the Partnership. If the assets of the Partnership remaining after the payment or discharge of the debts and liabilities of the Partnership is insufficient to return the Capital Account of any Partner, such Partner shall have no recourse against any other Partner.

ARTICLE X GENERAL PROVISIONS

10.1. Notices. Any notice, demand or other communication required or permitted to be given pursuant to this Agreement shall have been sufficiently given for all purposes if (a) delivered personally or by facsimile to the party or to an executive office of the party to whom such notice, demand or other communication is directed or (b) sent by registered or certified mail, postage prepaid, addressed to the Partner or the Partnership at his or its address set forth in this Agreement. Except as otherwise provided in this Agreement, any such notice shall be deemed to be given three business days after the date on which it was deposited in a regularly maintained receptacle for the deposit of United States mail, addressed and sent as set forth in this Section.

10.2. Books of Accounts and Records.

(a) At the expense of the Partnership, the Partners shall maintain at the Partnership's principal place of business, records and accounts of all operations and expenditures of the Partnership, including, without limitation, the following records: (i) a current list in alphabetical order of the name and mailing address of each holder of an Interest in the Partnership, their facsimile numbers and with respect to the holders of Interest in the Partnership, their respective shares of Net Profits and Net Losses, or information from which such shares can be derived;

(i) a current list of all IOLA accounts;

(ii) a copy of the Articles of Organization and all amendments thereto, together with executed copies of any powers of attorney pursuant to which any such amendment has been executed;

(iii) copies of the Partnership's Federal, state and local income tax returns and reports, if any, for the three most recent Fiscal Years;

(iv) copies of this Agreement, as in effect from time to time;

(v) any writings or other information with respect to each Partner's obligation to contribute cash, property or services to the Partnership, including, without limitation, the amount of cash so contributed and a description and statement of the value of the property or services so contributed or to be contributed;

(vi) any financial statements of the Partnership for the three most recent Fiscal Years;

(vii) minutes of every annual, special and court-ordered meeting of the Partners; and

(viii) any written consents obtained from the Partners for actions taken by the Partners without a meeting.

(b) Upon ten (10) days advance notice, during normal business hours, any Partner or its representatives may, at its expense, inspect and copy the records described in this Section for any purpose reasonably related to such Partner's Interest.

(c) Notwithstanding any provision of this Agreement, the Partners shall have the right to keep confidential, and not to disclose to the other Partners, (i) information relating to the Partnership reasonably believed by them to be in the nature of trade secrets, (ii) the disclosure of which is in good faith not believed to be in the best interests of the Partnership or (iii) required by law, the New York Code of Professional Responsibility, or by agreement with a third person to be kept confidential.

10.3. Amendments. This Agreement contains the entire agreement among the Partners with respect to the subject matter of this Agreement, and supersedes each course of conduct previously pursued or acquiesced in, and each oral agreement and representation previously made, by the

Partners with respect thereto, whether or not relied or acted upon. No usage of trade, whether or not relied or acted upon, shall amend this Agreement or impair or otherwise affect any Partner's obligations pursuant to this Agreement or any rights and remedies of a Partner pursuant to this Agreement. No amendment to this Agreement shall be effective unless made in writing duly executed by all Partners and specifically referring to the provision of this Agreement being amended.

10.4. Construction. Whenever the singular number is used in this Agreement and when required by the context, the same shall include the plural and vice versa, and the masculine gender shall include the feminine and neuter genders and vice versa.

10.5. Headings. The headings in this Agreement are for convenience only and shall not be used to interpret or construe any provision of this Agreement.

10.6. Waiver. No failure of a Partner to exercise, and no delay by a Partner in exercising, any right or remedy under this Agreement shall constitute a waiver of such right or remedy. No waiver by a Partner of any such right or remedy under this Agreement shall be effective unless made in writing duly executed by all partners and specifically referring to each such right or remedy being waived.

10.7. Severability. Whenever possible, each provision of this Agreement shall be interpreted in a manner as to be effective and valid under applicable law, including the New York Code of Professional Responsibility. However, if any provision of this Agreement shall be prohibited by or invalid under such law, it shall be deemed modified to conform to the minimum requirements of such law or, if for any reason it is not deemed so modified, it shall be prohibited or invalid only to the extent of such prohibition or invalidity without the remainder thereof or any other such provision being prohibited or invalid.

10.8. Binding. This Agreement shall be binding upon and inure to the benefit of all Partners, and each of the successors and assignees of the Partners, except that right or obligation of a Partner under this Agreement may be assigned by such Partner to another Person without first obtaining the written consent of all other Partners.

10.9. Counterparts. This Agreement may be executed in counterparts, each of which shall be deemed an original and all of which shall constitute one and the same instrument.

10.10. Governing Law. This Agreement shall be governed by, and interpreted and construed in accordance with, the laws of the State of New York applicable to the agreements and fully performed therein, and specifically the Act.

IN WITNESS WHEREOF, the entities signing this Agreement below conclusively evidence their agreement to the terms and conditions of this Agreement by so signing this Agreement. _____.

BY: _____
       _____

APPENDIX D-2

MODEL PARTNERSHIP AGREEMENT CHECKLIST

■ ■ ■

From *The Essential Formbook*, by Gary A. Munneke and Anthony E. Davis (1999)

Formation

- Intent of Partners
- Name of Partnership
- Names of Partners
- Addresses of Partner
- Signatures of Partners
- Purpose
- Term
- Principal Place of Business

Capital Contributions

- Original Partners
- Additional Capital
- Subsequent Partners
- Capital Accounts
- Loans to Partnership
- Goodwill

Allocation of Profits/Losses

- Shares/Points
- Formulas
- Two-tiered Partnerships
- Drawing Accounts

Management

- Powers
- Limits
- Committees, Designations

Voting

- Ordinary decisions
- Super-majorities
- Notice
- Meetings
- Proxies
- Adding/Removing partners

Withdrawal

- Voluntary
- Retirement
- Appointment to Bench, Government
- Other Practice Opportunities
- Involuntary
- Permanent Disability
- Suspension, Disbarment
- Bankruptcy
- Expulsion
- Reduction in Force
- Death

- Payments to Partner or Estate
- Capital
- Work on Progress
- Costs and Penalties
- Schedule

Process for Termination of Interest

- Reciprocal Duties
- Notice
- Draw to Date
- Allocation of Profits
- Billing and Collections
- "Gardening Leave"

Dissolution

- Winding Up
- Non–Dissolution if less than ___% leave
- Mediation/Arbitration

Financial

- Books/Accounts
- Method
- Fiscal Year
- Reimbursement of Expenses
- Right of Access to Books

Benefits

- Vacation
- Leave
- Sabbatical
- Retirement Plans

- Other benefits

Other

- Process to Add Partners
- Process to Amend Agreement
- Mediation/Arbitration
- Totality
- Severance
- Best Efforts
- Non-equity Partners
- No Non-compete
- Indemnification
- Fees and Billing
- Governing Law/Rules
- Ethical Practice
- Liability Insurance

Appendix E

Law Firm Questionnaire

■ ■ ■

What is the name of your firm?

Who are the partners?

Describe the special skills, experience and contacts possessed by each of the partners?

What business form will your firm operate under and why?

The casebook states that you will have $20,000 per partner available to finance your Firm.

- Do you think this will be enough?
- Where else will you go to look for capital?

Will the level of investment in the firm effect the voting rights of the partners?

What other factors will contribute to voting on partnership matters?

Will certain matters require a supermajority vote? Which ones?

How will you allocate decision-making authority in the firm?

- Will there be a managing partner, or other designated management responsibilities for specific partners?
- What responsibilities will the partners have to the practice?
- Who will be responsible for:
  ○ Financial matters?
  ○ Staff? Marketing?
  ○ The physical plant?
  ○ Computers and technology?
- Will these responsibilities be defined in the organizational agreement?

What limitations will you impose on individual partners' authority to act on behalf of and bind the firm?

How will you divide the profits and losses from your practice?

- What factors will govern your decisions?

- How will you make these decisions?
- What is your rationale?

What other benefits, in addition to compensation, do you intend to provide for the partners of the firm? How will these benefits be administered?

What accounting method will you use? Why?

What circumstances would lead to a termination of a partner's interest in the firm?

What procedures will you follow to terminate a partner's interest in the firm?

How will you compensate a terminated partner for the value of his/her interest in the firm? Will all terminated partners be treated the same? Why or why not?

How will you handle the clients and work of a terminated partner?

What provisions will you provide for the dissolution of the firm or other unanticipated practice interruption or termination?

How will you handle the responsibilities to the firm's clients in the event of a termination of the firm's practice?

What is your attitude toward long-term growth of the firm? Do you have a vision for the future of the practice?

How will you admit new partners to the firm? What kind of contribution will these new partners be required to make to join the firm?

Will you include permanent associates, staff attorneys, of counsel, and nonequity partners in your structure, in lieu of enlarging the partnership? Why or why not?

Appendix F

Law Firm Marketing Questionnaire

■ ■ ■

Describe the marketplace for legal services in the area where your firm will practice:
- Population/demographics
- Legal needs of the community
- Unique aspects of the local marketplace

Assess the competition:
- Who are the existing legal services providers in the area?
- What clients are well-served by these providers?
- What clients are not served or disserved by these providers?

Review your firm's strengths and weaknesses?
- What experience, talents, skills do lawyers in your firm bring to the table?
- What contacts/relationships do lawyers already have in the community?
- What are the practice interests of the lawyers in the firm (Typically, this is related to the answers to a. and b. above)
- What other resources are at your disposal that will give you a market advantage/leverage?
- What challenges do you face that could keep you from attaining your goals?

What is your market niche; i.e., what segment of the market do you propose to own? (Typically, this is related to the answers to 1., 2., and 3. above.)
- Describe your niche in terms of clients served and services provided.
- How will your practice be differentiated from those of other service providers?
- Message Platform: How will you succinctly articulate your niche to those not in the firm ("Our firm does _____.)

Explain what you will do to attract and retain the clients you expect to represent:

- Theme or concept
- Strategic marketing objectives (Specific things you can do to achieve your overall marketing goals; see the Marketing Checklist)
- Timetable
- Responsibility and accountability
- Resources required

Describe how you will assess the success of your marketing plan

Appendix G

Human Resources Plan Checklist

■ ■ ■

Who are the partners in your firm?

What specific responsibilities do they have for the management of the firm?

- Supervision of legal delivery staff (secretaries, paralegals)?
- Administrative assignments?
- Firm Management?
    - Finances?
    - Compensation/Benefits?
    - Human Resources?
    - Technology?
    - Strategic Planning?
    - Facilities?
- Client Relations?
- Marketing?

Describe your use of employed lawyers to leverage your services and enhance profitability? If you do not anticipate starting your practice with lawyer employees, what are your long range plans for recruiting and utilizing lawyers in the firm?

- Associates
- Of counsel, contract and other senior lawyers

Describe the support staff that you will require at start-up. How do you think your needs will change over time?

- Legal assistants
- Legal secretaries
- Law clerks
- Receptionists
- Bookkeepers

- Filing clerks, process servers, other clerical

Will you hire professional staff to handle management functions in the firm. If so, what positions will these professionals hold?
- Office manager?
- Information/Technology?
- Human Resources/Recruiting?
- Other employees ? (describe):_____

What functions will you outsource to contract services or consultants? Why?

Will you create a staff manual for the office, including:
- Policies and procedures?
- Job descriptions?
- Substantive Work Assignments?
- Compensation and Benefits?
- Disciplinary Procedures and Sanctions?
- Vacations and Leave Policies?
- Opportunities for Promotion and Professional Growth?
- Organizational chart?
- Other matters? (describe):

Describe the hiring process for your firm. Will the process be different for lawyers than it is for support staff? If so, how?
- Who interviews?
- How interviewed?
- Hiring Decisions:
    - Who makes them?
    - How are they made?

Describe how new employees in the firm are trained and evaluated:
- Orientation?
- Training:
- Who conducts training?
    - Training models:
    - Work Assignment/Feedback
    - Case Meetings
    - In-house Training
    - Continuing Education
    - Other? (describe):
- Evaluation:

- Frequency?
- Oversight of evaluation process?
- Who conducts the evaluation?
- Content of the evaluation?
- Employee input?
- Grievance/challenge mechanism?

How will you handle the discipline and termination of employees who do not meet standards?

- Procedures and process?
    - Grounds for disciplinary action?
    - Protection of employee rights?
    - Protection of the organization?
- Disciplinary actions
    - Warnings
    - Informal reprimand
    - Formal reprimand
    - Probation
    - Reduction of pay or rank
    - Docked pay or fine
    - Discharge for cause
    - Termination procedures
    - Payments to terminated employees

Describe the legal considerations that will you address in your human resources policies and procedures:

- Fair Labor Standards Act?
- Equal Employment Opportunity?
- Sexual Harassment in the Workplace?
- Occupational Safety and Health?
- Worker's Compensation
- Employees with Disabilities?
- Other (describe):

APPENDIX H–1

PHYSICAL RESOURCES PLAN (LAW OFFICE)

■ ■ ■

Describe the type of space your firm will use for its offices:
- Multi-story office building with general tenants?
- Lawyer suite within office complex?
- Sublease from a client, business, or another law firm?
- Converted residential property?
- Mall or suburban office property?
- Home office?
- Virtual office?
- Other (describe):

Prepare an illustrated floor plan for your law office, including:
- Client areas
- Work areas
    - Legal personnel
    - Support personnel
    - Administrative personnel
- Equipment/filing areas
- Conference space
- Reception
- Client flow patterns
- Security and protection of confidentiality
- Other areas (describe):

Where will your office be located?

Describe how your office will provide access the following:
- Clients, including those with disabilities?
- Courts and offices important to the firm's service?

- Parking and/or public transportation?

What will your office space cost?

$_____$/sq. ft. x No. sq. ft. _____ = Annual cost: $_____

- Building class
- Improvements, Carpeting
- Amenities
- Improvements, services, taxes and utilities not incorporated in the lease or mortgage
    - Janitorial
    - Maintenance
    - Security
    - Other (describe):

How will you finance your office space?

- Lease
    - Deposit: $_____
    - Monthly: $_____
    - Terms:_____
- Mortgage
    - Down Payment: $_____
    - Amount of mortgage: $_____
    - Interest rate: _____%/year
    - Number of years:_____
- Other? (describe):

APPENDIX H–2

PHYSICAL RESOURCES PLAN (EQUIPMENT AND FURNITURE)

■ ■ ■

What will be the cost of furniture and equipment for your office, including:

- Acquisition?
- Operation?
- Service/maintenance?
- Upgrades?
- Replacement?

How do you plan to finance the furniture and equipment for your office?

- Purchase?
- Lease?

Who will make decisions about what furniture and equipment to acquire:

- The Partners?
- Administrators?
- Consultants?
- Sales personnel?
- Research recommendations (e.g., books, magazines, blogs)

How will you evaluation vendors and products

- Stability/Longevity
- Training
- Support
- Value
- RFP
- Tax considerations

Describe the actual office equipment your firm will need to function efficiently, using the following categories as a guide:

(EQUIPMENT AND FURNITURE)

- Copiers
    - Digital
    - Multi-function
    - Collating, stapling
- Telephones
    - Centrex or other call management system
    - Wireless
    - Cellular
    - Smartphone
    - VOIP
- Fax (facsimile)
- Scanning, imaging
- Dictation/messaging
- Audiovisual
- Postage machine
- Safe
- Other (describe):

Describe your firm's computer system and network. To the extent that it is integrated with other office equipment, please indicate.

- Hardware
    - System, peripherals
    - Server(s)
    - Desktops
    - Laptops, tablets
    - Smartphones, PDAs
    - Network
    - Monitors
    - Fax/modem
    - Printers
    - DVD or other storage devices
    - Audio
    - Video
    - Backup
    - Other (describe):
- Software
    - Operating System

Appendix H-2

- ○ Office Suite
- ○ Word processing
- ○ Spreadsheet
- ○ Database
- ○ Personal Information Manager (calendar, contacts)
- ○ Presentation, graphics
- ○ Document assembly
- ○ Desktop publishing
- ○ Time and billing
- ○ Case/project management
- ○ Docket control/calendar
- ○ Client Database
- ○ Conflicts Checking
- ○ Records
- ○ Customer Relationship Management
- ○ Accounting, financial management
  - \> Accounts receivable
  - \> Accounts payable
  - \> Payroll
  - \> General ledger
  - \> Check writing
  - \> Client trust accounts
- ○ Communications/electronic mail
- ○ Substantive practice systems
- ○ Utilities
- ○ Antivirus, spam filter
- ○ Other (describe):

What furnishings will your office require?

- • Furniture
  - ○ Desks
  - ○ Chairs
  - ○ Tables
  - ○ Bookcases
  - ○ File cabinets
  - ○ Other (describe):

- Office furnishings:
  - Art, sculpture
  - Decoration (e.g., plants, fish, photos, documents)

Describe how you will address the following considerations in your office.
- Ergonomics and comfort of work stations
- Lighting
- Staff lounge, including kitchen/bar
- Firm Image
- Other (describe):

What supplies will your firm need in order to operate equipment and deliver legal services?

Appendix I

Model Law Office Floor Plan

■ ■ ■

Model Law Office Floor Plan

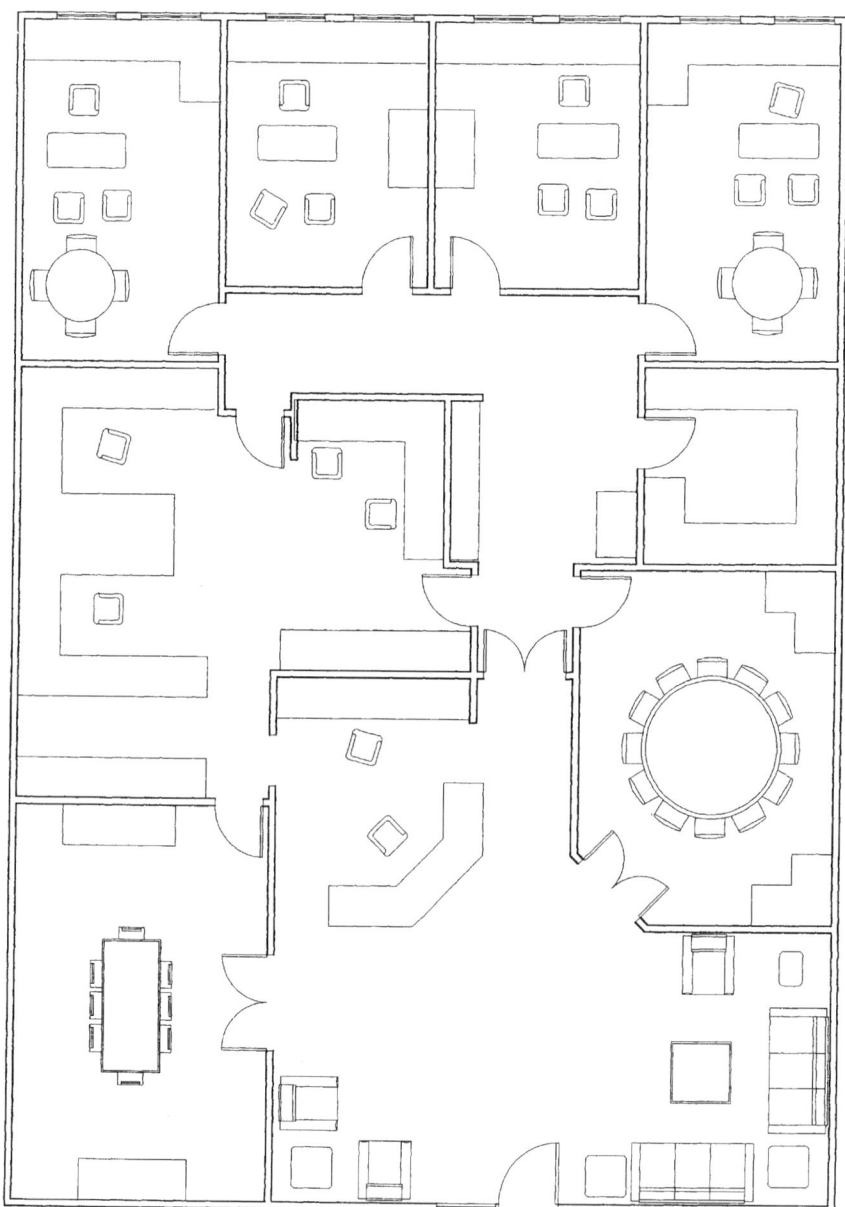

APPENDIX J

INFORMATION RESOURCES PLAN CHECKLIST

■ ■ ■

Who in the firm will make decisions about information resources?
- Who approves publications/orders?
- Who maintains information resources?

What electronic/on line resources will the firm use?
- Westlaw, Lexis
- Other search engines
- CD/DVD–ROM products
- Other online databases (describe):

What print resources will the firm retain?
- Professional journals
- Newspapers, magazines
- Jurisdictional materials
  - Rules of court
  - Statutes, or statutes annotated
  - Digest(s)
  - Pleadings and practice materials
- Reference materials
  - Forms
  - Continuing education materials
  - Directories

Describe your firm's Internet access, use, and data security protection

If you have a dedicated library/information resource center, what specific space will you need?
- Shelving
- Seating

- Administration
- Cost of space

What is the estimated cost of these information resources?
- Initial cost
- Update cost(s)
- Management costs
- System to charge research to clients

APPENDIX K

FINANCIAL PLAN CHECKLIST

■ ■ ■

Startup:
- Capital contribution(s)
- Financing
  - Amount(s)
  - Terms/conditions
  - Repayment philosophy vs. distributions to partners
- Cash on hand
- Startup expenses
  - Equipment
  - Supplies
  - Deposits
  - Licenses, permits
  - Insurance
  - Other (describe):
- Beginning Operating Balance: _____

Operating Expenses:
- Employee compensation
  - Salaries
  - How set?
  - How adjusted?
  - How frequently adjusted?
  - Grievance procedure
  - Benefits
  - Insurance
    - > Life
    - > Health

- > Dental
- > Disability
- > Unemployment
- > Social Security
- ○ Parking
- ○ Memberships
- ○ Special programs
- ○ Vacation, leave
    - > Vacation days
    - > Sick days
    - > Holidays
    - > Personal leave
    - > Medical leave
    - > Parental leave
    - > Sabbatical
- ○ Bonuses, incentives
- ○ Training, education
- Contract services
    - ○ Professional Fees
    - ○ Accounting
    - ○ Information technology
    - ○ Other (describe):
    - ○ Cleaning
    - ○ Security
    - ○ Other (describe):
- Office space
    - ○ Financing
    - ○ Lease
    - ○ Purchase
    - ○ Other (describe):
    - ○ Amenities
    - ○ Signage
    - ○ Maintenance
    - ○ Security
    - ○ Utilities
        - > Phone

- > Electrical, fuel
- > Water
- > Other (describe):
- Taxes
    - ○ Income (if corporate form)
    - ○ Property
    - ○ Other (describe)
- Insurance
    - ○ Malpractice
    - ○ General liability
    - ○ Property
    - ○ Business interruption
    - ○ Loss of key person
- Acquisition of new assets
    - ○ Equipment
    - ○ Furniture
    - ○ Art, Decoration
    - ○ Depreciation of capital assets
- Supplies
- Postage and express mail
- Information services
    - ○ Books
    - ○ Subscriptions
    - ○ Internet
    - ○ Other (describe):
- Marketing and entertainment
    - ○ Travel
    - ○ Client expenses
- Continuing education
    - ○ CLE for lawyers
    - ○ Training and education for staff
- Other, describe:

Fees and Income:
- Fee structure
    - ○ Hourly
    - ○ Hours worked by each lawyer

- ○ Billing rate of each lawyer
- ○ Write-offs and write-downs
- ○ Flat fees
- ○ Contingent fees
- ○ Blended or other value-based fees (describe):
- ○ Referral fees
  - ○ Outgoing
  - ○ Incoming
- ○ Reasonableness of fees under MR 1.5
  - ○ Reasonable to client
  - ○ Reasonable to attorney
  - ○ Reasonable to court
- ○ Written fee agreement
- • Billing structure
  - ○ Frequency of billing
  - ○ Form of billing
  - ○ Collecting accounts receivable
    - > Followup procedures
      - * 30–days
      - * 60–days
      - * 90–days
      - * Beyond 90 days
        - - Collection agencies
        - - Liens
        - - Negotiation and settlement
        - - Arbitration
        - - Lawsuit against client
      - * Write off as uncollectible
  - ○ Delay in collecting contingent fees
  - ○ Problem clients
  - ○ Interface with firm's accounting system
  - ○ Realization
  - ○ Value billing
  - ○ Basis for value billing structure
    - > Responsibility
    - > Expertise

- > Productivity
- > Risk
- > Blended Fees
- > Client-centered billing
  - Gross revenue from fees
  - Non-fee revenue (describe):
  - Reimbursements of client costs
  - Client trust accounts
  - Non-billable time

Budgeting and Planning:
  - Assumptions/Rationale/Discoveries
  - 2-Year period covered
  - Cash flow analysis
    - Final result after 2 years
    - Positive cash flow
    - Negative cash flow
    - Debt
      - > retired
      - > unretired
  - Profit and loss statement
  - Balance Sheet
    - Assets
    - Liabilities
    - Net Worth
  - Other considerations (describe):

Compensation of Owners:
  - Profits
    - Distribution
    - Retained earnings
    - Reinvestment
    - Credit/borrowing considerations
  - Draws of partners
    - Against what? (revenue/profits/billings)
    - How adjusted?
    - How frequently adjusted?

- Profit-sharing considerations
  - Who is eligible?
  - How much/how earned?
  - When earned?
  - When paid?
  - Contributions
    - > Partner
    - > Employee
  - Retirement plan
  - Other (describe):

APPENDIX L

MODEL LAW FIRM FINANCIAL REPORTS

■ ■ ■

Appendix L
Model Law Firm Financial Reports

Report # 1

The following example illustrates a typical summary of the basic start-up expenses and capital needed to start a three-attorney law firm.

Initial Capitalization	**Start-Up Expenses**
Partner # 1	$ 20,000
Partner # 2	20,000
Partner # 3	20,000
Bank Loan	100,000
Total Capitalization	**$ 160,000**

Start-Up Costs

Rent Security Deposit	$ 4,000
Desks & Chairs	2,100
Computers (5)	11,000
Laser Printers (5)	3,000
Fax (2)	1,200
Paper Shredder	200
Telephone System (6 lines)	3,000
Copy Machine	5,600
Sofa and Chairs (Reception area)	900
Stationary	800
Office Supplies	600
Tables/Chairs (Conference Room)	2,000
Artwork/Plant Service	400
Kitchen Accessories	500
Bookshelves (4)	640
Filing Cabinets (8)	1,600
Advertising	4,000
Miscellaneous	5,000
Total Expenses	**$ 46,540**
Available Cash on Hand	**$ 113,460**

Report # 2

The following example illustrates the typical projected revenue for the three-lawyer firm over a two year period.

Projected Revenue
Year 1

	1st Qtr	2nd Qtr	3rd Qtr	4th Qtr	Total Year
Hourly Rate	$160	$160	$160	$160	
Projected Average Billable Hours (3 Lawyers)	0	492	711	981	2184
Fees Billed/Earned	0	78,720	113,760	156,960	349,440
Less 5% Uncollectable	0	3,936	5,688	7,848	17,472
Total Fees Earned	**0**	**74,784**	**108,072**	**149,112**	**331,968**

Projected Revenue Year 2

	1st Qtr	2nd Qtr	3rd Qtr	4th Qtr	Total Year
Hourly Rate	$160	$160	$160	$160	
Projected Average Billable Hours (3 Lawyers)	941	960	988	1,018	3,907
Fees Billed/Earned	150,530	153,540	158,146	162,891	625,107
Less 5% Uncollectable	7,526	7,677	7,907	8,145	31,255
Total Fees Earned	**143,003**	**145,863**	**150,239**	**154,746**	**593,852**

Report # 3

The following example illustrates a typical summary of operating expenses for the three-lawyer firm which includes two secretaries. It assumes, also, that computers for the firm and a copier will be depreciated using the straight line method over a five year period. The first year always includes the start-up costs.

Projected Expenses
Year 1

	Start-Up	1st Qtr	2nd Qtr	3rd Qtr	4th Qtr	Total Yr. Including Start-Up	Total Yr. Excluding Start-Up
Support Salaries (2 Secretaries)		10,000	10,000	10,000	10,000	40,000	40,000
Benefits		2,400	2,400	2,400	2,400	9,600	9,600
Professional Fees		2,000	2,000			4,000	4,000
Accountant		500	500	500	500	2,000	2,000
Malpractice Insurance		3,000	3,000	3,000	3,000	12,000	12,000
Rent Security Deposit	4,000	6,000	6,000	6,000	6,000	28,000	24,000
Insurance		750	750	750	750	3,000	3,000
Desks & Chairs	2,100					2,100	0
Computers (5)	11,000	200	200	200	200	11,800	800
Computer Depreciation		550	550	550	550	2,200	2,200
Laser Printers (5)	3,000	320	300	300	300	4,220	1,220
Fax (2)	1,200	200	200	150	150	1,900	700
Paper Shredder	200					200	0
Telephone System (6 lines)	3,000	750	650	600	600	5,600	2,600
Copy Machine	5,600	240	200	250	270	6,560	960

Copier Depreciation						1,120	1,120
Sofa and Chairs (Reception area)	900					900	0
Stationary	800	280	280	280	280	1,300	500
Office Supplies	600	200	100		200	1,525	925
Tables/Chairs (Conference Room)	2,000	200	225	200	300	2,000	0
Artwork/Plant Service	400	150	150	150	150	1,000	600
Kitchen Accessories	500	200	200	150	150	1,200	700
Bookshelves (4)	640					640	0
Filing Cabinets (8)	1,600					1,600	0
Advertising/Promotions	4,000	300	200	600	600	5,700	1,700
Miscellaneous	5,000	1,000	1,000	1,000	1,000	9,000	4,000
Postage/Federal Express		300	300	200	250	1,050	1,050
Internet/West Law/AOL		300	350	450	500	1,600	1,600
Monthly Loan		3,931	3,931	3,931	3,931	15,724	15,724
Travel & Entertainment		2,000	1,500	1,000	2,000	6,500	6,500
Training (CLE and Computer)			1,500	2,000	2,000	5,500	5,500
Legal Books		3,000		3,000		6,000	6,000
Subscriptions		600		200		800	800
Total Expenses	**46,540**	**39,371**	**36,486**	**37,861**	**36,081**	**196,339**	**149,799**

APPENDIX L

Report # 4

The following example illustrates a typical summary of operating expenses for the second year of the three-lawyer firm which includes two secretaries. It assumes, also, that computers for the firm and a copier will be depreciated using the straight line method over a five year period. The expenses have been increased by 4% for inflation or adjusted when, anticipated to occur.

Projected Expenses/Pro Forma Statement
Year 2

	1st Qtr	2nd Qtr	3rd Qtr	4th Qtr	Total Year
Support Salaries (2 Secretaries)	10,500	10,500	10,500	10,500	42,000
Benefits	2,520	2,520	2,520	2,520	10,080
Professional Fees	3,000	2,000		1,000	6,000
Accountant	520	520	520	500	2,060
Malpractice Insurance	3,120	3,120	3,120	3,120	12,480
Rent/Security Deposit	6,000	6,000	6,000	6,000	24,000
Insurance	780	780	780	780	3,120
Desks & Chairs					0
Computers (5)	208	208	208	200	824
Computer Depreciation	550	550	550	550	2,200
Laser Printers (5)	333	333	333	333	1,331
Fax (2)	208	208	208	150	774
Paper Shredder					0
Telephone System (6 lines)	780	780	780	780	3,120
Copy Machine	250	250	250	250	998
Copier Depreciation	280	280	280	280	1,120

Sofa and Chairs (Reception area)					0
Stationary	208	208	150	200	766
Office Supplies	208	234	208	312	962
Tables/Chairs (Conference Room)					0
Artwork/Plant Service	156	156	156	156	624
Kitchen Accessories	208	208	208	208	832
Bookshelves (4)					0
Filing Cabinets (8)					0
Advertising/Promotions	312	300	624	700	1,936
Miscellaneous	1,000	1,000	1,000	1,000	4,000
Postage/Federal Express	200	250	200	250	900
Internet/West Law/AOL	350	375	450	550	1,725
Monthly Loan	3,931	3,931	3,931	3,931	15,724
Travel & Entertainment	2,000	1,900	2,000	2,200	8,100
Training (CLE and Computer)		1,500	2,000	2,000	5,500
Legal Books	1,000		2,000		3,000
Subscriptions	600		300		900
Total Expenses	**39,221**	**38,110**	**39,275**	**38,469**	**155,077**

Report # 5

The following example illustrates the Profit/(Loss) statement for the 3 attorney law firm. It includes the assumptions of the Revenue (Fees Earned) and Expenses from prior schedules.

Profit/(Loss) Statement
Year 1

	Start-Up	1st Qtr	2nd Qtr	3rd Qtr	4th Qtr	Total Yr. Including Start-Up	Total Yr. Excluding Start-Up
Fees Earned/Received	0	0	78,720	113,760	156,960	349,440	349,440
Less 5% Uncollectable	0	0	3,936	5,688	7,848	17,472	17,472
Total Collectable Fees	**0**	**0**	**74,784**	**108,072**	**149,112**	**331,968**	**331,968**
Support Salaries (2 Secretaries)		10,000	10,000	10,000	10,000	40,000	40,000
Benefits		2,400	2,400	2,400	2,400	9,600	9,600
Professional Fees		2,000	2,000			4,000	4,000
Accountant		500	500	500	500	2,000	2,000
Malpractice Insurance		3,000	3,000	3,000	3,000	12,000	12,000
Rent Security Deposit	4,000	6,000	6,000	6,000	6,000	28,000	24,000
Insurance		750	750	750	750	3,000	3,000
Desks & Chairs	2,100					2,100	0
Computers (5)	11,000	200	200	200	200	11,800	800
Computer Depreciation		550	550	550	550	2,200	2,200
Laser Printers (5)	3,000	320	300	300	300	4,220	1,220
Fax (2)	1,200	200	200	150	150	1,900	700

Paper Shredder	200				200	0
Telephone System (6 lines)	3,000	750	650	600	5,600	2,600
Copy Machine	5,600	240	200	270	6,560	960
Copier Depreciation		280	280	280	1,120	1,120
Sofa and Chairs (Reception area)	900				900	0
Stationary	800	200	100	200	1,300	500
Office Supplies	600	200	225	300	1,525	925
Tables/Chairs (Conference Room)	2,000		200		2,000	0
Artwork/Plant Service	400	150	150	150	1,000	600
Kitchen Accessories	500	200	200	150	1,200	700
Bookshelves (4)	640				640	0
Filing Cabinets (8)	1,600				1,600	0
Advertising/Promotions	4,000	300	200	600	5,700	1,700
Miscellaneous	5,000	1,000	1,000	1,000	9,000	4,000
Postage/Federal Express		300	300	200	1,050	1,050
Internet/West Law/AOL		300	350	450	1,600	1,600
Monthly Loan		3,931	3,931	3,931	15,724	15,724
Travel & Entertainment		2,000	1,500	1,000	6,500	6,500
Training (CLE and Computer)			1,500	2,000	5,500	5,500
Legal Books		3,000		3,000	6,000	6,000
Subscriptions		600		200	800	800
Total Expenses	**46,540**	**39,371**	**36,486**	**37,861**	**196,339**	**149,799**
Profit & (Loss)	**(46,540)**	**(39,371)**	**38,298**	**70,211**	**135,629**	**182,169**

Report # 6

The following example illustrates the Profit/(Loss) statement for the three-attorney law firm during its second year. It includes the assumptions of the Revenue (Fees Earned) and expenses from prior schedules.

Profit/(Loss) Statement
Year 2

	1st Qtr	2nd Qtr	3rd Qtr	4th Qtr	Total Year
Fees Received	150,530	153,540	158,146	162,891	625,107
Less 5% Uncollectable	7,527	7,677	7,907	8,145	31,255
Total Collectable Fees	**143,004**	**145,863**	**150,239**	**154,746**	**593,852**
Support Salaries (2 Secretaries)	10,500	10,500	10,500	10,500	42,000
Benefits	2,520	2,520	2,520	2,520	10,080
Professional Fees	3,000	2,000		1,000	6,000
Accountant	520	520	520	500	2,060
Malpractice Insurance	3,120	3,120	3,120	3,120	12,480
Rent/Security Deposit	6,000	6,000	6,000	6,000	24,000
Insurance	780	780	780	780	3,120
Desks & Chairs					0
Computers (5)	208	208	208	200	824
Computer Depreciation	550	550	550	550	2,200
Laser Printers (5)	333	333	333	333	1,331
Fax (2)	208	208	208	150	774
Paper Shredder					0

494 MODEL LAW FIRM FINANCIAL REPORTS

Telephone System (6 lines)	780	780	780	780	3,120
Copy Machine	250	250	250	250	998
Copier Depreciation	280	280	280	280	1,120
Sofa and Chairs (Reception area)					0
Stationary	208	208	150	200	766
Office Supplies	208	234	208	312	962
Tables/Chairs (Conference Room)					0
Artwork/Plant Service	156	156	156	156	624
Kitchen Accessories	208	208	208	208	832
Bookshelves (4)					0
Filing Cabinets (8)					0
Advertising/Promotions	312	300	624	700	1,936
Miscellaneous	1,000	1,000	1,000	1,000	4,000
Postage/Federal Express	200	250	200	250	900
Internet/West Law/AOL	350	375	450	550	1,725
Monthly Loan	3,931	3,931	3,931	3,931	15,724
Travel & Entertainment	2,000	1,900	2,000	2,200	8,100
Training (CLE and Computer)		1,500	2,000	2,000	5,500
Legal Books	1,000		2,000		3,000
Subscriptions	600		300		900
Total Expenses	**39,221**	**38,110**	**39,275**	**38,469**	**155,077**
Profit/(Loss)	**103,782**	**107,753**	**110,963**	**116,277**	**438,775**

Report # 7

The following example illustrates the Cash Flow Statement for the three-attorney firm. The Beginning Fund in Year # 1 refers to the $100,000 bank loan plus the $20,000 investment by each of the three partners. The Distribution in Year 2 assumes each partner will take out $60,000 as profit/income.

Cash Flow Analysis
Year 1

	Start-up	1st Qtr	2nd Qtr	3rd Qtr	4th Qtr
Beginning Fund (Capitalization)	160,000	113,460	74,089	112,387	182,598
Revenue (Fees earned)	0	0	74,784	108,072	149,112
Operating Expenses	(46,540)	(39,371)	(36,486)	(37,861)	(36,081)
Ending Balance	**113,460**	**74,089**	**112,387**	**182,598**	**295,629**

Cash Flow Analysis
Year 2

	Distribution	1st Qtr	2nd Qtr	3rd Qtr	4th Qtr
Beginning Fund Balance	295,629	160,000	263,782	371,545	482,509
Distribution to Partners	122,066	—	—	—	—
Retained Earnings	13,563	—	—	—	—
Revenue (Fees Earned)	—	143,003	145,863	150,239	154,746
Operating Expenses	—	(39,221)	(38,110)	(39,275)	(38,469)
Ending Balance	**160,000**	**263,782**	**371,545**	**482,509**	**598,786**

Report # 8

Balance Sheet
End of Year 1

Assets		Amount
Cash on Hand		295,269
Accounts Receivable (90 day collections)		149,112
Prepaid Rent		4,000
Furniture		7,240
Computer Equipment	11,000	
Less Accumulated Dep. (5 yr. SL)	(2,200)	
Computer Equipment		8,800
Office Equipment	7,400	
Copier	5,600	
Less Accumulated Dep. (5 yr. SL)	(1,120)	
Copier		4,480
Legal Books		6,000
Total Assets		**434,221**

Liabilities

Long-Term Debt (bank loan to be paid)		93,800
Initial Capital		
Partner # 1		20,000
Partner # 2		20,000
Partner # 3		20,000
General Payables (1 yr/12)		16,362
Total Liabilities		**170,162**

Net Worth/Equity

Total Assets		434,221
Total Liabilities		(170,162)
Total Net Worth		**305,099**

Report # 9

Balance Sheet
End of Year 2

Assets			Amount
	Cash on Hand		360,747
	Accounts Receivable (90 day collections)		150,239
	Prepaid Rent		4,000
	Furniture		7,240
	Computer Equipment	8,800	
	Less Accumulated Dep. (5 yr. SL)	(2,200)	
	Computer Equipment		6,600
	Office Equipment	7,400	
	Copier	4,480	
	Less Accumulated Dep. (5 yr. SL)	(1,120)	
	Copier		3,360
	Legal Books		6,000
	Total Assets		**538,186**

Liabilities			
	Long-Term Debt (bank loan to be paid)		86,965
	Initial Capital		
	Partner # 1		20,000
	Partner # 2		20,000
	Partner # 3		20,000
	General Payables (1 yr/12)		12,923
	Total Liabilities		**150,888**

Net Worth/Equity		
	Total Assets	538,186
	Total Liabilities	150,888
	Total Net Worth	**387,298**

Report # 10

The following schedule illustrates what each partner would get if they choose to draw a salary at the end of the year. The partners do not have to withdraw all profits, but can leave a certain percentage in as retained earnings which is reinvested for future growth.

Partnership Possible Draws
Year 1

	Amount
Year 1 Net Profit	135,629
10% to Retained earnings	13,563
Available for Draw	122,066
# of Partners	3
Share Per Partner	**$40,689**

Year 2

	Amount
Year 2 Net Profit	438,775
10% to Retained earnings	43,878
Available for Draw	394,898
# of Partners	3
Share Per Partner	**$131,633**

Appendix M

Substantive Practice System Checklist

■ ■ ■

Substantive System:

Describe the system for handling clients for one of the substantive areas that your firm will practice, including the following elements:
- Initial contact with the client
- Assignment of personnel to particular tasks
- Timing of tasks
- Performance of tasks (how done?)
- Contact back to client
- Retention or non-retention of the client
- Client interview or other information gathering
- Alternatives courses of action available
- Courses of action presented to client
- Client counseling
- Action items
- Exit interview
- Closing the file

Develop a flow chart to illustrate the system you just described.

Do you know about any software product(s) that you will be able to use with this system?

Document Assembly System:

Describe how your firm will produce one central document in your substantive system, including:
- Boilerplate language or template
- Standard clauses
- Special/specific clauses
- Case specific information

What instructions will you provide to help users to prepare this document
- How to use?
- When to use?
- Examples

What client, research or other extrinsic data will need to be incorporated into the document in order to make it case specific?

To what additional resources will you refer users who need help?

<u>Administrative Support Systems</u>:

Describe how your firm will handle each of the following administrative support functions in the substantive practice system you described above
- Calendar/Docket Control/Tickler System
- Filing and Retrieval System
- Conflicts Checking System
- Timekeeping/Billing System
- Client Trust Accounting System

How are these functions uniquely applied in your substantive system?

<u>Litigation Support System</u>:

Is your substantive system fundamentally a transactional practice system, a litigation system, or does it include elements of both? Explain your answer.

Will your firm handle litigation within the firm, or will you refer cases out to litigation specialists?

What will you do during the course of your representation of clients to protect their interests and rights in the event of litigation?

Appendix N

Student Experience and Skills Survey

■ ■ ■

Please complete the following survey of your background and experiences, as they relate to the course in Law Practice Management. If any of this information is confidential, that is, you do not wish it to be mentioned in class, please indicate on this form.

Name _____ E-mail:_____

Phone: _____(W) _____(H) _____(M)

What is your educational background?

- Degree?
- Professional certification?

Have you worked in a law firm?

- If so, how long?
- In what capacity?

Have you worked in another legal environment (e.g., corporate legal dept.)?

How long? In what capacity?

Have you owned or operated a business? What kind? What products/services did the business produce?

Have you held a management position in a business? How long? What kind of position? What fields?

- General organizational management
- System design and analysis
- Computers/IT
- Web design/e-commerce
- Human resources
- Benefits
- Staff supervision
- Tax/accounting
- Budgeting/strategic planning

- Economic modeling
- Writing/editing
- Marketing/advertising
- Sales
- Architecture/space design
- Real estate
- Information/knowledge management
- Teaching/training
- Other (describe)

Why did you take this course?

What do you expect to get out of it?

APPENDIX O

CAREER PLAN CHECKLIST

■ ■ ■

Please take a look at the following questions and return your answers to me electronically no later than Thursday, April 19, along with the most current copy of your resume. As you answer these questions, think about the individual questionnaire you filled out at the beginning of summer, the readings in Chapter 13 of the casebook, and our class discussions about trends in the practice of law. Try to limit your responses to no more than two sentences that capture the essence of your answers.

Name _____ E-mail:_____

Describe your post-law school career objective. In other words, what do you plan to do for the next couple of years after you graduate?

How has the economic outlook for the legal job market affected the decisions you have made about your career plans?

Describe why an employer should hire you, or if you plan to pursue entrepreneurial pursuits how you would convince potential investors that you are a good risk. In other words, what unique skills do you bring to the table that set you apart from other students?

What impediments to reaching your goals do you envision and what can you do to enhance your marketability?

What have you learned in this class about the practice of law and your own personal management skills that will help you in both the short term and long term with respect to your career?

Looking back at the Student Experience Survey you completed at the beginning of this course, what insights have you gained that will help you in the future?

When you die (hopefully, not soon), what would you like for the writer of your obituary to say about what you accomplished in life?

APPENDIX P

PROFILE OF WINTERS & SOMMERS, LLP

■ ■ ■

Winters & Sommers (W & S) is a prominent law firm with nine offices in seven U.S. states, including New York, California and Florida. W & S has approximately 600 lawyers, about half of whom practice at the firm's "home" office in Manhattan. Of the lawyers in the firm, there are 175 equity partners, another 60 non-equity partners, 15 lawyers who are designated as "of counsel," and the remaining 350 are associates.

W & S is also affiliated with Abogados Pastorales (AP), a law firm of 100 lawyers headquartered in San Jose, Costa Rica, with offices in Panama, Nicaragua, Honduras Guatemala and Belize. AP is organized as a closed corporation, with 20 members and 80 employed lawyers. AP is not too different from W & S fifteen years ago; it provides a number of somewhat unfocused services to a diverse but loyal client base. AP has grown much more deliberately than W & S, adding roughly 5 new associates each year, of whom 2–3 will become members.

Because W & S is so large, it is governed by a Management Committee comprised of fifteen lawyers, who are elected to three year terms, five members being elected each year, to which they may be re-elected once. The Management Committee separately elects a Chair each year, and the Chair can be re-elected an unlimited number of times. When the Chair is selected from the ranks of the Committee, another partner is elected to fill the new Chair's term on the Committee. The current Chair, Stormfield "Stormy" Weathers, has served in the position for the past 15 years, and despite occasional complaints from the dissidents, no one has challenged Weathers for the top spot.

W & S is a New York Limited Liability Partnership. The agreement, which is signed by all new equity partners, provides the basic governance structure for W & S. Among the features of the agreement are a lockstep system[1] for base compensation, a formula-based bonus system (factoring in billable hours, revenue generation, and client origination), and capital

---

1. A lockstep system, used by many firms establishes a base pay for all lawyers who joined the firm in a particular year; thus all the lawyers who are hired in 2012 will earn $160,000, and each year thereafter their raises are identical. Two lawyers who were hired in 1982 will still earn the same base salary. The bonuses that individual lawyers receive, on the other hand, will vary significantly.

contribution requirements based on a percentage of the net worth of the firm. All equity partners have one vote, but because of the size of the partnership most decisions are made by the Management Committee and ratified by the entire partnership. The non-equity partners are compensated according to a separate lockstep system (lower than the equity partners), and they receive smaller bonuses based solely on hours billed.

W & S recruits heavily for superstar prospects. These efforts generate several hundred applicants for the firm's summer associate program, out of which approximately 50 accept positions each year. Although summer associates are given interesting assignments and their work is reviewed for quality, it is generally assumed that anyone who makes it through the rigorous interview process possesses the intellectual and other skills to succeed at W & S. The summer program is realistically designed as an extended recruiting effort, an approach that has proven quite successful over the years. Starting salaries are competitive with other major New York firms ($160,000 USD in 3012). W & S conducts a rigorous training program for new associates in order to assure their early productivity at the firm. Associates are expected to bill 2,200 hours to client matters annually, and those who do not meet this expectation do not stay at the firm. Many of those who eventually are offered partnership regularly bill more than the 2,200 hour expectation.

Associates are also compensated under the lockstep system, with minimal bonuses recommended by their supervisors. Associates are eligible for equity partnership after eight years, but they may elect to withdraw from the equity partnership track at any time before their up-or-out year. If they withdraw, they are eligible to be considered for non-equity partnership in their ninth year, or later, if they have taken extended leave or worked part-time for an extended period. Historically, for every twenty new associates hired, two will become equity partners, one will become a non-equity partner, and 17 will leave the firm (most of these between years three and five).

Although women make up approximately half of the population of law students in the U.S., and W & S has hired approximately 50% women for the past decade, the attrition of women lawyers exceeds the attrition of males in the firm. Out of four associates being considered for equity partnership in the current year, none are women. So many women elect to pursue the non-equity partnership track that it is sometimes referred to as the "mommy track," because women who elect to have children often find this career path preferable to the demands of the equity track. Additionally, more women choose part-time work over full-time work, and others do not return to W & S at all after parental leave.

W & S has grown from about 50 lawyers in the early 1990s to its present size through a series of planned acquisitions and mergers. By hiring lateral partners to strengthen its core practice areas, while at the same time absorbing boutique firms in areas that complement the firm's core practice, W & S has managed to become a full-service corporate law firm.

The acquisition strategy has proven exceptionally productive for establishing branches in cities where W & S clients have legal needs. Mergers with somewhat smaller local firms has eliminated competition, while giving W & S a presence in the new location in much less time than it would take to build a branch office from the ground up. The acquisition process has also served as an occasion to get rid of less productive partners and practice areas at the acquired firms.

The client base of W & S has also evolved over the years. In 1990, the firm handled a few mid-sized corporations, many start-ups, and a variety of seemingly unrelated clients with a various needs. Prior to 1990, the partners, particularly a handful of rainmakers,[2] brought in new clients without much institutional attention to developing a coherent identity. The genius of Stormy Weathers as Chair of the Management Committee was that he recognized that the firm could not survive in a competitive environment by reacting to the marketplace; rather W & S needed to figure what services it would provide and develop a clientele for those services. Acting strategically, W & S now represents a solid lineup of medium-sized companies, and an increasing number of Fortune 100 companies, providing a carefully crafted lineup of services. Over the next decade, W & S plans to build client relationships with more of the top companies, and to get more businesses from those they already represent.

In recent years, the profit per partner at W & S has hovered at around $750,000, which is in line with other large New York firms, although not as high as some. This is considerably more than the profit per partner at the outset of Stormy Weathers' term as Management Committee Chair, when W & S began its current cycle of growth. Some lawyers complain that the billable hour requirements for associates and the demands of client development for partners has produced an unhealthy atmosphere at the firm, but no one wants to go back to the less profitable economic picture prior to 1990.

---

2. The term "rainmaker" refers to a lawyer who is able to attract new clients for the firm—a reference no doubt to native American medicine men whose magic could bring rain to water crops necessary for the survival of the tribe.

INDEX

References are to Pages

Accounts Receivable, 71
Administrative Lawyers, 188
Administrative Staff (see Support Staff)
Advertising (see Marketing)
Age Distribution of Lawyers, 19
Agency, 157
Alternative Dispute Resolution ("ADR"), 43
Alternative Fee Assignments (AFA), 8
Americans with Disabilities Act ("ADA"), 173
Ancillary Business, 6
Andrews, Lori (*Birth of a Salesman*), 129
Associate Lawyers, 36, 37, 61, 62, 63, 184–85
Association of Corporate Counsel, 101
Attorney–Client Relationship (see Lawyer–Client Relationship)
Balanced Life, 404
Benefits (see Human Resources Elements, Compensation and Benefits)
Boilerplate (see Practice Systems, Templates)
Bureau of Labor Statistics, 16, 17
Business Form (see Partnership)
Business Management, 4, 97
Business Plan (see Financing a Practice)
Business/Profession, 4, 39, 58
Business School Education, 97
Capital (see Financial Resources)
Career Paths, 386–88
Case Management, 357
Cash/Cash on Hand, 71
Client–Centered Lawyering (see Client Service)
Clients
    Base, 36–87
    Control, 156, 358
    Focus on, 315–16
    Relations, 167
    Satisfaction, 120, 156, 158, 159
    Service, 156
Clifford Chance, 17
Cloud Computing, 246, 252
Compensation (see Partner Compensation or Support Staff Compensation)
Competence, 291, 360, 384
Competition, 21, 103, 148
Commoditization, 32–33
Communication, 82, 162, 164, 375
Compensation of Owners/Partners, 35, 76
Computer Systems (see Technology)
Consultants, 141, 253, 294
Contract Lawyers, 188

Continuing Legal Education ("CLE"), 145, 150, 382, 383
Costs of Recruiting (see Human Resources Elements, Recruiting and Hiring)
Cross–Professional Practice, 50 (see also multi-disciplinary practice)
Davis, Anthony, 111, 162, 167
De-equitization, 64
Delegation, 177
Deming, C. Edwards, 301, 305
Demographics, 16, 147
Dinosaur, 104
Discipline, 116, 118
Disintermediation, 46, 239
Dissolution, 70–71
Drucker, Peter, 15, 97, 98
Economics, 34, 153
E-filing, 251
Employed Lawyers, 61, 62, 170, 186
Employment at Will, 173
Engagement Letters (see Fee Agreements)
Entrepreneurship, 198, 370
Enterprise Search, 251
Equal Employment Opportunity ("EEO"), 155, 173, 194
Equipment, 217
    Computer Systems (see Technology)
    Other Equipment, 224
    Phones/Fax, 222, 223
    Printing/Copying/Scanning, 223
Ewalt, Henry (*Through the Client's Eyes*), 158
Excellence, 290, 300
Extranets, 250
Fair Labor Standards Act ("FSLA"), 173
Fees
    Agreements, 160, 162
    Billing/Collections, 159, 160, 167, 267, 268, 279
    Communication about, 168
    Disputes, 162, 167
    Estimate, 166
    Unreasonable, 158, 164
Feng Shui, 224
Financial Management, Personal, 366
Financial Resources, 257
    Administration, 259
    Budgeting/Reporting, 271
    Capital/Capitalization, 70, 72, 262, 278
    Capital Account, 262
    Cash Flow, 282

INDEX

References are to Pages

Financial Resources—Cont'd
    Certified Public Accountant ("CPA"), 257, 272, 284, 342, 366
    Equity/Value/Net Worth, 264, 277
    Fixed Expenses, 265, 279
    Income, 266 (see also Fees)
    Management, 259
    Planning, 259, 266
    Profit/Loss, 266 (see also Profitability)
    Reinvestment of Profit, 271
    Realization, 268
    Operating Expenses, 265
    Start–Up Expenses, 264, 265, 282
    Variable Expenses, 265
Financing a Practice, 277
    Borrowing/Loans, 279
    Business Plan, 287
    Capitalization, 278
    Cash Flow, 282
    Senior Core of Retired Executives ("SCORE"), 287
    Start–Up Expenses, 281
Foonberg, 159, 167, 217, 281
Form Description, 124
Furniture/Fixtures, 70, 222, 224
Future Trends, 3, 8, 31, 40, 104, 221
General Practitioner, 52
Gigonomics, 67
Globalization, 31, 40
Goodwill, 70, 262
Greene, Robert, 305
Grella, Thomas C. (*The Lawyer's Guide to Strategic Planning*), 149
Hamel, Gary and C.K. Prahalad (*Competing for the Future*), 109
Hamilton (*Basic Business Concepts for Lawyers*), 258
Harr, Jonathon (*A Civil Action*), 283
Hierarchy, 61
Human Resources, 170
    Elements
        Recruitment/Hiring, 189, 191, 194
        Orientation/Training, 199
        Evaluation/Feedback, 200
        Compensation/Benefits, 201
        Discipline/Termination, 204
        Motivation, 208
Implied Partnership, 72
Information-based Business, 97, 238
Information Resources, 238, 251
Internet, 46, 219, 221, 225, 247, 305, 357
    Website, 48 145, 228, 232
Interest on Lawyer Trust Accounts ("IOLTA"), 349
Job Satisfaction, 208
Jones, Nancy Byerley (*Self-Audits for the Busy Lawyer*), 307
Knowledge Management (KM), 245, 252
Law Firm Administrators (see Support Staff)
Law Firms
    Ancillary Business, 6
    As Employer, 172
    Decline, 85
    Definition of, 63
    General Counsel, 187

Law Firms—Cont'd
    Institutional, 73
    Life Cycle, 84, 85
    Growth, 84, 85, 191
    Maturity, 86
    Multiprofessional, 74
    Pyramid, 61, 62, 63
    Space, 200, 209, 216
        Design, 210, 211
        Lease Purchase, 217
        Information Resources Center, 215
        Library, 213
        Security, 214
        Workspace, 210
    Start–Up, 85, 260, 262
Law Firm Management (see Law Practice Management)
Law of Law Practice, 151
Law Library (see Law Firms, Space, Library)
Law Office (see Law Firm)
Law Office Management (see Law Practice Management)
Law Practice Management
    Application of Model Rules of Professional Conduct, 116
    Class, Assumptions for Firm, 122–23
    Paradigm for Studying, 120
Lawyer–Client Relationship, 113
Lawyer Salaries, 76, 202
Lawyer Statistical Report, 3, 17, 20
Lawyers as Managers, 95, 171
Leadership, 169, 374
Legal Assistants (see Paralegals)
Legal Malpractice Insurance, 114
Legal Secretary (see Support Staff)
Legal Services Industry, 31
Legal Services Delivery Team, 310
Legal Research, 251
Legal Work, Definition of, 288, 309
Life Cycle of Law Firm (see Law Firm)
Limited Liability Partnership/Company ("LLP" "LLC"), 74
Litigation Support (see Technology, Computer Applications)
Leverage, 36, 37, 61, 295
MacCrate Report, 352, 359, 360, 378, 382, 383
Maister, David, 97
Malpractice, 111, 112, 114, 162, 336, 338
    Insurance (see Legal Malpractice Insurance)
Management Skills, 358
Management Theory, 97
Marketing Legal Services, 120
    Advertising, 127, 128
    Assess Marketplace, 147
    Commercial Speech, 128
    Assess Competition, 148
    Economics, 153
    Implementation, 149
    Niche, 149
    Planning, 127, 140
    Self–Assessment, 149
    Solicitation, 127
Marketplace for Legal Services, 16, 21, 26, 40, 147
Meyer, Charles (*Accounting for Lawyers*), 359

INDEX

References are to Pages

McCarthy, Dwight, 103
McLuhan, Marshall (*The Gutenburg Galaxy*), 238
Merger, 87
Metrics, 82
Missouri Bar Motivational Study, 159, 160
Mobile Law Office, 228
Mobility, 233
Model Code of Professional Responsibility, 159, 160
Model Rules of Professional Conduct, 8, 50, 57, 62, 75 92, 96, 114, 115, 116, 117, 118, 135, 159, 199, 247, 251, 264, 311, 341, 375
Morgan, J. Harris (*How to Drafft Bills that Clients Rush to Pay*), 159
Motivation, 100, 177
Multidisciplinary Practice ("MDP"), 40, 46, 49
Multijurisdictional Practice ("MJP"), 40, 45, 49
Munneke, Gary, 11, 27, 31, 40, 52, 228, 297, 389
Munneke's Pyramid, 400
National Association for Law Placement (see Lawyer Salaries)
New York Code of Professional Responsibility, 177
Niche, 151
Non-equity Partners, 63, 67, 187, 387
Nonlegal Careers, 26, 389
Nonlegal Personnel (see Support Staff)
Of Counsel, 187
Office Sharing, 72, 87
Organization, 103, 360, 367
Orwell, George (*Animal Farm*), 76
Overhead, 265
Paperless Office, 244, 246, 341, 344
Paralegals, 177, 180, 181
Part Time Lawyering, 66
Partner Compensation, 76, 77, 79, 80, 109, 268
    Distribution by Committee, 81
    Formula, 80
    Meritocracy, 78
    Under UPA, 71, 76
Partners, 69, 71, 76, 278
Partnership, 14, 59, 68, 69, 72
Partnership Agreement, 68, 69, 71
    Checklist, 70, 391
    Elements, 70, 91
    Written, 71, 92
Personal Digital Assistant (PDA), 341
Personal Management Skills (see Management Skills)
Personal Marketing Skills, 121
Peters, Tom (*Circle of Innovation*), 109
Physical Resources, 209
Pirsig, Robert (*Zen and the Art of Motorcycle Maintenance*), 292, 307
Practice Settings, 31
Practice Systems, 325
    Client (variable) Information, 315, 319, 330
    Components, 325
        Document Assembly, 326
        Substantive Practice Areas, 309
        Administrative Support Systems, 325

Practice Systems—Cont'd
    Components—Cont'd
        Administrative Support Systems—Cont'd
            Case Management, 353
            Calendar/Docket/Tickler, 335, 336, 339
            Conflicts, 345
            Filing/Retrieval, 3–10, 341
            Time and Billing, 348
            Trust Accounts, 349
        Litigation Management Systems, 351
    Creating, 318
    Implementing, 319
    Improving, 290, 320
    Instructions, 328
    Routinization, 322
    Templates, 327
Pro Bono, 78, 81, 159
Product Life Cycle (PLC), 84
Professional Corporation/Association ("PC" "PA"), 69, 74
Professional Development, 358
Professional Failure, 109–110
Professional Liability, 74, 111
Professional Managers, 181
Professional Negligence (see Malpractice)
Professional Staff (see Support Staff)
Professional Standards, 306
Professional Values, 39
Professionalism, 39
Profitability, 39, 61, 194, 266, 282
Quality, 110, 179, 291, 292, 293, 294, 295, 301, 305, 317
Quicken Family Lawyer, 22
Rainmaking, 87
Ramo, Roberta (*How to Create a System for the Law Office*), 318
Retirement/Death, 108
Revised Uniform Partnership Act ("RUPA") (see Uniform Partnership Act)
Risk/Risk Management, 110
Rosenthal, Arnold (*Lawyer and Client: Who's in Charge*), 157
Routinization of Legal Work, 31, 325
Salary Comparison, Law Graduate v. Banking Graduate, 36–37
Smart Phones, 222
Smith, Reginald Heber, 104, 105, 106
Socratic Method, 359
Social Media, 249
Solicitation (see Marketing)
Solo Practice/Practitioner, 17, 60, 161, 222, 311
Specialist/Specialization, 52, 63, 67
Staff Manual, 173, 199, 205
Standards for the Approval of Law Schools, 361–362
Statement of Fundamental Lawyering Skills (see MacCrate Report)
Stress, 408
Subchapter "S" Corporation, 74
Substantive Legal Skills, 380
Substantive Systems (see Practice Systems)
Supervisor/Supervision, 182, 374
Support Staff, 63, 170, 177, 208

Support Staff—Cont'd
   Assemblers, 181, 182
   Chief Executive Officer ("CEO"), 187
   Chief Financial Officer ("CFO"), 187
   Chief Operating Officer ("COO"), 187
   Compensation, 201
   Consultants/Contract Employees, 153
   Director of Human Resources, 187
   Director of Information Technology, 187
   Gatekeepers, 1, 182
   Law Firm Administrators, 178
   Legal Secretaries, 181
   Paralegals, 180
   Producers, 181, 182
   Professional Managers, 179
   Raises/Bonuses, 202
   Summer Associates/Law Clerks, 200
   Supervisors, 181
Survival, 3, 159
SWOT (Strengths/Weaknesses/Opportunities/Threats), 26
Systems, 104, 297, 309, 325
Task Force on the Future of the Legal Profession, 8, 66, 242, 405
Technology, 240, 295, 378
   Computer Applications, 240
      Accounting, 267
      Case Management, 241, 354
      Document Management, 242
      Litigation Support, 342, 351, 354
      Time and Billing, 240, 348
   Computer Systems, 218, 264
   Costs, 217
   DVD, 238

Technology—Cont'd
   Internet (see Internet)
   Intranets/Networks, 219, 221
   Merging Technologies, 219, 223
   Personal Digital Assistant ("PDA"), 337
   Software, 220, 240
   Skill, 3, 359
   Structured Query Language ("SQL"), 347
   Videoconferencing, 222
   Voice Recognition, 222, 223, 233, 236
Telecommuting, 235
Time, 105
   Management, 363
   Records, 160
   Timekeeping, 108, 160, 223, 240, 348
Title VII of the Civil Rights Act of 1964 (see Equal Employment Opportunity)
Toffler, Alvin (*Future Shock*), 238
Total Quality Management ("TQM") (see Quality)
Trust Accounts, 349
Unauthorized Practice of Law/Monopoly, 22, 23, 26, 46
Uniform Partnership Act ("UPA"), 69, 70, 71, 76
Virtual Office, 226, 248
Voice Recognition Software, 223
Virtual Private Network (VPN), 34
Website (See Internet)
Winters & Sommers, LLP, 28
Women
   Lawyers, 19, 65
   Role of, 181
Yin and Yang, 290

†